50

DETECTIVE FICTION

To the memory of my father,
Herbert Wallace Cooper (1917–93)

R. J. C.

To Dorothy, Karl and John

B.A.P.

DETECTIVE FICTION

The Collector's Guide

Second Edition

JOHN COOPER
and
B. A. PIKE

SCOLAR PRESS

Published by
SCOLAR PRESS
Gower House
Croft Road
Aldershot
Hants GU11 3HR
England

Ashgate Publishing Company
Old Post Road
Brookfield
Vermont 05036
USA

British Library Cataloguing in Publication Data

Cooper, John
    Detective Fiction: Collector's Guide. –
    2Rev.ed
    I. Title II. Pike, Barry
    016.80883872

ISBN 0–85967–991–8

Phototypeset in 9 point Times by Intype,
London and printed in Great Britain at
The University Press, Cambridge

CONTENTS

ABBREVIATIONS

AHMM	*Alfred Hitchcock's Mystery Magazine* (New York)
a.k.a.	also known as
BL	British Library
CC	*Catalogue of Crime*, by Jaques Barzun and Wendell Hertig Taylor (New York, Harper & Row, 1971)
Cook	*Monthly Murders* by Michael L. Cook (Greenwood 1982)
Cook & Miller	*Mystery, Detective and Espionage Fiction* by Michael L. Cook & Stephen T. Miller, 2 vols, (Garland 1988)
CWA	Crime Writers Association (UK)
DBC	Detective Book Club (USA)
ECB	*The English Catalogue of Books*
EMD	Encyclopaedia of Mystery and Detection by Chris Steinbrunner and Otto Penzler (McGraw Hill 1976, Routledge 1987)
EN	Evening News (London)
EQA	Ellery Queen's Anthology
EQMM	Ellery Queen's Mystery Magazine (New York)
ES	*Evening Standard* (London)
EWMM	Edgar Wallace Mystery Magazine (UK)
GMP	Gay Men's Press (London)
Hubin	*Crime Fiction 1749–1980* by Allen J. Hubin (New York, Garland 1984) (the comprehensive bibliography of the genre)
JCMM	*John Creasey Mystery Magazine* (UK)
LMM	*London Mystery Magazine*
MSMM	*Mike Shayne's Mystery Magazine*
MWA	Mystery Writers of America
NAL	New American Library
n.d.	not dated
NEL	New English Library
OUP	Oxford University Press
pb	paperback
Reilly	*Twentieth-Century Crime and Mystery Writers* edited by John M. Reilly (New York, St Martin's Press 1980); second edition (New York, St Martin's Press/London, St James Press 1985)
SF	Science Fiction
TAD	*The Armchair Detective* (New York, Mysterious Press: founder-editor Allen J. Hubin)
UK	United Kingdom
ULP	University of London Press
USA	United States (of America)
V & A	Victoria & Albert Museum (London)

ACKNOWLEDGMENTS

In assembling the second edition of this guide we have had a great deal of help from a large number of people. The authors who responded directly to our appeals for information about their work are: Catherine Aird, Robert Barnard. J. S. Borthwick, Simon Brett, W. J. Burley, Roger Busby, Gwendoline Butler, Ann Cleeves, Amanda Cross, Colin Dexter, Peter Dickinson, Elizabeth Ferrars, Anthea Fraser, Antonia Fraser, Michael Gilbert, Caroline Graham, Joseph Hansen, Roy Hart, Reginald Hill, P. D. James, H. R. F. Keating, Peter Lovesey, Charlotte Macleod, Jill McGown, James Melville, Magdalen Nabb, Ian Rankin, Ruth Rendell, Peter Robinson, John Rossiter, Dorothy Simpson, Julian Symons, June Thomson, David Williams and R. D. Wingfield. We are grateful to them all.

For information of all kinds we thank Robert Adey, Jack Adrian, Geoff Bradley, Jon L. Breen, Nicholas Cawdry, J. C. Critchley, William F. Deeck, Karen Ende, Karen Godfrey, Douglas G. Greene, Lyndsey Greenslade, John Hines, Ian Hughes, Maxim Jakubowski, John Jeffries, Roger Johnson, James Lay, Stephen Leadbeatter, Tony Medawar, Ellen Nehr, Barbara Peters, Maria Rejt, Marion Richmond, Philip Scowcroft, Ralph Spurrier, Jamie Sturgeon, Pat Watt and Julia Wisdom. We are indebted to them all, to some enormously so.

We again acknowledge the help of Mr Charles Gordon Clark for information about the work of his father, the late Cyril Hare, and we are grateful too, to Miss Joyce Allingham, sister of the late Margery Allingham, for a considerable contribution to this book. As before, we express particular thanks to Nina Evans and her staff at the British Library.

The published sources we have tapped include works by: Michael Cook (*Monthly Murders*, Greenwood 1982); Michael Cook and Stephen Miller (*Mystery, Detective and Espionage Fiction*, Garland 1988); Norman Donaldson (*In Search of Doctor Thorndyke*, Popular Press 1971); Colleen Gilbert (*Bibliography of the Works of Dorothy L. Sayers*, Macmillan 1979); Richard Lancelyn Green and John Michael Gibson (*A Bibliography of A. Conan Doyle*, OUP 1983); John McAleer et al. (*Rex Stout: An Annotated Primary and Secondary Bibliography*, Garland 1980); Ellen Nehr (*Doubleday Crime Club Compendium, 1928–1991*, Offspring Press 1992); John J. Sullivan (*G. K. Chesterton: A Bibliography*, ULP 1958); and David Jasen and Otto Penzler (contributions to *TAD*, on Craig Rice by the former and on collecting mystery fiction by the latter). Allen Hubin's bibliography has been a continual resource; so, too, has *Twentieth-Century Crime and Mystery Writers*, initially edited by John Reilly, most recently by Lesley Henderson (third edition, St James' Press 1991).

Karl Pike is working on the bibliography of Dame Agatha Christie and has generously shared with us important information regarding the primacy of certain American editions over the British.

Finally, we thank Margaret Cooper, who first suggested we write this guide and helped in many ways to bring it to fruition.

John Cooper
B. A. Pike

The authors would be glad to hear from readers with suggested corrections or additions to the information contained in this book. Please get in touch by writing c/o the publisher.

INTRODUCTION

This book is intended as a handbook for collectors of detective fiction, and it seeks to include practical advice on all aspects of assembling and maintaining such a collection. It is also a celebration of the mystery or detective story, and largely disregards hard-boiled, Gothic, espionage, thriller, adventure, and psychological suspense fiction. This is not from contempt for any of these fields, but from enthusiasm for the genuine whodunit, which is too seldom given its due.

The first edition concentrated on Golden Age authors and their modern successors, but we have cast our net much more widely in this expanded sequel. Conan Doyle is now included, as are G. K. Chesterton and R. Austin Freeman, both of whom were in need of revised documentation. We have also included a token representation of both the classic hard-boiled school and the present-day female private eyes, partly in response to requests and partly to acknowledge that collecting traditional whodunits does not necessarily exclude collecting much else besides.

Authors are featured under the names by which they are primarily known within the crime fiction genre, even where their real names were also used for mysteries. Thus, Anthony Berkeley takes precedence over A. B. Cox, and Ellis Peters over Edith Pargeter. All featured authors are listed at the beginning of Chapter 5 with their pseudonyms.

Because we are concerned with crime fiction, we have generally ignored works by our chosen authors in other areas of literature. In such a context, *Blackkerchief Dick, Nurse Matilda,* and *English Farming and Why I Turned It Up* are irrelevant. Reference is made to some works outside the genre, where their status needs to be clarified: *The Three Cornered Halo* is a good example of this. We have tried to avoid excessive factual detail in the discussions of writers, though some, inevitably, are heavily weighted with information. In general, the author entries are intended to give a complete survey of the writers' books and stories within the crime fiction genre, with descriptions of first editions and their dust-wrappers and some account of series characters and their frequency. There are, however, exceptions to this. JC has chosen to disregard the Gothic novels of Jennie Melville and the thrillers of John Rossiter, for instance; and BP's entries on A. E. W. Mason and Roy Vickers are selective, the latter extremely so, since it deals only with Vickers' later stories. The checklists are designed to give as much as possible of the significant information, and to provide complementary detail to the text.

In our descriptions of books, we have aimed to limit ourselves to what we know and have seen. Where we have given in to the temptation to speculate, we hope to have made it clear that this is what we have done. Checklists are based on books we have seen rather than on previously published lists, and we can vouch for the datings of all British first editions given here, which we have, almost without exception, verified by reference to the books themselves. Where books are undated, we have relied initially on the advertisement sections and printers' codes many of them contain; and where these are not present, we have consulted the *English Catalogue of Books (ECB)* or visited the British Library (which almost always agree in their dating of first editions). We cannot, unfortunately, vouch for the dating of American books in the same way, since we have had access to relatively few US texts. Here, our principal authority has been Allen J. Hubin, whose bibliography of crime fiction will always be indispensable to collectors.

Accuracy is obviously crucial in a book of this

kind, but we are of course subject to human fallibility. Where the word 'known' occurs in the text, it means known to us or to one of us. The claim that 'no variant bindings are known' of an author's first editions means, specifically, that we have never encountered any. With the older authors, in particular, we have aimed to pass on all we know and have learnt; but for current authors, we have been more selective (very few modern dust-wrappers, for instance, are worth describing).

We are amateurs in bibliography, with no training or specialized knowledge of this field (as, perhaps, will be painfully apparent to those with such expertise). However, we have tried, conscientiously and responsibly, to describe accurately all the books included in this survey. Appendix E assembles many of the terms we have consistently used, with indications of what we understand and intend them to mean. In the matter of colour description we have found a major area of uncertainty, especially since we cannot always agree between ourselves (JC maintains that pre-war Gollancz books are lettered in red, but BP persists in regarding this colour as orange). The binding colours given in this book are accurate in essentials, in that no green books are said to be red; but we are as fallible as anyone when the finer shades are in question, and whether a binding is purple or maroon, pink or mauve, fawn or beige or sand-coloured, depends on, and varies with, the individual.

In general, we do not mention that the publisher is named on the spine of the book, since this is standard publishing practice. 'Spine lettering' may be taken to include title, author, and publisher. Title and author are often singled out, however, since they occur jointly on many front covers, in a way that publishers, as a rule, do not.

In a few checklists, some months of publication are given, as well as the years. This may indicate that the months are stated in the books, as with Patricia Wentworth; but it is more often intended to establish exact chronology when two or more books appeared in the same year (particularly where a checklist is divided between novels and story collections). Authors who benefit from this kind of precision include H. C. Bailey, Philip MacDonald, and Rex Stout. It has not always been possible to establish the exact order of publication for all an author's books.

We have tried to ensure that publishers are named in full when they first appear in a checklist (e.g. Hodder and Stoughton), but for later references we have adopted the convenient shorter form (e.g. Hodder). Since Collins' crime fiction appeared both under the firm's general imprint and within the Crime Club series, books from this house are identified either as Collins or as Crime Club books. The Crime Club formula is used here exclusively for Collins books, and never for those from the US Crime Club, which are invariably attributed to their publisher, Doubleday.

We have not given the place of publication in checklists, since we believe that doubts about which are British and which are American publishers may be dispelled by reference to the text. We are uncertain of the distinction between the US publishers British Book Centre and London House, which at times appear to be interchangeable. Where they occur in a checklist, they follow Hubin exactly.

We make the common assumption that books by British authors were first published in Britain, and that books by American authors first appeared in the US, except where we know this to be untrue. If a number of books in sequence have bindings and letterings in a variety of colours, it has sometimes been judged wise to include such details in the checklist, rather than in the text of the essay. 'Red, green' after a title indicates that the book has a red binding with green lettering on the spine (and the text will confirm whether it is also on the front cover). If these details are not present for any title in a checklist, they will be found in the course of the entry on the author.

We have tried to make checklists complete and, with authors currently active, as up-to-date as possible. We regard uncollected stories as of prime importance, and have listed many that were previously little known or unknown. They are listed according to the earliest known appearance of each story. Ideally, we have given details of the first publication, and also of the first book appearance, if this is different. In many cases, we have listed additional appearances, where these occur in books or journals likely to be more generally accessible to collectors than the others listed: we have, for example, usually listed details of publication in *EQMM*. In many cases we have *not* listed all known appearances of a story, particularly since space is limited. When two months are given in a checklist for the *Saint* magazine, the former is the US date, and the latter the UK.

Series characters contribute greatly to the appeal of the mystery novel, and their characters are indicated in checklists accordingly. Some indication of series characters' contributions to story collections is usually given, and the uncollected stories have also largely been checked for the presence or absence of series detectives.

Appendices are provided for various aspects of collecting, and to illustrate and enlarge upon points made in the opening chapters. Of particular importance is Appendix I, which lists other authors who deserve presentation in a book such as this but have been excluded for reasons of space. Many of these are excellent performers, and all have something to offer the followers of the civilized mystery. Many also deserve to be far better known than they are.

It will be apparent, not only from the title-page and from the dominant pronoun in this introduction, that this book is a collaboration. There have been two of us involved, each with his own distinctive ideas and objectives. We began with the intention to present our information formally, according to a standard pattern; but it became increasingly obvious that our approaches were essentially different, particularly with regard to the main business of the book, the discussions of individual authors. Accordingly, we have gone our separate ways, though always with the sole desire to be informative, interesting, accurate, and helpful. It has seemed advisable to attribute each discussion of a writer to its author, so that readers know in every case with whom they have to reckon. Though we hope that the checklists are standardized, we know that the author discussions are not.

Alice in Wonderland felt that a book without pictures was of no use. Since we sympathize with her, we have included as many illustrations as could be accommodated within these pages.

APPROACHES TO COLLECTING 1

Collections of crime fiction vary, like those who cater for them, from the high-powered to the unassuming. The level at which you operate depends on your temperament and your financial resources. For a number of admirable reasons, most collectors now prefer to have the books of their favoured authors in first editions; but there is a world elsewhere, and, for those who inhabit it, the range of crime writing available in paperback is wider now than for many years past, and there are many reissues available on the second-hand market. There are also vast numbers of dilapidated ex-library books still circulating, for collectors unconcerned about the condition of their acquisitions.

This book, however, is intended for the committed collector, who gets high on detective fiction first editions, craving them as others long for drugs or casinos or soap operas or alcohol. It pays tribute to the power of the first edition, to its status as an antique, as a survivor, as a part of man's cultural history, like the Sheraton sideboard or the long-case clock. It acknowledges that a reproduction must always be inferior to the original, and that rarity imparts an additional lustre to an already desirable object.

First editions can, and often do, increase in monetary value. Ten years ago, an Agatha Christie first from the 1930s cost about £20 without its dust-wrapper. Nowadays it is more likely to cost £50. Colin Dexter's first book sold for £2.50 in 1975, on first publication; recently, a copy was sold for £175. P. D. James' first book is now worth about 300 times what it originally cost in 1961. It is important to remember, however, that *Cover Her Face* is desirable only partly because it is rare. The chief reason is that it is the distinguished first novel of a major writer. Those who collect purely as an investment are surely missing this point and, perhaps, also much of the fun. The rules of their particular game permit them to collect only fashionable authors, who are

not necessarily the best. Since investors intend eventually to sell what they acquire, they distance themselves from reader-collectors, who would always rather have the book than the money it might raise.

Restricting oneself to first editions has certain advantages. It limits the rate at which one acquires books; it makes each acquisition a cause for celebration; and it imposes worthwhile standards from the outset. It would be easy and still quite cheap to amass a large collection of ex-library books or second-hand paperbacks; and if this would satisfy you, it is the obvious path to follow. But it is also very easy to become disenchanted with inferior copies, and the itch to replace them with better ones tends to make itself felt. When you find yourself buying the same book twice, or even three times, you will know that the curse of the upgrader is well and truly upon you.

It is better by far to get the perfect copy of a book you want the first time around – or, if not a perfect copy, at least one that will continue to satisfy you and will not demand to be replaced. The more elusive a book, the more absorbing the business of trying to track it down – and the more rewarding its eventual acquisition. Some books are more elusive than others, largely because the original editions were smaller. Agatha Christie's first novel was published in an edition of 2,000 copies, so it is inevitably much harder to find than a later work like *A Murder Is Announced*, of which 50,000 copies were printed. Many modern crime novels have smaller print-runs than might reasonably be expected: 1,250 or 2,500 copies in many cases. Most of these will be bought for libraries, so that relatively few will survive for collectors. It has become advisable to acquire as they appear new books by the writers one collects, since they may not surface again later. Anyone now seeking the original editions of Ruth Rendell's and P. D. James' first novels will know what rarity means.

First edition collections, inevitably, vary with the individual collector. Some meticulously follow the recommendations of accredited gurus, regardless of personal taste and judgement. James Sandoe's *Readers' Guide to Crime* and the Haycraft-Queen 'definitive library' of cornerstones of mystery fiction are two such influential listings. A third, *Queen's Quorum*, claims to identify 'the 106 most important books' of short crime stories, for those who like to have these things cut and dried. Some collectors aim to assemble the books that have won awards from the professional associations of crime writers (see Appendix C). Others try to find all the crime fiction issued by a particular publisher. Each of these procedures must surely entail the acquisition of some items one would not otherwise have wanted; but substantial collections of books from the major publishers would undoubtedly be of considerable interest.

Some collections are limited to a particular period of time, such as the 'Golden Age' between the wars. This means that only the earlier works of many writers are collected, and the collector hardly knows the pleasure of a complete collection of an admired author's work. Single-author collections are also known, especially with Sir Arthur Conan Doyle as their subject (or, rather, Sherlock Holmes, since interest appears to be centred on the character rather than his creator). Anyone aiming to acquire every item relating to Holmes has a lifetime's pleasurable endeavour ahead. A common setting for a group of novels can be the basis of a collection: the English country house or village, a boat or train, a hospital or theatre, London or New England. Locked-room mysteries and impossible crime are widely and keenly sought. Feminists seek and study the cases of women detectives, and there is an increasing interest in the 'ethnic' investigators, especially those with a distinctive culture, defined in the course of a series. Police procedural novels are popular, and so are the historical crime novels, ranging through time from the classical Greece of Margaret Doody to the early twentieth century of Peter Lovesey. (See Appendix A).

The stories of a chosen author can be fascinating to the collector, particularly if they have not been brought together and published in volume form. Ideally, an author's stories should all be available in this way, or at least in mixed anthologies with the work of other writers, but in practice this is seldom so and many stories remain uncollected in book form. All Dorothy L. Sayers' stories have now been collected together and all Ngaio Marsh's, but these are exceptions rather than the rule. Two established annual anthologies are the *Winter's Crimes* series, originated in 1969, and the CWA collections, now in their thirty-second year. The former is published by Macmillan and contains stories new to Britain. The latter are now edited by Liza Cody and Michael Z. Lewin and published by Chatto & Windus, with a mixture of reprints and new material. Two more recent series have begun to establish themselves: *Midwinter Mysteries*, edited by Hilary Hale and published by Little, Brown; and *New Crimes* edited by Maxim Jakubowski and published by Constable. The MWA also issue an annual collection. *EQMM* is published monthly by Dell in New York, with Janet Hutchings as editor. A complete collection is a pearl of great price.

Personal taste is, of course, the ultimate criterion for any collector, and it is generally safe to assume that one doesn't buy something one doesn't expect to enjoy. Problems arise when a favoured writer changes direction: do you, or do you not, follow? Julian Symons, for instance, began with entertaining detective novels in the grand tradition, but later diversified into a bewildering range of styles and themes; and Ruth Rendell's more recent novels and stories are deeply disconcerting to admirers of her earlier work. A selective collection is the obvious answer in such cases, but it is hard to abandon an author in mid-stream, and there is always the hope that normal service will be resumed. The possibilities are infinite: all the collector has to do is make the decisions (and pay for the books). John Dickson Carr rightly regarded mystery fiction as 'the grandest game in the world', and its collection is an enthralling activity. For its devotees, the game is continually afoot.

FORMING A COLLECTION 2

Any potential repository of books should be investigated, however unpromising: charity shops, antique markets, auction rooms, car boot sales, or church fêtes. With sufficient energy and resilience to tackle anything, the determined collector has a better chance of making worthwhile discoveries than those of us who wait for books to come to them. Though the stock of most second-hand bookshops is depressingly static, significant acquisitions are still made, particularly by dealers, who are often able to hunt more assiduously than most collectors. The number of bookshops stocking second-hand crime fiction seems, sadly, to be dwindling (though the remarkable concentration of booksellers in Hay-on-Wye appears still to be flourishing).

Because many book-dealers have short business lives, it is advisable to phone in advance of a visit, to confirm opening hours, and even to establish if the concern is still active. It is very disheartening to track down a bookshop and find it with whitewash on the windows, or an announcement that the premises will shortly reopen as a burger bar. Three publications list the country's bookshops and dealers, with details of specialization: Sheppard's *Book Dealers in the British Isles*, Richard Joseph 1993; Cole's *Register of Antiquarian Booksellers*, The Clique 1993; and *Driff's Guide*, Drif Field 1992.

Joseph also publishes Sheppard's *Book Dealers in North America* and *European Booksellers*. Some dealers offer a book-search service, but it has to be said that they are no more likely to locate elusive books than anyone else, without untapped resources unknown to the rest of us. More reliable sources of supply must be book fairs and auctions, which are continually advertised in the specialist press. Collectors may themselves advertise in the *Book and Magazine Collector*, a monthly journal first published in 1984.

The market in crime fiction tends to centre nowadays on specialist dealers, who will almost certainly charge more for desirable books, but will also have a better chance than most of actually locating some (see Appendix D). Dealers' catalogues are the most likely regular source of decent second-hand crime fiction, and the collector should aim to figure on as many mailing lists as possible. Catalogues are a mixed blessing, since they spare one the necessity of trudging round the country in an often futile search, but put collectors directly into competition with each other for the more desirable items. Whether or not one secures a book from a list largely depends on the speed at which the local postal service delivers the list. Most dealers profess to work on their customers' wants lists, but few actually do so. It is a common occurrence to see books from one's wants list advertised for sale in the catalogues of dealers who ought to have offered them to you – and it is deeply irritating to ring and find them sold.

The condition of books has increased in importance, and collectors generally are becoming more demanding in this respect. Ideally a book should be in the same state as when it was published, but it is unrealistic to expect this in most cases; and it is reasonable to tolerate in an older book faults that would be unacceptable in a more recent one. Defective copies are especially undesirable: whatever else may have happened to a book, all its pages, including both free endpapers, should be intact. People tend to read detective novels during meals, so that food-stains and greasy thumbmarks are always a danger, to be avoided if possible. Ex-library books are wholly unacceptable to a serious collector, since not only are they too heavily read, but they also carry the inevitable stigmata of public ownership. In particular, they are often rebound for library circulation, and a book without its original binding is worthless to a collector. Heavy foxing is a disfigurement more tolerable to some collectors than others: the more scrupulous will insist that it is light or, preferably, non-existent. A book with bumped corners, caused by some collision, is also essentially undesirable to the fastidious. Inscriptions in general are unwelcome to a collector, particularly those that take over a front free endpaper (unless, like Helene Hanff, you cherish them as part of the individual history of each book). Only when the inscription is in the hand of the author is it an asset. A writer's signature is desirable, but presentation inscriptions are obviously more so. The more considered an inscription, the more enthralling it is to the collector. An inscription at the time of publication is more desirable than a later one, but both are enhancements. Best of all is a written dedication to reinforce a printed one.

Dust-wrappers have become increasingly important to first-edition collectors, to such an extent that a book with the wrapper may be worth much more than the same book without it.

Because they tend to be scarce, dust-wrappers for books published before the 1950s make a considerable difference to the book's value.

Even collectors who are unhappy about this price differential do not deny the appeal of the dust-wrapper, and accept that, as a collector's item, a book without it is deficient. It is part of the book as first issued and so, in an ideal world, inseparable from it. It can also be a source of aesthetic pleasure or invaluable information. Some wrappers have little or no appeal beyond the fact that they belong with the books, but others are works of art in themselves, with something of the dignity of collaboration about them. It is to be regretted that so many modern wrappers derive from the photographer rather than the graphic artist.

It is advisable to set limits as to what is and is not acceptable without the dust-wrapper. It might be foolish to insist on it for pre-war books, since relatively few have survived in this state (and are highly priced, accordingly); but, for post-war books the chances are usually better, and the collector may well live to regret the acquisition of a book without its wrapper when a copy with the wrapper turns up. Most collectors and dealers switch wrappers from inferior to better copies of books. Sometimes the wrapper of a later impression is identical to that of the first, so that it may reasonably (and, surely, legitimately) be transferred to the first edition. If a later wrapper carries reviews of the book or new

publicity for the publisher it should be regarded only as a makeshift substitute for the genuine article. The ultra-fastidious collector prefers dust-wrappers with the price still present, but the rest of us tend to consider this unrealistic.

Booksellers' lists define books according to a common code (which is, none the less, variously interpreted by different dealers). A 'fine' book should be virtually as new, and a 'very good' one ought to be in a decent state, with no serious blemishes. The word 'good', in relation to second-hand books, in fact means 'not good', and the discerning collector should avoid anything so described. Reading copies are precisely that – for reading only, and worth no more than a pound or so at the outside.

Collectors need to be wary of false first editions, those which appear to make the claim but are not actually doing so. Ward Lock, Bles, Longmans Green, Constable, Gollancz, Methuen, and Collins Crime Club all issued certain books in cheaper-edition form without making that distinction clear in the books themselves (though presumably they did so on the dust-wrappers). If a book states that it was first published in a particular year, there is no reason to doubt the truth of that statement: but it does not necessarily mean that the copy in question is the first edition. In some cases, it is merely recording the year of first publication, rather than staking a claim to be the original edition. It is hoped that our discussions of individual authors will make this point more clearly and forcibly, since no single issue causes greater confusion. (For a general guide to publishers' practice, see Appendix F.) Later issues of first editions are also very problematical. If a printer bound some copies of a book in one colour and some in another, who is to say which is the 'true' first edition? We have invariably assumed that the British Library has the primary issue, especially if the Library's dating coincides with the *English Catalogue of Books*, as is usually the case.

British book club editions are easily identified, since they state clearly that this is what they are; but US book clubs are trickier. Unfortunately, the original publisher is named on both title-page and spine of American book club editions, so that mistakes are easily made. If it is slim, with shiny covers and cheap paper, an American book may well be a book club issue. Confirmation will be found on the dust-wrapper, unless some unscrupulous person has removed the evidence; where British books show the price, the words 'Book Club edition' appear, so that the obvious assumption for a British collector is that the price has been removed from a first edition wrapper. Some cheaply produced firsts from publishers like St Martin's Press and Doubleday are virtually indistinguishable from book club editions: only the magic words 'first edition' within separate the sheep from the goats. Doubleday books always state the fact if they are first editions: if they do not, they are not. In Britain, Collins Crime Club is an authentic imprint, under which many important writers have had their books first published.

Another particular feature of some US books that causes confusion is the system of numbering whereby the status of the issue is indicated. In general, it seems to be true that a book is a first edition if all the numbers from one to ten appear with the copyright details on the reverse of the title-page. In some cases, however, the lowest figure in the first edition is a two, so this is not a hard-and-fast rule. Often the figure 2 shows that the book is a second issue (and a 3 that it is the third, and so on). Sometimes the words 'first printing' appear, even when the numbers indicate that it is no such thing. Random House is known for books where the lowest figure in the printer's key is a 2. In recent years some British books have acquired printer's keys: See Appendix F.

MAINTAINING A COLLECTION

Once a book is in your possession, you can, of course, do what you like with it in an attempt to restore to it some of its former glory. If a page is loose, you can stick it back in, discreetly, with a thread of Prittstick, for preference. Covers may be cleaned with Backus Bookcloth Cleaner (obtainable from Edgar Backus Ltd, 44–6 Cank Street, Leicester). Inscriptions by and to previous owners may irritate you to the point where you wish to remove them, but if so, you should be aware that you will also remove the surface of the paper, however gently you proceed. Despite this, gratifying results can be obtained, if the paper is thick enough, and if an ink-rubber or a typewriter-rubber is applied with a featherlight pressure and unlimited patience. Labels and bookplates may be removed from the pastedown of a book by painting them with water, and leaving this to penetrate, before lifting them clear. The wet paintbrush may be used to wipe away any remaining gum, and the damp area should be dried with absorbent paper. This is much less likely to work with labels attached to the front free endpaper of a book, since the paper will almost certainly buckle. Chipped and defective dust-wrappers may be repaired internally with sticky white or brown paper, but never with sellotape, which deteriorates with the passage of time. The ideal way to make good a wrapper's deficiencies is, perhaps, to enshroud it in protective, unshrinkable plastic and to stick the paper to this rather than to the wrapper itself. If you use ordinary commercial cellophane, you should fold it clear of the top edge of the wrapper, to allow for shrinkage.

In comparison with stamps or porcelain, books are robust, but they are still vulnerable in a number of ways – to sunlight, to damp, to radiators, and to careless handling. Damp is probably the arch-enemy, but clumsy handling is perhaps more insidious (and must be more widespread). Glass-fronted bookcases, adequately ventilated, are the ideal storage places, but since these are so hideously expensive, most books take their chance, like many cars, out in the open. Books should support each other on the shelf, without being so tightly packed that there is difficulty in removing one. Split spines result from careless removal of a book from the shelf. The grasp should encompass the spine; this is built to stand the pressure, while the top of the spine is not. Most readers, and even some collectors read books clumsily, creasing, thumbing, and generally bashing the pages about in the process of getting from start to finish. It is possible to re-read a book several times without leaving a trail of devastation – or to maul it once, sufficiently to mark it for ever. The pleasure of reading is the primary reason for collecting books, and a scornful reader who does not also collect might regard this book and all it celebrates as window-dressing. Those of us who do collect seriously know better. To the pleasures of reading are added the pleasures of collecting, and both are infinite. As a purpose in life or a relief from its pressures, book-collecting has a great deal to recommend it. Books do not only furnish a room, as Lindsay Bagshaw has it in Anthony Powell's novel: they also entertain, instruct, transport, and give delight.

SECONDARY ACTIVITIES

As enthusiasm for the mystery has grown, many supplementary activities and amenities have become available to readers and collectors.

Societies exist to celebrate the lives and works of specific authors. Pre-eminent among these are the Sherlockian societies, which are legion. The Wolfe Pack in the USA and the Sayers Society in the UK are other flourishing groups. A comprehensive listing appears in Appendix H. Mystery Readers International is a general society, run with energy and imagination by Janet A. Rudolph, for the benefit of those defined by its name. The CWA and MWA are professional associations for authors, rather than for those who read and collect their work. It is open to 'fans' to join the MWA as affiliated members, but to join the CWA one needs some kind of professional credential. The mass of members are, naturally, fiction writers, but critics and reviewers, true-crime writers, publishers, agents, and dealers, can and do join. Members of both organizations receive newsletters, *The Third Degree* for the MWA, *Red Herrings* for the CWA. Awards are presented at an annual dinner: Edgars (after Poe) in America, and Gold and Silver Daggers in Britain. Sustained excellence is recognized by both associations: the MWA through its Grand Master awards, and the CWA through its Diamond Daggers.

Since 1970, an annual convention for mystery enthusiasts has been held. It is known as the Bouchercon and is named after the late Anthony Boucher. Until 1990, the Bouchercons were exclusive to the USA, but the twenty-first convention was held in London in that year and the twenty-third in Toronto in 1992. Malice Domestic, a convention for lovers of the traditional or 'cosy' mystery, was founded in 1989 and has taken place in Washington in the spring of each year since. West Coast Crime was first held in Omaha, with the emphasis on the tougher tradition. Shots on the Page is a British convention, launched in Nottingham in 1992 as an offshoot of a film noir festival. It is now established as an annual event. Seattle is the selected venue for the 1994 Bouchercon and Nottingham is the venue for the 1995. At Bouchercons, at least, alternative programmes run simultaneously, so that those who attend have a choice of diversion. Talks, films, author interviews, discussions, signing sessions, and book sales are among the events on offer.

Specialist magazines come and go, according to the waxing or waning of their resources or readership or the editor's enthusiasm. Most welcome contributions from readers and collectors – who should not expect to be paid for their efforts, since no one gets rich on publishing a fan magazine. The veteran in the field is *The Armchair Detective*, founded in 1967 by Allen J. Hubin, and now, in its twenty-seventh year, published by Otto Penzler and edited by Kate Stine. Britain has one magazine, the USA many more. A selective listing appears in Appendix G.

There is much more supplementary activity in the USA than in the UK. Courses in crime fiction are on offer at certain American colleges. American bookshops arrange regular promotional sessions, at which authors and their admirers may meet. Certain hotel chains and bookshops organize 'murder weekends' for those who wish actively to engage in a mystery scenario. Mystery tours and other social events also occur.

The opportunities for tributary collections are considerable, and range from postage stamps and theatre programmes to games and Doulton china. Films and TV and radio transmissions are increasingly available to collectors. The more ambitious will seek unique material: holograph manuscripts and letters, original illustrations and cover art. On such a tide of activity, the books might get forgotten – except that none of it would mean very much without them.

9

Anthony Abbot
Catherine Aird
Margery Allingham/Maxwell March
Marian Babson
H. C. Bailey
Robert Barnard/ Bernard Bastable
Josephine Bell
E. C. Bentley
Anthony Berkeley/(A. B. Cox)/A. Monmouth
    Platts/Francis Iles
Nicholas Blake
John and Emery Bonett
J. S. Borthwick
Anthony Boucher/H. H. Holmes
Dorothy Bowers
Ernest Bramah
Pamela Branch
Christianna Brand
Lilian Jackson Braun
Simon Brett
Lynn Brock
Douglas G. Browne
Leo Bruce
W. J. Burley
Roger Busby
Christopher Bush/Michael Home
Gwendoline Butler/Jennie Melville
Joanna Cannan
John Dickson Carr/Carter Dickson/Roger
    Fairbairn
Sarah Caudwell
Raymond Chandler
G. K. Chesterton
Agatha Christie
Ann Cleeves
V. C. Clinton-Baddeley
G. D. H. and M. Cole
J. J. Connington
Patricia D. Cornwell/Patricia Daniels Cornwell
Edmund Crispin

Freeman Wills Crofts
Amanda Cross
Elizabeth Daly
Clemence Dane and Helen Simpson
Glyn Daniel/Dilwyn Rees
Lillian de la Torre
The Detection Club
D. M. Devine/Dominic Devine
Colin Dexter
Peter Dickinson
Arthur Conan Doyle
Margaret Erskine
Elizabeth Ferrars/ E. X. Ferrars
Mary Fitt/Kathleen Freeman/Stuart Mary Wick
Joan Fleming
Leslie Ford/David Frome
Anthea Fraser
Antonia Fraser
James Fraser
R. Austin Freeman/Clifford Ashdown
Elizabeth George
Val Gielgud
Anthony Gilbert/J. Kilmeny Keith/Anne
    Meredith
Michael Gilbert
B. M. Gill
Sue Grafton
Caroline Graham
Dashiell Hammett/Peter Collinson/Samuel
    Dashiell/Mary Jane Hammett
Joseph Hansen/Joseph Colton
Cyril Hare/T. G. Clark
Roy Hart
John Harvey
Keith Heller/Allan Lloyd
Georgette Heyer
Reginald Hill/Patrick Ruell
Tony Hillerman
John Buxton Hilton/John Greenwood
Michael Innes

P. D. James
Lucille Kallen
H. R. F. Keating/ Evelyn Hervey
Harry Kemelman
C. Daly King
Ronald A. Knox
Jane Langton
Emma Lathen/R. B. Dominic
Elizabeth Lemarchand
E. C. R. Lorac/Carol Carnac
Peter Lovesey
Philip MacDonald/Martin Porlock/Anthony
    Lawless
Charlotte Macleod/Alisa Craig
Jessica Mann
Ngaio Marsh
A. E. W. Mason
Helen McCloy
Jill McGown/Elizabeth Chaplin
James Melville/Hampton Charles
Gladys Mitchell/Malcolm Torrie
Gwen Moffat
Anne Morice
Arthur Morrison
Patricia Moyes
Magdalen Nabb
Beverley Nichols
Gil North
Anthony Oliver
Baroness Orczy
Emma Page/Honoria Tirbutt
Stuart Palmer/Jay Stewart
Sara Paretsky
Ellis Peters/Edith Pargeter/Jolyon Carr/John
    Redfern
Joyce Porter
E. R. Punshon/Robertson Halkett
Ellery Queen/Barnaby Ross
Sheila Radley
Ian Rankin/Jack Harvey
Clayton Rawson/Stuart Towne
Ruth Rendell/Barbara Vine
Louisa Revell
John Rhode/Miles Burton
Craig Rice/Michael Venning/Daphne Sanders
Peter Robinson
Jonathan Ross/(John Rossiter)
Dorothy L. Sayers
A. and P. Shaffer/Peter Antony

Dorothy Simpson
C. P. Snow
Rex Stout
Julian Symons
Phoebe Atwood Taylor/Alice Tilton/Freeman
    Dana
Josephine Tey/Gordon Daviot
June Thomson
John Trench
S. S. Van Dine
Robert Van Gulik
Roy Vickers/David Durham/Sefton Kyle/John
    Spencer
Henry Wade
R. A. J. Walling
Thurman Warriner/Simon Troy/John Kersey
Colin Watson
Patricia Wentworth
David Williams
R. D. Wingfield/Rodney Wingfield
Clifford Witting
Sara Woods/Anne Burton/Mary Challis/
    Margaret Leek
Margaret Yorke

Anthony Abbot (1893–1952)

Anthony Abbot was the criminous *alter ego* of the journalist and author Fulton Oursler, whose son, Will Oursler, also wrote crime fiction. All eight of Abbot's novels and two stories feature Thatcher Colt, Commissioner of Police for New York City, a dashing figure, handsome, wealthy, cultured and well connected. The Colt books are characteristic Golden Age products, complex and clever, designed to deceive and, in doing so, to satisfy.

All were first published in America, initially by Covici, Friede, later by Farrar & Rinehart. Four titles are known. *About the Murder of the Clergyman's Mistress* and *About the Murder of the Night Club Lady* are tall yellow books with purple lettering. The front covers have the title along the top and 'A Thatcher Colt Mystery' along the spine edge, each underlined by an extended purple rule, joining towards the top

left corner. The other two Covici titles may be uniform with these. *The Creeps* has a red binding and *The Shudders* is blue-green. Both have black lettering on the spine and front cover. All four books are dated by the copyright notice only. The blue wrapper for *The Shudders* is by Robert Graves and shows a dark, robotic figure and a left hand depressing a hypodermic syringe.

In Britain the Crime Club published the entire run, all in orange bindings with black lettering on the spine and the date on the copyright page. The four titles to *The Murder of the Circus Queen* have heavy black lettering, including title and author on the front cover. *The Murder of Geraldine Foster* also has a single black border on the front cover. All except the last book have advertisements at the rear. *Murder at Buzzards Bay* is correctly written with no apostrophe. The black wrapper for *The Murder of the Circus Queen* features a photograph of the woman in question poised for action. *The Murder of a Man Afraid of Women* has an apple-green wrapper with the head of a young woman (also on the spine). *Murder at Buzzards Bay* has a view of a large house under snow, with a skull looming over it. *Deadly Secret* has a decorative cloth with a brown plant design on it.

Two Colt stories only are known, but *EMD* records an eleventh case for Colt: the film *The Panther's Claw*. Other 'stories' attributed to Abbot are either true-crime pieces ('The Ship of Sleepless Men', 'The Face from Beyond') or not by him ('Hula Homicide' by his son Will). Fulton Oursler contributed the preface and Anthony Abbot the third chapter to *The President's Mystery Story* (see S. S. Van Dine).

Thatcher Colt novels

About the Murder of Geraldine Foster Covici, Friede 1930
a.k.a. *The Murder of Geraldine Foster* Crime Club March 1931
About the Murder of the Clergyman's Mistress Covici 1931
a.k.a. *The Crime of the Century* Crime Club October 1931
a.k.a. *The Murder of the Clergyman's Mistress* Popular Library 1950

About the Murder of the Night Club Lady Covici 1931

a.k.a. *The Murder of the Night Club Lady* Crime Club April 1932

a.k.a. *The Night Club Lady* Grosset & Dunlap 1932, Detective Story Club n.d. (1932)

About the Murder of the Circus Queen Covici 1932

a.k.a. *The Murder of the Circus Queen* Crime Club March 1933

About the Murder of a Startled Lady Farrar & Rinehart 1935

a.k.a. *Murder of a Startled Lady* Crime Club May 1936

About the Murder of a Man Afraid of Women Farrar 1937

a.k.a. *Murder of a Man Afraid of Women* Crime Club July 1937

The Creeps Farrar 1939

a.k.a. *Murder at Buzzards Bay* Crime Club October 1940

The Shudders Farrar 1943

a.k.a. *Deadly Secret* Crime Club November 1943

Thatcher Colt stories

'About the Disappearance of Agatha King' (in *The Mystery Book* Farrar 1939)

'About the Perfect Crime of Mr. Digberry' (in *The Second Mystery Book* Farrar 1940; in *EQMM*, Fall 1941 and November 1950; in *To The Queen's Taste* Little, Brown 1946, Faber 1949)

Collaborative novel

The President's Mystery Story Farrar 1935, Bodley Head 1936 (Chapter 3 is by Anthony Abbot) *BP*

Catherine Aird (b. 1930)

Catherine Aird is the pseudonym of Kinn Hamilton McIntosh, who has written fifteen novels and eight stories. Set in the English county of Calleshire, the books reflect the author's acutely witty perception of the human condition. With the exception of *A Most Contagious Game*, the

series characters of Inspector C. D. Sloan, Detective-Constable William Crosby, Superintendent Leeyes, and Dr Dabbe appear in all the books. Sloan is a quiet, steady family man, who manages to bring criminals to justice despite a smug superior and bungling assistant. Crosby is not very bright but full of enthusiasm, and his performance behind the wheel of his police car would lead one to suspect that he is trying to increase the road accident statistics. Leeyes, a fount of often useless information gleaned from assorted night-school courses, frequently throws at the unfortunate Sloan quotations which he fondly imagines will point him in the right direction for solving the crime. Dabbe, the pathologist, has a sense of humour which enlivens the otherwise deadly business of autopsies. Some of these characters use their detective skills in four of the stories.

The UK editions are in all cases the true firsts and are clearly dated. There is one variant title: *The Complete Steel* becomes in the USA *The Stately Home Murder*. Catherine Aird's first four novels were published by Macdonald and, with one exception, were issued in black cloth, with silver lettering on the spine. *Henrietta Who?* was issued in green cloth, with the spine lettered gilt. From 1970 to 1986, all the books were published by Collins Crime Club, in red cloth, with the spines lettered gilt. Pictorial endpapers showing a map of Calleshire are found in the four Macdonald first editions but, unfortunately, only in one Collins title, *His Burial Too*. The map in the Collins book contains additional detail of Calleshire. The two more recent books were published by Macmillan, *The Body Politic* in beige cloth, *A Going Concern* in red. Both have gilt spine lettering.

The wrapper for *The Religious Body* depicts a bunch of keys, below which is a line of six nuns' heads, while that for *A Most Contagious Game* shows a skeleton and female corpse, head to toe. Edward Hughes designed the very plain green wrapper with black and white lettering for *Henrietta Who?* Edwin Paddock produced the striking silver and black wrapper for *The Complete Steel*, depicting a head in chain mail, with piercing blue eyes. The later wrappers are all photographic. One which merits special attention is Peter Thuring's photo for *A Late Phoenix*, showing the skeleton being unearthed.

A Foreign Office official, Henry Tyler, has appeared in two stories.

The most difficult first edition to locate is *Henrietta Who?*

Novels

(with Sloan, except as stated)

The Religious Body Macdonald 1966, Doubleday 1966
A Most Contagious Game Macdonald 1967, Doubleday 1967 (not Sloan)
Henrietta Who? Macdonald 1968, Doubleday 1968
The Complete Steel Macdonald 1969
a.k.a. *The Stately Home Murder* Doubleday 1970
A Late Phoenix Collins Crime Club 1970, Doubleday 1971
His Burial Too Crime Club 1973, Doubleday 1973
Slight Mourning Crime Club 1975, Doubleday 1976
Parting Breath Crime Club 1977, Doubleday 1978
Some Die Eloquent Crime Club 1979, Doubleday 1980
Passing Strange Crime Club 1980, Doubleday 1981
Last Respects Crime Club 1982, Doubleday 1982
Harm's Way Crime Club 1984, Doubleday 1984
A Dead Liberty Crime Club 1986, Doubleday 1987
The Body Politic Macmillan 1990, Doubleday 1991
A Going Concern Macmillan 1993

Stories

(with Sloan or Tyler, as stated)

'The Scales of Justice' (*Argosy*, Feb. 1974) (non-series)
'Home is the Hunter' (*John Creasey's Crime Collection* 1988, Gollancz 1988) (Sloan)

'Cause and Effects' (*A Classic English Crime*, Pavilion 1990) (Tyler)
'The Hard Sell' (*Crime Waves 1*, Gollancz 1991) (Sloan)
'Lord Peter's Touch' (*Encounters with Lord Peter*, Dorothy L. Sayers Society 1991) (Sloan)
'The Man Who Rowed for the Shore' (*The Man Who . . .* Macmillan 1992) (not Sloan – until the end)
'Steady as She Goes' (*1st Culprit*, Chatto & Windus 1992) (Sloan)
'Slight of Hand' (*2nd Culprit*, Chatto 1993) (Tyler)   *JC*

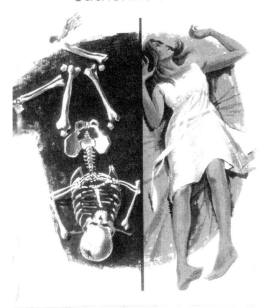

Margery Allingham (1904–1966) **a.k.a. Maxwell March**

Margery Allingham was a writer of high talent, whose work was intended for 'the connoisseur of detective fiction'. A vivacious narrator and a masterly contriver, she moved with the times and continually tested her considerable range. From her early fantastical phase, she went on to bring to the mystery the refinements of the novel of manners. After the war, her work gained remarkably in density and depth.

She wrote twenty-four crime novels, three of which appeared under the pseudonym Maxwell March. Of her sixty mystery stories, two only have not appeared in a collection. Her last novel, *Cargo of Eagles*, was completed after her death by her husband, Philip Youngman Carter, who also continued her series with two elegant, idiomatic sequels. There are eight story collections, two books of paired novellas, three significant omnibus volumes and a long magazine story. At least four books first appeared in the USA: *Black Plumes, Deadly Duo, The China Governess*, and *The Mind Readers*. Nineteen of the novels and thirty-one of the stories feature Albert Campion, Miss Allingham's high-born detective, one of the subtlest operators in the field, whose understated portrait by Youngman Carter appears on the wrapper of *Mr. Campion and Others*. Although long-established as a major figure, he is still not as widely celebrated as he should be. The Lady Amanda Fitton, Magersfontein Lugg, Stanislaus Oates, and Charlie Luke are others who recur, to memorable effect. The three Maxwell March novels are romantic thrillers in a more lurid vein than the Allingham books. They are none the less the work of a professional, written to formula under strict editorial supervision, for serialization in *Answers*.

Four books were published by Jarrolds between 1928 and 1931. *The White Cottage Mystery* has a purple binding with orange lettering on the spine and front cover. There are decorative orange bands at each end of the spine and the front cover has a decorative orange border. At the rear is an advertisement section dated Spring 1928. *The Crime at Black Dudley* is not available at the BL, but a helpful correspondent reports that it has a pinkish-tan binding, with black lettering on the spine and front cover, the latter with a decorative black border. *Mystery Mile* is red with black lettering and *Look to the Lady* black with green lettering, on the spine only in each case. All four books are undated. *Mystery Mile* has one map and *Look to the Lady* has two.

The only other undated book in the sequence is the story collection *Mr. Campion and Others*, which William Heinemann published in 1939. Heinemann was Margery Allingham's principal British publisher from 1931 to 1949, and eleven titles appeared under his imprint. They are variously coloured, both in binding and lettering, and all have blank front covers and the publisher's windmill on the back cover, usually blind-stamped but occasionally in the colour of the lettering. The black lettering of *Sweet Danger* is set against a red triangle. *The Fashion in Shrouds* is taller than the rest of the sequence. From *Police at the Funeral* to *Dancers in Mourning*, the books have stylish endpapers by Alan Gregory: of Socrates Court for *Police at the Funeral*; of Pontisbright for *Sweet Danger*; of the Lafcadio House in Little Venice for *Death of a Ghost*; of the Barnabas family tree for *Flowers for the Judge*; and of White Walls for *Dancers in Mourning*. He also drew the frontispiece of the Mill at Pontisbright for *Sweet Danger*. The unattributed endpapers of *More Work for the Undertaker* feature a map of Apron Street and its environs. This book is dated 1948 but did not, in fact, appear until February 1949.

The Fashion in Shrouds and *Mr. Campion and Others* have green endpapers. A blue binding for *Dancers in Mourning*, with gilt lettering, is also recorded.

The Case of the Late Pig came from Hodder & Stoughton in 1937 in a series of tall paperbacks called 'New at Ninepence'. It has a yellow cover, with the title and an unattributed illustration in blue. The spine is black with yellow lettering. The cover illustration recurs within, with a second, both preceding the text; and Effie Rowlandson's head from the repeated illustration is featured a third time on the title-page.

Except for the two books of novellas, which were issued by World's Work, a division of Heinemann, and a final round-up of stories from Hodder & Stoughton, Margery Allingham's later books were published by Chatto & Windus. The books in this sequence are taller than most of their predecessors. They have bindings in various colours but have gilt lettering in common, on the spine only. The title of *The China Governess* shows against a mauve background within a gilt framework. All three omnibus volumes are red. Besides completing *Cargo of Eagles*, Youngman Carter designed its wrapper and the splendid preliminary map of Saltey.

Both novella volumes have black spine lettering. *Take Two at Bedtime* is blue and *No Love Lost* is green. The former contains 'Wanted: Someone Innocent' and 'Last Act', and the latter 'The Patient at Peacocks Hall' and 'Safer than Love'. 'Uncle' Fred South, who recurs in *The Beckoning Lady*, makes his first appearance in 'Safer than Love'.

The Return of Mr. Campion, issued in 1989 by Hodder, is a blue book with gilt lettering on the spine.

The Doubleday edition of *Black Plumes* is a handsome yellow book with black lettering on the spine and a skeletal horse's head surmounted by black plumes, overlapping on to both covers. The front cover also has the Crime Club gunman and 'Crime Club Selection' in the upper right corner. The title-page is decorated with the horse's skull and the plumes, white like the lettering, within a black panel. The date is on the title-page and the copyright page states 'First edition'. *The China Governess* was published by Doubleday outside the Crime Club and has a red binding with gilt lettering along the spine. The title-page is both decorated and dated and the copyright page states 'First edition'. The fore-edge is roughly trimmed.

The Maxwell March novels were all published by Collins, the last in the Crime Club series. The earlier titles are mauve, with silver spine lettering; and the Crime Club book is orange, with black spine lettering. All three are dated.

The eight story collections contain fifty-seven stories within or edging on the genre and eight other items, with some overlapping. *Mr. Campion Criminologist*, *Wanted: Someone Innocent*, and *The Case Book of Mr. Campion* appeared only in America. *Mr. Campion Criminologist* includes *The Case of the Late Pig*, which was not then published separately in the USA. The other two are paperbacks: *Wanted: Someone Innocent*, no. 56 in the Pony Book series pub-

lished by Stamford House, and *The Case Book of Mr. Campion*, no. 12 of the Mercury Mysteries, published by Spivak, with an introduction by Ellery Queen. In Britain *Mr. Campion and Others* had two editions: the original Heinemann hardback of 1939, which contains fourteen stories, and the Penguin of 1950, which substitutes five new stories for six omitted from the earlier edition. 'The Danger Point' is collected only in the Penguin. *The Mystery Man of Soho* is a long story which appeared as no. 207 of the *Thriller* magazine in 1933, and recurs in *The Allingham Minibus* as 'A Quarter of a Million'. Thos. Knapp, well known to Campion, makes a solo appearance.

Both Chatto collections have stories collected for the first time and reprints from earlier collections. 'The Pioneers', in *The Allingham Minibus*, is not a crime story. *The Return of Mr. Campion* has entirely new material: four Campion stories, two essays about him, two ghost/horror stories and five others. Some textual revision is apparent in at least four stories: three with Campion – 'The Case is Altered', 'The Dog Day' and 'The Curious Affair in Nut Row' – and 'The Wind Glass'. The US edition has a brief 'introduction' by Agatha Christie. Many stories appear in more than one collection: 'The Borderline Case', for instance, is in no fewer than three. No story appears only in an American collection: but all the British collections contain at least one item that does not appear in any other volume.

Two American omnibus volumes merely reprint three novels apiece and are not important, but a late British series from Chatto & Windus has significant features: two otherwise uncollected stories, two introductions by the author, her heavily edited version of *The Fashion in Shrouds* and, after her death, an illuminating memoir by her husband. 'On Christmas Day in the Morning' is included in *The Mysterious Mr. Campion* and 'Word in Season', a brief fantasy adapted for Campion from a non-series original in *Tatler* for 11 Nov. 1955, in *Mr. Campion's Lady*.

Many Allingham novels were abridged at various times, and it is not always apparent that this is so. Penguin editions of *Mystery Mile* after 1968 have the abridged text that first appeared in *Mr.*

Campion's Clowns, and this also appears in *The Allingham Omnibus* of 1982. Some American paperbacks also have abridged text. Many of the books have variant titles in America; and *Pearls Before Swine* even has a different closing sentence from its British counterpart, *Coroner's Pidgin*.

In 1990 Youngman Carter's *Mr. Campion's Farthing* was issued in paperback by Carroll & Graf as 'Margery Allingham's *Mr. Campion's Farthing'*.

Most of the dust-wrappers for Margery Allingham's books were the work of her husband, who also contributed ideas and jokes to her narratives. Among much that is stylish and appealing, the design for *The Beckoning Lady* is especially memorable, focusing on the novel's most brilliant moment, as Tonker's macabre beauty masks float down the stream towards the house and the party.

Earlier images include the conjuror and the red chess knight for *Mystery Mile*; the map of Sanctuary for *Look to the Lady*; the question-mark of mourners for *Police at the Funeral*; the invitation card for Campion over the portrait of John Lafcadio for *Death of a Ghost*; the judge with his nosegay for *Flowers for the Judge*; a funereal dancer for *Dancers in Mourning*; and horse-drawn funeral carriages for both *Black Plumes* and *More Work for the Undertaker*. The American *Black Plumes* has the skeletal horse, white with black plumes against a yellow background. In both editions of *The China Governess* the pottery group of Thyrza Caleb and her charges is portrayed, more plausibly in Youngman Carter's pastel shades than in Saul Lambert's harsher colours. Two of the March wrappers are signed by Youngman Carter. That for *Rogues' Holiday* shows the moment when Judy Wellington is transferred from her rowing boat to the dubious safety of her rescuer's boat; and that for *Shadow in the House* has a vivid portrait of Mary Coleridge, in blue. The lorries grimly assembled on the wrapper of *Traitor's Purse* are by C. W. Bacon and the Mephistophelean face from *Take Two at Bedtime* is by James McConnell.

Room to Let is an original radio play, broadcast on 12 November 1947. It combines a locked room mystery with Jack the Ripper and was adapted as a film.

Novels by Margery Allingham

(With Campion, except as stated. Details of bindings and letterings refer to British editions.)

The White Cottage Mystery   Jarrolds n.d. (1928), Carroll & Graf 1990 (abridged) (not Campion)

The Crime at Black Dudley   Jarrolds n.d. (1929) a.k.a. *The Black Dudley Murder* Doubleday 1930

Mystery Mile   Jarrolds n.d. (1930), Doubleday 1930

Look to the Lady   Jarrolds n.d. (1931) a.k.a. *The Gyrth Chalice Mystery* Doubleday 1931

Police at the Funeral   Heinemann 1931, Doubleday 1932 (blue binding, yellow lettering)

Sweet Danger   Heinemann 1933 (pale yellow) a.k.a. *Kingdom of Death*   Doubleday 1933 a.k.a. *The Fear Sign*   McFadden 1961

Death of a Ghost   Heinemann 1934, Doubleday 1934 (blue, silver)

Flowers for the Judge Heinemann 1936, Doubleday 1936 (red, gilt) a.k.a *Legacy in Blood*   Mercury 1949

Dancers in Mourning Heinemann 1937, Doubleday 1937 (black, gilt) a.k.a. *Who Killed Chloe?*   Avon 1943

The Case of the Late Pig   Hodder & Stoughton 1937, Avon 1989

The Fashion in Shrouds Heinemann 1938, Doubleday 1938 (green, gilt)

Black Plumes Doubleday Oct. 1940, Heinemann Nov. 1940 (not Campion) (fawn, black)

Traitor's Purse Heinemann 1941, Doubleday 1941 (orange, black) a.k.a. *The Sabotage Murder Mystery*   Avon 1942

Coroner's Pidgin Heinemann 1945 (black, silver) a.k.a. *Pearls Before Swine*   Doubleday 1945

More Work for the Undertaker Heinemann 1948, Doubleday 1949 (black, silver)

The Tiger in the Smoke   Chatto & Windus 1952 Doubleday 1952 (red binding)

The Beckoning Lady   Chatto 1955 (blue)
a.k.a. *The Estate of the Beckoning Lady* Doubleday 1955
Hide My Eyes   Chatto 1958 (orange)
a.k.a. *Tether's End*   Doubleday 1958
a.k.a. *Ten Were Missing*   Dell 1961
The China Governess   Doubleday 1962, Chatto
   1963 (sage)
The Mind Readers   Morrow 1965, Chatto 1965
   (black)
Cargo of Eagles   Chatto 1968, Morrow 1968
   (mauve) (completed by Youngman Carter)

Campion novels by Youngman Carter

Mr. Campion's Farthing   Heinemann 1969,
   Morrow 1969
Mr. Campion's Falcon   Heinemann 1970
a.k.a. *Mr. Campion's Quarry*   Morrow 1971

Novels by Maxwell March

Other Man's Danger   Collins 1933
a.k.a. *The Man of Dangerous Secrets*   Doubleday 1933
Rogues' Holiday   Collins 1935, Doubleday 1935
The Shadow in the House   Collins Crime Club
   1936, Doubleday 1936

Story and novella collections

Mr. Campion: Criminologist   Doubleday 1937
   (*The Case of the Late Pig*   and 6 Campion
   stories)
Mr. Campion and Others   Heinemann n.d.
   (1939) (14 stories, 9 with Campion) (green,
   gilt)
Wanted: Someone Innocent   Stamford House
   1946 (1 novella and 3 stories)
The Case Book of Mr. Campion   Spivak 1947
   (7 Campion stories)
Deadly Duo   Doubleday 1949 (2 novellas)
a.k.a. *Take Two at Bedtime*   World's Work 1950
Mr. Campion and Others   Penguin 1950 (13
   Campion stories)
No Love Lost   World's Work 1954, Doubleday
   1954 (2 novellas)
The Allingham Casebook   Chatto 1969,

Morrow 1969 (18 stories, 10 with Campion)
   (light brown binding)
The Allingham Minibus   Chatto 1973, Morrow
   1973 (18 stories, 3 with Campion) (mauve)
a.k.a. *Mr. Campion's Lucky Day*   Penguin 1992,
   Carroll & Graf 1992
The Return of Mr. Campion   Hodder 1989, St
   Martin's 1990 (13 items, 6 with Campion)

Magazine story

'The Mystery Man of Soho' (Amalgamated
   Press, 1 Apr. 1933)
a.k.a. 'A Quarter of a Million' (in *The Allingham
   Minibus*)

Omnibus volumes

The Mysterious Mr. Campion   Chatto & Windus
   1963
Mr. Campion's Lady   Chatto 1965
Mr. Campion's Clowns   Chatto 1967, with a
   memoir by Youngman Carter

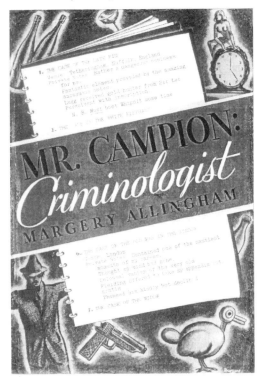

Uncollected stories

'A Proper Mystery' (*Town and Country Review*, July 1946; *MacKill's*, Feb. 1954; *Essex Countryside*, Oct. 1986)

'The Day of the Demon' (1951; *Essex Countryside*, Nov. 1986)   *BP*

Marian Babson

Marian Babson is the pseudonym of a writer whose thirty-four novels to date display a refreshing variety of storylines and settings. Douglas Perkins, a public relations officer, appears in four books. A pair of elderly actresses, Evangeline Sinclair and Trixie Dolan, play detective in four more. *A Trail of Ashes* and *Death Swap* are linked books involving holiday house-swapping between an English and an American family and the crimes that they become involved in. Two books, *Tourists are for*

Trapping and *In the Teeth of Adversity*, were published in the USA by St Martin's, both with black cloth and gilt spine lettering. Otherwise the books were all first published in London by Collins Crime Club in red cloth with gilt lettering on the spine. They are all dated and have printers' keys on the copyright page from *Shadows in their Blood*. Some books, like *Queue Here for Murder*, have alternative titles in America, and seven titles have been published only in Britain. All the dust-wrappers are of the modern photographic type.

Novels

(with Perkins or Sinclair and Dolan, as stated)

Cover-up Story   Collins Crime Club 1971, St Martin's 1988 (Perkins)

Murder on Show   Crime Club 1972 (Perkins)
a.k.a. *Murder at the Cat Show*   St Martin's 1989

Pretty Lady   Crime Club 1973

The Stalking Lamb   Crime Club 1974

Unfair Exchange   Crime Club 1974, Walker 1986

Murder Sails at Midnight   Crime Club 1975

There Must Be Some Mistake   Crime Club 1975, St Martin's 1987

Untimely Guest   Crime Club 1976

The Lord Mayor of Death   Crime Club 1977, Walker 1979

Murder, Murder, Little Star   Crime Club 1977, Walker 1980

Tightrope for Three   Crime Club 1978, Walker 1990

So Soon Done For   Crime Club 1979, Walker 1988

The Twelve Deaths of Christmas   Crime Club 1979, Walker 1980

Dangerous to Know   Crime Club 1980, Walker 1981

Queue Here for Murder   Crime Club 1980
a.k.a. *Line Up for Murder*   Walker 1981

Bejewelled Death   Crime Club 1981, Walker 1982

Death Warmed Up   Crime Club 1982, Walker 1982

Death Beside the Seaside   Crime Club 1982
a.k.a. *Death Beside the Sea*   Walker 1983

A Fool for Murder   Crime Club 1983, Walker 1984

The Cruise of a Deathtime   Crime Club 1983, Walker 1984

A Trail of Ashes   Crime Club 1984, Walker 1985

Death Swap   Crime Club 1984, Walker 1985

Death in Fashion   Crime Club 1985, Walker 1985

Weekend for Murder   Crime Club 1985

a.k.a. *Murder on a Mystery Tour*   Walker 1987

Reel Murder   Crime Club 1986, St Martin's 1987 (Sinclair & Dolan)

Fatal Fortune   Crime Club 1987

Guilty Party   Crime Club 1988, St Martin's 1991

Encore Murder   Crime Club 1989, St Martin's 1990 (Sinclair & Dolan)

Tourists are for Trapping   St Martin's 1989 (Perkins)

Past Regret   Crime Club 1990, St Martin's 1992

In the Teeth of Adversity   St Martin's 1990 (Perkins)

Shadows in their Blood   Crime Club 1991, St Martin's 1993 (Sinclair & Dolan)

Nine Lives to Murder   Crime Club 1992

Even Yuppies Die   Crime Club 1993 (Sinclair & Dolan)   *JC*

H. C. Bailey (1878–1961)

H. C. Bailey's lasting fame rests securely on his twelve collections of Reggie Fortune stories, which are remarkable: complex and oblique, with an elegant surface and a savage undertow. Besides the eighty-four collected stories, there are nine Fortune novels and an uncollected story in which he appears – 'The Thistle Down' – so that the total number of his investigations is ninety-four. Eleven novels involve Joshua Clunk, a tricky lawyer given to praising the Lord, and there is one non-series novel. No Clunk stories are recorded.

Bailey began with Methuen, who published four Mr Fortune collections and the first Clunk novel, *Garstons*. All five books have title and author blind-stamped on the front cover, within a matching decorative framework. On the spines, these features recur in gilt. *Call Mr. Fortune* is blue and the others are red (but a blue variant for *Garstons* is also known). Conflicting claims

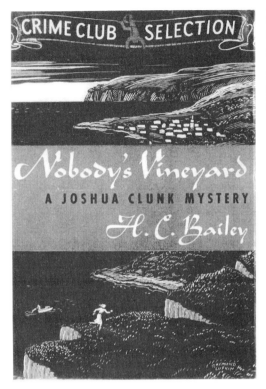

bedevil the date of *Call Mr. Fortune*, which is generally on record as 1920. The BL copy is so dated and is also stamped with the accession date: 31 January 1920. At the end of the book a further date – 27/6/19 – suggests that printing was completed six months ahead of publication in January 1920. However, at least one reissue of the book puts initial publication in January 1919, and the Fortune omnibus of 1936 asserts that Reggie 'made his bow to the public in 1919' specifying as the exact date of his debut 29 January in that year. In the absence of a copy actually dated 1919, it is not easy to accept these claims.

Mr. Fortune's Practice is dated only by the publisher, but the three later Methuen books also have a printer's code at the end, which should accord with the publisher's dating. If *Mr. Fortune's Trials* has 1026, it cannot be a true first edition, since the book came out in 1925. The first-edition code is 425: 1026 indicates the October printing of the cheap edition of January 1927, as does the grey binding. The code for *Mr. Fortune, Please* is 1026 and for *Garstons* 530.

Mr. Fortune's Practice is known with varying undated advertisement sections at the rear. Priority between or among these remains a moot point.

Ward Lock also published four Fortune collections and a Clunk novel, *The Red Castle*. The Fortune books all have dark bindings of green or greenish-brown, but the novel, appropriately, is red. All five have black spine lettering, with title and author and a border, also in black, on the front cover. The publisher's device on the cover features only on later issues, and red bindings for the Fortune books generally indicate a later printing. However, a red variant of *Case for Mr. Fortune* and an orange variant of *The Red Castle* are known, each identical to the accepted first edition in every other respect. *The Man in the Cape*, the non-series book, was published by Benn in 1933. It is red, with black lettering on the spine.

The first Fortune novel, *Shadow on the Wall*, was published in 1934 by Gollancz, who brought out fifteen more of Bailey's books, the last, *Slippery Ann*, in 1944. From *Shadow on the Wall* to *Mr. Fortune Here* the series is black, with orange lettering on the spine: black lettering on a red or blue binding indicates a later issue. From *The Bishop's Crime*, the books are blue, at first with dark blue lettering, but from *Mr. Fortune Finds a Pig* with gilt.

Many Gollancz reissues are identified internally, and the disappearance of the date from the title-page is a further sign of a later impression.

Bailey's last publisher was Macdonald, who issued the final run of six novels, which appear to exist in first-edition form only. Five have silver spine lettering, but *Shrouded Death* has black. *Honour Among Thieves* also has black decoration and *Saving a Rope* has a representation of a noose, in black. *Dead Man's Effects* and *The Wrong Man* are black books, *Saving a Rope* is blue, and the others are red. Except for *Dead Man's Effects* and *The Wrong Man*, all Bailey's British first editions are dated. All the books are of uniform size.

The US editions are the true firsts of two of Bailey's books: *The Cat's Whisker* and *The Wrong Man*. The text of the former was revised for British publication as *Dead Man's Effects*, and there are textual differences between the two editions of *The Wrong Man*. Most of the Clunk novels were retitled for the American market. The Doubleday edition of *Mr. Fortune Wonders* is illustrated by Frederic Dorr Steele.

In addition to his own eleven cases, Mr Clunk figures in two of Reggie's: briefly in *The Great Game*, and very briefly in *Shadow on the Wall*. In his turn, Reggie is called on in the course of *Clunk's Claimant*, *The Veron Mystery* and *The Wrong Man*, which are Clunk cases. The Hon. Sidney Lomas and Superintendent Bell of Scotland Yard are featured throughout, happier, in the main, with Reggie than with Josh, but frequently exasperated by both. The blurb for *The Red Castle* promotes Bell as the central figure, suggesting that Mr Clunk was not originally intended as an alternative series character to Mr Fortune, but took matters into his own hands.

Many of Bailey's dust-wrappers are victims of the yellow peril dictated by Victor Gollancz, but his earlier and later publishers were, blessedly, less austere. Frank Wright's design for *Mr. Fortune's Practice* illustrates 'The Unknown Murderer', and shows Reggie grappling with his improbable temporary chauffeur. Abbey's wrapper for *Mr. Fortune Speaking* has him with a telephone to his ear, with a frieze of shady characters beyond him; and for *Mr. Fortune Explains* the same artist involves him in a further struggle, as 'The Picnic' approaches its climax. *The Red Castle* has the castle looming in the background and the Luel Cup prominent in the foreground. *Mr. Fortune Wonders* has an elegant view of Reggie in an armchair, in conversation with a standing woman, surely his wife Joan. The artist, John Campbell, shows him on the spine in sleek, handsome profile, his hands up at his lapels. Reggie looks benign on the jaunty wrapper for *Dead Man's Effects*, while his associates peer bemusedly at a set of false teeth. The other Macdonald books have wrappers by Stein in a uniform style. *Shrouded Death* shows Josh lurking outside the Kottos factory, while a veiled figure drifts provocatively past.

Novels

(with Fortune or Clunk, as stated)

Garstons Methuen July 1930 (Clunk)
a.k.a. *The Garston Murder Case* Doubleday 1930
The Red Castle Ward Lock Sept. 1932 (Clunk)
a.k.a. *The Red Castle Mystery* Doubleday 1932
The Man in the Cape Benn Oct. 1933
Shadow on the Wall Gollancz 1934; Doubleday 1934 (Fortune)
The Sullen Sky Mystery Gollancz Sept. 1935, Doubleday 1935 (Clunk)
Black Land, White Land Gollancz Jan. 1937, Doubleday 1937 (Fortune)
Clunk's Claimant Gollancz Sept. 1937 (Clunk)
a.k.a. *The Twittering Bird Mystery* Doubleday 1937
The Great Game Gollancz Feb. 1939, Doubleday 1939 (Fortune)
The Veron Mystery Gollancz June 1939 (Clunk)
a.k.a. *Mr. Clunk's Text* Doubleday 1939
The Bishop's Crime Gollancz 1940, Doubleday 1941 (Fortune)
The Little Captain Gollancz 1941 (Clunk)
a.k.a. *Orphan Ann* Doubleday 1941
No Murder Gollancz 1942 (Fortune)
a.k.a. *The Apprehensive Dog* Doubleday 1942
Dead Man's Shoes Gollancz 1942 (Clunk)
a.k.a. *Nobody's Vineyard* Doubleday 1942
Mr. Fortune Finds a Pig Gollancz 1943, Doubleday 1943 (Fortune)
Slippery Ann Gollancz 1944 (Clunk)
a.k.a. *The Queen of Spades* Doubleday 1944
The Cat's Whisker Doubleday 1944 (Fortune)
a.k.a. *Dead Man's Effects* Macdonald n.d. (1945)
The Wrong Man Doubleday 1945, Macdonald n.d. (1946) (Clunk)
The Life Sentence Macdonald 1946, Doubleday 1946 (Fortune)
Honour Among Thieves Macdonald 1947, Doubleday 1947 (Clunk)
Saving a Rope Macdonald 1948 (Fortune)
a.k.a. *Save a Rope* Doubleday 1948
Shrouded Death Macdonald 1950 (Clunk)

Fortune story collections

Call Mr. Fortune Methuen 1920, Dutton 1921 (6 stories)
Mr. Fortune's Practice Methuen 1923, Dutton 1924 (7 stories)
Mr. Fortune's Trials Methuen 1925, Dutton 1926 (6 stories)
Mr. Fortune, Please Methuen 1927, Dutton 1928 (6 stories)
Mr. Fortune Speaking Ward Lock 1929, Dutton 1931 (8 stories)
Mr. Fortune Explains Ward Lock April 1930, Dutton 1931 (8 stories)
Case for Mr. Fortune Ward Lock May 1932, Doubleday 1932 (8 stories)
Mr. Fortune Wonders Ward Lock Nov. 1933, Doubleday 1933 (8 stories)
Mr. Fortune Objects Gollancz Apr. 1935, Doubleday 1935 (6 stories)
Clue for Mr. Fortune Gollancz 1936 (6 stories)
a.k.a. *A Clue for Mr. Fortune* Doubleday 1936
This is Mr. Fortune Gollancz 1938, Doubleday 1938 (6 stories)
Mr. Fortune Here Gollancz 1940, Doubleday 1940 (9 stories)

Uncollected stories

'The Country Cottage' (*Grand*, Aug. 1921)
'A Good Place' (*Pan*, Jan. 1922)
'Mr. Bowley's Sunday Evening' (*Detection Medley*, Hutchinson n.d. (1939); *Rogue's Gallery*, Little, Brown 1945, Faber 1947)
'The Thistle Down' (*The Queen's Book of the Red Cross*, Hodder & Stoughton 1939; *EQMM*, May 1943)
'Victoria Pumphrey' (*Holly Leaves*: Christmas Number of *The Illustrated Sporting and Dramatic News*, 1939; *EQMM*, Feb. 1961 and *EQA*, mid-year 1968, Davis 1968 as 'A Matter of Speculation') *BP*

Robert Barnard (b. 1936)
a.k.a. Bernard Bastable

Robert Barnard is a fluent, engaging writer of light, lively detective fiction, notable for a waspish narrative manner. He has three series detectives, all policemen: Idwal Meredith, an agreeable Welshman; Perry Trethowan, a rather laid-back aristocrat; and Mike Oddie, a more robust figure than either of his predecessors. His earlier work was published by the Crime Club, who brought out twenty-four novels and a collection of sixteen stories, the first in 1974, the last in 1989. From 1990 he has been with Bantam, who have published the Oddie novels. A pseudonymous series, as by Bernard Bastable, was launched by Macmillan in 1993, with *To Die like a Gentleman*. The Crime Club books are red with gilt lettering on the spine, the date on the copyright page and routine photographic wrappers of minimal interest. *Death of a Chaste Apprentice* and *Death of a Salesperson* are taller than the rest. According to Ralph Spurrier in Post Mortem Books' Catalogue 33, *At Death's Door* was published in August 1988 at £9.95 and reprinted in October that year for reissue in January 1989. A revised price of £10.95 is the only indication of the reissue. *A Scandal in*

Belgravia has a blue binding; *A City of Strangers* and *A Fatal Attachment* are red. All three have gilt spine lettering and white wrappers in a uniform style with attractive illustrations by Gary Benfield. *A Hovering of Vultures* is blue with gilt lettering on the spine and a blue photographic wrapper. The Bantam books have dated copyright pages. *To Die like a Gentleman* is grey with gilt lettering on the spine, dated copyright page and a printer's key, 10–1. Several books have variant US titles, invariably less subtle than the British. One of the uncollected stories features Perry Trethowan: 'The Dangling Man'.

Novels

(with Trethowan, Meredith or Oddie, as stated)

Death of an Old Goat Collins Crime Club 1974, Walker 1977

A Little Local Murder Crime Club 1976, Scribner 1983

Death on the High C's Crime Club 1977, Walker 1978

Blood Brotherhood Crime Club 1977, Walker 1978

Unruly Son Crime Club 1978 (Meredith)
a.k.a. *Death of a Mystery Writer* Scribner 1979

Posthumous Papers Crime Club 1979
a.k.a. *Death of a Literary Widow* Scribner 1980

Death in a Cold Climate Crime Club 1980, Scribner 1981

Mother's Boys Crime Club 1981
a.k.a. *Death of a Perfect Mother* Scribner 1981

Sheer Torture Crime Club 1981 (Trethowan)
a.k.a. *Death by Sheer Torture* Scribner 1982

Death and the Princess Crime Club 1982, Scribner 1982 (Trethowan)

The Missing Bronte Crime Club 1983 (Trethowan)
a.k.a. *The Case of the Missing Bronte* Scribner 1983

Little Victims Crime Club 1983
a.k.a. *School for Murder* Scribner 1984

A Corpse in a Gilded Cage Crime Club 1984, Scribner 1984

Out of the Blackout Crime Club 1985, Scribner 1985

The Disposal of the Living Crime Club 1985

a.k.a. *Fete Fatale*   Scribner 1985

Political Suicide   Crime Club 1986, Scribner 1986

Bodies   Crime Club 1986, Scribner 1986 (Trethowan)

Death in Purple Prose   Crime Club 1987 (Trethowan)

a.k.a. *The Cherry Blossom Corpse*   Scribner 1987

The Skeleton in the Grass   Crime Club 1987, Scribner 1988

At Death's Door   Crime Club 1988, Scribner 1988 (Meredith)

Death and the Chaste Apprentice   Crime Club Oct. 1989, Scribner 1989

A City of Strangers   Bantam 1990, Scribner 1990 (Oddie)

A Scandal in Belgravia   Bantam 1991, Scribner 1991

A Fatal Attachment   Bantam 1992, Scribner 1992 (Oddie)

A Hovering of Vultures   Bantam 1993, Scribner 1993 (Oddie)

Story collection

Death of a Salesperson   Crime Club Jan. 1989, Scribner 1990

Novel as Bernard Bastable

To Die like a Gentleman   Macmillan 1993, St Martin's 1993

Uncollected stories

'Happy Christmas' (*Ellery Queen's Prime Crimes 4*, Davis 1986; *Crime Waves 1*, Gollancz 1991)

'Perfect Honeymoon' (*EQMM*, Aug. 1987; *Murder Takes a Holiday*, O'Mara 1989)

'More Final than Divorce' (*EQMM*, Oct. 1988; *Under the Gun*, NAL 1990)

'The Face of Violence' (*EQMM*, Feb. 1989)

'Not Much of a Life' (*EQMM*, Mar. 1989)

'Post Mortem' (*EQMM*, May 1989; *Winter's Crimes 21*, Macmillan 1989)

'Divine Anger' (*EQMM*, July 1989)

'Family Ties' (*New Crimes*, Robinson 1989; *EQMM*, Dec. 1989 as 'A Good Turn')

'The Nick of Time' (*EQMM*, Jan. 1990)

'An Exceptional Night' (*EQMM*, Mar. 1990)

'Cupid's Dart' (*EQMM*, May 1990)

'Good Time Had by All' (*A Classic English Crime*, Pavilion 1990)

'The Dangling Man' (*A Suit of Diamonds*, Crime Club 1990)

'Living with Jimmy' (*Winter's Crimes 22*, Macmillan 1990; *EQMM*, Nov. 1990)

'The Stuff of Nightmares' (*EQMM*, Dec. 1990; *Midwinter Mysteries 1*, Scribner 1991)

'The Habit of Widowhood' (*EQMM*, July 1991; *Winter's Crimes 23*, Macmillan 1991)

'A Political Necessity' (*Christmas Stalkings*, Mysterious Press 1991, Harper Collins 1992)

'A Child is Born' (*Woman*, 20 Jan. 1992)

'A Sure-fire Speculation' (*Northern Blood*, Didsbury Press 1992; *EQMM*, June 1992)

'Soldier from the Wars Returning' (*1st Culprit*, Chatto & Windus 1992)

'A Hotel in Bucharest' (*EQMM*, mid-Dec. 1992)

'Balmorality' (*EQMM*, Feb. 1993; *Royal Crimes*, Penguin (US) 1994)

'A Statesman's Touch' (*EQMM*, Mar. 1993; *Royal Crimes*, Penguin (US) 1994)

'Dog Television' (*Malice Domestic 2*, Pocket Books 1993)

'Keep Taking the Tabloids' (*2nd Culprit*, Chatto 1993)   *BP*

Josephine Bell (1897–1987)

In the forty-five years between 1937 and 1982, Josephine Bell published forty-three crime novels, on a wide range of themes and with varying success. Because she eschewed formula, her books lack the immediate reassurance of a familiar style and ambience (though several have a medical background, deriving from her own experience as a doctor). As she grew older, she dealt increasingly with the problems of elderly people under threat. Like Dorothy L. Sayers, she attended the Godolphin School at Salisbury. In *Murderess Ink* (Workman 1979), she recalls encounters with her fellow crime writer, both at school and later in life.

Twelve of her earlier novels feature a doctor,

David Wintringham, whom she abandoned after *The Seeing Eye* in 1958. Later she used a barrister, Claud Warrington-Reeve, for three books, and another doctor, Henry Frost, for two more. Her last detective is Amy Tupper, a doughty old actress whose investigations enliven her retirement. Steven Mitchell, the series policeman, collaborates with all except Miss Tupper, besides having an early case of his own. David Wintringham also features in at least twenty-one stories. He does not, however, appear in *Trouble at Wrekin Farm*, though listed as doing so by Allen Hubin, who was misled by a correspondent. This book features Ted Barnes and Elsie Little, who are also in *All is Vanity*.

Josephine Bell's first publishers were Longmans, Green, who brought out ten of her novels. Nine have title and author in bold capitals on the front cover, as well as on the spine. Binding and lettering colours vary, but this pattern is consistent. It is the mark of the true Longman firsts and any book without it must be a later

issue. The tenth book, *Death in Clairvoyance*, is green, with gilt spine lettering.

Five books from Methuen followed, in a uniform format, with gilt lettering in a scalloped framework on the spine. *Bones in the Barrow* is red, and the others are blue. In 1956 Hodder & Stoughton launched a long series of twenty-eight novels, with *The China Roundabout* one of only two books slightly taller than the rest (the other is *A Flat Tyre in Fulham*). The books in this sequence are bound in various colours, but they all have gilt lettering on the spine. All Josephine Bell's books are dated.

Murder in Hospital and *Death on the Borough Council* have uniform wrappers, each with a scene from the action within a circle placed centrally to the left of the panel.

Death at Half-Term, All Is Vanity, and *Trouble at Wrekin Farm* are also uniform, with emphatic lettering set against shades of blue, green, and yellow.

Death At the Medical Board breaks the pattern with a thematic design by Bruce Roberts; and two masked harlequins hint at the confusions of *Death in Clairvoyance*. Ramsay's wrapper for *The Summer School Mystery* features the timpani of the Falconbury School orchestra, and Oliver Carson's for *To Let. Furnished* shows an aspect of Wentworth Grange. Joan Kiddell Monroe designed the picturesque horses and riders for *The China Roundabout*, the sinister profiles for *Double Doom*, and the ladder over swirling water for *The House Above the River*. Auguste von Briesen's powerful design for *New People at the Hollies* shows Mr Coltman looking frightened in the garden of the nursing home. Victor Reinganum's elegant wrapper for *Death on the Reserve* creates a vivid pattern from an open-air scene, from a beach and birds and a runner on the sands.

A Flat Tyre in Fulham has two new titles in the USA, and the first US editions of four other novels are paperbacks. *The Alien* and *Backing Winds* are sometimes listed, wrongly, as crime fiction. *Crime in our Time* (1961) is a true-crime study.

There are twenty-nine known stories, all uncollected. Twenty-one of them feature David Wintringham, often with Steven Mitchell, who is on his own in 'You Need the Luck for the Job'. The non-series items are 'Easy Money', 'The Sea Decides', 'A Case of Hiccups', 'The Commuters', 'The Unfinished Heart', 'The Alibi', and 'The Carol Singers'. A non-series novella, *The Silver Snuffbox*, originally in *Everywoman*, appeared in *AHMM*, mid-Dec. 1992.

Novels

(with Wintringham and/or others, as stated. Details of bindings refer to British editions.)

Murder in Hospital Longmans, Green 1937 (Wintringham) (yellow-brown binding, red lettering)

Death on the Borough Council Longman 1937 (Wintringham) (deep red, black)

Fall Over Cliff Longman 1938, Macmillan 1956 (Wintringham) (blue, black)

The Port of London Murders Longman 1938, Macmillan 1958 (Mitchell) (red, black)

Death at Half-term Longman 1939 (Wintringham) (blue, black)

a.k.a. *Curtain Call for a Corpse* Macmillan 1965, White Lion 1976

From Natural Causes Longman 1939 (Wintringham) (red, black)

All Is Vanity Longman 1940 (Wintringham, Barnes, Little) (blue, black)

Trouble at Wrekin Farm Longman 1942 (Barnes, Little) (yellow-brown, red)

Death at the Medical Board Longman 1944, Ballantine 1964 (Wintringham) (green, red)

Death in Clairvoyance Longman 1949 (Wintringham)

The Summer School Mystery Methuen 1950 (Wintringham)

To Let. Furnished Methuen 1952

a.k.a. *Stranger on a Cliff* Ace 1964

Bones in the Barrow Methuen 1953, Macmillan 1955 (Wintringham)

Fires at Fairlawn Methuen 1954

Death in Retirement Methuen 1956, Macmillan 1956

The China Roundabout Hodder & Stoughton 1956 (Wintringham) (blue binding)

a.k.a. *Murder on the Merry-go-round* Ballantine 1965

Double Doom Hodder 1957, Macmillan 1958 (dark blue)

The Seeing Eye Hodder 1958 (Wintringham) (dark blue)

The House Above the River Hodder 1959 (maroon)

Easy Prey Hodder 1959, Macmillan 1959 (Warrington-Reeve) (dark red)

A Well-Known Face Hodder 1960, Ives Washburn 1960 (Warrington-Reeve) (blue-green)

New People at the Hollies Hodder 1961, Macmillan 1961 (green)

Adventure with Crime Hodder 1962 (green)

A Flat Tyre in Fulham Hodder 1963 (Warrington-Reeve) (dark red)

a.k.a. *Fiasco in Fulham* Macmillan 1963

a.k.a. *Room for a Body* Ballantine 1964

The Hunter and the Trapped Hodder 1963 (orange)

The Upfold Witch Hodder 1964, Macmillan 1964 (Frost) (dark blue)

No Escape Hodder 1965, Macmillan 1966 (dark blue)

Death on the Reserve Hodder 1966, Macmillan 1966 (Frost) (dark blue)

The Catalyst Hodder 1966, Macmillan 1967 (dark blue)

Death of a Con Man Hodder 1968, Lippincott 1968 (maroon)

The Wilberforce Legacy Hodder 1969, Walker 1969 (green)

The Fennister Affair Hodder 1969, Stein & Day 1977 (black)

A Hydra with Six Heads Hodder 1970, Stein & Day 1977 (blue)

A Hole in the Ground Hodder 1971, Ace 1973 (blue)

Death of a Poison-Tongue Hodder 1972, Stein & Day 1977 (maroon)

A Pigeon Among the Cats Hodder 1974, Stein & Day 1977 (blue)

Victim Hodder 1975, Walker 1976 (black)

The Trouble in Hunter Ward Hodder 1976, Walker 1977 (red)

Such a Nice Client Hodder 1977 (blue)

a.k.a. *The Stroke of Death* Walker 1977

A Swan-Song Betrayed Hodder 1978 (maroon)

a.k.a. *Treachery in Type* Walker 1980

Wolf! Wolf! Hodder 1979, Walker 1980
(Tupper) (dark blue)

A Question of Inheritance Hodder 1980,
Walker 1981 (Tupper) (black)

The Innocent Hodder 1982 (blue-green)
a.k.a. *A Deadly Place to Stay* Walker 1983

Novella

The Silver Snuffbox (*AHMM*, mid-Dec. 1992)

Uncollected stories

'Gale Warning' (*ES*, 30 Nov. 1949; *The Evening Standard Detective Book* (*ESDB*), Gollancz 1950)

'Death in Ambrose Ward' (*ES*, 8 Dec. 1949; *ESDB*, Gollancz 1950)

"The Case of the Faulty Drier' (*ES*, 19 Dec. 1949; *ESDB*, Gollancz 1950; *The Mystery Bedside Book*, Hodder & Stoughton 1960, as 'Wash, Set – and Murder')

'Death in a Cage' (*ES*, 19 Jan. 1950; *ESDB*, Gollancz 1950)

'The Thimble River Murder' (*ES*, 8 May 1950; *ESDB*, Gollancz 1950; *Butcher's Dozen*, Heinemann 1956, as 'The Thimble River Mystery')

'The Surgeon's Towel' (*ES*, 29 June 1950)

'The Packet Boat Murder' (*ES*, 5 Oct. 1950; *ESDB*, series 2, Gollancz 1951)

'The Case of the Murdered Cellist' (*ES*, 19 Oct. 1950)

'The Fatal Concerto' (*ES*, 27 Dec. 1950)

'The Dead Bed' (*ES*, 17 Jan. 1951)

'Dead Man's Mouth' (*ES*, 18 May 1951)

'Man Overboard' (*ES*, 3 July 1951)

'The Missing Key' (*ES*, 6 Sept. 1951)

'Yacht in Distress' (*ES*, 28 Sept. 1951)

'Money Box Murder' (*ES*, 23 Feb. 1952)

'Death in a Crystal' (*ES*, 26 Apr. 1952)

'Man in the Water' (*ES*, 27 May 1953)

'Easy Money' (*ES*, 11 Jan. 1954)

'A Question of Fouling' (*JCMM*, Jan. 1957)

'You Need the Luck for the Job' (*JCMM*, Sept. 1958)

'The Sea Decides' (*Planned Departures*, Hodder 1958)

'A Case of Hiccups' (*EN*, 10 July 1961)

'The Unfinished Heart' (*EN*, 26 Sept. 1961; *John Creasey's Mystery Bedside Book 1974*, Hodder 1973)

'Follow My Leader' (*EN*, 20 Oct. 1961; *Crime Writer's Choice*, Hodder 1964, as 'A Case of Fugue')

'Murder Delayed' (*EN*, 1 Dec. 1961; *Crimes Across the Sea*, Harper 1964, Harrap 1965)

'Experiment – If You Want to Learn the Exact Truth' (*ES*, 11 June 1964; *Saint*, Oct. 1965 (UK) as 'Experiment')

'The Carol Singers' (*Illustrated London News*, 16 Nov. 1964; *John Creasey's Crime Collection 1979*, Gollancz 1979)

'The Commuters' (*EWMM*, Oct. 1965; *John Creasey's Mystery Bedside Book*, Hodder 1966)

'The Alibi' (*John Creasey's Mystery Bedside Book 1975*, Hodder 1974)   *BP*

E. C. Bentley (1875–1956)

Despite the paucity of his output, E. C. Bentley is assured of classic status by his first book, *Trent's Last Case*. He wrote three more books and three uncollected stories, and contributed to two short novels, collectively written by members of the Detection Club (q.v.).

It is not clear from published sources whether the British or the American edition of *Trent's Last Case* is the true first; and by leaving the book undated, Nelson may have done its students a disservice. A. E. Murch, in *The Development of the Detective Novel* (1958), asserts that the 'original publishers' were 'the Century Company of New York', who brought it out in 1912, under the title *The Woman in Black*. She further states that the British edition did not appear until March 1913, with the title *Trent's Last Case*. *CC* reverses these dates, assigning the British edition to 1912 and the American to 1913. In his introduction to the Mystery Library edition of 1977, Aaron Marc Stein claims that the book 'was published in both countries in March 1913'. The BL copy of the Nelson edition is stamped 29 March 1913, but the *ECB* gives the publication date as 13 February 1913.

Nelson bound the book handsomely in blue, with title and author blind-stamped on the front cover, within an elaborate decorative framework

written in collaboration with H. Warner Allen, whose own detective, the oenophile Mr Clerihew, figures briefly in the action. It is an orange book, dated within and with ornate blue lettering on both cover and spine. The top edge is coloured blue. Though the title-page accords equal status to both authors, Warner Allen's name is less prominent on the cover and spine and much reduced on the wrapper. A later issue of the first edition gives both men identical prominence at all points on the book itself. On the cover and spine the co-author is named as 'Warner Allen', but he retains his preliminary 'H.' on the title-page. The later issue also has a tipped-in note of apology to the Association for Moral and Social Hygiene, regarding a reference on page 160 which might forgiveably be 'taken to reflect upon the reputation of the Association or those concerned with it'.

Trent Intervenes collects twelve of Trent's shorter cases. It is a blue book, dated June 1938 and lettered in white on the spine. The wrapper shows Trent and Mrs Langley gazing at 'the genuine tabard' that gives its name to the first story in the collection.

Elephant's Work, a late non-series thriller, variously regarded, is dated 1950 and bound in maroon, with white lettering on the spine. The plain dust-wrapper is by Roy Sanford.

The uncollected stories are a parody of Dorothy L. Sayers called 'Greedy Night'; 'The Ministering Angel', a Trent story; and 'The Feeble Folk', described by Charles Shibuk as 'more horror than crime fiction'. For its original appearance, 'Greedy Night' was illustrated by the author's son Nicolas, a prolific graphic artist, who also wrote crime fiction in the course of his career. Regrettably the American omnibus, *Trent's Case Book*, missed the chance to take in 'The Ministering Angel'. The late story 'Flying Visit' (*ES*, 31 Mar. 1953) is not crime fiction.

Bentley contributed to both novels written by members of the Detection Club for serial broadcasting in 1930 and 1931. The episodes were published in *The Listener*: Chapter 5 of *Behind the Screen* on 16 July 1930 and Chapters 3 and 8 of *The Scoop* on 28 January and 11 March 1931. The episode for *Behind the Screen* is untitled, but the chapters for *The Scoop* have

extending over most of the surface. The spine has gilt lettering and a further blind-stamped decorative panel. As frontispiece the book has a portrait by Hickling of Mrs Manderson as Trent first sees her, 'her arms about her drawn-up knees, her eyes fixed on the trailing smoke of a distant liner, her face full of some dream'. This portrait also features on the dust-wrapper. The endpapers disconcertingly suggest a series reissue rather than a first edition; and there is a dedicatory letter to G. K. Chesterton. In his bibliography to the Mystery Library volume, Charles Shibuk records a revised edition, published by Knopf in 1929 and by Nelson in 1936, though without specifying the nature of the revisions. Another view of Mabel Manderson, this time with Trent on the cliff above her, appears on the wrapper of *The Woman in Black*.

Trent's Own Case appeared in 1936 and was

names attached: 'Fisher's Alibi' and 'The Sad Truth About Potts'.

Trent books

Trent's Last Case   Nelson n.d. (1913)
a.k.a. *The Woman in Black*   Century 1913
Trent's Own Case   Constable 1936, Knopf 1936 with H. Warner Allen
Trent Intervenes   Nelson 1938, Knopf 1938 (12 stories)

Other novel

Elephant's Work   Hodder & Stoughton 1950, Knopf 1950
a.k.a. *The Chill*   Dell 1953

Novels with other members of the Detection Club (q.v.)

The Scoop and *Behind the Screen* Gollancz 1983

Uncollected stories

'Greedy Night' (*Parody Party*, Hutchinson 1936; *EQMM*, Jan. 1943; *Lord Peter*, Harper 1972)
'Trent and the Ministering Angel' (*Strand*, Nov. 1938; *EQMM*, Sept. 1943 and *To the Queen's Taste*, Little, Brown 1946, Faber 1949 as 'The Ministering Angel')
'The Feeble Folk' (*EQMM*, Mar. 1953)   BP

Anthony Berkeley (A. B. Cox (1893–1971)) a.k.a. A. Monmouth Platts a.k.a. Francis Iles

Anthony Berkeley Cox used his own name for one crime novel, but generally wrote under pseudonyms. He produced nineteen novels and twelve uncollected stories, besides contributing to five collaborations written by various members of the Detection Club (of which he was the founder).

As Anthony Berkeley he wrote several outstanding detective novels, including *The Poisoned Chocolates Case, Murder in the Basement*, and *Trial and Error*. He created two amateur sleuths who figure in several of his books. Roger

Sheringham, popular novelist turned amateur detective, appears in ten novels and five stories. At the beginning of his career he is rather offensive, but in the later books he has mellowed to become a well-liked champion of justice. A confirmed bachelor, the nervous, mouse-like Ambrose Chitterwick features in three novels. He pops out of his quiet house, solves the problems with his quick intellect, and then retreats to comfortable obscurity once again. Inspector Moresby of Scotland Yard figures in six novels and four stories, once on his own.

As Francis Iles, A. B. Cox wrote three novels, two of which, *Malice Aforethought* and *Before the Fact*, are brilliant inverted tales. As A. Monmouth Platts he wrote one mystery novel, *Cicely Disappears*, which was not published in the USA. It originally appeared as a serialised competition story in the *Daily Mirror* from 1 Mar. to 6 Apr. 1926 as 'The Wintringham Mystery' by A. B. Cox. *Mr. Priestley's Problem* was issued under his own name. The books in all four names were first published in London. Several have variant titles in the USA.

The first Anthony Berkeley novel, *The Layton Court Mystery*, was written anonymously and published by Herbert Jenkins in a green pictorial cloth. The spine and front cover are lettered in black. Also featured in black on the front cover are four men pushing at a door. The book is dated MCMXXV on the title-page. It was issued in an attractive wrapper which shows a hand reaching out towards a window-latch.

The next three Berkeley books and the Cox book *Mr. Priestley's Problem* were all published by Collins in blue cloth, lettered in red on the spine and front cover. *The Wychford Poisoning Case* and *Roger Sheringham and the Vane Mystery* have a double red border on the front cover and at the top and base of the spine, and the others have a single red border. Pale blue cloth with black lettering indicates a later issue. All four books are dated on the reverse of the title page. *The Wychford Poisoning Case* was, again, written anonymously, though the author is identified on the spine and front cover as having written *The Layton Court Mystery. The Poisoned Chocolates Case* and *The Piccadilly Murder* were published by Collins in black cloth, lettered in red on the spine and front cover, which also has a red border. There are red rules at the head and foot of the spine. Both books are clearly dated. *The Piccadilly Murder* is the only Collins title by Berkeley without publishers' advertisements at the back. All the remaining Anthony Berkeley titles were published by Hodder & Stoughton, with one exception in blue cloth, with black lettering on the spine and the title in black on the front cover. The exception is the last book, *Death in the House*, which was first serialised in *John O'London's*. This has red cloth lettered gilt within a double gilt border towards the top of the spine. The first three Hodder books also have the initials A. B. in black in the lower right-hand corner of the front cover. There are two undated books in the Hodder series: *The Second Shot* and *Top Storey Murder*. The former was published with a pictorial front endpaper of a map of Minton Deeps Farm and the surrounding countryside. The supposed positions of various people at 3.30 p.m. are marked. This book also has eight pages of publisher's advertisements at the back. *Panic Party* and *Trial and Error* are slightly taller than the other titles. A new edition of *Trial and Error* with an introduction by the author was published by Penguin in 1947. The Doubleday edition of *Dead Mrs. Stratton* (*Jumping Jenny* in the UK) contains a short biography of Roger Sheringham, which is reproduced in the recent British edition with this title.

The first Francis Iles novel, *Malice Aforethought*, was published as a paperback in 1931 by Victor Gollancz, under the Mundanus imprint. It has yellow paper covers, fading to fawn, and is lettered in black on the spine and front cover, which also show the price of three shillings. The front cover also has an orange rectangle enclosing the title. A short résumé of the plot appears on the back cover. This paperback is the true first edition. A hardback edition was issued later, probably for libraries. It has orange cloth and is dated 1931, on the title-page. Unusually, the author is identified on the spine by his surname only. The book was issued in a yellow wrapper with 'Circulating Library Edition' printed at the top of the front panel.

Before the Fact was published by Gollancz in black cloth with green lettering on the spine. It is dated on the title-page and has the typical yellow wrapper. A copy with gilt lettering is reported.

The last Iles book was published by Jarrolds in black cloth with the spine lettered gilt. There is a blind-stamped vertical line on the front cover. The book is undated and was issued in a blue and yellow wrapper. Blue and orange cloth with black lettering are later issues. A revised edition of *Before the Fact* was published by Pan in 1958.

The book written under the pseudonym A. Monmouth Platts, *Cicely Disappears*, was published by John Long in red cloth, and dated on page 286. The spine is lettered in black with two black lines across its top and base. There is a double border blind-stamped on the front cover.

Ellen Edwards' wrapper for *The Wychford Poisoning Case* is dominated by a woman's face partly covered by a large blue hat, with two smaller scenes superimposed on the hat. E. P. produced a black and blue design of a hand, question mark and horror-stricken female for *Roger Sheringham and the Vane Mystery*. 'Nick' drew three men in black, silhouetted against a red background, for *Mr. Priestley's Problem*. C. Morse's wrapper for *The Silk Stocking Murders* has the title in large blue letters with the author's name in black and 'A Roger Sheringham Detective Novel' in blue. Beneath is an illustration of a man carrying a fainting woman in his arms. Beneath this is the Collins detective novels logo with a description of the book as 'The story of a crime which baffled Scotland Yard!'. A woman in a long blue dress watches as poison is dropped into a box of chocolates for *The Poisoned Chocolates Case*. Mee's wrapper for *The Piccadilly Murder* has a hand dropping a sinister something into a cup of coffee. 'A New Roger Sheringham Novel' is announced at the top of the blue-grey wrapper for *The Second Shot*. Below this, three observers peer through trees at a man reeling from the impact of a bullet. Hastain's eye-catching design for *Top Storey Murder* shows a cleaning lady holding her broom aloft in terror as she stands at the top of a black flight of stairs. A dark figure silhouetted against a magenta background climbs the stairs towards her. Eight suspects are listed on the lower front cover. For *Murder in the Basement* a young woman in a floor-length robe reels back aghast at the foot of the basement steps. A pick-axe lies amid the rubble at her feet. A black-and-white study of a hangman's noose suspended from a gibbet features on the wrapper for *Jumping Jenny*. *Panic Party*'s largely dark pink wrapper shows Guy Pidgeon's body falling backwards over a cliff, silhouetted against the moon and framed by trees. The predominantly blue wrapper of *Not To Be Taken* has row upon row of poison bottles, with a panel containing title and author laid across them. *Death in the House* has a blue wrapper with Big Ben rising out of the mist.

There are twelve uncollected stories, nine by Anthony Berkeley and three by Francis Iles. Roger Sheringham is in all the Berkeley stories except 'Unsound Mind', 'Mr. Simpson Goes to the Dogs' 'Publicity Heroine' and 'The Policeman Only Taps Once' (which is a parody of *The Postman Always Rings Twice*). 'The Avenging Chance' is the basis of *The Poisoned Chocolates Case*, without all the novel's different solutions. 'Holmes and the Dasher', from *The Misadventures of Sherlock Holmes* (Little, Brown 1944), was originally published as Chapter 19 of the A. B. Cox book *Jugged Journalism* (Jenkins 1925). The Iles story 'Outside the Law' was reprinted as by Anthony Berkeley.

A radio play, *Red Anemones*, featuring Roger Sheringham, was broadcast in two parts on 1 and 8 June 1940. It was later adapted as the story 'Mr. Bearstowe Says . . .' An adaptation of Berkeley's *Trial and Error*, as by Francis Iles, was broadcast on 12 Dec. 1957. A true-crime radio play, *The Case of Serafino Pelizzioni*, was broadcast on 19 December 1957. A stage play, *Mr. Priestley's Problem*, was performed in Brighton and London in 1928.

The most difficult books to find in first edition are *Cicely Disappears, Roger Sheringham and the Vane Mystery*, and *Murder in the Basement*.

Novels by Anthony Berkeley
(with Sheringham, except as stated)

The Layton Court Mystery   Jenkins 1925, by ?; Doubleday 1929 (US editions were issued as by Anthony Berkeley)

The Wychford Poisoning Case   Collins 1926, by the author of *The Layton Court Mystery*; Doubleday 1930

Roger Sheringham and the Vane Mystery   Collins 1927

a.k.a. *The Mystery at Lovers' Cave*   Simon & Schuster 1927

The Silk Stocking Murders   Collins 1928, Doubleday 1928

The Poisoned Chocolates Case   Collins 1929, Doubleday 1929 (also with Chitterwick)

The Piccadilly Murder   Collins 1929, Doubleday 1930 (Chitterwick)

The Second Shot   Hodder & Stoughton 1930, Doubleday 1931

Top Storey Murder   Hodder 1931

a.k.a. *Top Story Murder*   Doubleday 1931

Murder in the Basement   Hodder 1932, Doubleday 1932

Jumping Jenny   Hodder 1933

a.k.a. *Dead Mrs. Stratton*   Doubleday 1933, Hogarth 1984

Panic Party   Hodder 1934

a.k.a. *Mr. Pidgeon's Island*   Doubleday 1934

Trial and Error   Hodder 1937, Doubleday 1937 (Chitterwick)

Not To Be Taken   Hodder 1938 (not Sheringham)

a.k.a. *A Puzzle in Poison*   Doubleday 1938

Death in the House   Hodder 1939, Doubleday 1939 (not Sheringham)

Novels by Francis Iles

Malice Aforethought   Gollancz (Mundanus) 1931, Harper 1931

Before the Fact   Gollancz 1932, Doubleday 1932

As for the Woman   Jarrolds n.d. (1939), Doubleday 1939

Novel by A. Monmouth Platts

Cicely Disappears   John Long 1927

Novel by A. B. Cox

Mr. Priestley's Problem Collins 1927
a.k.a. *The Amateur Crime* Doubleday 1928;
Penguin 1947 as by Anthony Berkeley.

Novels with other members of the Detection Club (q.v.)

The Floating Admiral Hodder n.d. (1931),
Doubleday 1932
Ask a Policeman Arthur Barker n.d. (1933),
Morrow 1933
The Scoop and *Behind the Screen* Gollancz
1983

Uncollected stories by Anthony Berkeley

'The Avenging Chance' (*Best Detective Stories
of the Year 1929*, Faber 1930/*Best English
Detective Stories of the Year*, Liveright 1930;
Tales of Detection, Dent 1936; *Great Stories of
Detection*, Arthur Barker 1960)
'Perfect Alibi' (*Radio Times*, 1 Aug. 1930;
revised as 'The Perfect Alibi', *ES*, 11 Mar.
1953; *TAD*, Summer 1992)
'Unsound Mind' (*Time and Tide*, 14 and 21 Oct.
1933) (Moresby)
'Mr Simpson Goes to the Dogs' (*Strand*, June
1934; *EQMM*, Feb. 1946)
'The Policeman Only Taps Once' (*Six Against
the Yard*, Selwyn & Blount n.d. (1936)/*Six
Against Scotland Yard*, Doubleday 1936; *Thir-
teen Ways to Kill a Man*, Faber 1966)
'Publicity Heroine' (*Missing From Their Homes*,
Hutchinson 1936)
'White Butterfly' (*ES*, 28 Aug. 1936; *Fifty
Famous Detectives of Fiction*, Odhams n.d.
(1938); *EQMM*, Dec. 1982)
'The Wrong Jar' (*Detective Stories of Today*,
Faber 1940; *EQMM*, Mar. 1947)
'Mr. Bearstowe Says...' (*Saturday Book 3*,
Hutchinson 1943; *EQA Mid-year 1965*, Davis
1965)

Uncollected stories by Francis Iles

'Outside the Law' (*Strand*, July 1934; *Fifty Masterpieces of Mystery*, Odhams 1937, as by
Anthony Berkeley; *EQMM*, June 1949)

'Dark Journey' (*A Century of Horror Stories*,
Hutchinson 1935; *To the Queen's Taste*, Little,
Brown 1946, Faber 1949)
'It Takes Two to Make a Hero' (*Collier's*, 4 Sept.
1943; *Saturday Book 3*, Hutchinson Oct. 1943;
EQMM, Jan. 1953 and *EQA 3*, Davis 1963, in
variant text, as 'The Coward') *JC*

Nicholas Blake (1904–1972)

Nicholas Blake was the pseudonym of Cecil Day
Lewis, who was Poet Laureate at the time of his
death. He wrote twenty novels and five uncollected stories; only *The Deadly Joker* has not
appeared in the USA. Whether writing detective
stories like *Minute for Murder*, thrillers like *The
Smiler with the Knife*, or psychological crime
novels like *A Tangled Web*, he always writes with
style and scholarship, and often with humour.

Blake created the likeable Nigel Strangeways,
partly based on his friend W. H. Auden. He
appears in sixteen novels and three stories.

Besides being a dabbler in literature, he is a keen amateur sleuth. He marries the famous explorer Georgia Cavendish, who features in five novels before being killed by a bomb in the Blitz. Clare Massinger, a celebrated sculptor, later becomes Nigel's lover and is also involved in five of his investigations. The Scottish Inspector Blount works with Nigel on seven cases.

All Nicholas Blake's books were first published in London by Collins, and they are all dated. Some, like *Malice in Wonderland* and *A Tangled Web*, have alternative titles in America. All the Collins titles were published in orange or red cloth, with the exception of *A Tangled Web*, which is bound in black cloth. It is also the only book not in the Crime Club series. The first book, *A Question of Proof*, is lettered in black on the spine and front cover. The remaining titles have black lettering on the spine only, until the final group of three, from *The Sad Variety*, which have gilt lettering. *Thou Shell of Death, There's Trouble Brewing, The Beast Must Die, A Tangled Web*, and *The Private Wound* are taller than the other titles. Normally, the masked gunman on the title-page of Crime Club books faces to the left, but he looks to the right in *The Smiler with the Knife*, and he is absent from *Thou Shell of Death*. With the exception of *Thou Shell of Death*, all the pre–1947 titles have the publisher's advertisements at the back. This title also has the page edges at the top coloured orange. Collectors of first editions should beware of an undated *Smiler with the Knife*, which is otherwise identical to the dated first edition.

The wrapper of *A Question of Proof* shows a noose and a gun beneath the title, which is drawn to give a three-dimensional effect. *Thou Shell of Death* is dominated by a death-mask on a blue background, and *There's Trouble Brewing* has an arrangement of casks fading into a brown cellar. *The Beast Must Die* has Felix Lane writing his diary by the light of his desk lamp, surrounded by darkness. Lowen's design for *The Smiler with the Knife* has a map of England with a grey cobweb over it, representing the spy network in the book. Various area headquarters are marked, as are warships in the channel and old-fashioned guns on the coast. *Malice in Wonderland* has a head-and-shoulders portrait of a sinister-looking Mad Hatter. Thompson's snowman for *The Case of the Abominable Snowman* is modelled on Queen Victoria. Beneath is a banner with the lines: 'A neck God made for other use/Than strangling with a string!'. *Minute for Murder* shows a retreating bowler-hatted figure silhouetted against an illuminated building, at night. *Head of a Traveller* has an injured figure making his way over the brow of a country hill, leaving behind bloodstains. Most of the later dust-wrappers have the title in bold colours printed on black, though the background is red for *The Dreadful Hollow*. Two notable exceptions are designed by Kenneth Farnhill: *A Tangled Web* has an elongated Siamese cat set below title and author on a pink background, and *The Private Wound* shows an open penknife, grey on white, both on the spine and the front cover of the wrapper.

Calling James Braithwaite is an unpublished two-part radio play featuring Nigel Strangeways, broadcast on 20 and 22 July 1940.

Malice in Wonderland seems to be the most difficult first edition to find.

Novels

(with Strangeways, except as stated: other series characters as stated)

A Question of Proof Collins Crime Club 1935, Harper 1935

Thou Shell of Death Crime Club 1936 (Cavendish, Blount)

a.k.a. *Shell of Death* Harper 1936

There's Trouble Brewing Crime Club 1937, Harper 1937 (Cavendish)

The Beast Must Die Crime Club 1938, Harper 1938 (Cavendish, Blount)

The Smiler with the Knife Crime Club 1939, Harper 1939 (Cavendish)

Malice in Wonderland Crime Club 1940

a.k.a. *The Summer Camp Mystery* Harper 1940

a.k.a. *Malice with Murder* Pyramid 1964

a.k.a. *Murder with Malice* Carroll & Graf 1987

The Case of the Abominable Snowman Crime Club 1941 (Cavendish, Blount)

a.k.a. *The Corpse in the Snowman* Harper 1941

Minute for Murder Crime Club 1947, Harper 1948 (Blount)

Head of a Traveller Crime Club 1949, Harper 1949 (Blount)

The Dreadful Hollow Crime Club 1953, Harper 1953 (Blount)

The Whisper in the Gloom Crime Club 1954, Harper 1954 (Massinger, Blount)

a.k.a. *Catch and Kill* Bestseller 1955 (abridged)

A Tangled Web Collins 1956, Harper 1956 (not Strangeways)

a.k.a. *Death and Daisy Bland* Dell 1960

End of Chapter Crime Club 1957, Harper 1957 (Massinger)

A Penknife in My Heart Crime Club 1958, Harper 1959 (not Strangeways)

The Widow's Cruise Crime Club 1959, Harper 1959 (Massinger)

The Worm of Death Crime Club 1961, Harper 1961 (Massinger)

The Deadly Joker Crime Club 1963 (not Strangeways)

The Sad Variety Crime Club 1964, Harper 1964 (Massinger)

The Morning After Death Crime Club 1966, Harper 1966

The Private Wound Crime Club 1968, Harper 1968 (not Strangeways)

Uncollected stories

(all except 'The Snow Line' and 'Sometimes . . . the Blind See the Clearest' with Strangeways)

'A Slice of Bad Luck' (*Bystander*, 22 Nov. 1935; *Detection Medley*, Hutchinson n.d. (1939); *EQMM*, Mar. 1945, *Murder for the Millions*, Fell 1946 & *The Fifth Bedside Book of Great Detective Stories*, Barker 1981 as 'The Assassins' Club')

'Mr Prendergast and the Orange' (*Sunday Dispatch*, 27 Mar. 1938; *Great Stories of Detection*, Barker 1960; *EQMM*, Jan. 1962 as 'Conscience Money')

'It Fell to Earth' (*Strand*, June 1944; *Armchair Detective Reader*, Boardman 1948; *EQMM*, Feb. 1964 and *Ellery Queen's 20th Anniversary Annual*, Random House 1965, Gollancz 1966, as 'Long Shot')

'The Snow Line' (*Strand*, Feb. 1949, illustrated by Illingworth; *EQMM*, May 1949 and *The Queen's Awards 4*, Little, Brown 1949, Gollancz 1951, as 'A Study in White'; *Crime at Christmas*, Equation 1988, as 'A Problem in White')

'Sometimes . . . the Blind See the Clearest' (*ES*, 18 Mar. 1963; *Saint*, July 1964 (UK), as 'Sometimes the Blind') *JC*

John and Emery Bonett (b. 1906 and 1907)

John and Emery Bonett wrote between them ten detective novels, one each and eight in collaboration. Three feature Professor Mandrake, an early specimen of the TV pundit, and six Salvador Borges, a dapper Spanish policeman with violet eyes. The books are custom-made detective stories, relaxed and charming, meticulously designed as intelligent entertainment. Some titles vary between Britain and America and *No Grave for a Lady*, at least, appeared first in the USA. The sequence began with Emery Bonett's solo novel, *High Pavement*, published by Heinemann in 1944. It is a red book with silver lettering on the spine and beige endpapers. It is dated on the copyright page. The rear cover has the Heinemann windmill, blind-stamped.

Dead Lion launched both the collaboration and Professor Mandrake, who is ugly but engaging. It is the first of six books published by Joseph, all in black bindings except for *The Private Face of Murder*, which is green, and *This Side Murder?*, which is mauve. All are dated on the copyright page and lettered on the spine only: *Better Dead* in white, *No Grave for a Lady* and *The Private Face of Murder* in gilt, the others in silver. *Dead Lion* and *A Banner for Pegasus* have extra spinal features: the head of Cyprian Druse and the winged horse, respectively, both in silver.

Two further books were published by Harrap: *The Sound of Murder* in a black binding with silver lettering and rules on the spine; *In Time for Murder* in a pale-brown binding with white lettering and rules on the spine and the publisher's circular logo in white at the lower corner of the front cover. Both are dated on the copyright page, and the former has a preliminary plan of the Corsairs' flat. The final novel, by John alone, is *Perish the Thought*, published by Hale in 1984 in a black binding with silver lettering on the spine and dated copyright page.

The most attractive of the Bonetts' wrappers is by Olga Lehmann, for *Dead Lion*. An arresting design centres on the dead head of Cyprian Druse and an elegant, enigmatic woman. *A Banner for Pegasus* has a rampant Pegasus and *No Grave for a Lady* a woman in sunglasses and a magnolia wilting under a blazing sun. Later wrappers are increasingly photographic.

Besides the novels, John Bonett published a number of stories, twenty-six in the *Evening Standard* and one in *Argosy* (1950–1960).

Novel by Emery Bonett

High Pavement   Heinemann 1944
a.k.a. *Old Mrs. Camelot*   Blakiston 1944

Professor Mandrake novels in collaboration

Dead Lion   Joseph 1949, Doubleday 1949
A Banner for Pegasus   Joseph 1951
a.k.a. *Not in the Script*   Doubleday 1951
No Grave for a Lady   Doubleday 1959, Joseph 1960

Inspector Borges novels in collaboration

Better Dead   Joseph 1964
a.k.a. *Better Off Dead*   Doubleday 1964
The Private Face of Murder   Joseph 1966, Doubleday 1966
This Side Murder?   Joseph 1967
a.k.a. *Murder on the Costa Brava*   Walker 1968
The Sound of Murder   Harrap 1970, Walker 1971
No Time to Kill   Harrap 1972, Walker 1972

Inspector Borges novel by John Bonett

Perish the Thought Hale 1984

Non-series stories by John Bonett

'A Bath Before Dinner' (*ES*, 18 Oct. 1950)
'The Five Miss Forthrights' (*ES*, 8 Dec. 1950)
'Explosive Matter' (*ES*, 8 Jan. 1951)
'Return Journey' (*ES*, 22 Feb. 1951)
'Children May Play' (*ES*, 21 Jun. 1951)
'Footsteps to the Gallows' (*ES*, 29 Jun. 1951)
'Stiff with Diamonds' (*ES*, 4 Sept. 1951)
'Eunice Dead' (*ES*, 10 Sept. 1951)
'Holly Blue' (*ES*, 17 Sept. 1951)
'Questionnaire' (*ES*, 9 Oct. 1951)
'Intruder's End' (*ES*, 13 Oct. 1951)
'Purpleheart' (*ES*, 3 Dec. 1951)
'Atalanta Vanquished' (*ES*, 8 Feb. 1952)
'Room 666' (*ES*, 3 Apr. 1952)
'Detective on the Scent' (*ES*, 17 Apr. 1952)
'Light Exposure' (*ES*, 24 May 1952)
'Spots on the Dandy Roll' (*ES*, 5 Jun. 1952)
'Wax in his Hands' (*ES*, 1 Dec. 1952)
'Pretty Boy' (*ES*, 12 Jan. 1953)
'The Snow-White Feather' (*ES*, 20 Aug. 1953)
'Dinner for Two' (*ES*, 22 Jul. 1954)
'Cottage by the River' (*ES*, 31 Jul. 1954)
'Climbing Rose' (*ES*, 8 Oct. 1954)

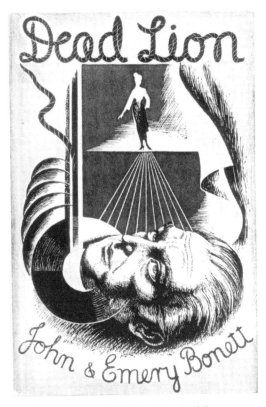

'A Blooming Lyre' (*ES*, 11 Nov. 1954)
'Toll Call' (*ES*, 7 Dec. 1954)
'I'll Consider Your Offer' (*ES*, 15 Jan. 1955)
'Night Call' (*Argosy*, Jan. 1960)   *BP*

J. S. Borthwick (b. 1923)

J. S. Borthwick is a graceful recruit to the high literate tradition of the detective novel. She is spirited, stylish and erudite, with a confident eye to character and a sure sense of place: her communities come alive, as do the tensions within them. All her books feature Sarah Deane, a young English teacher, and Alex McKenzie, the slightly older doctor who will surely become her husband.

Only her first book has been published in Britain: *The Case of the Hookbilled Kites*, a typical Gollancz product of its era, red with gilt lettering on the spine and dated title-page. A drawing in silhouette of two kites on a branch appears on the half-title and title-page and also marks divi-

sions in the narrative. This and the preliminary map of the Dona Clara National Wildlife Refuge are by the author's daughter, Margaret Creighton.

The book was first published in America by St Martin's, who also brought out the later books in the series: *The Down East Murders* and *Bodies of Water* in blue bindings, *The Student Body* and *Dude on Arrival* in black. All four are dated on the copyright page, which also has 'First Edition' and a printer's key. *Bodies of Water* is lettered on the spine in silver, the others in gilt, *Dude on Arrival* with a gilt silhouette of a man on a horse within a rectangular gilt frame. The books are all decorated: *The Down East Murders* and *The Student Body* with preliminary maps by Margaret Creighton, the entire series with vignettes of locations and properties that serve as chapter headings by the author's son Alec. *Bodies of Water* also has a preliminary plan by Alec Creighton. Two title-pages are decorated: that for *Bodies of Water* with a frothing

grey and white sea and that for *Dude on Arrival* with cacti among rocks.

Margaret Creighton's wrapper for *The Down East Murders* shows a waterside scene with a lighthouse throwing its beam and *The Student Body* has her drawing of Bowmouth College seen through bare winter trees. For *Bodies of Water* Bob Newman shows the sloop *Pilgrim* in full sail, with a lighthouse beyond her and, in the foreground, the corpse of Billy Brackett, supine on rocks. Willette Brown's wrapper for *Dude on Arrival* shows the man on horseback from the spine of the book in black and white and in a wider landscape. Even the Gollancz wrapper for *Hookbilled Kites* enlivens the standard yellow with Margaret Creighton's kites in silhouette, adapted from the design for the American edition, which has them much enlarged in brown.

Sarah Deane novels

The Case of the Hookbilled Kites St Martin's
   1982, Gollancz 1983
The Down East Murders St Martin's 1985
The Student Body St Martin's 1986
Bodies of Water St Martin's 1990
Dude on Arrival St Martin's 1992   *BP*

Anthony Boucher (1911–1968)
a.k.a. H. H. Holmes

Anthony Boucher's seven detective novels, including two as by H. H. Holmes, are distinguished examples of the detective novel as intellectual game, erudite, eventful, ingenious and high-spirited. *Nine Times Nine*, in particular, is an altogether dazzling performance. Four of the novels feature Fergus O'Breen, an Irish-American private detective. Other series characters are Sister Ursula of the Order of Martha of Bethany and Nick Noble, an alcoholic ex-policeman. All three operate in Los Angeles. Besides his own novels, Boucher contributed to a collaborative novel published as by Theo Durrant. There are also three collections of stories, two of which were posthumous and sixteen uncollected stories with some claim to be considered criminous. *Exeunt Murderers* collects the bulk of the shorter

crime fiction; the other two collections, despite the occasional presence of Fergus O'Breen, are largely SF.

All five Boucher novels were originally published by Simon & Schuster, *The Case of the Seven of Calvary* in 1937 in a black binding with gilt lettering on the spine. The front cover has the logo for the Inner Sanctum Mysteries blind-stamped on it. The endpapers are buff and the front pastedown has an ecstatic preamble from the publisher. There is no half-title page, though it looks as if one might have been removed. This is not so, however. The brown wrapper features the device of the Seven of Calvary. The UK edition was published by Hamish Hamilton, also in 1937, in a yellow binding with red lettering on the spine and double red rules at either end. This edition is dated on the copyright page. The novel is virtually non-series, except that Martin

Lamb, who investigates with his teacher, Dr Ashwin, recurs in three stories.

Fergus O'Breen appeared two years later in *The Case of the Crumpled Knave*, an orange book with dark-blue lettering on the spine and the Inner Sanctum logo on the front cover, also dark blue. The wrapper design features playing cards. The Harrap edition of the same year has a blue binding with the lettering and the publisher's prison bar logo showing blue through yellow rectangular panels. The front cover has a blind-stamped border and the copyright page is dated. The wrapper shows a crumpled Jack of Diamonds. Despite the statement 'First published in 1939' in copies with a brown binding and black panels, these are part of the cheaper reissue.

The Case of the Baker Street Irregulars appeared in 1940 in a red binding with black lettering on the spine. The front cover has a black profile silhouette of Sherlock Holmes, placed centrally. The black wrapper has Holmes' dancing men at top and bottom and the Holmes silhouette within a yellow disc in the centre. To interpret the message, readers are referred to Chapter V. *The Case of the Solid Key* followed in 1941, in a red binding with gilt spine lettering, the title within double gilt rules notched at the centre. Neither this nor its immediate predecessor was published in Britain.

The Case of the Seven Sneezes is the last Boucher novel. It was published in 1942 in a black binding with gilt lettering on the spine. Its British edition, from United Authors in 1946, has a grey binding with gilt lettering on the spine and dated copyright page. The blue wrapper has a cat on a yellow handkerchief. All the Simon & Schuster books have a ruled framework and the date on the title-page.

The Holmes novels, also, were not separately published in Britain, though they did appear in a Black Box collection from Zomba in 1984, with an excellent introduction by David Langford. They were originally published by Duell, Sloan & Pearce, *Nine Times Nine* in 1940, *Rocket to the Morgue* in 1942. Both books are black with blank covers and are dated by the copyright notice, with 'first edition' on the copyright page. *Nine Times Nine* has the title showing black through a ragged yellow patch on the spine, with the other lettering and the publisher's bloodhound motif in yellow. *Rocket to the Morgue* has lettering and bloodhound in blue and a blue wrapper with the title white against a rocket trail. A handsome Phantom paperback, also dated 1942 and stating 'first edition', has reviews on its back cover that suggest otherwise.

Far and Away includes nine SF stories, a Martin Lamb story, 'The Anomaly of the Empty Man', and a Fergus O'Breen story, 'Elsewhen'. It is a paperback original, published by Ballantine in 1955. *The Compleat Werewolf* was published in Britain in 1970, a year later than its US edition. It contains eight SF stories and two SF mysteries with O'Breen. The Allen edition is blue with gilt lettering on the spine and dated title-page.

Exeunt Murderers, an invaluable collection, is quarterbound in fawn boards with a red spine and adjacent cover strips and silver lettering on the spine. The endpapers are a darker fawn than the boards. The date is in the copyright notice. The introduction and checklist are by Francis M. Nevins, Jr. All nine of the Nick Noble stories are collected here, as well as one of the two Sister Ursula novellas and a brief O'Breen story. The uncollected stories include a Sherlock Holmes pastiche, two more Martin Lamb stories, a fourth case for Sister Ursula and four more O'Breen stories. 'The Clue of the Knave of Diamonds' is the first version of *The Case of the Crumpled Knave*.

The Marble Forest was the result of a collaboration among twelve members of the MWA in California, with Boucher and Lenore Glen Offord acting as controlling editors. The UK edition is blue-green with gilt lettering on the spine and dated copyright page. The title-page calls the author 'Theo Durrant', the spine 'Theo Durant'. The latter form appears also on the wrapper, which is a grim affair with a graveyard and a coffin.

Novels

(with Fergus O'Breen, except where stated)

The Case of the Seven of Calvary   Simon &
Schuster 1937, Hamilton 1937 (Lamb)
The Case of the Crumpled Knave   Simon 1939,
Harrap 1939
The Case of the Baker Street Irregulars   Simon
1940 abridged as *Blood on Baker Street*   Mer-
cury 1953
The Case of the Solid Key   Simon 1941
The Case of the Seven Sneezes   Simon 1942,
United Authors 1946

Sister Ursula novels by H. H. Holmes

Nine Times Nine   Duell, Sloan & Pearce 1940
Rocket to the Morgue   Duell 1942

Story collections

Far and Away   Ballantine 1955 (11 stories)
The Compleat Werewolf   Simon 1969, Allen
1970 (10 stories)
Exeunt Murders   Southern Illinois University
Press 1983 (22 stories)

Collaboration as by Theo Durrant

The Marble Forest   Knopf 1951, Wingate 1951
a.k.a. *The Big Fear*   Popular Library 1953

Uncollected stories

'Murder by Jove' (*Look*, 6 Sept. 1944)
'The Way I Heard It' (*Acolyte*, Fall 1944)
(Lamb)
'Arsene Lupin vs. Colonel Linnaus' (*EQMM*,
Nov. 1944)
'Toy Cassowary' (*Acolyte*, Winter 1944) (Lamb)
'The Adventure of the Illustrious Imposter' (*The
Misadventures of Sherlock Holmes*, Little,
Brown 1944)
'Murder on V-Day' (*Look*, Jan. 1945)
'The Chronokinesis of Jonathan Hull'
(*Astounding Science Fiction*, June 1946; *Great
Stories of Science Fiction*, Random House
1951, Cassell 1953) (O'Breen)

'Transcontinental Alibi' (*Mystery Book Maga-
zine*, Spring 1950)
'Nine-finger Jack' (*Esquire*, May 1951; *Twenty
Great Tales of Murder*, Random House 1951,
Hammond 1952; *EQMM*, Sept. 1964)
'Gandolphus' (*Other Worlds Science Stories*, Jun.
1952; *A Decade of Fantasy and Science Fiction*,
Doubleday 1960, Gollancz 1962) (O'Breen)
'Public Eye' (*Thrilling Wonder Stories*, Apr.
1953; *Best Detective Stories of the Year 1953*,
Dutton 1953, Boardman 1954)
'The Last Hand' (*EQMM*, Sept. 1958; *Masters
of Mayhem*, Morrow 1965 as 'A Little Honest
Stud') (O'Breen)
'The Clue of the Knave of Diamonds' (*EQMM*,
May 1963) (O'Breen)
'A Kind of Madness' (*EQMM*, Aug. 1972; *Ellery
Queen's Crookbook*, Random House 1974,
Gollancz 1975)

Novella by H. H. Holmes

Vacancy with Corpse (*Mystery Book Magazine*,
Feb. 1946) (Ursula)

Story by William A. P. White

'Ye Goode Olde Ghoste Storie' (*Weird Tales*,
Jan. 1927)   *BP*

Dorothy Bowers (b. 1904)

Dorothy Bowers is an unsung crime writer
whose career began just before the Second
World War and ended abruptly just after it. Perhaps she ran out of steam, though the quality of
her last book suggests powers in a confident
ascendant. She published five novels between
1938 and 1947, all from Hodder & Stoughton
in Britain, all save the first from Doubleday in
America. The two variant titles contain adjust-
ments rather than changes.

Inspector Dan Pardoe investigates in all
except *The Bells at Old Bailey*, assisted
invariably by Sergeant Salt. Despite their presence in *Fear for Miss Betony*, this is more a
novel of angst and atmosphere than a detective
story. The others are handmade whodunits, rising
in range and accomplishment to the high

achievement of *A Deed Without a Name* and *The Bells at Old Bailey*.

Postscript to Poison is a blue book with the title in black on the front cover and black spine lettering. The endpapers are also blue. The dust-wrapper has a drab photo of a medicine bottle and glass on a white table. *Shadows Before* is red with gilt spine lettering, all contained within a double border high on the spine. *A Deed Without a Name* and *Fear for Miss Betony* share this format, but with blue-black lettering and borders on a blue binding. *A Deed Without a Name* also has an advertisement section at the back. The black wrapper for *Shadows Before* has a vivid portrait of a gipsy woman cooking over a fire. That for *A Deed Without a Name* is brown, with a black blunt instrument and a white plaster bird. *The Bells at Old Bailey* is a deep-red book with black spine lettering and the title on the cover, also in black. Its attractive wrapper shows

the 'bells of London' sampler hung by Bertha Tidy on the wall of the Minerva in Ravenchurch. All five books are dated, *Fear for Miss Betony* and *The Bells at Old Bailey* with the month of printing.

In *More Monmouthshire Writers* (1948), W. J. Townsend-Collins states that Dorothy Bowers' first story was published in 1936, but he does not identify it or establish whether it was a crime story. The reference to a 'first' story also implies, of course, that there were others.

Novels

(with Pardoe and Salt, except as stated)

Postscript to Poison   Hodder & Stoughton 1938
Shadows Before   Hodder 1939, Doubleday 1940
A Deed Without a Name   Hodder 1940, Doubleday 1940
Fear for Miss Betony   Hodder 1941
a.k.a. *Fear and Miss Betony*   Doubleday 1942
The Bells at Old Bailey   Hodder 1947 (not Pardoe and Salt)
a.k.a. *The Bells of Old Bailey*   Doubleday 1947
BP

Ernest Bramah (1868–1942)

All Ernest Bramah's crime fiction involves the blind detective Max Carrados, formerly Wynn. His blindness is not seen as a handicap in detection, or even, much, in life, and occasionally, as in 'The Game Played in the Dark', it is an advantage. He is leisured and learned, with a particular expertise in numismatics. He appears in one novel and twenty-six stories, spread over four collections. An American reprint anthology appeared in 1972. *CC* describes Bramah as a 'secretive man with a dash of sadistic pruriency in his make-up'; but Hugh Greene claims that he was 'a small bald man with twinkly black eyes, and a reputation for immense kindness of heart'. The belief that he lived in China (the setting for his Kai Lung stories) has been shown to be false (*TAD*, May 1975). Joshua Goldberg wrote brilliantly on Bramah in *TAD* of February 1974.

The first book, *Max Carrados*, appeared in

January 1914, according to the *ECB*, and Bramah later confirmed that publication occurred 'in the spring of 1914'. The format is similar to that later used by Methuen for H. C. Bailey's Fortune books: a red binding, with title and author blind-stamped on the front cover and gilt on the spine, each within a corresponding patterned framework. The book is dated and carries advertisements from the previous year in two distinct sections: eight pages of Methuen's Popular Novels for Autumn 1913, and thirty-one pages of A Selection of Books from the publisher's list, dated September 1913. A later issue of the first edition, in the identical format, carries an advertisement section dated Spring 1915. The cheap edition appeared in November 1917, in a smaller format.

The Eyes of Max Carrados is a handsome blue book, dated in roman numerals on the title-page, and lettered in blue-black on front cover and spine. The extended introduction redefines Carrados for the reader, and goes on to discuss the achievements of eminent blind men and women, in support of the attribution to Carrados of certain of his powers.

The Specimen Case is a mixed collection of stories, essential to Carrados enthusiasts for 'The Bunch of Violets', included to help the author achieve his determination to have Carrados and Kai Lung 'between one pair of covers'. His avoidance of publicity and his stylistic diversity were seen as evidence of both non-existence and dual existence, and he wished to 'confound the non-existers and the dualists alike'. The title refers to the collection as a whole, which features stories from three decades of writing. 'The Bunch of Violets' is the fifth of twenty-one stories, recounting 'An Episode in the War-time Activities of Max Carrados'. It was first published in *The Strand Magazine* of July 1924, and it is reprinted in *The Detective in Fiction: A Posse of Eight* (Bell 1931) and in *EQMM* for September 1943.

The Specimen Case is bound in red, with plain black lettering on the spine. The front cover has a blind-stamped border round its edges. At the top, title and author appear in red against a black rectangular background stamped into the cover: the lettering is formed by the raised areas,

as if designed to be read by Carrados himself. The title is in larger letters than those naming the author, and a short red line divides them. The central black area and its lettering are contained within four borders, the innermost of which is a thin, red one, comparable in thickness to the line dividing title and author. The other three, alternating black and red, are broader. The entire pattern is thus enclosed within the outer of the two black bands. All the black areas are stamped, throwing the red into relief. The book has a segmented, undated title-page, on the reverse of which is the legend 'Made and printed in Great Britain 1924', with the printer's name and address beneath. A later issue dispenses with the black framework and borders on the front cover and simply states 'Copyright 1924' on the reverse of the title-page. The BL copy is stamped 23 October 1924.

Max Carrados Mysteries is the standard blue Hodder product of the 1920s and 1930s, lettered in black on the spine, and with Bramah's initials and the title on the cover, also in black. The BL copy is stamped 12 September 1927, but the book itself is undated. *The Bravo of London* marks Carrados' last appearance and gives him the only full-length case of his career, a lurid affair involving an evil antique-dealer with a 'monstrous distortion' of a face. The book was published by Cassell, and is dated, with a green binding and exotic gilt lettering on the spine.

The wrapper for *Max Carrados* illustrates the last scene in the book, at the climax of 'The Game Played in the Dark'. Carrados sits at the table, confronting the astonished Inspector and his men, as they break into the room overlooking Heronsbourne Park: beyond him, Mme Dompierre buries her head in the cushions. *The Eyes of Max Carrados* has a graceful portrait of the detective by Peacock, who shows him standing with folded arms, his slender right hand to the fore, with a ring on the little finger. The coin on the wrapper of *Max Carrados Mysteries* is perhaps the vanished petition crown of the second story in the collection; if so, the woman peering over the top of it must be Miss Frensham. *The Specimen Case* has an Ellen Edwards wrapper with a blonde woman about to step into a glass-fronted cabinet, to avoid the figure cast-

The Bunch of Violets

'The Bunch of Violets', The *Strand Magazine*, Jul. 1924. Illustration by J. Dewar Mills.

ing a menacing shadow over the foreground. She must be Sybil, from the bravura spoof spy story, 'Smothered in Corpses'. Conrad Leigh's arresting wrapper for *The Bravo of London* shows the hideous Julian Joolby in his Padgett Street shop, brooding over a piece of Dresden, with his assistant, Won Chou, looking on, the image of Oriental inscrutability.

Checklist

Max Carrados Methuen 1914, Hyperion 1975
   (8 stories)
The Eyes of Max Carrados Grant Richards
   1923, Doran 1924 (9 stories)
The Specimen Case Hodder & Stoughton 1924,
   Doran 1925 (includes 'The Bunch of Violets')
Max Carrados Mysteries Hodder n.d. (1927),
   Penguin (Baltimore) 1964 (8 stories)
The Bravo of London Cassell 1934 (novel)
Best Max Carrados Stories Dover 1972

BP

Pamela Branch (1920–1967)

The work of Pamela Branch deserves a wider fame. She was not published in America and is still a minority taste in Britain. Her four novels are distinguished by amoral energy, exact, untir-

ing wit, and impressive unity of tone. Having resolved to see murder as a topic for humour, she sets about persuading the reader to share her view with irresistible effrontery. Her control of her chosen manner is absolute: she is wickedly, lethally funny. A comparison with Joe Orton might be rewarding, but, essentially, there is no one quite like her.

Two of her books involve the Asterisk Club in Chelsea, a residential club for acquitted murderers, established by Clifford Flush and a group of kindred spirits. They first appear in *The Wooden Overcoat* and surface again in *Murder Every Monday*, setting up shop at Dankry Manor in Dorset.

All four books were published by Hale, in black bindings, lettered in green on the spine. They are all dated. At least two of the dustwrappers are by Sax, whose spirited designs mirror the eccentric world within. *Lion in the Cellar* shows Roarer rampant, with a blood-stained axe propped against a beer-barrel, and

the protruding legs of Marigold Tossit. *Murder Every Monday* has Clifford Flush, revolver in hand, stepping fastidiously through the scattering of blood-stained Chicago gangsters who clutter his progress.

Murder Every Monday is dedicated to Christianna Brand and *Murder's Little Sister* to Francis Iles.

Novels

The Wooden Overcoat   Hale 1951 (Flush)
Lion in the Cellar   Hale 1951
Murder Every Monday   Hale 1954 (Flush)
Murder's Little Sister   Hale 1958   *BP*

Christianna Brand   (1907–1988) a.k.a. Mary Ann Ashe

Christianna Brand is the principal pseudonym of Mary Christianna Lewis, who also wrote as Mary Ann Ashe. Her other pseudonyms, China Thompson, Annabel Jones, and Mary Roland, were not used for her crime fiction. She wrote thirteen crime novels, eight of which are classical detective stories, justly famous for their ingenuity and their last-minute surprises. She also contributed the final three chapters to the collaborative novella *No Flowers by Request*, and she wrote the closing sequence of a story written with Dick Francis, Gavin Lyall, and Miles Tripp, 'The Diamonds Are Forever Amber Mystery'. The Mystery Library edition of Anthony Berkeley's *The Poisoned Chocolates Case* includes a new dénouement to this novel by Christianna Brand. Thirty of her stories are collected in three volumes, and there are nine uncollected stories.

Her main series character (based on her father-in-law) is the sparrow-like Inspector Cockrill ('Cockie') of the Kent County Police, who appears in six novels and eight stories. Others are Chief Inspector Charlesworth of Scotland Yard, who is in four novels and goes on to become a chief-superintendent; the Welsh Detective-Inspector Chucky, in two novels; and the dress designer Mr Cecil, also in two novels. Miss Cockrill, Cockie's sister, features in *The Three-Cornered Halo*, but this is not strictly a crime novel. Three books had their first publication in the USA: *Green for Danger, The Crooked Wreath (Suddenly At His Residence)*, and *Death of Jezebel*. Six books have not been published in the USA, and *London Particular* also has an alternative American title.

The British first editions of Christianna Brand's books are all dated. The first five were published by the Bodley Head. *Death in High Heels* has orange cloth, with silver lettering on the spine. *Heads You Lose* has blue cloth, is lettered on the spine in black and has pictorial endpapers of Pigeonsford House and its surroundings. A variant edition is known with plain white endpapers. The wrapper for *Death in High Heels* is grey, red and black and shows the legs of an elegant woman in high heels approaching a sweeping staircase and two armchairs. The heels recur on the spine. *Heads You Lose* has a blue and black wrapper, with Stephen Pendock standing in snow and staring in horror at the scene illuminated by his bowler-hatted butler's torch. The dachshund Aziz is on the spine. *Green for Danger* has green cloth, with the spine lettered in black, and with a black bloodhound sniffing footprints on the spine and front cover. The green, black, and white dust-wrapper, with the designer's initials, P. M., depicts a scene under the bright light of the operating theatre at Heron's Park. *Suddenly At His Residence* was issued in blue cloth, with the spine lettered in red. The wrapper is again green, black, and white, and shows the house Swanswater, with a coffin being carried away down the drive. Swanswater and its drive, and the Marsh family tree, appear on the front endpapers. *Death of Jezebel* has green cloth lettered in red on the spine, with a red bloodhound sniffing on the spine and front cover. A knight in armour on the stage at the Assembly Rooms appears on the wrapper.

The next three books were published by Michael Joseph, *Cat and Mouse* in grey cloth, lettered gilt on the spine. The design for the wrapper shows a man in black running from a house towards a blindfolded girl, down an avenue of bare trees. A white cat toys with a mouse on the spine. There are differences in the texts of the UK and US editions of this book. *London Particular* and *Tour de Force* have black cloth, with the spine lettered gilt. The former has the title printed on a red band. Both have wrappers by Freda Nichols. The atmospheric design for *London Particular* shows Tedward and Rosie outside the open doorway of the house in Maida Vale, looking down at the body of Raoul Vernet, while the London fog swirls around them. *Tour de Force* shows the body of Vanda Lane in her blood-spattered kimono, lying on a red shawl on her bed.

Alas, for Her that Met Me! and *A Ring of Roses* were written under the pseudonym Mary Ann Ashe, and both appeared first as paperbacks published by Star Books. A hardback edition of *A Ring of Roses* was published later in the same year by W. H. Allen, as by Christianna Brand, and with the same design of a doll's head resting on roses on the wrapper. This publisher also issued *The Honey Harlot*, in blue cloth, with the spine lettered gilt. The wrapper illustration by Brian Lewis depicts the square-rigger *Mary Celeste*, dominated by the face of a young girl.

For her last detective novel, the author returned to Michael Joseph. *The Rose in Darkness* has black cloth, with gilt spine lettering. Clare Hatcher's design for the wrapper has a pair of hands pulling petals from a red rose, on a black background. The final Brand novel is a Gothic mystery, *The Brides of Aberdar*, in black cloth, with gilt lettering on the spine. Clair (sic) Hatcher's wrapper shows Miss Tetterman standing before Aberdar Manor.

The earlier collections of stories were also published by Michael Joseph, *What Dread Hand* in blue cloth, lettered gilt on the spine, in a wrapper designed by Laurence Cutting, and *Brand X* in black cloth, with the spine lettered gilt and a plain blue wrapper. Collectors should be aware that eight stories in the latter collection are not crime fiction. Both collections contain the story 'The Kite'. *Buffet for Unwelcome Guests*, published by the Southern Illinois University Press, contains only six stories not previously collected (including one with Cockrill). The book has pale-blue boards, with a grey cloth spine lettered in black, and it is dated. It includes an introduction and a checklist by Robert E. Briney. The wrapper is dominated by a bat with spread wings.

Certain works by Christianna Brand have not appeared in book form: *Shadowed Sunlight*, a novel; *The Witch*, a Gothic novella; and two newspaper serials.

Novels by Christianna Brand

(with series characters, as stated)

Death in High Heels Bodley Head 1941, Scribner 1942 (Charlesworth, Cecil)
Heads You Lose Bodley Head 1941, Dodd, Mead 1942 (Cockrill)
Green for Danger Dodd 1944, Bodley Head 1945 (Cockrill)
The Crooked Wreath Dodd 1946 (Cockrill)
a.k.a. *Suddenly At His Residence* Bodley Head 1947
Death of Jezebel Dodd 1948, Bodley Head 1949 (Cockrill, Charlesworth)
Cat and Mouse Joseph 1950, Knopf 1950 (Chucky)
London Particular Joseph 1952 (Cockrill, Charlesworth)
a.k.a. *Fog of Doubt* Scribner 1953
Tour de Force Joseph 1955, Scribner 1955 (Cockrill, Cecil)
The Honey Harlot Allen 1978
The Rose in Darkness Joseph 1979 (Charlesworth)
The Brides of Aberdar Joseph 1982, St Martin's 1983

Novels by Mary Ann Ashe

Alas, for Her that Met Me! Wyndham 1976
A Ring of Roses Wyndham 1977 (Chucky); Allen 1977 as by Christianna Brand

Story collections by Christianna Brand

What Dread Hand Joseph 1968 (15 stories, 3 with Cockrill)
Brand X Joseph 1974 (18 stories, 8 not criminous)
Buffet for Unwelcome Guests Southern Illinois University Press 1983 (16 stories, 4 with Cockrill)

Collaborations by Christianna Brand and others

(see also under Detection Club)

'The Diamonds Are Forever Amber Mystery' (*TV Times*, 12 July 1973)

The Poisoned Chocolates Case and 'The Avenging Chance' by Anthony Berkeley, with a new dénouement to the novel by Christianna Brand, University of California 1979

No Flowers by Request Gollancz 1984 (with *Crime on the Coast*)

Magazine and newspaper fiction

Shadowed Sunlight (*Woman*, 7 Jul.–4 Aug. 1945)

Cyanide in the Sun (*Daily Sketch*, 4–8 Aug. 1958)

A Shot in the Sun (*Daily Sketch*, 3–7 Aug. 1959)

The Witch (*Woman's Journal*, Aug. 1962)

Uncollected stories

'The Last Short Story' (*EQMM*, Jan. 1973) (Cockrill)

'The Kissing Cousin' (*Woman*, 2 June 1973) (Cockrill)

'Over my Dead Body' (*EQMM*, Aug. 1979)

'Cloud Nine' (*Verdict of Thirteen*, Faber 1979, Harper 1979)

'A Piece of Cake' (*EQMM*, Jan. 1983)

'And She Smiled at Me' (*EQMM*, May 1983)

'To the Widow' (*Saint*, June. 1984)

'The Rocking Chair' (*Saint*, Aug. 1984; *EQMM* May 1989) (Cockrill)

'The Man on the Roof' (*EQMM*, Oct 1984; *English Country House Murders*, Mysterious Press 1988/ *Country House Murders*, O'Mara 1989) (Cockrill)   *JC*

Lilian Jackson Braun

Lilian Jackson Braun had a brief career as a detective novelist in the 1960s but thereafter vanished from view for nearly twenty years. Since her return in 1986 she has become very popular, benefiting from a swing in public taste as, earlier, she had suffered from one (like Barbara Pym in the mainstream). All her novels prominently feature cats, not just as set decoration but as participants in the mysteries and their solution. Two Siamese feature, throughout in the case of the male, Koko, from the third in the series in the case of the female, Yum Yum. Their owner is Jim Qwilleran, a seasoned newspaperman, good-humoured and adaptable, who later comes into big money.

The books are of three distinct types: the early trio from Dutton in America and the Crime Club in Britain; five paperback originals from Jove, when the tide turned; and, since then, a series of hefty hardback slabs from Putnam, who believe that big is beautiful. In Britain, several later titles have appeared from Headline, most as paperback originals. Headline hardbacks exist but some, at least, appear to be later issues.

The Crime Club books are from the transitional era of this publisher when, simultaneously, the books grew bigger, went photographic and lost character. *The Cat Who*

Could Read Backwards is one of the last Crime Club books in the old, sensible, standard size. It has a red binding overlaid with a fine black mesh and gilt lettering on the spine. Kenneth Farnhill's wrapper has a pattern of mauve, orange and dark red triangles among which two black cat's eyes appear. *The Cat Who Ate Danish Modern* and *The Cat Who Turned On and Off* are taller books with red bindings and gilt spine lettering. All three are dated by the copyright notice. The Jove paperbacks began with *The Cat Who Saw Red* and include three more novels and a collection of fourteen non-series cat mysteries. These books all have bright pictorial covers, each featuring a bloodstained object and feline pawprints. They are all dated on the copyright page and the three titles from December 1987 also have printer's keys running from 1. All except *The Cat Who Saw Red* have a yellow fore-edge and *The Cat Who Played Post Office* has the other edges yellow, too.

The Putnam series continues in the visual tradition set by the paperbacks, with dust-wrappers by Jill Bauman in the style of their covers, which, surely, she must also have designed. The books are thumping great tomes, quarterbound in various colours and with gilt lettering on the spine, except for *The Cat Who Talked to Ghosts*, which has silver spine lettering. They are all dated by the copyright notice only and have printers' keys running from 1 on the copyright page. From *The Cat Who Moved a Mountain* the front covers have three gilt pawprints and the lettering on the front of the dust-wrapper is embossed. Within, black pawprints abound.

Qwilleran novels

(Binding details refer to Putnam editions)

The Cat Who Could Read Backwards Dutton 1966, Crime Club 1967

The Cat Who Ate Danish Modern Dutton 1967, Crime Club 1968

The Cat Who Turned On and Off Dutton 1968, Crime Club 1968

The Cat Who Saw Red Jove 1986, Headline 1990

The Cat Who Played Brahms Jove Jun. 1987

The Cat Who Played Post Office Jove Dec. 1987

The Cat Who Knew Shakespeare Jove Jun. 1988

The Cat Who Sniffed Glue Putnam Sept. 1988, Headline pb 1990 (mauve boards, cream spine)

The Cat Who Went Underground Putnam 1989 (cream, dark pink)

The Cat Who Talked to Ghosts Putnam 1990, Headline pb 1990 (deep red, black)

The Cat Who Lived High Putnam 1990, Headline pb 1991 (blue, blue)

The Cat Who Knew a Cardinal Putnam 1991, Headline pb 1991 (sand, fawn)

The Cat Who Moved a Mountain Putnam 1992, Headline 1992 (white, blue-green)

The Cat Who Wasn't There Putnam 1992 (blue, dark blue)

The Cat Who Went into the Closet Putnam 1993, Headline pb 1993 (white, green)

Story collection

The Cat Who Had 14 Tales   Jove Mar. 1988
(fourteen stories)   *BP*

Simon Brett (b. 1945)

Simon Brett's bent is for light entertainment, both in TV and radio, where he made his primary career, and more recently in his detective novels, particularly those with Charles Paris as protagonist. Since Paris is an actor, scratching a living rather than making a name, the seedier reaches of the theatrical world are explored in the course of the series. It is this enticing ambience that gives these books their special savour, rather than any particular cunning in their devising. Though agreeably lightweight as narratives, they sometimes lack the 'element of satisfaction' that Margery Allingham demanded of the classic mystery novel.

After ten Paris books published by Gollancz, Simon Brett changed direction with two inverted novels from a new publisher, Macmillan. This departure was deplored by Anthony Lejeune on the grounds that an expert light entertainer is ill advised to air a darker side; but the author, understandably, sees it as extending his range. A third novel from Macmillan introduced a new detective, Melita Pargeter, the widow of an upmarket burglar, whose astute and attractive personality clearly destined her for a series of her own.

The Gollancz books to 1987 are all red with gilt lettering on the spine. *A Series of Murders* and *Corporate Bodies* are black, the former with gilt spine lettering, the latter with silver. The Macmillan books vary both in binding and lettering colours. Both series are dated, the Gollancz on the title-page, the Macmillan on the copyright page. Neither has interesting wrappers: the Gollancz are standard yellow for most of the run, the Macmillans photographic, with red and white spines. From *Corporate Bodies* the books are taller. *Mrs. Pargeter's Pound of Flesh* has a printer's key from 1 on the copyright page: no '1' means a later impression.

The Christmas Crimes at Puzzel Manor provides 'Festive fun for the criminally minded'.

The book has laminated covers and many puzzles, plans and diagrams to enhance the narrative. The front cover has a fine picture of the manor under snow, with all lights blazing.

The Charles Paris books continue to appear from Gollancz, who also brought out a collection of twelve crime stories, *A Box of Tricks*, the first of three books published in 1985. The final story, 'The Haunted Actress', features Charles Paris, who also appears in 'Who Killed Terry Wogan?' and in 'Murder in the Grotto', both uncollected. 'Easier in the Abstract', in *EQMM* for July 1986, is not a story, but an extract from *A Shock to the System*. 'A Little Learning', in *A Classic English Crime*, Pavilion 1990, is a spoof scholarly essay on Agatha Christie.

Novels

(with Paris, except as stated or as a title indicates)
(Binding details refer to Macmillan editions)

Cast, in Order of Disappearance   Gollancz 1975, Scribner 1976
So Much Blood   Gollancz 1976, Scribner 1977
Star Trap   Gollancz 1977, Scribner 1978
An Amateur Corpse   Gollancz 1978, Scribner 1978
A Comedian Dies   Gollancz 1979, Scribner 1979
The Dead Side of the Mike   Gollancz 1980, Scribner 1980
Situation Tragedy   Gollancz 1981, Scribner 1981
Murder Unprompted   Gollancz 1982, Scribner 1982
Murder in the Title   Gollancz 1983, Scribner 1983
Not Dead, Only Resting   Gollancz 1984, Scribner 1984
A Shock to the System   Macmillan 1984, Scribner 1985 (not Paris) (brown, gilt)
Dead Romantic   Macmillan 1985, Scribner 1986 (not Paris) (red, silver)
Dead Giveaway   Gollancz 1985, Scribner 1986
A Nice Class of Corpse   Macmillan 1986, Scribner 1986 (Pargeter) (light brown, gilt)
What Bloody Man Is That?   Gollancz 1987, Scribner 1987

Mrs., Presumed Dead Macmillan 1988, Scribner 1988 (Pargeter) (blue, silver)

A Series of Murders Gollancz 1989, Scribner 1989

Mrs. Pargeter's Package Macmillan 1990, Scribner 1991 (maroon, silver)

Corporate Bodies Gollancz 1991, Scribner 1992

Mrs. Pargeter's Pound of Flesh Macmillan 1992, Scribner 1993 (green, gilt)

A Reconstructed Corpse Gollancz 1993, Scribner 1994

'Puzzle' novel

The Christmas Crimes at Puzzel Manor Hodder & Stoughton 1991, Delacorte 1992

Story collection

A Box of Tricks Gollancz 1985 (12 stories) a.k.a. *Tickled to Death* Scribner 1985

Uncollected stories

'Letter to his Son' (*Winter's Crimes 18*, Macmillan 1986, St Martin's 1987)

Who Killed Terry Wogan?' (*Sunday Express Magazine*, 21 Dec. 1986)

'Murder in the Grotto' (*Sunday Express Magazine*, 20 Dec. 1987)

'Stardust Kill' (*Raymond Chandler's Philip Marlowe*, Knopf 1988)

'An Unmentionable Death' (*Winter's Crimes 20*, Macmillan 1988)

'The Battered Cherub' (*Winter's Crimes 21*, Macmillan 1989)

'False Scent' (*Midwinter Mysteries 1*, Scribner 1991)

'The Man Who Got the Dirt' (*The Man Who . . .* Macmillan 1992)

'The Christmas Crimes at "Cinderella" ' (*1st Culprit*, Chatto & Windus 1992)

'Death at the Office Party' (*Daily Mail*, 24, 26, 28 & 29 Dec. 1992) *BP*

A BOX OF TRICKS

The first collection of short stories by
SIMON BRETT

Gollancz
Detection

Lynn Brock (1877–1943)

Lynn Brock was a pseudonym of Alister McAllister, who wrote eleven detective novels under this name. These books are noted for their intricate plots. *Nightmare* combines murder with a psychological study. The books written as by Anthony Wharton are not concerned with detection (and this includes *The Two of Diamonds*, later published under the Brock pseudonym). Brock's most important series character is Colonel Wickham Gore, ex-Indian Army, who sets up a detective agency and features in seven novels. In five of these, Barbara Lethbridge, who is known as Pickles and marries Dr Melhuish, either appears or is referred to in a letter. Sergeant Venn and Detective-Constable Kither – the tortoise and hare of Scotland Yard – solve two cases together. Venn goes solo for *The Riddle of The Roost.*

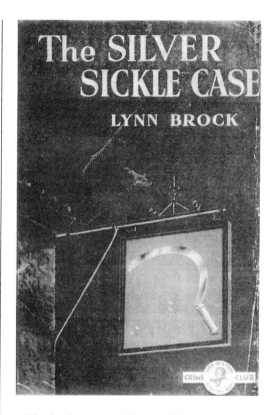

The SILVER
SICKLE CASE

LYNN BROCK

The books were all first published in London by Collins and are all clearly dated. The last five titles were not published in the USA. Four books have alternative US titles. *Q.E.D./Murder on the Bridge* is a sequel to *The Mendip Mystery/ Murder at the Inn*.

The first four titles all have dark-blue cloth with red lettering on the spine and title and author in red on the front cover. Of these, the first two also have a double red border and the second two have a single red border, on the front cover in each case. There are corresponding rules at the top and base of each spine. *The Dagwort Coombe Murder* and *The Mendip Mystery* have black cloth with red spine lettering and title and author in red on the front cover. Both front covers have a single red border with single red rules at the top and base of the spine. *Nightmare* has green cloth with red lettering on the spine and front cover. The five remaining titles are all Crime Club books with orange/red cloth and black lettering on the spine. *Q.E.D.*

has title and author in black lettering on the front cover with a single black border. The other four titles have blank front covers. Apart from *Nightmare*, all the books have pages of advertisements at the rear. The Crime Club gunman faces right on the title-page of *The Riddle of the Roost*.

Colonel Gore's Second Case is one of several books which contain maps. Its wrapper, by Ellen Edwards, shows an anxious young woman looking over her shoulder at a broken window. The wrapper for *The Dagwort Coombe Murder* has a honeycomb design in orange and black. Wilkins' design for *Murder on the Bridge* shows the body of Dr Melhuish falling from the Westmouth Suspension Bridge. The wrapper for *The Silver Sickle Case* has the hanging sign of a silver sickle on a blue background. *Nightmare* has a striking blue-green wrapper with the features of two faces outlined in red and black.

'Peter Poppy's Passions', a series of six stories with Mr Poppy as detective, appeared in 1928.

Novels

(with Gore or Venn, as stated)

The Deductions of Colonel Gore Collins 1924, Harper 1925
a.k.a. *The Barrington Mystery* Collins 1932
Colonel Gore's Second Case Collins 1925, Harper 1926
Colonel Gore's Third Case: The Kink Collins 1925, Harper 1927
The Slip-Carriage Mystery Collins 1928, Harper 1928 (Gore)
The Dagwort Coombe Murder Collins 1929
a.k.a. *The Stoke Silver Case* Harper 1929
The Mendip Mystery Collins 1929 (Gore)
a.k.a. *Murder at the Inn* Harper 1929
Q.E.D. Collins Crime Club 1930 (Gore)
a.k.a. *Murder on the Bridge* Harper 1930
Nightmare Collins 1932
The Silver Sickle Case Crime Club 1938 (Venn)
Fourfingers Crime Club 1939 (Venn)
The Riddle of the Roost Crime Club 1939 (Venn)
The Stoat Crime Club 1940 (Gore)

Stories

Peter Poppy's Passions, *The Sketch* 1928
'The Dishonest Landlady' (7 Mar.)
'The Bed-Fellows' (14 Mar.)
'Vanitas, Puritas' (21 Mar.)
'The Bower of Bliss' (28 Mar.)
'Colonel Sydenham's Nerves' (4 Apr.)
'The Eye Rock Affair' (11 Apr.)   *JC*

Douglas G. Browne (1884–1963)

Douglas Gordon Browne was the son of Gordon Browne, the artist, and grandson of 'Phiz', the Dickens illustrator. His earlier work is various and unreliable, but he hit his stride with the Harvey Tuke series, launched in the war and eventually seven-strong. Two other detectives are underdeveloped: Major Maurice Hemyock (in three novels and a story) and Inspector Horatio Thew (in two novels): but Mr Tuke, canny and urbane, has his own distinctive savour and the series he graces is substantial fare.

Browne began with a story collection, *Uncle William*, published by Blackwood in 1930 in a red binding. The first issue has gilt lettering on the spine and title and author in gilt on the front cover, which also has a blind-stamped border. A later issue has black lettering on the spine only. Both are dated on the title-page. The four stories include a historical novella, 'Hearse House', and the first Hemyock title, 'The Whistle'.

Five books were published by Methuen, including two with Hemyock and both with Thew. *The Dead Don't Bite* has decorated black lettering on the spine and *Plan XVI* and *The 'Looking Glass' Murders* have black lettering with a dagger in relief against a black diamond shape. All have title and author in black on the front cover. *Plan XVI* has a blue binding, the others are red. *The Cotfold Conundrums* has a red-brown binding with gilt lettering on the spine only and *The Stolen Boat-Train* has a pale yellow-grey binding with heavy dark-red lettering, including title and author on the front cover. The front endpapers of the latter have an unsigned map of the Kentish countryside between Lydden and Frythe with, inset, a plan of the North Part of Saltmarshe Works. All the

Methuen books are dated on the copyright page and each has an advertisement section at the end with a final printer's code (in order of publication: 332, 133, 530 (*sic*), 934 and 835).

The May Week Murders is an isolated Longman book with an apple-green binding and red lettering on the spine and front cover (the title at the top and the author's name at the lower right corner). It is dated on the copyright page (and features, for the last time, Major Hemyock). *The House of the Sword* and *Death Wears a Mask* were published by Hutchinson (the latter introducing Harvey Tuke). Both are undated and have the publisher's name slanted across the lower right corner of the front cover, in black for the former, in red for the latter. *The House of the Sword* is red with black lettering on the spine and undated advertisements at the rear. *Death Wears a Mask* is pale blue with red lettering on the spine.

The remaining Tuke novels were published by Macdonald, *Too Many Cousins* in a red binding, the final pair in black and the other three in blue. Their spine lettering varies: black for *Too Many Cousins*; red with a criss-cross decoration in yellow for *Rustling End*; gilt/yellow with single rules for *Death in Perpetuity*; and yellow for the final pair. *What Beckoning Ghost* has title and author in green within a black rectangular block. All the Macdonald books are dated on the copyright page, except *Too Many Cousins*, which is undated.

Apart from the stories in *Uncle William*, two other stories are known. More must exist, since the blurb for *Too Many Cousins* refers to Browne's 'numerous short stories in *The Cornhill* and similar magazines'.

The wrapper for *Uncle William* is by the author himself and shows William Sheaffe in the doorway of the studio at his brother's house. *The Cotfold Conundrums* has a frenzied man loomed over by a huge blue caveman, both wielding battle-axes. *Plan XVI* shows an ocean-going liner lifted clear of the water by a giant hand. *The Stolen Boat-Train* has the tunnel into which the train vanished on the front panel and the spine shows a bald, bespectacled man looking down on another man lying under railway sleepers, with a telephone on the rail. *The House of* the *Sword* features a mountain scene with a couple on skis and, looming beyond and stretching his hand towards them, a large bald man, scowling and looking threatening. The blue wrapper of *Death Wears a Mask* has a large skeletal hand supporting a man on a stretcher, with an even larger gas-mask on the right of the panel. The six Shearsby cousins figure on the wrapper for *Too Many Cousins* and *What Beckoning Ghost* has the Hyde Park Ghost in naval combat gear. *Rustling End* also has its ghost, this time in Elizabethan male costume; an ominous male shadow in modern dress occupies the other half of the panel.

Novels

(with series characters as indicated)

The Dead Don't Bite   Methuen February 1933 (Hemyock)
The Cotfold Conundrums Methuen October 1933 (Thew)
Plan XVI Methuen 1934, Doubleday 1934 (Thew)
The 'Looking Glass' Murders Methuen January 1935 (Hemyock)
The Stolen Boat-Train Methuen October 1935
The May Week Murders Longman 1937 (Hemyock)
The House of the Sword Hutchinson n.d. (1939)

Harvey Tuke novels

Death Wears a Mask   Hutchinson n.d. (1940), Macmillan 1954
Too Many Cousins Macdonald n.d. (1946), Macmillan 1953
What Beckoning Ghost Macdonald 1947
Rustling End Macdonald 1948
Death in Perpetuity Macdonald 1950
Sergeant Death Macdonald 1955
Death in Seven Volumes Macdonald 1958

Story collection

Uncle William   Blackwood 1930

Uncollected stories

'Eight O'clock' (*The Sketch*, 24 Sept. 1930)
'The Queer Door' (*Great Short Stories of Detection, Mystery and Horror, Second Series*, Gollancz 1931)   *BP*

Leo Bruce (1903–1979)

Besides a prolific output in his own name, Rupert Croft-Cooke wrote thirty-one detective stories as Leo Bruce. His adherence to the classic form makes him rare among crime writers. A detractor might dismiss his work as formula fiction, but who would wish to detract from so rich an achievement, so cunningly sustained?

The earlier of his two detectives is Sergeant Beef, a beer-swilling village policeman, who leaves the force to set up his plate as a private investigator in Lilac Crescent, near Baker Street. His first case pits him against the three detectives of its title: Lord Simon Plimsoll, Amer Picon, and Monsignor Smith. He succeeds where they fail, and his career is launched. Sadly, the war stopped him in his tracks. He had fewer post-war cases and none after his eighth in 1952. Three years later Carolus Deene took the floor, to hold it steadily through twenty-three investigations. A public schoolmaster, removed from the constraints of professional poverty by a substantial private income, he has a fine war record and runs a Bentley Continental. Irresistibly, over the years, certain rituals accumulate: the headmaster's protests, the housekeeper's threats of resignation, the unwelcome intrusions of the schoolboy Watson. Few writers ring the changes on the formal pattern so adroitly and resourcefully, and yet provide so reassuringly the mixture as before.

All Bruce's first editions are dated, and, since the books were seldom reprinted, there are few problems of identity. The earliest books, from Geoffrey Bles, give the most trouble, since only the bindings distinguish first from later issues. All three books are bound in red, with the title stamped in white on the cover and the spine lettering also in white. Variant bindings and black lettering invariably indicate later issues. The Bles dust-wrappers are photographic. Beef's hands figure on *Case without a Corpse*, the left holding a pint of beer, the right removing darts from a board. *Case with No Conclusion* has them beginning a letter to a client.

Beef's fourth case was published by Peter Davies, who later brought out many of the Deene books: *Case with Four Clowns* is bound in blue, with black spine lettering. His fifth and sixth cases came from Nicholson & Watson, one before and one after the war. *Case with Ropes and Rings* is an orange book, lettered in black on the spine. On the half-title a bull curvets within a circle surmounted by a pair of arching horns: beneath is the legend 'Sergeant Beef scores a bull'. The post-war reissue of this book causes confusion, since its claim to have been first published in 1949 implies a first edition. The reissue is a red book, with silver lettering on the spine, the title within a black frame. The second Nicholson book is *Case for Sergeant Beef*, a slim blue book with gilt spine lettering in disconcertingly small print. The two Gollancz books mark the closing stage in Beef's career. Both are red, *Neck and Neck* with black spine lettering, and *Cold Blood* with gilt, and both have the standard yellow wrappers of this publisher. *Case for Sergeant Beef* has a Bruce Roberts wrapper showing Beef in a brown suit, surveying the terrain.

Carolus Deene's career began with Hamish Hamilton, who issued *At Death's Door* in 1955. The blurb 'introduces us to a new, more sophisticated detective', 'an elegant schoolmaster, rather in the Peter Wimsey tradition': if you can't beat 'em, join 'em. The book is black, with silver spine lettering, and the plain dust-wrapper has large black letters on an orange background.

All but one of the Davies books are identical in format, with uniform spine lettering, the title and publisher in lower case, and the author in capitals. *Dead for a Ducat, Our Jubilee is Death, Furious Old Women*, and *Nothing Like Blood* have gilt lettering, the others silver. *Death of Cold* is distinguished by black cursive lettering. The Davies bindings are in various colours, and, variants are known for *A Louse for the Hangman*, which is maroon or black, and *A Bone and a Hank of Hair*, which is orange or blue. The wrappers for the series, at least from *Dead for a Ducat*, are in a uniform style devised by Val Biro. Each is individualized by an enticing detail from the text, and together they make an arresting show. All the Davies books have the publisher's initials blind-stamped on the rear cover. *Dead Man's Shoes* is wrongly described by the publisher as Deene's fifth case, and, from this book on, *Cold Blood* is attributed to him and not to Beef.

The Allen books are less appealing, though Peter Barrett launches them well with his gloomy evocation of Albert Park, and Gill Speirs' design for *Death in the Middle Watch* includes the only portrait of Carolus, looking at once both dapper and pensive. Most of the others have glossy photographic wrappers, and from *Death of a Commuter* the books are slightly taller. All the Allen books have gilt spine lettering, except the last, which has red. This publisher's attempt to establish a separate identity for the books he issued – as the 'Carolus Deene "Death" Books' – seems pointless, since they simply continue the existing series: what he actually means is that they all have 'Death' in their titles.

All Leo Bruce's known stories were collected as *Murder in Miniature* in 1993. The book, from Academy Chicago, has red boards, yellow spine and cover strips and purple spine lettering. Though dated 1992 by the copyright notice, it did not appear until 1993. Each of the twenty-eight stories has a preliminary illustration by Barbara Spann. Beef appears in ten stories, Detective-Sergeant Grebe, a new policeman, in eight. 'Bloody Moon', listed previously, is not by Leo Bruce.

Some of the novels written in the author's real name deal with crime and criminals but are in a wholly different vein.

Beef novels

Case for Three Detectives Bles 1936, Stokes 1937
Case without a Corpse Bles 1937, Stokes 1937
Case with No Conclusion Bles 1939, Academy Chicago 1984
Case with Four Clowns Davies 1939, Stokes 1939
Case with Ropes and Rings Nicholson & Watson 1940, Academy 1980
Case for Sergeant Beef Nicholson 1947, Academy 1980
Neck and Neck Gollancz 1951, Academy 1980
Cold Blood Gollancz 1952. Academy 1980

Deene novels

(Details of bindings refer to British editions)

At Death's Door Hamish Hamilton 1955
Death of Cold Davies 1956 (blue-green binding)
Dead for a Ducat Davies 1956 (blue)

Dead Man's Shoes Davies 1958, Academy 1987 (red)
A Louse for the Hangman Davies 1958
Our Jubilee Is Death Davies 1959, Academy 1986 (red)
Jack on the Gallows Tree Davies 1960, Academy 1983 (red)
Furious Old Women Davies 1960, Academy 1983 (green)
A Bone and a Hank of Hair Davies 1961, Academy 1985
Die All, Die Merrily Davies 1961, Academy 1986 (green)
Nothing Like Blood Davies 1962, Academy 1985 (blue)
Crack of Doom Davies 1963 (red)
a.k.a. *Such Is Death* London House 1963
Death in Albert Park Allen 1964, Scribner 1979 (red)
Death at Hallows End Allen 1965 (black)
Death on the Black Sands Allen 1966 (blue)

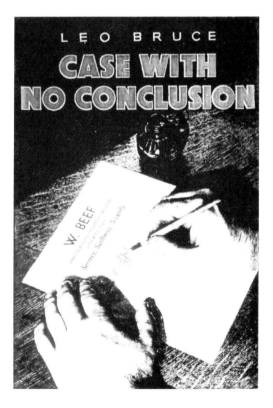

Death at St. Asprey's School   Allen 1967, Academy 1984 (black)

Death of a Commuter   Allen 1967, Academy 1988 (blue)

Death on Romney Marsh   Allen 1968 (blue)

Death with Blue Ribbon   Allen 1969, London House 1970 (blue)

Death on Allhallowe'en   Allen 1970, Academy 1988 (maroon)

Death by the Lake   Allen 1971 (dark red)

Death in the Middle Watch   Allen 1974 (dark blue)

Death of a Bovver Boy   Allen 1974 (black)

Story collection

Murder in Miniature   Academy 1992 (1993) (28 stories, 10 with Beef, 8 with Grebe)   *BP*

W. J. Burley (b. 1914)

William John Burley has written twenty-four novels to date, but remains an absurdly undervalued writer. He deserves a far wider appreciation, as those who have already discovered him will confirm. A particularly good example of his work is *Death in a Salubrious Place*. Chief Superintendent Charles Wycliffe, who appears in nineteen novels, is a West Country detective with his heart very much in his job. His interest extends to the people involved and the reasons behind their crimes. Dr Henry Pym, criminologist and professor of zoology, is featured in two early novels.

Burley's books were first published in London by Gollancz, all dated on the title-page and with gilt lettering on the spine. The nineteen titles to 1987 have red cloth but from *Wycliffe and the Tangled Web* to *Wycliffe and the Last Rites* they are black. *Wycliffe and the Dunes Mystery* has a blue binding. Towards the end of *Wycliffe and the Cycle of Death* in its Corgi paperback edition (1991) there are some differences from the text of the first edition. All but the two most recent titles, which are taller than the rest, have yellow wrappers. Nadine Wickenden designed Burley's first UK pictorial wrapper for *Wycliffe and the Last Rites*, depicting an attractive tranquil scene of St Julian's church and graveyard. *Wycliffe and the Dunes Mystery* has another illustration by this artist, showing the dead hand of Cochran Wilder emerging from the St Ives sand. Two titles were not published in the USA: *A Taste of Power* and *Three-toed Pussy*. *Charles and Elizabeth* and *The House of Care* are Gothic suspense novels. *The Sixth Day* is a SF novel.

The most difficult first edition to find is the author's first book, the Pym novel *A Taste of Power*.

Novels

(with Wycliffe, except as stated)

A Taste of Power   Gollancz 1966 (Pym)

Three-toed Pussy   Gollancz 1968

Death in Willow Pattern   Gollancz 1969, Walker 1970 (Pym)

To Kill a Cat   Gollancz 1970, Walker 1970

Guilt Edged   Gollancz 1971, Walker 1972

Death in a Salubrious Place   Gollancz 1973, Walker 1973

Death in Stanley Street   Gollancz 1974, Walker 1974

Wycliffe and the Pea-green Boat   Gollancz 1975, Walker 1975

Wycliffe and the Schoolgirls   Gollancz 1976, Walker 1976

The Schoolmaster   Gollancz 1977, Walker 1977 (not Wycliffe)

Wycliffe and the Scapegoat   Gollancz 1978, Walker 1978

Charles and Elizabeth   Gollancz 1979, Walker 1981 (not Wycliffe)

Wycliffe in Paul's Court   Gollancz 1980, Doubleday 1980

The House of Care   Gollancz 1981, Walker 1982 (not Wycliffe)

Wycliffe's Wild-goose Chase   Gollancz 1982, Doubleday 1982

Wycliffe and the Beales   Gollancz 1983, Doubleday 1984

Wycliffe and the Four Jacks   Gollancz 1985, Doubleday 1986

Wycliffe and the Quiet Virgin   Gollancz 1986, Doubleday 1986

Wycliffe and the Winsor Blue   Gollancz 1987, Doubleday 1987

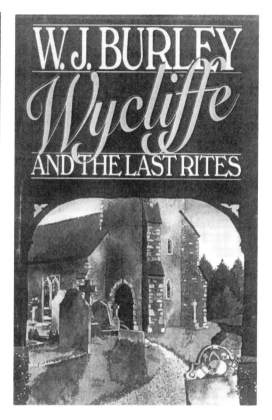

turing in five books. Leric's rough and ready approach to life does not endear him to his fellow officers but in no way impedes his efficiency. Detective-Sergeant Tony Rowley of Scotland Yard has appeared to good effect in three books containing linked stories.

Roger Busby's books were all first published in London and they are all dated. The collaboration, *Main Line Kill*, centred on a Birmingham nightclub, was published by Cassell in black cloth with white lettering on the spine. It is one of three titles published in the USA. *Fading Blue* is a paperback, published by the *Police Review* and humorously illustrated by John Whittaker. This book is written in the form of anecdotes, some humorous, some tragic. 'The Arrow Bridge Jumper' was expanded into the novel *High Jump*. The remaining books have been published by Collins Crime Club in red cloth with gilt lettering on the spine. *High Jump* has a printer's key on the copyright page. Alan Burton designed the striking yellow wrapper for *A Reasonable Man*, showing the double-bass case in which part of a human corpse is found.

The most difficult title to find is the collaboration *Main Line Kill*.

Wycliffe and the Tangled Web   Gollancz 1988, Doubleday 1989
Wycliffe and the Cycle of Death   Gollancz 1990, Doubleday 1991
Wycliffe and the Dead Flautist   Gollancz 1991, Doubleday 1992
Wycliffe and the Last Rites   Gollancz 1992, St Martin's 1993
Wycliffe and the Dunes Mystery   Gollancz 1993   *JC*

Roger Busby (b. 1941)

Roger Busby has written thirteen books, the first in collaboration with Gerald Holtham. He is one of the leading writers of British police procedural novels, with authentic backgrounds arising from his own involvement in police work. *A Reasonable Man* and *Pattern of Violence* are fine examples of his work. Detective-Sergeant (later Inspector) Leric is his first series character, fea-

Novels

(with Leric or Rowley, as stated)

Main Line Kill   Cassell 1968, Walker 1968 with Gerald Holtham.
Robbery Blue   Collins Crime Club 1969 (Leric)
The Frighteners   Crime Club 1970 (Leric)
Deadlock   Crime Club 1971 (Leric)
A Reasonable Man   Crime Club 1972 (Leric)
Pattern of Violence   Crime Club 1973 (Leric)
New Face in Hell   Crime Club 1976
Garvey's Code   Crime Club 1978
The Hunter   Crime Club 1985, Doubleday 1989 (Rowley)
Snow Man   Crime Club 1987, Doubleday 1989 (Rowley)
Crackshot   Crime Club 1990 (Rowley)
High Jump   Crime Club 1992

Fading Blue   *Police Review*   1984   *JC*

FADING BLUE

ROGER BUSBY

Christopher Bush (1885–1973) a.k.a. Michael Home

For over forty years, Christopher Bush was one of the most reliable and resourceful of true detective writers, author of sixty-three novels marked by a quirky ingenuity, a craftsman's control, and a well-bred, clubman's restraint. Much of his earlier work is Golden Age baroque, rendered remarkable by some extraordinary flights of fancy. His later work is absorbing rather than exciting, the style easy and urbane. The narratives advance sedately, and much cunning is expended on the demolition of inconvenient alibis.

All Bush's novels and four of his stories feature a reassuring toff called Ludovic Travers, the least showy of men despite considerable gifts of taste and intellect. Of his several recurring associates, two are particularly important:

George Wharton, the ebullient Scotland Yard man, known to friends and associates as 'the General'; and, in the later books, Chief Inspector Jewle, a less flamboyant figure. Wharton appears in the second book, *The Perfect Murder Case*, and he recurs in well over half the series, for the last time in *The Case of the Flowery Corpse*, which is really Jewle's case. Reference is made to him at the outset of *The Case of the Russian Cross*, but he does not in fact become involved in it. Travers proposes to his future wife, the dancer Bernice Haire, in *The Case of the Leaning Man*. His war service – as a captain and later as a major – accounts for a run of military titles. From *The Case of the Kidnapped Colonel*, he acts as his own narrator. *The Case of the Flying Ass* and *The Case of the Climbing Rat* are unusual in being set in France.

Bush began with Jarrolds, who published *The Plumley Inheritance* in 1926. The book is undated, with a frontispiece plan of Hainton village. The binding is purple and the spine has orange lettering and decoration at both ends. The front cover has title and author and a decorative border, all in orange. In the lower right corner is a masked man, purple within an orange rectangular block. An advertisement section at the end is dated Spring 1926. The next book and the five after it came from Heinemann, who bound them all in black and dated them. The first of this sequence, *The Perfect Murder Case*, has yellow lettering on the spine. The front cover has the title at the top and the author's name at the bottom, and the rear cover has the Heinemann windmill, all in yellow. The later Heinemann books have gilt lettering on the spine only and blind-stamped borders edging their front covers. The Heinemann windmill is blind-stamped on their rear covers. *Murder at Fenwold* has a gilt band at the top of the spine and another at the foot; it also has a frontispiece plan of Fenwold village. *Cut Throat* has the title and the publisher's windmill in red on the title-page.

Evidence suggests that *The Death of Cosmo Revere* antedates its British equivalent, *Murder at Fenwold*, by six months. The BL has a copy of the Doubleday first edition, with a cancel title-page inserted by Heinemann, suggesting that a makeshift British edition may have had some currency in advance of the independent Heinemann issue with its different title. The *ECB*, however, does not list such an edition, and, in any case, the possibility seems remote. The adapted Doubleday edition is stamped 23 May 1930, and *Murder at Fenwold* has the later stamp, 18 November 1930. The *ECB* confirms November for the latter.

After *Cut Throat*, Bush was published by Cassell, who issued twenty-two of his books, the last in 1945. The six books from *The Case of the Unfortunate Village* to *The Case of the Chinese Gong* are variously coloured, but their spines have uniform lettering, with a line ruled at top and bottom. *The Case of the Monday Murders* has similar lettering but no rules. *The Case of the Unfortunate Village* has a blind-stamped border on the front cover. *The Case of the Dead Shepherd* has two plans of Woodgate Hill County School as a double frontispiece.

The books from *The Case of the Tudor Queen* to *The Case of the Fighting Soldier* have spines with three lines ruled over the title and repeated under the author's name. Five of this run are green, generally with black lettering, but blue for *The Case of the Kidnapped Colonel*. *The Case of the Leaning Man* and *The Case of The Green Felt Hat* are red with black lettering, and *The Case of the Flying Ass* is brown with green. *The Case of the Green Felt Hat* has a frontispiece plan of Pettistone.

The final run of Cassell books is uniform in all respects, with green bindings and the titles in black, running along the spine, with the base of the lettering towards the front cover. The author's and publisher's names are printed upright, at the head and foot, respectively. All the Cassell books are dated, and all have a printer's date code on the reverse of the title-page. *The Case of the Corporal's Leave* has no rear endpaper.

All Bush's post-war books were published by Macdonald, the twenty-three from *The Case of the Corner Cottage* to *The Case of the Jumbo Sandwich* in a uniform format of black binding and yellow spine lettering, with a yellow dagger over the publisher's name. Only five of the Macdonald books are not black: *The Case of the*

Haven Hotel and *The Case of the Happy Warrior*, which are blue; and *The Case of the Missing Men*, *The Case of the Second Chance*, and *The Case of the Seven Bells*, which are red. *The Case of the Second Chance* has black spine lettering against a green panel, surmounted by three wavy black lines in a decorative flourish. All except the first of the Macdonald books are dated. From *The Case of the Happy Medium* to *The Case of the Jumbo Sandwich*, all but one of the books (*The Case of the Three Ring Puzzle*) have a portrait of Ludovic Travers on the half-title (which recurs on the rear dust-wrapper panel of several of the sequence).

The wrapper for *The Case of the Dead Shepherd* shows the prone corpse of the unpleasant headmaster of Woodgate Hill School. *The Case of the Chinese Gong* has a bronze gong suspended on red cords and *The Case of the Monday Murders* (by James E. McConnell) features a newsboy touting for custom. *The Case of the Tudor Queen* has an elegant lettered wrapper, with red bands and blue lettering on a cream base. *The Case of the Green Felt Hat* offers a vivid impression of Molly Pernaby with the significant headgear; and Mays' design for *The Case of the Climbing Rat* presents a sinister hooded trapeze artist with a rat on his shoulder.

Jack Matthew's wrapper for *The Case of the Running Mouse* shows the rodent in question, with Peter Worrack lying dead in a chair and one of the smart women at his gaming club on the night he died. The initials J. M. suggest that the same artist worked on *The Case of the Kidnapped Colonel*, depicting the encounter between the shepherd and the exhausted colonel. Crispin's designs for several of the earlier Macdonald books include the rainswept sign of the East End pub for *The Case of the Seven Bells*. *The Case of the Purloined Picture* shows Corbit's antique shop, with the fatal pestle in its mortar prominently displayed.

C. W. Bacon's design for *The Case of the Burnt Bohemian* is, properly, like 'a stage setting for some corner of an operatic Bohemia'; and for *The Case of the Red Brunette* he provides an uncharacteristic view of Travers, looking severely rattled by his discovery of Vera Millmay's body. Since *The Case of the Silken Petticoat* comes between these in the sequence, Bacon may also have shown the encounter between Clement Foorde and the elusive blonde who berates him, while Travers – round the corner, on the spine – looks on. Travers features on a number of the later wrappers, most notably on H. Johns' landscape for *The Case of the Amateur Actor*, which shows him with Chief Constable Gilson, approaching the ditch in which Richard Alton's body was found.

Two of Bush's American publishers evidently took against his unyielding title formula and substituted their own variants. Cherry Tree and Mellifont issued abridgements of six of his novels in the 1940s and early 1950s. Six of the books he wrote as Michael Home are listed as 'Novels of Military Intelligence'; and two are certainly mysteries, with a real detective, Captain John Benham of MI5, to unravel them. The others were described by J. B. Priestley as in the manner of A. E. W. Mason and John Buchan.

Of the five known stories, all but one feature Ludovic Travers: the exception is 'The Hampstead Murder', which exists in two versions. Three stories are condensed versions of earlier novels: 'Murder of a Maharajah' of *The Case of the Leaning Man*, 'The Holly Bears a Berry'/'Murder at Christmas' of *The Case of the Green Felt Hat* and 'Wings of Death' of *The Case of the Flying Ass*. 'A Drop Too Much' has links with *The Case of the Magic Mirror*, but since it antedates the novel it cannot be a condensation of it. 'Tears for the Jury', the later version of this story, may perhaps owe something to the novel.

Travers novels

(Details of bindings refer to British editions.)

The Plumley Inheritance Jarrolds n.d. (1926)
The Perfect Murder Case Heinemann 1929, Doubleday 1929
Dead Man Twice Heinemann 1930, Doubleday 1930
The Death of Cosmo Revere Doubleday 1930
a.k.a. *Murder at Fenwold* Heinemann 1930
Dancing Death Heinemann 1931, Doubleday 1931

Dead Man's Music Heinemann 1931, Doubleday 1932
Cut Throat Heinemann 1932, Morrow 1932
The Case of the Unfortunate Village Cassell 1932 (blue binding, dark blue lettering)
The Case of the April Fools Cassell 1933, Morrow 1933 (light green, dark green)
The Case of the Three Strange Faces Cassell 1933 (grey-blue, dark blue)
a.k.a. *The Crank in the Corner* Morrow 1933
The Case of the 100% Alibis Cassell 1934 (red, black)
a.k.a. *The Kitchen Cake Murder* Morrow 1934
The Case of the Dead Shepherd Cassell 1934 (fawn-yellow, blue)
a.k.a. *The Tea-tray Murders* Morrow 1934
The Case of the Chinese Gong Cassell 1935, Holt 1935 (grey-green, red)
The Case of the Monday Murders Cassell 1936 (green, red)
a.k.a. *Murder on Monday* Holt 1936
The Case of the Bonfire Body Cassell 1936 (orange, black)
a.k.a. *The Body in the Bonfire* Holt 1936
The Case of the Missing Minutes Cassell 1937 (green, yellow)
a.k.a. *Eight O'clock Alibi* Holt 1937
The Case of the Hanging Rope Cassell 1937 (red, black)
a.k.a. *The Wedding Night Murder* Holt 1937
The Case of the Tudor Queen Cassell 1938, Holt 1938
The Case of the Leaning Man Cassell 1938
a.k.a. *The Leaning Man* Holt 1938
The Case of the Green Felt Hat Cassell 1939, Holt 1939
The Case of the Flying Ass Cassell 1939
The Case of the Climbing Rat Cassell 1940
The Case of the Murdered Major Cassell 1941
The Case of the Kidnapped Colonel Cassell 1942
The Case of the Fighting Soldier Cassell 1942
The Case of the Magic Mirror Cassell 1943
The Case of the Running Mouse Cassell 1944
The Case of the Platinum Blonde Cassell 1944, Macmillan 1949
The Case of the Corporal's Leave Cassell 1945
The Case of the Missing Men Macdonald n.d. (1946), Macmillan 1947 (black lettering)

The Case of the Second Chance Macdonald 1946, Macmillan 1947

The Case of the Curious Client Macdonald 1947, Macmillan 1948 (gilt)

The Case of the Haven Hotel Macdonald 1948 (silver)

The Case of the Housekeeper's Hair Macdonald 1948, Macmillan 1949 (green)

The Case of the Seven Bells Macdonald 1949, Macmillan 1950 (gilt)

The Case of the Purloined Picture Macdonald 1949, Macmillan 1951 (yellow)

The Case of the Happy Warrior Macdonald 1950 (gilt)

a.k.a. *The Case of the Frightened Mannequin* Macmillan 1951

The Case of the Corner Cottage Macdonald 1951, Macmillan 1952

The Case of the Fourth Detective Macdonald 1951

The Case of the Happy Medium Macdonald 1952, Macmillan 1952

The Case of the Counterfeit Colonel Macdonald 1952, Macmillan 1953

The Case of the Burnt Bohemian Macdonald 1953, Macmillan 1954

The Case of the Silken Petticoat Macdonald 1953, Macmillan 1954

The Case of the Red Brunette Macdonald 1954, Macmillan 1955

The Case of the Three Lost Letters Macdonald 1954, Macmillan 1955

The Case of the Benevolent Bookie Macdonald 1955, Macmillan 1956

The Case of the Amateur Actor Macdonald 1955, Macmillan 1956

The Case of the Extra Man Macdonald 1956, Macmillan 1957

The Case of the Flowery Corpse Macdonald 1956, Macmillan 1957

The Case of the Russian Cross Macdonald 1957, Macmillan 1958

The Case of the Treble Twist Macdonald 1958

a.k.a. *The Case of the Triple Twist* Macmillan 1958

The Case of the Running Man Macdonald 1958, Macmillan 1959

The Case of the Careless Thief Macdonald 1959, Macmillan 1960

The Case of the Sapphire Brooch Macdonald 1960, Macmillan 1961

The Case of the Extra Grave Macdonald 1961, Macmillan 1962

The Case of the Dead Man Gone Macdonald 1961, Macmillan 1962

The Case of the Three-Ring Puzzle Macdonald 1962, Macmillan 1963

The Case of the Heavenly Twin Macdonald 1963, Macmillan 1964

The Case of the Grand Alliance Macdonald 1964, Macmillan 1965

The Case of the Jumbo Sandwich Macdonald 1965, Macmillan 1966

The Case of the Good Employer Macdonald 1966, Macmillan 1967 (silver)

The Case of the Deadly Diamonds Macdonald 1967, Macmillan 1969 (silver)

The Case of the Prodigal Daughter Macdonald 1968, Macmillan 1969 (gilt)

Novels by Michael Home

(with John Benham, as stated)

The Place of Little Birds Methuen 1941
The House of Shade Methuen 1942
City of the Soul Methuen 1943
The Cypress Road Methuen 1945
The Strange Prisoner Methuen 1947 (Benham)
The Auber File Methuen 1953 (Benham)

Uncollected stories

'The Hampstead Murder' (*A Century of Detective Stories*, Hutchinson n.d. (1935); variant text in *Saint*, Aug./Nov. 1955)

'A Drop Too Much' (*ES*, 18 Aug. 1936; *Fifty Famous Detectives of Fiction*, Odhams n.d. (1938); variant text in *Saint*, June 1956/Feb. 1957, as 'Tears for the Jury')

'The Holly Bears a Berry' (*Illustrated London News*, 15 Nov. 1951; *Saint*, Feb. 1956 (UK) as 'Murder at Christmas')

'Wings of Death' (*Saint*, Oct. 1956 (USA))

'Murder of a Maharajah' (*Saint*, Feb. 1957 (USA))

BP

Gwendoline Butler (b. 1922) a.k.a. Jennie Melville

Gwendoline Butler is an undervalued writer, whose books are full of atmosphere and tension, besides being cleverly plotted. She has written twenty-seven crime novels in her own name and a further twenty-five as Jennie Melville; and there are eleven uncollected stories. She was one of the collaborators in a 'consequences'-style murder story, 'A Slight Case of Scotch', published in 1979. Good examples of her work are *Coffin on the Water* and *A Coffin from the Past*.

Her main series character is Sergeant John Coffin, whose investigations take him through twenty-one novels and one story – and to the rank of Chief Commander of the Second City of London police force, including responsibility for the Docklands area. He was born in South London and joined the local metropolitan force.

A tough, ambitious policeman, in his early days he works under the disciplinarian Inspector (later Superintendent) William Winter, who features in four books. In his later career Coffin is assisted in several cases by Inspector William Dove. Laetitia Bingham, Coffin's half-sister, who has converted a derelict church in the docklands into a theatre, and Stella Pinero, an actress, who eventually becomes his second wife, appear in several novels.

Three of Gwendoline Butler's crime novels have a historical setting: *A Coffin for Pandora, The Vesey Inheritance*, and *The Brides of Friedberg*. *The Red Staircase* is not a crime novel. Eight titles were not published in the USA. Several have alternative American titles: *A Coffin for the Canary*, for instance, becomes *Olivia*. Apart from *The Vesey Inheritance*, the books were first published in London.

The first fifteen books were published by Bles. They are all dated and lettered on the spine only. *Receipt for Murder* was published in green cloth, lettered in red. 'Eagle Detective' appears over the publisher's colophon. Black lettering indicates a later issue. *Dead in a Row* has orange cloth and is lettered in black. The later issue has red cloth with black lettering. *The Dull Dead* was issued in brown cloth with blue lettering, and *The Murdering Kind* in red with silver lettering.

The wrapper design for *Dead in a Row* is a sketch of part of the Georgian shop fronts on Bartholomew Row. The other three all have black-and-white photographs on the cover, overlapping on to the spine, with coloured lettering. *Receipt for Murder* has a wooden pencil box, part of a handbag, and a scattering of beads, and *The Dull Dead* shows a dropped glove, a bus ticket, and a two-shilling piece. A caged cat features on *The Murdering Kind*. *The Interloper* has maroon cloth with silver lettering, and *Death Lives Next Door* is blue and lettered in red, with a wrapper showing an angry cat being held by the scruff of the neck. *Make Me a Murderer* and *Coffin in Oxford* have blue cloth and silver lettering. Both wrappers are by Joseph Gross, the former showing a green face covered by a purple cobweb, the latter two pairs of shoes. *Coffin for Baby* has a light tan cloth, lettered in black. Beverley Lebarrow's design shows Mary Ellen and her double, both clutching parcels, sitting on benches in the old cemetery of St Bride's Church. *Coffin Waiting* has maroon cloth, *Coffin in Malta* dark green, *A Nameless Coffin* black, and *Coffin Following* red. They are lettered alternately in white and gilt. *Coffin's Dark Number* is blue with gilt lettering and an effective wrapper by Brian Ashpool, on which a large black hand almost covers the body of a small girl, against a blue background. *A Coffin from the Past* was issued in dark green cloth with gilt lettering. The attractive wrapper by Salim Patell shows a figure in brown studying a gravestone in a cemetery, and covers the whole of the wrapper except the inside flaps.

The author's next four titles were published by Macmillan, in various colours: red, yellow, blue, and dark brown. The first two are lettered in black and the latter two in white. All four are dated. Charles Geer's wrapper for *The Vesey Inheritance* shows Errol Vesey crossing Masham Square. The design is continued on to the back cover. *The Brides of Friedberg* has illustrated endpapers showing the family trees of the House of Saxe-Coburg and the House of Hohenzollern. Yvonne Gilbert's wrapper design shows the present Bride of Friedberg and ghost of the previous one.

The last eight titles were published by Collins Crime Club in red cloth lettered gilt. They are all dated and became taller with *Coffin in the Black Museum*. From *Cracking Open a Coffin* the books have a printer's key on the copyright page.

The books written under the pseudonym Jennie Melville fall into three categories: police procedural, psychological crime, and gothic thrillers. The last-mentioned are not in the scope of this book. The police procedural stories feature the young woman Sergeant (later Inspector) Charmian Daniels of Deerham Hills CID, which is 40 miles from London. In the last six books, Charmian Daniels has been working in Windsor and has been promoted to Chief Superintendent, in charge of Southern Register, Documentation and Index of Crime. Five of these books also feature her god-daughter, Kate Cooper. In several of the thirteen books, patient, clever,

observant Charmian is almost engulfed by her deep involvement in the case. She also figures in one story.

The first four Daniels novels were all published by Michael Joseph. They are all dated and have blank front covers, with gilt lettering on the spine. The first pair are black, the second pair grey. In addition, *Murderers' Houses* has a black hand-shaped tree on the spine and *Come Home and Be Killed* has a red rose on the spine, below the title. Broom Lynne's wrapper for *Murderers' Houses* has many houses interspersed with more hand-shaped trees. His design for *Come Home and Be Killed* depicts a skull with a red rose between its teeth. For *There Lies Your Love*, his simple but effective design is of a blonde wig on a black stand, against a green background. *A Different Kind of Summer* and *A New Kind of Killer, an Old Kind of Death* were published by Hodder & Stoughton. The first has black cloth, the second red, both with gilt spine lettering. Both books are dated. The last seven Daniels novels have been published by Macmillan, with bindings and lettering in various colours. All books are dated and become taller with *Footsteps in the Blood*. *Whoever has the Heart* has a printer's key on the copyright page.

The first of the psychological novels is *Nell Alone*, published by Michael Joseph in charcoal grey cloth, with gilt spine lettering, and dated. The wrapper design by Ivan Lapper shows Nell Hilton. *The Hunter in the Shadows* and *The Summer Assassin* are published by Hodder & Stoughton, dated, bound in blue and black cloth, respectively, and lettered in gilt. *Listen to the Children* and *Death in the Garden* were published by Macmillan, the first in green cloth, the second in light blue. Both have silver lettering and are dated. Sharon Finmark's wrapper illustration for *Death in the Garden* is of the shopping arcades in present-day Covent Garden.

The most difficult titles to obtain in first edition seem to be *Coffin in Oxford* and *Come Home and Be Killed*.

Novels by Gwendoline Butler

(with Coffin, except as stated)

Receipt for Murder   Bles 1956 (Winter)
Dead in a Row   Bles 1957 (Winter)
The Murdering Kind   Bles 1958, Roy 1964 (Winter)
The Dull Dead   Bles 1958, Walker 1962 (also with Winter)
The Interloper   Bles 1959
Death Lives Next Door   Bles 1960
a.k.a. *Dine and Be Dead*   Macmillan 1960
Make Me a Murderer   Bles 1961
Coffin in Oxford   Bles 1962
Coffin for Baby   Bles 1963, Walker 1963
Coffin Waiting   Bles 1964, Walker 1964
Coffin in Malta   Bles 1964, Walker 1965
A Nameless Coffin   Bles 1966, Walker 1967
Coffin Following   Bles 1968
Coffin's Dark Number   Bles 1969
A Coffin from the Past   Bles 1970
A Coffin for Pandora   Macmillan 1973 (not Coffin)
a.k.a. *Sarsen Place*   Coward 1974
A Coffin for the Canary   Macmillan 1974
a.k.a. *Olivia*   Coward 1974
The Vesey Inheritance   Coward 1975, Macmillan 1976 (not Coffin)
The Brides of Friedberg   Macmillan 1977 (not Coffin)
a.k.a. *Meadowsweet*   Coward 1977
Coffin on the Water   Collins Crime Club 1986, St Martin's 1989
Coffin in Fashion   Crime Club 1987, St Martin's 1990
Coffin Underground   Crime Club 1988, St Martin's 1989
Coffin in the Black Museum   Crime Club 1989
a.k.a. *Coffin in the Museum of Crime*   St Martin's 1990
Coffin and the Paper Man   Crime Club 1990, St Martin's 1991
Coffin on Murder Street   Crime Club 1991, St Martin's 1991
Cracking Open a Coffin   Crime Club 1992, St Martin's 1993
A Coffin for Charley   Crime Club 1993

Novels by Jennie Melville

(with Daniels, as stated)

Come Home and Be Killed   Joseph 1962, British Book Centre 1964 (Daniels)
Burning Is a Substitute for Loving   Joseph 1963, British Book Centre 1964 (Daniels)
Murderers' Houses   Joseph 1964 (Daniels)
There Lies Your Love   Joseph 1965 (Daniels)
Nell Alone   Joseph 1966
A Different Kind of Summer   Hodder & Stoughton 1967 (Daniels)
The Hunter in the Shadows   Hodder 1969, McKay 1970
A New Kind of Killer, an Old Kind of Death   Hodder 1970 (Daniels)
a.k.a. *A New Kind of Killer*   McKay 1971
The Summer Assassin   Hodder 1971
Murder Has a Pretty Face   Macmillan 1981, (Daniels) (tan, silver) St Martin's 1989
Listen to the Children   Macmillan 1986
Death in the Garden   Macmillan 1987
a.k.a. *Murder in the Garden*   St Martin's 1989
Windsor Red   Macmillan 1988, St Martin's 1988 (red, silver) (Daniels)
A Cure for Dying   Macmillan 1989 (green, silver) (Daniels)
a.k.a. *Making Good Blood*   St Martin's 1990
Witching Murder   Macmillan 1990, St Martin's 1991 (tan, gilt) (Daniels)
Footsteps in the Blood   Macmillan 1990 (black, gilt) (Daniels)
Dead Set   Macmillan 1992, St Martin's 1993 (pale orange, gilt) (Daniels)
Whoever has the Heart   Macmillan 1993 (grey, gilt) (Daniels)

NB. Jennie Melville has also published seven Gothic novels.

Uncollected stories by Gwendoline Butler

'The Sisterhood' (*EQMM*, Oct. 1968; *Ellery Queen's Murder Menu*, World 1969, Gollancz 1969)
'Time Bomb' (*Winter's Crimes 4*, Macmillan 1972)
'Older than the Rocks' (*Winter's Crimes 6*, Macmillan 1974, St Martin's 1974)

'North Wind' (*Winter's Crimes 11*, Macmillan 1979, St Martin's 1979)

'The Rogue's Twist' (*Verdict of Thirteen*, Faber 1979, Harper 1979) (Coffin)

'Ladies who Lunch' (*A Suit of Diamonds*, Crime Club 1990)

'The Child Cannot Speak' (*Midwinter Mysteries 2*, Little, Brown 1992)

Uncollected stories by Jennie Melville

'Hand in Glove' (*Winter's Crimes 6*, Macmillan 1974, St Martin's 1974)

'What I Tell You Twice Times Two Is True' (*Winter's Crimes 13*, Macmillan 1981, St Martin's 1981)

'Chicken Feed' (*Winter's Crimes 17*, Macmillan 1985, St Martin's 1986)

'Pray Tell Me, Sir, Whose Dog Are You?' (*Winter's Crimes 22*, Macmillan 1990) (Daniels)

Story with other writers, by Gwendoline Butler

'A Slight Case of Scotch', by Divers Hands (in *The Bell House Book*, Hodder 1979)   *JC*

Joanna Cannan (1898–1961)

Joanna Cannan turned to detective fiction in 1939, after some years as a mainstream novelist. Her work is orderly and observant, with subtle tensions and a rather disdainful wit. Her themes and settings echo her enthusiasms, which tend to be literary, equestrian, or mountainous. Some of her mainstream novels have criminous elements, though none is a detective story. *No Walls of Jasper* (Benn 1930) and *Frightened Angels* (Gollancz 1936) both show a murderer's decline to suicide. *A Hand to Burn* (Hodder 1936) is a novel of pursuit.

There are two series detectives, both policemen, but otherwise wholly different. Guy Northeast is young and fallible, and has his author's approval; but she makes relentless fun of Ronald Price, who is a product of her bias against the post-war welfare state. He is saddled with a shrill, pretentious wife, and is himself mean-spirited, small-minded, and neurotically insecure. Both detectives undertake meticulous formal detection in the approved tradition, but the later series derives an additional comic impetus from the tensions raging within Price himself.

All seven detective novels were published by Gollancz, the first in 1939, the last in 1962. The two Northeast books are more substantial in appearance than the later run with Price. *They Rang Up the Police* is blue with dark-blue lettering on the spine; but *Death at the Dog*, which succeeded it, reverts to pre-war black, with orange lettering. The red binding of *Murder Included* has a brownish tinge and its lettering is black, but the later Price novels are all unambiguously red, with gilt spine lettering. All seven books are dated and have the dingy yellow wrappers dictated by their publisher. Only *Death at the Dog* and *Murder Included* found American publishers, the latter with a title-change.

Northeast novels

They Rang Up the Police   Gollancz 1939
Death at the Dog   Gollancz 1940, Reynal 1941

Price novels

Murder Included   Gollancz 1950
a.k.a. *Poisonous Relations*   Morrow 1950
a.k.a. *The Taste of Murder*   Dell 1951
Body in the Beck   Gollancz 1952
Long Shadows   Gollancz 1955
And Be a Villain   Gollancz 1958
All is Discovered   Gollancz 1962   *BP*

JOANNA CANNAN'S
first detective Story

THEY RANG UP THE POLICE

John Dickson Carr (1906–1977)
a.k.a. Carr Dickson;
a.k.a. Carter Dickson;
a.k.a. Roger Fairbairn;
a.k.a. Robert Southwell

John Dickson Carr wrote forty-six detective novels, one of which, *The Murder of Sir Edmund Godfrey*, is a fictional account of an actual historical murder (described by the author himself as 'a detective story built on facts'). His twenty-nine stories are collected in seven volumes, and include six Sherlock Holmes pastiches written in collaboration with Adrian Conan Doyle. Radio plays are also included in four collections, and a posthumous collection of nine radio plays was published in 1983. Carr also wrote the first two chapters of the collaborative novella *Crime on the Coast* (see under 'Detection Club') and there is one non-series story still uncollected. As Carter Dickson, he wrote twenty-five novels, one of which is a collaboration with John Rhode. *The Bowstring Murders* was first published in the USA as by Carr Dickson. A collection of eleven stories and a novella, *The Third Bullet*, were also published in the Carter Dickson name. The pseudonym Roger Fairbairn was used for the historical mystery, *Devil Kinsmere* (later the basis of the Carr novel *Most Secret*).

John Dickson Carr is one of the giants of the genre. His books are always entertaining, with strong atmosphere and brilliant plots that verge on the supernatural, but are always logically explained. His detectives are given impossible crimes to solve, in the 'locked-room' novels for which he is famous (several with a very authentic historical background).

He created two great detectives, Dr Gideon Fell and Sir Henry Merrivale. Dr Fell is a former teacher and historian, who acts as an adviser to Scotland Yard. He is stout and red-faced, with three chins and a bandit's moustache. He walks with two canes, and wears a cape and a shovel hat, and he is famous for his quaint expletives ('Archons of Athens!'). This great eccentric appears in twenty-three novels, five stories and four radio plays. Chief Inspector David Hadley of the CID also features in ten of these novels and two of the stories. In *The Plague Court*

Murders Carter Dickson introduced Sir Henry Merrivale, nicknamed Mycroft, but usually known as HM. He is a veteran of Military Intelligence at the War Office, with degrees in both law and medicine. He is bald and barrel-shaped, very garrulous, but also very astute. He figures in twenty-two novels and two stories, assisting the burly, bowler-hatted Chief Inspector Humphrey Masters of New Scotland Yard in thirteen full-length cases and one shorter one.

In his own name, Carr also created the flamboyant Frenchman, Henri Bencolin, an adviser to the courts and director of the Paris police. He is tall, with black hair parted in the middle, a small moustache, and a black pointed beard. He appears in five novels and four stories. The first four novels are narrated by the journalist, Jeff Marle. Bencolin officially retires in 1932, but reappears to solve the murders in *The Four False Weapons*. An Irish barrister, Patrick Butler, figures in two novels, and the large, amiable Head of D–3, Colonel March of Scotland Yard, is

given nine impossible crimes to solve, all in the shorter form. The character of Colonel March was based on Carr's friend and co-writer, John Rhode.

Most of Carr's books were first published in the USA. Fourteen titles, however, had their first publication in the UK (see checklist, where UK edition appears first). Many books have alternative titles in the UK, and there are some differences between the texts of the two versions of *The Judas Window*: e.g. Mr. Justice Bodkin (US)/ Rankin (UK).

Several books contain a map or plan, *The Mad Hatter Mystery, The Three Coffins, To Wake the Dead*, and *The Judas Window* among them. The UK *The Man Who Could Not Shudder* has a plan of the study at Longwood House that is not in the US edition. Except for *Captain Cutthroat, Most Secret* and *The Witch of the Lowtide* (US) the historical mysteries all have a section 'Notes for the Curious' at the end of the book. Many of the US editions contain seals, and were sold as sealed mysteries. Only two UK editions have seals: *It Walks By Night* and *The Lost Gallows*. The Harper edition of *The Murder of Sir Edmund Godfrey* and the Heinemann edition of *Drop to His Death* are the only firsts by this author to be undated. All the UK editions, except *It Walks by Night*, are dated on the reverse of the title-page. The Morrow titles are all dated on the title-page, as are the Harper books, until the publication of *The Man Who Could Not Shudder*. After this title, they are dated on the reverse of the title-page.

The US editions of the John Dickson Carr books all have author, title, and publisher on the spine, and for the four books from *It Walks by Night* to *The Corpse in the Waxworks*, and for *The Eight of Swords*, these details also appear on the front cover. The title and author, but not the publisher, appear on the front cover of the books from *Poison in Jest* to *The Mad Hatter Mystery* and from *The Blind Barber* to *The Emperor's Snuffbox*. *Till Death Do Us Part* is lettered on the spine only, but *He Who Whispers* also has title and author on the front cover. From *Below Suspicion*, the spines only are lettered. From this book, also, most of the Harper books have the publisher's logo on the front cover, but this feature is not present on *The Devil in Velvet, The Third Bullet and other stories, The Men Who Explained Miracles*, and *Papa La-bas*. The logo appears blind-stamped or in one of several colours. The covers of *The Exploits of Sherlock Holmes* and *The Dead Sleep Lightly* are also blank. From *The Mad Hatter Mystery* to *The Arabian Nights Murder*, the books are black with orange lettering. From *The Devil in Velvet*, the Harper books have spines in one colour and sides in another. *The Exploits of Sherlock Holmes* also has spine and side boards distinct from each other.

It Walks by Night has the publisher's colophon on the rear cover. *Hag's Nook* has black lettering, with a gallows, also in black, on an orange rectangle, on both the front cover and the spine. *The Eight of Swords* has two vertical orange lines to the left of the front cover lettering. *Death Watch* has the hands of a clock in red, showing the time as twenty to five. *To Wake the Dead* has orange cloth, with three horizontal blue lines on both spine and front cover, on which the lettering appears in orange. *The Problem of the Green Capsule* has orange cloth, with a large green capsule on both spine and front cover, within which the lettering, also in orange, appears. *He Who Whispers* has a pattern in blue, like the edge of a saw pointing upwards, separating the title from the author's name on the front cover. *The Sleeping Sphinx* has title and author separated by a black pattern resembling battlements on the front cover. There are two silver keys at the top of the spine of *The Dead Man's Knock*, and *The Witch of the Low-tide* has two beach-huts on the spine, below the title. *Papa La-bas* has a red, scroll-like decoration on the front cover. *The Devil in Velvet* (US) has pictorial endpapers by Douglas Ash, depicting a duel between two swordsmen and a man peering over a water-trough.

Variant issues of *The Sleeping Sphinx* in drab yellow and light brown and *The Bride of Newgate* in red cloth with black spine lettering, are known. From *The Sleeping Sphinx*, the Harper books become taller. A variant UK edition from Harper of *The Murder of Sir Edmund Godfrey* also exists. Both editions have the identical binding of black cloth with title, author and publisher

in gilt on the spine and front cover. The UK variant is dated 1936 at the base of the title page, which states on its verso 'Printed in Guernsey, Channel Islands, British Isles by the Star and Gazette Limited'. The US variant is undated and on the verso of the title-page has 'Printed in the United States of America, First Edition'. In fact, the Harper UK variant precedes the Harper US variant.

Dr Fell, Detective is a paperback, with fawn wrappers, with a pink and white rectangle on the front cover, in the form of a postage stamp. Within this appears a design by Salter, of part of a liner, which contains author and title. The front cover also carries a quotation from J. B. Priestley and the price. The book is in the American Mercury series, with an introduction by Ellery Queen. *The Door to Doom, The Dead Sleep Lightly, Fell and Foul Play* and *Merrivale, March and Murder* are posthumous collections edited and introduced by Douglas G. Greene. Each of the latter pair has a small portrait of the featured detective on the spine, Dr Fell in red, HM in black, similar to their appearance on the wrappers.

It Walks by Night was published by Harper in London as well as New York, with the same binding and lettering as the US edition and with a cancel title-page tipped in. From *The Lost Gallows*, the British editions were published by Hamish Hamilton, except for *Castle Skull* and *The Exploits of Sherlock Holmes. Castle Skull* was not published in Britain until 1973, when Tom Stacey issued it. This edition was taken over by Severn House, who put in their own cancel title-page, dated 1976, and provided a new dust-wrapper.

Five books have the title on the front cover, in the same colour as the lettering on the spine: *The Lost Gallows, The Black Spectacles, The Problem of the Wire Cage, The Man Who Couldn't Shudder*, and *The Case of the Constant Suicides*. The author's name is not on the spine or the front cover of the last of these. *The Eight of Swords* has the author and title on the front cover, in black. Otherwise the front covers are blank. *Dark of the Moon, Deadly Hall*, and *The Hungry Goblin* all have coloured top edges: red, grey, and magenta, respectively. *The Murder of*

Sir Edmund Godfrey is much taller than the rest of the earlier books. It has a frontispiece portrait of the victim and thirteen pages of illustrations, which show a complete pack of playing cards depicting 'the panorama of the plot, seen through contemporary eyes'. Six variant issues are known: *The Lost Gallows* in an orange binding, *Captain Cut-throat* in a red binding, *Patrick-Butler* in a light-blue and also a fawn binding, *Panic in Box C* in a pink binding, and *The Witch of the Low-tide* with black lettering.

Most of the US first editions of the Carter Dickson books were issued by Morrow, who published *The Bowstring Murders* under the name Carr Dickson. This book, *The Plague Court Murders*, and *The White Priory Murders* all have author, title, and publisher on the spine and front cover. *The Bowstring Murders* has a pair of gauntlets in orange on the spine, and *The Plague Court Murders* has a red noose on the front cover. *The Red Widow Murders* has a red rectangle on the front cover containing the title in black. Below this is the author's name in red.

The Unicorn Murders has a pictorial cover designed by Gorska, in black and white. It shows the Marseilles-Paris plane flying over the Château de l'Ile near the River Loire. The head of a red unicorn is superimposed on the design and also features on the spine, below the title and author's name in white. The publisher's logo on the spine and the title and author on the front cover are also in white. The back cover is plain black.

The Morrow edition of *The Punch and Judy Murders* appeared after the British, which was called *The Magic Lantern Murders*. It features a red drawing of Punch and Judy on the front cover and spine, but is lettered only on the spine. *The Peacock Feather Murders* is lettered red on the spine, the title enclosed in a single red border. On the front cover, again in red, the title is superimposed on a red peacock feather. A smaller feather decorates the middle of the spine. *The Judas Window* has a red line drawing of Sir Henry Merrivale in a top hat and waving a closed umbrella on both front cover and spine. The title appears black within a red rectangle superimposed across HM on the front cover. *Death in Five Boxes* has the title black against

a green rectangle on the front cover. Five green boxes appear with the green lettering on the spine. *The Reader is Warned* has red and green lettering on the spine and front cover and the portrait from *The Judas Window* on the spine (of HM waving his umbrella). Except for *The Unicorn Murders*, the Morrow books all have black cloth to *The Reader is Warned* and most of them have red lettering and decoration. For *The Bowstring Murders* these are orange, for *The White Priory Murders* yellow, for *Death in Five Boxes* green and for *The Reader is Warned* red and green. Some of the pre-war Morrow titles have coloured top edges.

The books after 1939 have less decoration and most are lettered on the spine only. *And So To Murder* has a steaming cup of coffee between the title and author on the spine, and the title is printed within frames of a motion picture film. The top of the spine of *The Gilded Man* has a hand pointing downwards and *She Died a Lady* has a black vignette of a bungalow with steps leading from it in the same position. The spine of *Seeing is Believing* has title and publisher in green with the author named in yellow against a green rectangle, a yellow dagger on a green rectangle and a green dagger on a yellow rectangle. The binding is yellow. *He Wouldn't Kill Patience* has a reaching hand printed on the spine between title and author. The spine of *The Curse of the Bronze Lamp* is lettered red and grey. *Fear is the Same* has yellow board sides with a blue cloth spine lettered yellow. *Behind the Crimson Blind* and *Fear is the Same* are in a larger format. The publisher of *He Wouldn't Kill Patience* is 'The Hampton Publishing Co. distributed by Morrow' on the title-page but 'Morrow' only appears on the spine, which also shows a hand between title and author.

Grey, blue or red-brown variants of *Skeleton in the Clock* are Book Club editions, undated on the title-page and lacking the list of the author's previous publications. The red cloth undated edition of *Behind the Crimson Blind* is also a Book Club edition. *Fatal Descent* was published by Dodd, Mead in 1939, after the British edition of January 1939. It has yellow cloth, with the spine and front cover lettered in black. The front cover also shows a lift floor indicator, in black.

The Third Bullet is a paperback novella, published by Hodder & Stoughton in the New at Ninepence series. It has a black spine, lettered in yellow. A black-and-white pictorial design appears on the front cover, below the title, author, and price, which are shown against a yellow background. Kenneth Inns' design shows Judge Mortlake slumped across his desk, with Gabriel White holding a revolver and Inspector Page entering through the window. This design is repeated over two full pages, after the title-page. Between this and the title-page is a second black-and-white illustration by Kenneth Inns, showing Carolyn Mortlake being interviewed by Colonel Marquis, who is sitting bolt upright, his gloved hands folded over his cane, while Inspector Page stands by his side. The same head-and-shoulders portrait of Carolyn Mortlake is reproduced on the title-page below the author's name. The yellow back cover has an advertisement on it.

All Carter Dickson's other books were published in Britain by Heinemann. Except for *A Graveyard to Let*, which has the title in black on the front cover, they are lettered on the spine only. From *The Bowstring Murders* to *Drop to His Death*, the books have black cloth bindings, and from *The Reader Is Warned* to *She Died A Lady* the bindings are in blue cloth. From *He Wouldn't Kill Patience* to *A Graveyard to Let*, the bindings are in various colours. The four books from *Night at the Mocking Widow* have black cloth, with gilt lettering on the spine. *Fear is the Same* is taller than the earlier books.

All the Heinemann books have the publisher's windmill colophon on the back cover. On twelve titles this is blind-stamped: *The Red Widow Murders, The Ten Teacups, The Judas Window, Death in Five Boxes, Drop to His Death, Lord of the Sorcerers, My Late Wives*, and the five books from *A Graveyard to Let*. On the other fourteen, the colophon is the same colour as the lettering.

From *The Magic Lantern Murders* to *Drop to His Death*, the books have maroon endpapers. *The Reader is Warned, Murder in the Submarine Zone*, and *The Department of Queer Complaints* have blue endpapers. A small blue skull-and-crossbones on a black rectangle appears on the spine of *The Skeleton in the Clock*. *Night at*

the *Mocking Widow, Behind the Crimson Blind*, and *The Cavalier's Cup* have the same spine decoration of a black prostrate body on a gilt background. A blue cloth edition of *Drop to His Death* with the spine lettered in black is a later issue.

Devil Kinsmere, the Roger Fairbairn title, was issued in green cloth, with the spine lettered in black, by Hamish Hamilton in 1934. The Harper edition appeared the same year, and has black cloth with the spine lettered in yellow and the publisher's logo blind-stamped on the front cover.

The pseudonym Robert Southwell was used for a radio play broadcast on 11 September 1941, *Lord of the Witch Doctors*.

John Dickson Carr was served well by the various artists who designed the wrappers for his books, and they form a most attractive collection. The weirdly constructed Schloss Schadel appears to have blank eyes and teeth on the wrapper for *Castle Skull* (US). A disembodied face stares from behind bars to the left of *Poison in Jest* (US) while poison drips into a glass on the right. *Hag's Nook* (US) shows Martin Starberth's falling body. J. L. Carstairs' stylish design for *The Mad Hatter Mystery* (UK) shows (in blue, black and white) Traitors' Gate at the Tower, with an axe embedded in a block and a top hat hanging from its handle. The pink wrapper by Manso for *The Three Coffins* has three coffins in black outline, with a white hand with three raised fingers laid over them. *The Hollow Man* has a mysterious figure in a mask in the foreground and Stuart Mills looking startled in a doorway behind him. The masked man recurs on the spine in a wide-brimmed black hat. Vernon Soper's design for *The Arabian Nights Murder* (UK) depicts Police Constables Collins and Martin opening a lead coffin inside the pillared Wade Museum. The coffin's packing case lies nearby and seven onlookers (including Detective-Inspector John Carruthers) gaze into the open coffin. A startled-looking man with side-whiskers and a top hat stares out from the spine. The US wrapper for this book shows a policeman looking at the body of a stabbed man within an early nineteenth-century travelling carriage. The green wrapper for *The Four False Weapons*

(UK), attributed to B., shows a pistol, a razor, a box of tablets and a stiletto. The four words of the title show red on white labels attached to the exhibits. *To Wake the Dead* (UK) has the door of bedroom 707 at the Royal Scarlet Hotel with a 'Do Not Disturb' notice hanging from the door knob, with 'Dead Woman' scrawled across it in red. A pair of brown shoes has been placed outside the door for cleaning. This design recurs on the US wrapper. *The Crooked Hinge* (UK) has Abbey's silhouette in black of Dr Fell against an ornamental hedge at Fernleigh Close. The same artist's design for *The Black Spectacles* pictures the three witnesses looking through the doorway into Marcus Chesney's office, where he sits at his desk, with a figure in a black top hat standing over him. *The Problem of the Wire Cage* (UK) has Frank Dorrance's body sprawled on a tennis court with one set of footprints leading towards him. *The Man Who Could Not Shudder* (UK) shows the study of Longwood House, with a figure holding a typewriter on a table and rows of pistols above the red-brick chimney. The US wrapper for this book depicts Longwood House with a ghost-like figure coming up the chimney into the Essex night sky. *The Case of the Constant Suicides* (UK) is distinguished by Hookway Cowles' excellent illustration of the Castle of Shira, with its round tower, at the bottom of which Colin Campbell lies prone in red and white pyjamas, while Alan Campbell stands anxiously by. Mr Justice Ireton dominates the turquoise, red, black and white wrapper for *The Seat of the Scornful*; and *The Emperor's Snuffbox* (UK) has Hookway Cowles' view of Ned Atwood walking down the Rue des Anges at night. Cowles also designed the attractive wrapper for *Till Death Do Us Part* (UK), showing Dick Markham, Major Price and Dr Middlesworth standing in the grounds of Ashe Hall outside the red-and-white-striped fortune teller's tent, within which the shadows of two people can be seen. The US wrapper for this title was the work of P. K. Jackson, again with the striped tent in the foreground and with Ashe Hall among trees in the background and lightning overhead.

On the wrapper of *He Who Whispers* (US), the tower of Henry the Fourth, next to the River Eure, is shown in black and white. The doorway of the tower is illuminated by a yellow light. For the UK edition, Hookway Cowles shows Professor Rigaud discovering the dying Howard Brooke, with a swordstick lying by his side, at the top of the tower. Herlstman's black wrapper, with the title *The Sleeping Sphinx* in yellow, also features a mask near the lower right-hand corner. Cowles' design for the British edition has Inspector Crawford reaching for a bottle of poison, in a niche in the wall of a vault, surrounded by four coffins. C. W. Bacon's black picture of Abbot's House illustrates *Below Suspicion* (UK).

For *The Bride of Newgate*, both Galdone (US) and James Arnold (UK) have Caroline Ross in her white gown, visiting Dick Darwent in his cell at Newgate prison. Arnold has replaced the grey cape with a grey shawl. Professor Fenton holds a chair aloft, while Meg and Lydia cower by a roaring fire, on the wrapper for *The Devil in Velvet* (UK). C. W. Bacon's design for *The Nine Wrong Answers* (UK) is outstanding. On the front panel, Bill Dawson and Gaylord Hurst are seated at a dining table, while the butler, Hatto, on the spine, carries a silver serving-dish.

Biro's illustration for *The Third Bullet and other stories* (UK) has the body of Mr Justice Mortlake lying across a desk. For *Patrick Butler for the Defence* (US) Rus Anderson's wrapper depicts a pair of white-gloved hands, smeared with blood, against a black background. For the UK edition, C. W. Bacon shows a figure in a green fez, crossing a road in Lincoln's Inn Fields on a foggy November afternoon. Arnold Saks produced a simple design of two keys on a white background for the US edition of *The Dead Man's Knock*, but Biro, for the UK edition, created a marvellous portrait of Dr Fell. Biro went on to produce excellent period wrappers for Carr's next four historical novels, as well as a stylized design for *The Men Who Explained Miracles* (all UK).

Luiz Woods' illustration for *Panic in Box C* shows the head and shoulders of a woman, with the face replaced by a skull. This was used for both the US and the UK editions. The mainly grey cover design by Castle, Chappell for *Castle*

Skull (UK) shows Schloss Schadel, set high in the mountains over the Rhine.

Youngman Carter's design for *The Bowstring Murders* shows a man in armour, with a plumed helmet, mounted on a horse, caparisoned as if for a tournament. The victim lies dead nearby, the cowl and robe he wore falling away from his body. The UK wrapper for *The Plague Court Murders* shows the head of Roger Darworth against the flames, his eyes staring, his mouth 'wrenched back in agony'. *The White Priory Murders* (US) shows a figure with an upraised arm silhouetted against the doorway of the Queen's Mirror pavilion, set amid fir trees and snow. *The Unicorn Murders* (UK) has the Château de l'Ile in a romantic landscape with, over it, a unicorn's head on which the title is superimposed. *The Magic Lantern Murders* has a Youngman Carter design with a red figure wearing a fez against a black background with shafts of white and red light. On the spine a policeman enters a doorway. *The Punch and Judy Murders* is black and white, with Gorska's aerial view of The Larches in Valley Road and the rest of Moreton Abbot. A red line-drawing of Mr Punch beating Judy is superimposed on the village (and recurs on both the spine and the front cover of the book). Barlow's wrapper for *The Ten Teacups* has a circle divided into two: half white with five black cups and half black with five white ones. The spine has one more cup and the background is orange. *The Judas Window* (UK) and *Death in Five Boxes* (UK) have designs by Youngman Carter. The former has a pink crossbow with the arrow penetrating Avory Hume's body (and the crossbow recurring on the spine); and the latter shows five white, parcel-like boxes in the shape of a question-mark, against a background which is three-quarters brown and, at the top, one quarter black. The brown area is like a game-board, in which alternate squares contain fives and question marks. The US edition of *Death in Five Boxes* has a pale green wrapper by Manso, on which a skeletal hand tries to grasp five cardboard boxes, each lettered with a different name. Youngman Carter also provided the wrapper for *Drop to His Death*, which shows newsboys in a busy

London street announcing the sudden death of Sir Ernest Tallant.

The Reader is Warned (UK) has a photograph of Sam Constable, fallen across the top of the banisters of the stairs at Fourways, while Mina Constable looks on in horror. Manso's design for *And so to Murder* (US) has a skeletal hand hovering over a cup of coffee, with a burning cigarette in the saucer, on a red and yellow background. *Nine – and Death Makes Ten* has nine passengers shown in outline, walking up the gangplank of the M. V. *Edwardic*. Chester's design for *The Department of Queer Complaints* (US) has a gloved hand holding a revolver pointed at an open doorway, but the UK edition has a plain grey wrapper lettered in black and red. *Seeing is Believing* (US) is lettered in yellow against a green background. A scene outlined in the shape of an eye shows the hypnotized Victoria Fane, holding a dagger and walking towards Arthur Fane, who is seated in a chair. The large bungalow 'Mon Repos', with footsteps going towards Lovers' Leap, appears on the wrapper of *She Died a Lady* (US). Lady Helen Loring, holding a bronze lamp behind her and opening the door to Severn Hall is shown on *The Curse of the Bronze Lamp*. *And So To Murder* and the next six UK wrappers are all plain, with a central coloured band containing the title. The author's name appears above the band and earlier titles below. *My Late Wives* (UK) is grey, lettered in black and red.

The pale-blue wrapper of *The Skeleton in the Clock* (UK) has a grandfather clock, with the hand of a skeleton protruding from the pendulum case. Charles Lofgren's design for *A Graveyard to Let* (US) has a scantily dressed woman seated on a gravestone, and the UK edition shows a graveyard scene, with a figure pointing a gun. The wrappers of *Night at the Mocking Widow*, by Lofgren (US) and Stein (UK) offer different visual interpretations of the stone ruin outside the village of Stoke Druid. Stein also produced the wrappers for the last two Merrivale titles in the UK. Arthur Barbosa's design for *Fear is the Same* (UK) shows a dramatic Regency scene, with lightning flashing overhead.

There are four unpublished stage plays, two

written with Val Gielgud: *Inspector Silence Takes the Air* and *Thirteen to the Gallows*.

The most difficult first editions to find seem to be *Devil Kinsmere, The Eight of Swords, The Burning Court, The Department of Queer Complaints*, and the paperback, *The Third Bullet*.

Novels by John Dickson Carr

(with series detectives as stated)

It Walks by Night Harper (New York & London) 1930 (dark blue binding, pale blue lettering) (Bencolin)

The Lost Gallows Harper 1931 (orange, black), Hamish Hamilton 1931 (green, black) (Bencolin)

Castle Skull Harper 1931 (black, salmon-pink), Tom Stacey 1973 (maroon, silver) (Bencolin)

The Waxworks Murder Hamilton 18 Mar. 1932 (red, black)

a.k.a. *The Corpse in the Waxworks* Harper 23 Mar. 1932 (black, pale blue) (Bencolin)

Poison in Jest Harper 1932 (black, turquoise) Hamilton 1932 (red, black)

Hag's Nook Harper 1933 (black binding), Hamilton 1933 (green, black) (Fell)

The Mad Hatter Mystery Harper 1933, Hamilton 1933 (yellow, black) (Fell)

The Eight of Swords Harper 1934, Hamilton 1934 (blue, black) (Fell)

The Blind Barber Harper 1934, Hamilton 1934 (salmon-pink/orange, yellow) (Fell)

Death Watch Hamilton Mar. 1935 (blue, white), Harper Apr. 1935 (Fell)

The Three Coffins Harper 1935 (Fell)

a.k.a. *The Hollow Man* Hamilton 1935 (orange, silver)

The Arabian Nights Murder Hamilton Feb. 1936 (dark blue, red), Harper Mar. 1936 (Fell)

The Murder of Sir Edmund Godfrey Hamilton Oct. 1936 (black, green), Harper ? Nov. 1936 (black, gilt)

The Burning Court Hamilton 1 Apr. 1937 (green, red), Harper 21 Apr. 1937 (black, orange)

The Four False Weapons Harper 1937 (green, blue), Hamilton 1938 (green, red) (Bencolin)

To Wake the Dead Hamilton 1937 (orange/yellow, black), Harper 1938 (Fell)

The Crooked Hinge Harper 1938 (red, blue), Hamilton 1938 (green, black) (Fell)

The Problem of the Green Capsule Harper 1939 (Fell)

a.k.a. *The Black Spectacles* Hamilton 1939 (fawn, red)

The Problem of the Wire Cage Harper 1939 (orange, black), Hamilton 1940 (blue/grey, green) (Fell)

The Man Who Could Not Shudder Harper 1940 (dark blue, red), Hamilton 1940 (fawn, blue) (Fell)

The Case of the Constant Suicides Harper 1941 (blue, green), Hamilton 1941 (fawn, green) (Fell)

Death Turns the Tables Harper 1941 (blue, white) (Fell)

a.k.a. *The Seat of the Scornful* Hamilton 1942 (fawn, black)

The Emperor's Snuffbox Harper 1942 (red, black), Hamilton 1943 (fawn, blue)

Till Death Do Us Part Harper 1944 (blue, dark blue), Hamilton 1944 (grey/blue, blue) (Fell)

He Who Whispers Harper 1946 (grey, blue), Hamilton 1946 (cream, red) (Fell)

The Sleeping Sphinx Harper 1947 (turquoise, black), Hamilton 1947 (dark blue, gilt) (Fell)

Below Suspicion Harper 1949 (black, red), Hamilton 1950 (blue, gilt) (Fell, Butler)

The Bride of Newgate Harper 1950 (fawn, blue), Hamilton 1950 (red, gilt)

The Devil in Velvet Harper 1951 (brown spine, blue boards, silver lettering), Hamilton 1951 (green, gilt)

The Nine Wrong Answers Harper 1952 (brick-red, grey, silver), Hamilton 1952 (blue, silver)

Captain Cut-throat Harper 1955 (black, blue, gold and blue), Hamilton 1955 (black, gilt)

Patrick Butler for the Defence Harper 1956 (black, red, red), Hamilton 1956 (black, silver) (Butler)

Fire, Burn! Harper 1957 (black, grey/pink, silver), Hamilton 1957 (red, gilt)

The Dead Man's Knock Harper 1958 (black, blue, silver), Hamilton 1958 (green, gilt) (Fell)

Scandal at High Chimneys Harper 1959 (pink,

dark grey, black, white), Hamilton 1959 (black, silver)

In Spite of Thunder Harper 1960 (brown, blue, black, white), Hamilton 1960 (black, gilt) (Fell)

The Witch of the Low-tide Harper 1961 (cream, dark blue, black, blue), Hamilton 1961 (blue, gilt)

The Demoniacs Harper 1962 (dark blue, mottled blue, silver), Hamilton 1962 (salmon-pink, gilt)

Most Secret Harper 1964 (black, dark pink, gold), Hamilton 1964 (lilac, silver)

The House at Satan's Elbow Harper 1965 (grey, black, blue), Hamilton 1965 (green, silver) (Fell)

Panic in Box C Harper 1966 (black, black, green), Hamilton 1966 (light blue, gilt) (Fell)

Dark of the Moon Harper 1967 (black, orange, silver), Hamilton 1968 (blue, gilt) (Fell)

Papa La-bas Harper 1968 (blue-green, blue, dark blue), Hamilton 1969 (brown, gilt)

The Ghosts' High Noon Harper 1969 (light grey, dark grey, dark grey), Hamilton 1970 (red, gilt)

Deadly Hall Harper 1971 (purple, white, white), Hamilton 1971 (red, gilt)

The Hungry Goblin Harper 1972 (mustard, dark pink), Hamilton 1972 (blue, silver)

Story collections

Dr. Fell, Detective Spivak 1947 (8 items, 5 with Fell)

The Third Bullet and other stories Harper 1954 (black, yellow, silver), Hamilton 1954 (blue, gilt) (a novella and 6 stories, 3 with Fell, 1 with HM)

The Exploits of Sherlock Holmes Random House 1954 (brown, marbled brown, with purple cast, gold), Murray 1954 (red, gilt) (12 Sherlock Holmes pastiches, with Adrian Conan Doyle)

The Men Who Explained Miracles Harper 1963 (yellow, black, black), Hamilton 1964 (green, gilt) (7 stories, 2 with Fell, 2 with March, 1 with HM)

The Door to Doom Harper 1980 (blue, blue, silver), Hamilton 1981 (red, gilt) (18 items,

including 4 Bencolin stories and a Fell radio play)

Fell and Foul Play International Polygonics 1991 (light brown, red) (15 items including 5 Fell stories, 4 Fell radio plays, 5 other stories, 1 novella; 2 plays and 1 story new)

Merrivale, March and Murder International Polygonics 1991 (beige, black, black) (18 items including 2 HM stories, 9 March stories, 6 other stories, 1 radio script; 3 stories new)

Radio Plays

The Dead Sleep Lightly Doubleday 1983 (brown binding, black lettering) (9 radio plays, 2 with Fell)

Novel by Carr Dickson

The Bowstring Murders Morrow 1933; as by Carter Dickson: Heinemann 1934 (red lettering)

Novels by Carter Dickson

(with HM, except as stated)

The Plague Court Murders Morrow 1934, Heinemann 1935 (red)

The White Priory Murders Morrow 1934, Heinemann 1935 (red)

The Red Widow Murders Morrow 1935, Heinemann 1935 (white)

The Unicorn Murders Morrow 1935, Heinemann 1936

The Magic Lantern Murders Heinemann 1936 (green)

a.k.a. *The Punch and Judy Murders* Morrow 1937

The Peacock Feather Murders Morrow 1937

a.k.a. *The Ten Teacups* Heinemann 1937 (gilt)

The Judas Window Morrow 1938, Heinemann 1938 (gilt)

a.k.a. *The Crossbow Murder* Berkley 1964

Death in Five Boxes Heinemann 19 Sept. 1938 (gilt), Morrow 28 Sept. 1938

Drop to His Death Heinemann n.d. (1939) (gilt) (not HM)

a.k.a. *Fatal Descent*   Dodd, Mead 1939, with John Rhode

The Reader is Warned   Heinemann Jul. 1939 (black), Morrow Aug. 1939

And So To Murder   Morrow 1940 (grey binding, red and brown lettering), Heinemann 1941 (black lettering)

Murder in the Submarine Zone   Heinemann Aug. 1940 (black)

a.k.a. *Nine – and Death Makes Ten*   Morrow 1940 (blue, yellow), Chivers 1991

a.k.a. *Murder in the Atlantic*   World 1959

Seeing is Believing   Morrow 1941, Heinemann 1942 (black)

a.k.a. *Cross of Murder*   World 1959

The Gilded Man   Morrow 1942 (purple, gilt) Heinemann 1942 (red)

a.k.a. *Death and the Gilded Man*   Pocket Books 1947

She Died a Lady   Morrow 1943 (orange, black), Heinemann 1943 (red)

He Wouldn't Kill Patience   Morrow (Hampton) 1944 (peach-orange, purple), Heinemann 1944 (pink, black)

The Curse of the Bronze Lamp   Morrow 1945 (grey, red)

a.k.a. *Lord of the Sorcerers*   Heinemann 1946 (green, gilt)

My Late Wives   Morrow 1946 (grey, blue), Heinemann 1947 (black, silver)

The Skeleton in the Clock   Morrow 1948 (cream, red), Heinemann 1949 (blue, black)

A Graveyard to Let   Morrow 1949 (blue, red), Heinemann 1950 (brown, black)

Night at the Mocking Widow   Morrow 1950 (maroon, black), Heinemann 1951

Behind the Crimson Blind   Morrow 1952 (grey, blue), Heinemann 1952

The Cavalier's Cup   Morrow 1953 (yellow, red), Heinemann 1954

Fear is the Same   Morrow 1956, Heinemann 1956 (not HM)

Novella by Carter Dickson

The Third Bullet   Hodder & Stoughton 1937 (not HM)

Story collection by Carter Dickson

The Department of Queer Complaints   Heinemann Sept. 1940 (black lettering) Morrow Dec. 1940 (red, black) (11 stories, 7 with March)

Novel by Roger Fairbairn

Devil Kinsmere   Hamish Hamilton 1934, Harper 1934

Novella by John Dickson Carr and others

(see under 'Detection Club')

Crime on the Coast   Gollancz 1984 (with *No Flowers by Request*)

Uncollected story by John Dickson Carr

'Harem Scarem' (*Daily Mail*, 24 Mar. 1939)

Uncollected plays by John Dickson Carr

'Mr Markham, Antique Dealer' (*Rogues' Gallery*, Little, Brown 1945, Faber 1947)

'The Customers Like Murder' (*EQMM*, April 1952)

'Flight from a Razor in Fleet Street' (*LMM* Feb./Mar. 1952; *The Art of the Impossible* Xanadu 1990 as 'A Razor in Fleet Street')   *JC*

Sarah Caudwell (b. 1939)

Sarah Caudwell is the daughter of Claud Cockburn. She was a barrister before becoming a writer and her conclave of detectives includes five young barristers, two female, three male, and the Tutor in Legal History at St George's College, Oxford, whose gender was not finally established until a radio reading in the first person by a male actor. The books are meticulously composed and few and far between. They are complex and artful, with wit and a fastidious style.

The first book appeared from Collins Crime Club in 1981 in a red binding with gilt lettering on the spine and the date on the copyright page. Its successors have the same features but *The Sirens Sang of Murder* is taller. The wrappers are all photographic, each with a barrister's wig and an individually relevant item.

A Tamar story appeared in 1990. Sarah Caudwell also contributed to a collaborative work, *The Perfect Murder*, devised by Jack Hitt.

Tamar novels

Thus was Adonis Murdered Collins Crime Club 1981, Scribner 1981

The Shortest Way to Hades Crime Club 1984, Scribner 1985

The Sirens Sang of Murder Crime Club 1989, Delacorte 1989

Tamar story

'An Acquaintance with Mr. Collins' (*A Suit of Diamonds*, Crime Club 1990)

Collaboration

The Perfect Murder HarperCollins 1991 *BP*

Raymond Chandler (1888–1959)

Raymond Chandler is without doubt one of America's finest detective writers. He crafted his stories with a skilled use of the American vernacular, which lent authenticity to his portrayal of the tough world of the West Coast. His dialogue is often terse and rich in sardonic humour, which complements the action and suspense of the stories. Chandler clearly had an acute ear for the apt phrase and an eye for detail. He lovingly evokes the vibrant world of the California of the 1930s and 1940s in his novels and many of his short stories. His characters often favour strong-arm methods in obtaining justice and are no strangers to lethal weapons and sudden death. They are vivid, closely observed people.

Raymond Chandler wrote seven novels, one unfinished novel and twenty-four collected stories, one of which, 'English Summer', is a Gothic romance and is collected in *The Notebooks of Raymond Chandler*. One uncollected story, 'Professor Bingo's Snuff', was published in the USA in *Park East* (June-Aug. 1951). The screenplays for the films *The Blue Dahlia* and *Playback* have also been published. Many short stories first appeared in the pulp magazines *Black Mask, Detective Fiction Weekly* and *Dime Detective Monthly*. The first story, 'Blackmailers Don't Shoot', was published in *Black Mask* in Dec. 1933. Raymond Chandler's private detective Philip Marlowe appears in seven novels and the unfinished novel, *The Poodle Springs Story*. Only one story, 'The Pencil' (or 'Philip Marlowe's Last Case'), collected in *The Smell of Fear*, was originally written about Marlowe. All the 'Marlowe' stories in *The Simple Art of Murder* were reprinted from previous collections with the detective's name changed to Marlowe.

Philip Marlowe is physically attractive, with a tall, lean frame and brown hair and eyes. He inhabits a tough world but maintains his integrity and a passionate belief in justice. Until he meets Linda Loring in *The Long Goodbye* and marries

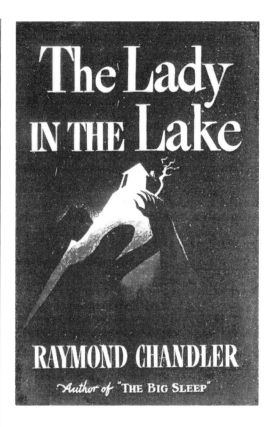

her at the beginning of *The Poodle Springs Story*, he is a loner, who seeks solace in the beauties of classical music and art. He sharpens his brain by solving chess problems. He is very much an individual and lost his job in the District Attorney's office because his attitude was considered insubordinate. He does his best for his clients and frequently endangers himself in the course of duty. His courage and physical strength, however, always allow him to redeem the most dangerous situation. His one-man detective agency is located in the Cahuenga Building on Hollywood Boulevard and his trench-coat and hat are unmistakable on the mean streets of Los Angeles. He speaks fluent Spanish and is intelligent, sympathetic, indestructible and utterly incorruptible. With an unforgettable line in wisecracks, he is arguably the greatest figure in American detective fiction.

Three novels, *The Little Sister*, *The Long*

Goodbye and *Playback*, were first published in the UK, as were the story collection *Killer in the Rain* and *Raymond Chandler Speaking*. The story collection *The Smell of Fear*, which contains the first book appearance of 'The Pencil', has been published only in the UK. All other novels and story collections made their first appearance in the USA.

Raymond Chandler's first four novels were published in the USA by Knopf. They are all dated, with lettering on the spine and both covers. The cloth for *The Big Sleep* is orange-brown and the lettering blue; for *Farewell, My Lovely*, salmon-pink with blue lettering; for *The High Window*, grey with burgundy lettering; and for *The Lady in the Lake* green with dark green lettering. The front cover of *Farewell, My Lovely* has the author's name and title inside a lozenge; a further lozenge on the spine encloses only the title. The spine also has a curled blue line over the publisher's name. All four books state 'First edition' on the copyright page. Even copies of *The Big Sleep* and *The Lady in the Lake* stating 'second printing before publication' on the copyright page do not qualify as first editions.

Chandler's British publisher was Hamish Hamilton and all his books are dated. *The Big Sleep* has black cloth with a double red border on the front cover and the publisher's initials in red in each corner. There is a similar pattern on the back of the book. The front cover also has title and author in red. The spine has two red rules at the top and base, with the title, author and publisher in red. For *Farewell, My Lovely* the cloth is yellow, the spine is lettered red and the front cover has the title in red. *The High Window* has orange-red cloth and gilt lettering on the spine and *The Lady in the Lake* is orange-yellow with red spine lettering. The latter two titles have blank covers.

The Little Sister (UK) has red cloth with gilt spine lettering. The US edition was published by Houghton Mifflin, who also published the remaining novels and hardback story collections. All the Houghton books are dated. *The Little Sister* (US) was issued in orange cloth with blue lettering on front cover and spine. The first edition has the date of publication, 'September 26, 1949' on the title-page. Later editions omit the date. A yellow cloth binding is known but is later than the orange. The cloth for *The Long Goodbye* (UK) is maroon with silver spine lettering. The US edition has a blue spine with the covers half blue, half green and with dark-green lettering on both front cover and spine. The first edition has the publication date 'March 1, 1954' on the title-page. *Playback* (UK) has red cloth with the spine lettered silver. The US *Playback* has tan cloth with brown lettering on spine and front cover. The first edition has the date of publication 'October 16, 1958' on the title-page. Three important story collections were published only in the USA, as paperbacks from Avon, $7\frac{5}{8}$ × $5\frac{1}{4}$ inches in size. All state 'Murder Mystery Monthly' on the pictorial front cover. Later editions state 'New Avon Library' and are of normal paperback size. *Five Murderers* was published in 1944 and the cover depicts a startled blonde with four assorted men looking over her shoulder. The stories collected are: 'Goldfish', 'Spanish Blood', 'Blackmailers Don't Shoot', 'Guns at Cyrano's', 'Nevada Gas'. *Five Sinister Characters* was issued in 1945, with a cover showing a central portrait of a smart young woman surrounded by three sinister men and a mysterious older woman wearing a hat. The contents are: 'Trouble is My Business', 'Pearls are a Nuisance', 'I'll be Waiting', 'The King is Yellow', 'Red Wind'. In 1946 the collection *The Finger Man* was published, with a glamorous brunette on the cover, posing before a roulette wheel, flanked by the heads and shoulders of two men. This collection has three stories: 'Finger Man', 'The Bronze Door' and 'Smart-Aleck Kill', together with the non-fiction item, 'The Simple Art of Murder'. All but one of the Avon stories – 'Blackmailers Don't Shoot' – were included in the US hardback collection *The Simple Art of Murder*: thus, it contains twelve stories besides the title essay. The book has grey cloth, with spine and front cover lettered orange and yellow. The UK edition has only seven stories and the essay: it has dark-red cloth and gilt spine lettering. Eight more pulp stories were collected in the UK in *Killer in the Rain*, issued in dark-red cloth with gilt-lettered spine. The US edition has blue cloth with white spine and front cover lettering. The UK collection *The Smell of Fear* contains fourteen stories, including 'The Pencil' and 'Blackmailers Don't Shoot'. This book has grey cloth with gilt spine lettering, and the author's name on the spine is enclosed in a decorative gilt framework.

The unfinished novel *The Poodle Springs Story* first appeared in *Raymond Chandler Speaking* (UK), which has red-purple cloth and gilt spine lettering. Blue and red dots appear on the spine above and below the title. The US edition is bound in blue cloth with red lettering on the spine and front cover. The title-page is dated 'April 24, 1962'. The novel was completed by Robert B. Parker and published in 1989.

The screenplay for *The Blue Dahlia* was first published by the Southern Illinois University Press, in blue cloth, lettered dark blue on the front cover and silver on the spine. A simultaneous paperback edition has the dust-wrapper illustration on the front cover. This reproduces the poster for the film, featuring Alan Ladd, Veronica Lake and William Bendix. The UK edition was published by Elm Tree Books. *Raymond Chandler's Unknown Thriller: the Screenplay of 'Playback'* was published in 1985 by Mysterious Press in the USA and Harrap in the UK.

Collectors should note that the US story collections *Red Wind* and *Spanish Blood* contain reprinted stories only.

Chandler was well served by his publishers, especially Hamish Hamilton, who produced many attractive dust-wrappers, designed by distinguished artists. The US edition of *The Big Sleep* has the title and its reflection set at a slant on a white, red and blue background. The British *Big Sleep* has an orange wrapper with a hand holding a smoking brown gun and yellow lettering. The US *Farewell, My Lovely* has the first word of the title in two-toned block capitals, with 'My Lovely' underneath in script. H. C.'s wrapper for the UK edition has a line drawing of a couple embracing on a sofa, with a decanter and two glasses in the foreground. The background is red, lettered white. The spine carries a full-length drawing of a man in a blue suit firing a gun.

The US *High Window* features a man plunging from a window towards a surreal design including scales and a magnifying glass. Hewitt's yellow wrapper for the UK edition has a long-legged blonde in a tight-fitting blue dress kicking at a gun which appears to have fallen from a man's hands. She is bisected by a red panel containing the title in white.

The Lady in the Lake has the same design for both US and UK wrappers (except for the wording under the author's name). The shadow of an elongated figure lies on a hill topped by a lone house and a bare tree. The background is indigo, with pink lettering. The US *Little Sister* has the title in large script at the top of the wrapper with a fly beneath. There is an ingenious design of drapes suspended from a woman's finger and falling into the shape of a face surmounted by dark spectacle frames. A smooth-handled tool penetrates vertebrae in the right corner, while supporting the drapes. C. W. Bacon's design for the UK *Little Sister* shows a prim, bespectacled woman in an olive suit with matching hat and gloves opening the door of Philip Marlowe's office. Marlowe gapes at her from the spine.

Cadaverous hands hold a palette and brush on the wrapper for the US *Simple Art of Murder*. Bacon's UK wrapper is dark, with red and white letters and a firing gun. The US *Long Goodbye* has an eye in the centre, with the lower half of a figure carrying a case on the left and a totem carving in the right foreground. Fritz Wegner's design for the UK *Long Goodbye* is a view seen through an open doorway of a brunette's body draped over the bed in an elegant room. A blue wrap has been thrown over a chair. The US *Playback* features two reels with the author's name on a broad band between them. The UK wrapper is plain black with red and white lettering.

The US *Raymond Chandler Speaking* sets the title in an irregular box. The UK version is two-toned, the top purple with the author in white, the lower half lime green with a photograph of Chandler and a list of contents. *Killer in the Rain* (US) shows a man holding a gun behind his back while sheltering under an umbrella. Andrew's UK wrapper has a dagger on a blue background covered in raindrops. Youngman Carter's design for *The Smell of Fear* has a background of red

skyscrapers and a tough-looking gunman in trench coat and sunglasses in the foreground.

Marlowe novels

The Big Sleep Knopf 1939, Hamish Hamilton 1939
Farewell, My Lovely Knopf 1940, Hamilton 1940
The High Window Knopf 1942, Hamilton 1943
The Lady in the Lake Knopf 1943, Hamilton 1944
The Little Sister Hamilton 1949, Houghton Mifflin 1949
a.k.a. *Marlowe* Pocket Books 1969
The Long Goodbye Hamilton 1953, Houghton 1954
Playback Hamilton 1958, Houghton 1958
Poodle Springs: in *Raymond Chandler Speaking* Houghton 1962, Hamilton 1962; completed by Robert B. Parker, Putnam 1989, Macdonald 1990

Story collections

Five Murderers Avon 1944 (5 stories)
Five Sinister Characters Avon 1945 (5 stories)
Finger Man Avon 1946 (3 stories, 1 essay)
The Simple Art of Murder Houghton Mifflin 1950 (12 stories, 1 essay); Hamilton 1950 (7 stories, 1 essay)
Killer in the Rain Houghton 1964, Hamilton 1964 (8 stories)
The Smell of Fear Hamilton 1965 (14 stories)

Uncollected story

'Professor Bingo's Snuff' (*Park East*, June-Aug. 1951)

Screenplays

The Blue Dahlia Southern Illinois University Press 1976, Elm Tree 1976
Raymond Chandler's Unknown Thriller: The Screenplay of 'Playback' Mysterious Press 1985, Harrap 1985

JC

G. K. Chesterton 1874–1936

As a detective writer G. K. Chesterton is *sui generis*, his own man on an impressive scale. His work combines imagination and intellect in a wholly original manner, imposing its own conditions with bizarre but irresistible logic.

Chesterton's major criminous works are collections of stories. None of his novels falls strictly within the genre (but *The Man Who Was Thursday* has some claims and is included here).

His first collection was published by Harper in 1905, five years before the advent of Father Brown. *The Club of Queer Trades* concerns a club of which the aspirant member 'must have invented the method by which he earns his living'. The six stories all feature Basil Grant, whose detective brother, Rupert, also figures in three. The book is dark red with gilt lettering on the spine, which also has black rules at top and bottom. The front cover has title and author in black over the central figure from the illustration facing page 119, also in black (Basil Grant 'advancing with blazing eyes', for 'The Awful Reason of the Vicar's Visit'). Enclosing everything is a single black border. The title-page is dated. The text has thirty-two black-and-white drawings by the author, paired opposite page 258, singly otherwise. There are four pages of advertisements at the rear. The New York edition followed a month later with illustrations by W. E. Mears.

The first Father Brown story appeared in September 1910 and the first collection in July 1911, from Cassell, who published all Chesterton's later collections to 1937. *The Innocence of Father Brown* has a red binding with gilt lettering on the spine and title and author in gilt on the front cover, which also has a blind-stamped border. It is dated on the title-page. Eight full-page illustrations by Sydney Seymour Lucas, including a frontispiece, show scenes from six of the twelve stories ('The Invisible Man' and 'The Eye of Apollo' have two each). The US edition, again, has variant illustrations, by Will F. Foster. *The Wisdom of Father Brown* also has twelve stories. It has a blue binding with the spine lettered in gilt and the front cover with title and author blind-stamped and a blind-stamped border. The

BL copy is dark blue and a lighter variant is recorded, identical except for the variant shade. The book is dated on the title-page and has a coloured frontispiece by Sydney Seymour Lucas, for 'The Man in the Passage'. *The Man Who Knew Too Much* contains eight stories with Horne Fisher, whose particular knowledge in excess affects the resolution of some of his cases. The original British edition of 1922 also has four non-series stories, of which only the first is included in the US edition: 'The Trees of Pride', 'The Garden of Smoke', 'The Five of Swords' and 'The Tower of Treason'. The book is dark green with dark-blue lettering on the spine and title and author and a border in dark blue on the front cover. It is dated on the copyright page and there is a printer's code at the end: F40.1022. The US edition has a frontispiece by W. Hatherell illustrating 'The Bottomless Well'.

The Incredulity of Father Brown, which has eight stories, appeared in 1926 in a black binding with red lettering and decorative borders on the spine and front cover. The spinal border is wavy at top and bottom and straight at the sides; that on the cover is wavy all round and is contained within a straight, close, blind-stamped border. In the upper half of the front cover, title and author appear within an intricate decorative framework, with straight and wavy lines, partly red and partly blind-stamped. The book is dated on the copyright page and a printer's code appears at the end: F75.426.

The Secret of Father Brown, *The Poet and the Lunatics* and *Four Faultless Felons* have the same format: black binding, spine lettered in gilt and with single gilt rules at either end, blind-stamped border on the front cover, dated copyright page and printer's code at the end: 807.27, F60.629 and F60.730, respectively. *The Secret of Father Brown* has ten stories including the framing narratives of Father Brown and Flambeau; *The Poet and the Lunatics* consists of eight mysteries of 'the sort . . . more attractive to a mystic', all with the painter and poet, Gabriel Gale; and *Four Faultless Felons* has a prologue and epilogue framing four long stories about the Club of Men Misunderstood, who devote themselves to 'a new sort of detective story', hunting not 'for crimes but for concealed virtues'. The

Harper edition of *The Secret of Father Brown* has illustrations by Frederic Dorr Steele.

The Scandal of Father Brown has a dark-blue binding with gilt lettering and a single gilt rule at both top and bottom of the spine. It is dated on the copyright page, which also has the printer's code F60.235. *The Paradoxes of Mr. Pond* has a black binding with mauve lettering on the spine. It is undated but the copyright page has the printer's code F.1236. *ECB* gives March 1937 as the month of publication. Mr Pond, a 'Government official', solves eight mysteries in a strongly individual fashion.

The Scandal of Father Brown contains eight stories, bringing the tally to fifty. Three other Father Brown stories have since appeared in collected form: 'The Vampire of the Village' in *The Father Brown Omnibus* (Dodd, Mead 1951), *The Father Brown Stories* (Cassell 1953) and *The Scandal of Father Brown* (Penguin 1978); 'The Donnington Affair', written with Max Pemberton, in *Thirteen Detectives* (Xanadu 1987); and 'The Mask of Midas', issued separately by Classica in January 1991. Two other uncollected stories have also been absorbed into Chesterton collections: 'The White Pillars Murder' into *Thirteen Detectives* and 'The Man Who Shot the Fox' into *Seven Suspects* (Xanadu 1990). The Penguin *Scandal*, in orange wrappers, has a cover photograph of Kenneth More as Father Brown. *Thirteen Detectives* has a blue binding and *Seven Suspects* is maroon. Both have gilt lettering on the spine and dated copyright page. Besides the seven stories the contents of the latter also include Chesterton's 'Defence of Detective Stories'. Both Xanadu collections were edited by Marie Smith.

The Mask of Midas was published in a limited edition of 1000 copies, of which numbers 1–50 are leather-bound. The rest are in a dark red-brown binding with silver lettering on the spine and dated title-page. The front cover has the title, in decorative lettering, in silver and the rear cover has a vignette of Father Brown, also in silver. The limitation appears on the page opposite the title and is signed and numbered by the illustrator, Noralf Husby. There is a preface by Geir Hasnes and there are four illustrations, one half-page and three full-page, all in black and white. Notes and a bibliography complete the volume.

A sixteen-page pamphlet of 'The Donnington Affair' with Chesterton's sequel was issued by the 'Pember-Chess Press, New York' 'on 25 December 1979, for friends of the publisher'. The last page states 'First printing' and gives the limitation as one hundred numbered copies.

The Man Who Was Thursday was published in 1908 in a dark-red binding with gilt lettering on the spine. The front cover has title and author in black, together with the subtitle 'A Nightmare' (also on the title-page). The book is dated on the copyright page and there are two pages of advertisements at the rear.

'The Tremendous Adventures of Major Brown', collected in *The Club of Queer Trades*, was separately published by Shurmer Sibthorp, to establish copyright, in December 1903. 'The Perishing of the Pendragons' was also published separately, by Paget in 1914 (and is collected in *The Wisdom of Father Brown*). Dodd, Mead published three of the long stories that make up *Four Faultless Felons*: 'The Moderate Murderer' and 'The Honest Quack' in tandem in 1929 and 'The Ecstatic Thief' on its own in 1930.

In addition, Chesterton contributed a Prologue, 'The Three Pipe-Dreams', to *The Floating Admiral* (see 'The Detection Club').

Otto Penzler states (in *TAD*, Summer 1983) that a variant version of *The Innocence of Father Brown* exists, in a brown binding with black lettering on the spine and front cover, the latter also with a large full-colour illustration pasted to it. He also records a variant for *The Wisdom of Father Brown*: in a dark-blue binding with gilt lettering and heavy gilt ornamentation on the spine, the front cover with title and author in gilt, a blind-stamped border and a blind-stamped leaf ornament at each corner.

Three of the elusive non-series stories from *The Man Who Knew Too Much* recur in the late posthumous collections: 'The Garden of Smoke' in *Thirteen Detectives* and 'The Five of Swords' and 'The Tower of Treason' in *Seven Suspects*.

Father Brown features on at least three of Chesterton's dust-wrappers: looking cherubic and counting on his fingers for *The Incredulity*, and for *The Scandal* in a portrait by Noel Syers, enigmatic of expression and holding his umbrella with both hands. The cream wrapper for *The Mask of Midas* has a fifth illustration by Noralf Husby, with Father Brown outside the Casterville and County Bank. *The Man Who Knew Too Much* has a man shrinking from an unseen threat behind him, to his left. *The Poet and the Lunatics* shows Gale and two associates startled by a hideous face at the window. *The Paradoxes of Mr. Pond* offers a splendid view of Mr Pond in an armchair, his fingertips together and his two friends looking towards him, with their backs to us. The wrappers for *Thirteen Detectives* and *Seven Suspects* reproduce black-and-white drawings by Frederic Dorr Steele.

Other items of interest include the World's Classics selection *Father Brown* (OUP 1955) introduced by Ronald Knox; *Father Brown Stories* (Folio Society 1959) illustrated by Edward Ardizzone; and *The Annotated Innocence of Father Brown* with introduction and notes by Martin Gardner (OUP 1987).

Novel

The Man Who Was Thursday Arrowsmith 1908, Dodd, Mead 1908

Story collections

(with Father Brown as titles indicate)

The Club of Queer Trades Harper (London) March 1905, (New York) April 1905.
The Innocence of Father Brown Cassell July 1911, Lane 1911
The Wisdom of Father Brown Cassell October 1914, Lane 1915
The Man Who Knew Too Much Cassell November 1922 (12 stories) Harper 1922 (9 stories)
The Incredulity of Father Brown Cassell June 1926, Dodd 1926
The Secret of Father Brown Cassell September 1927, Harper 1927
The Poet and the Lunatics Cassell July 1929, Dodd 1929
Four Faultless Felons Cassell August 1930, Dodd 1930

The Scandal of Father Brown Cassell March 1935, Dodd 1935; with 'The Vampire of the Village' Penguin 1978
The Paradoxes of Mr. Pond Cassell n.d. (March 1937), Dodd 1937
Thirteen Detectives Xanadu 1987 (includes one Father Brown story written with Max Pemberton)
Seven Suspects Xanadu 1990

Separately published stories

The Tremendous Adventures of Major Brown Shurmer Sibthorp 1903
The Perishing of the Pendragons Paget 1914
The Moderate Murderer and the Honest Quack Dodd 1929
The Ecstatic Thief Dodd 1930
The Donnington Affair (with Max Pemberton) Pember-Chess Press 1979

The Mask of Midas Classica 1991

Novel with other members of the Detection Club (q.v.)

The Floating Admiral Hodder & Stoughton n.d. (1931), Doubleday 1932 *BP*

Dame Agatha Christie (1890–1976)

Agatha Christie wrote sixty-six crime novels and thirteen plays, one of which was written in collaboration. Her 154 stories have largely been collected in sixteen volumes in the UK and thirteen in the USA. She also contributed to three collaborative novels. She was one of the best and most popular of detective writers and her influence on crime fiction has been considerable. She created some of the most ingenious plots in the history of the genre, and she remains one of the most collected of writers.

The first of her two great detectives is the Belgian, Hercule Poirot, whose debut was in 1920, in *The Mysterious Affair at Styles*. Before his death in *Curtain*, he appeard in thirty-three novels and fifty-four stories. He is very short, with an egg-shaped head and a large waxed moustache. He is always immaculately dressed, and usually wears pointed black patent-leather shoes. His technique relies heavily on order and method, and his 'little grey cells' are used to great effect in his many cases.

The second is the elderly spinster Miss Jane Marple, tall, thin, and white-haired. She lives in St Mary Mead and becomes a connoisseur of human nature, bringing her experience of many years of village life to bear on the cases in which she becomes involved. She first appeared in a story, 'The Tuesday Night Club', included in *The Best Short Stories of the Year 1928*, published by Faber in 1929. She went on to figure in twelve novels and twenty stories.

Other important series characters in Agatha Christie's work are: Tommy and Tuppence Beresford, a husband and wife, who appear in four novels and a story collection; Ariadne Oliver, who provides much humour and some detection, besides eating many apples, in the course of the eight books in which she appears;

Chief Inspector James Japp, of Scotland Yard, who collaborates with Poirot on eleven cases; Captain Arthur Hastings, OBE, who acts as Poirot's Watson in eight novels and twenty-six stories; Superintendent Battle, also of Scotland Yard, who features in five investigations; Colonel Johnny Race, a secret service agent with four cases; Parker Pyne, a private detective, who appears in two collections of stories; Mr Satterthwaite, a lover of the fine arts, who assists in four books and one story; and Harley Quin, whose magical powers are seen in fourteen stories.

For most of the novels, the British editions are the true firsts. There are twenty exceptions (see checklist where US publisher has precedence). *The Moving Finger* and *Death Comes as the End* underwent changes for their British editions. Many books have variant titles in the USA, and even some of the stories are retitled, like 'Wireless', which became 'Where There's a Will'. In the UK, Agatha Christie's first six books were published by the Bodley Head. Odhams published *The Hound of Death* in 1933, and the rest of the novels and story collections were brought out by Collins. All the books are dated, except for *The Mystery of the Blue Train*, which simply states 'Copyright' on the reverse of the title page. *After the Funeral* is dated on page 192.

The Bodley Head first editions have decorated cloth in different colours, and they all have the title and author's name on the front cover, as well as on the spine. *The Mysterious Affair at Styles* has brown cloth, with a black decorative pattern. *The Secret Adversary* is dark green and the pattern is light green. *The Murder on the Links* has orange cloth, with the same decorative pattern, in black, as *The Mysterious Affair at Styles*. Both *Poirot Investigates* and *The Man in the Brown Suit* have the same decoration, but the former has yellow cloth, with the pattern in dark blue, while the latter is light brown, with dark brown decoration. *The Secret of Chimneys* has pale blue cloth, with the pattern in black. *Poirot Investigates* is slightly taller than the others.

The first three Collins titles have dark-blue cloth, lettered in red on the spine, and with title and author in red on the front cover. The first two also have a double red border on the front cover and double rules at the top and base of the spine. The third has a single border and single rules, all in red. Copies with pale-blue cloth lettered in black are later issues. *The Seven Dials Mystery, Partners in Crime*, and *The Mysterious Mr. Quin* have black cloth, with red spine lettering, and title and author in red on the front cover. All three covers have a single red border, and the first two have single red rules at the top and bottom of the spine (but these are not present on *The Mysterious Mr. Quin*). *Murder at the Vicarage*, published in 1930, was one of the earliest Crime Club books from Collins. All the Christie Crime Club books have orange or red cloth, until *Postern of Fate* appeared in 1973 with green cloth. Any editions published between these dates with black cloth lettered in red, or purple cloth lettered in green, are later issues. *By the Pricking of My Thumbs* was issued in red and in green cloth. The early Crime Club books are lettered in black on the spine, with title and author's name in black on the front cover. From *Death in the Clouds*, the front covers are blank. *Murder at the Vicarage* has a single black border on the front cover. From the publication of *A Caribbean Mystery* in 1964, the black spine lettering was replaced with gilt. *The Listerdale Mystery* and *Parker Pyne Investigates* were issued by Collins, as opposed to the Crime Club, in mauve cloth, with silver lettering on the spine. *Poirot's Early Cases* has brown cloth and *Miss Marple's Final Cases* has red, both with the spine lettered gilt. *Curtain, Sleeping Murder*, and *The Agatha Christie Hour* all have black cloth, with gilt lettering on the spine, while *Problem at Pollensa Bay* has claret cloth with the spine lettered gilt.

The Crime Club gunman, who usually faces left, faces right on the title-pages of *N or M?* and *Ten Little Niggers*. *Death on the Nile* and *Sleeping Murder* have no gunman on the title-page. 'A Poirot Story' appears in black below the author's name on the spine of *Murder in Mesopotamia*. All the books before *N or M?* have advertisement sections at the rear, except *The Mysterious Affair at Styles, The Murder of Roger Ackroyd, The Big Four, The Mystery of the Blue Train, The Mysterious Mr. Quin, The*

Hound of Death, and *Cards on the Table*. There is a variant title-page for *Passenger to Frankfurt* and *Endless Night*, with a modified address for the publisher: Collins, London-Sydney, instead of the usual Collins, St James' Place, London. The true first edition of *Hercule Poirot's Christmas* has the top of 'Hercule' 7mm from the top of the spine, whereas for a later impression the word is set 14 mm down from the top. From *Cards on the Table* to *Hercule Poirot's Christmas* the books are taller than the others, and the titles after 1966 are also taller. Collectors should be wary of an undated *Ten Little Niggers*, which is otherwise identical to the dated first edition. *The Hound of Death* has maroon cloth, with the spine lettered gilt. Odhams also published a blue cloth edition of *Murder in the Mews*, which is sometimes mistakenly thought to be the first.

The US version of *Why Didn't They Ask Evans?* was entitled *The Boomerang Clue* and first appeared in book form in the USA as a quarto-sized hardback, published by the *Redbook Magazine* in March/April 1934. The book has red boards with black cloth spine. There is no lettering on the spine but 'Six Redbook Novels' appears in gilt on the front cover. Below this, in a square, is a stylish female figure with, behind her, a male silhouette, both red against a gilt background. *The Boomerang Clue* is one of six abridged magazine novels bound into one volume. Another of the six is Dashiell Hammett's *The Thin Man*.

Penguin issued ten Christie titles in 1953, with introductions specially written for these editions by the author.

Unfortunately, not all the stories were published in book form both in London and New York, and collectors in the UK and the USA need to be aware of stories they may be missing. British collectors need all the UK story collections, except *Thirteen for Luck!*. They will also need *The Regatta Mystery* for 'The Mystery of the Baghdad Chest' and *Three Blind Mice* for the title story. American collectors need the US collections, except *Thirteen for Luck!, Surprise! Surprise!, 13 Clues for Miss Marple* and *Hercule Poirot's Early Cases*. They will also need: *The Adventure of the Christmas Pudding* for the Poirot story 'The Mystery of the Spanish Chest', an expanded version of 'The Mystery of the Baghdad Chest'. Collectors generally will need *Agatha Christie*, the official centenary celebration book, for 'A Trap for the Unwary'; *The Problem at Pollensa Bay*, a war-time Polybook (a sixteen-page pamphlet produced during the Second World War), which contains 'Christmas Adventure', a Poirot story later rewritten as 'The Adventure of the Christmas Pudding' (and originally in the *Sketch* for 12 Dec. 1923 as 'Christmas Adventure'); and *Poirot and the Regatta Mystery*, another wartime product from Bantam in 1943, containing a variant version of 'The Regatta Mystery' with Poirot instead of Parker Pyne (and originally in *The Strand* for June 1936). Two stories, 'The First Wish' (*Grand Magazine*, Dec. 1923) and 'Publicity' (*Hutchinson's*, Feb. 1928) were adapted for *Partners in Crime*. Other uncollected stories, not all dealing with crime or mystery, are 'While the Light Lasts', 'Within a Wall', 'The House of Dreams', 'The Lonely God', 'The Edge' and 'Manx Gold'. 'Manx Gold' first appeared in five short instalments in the *Daily Dispatch* on 23, 24, 26, 27 and 28 May 1930 and then in a booklet entitled 'June in Douglas, Isle of Man'. The story was used as the basis for a treasure hunt to attract visitors to the island.

The Problem at Pollensa Bay is a paperback, with an attractive illustrated front endpaper by Frank R. Grey, showing Poirot kneeling in the snow by a corpse. *Poirot and the Regatta Mystery* is a similar pamphlet, also with a frontispiece by Frank R. Grey. There are two collections of stories published in the UK and the USA with identical titles but varying contents. The US edition of *Poirot Investigates* contains three stories not in the British original: 'The Veiled Lady', 'The Lost Mine', and 'The Chocolate Box'. The Dodd, Mead edition of *Thirteen for Luck!* contains 'The Veiled Lady', 'Tape Measure Murder', 'The Regatta Mystery', and 'Problem at Pollensa Bay'; but Collins substituted for these 'Greenshaw's Folly', 'The Witness for the Prosecution', 'Where There's a Will', and 'The Mystery of the Spanish Shawl'. The other nine stories are common to both editions.

The story 'The Under Dog' was first published in the *London Magazine* for Oct. 1926 and its first book publication was by the Readers' Library in 1929, together with E. Phillips Oppenheim's 'Blackman's Wood'. The book is entitled *Two New Crime Stories* on the spine and front cover, and the authors' surnames also appear at these points. The words 'Copyright edition' appear on the reverse of the title-page, and the book is undated. It is a small maroon book, with the spine and front cover lettered and decorated gilt. The wrapper for the first edition has a description of the stories on the front flap, whereas later editions have a list of titles in the Readers' Library. *The Sunningdale Mystery* is a 1933 Collins reprint of part of *Partners in Crime*. Reilly and Hubin disagree about the first publisher and even the original title of *The Mousetrap/Three Blind Mice*. The checklist follows Hubin.

All Agatha Christie's first editions were published with dust-wrappers. Lawrence Cavendish, holding a candle, accompanied by other residents, is seen in Mrs Inglethorp's bedroom on the wrapper of *The Mysterious Affair at Styles*. *Poirot Investigates* has W. Smithson Broadhead's full-length black and white portrait of Poirot. Ellen Edwards' design for *The Murder of Roger Ackroyd* shows a desk on which is a telephone, with a young woman looking at some documents. C. Morse's wrapper for *the Mystery of the Blue Train* depicts the dead Ruth Kettering, lying on a berth in a train compartment with two puzzled gendarmes looking on. A head-and-shoulders portrait of Hercule Poirot appears in the middle of the blue spine, below the title and above the price, 7/6d. *Partners in Crime* (UK) has the bright young things, Tommy holding a gun and Tuppence holding a magnifying glass, both in evening dress, with a trusting bloodhound. Behind, a literally beaming moon looks down through a window, while a threatening shadow looms over Tommy. For *Partners in Crime* (US) an elegant couple dance against a blue background, entwined within red coils extending from the letter *R* of *Crime*. *Peril at End House* has a figure carrying a lantern against a blue-green background. The green wrapper of *The Thirteen Problems* has three masked gunmen on the front panel and another on the spine. Lambart's blue and white design for *Lord Edgware Dies* shows Lord Edgware slumped across his desk, stabbed through the neck, while a seated man, perhaps Inspector Japp, studies the body. The spine shows Lady Edgware walking through a doorway. The lettering is in red. Dermonay drew a sinister green hound, depicted against a background of a ruined convent, for the green, black, and blue wrapper for *The Hound of Death*. A black hound's head appears on the spine, below the author's name. *Murder on the Orient Express* shows the engine of the train, with a glowing fire illuminating the driver and stoker. *The Listerdale Mystery* has author and title caught in the beam of a hand-held torch, shining upwards from the lower left corner. A head-and-shoulders portrait of the dead Alec Pritchard by Gilbert Cousland appears on the front panel of the wrapper for *Why Didn't They Ask Evans?*, with Bobby Jones' hands holding a photograph on the spine. *Parker Pyne Investigates* has a benevolent portrait by B. of Mr Parker Pyne, set against a pair of handcuffs. Robin Macartney's wrapper for *Murder in the Mews* shows the front of a car parked in Bardsley Garden Mews at night, with the back of the same car on the spine. *Death in the Clouds* has the title in a blue sky, formed from the vapour trail of a biplane. Three wineglasses appear on the front and spine of the wrapper for *Three Act Tragedy*, and a yellow *ABC* railway guide illustrates *The ABC Murders*.

The architect and painter Robin Macartney, who took part in archaeological expeditions with Agatha Christie and her husband, created some distinctive wrappers, including one showing labourers excavating near a river, watched by a figure on horseback, for *Murder in Mesopotamia*. He also painted the SS *Karnah*, sailing down the Nile past two vast carved Pharaohs, for *Death on the Nile*. In a similar vein, and perhaps by the same artist, is the wrapper for *Appointment with Death*, which has a bedouin perched high on a mountain, looking across a valley in Palestine. A run of twelve playing cards, with the ace of spades at the top, is spread across a green background for *Cards on the Table*. The brown wrapper for *Dumb Witness* is notable for the photographs, on both spine and front panel, of the author's wire-haired terrier Peter, to whom

the book is dedicated. *Hercule Poirot's Christmas* has a red wrapper covered in white snowflakes. The wrapper of *Murder Is Easy* is green with a witch's broom superimposed on a cloud. The green wrapper, lettered in red, for *Ten Little Niggers* shows a hand hovering over one of the ten black figures displayed on a circular glass stand. Barlow's wrapper for *Sad Cypress* is blue and lettered in yellow, with a black cypress tree. Ten scenes from the nursery rhyme decorate the brown and green wrapper of *One, Two, Buckle My Shoe*. For *Evil Under the Sun*, Rose produced a stylized drawing of rocks and sea under a burning sun.

Stead created two particularly striking wrappers: picking out the title of *The Body in the Library* on the spines of books arranged on three shelves; and showing a green skull, leering behind a glass of effervescent wine, for *Sparkling Cyanide*. Line-drawings of nursery-rhyme pigs on a yellow background alternate with the words of the title, in pink, for *Five Little Pigs*. The green wrapper of *The Moving Finger* is lettered in red and features a cobweb, in which people and objects from the novel are caught. A golf-club and a bell feature prominently in J. Z. Atkinson's design for *Towards Zero*. The body of an ancient Egyptian is towed in a funeral barge across the grey, blue, and gold wrapper of *Death Comes as the End*. A green pekingese, Shan Tung, dominates the black wrapper of *The Labours of Hercules*, while Hercules himself appears on the spine, below the author's name. Rough seas and a stormy sky rage across *Taken at the Flood*: and Birtwhistle's surreal design of a crazy house in a midnight wood illustrates *Crooked House*. The clock on the blue-green wrapper of *A Murder Is Announced* stands at 6.30 p.m., the time set for the murder to occur at Little Paddocks.

The wrappers for *The Hollow* and for the fourteen books from *They Came to Baghdad* are all very similar, with the title and the author's name set against a coloured background. *The Clocks* appeared in 1963 with a wrapper by Michael Harvey, showing the black hands of a clock against a pattern of blue circles. This particular dust-wrapper has proved elusive in pristine condition. The wrappers for the rest of the canon after this date are regrettably unimaginative.

The actual locations for several books are known: 'End House' was in reality 'Rockend', next to the Imperial Hotel in Torquay (known in the book as 'The Majestic'); Sidmouth is the location for *Sleeping Murder*; Burgh Island off the south Devon coast is the main setting for *Evil Under the Sun* and, perhaps, *Ten Little Niggers*; and the grounds and boat-house of the author's home, Greenway House, in Devon, were used for *Dead Man's Folly*.

Fiddlers Three is the only one of Agatha Christie's stage plays still unpublished. Three TV plays have been broadcast: *The Wasp's Nest* on 18 June 1937; *Three Blind Mice* on 21 Oct. 1947; and *Ten Little Niggers* on 10 June 1949. There are also three unpublished radio plays: *Butter in a Lordly Dish*, *Three Blind Mice*, and *Personal Call* (featuring Inspector Narracott from *The Sittaford Mystery*). Five first editions seem particularly difficult to locate: *Murder on the Links, The Thirteen Problems, Parker Pyne Investigates, The Mysterious Affair at Styles*, and *The Secret Adversary*.

Novels

(with series characters, as stated)

The Mysterious Affair at Styles Lane 1920, Bodley Head 1921 (Poirot, Hastings)

The Secret Adversary Bodley Head 1922, Dodd, Mead 1922 (Beresford)

The Murder on the Links Dodd 1923, Bodley Head 1923 (Poirot, Hastings)

The Man in the Brown Suit Bodley Head 1924 Dodd 1924 (Race)

The Secret of Chimneys Bodley Head 1925, Dodd 1925 (Battle)

The Murder of Roger Ackroyd Collins 1926, Dodd 1926 (Poirot)

The Big Four Collins 1927, Dodd 1927 (Poirot, Hastings)

The Mystery of the Blue Train Collins n.d. (1928), Dodd 1928 (Poirot)

The Seven Dials Mystery Collins 1929, Dodd 1929 (Battle)

The Murder at the Vicarage Collins Crime Club 1930, Dodd 1930 (Marple)

The Murder at Hazelmoor Dodd 1931

a.k.a. *The Sittaford Mystery* Crime Club 1931

Peril at End House Crime Club 1932, Dodd 1932 (Poirot, Hastings)

Lord Edgware Dies Crime Club 1933 (Poirot, Hastings)

a.k.a. *Thirteen at Dinner* Dodd 1933

Murder on the Orient Express Crime Club 1934 (Poirot)

a.k.a. *Murder in the Calais Coach* Dodd 1934

Why Didn't They Ask Evans? Crime Club 1934

a.k.a. *The Boomerang Clue* Dodd 1935

Murder in Three Acts Dodd 1934 (Poirot, Satterthwaite)

a.k.a. *Three-Act Tragedy* Crime Club 1935

Death in the Air Dodd 1935 (Poirot)

a.k.a. *Death in the Clouds* Crime Club 1935

The ABC Murders Crime Club 1936, Dodd 1936 (Poirot, Hastings)

a.k.a. *The Alphabet Murders* Pocket Books 1966

Murder in Mesopotamia Crime Club 1936, Dodd 1936 (Poirot)

Cards on the Table Crime Club 1936, Dodd 1937 (Poirot, Battle, Race, Oliver)

Dumb Witness Crime Club 1937 (Poirot, Hastings)

a.k.a. *Poirot Loses a Client* Dodd 1937

Death on the Nile Crime Club 1937, Dodd 1938 (Poirot, Race)

Appointment with Death Crime Club 1938, Dodd 1938 (Poirot)

Hercule Poirot's Christmas Crime Club 1939 (Poirot)

a.k.a. *Murder for Christmas* Dodd 1939

a.k.a. *A Holiday for Murder* Avon 1947

Murder Is Easy Crime Club 1939 (Battle)

a.k.a. *Easy to Kill* Dodd 1939

Ten Little Niggers Crime Club 1939

a.k.a. *And Then There Were None* Dodd 1940

a.k.a. *Ten Little Indians* Pocket Books 1965

Sad Cypress Crime Club 1940, Dodd 1940 (Poirot)

One, Two, Buckle My Shoe Crime Club 1940 (Poirot)

a.k.a. *The Patriotic Murders* Dodd 1941

a.k.a. *An Overdose of Death*   Dell 1953

Evil Under the Sun   Crime Club 1941, Dodd 1941 (Poirot)

N or M? Dodd 1941, Crime Club 1941 (Beresford)

The Body in the Library   Dodd 1942, Crime Club 1942 (Marple)

Murder in Retrospect   Dodd 1942 (Poirot)

a.k.a. *Five Little Pigs*   Crime Club 1942

The Moving Finger   Dodd 1942, Crime Club 1943 (Marple)

Towards Zero   Dodd 1944, Crime Club 1944 (Battle)

Death Comes as the End   Dodd 1944, Crime Club 1945

Remembered Death   Dodd 1945 (Race)

a.k.a. *Sparkling Cyanide*   Crime Club 1945

The Hollow   Dodd 1946, Crime Club 1946 (Poirot)

a.k.a. *Murder After Hours*   Dell 1954

There is a Tide . . .   Dodd 1948 (Poirot)

a.k.a. *Taken at the Flood*   Crime Club 1948

Crooked House   Dodd 1949, Crime Club 1949

A Murder Is Announced   Crime Club 1950, Dodd 1950 (Marple)

They Came to Baghdad   Crime Club 1951, Dodd 1951

Mrs. McGinty's Dead   Dodd 1952, Crime Club 1952, (Poirot, Oliver)

a.k.a. *Blood Will Tell*   DBC 1952

Murder with Mirrors   Dodd 1952 (Marple)

a.k.a. *They Do it With Mirrors*   Crime Club 1952

Funerals Are Fatal   Dodd 1953 (Poirot)

a.k.a. *After the Funeral*   Crime Club 1953

a.k.a. *Murder at the Gallop*   Fontana 1963

A Pocket Full of Rye   Crime Club 1953, Dodd 1954 (Marple)

Destination Unknown   Crime Club 1954

a.k.a. *So Many Steps to Death*   Dodd 1955

Hickory, Dickory, Dock   Crime Club 1955 (Poirot)

a.k.a. *Hickory, Dickory, Death*   Dodd 1955

Dead Man's Folly   Crime Club 1956, Dodd 1956 (Poirot, Oliver)

4.50 from Paddington   Crime Club 1957 (Marple)

a.k.a. *What Mrs. McGillicuddy Saw!*   Dodd 1957

a.k.a. *Murder, She Said*   Pocket Books 1961

Ordeal by Innocence   Crime Club 1958, Dodd 1959

Cat Among the Pigeons   Crime Club 1959, Dodd 1960 (Poirot)

The Pale Horse   Crime Club 1961, Dodd 1962 (Oliver)

The Mirror Crack'd from Side to Side   Crime Club 1962 (Marple)

a.k.a. *The Mirror Crack'd*   Dodd 1963

The Clocks   Crime Club 1963, Dodd 1964 (Poirot)

A Caribbean Mystery   Crime Club 1964, Dodd 1965 (Marple)

At Bertram's Hotel   Crime Club 1965, Dodd 1966 (Marple)

Third Girl   Crime Club 1966, Dodd 1967 (Poirot, Oliver)

Endless Night   Crime Club 1967, Dodd 1968

By the Pricking of My Thumbs   Crime Club 1968, Dodd 1968 (Beresford)

Hallowe'en Party   Crime Club 1969, Dodd 1969 (Poirot, Oliver)

Passenger to Frankfurt   Crime Club 1970, Dodd 1970

Nemesis   Crime Club 1971, Dodd 1971 (Marple)

Elephants Can Remember   Crime Club 1972, Dodd 1972 (Poirot, Oliver)

Postern of Fate   Crime Club 1973, Dodd 1973 (Beresford)

Curtain   Crime Club 1975, Dodd 1975 (Poirot, Hastings)

Sleeping Murder   Crime Club 1976, Dodd 1976 (Marple)

Story collections

Poirot Investigates   Bodley Head 1924 (11 Poirot stories), Dodd 1925 (14 Poirot stories)

Partners in Crime   Dodd 1929, Collins 1929 (14 Beresford stories), partly reprinted as

The Sunningdale Mystery   Collins 1933

Two New Crime Stories   Readers' Library 1929 (1 Poirot story), with E. Phillips Oppenheim

The Mysterious Mr. Quin   Collins 1930, Dodd 1930 (12 Quin and Satterthwaite stories)

The Thirteen Problems   Collins Crime Club 1932 (13 Marple stories)

a.k.a. *The Tuesday Club Murders* Dodd 1933

The Hound of Death Odhams 1933 (12 stories)

The Listerdale Mystery Collins 1934 (12 stories)

Parker Pyne Investigates Collins 1934 (12 Pyne stories, 1 with Oliver)

a.k.a. *Mr. Parker Pyne, Detective* Dodd 1934

Murder in the Mews Crime Club 1937 (4 Poirot stories)

a.k.a. *Dead Man's Mirror* Dodd 1937

The Regatta Mystery Dodd 1939 (9 stories, 5 with Poirot, 2 with Pyne, 1 with Marple)

The Mystery of the Crime in Cabin 66 Todd (Bantam) Apr. 1943 (contains the Poirot story 'Problem at Sea' with a new title)

The Regatta Mystery Todd (Bantam) Apr. 1943 (contains 'Poirot and the Regatta Mystery')

The Mystery of the Baghdad Chest Todd (Bantam) May 1943 (contains this one Poirot story)

Problem at Pollensa Bay and Christmas Adventure Todd (Polybooks) June 1943 (with Pyne and Poirot, respectively)

Poirot on Holiday Todd (Polybooks) Nov. 1943 (contains two Poirot stories, 'The Regatta Mystery' and 'The Crime in Cabin 66', a.k.a. 'Problem at Sea')

The Veiled Lady and The Baghdad Chest Hodgson (Polybooks) Apr. 1944 (contains two Poirot stories)

Poirot and the Regatta Mystery Vallancey n.d. (1944) (contains this one story)

Crime in Cabin 66 Vallancey n.d. (1944) (contains the Poirot story 'Problem at Sea' with its variant title)

The Mystery of the Baghdad Chest Vallancey (1945) (contains this one Poirot story)

Poirot Knows the Murderer Polybooks March 1946 (contains 3 Poirot stories: 'The Mystery of the Baghdad Chest', 'Crime in Cabin 66' (a.k.a. 'Problem at Sea'), 'Christmas Adventure')

Poirot Lends a Hand Polybooks Mar. 1946 (contains 3 stories: 'Problem at Pollensa Bay' (with Pyne), 'The Regatta Mystery', 'The Veiled Lady' (both with Poirot))

The Labours of Hercules Dodd 1947, Crime Club 1947 (12 Poirot stories)

The Witness for the Prosecution Dodd 1948 (11 stories, 1 with Poirot)

Three Blind Mice Dodd 1950 (9 stories, 3 with Poirot, 4 with Marple, 1 with Quin)

a.k.a. *The Mousetrap* Dell 1960

The Under Dog Dodd 1951 (9 Poirot stories)

The Adventure of the Christmas Pudding Crime Club 1960 (6 stories, 5 with Poirot, 1 with Marple)

Double Sin Dodd 1961 (8 stories, 4 with Poirot, 2 with Marple)

Thirteen for Luck! Dodd 1961 (13 stories)

Surprise! Surprise! Dodd 1965 (13 stories)

Thirteen for Luck! Collins 1966 (13 stories)

13 Clues for Miss Marple Dodd 1966 (13 Marple stories)

The Golden Ball Dodd 1971 (15 stories)

Poirot's Early Cases Crime Club 1974 (18 Poirot stories)

a.k.a. *Hercule Poirot's Early Cases* Dodd 1974

Miss Marple's Final Cases Crime Club 1979 (8 stories, 6 with Marple)

The Agatha Christie Hour Collins 1982 (10 stories, 2 with Pyne)

Agatha Christie: Official Centenary Celebration 1890–1990 Belgrave 1990 (a large format paperback, 27.5 cm × 20.5 cm) (contains 'A Trap for the Unwary', non-series story)

Problem at Pollensa Bay HarperCollins 1991 (8 stories, 2 with Poirot, 2 with Pyne, 2 with Quin and Satterthwaite)

Novels with other members of the Detection Club (q.v.)

The Floating Admiral Hodder & Stoughton n.d. (1931), Doubleday 1932

The Scoop and *Behind the Screen* Gollancz 1983

Uncollected stories

'While the Light Lasts' (*Novel Magazine*, Apr. 1924)

'Within a Wall' (*Royal Magazine*, Oct. 1925)

'The House of Dreams' (*Sovereign Magazine*, Jan. 1926)

'The Lonely God' (*Royal Magazine*, Jul. 1926)

'The Edge' (*Pearson's Magazine*, Feb. 1927)

MURDER IN MESOPOTAMIA
AGATHA CHRISTIE
A NEW POIROT STORY

'Manx Gold' (*Daily Dispatch*, 23, 24, 26, 27, 28 May 1930; also in a booklet 'June in Douglas', Isle of Man')   *JC*

Ann Cleeves (b. 1954)

Ann Cleeves is a most attractive writer, whose work combines the traditional pleasures of the detective story with the range and intensity of the modern crime novel of character. She has two series detectives: George Palmer-Jones, a retired Home Office official who is also a seasoned naturalist, and Stephen Ramsay, a Northumbrian policeman in mid-career. Besides her ten novels to date, she has published one story featuring Ramsay.

The earlier books were published by Century, in various phases of its complex evolution. Except for *Murder in my Back Yard*, which has a grey binding, they are all black; and all but *A Bird in the Hand*, which has silver spine letter-ing, have gilt lettering on the spine. The three Century-cum-Mysterious Press books have red endpapers with a pattern formed from multiple repetitions of the Press logo in black. From *Murder in Paradise*, the books are taller.

In 1991 the fifth Palmer-Jones novel was published in America by Fawcett, as a Gold Medal paperback original. The book has dark-blue covers and yellow edges. The vivid cover drawing shows bird-watching and martime impedimenta in a cabin on the *Jessie Ellen*. A lighthouse and a stormy sea are seen through a porthole. The book is dated 'October 1991' on the copyright page. The British edition was delayed until 1993, when Macmillan brought it out in hard covers.

From 1992 the books have been published by Macmillan, in various colours. They all have gilt lettering on the spine. All the books from both publishers are dated on the copyright page and *Killjoy* also has a printer's key 9–1.

The Century wrappers are all pictorial and the books look well on the shelf. Birds feature prominently on the earlier titles, reflecting Palmer-Jones' ornithological expertise. Trevor Scobie's falcon for *A Prey to Murder* is especially handsome. He also provided the striking designs for the earlier Ramsay novels: for *A Lesson in Dying*, the school by the river with a grotesque mask on a tree; and for *Murder in my Back Yard* a snowbound grave with a funeral urn spilling dead flowers and a dagger. Predictably, all this went out of the window with the move to Macmillan.

Novels

(with Palmer-Jones or Ramsay, as stated)
(Binding details refer to Macmillan editions)

A Bird in the Hand   Century 1986, Fawcett 1986 (Palmer-Jones)
Come Death and High Water   Century 1987, Fawcett 1987 (Palmer-Jones)
Murder in Paradise   Century/Mysterious Press 1988, Fawcett 1989 (Palmer-Jones)
A Prey to Murder   Century/Mysterious Press 1989, Fawcett 1989 (Palmer-Jones)

A Lesson in Dying Century/Mysterious Press 1990, Fawcett 1990 (Ramsay)
Murder in my Back Yard Random Century 1991, Fawcett 1991 (Ramsay)
Sea Fever Fawcett 1991, Macmillan 1993 (Palmer-Jones) (blue)
A Day in the Death of Dorothea Cassidy Macmillan 1992, Fawcett 1992 (Ramsay) (light brown)
Another Man's Poison Macmillan 1992, Fawcett 1993 (Palmer-Jones) (yellow)
Killjoy Macmillan 1993 (Ramsay) (blue)

Story

'A Winter's Tale' (*Northern Blood*, Didsbury Press 1992) (Ramsay)   *BP*

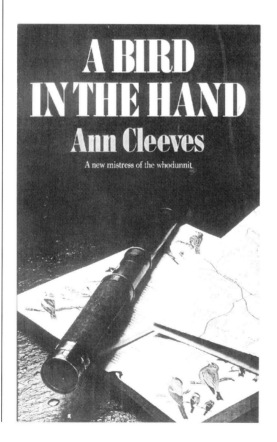

DEATH'S BRIGHT DART

The first thriller, set in a Cambridge college, by an author already distinguished in other literary fields

V.C. CLINTON-BADDELEY

V. C. Clinton-Baddeley (1900–1970)

V. C. Clinton-Baddeley wrote five novels, the last of which, *To Study a Long Silence*, was only belatedly published in the USA. Like his famous actress cousins Angela ('Mrs Bridges') and Hermione Baddeley, he also appeared on the London stage. He came, unfortunately, very late in life to writing detective fiction, but has left us a marvellous legacy. His books are delightfully nostalgic, elegant, charming, and civilized – essential reading for all connoisseurs of detective fiction. Dr R. V. Davie of St Nicholas's College, Cambridge, is one of the most likeable of fictional dons and appears in all five books. He is constantly reminding us of his happy memories of days gone by, at the same time continuing to enjoy life to the full.

The books were all first published in London by Gollancz and are dated. They all have red cloth with gilt lettering on the spine. All were issued in yellow dust-wrappers, with red and black lettering. *Death's Bright Dart* has a plan of Davie's college and is smaller in size than the others. *To Study a Long Silence* was left unfinished when the author died and was completed by his nephew, Mark Goullet.

The most difficult first edition to find is the first book, *Death's Bright Dart*.

Davie novels

Death's Bright Dart Gollancz 1967, Morrow 1970

My Foe Outstretch'd Beneath the Tree Gollancz 1968, Morrow 1968

Only a Matter of Time Gollancz 1969, Morrow 1970

No Case for the Police Gollancz 1970, Morrow 1970

To Study a Long Silence Gollancz 1972, (completed by Mark Goullet) Perennial 1984

JC

G. D. H. and M. Cole (1889–1959 and 1893–1980)

G. D. H. Cole was a left-wing intellectual, eminent in his time as economic and political theorist. His wife, Dame Margaret Cole, was Raymond Postgate's sister: she, too, was a prominent Socialist, long active in public life. They found time to write twenty-eight detective novels and four collections of stories. A further story was published separately; another appeared with reprinted material; and a third is uncollected. The Coles also contributed to *The Floating Admiral* (see 'The Detection Club'). Four titles were changed for US publication and a fifth is a phantom: *Murder in Four Parts*, listed by Hubin and Reilly, was published as *Death in the Quarry*.

The Coles' books are wholly traditional: despite some social criticism and satire, they seek to amuse their audience, not to unsettle it. They took turns to write their novels, but who wrote which titles is not established. Twenty-one novels and twenty-four stories feature Henry Wilson, a Scotland Yard man and occasional private investigator. Most of the Coles' other detectives work with him: the Hon. Everard Blatchington on three occasions, Dr Benjamin Tancred and Inspector Tom Fairford twice each. Dr Tancred appears in the uncollected story and Everard Blatchington, a toff with a yen for criminal investigation, has three cases of his own. Elizabeth Warrender collaborates with her son James in a novel and a collection of stories.

The major run of the Coles' titles was published by Collins, in the Crime Club format from *Burglars in Bucks*. The first in the series is *The Brooklyn Murders*, published as by G. D. H. Cole only, though reissued in 1933 in both names. Seven books appeared before the Crime Club was launched. Of these, five have a dark-blue binding and the final pair is black. All have orange lettering on the spine and title and authors in orange on the front cover, in capitals except for the two black books, which have largely lower-case lettering. From *The Brooklyn Murders* to *The Blatchington Tangle* the spines have double orange rules at either end and the front covers have double orange borders. The four later titles have single rules and borders. All except *Superintendent Wilson's Holiday* have advertisements at the rear. From *The Death of a Millionaire* to *The Murder at Crome House* the books are invariably attributed to G. D. H. and Margaret Cole, but *The Man from the River* has 'Margaret' externally and 'M' within and the reverse is true of *Poison in the Garden Suburb*. *Superintendent Wilson's Holiday* has 'M' at all points.

From *Burglars in Bucks* the books were published by Collins' Crime Club, all in orange bindings, with black lettering on the spine. Those to *Dr. Tancred Begins* also have title and author in black on the front cover (with a single black border for the three titles to *The Great Southern Mystery*). *Burglars in Bucks* and the books from *Scandal at School* have lighter lettering than the intervening run. Most titles have advertisements at the end but *Burglars in Bucks, The Great Southern Mystery, Knife in the Dark* and *Toper's End* do not. 'Margaret' comes and goes on title-pages but externally the books are always credited to G. D. H. and M. Cole. A few titles have preliminary plans: *Burglars in Bucks* of the grounds of Headingham Manor; *Dr. Tancred Begins* of 'the District round Polruan' spread over two pages; *Murder at the Munition Works* of the Anchor Works; and *Toper's End* of Excalibur House. *Last Will and Testament* has two preliminary maps of the St Blaizey country. All the Collins/Crime Club books are dated (by the copyright notice). A single short novel was published by Hodder & Stoughton in 1937 as a 'New at Ninepence' paperback: *Disgrace to the College*, illustrated by Kenneth Inns and with Everard Blatchington as dectective. The top quarter of the front cover is yellow and contains the lettering: the rest has a blue illustration of Samuel Barrett and Dr Preedy with the caption, 'I'm going to marry her'. This recurs in black and white as the second of two double-page illustrations preceding the title-page: the first shows the discovery of Percy Symonds' dead body. The title-page has the head of Samuel Barrett facing in the opposite direction from that shown in the full drawing. The book has a black spine with yellow lettering and is dated on the copyright page.

Nineteen subsidiary items were published between 1943 and 1948, all with stories reprinted from the main collections. Two more have original material: *Death of a Bride*, a non-series story published separately by Vallancey in 1945, and *Birthday Gifts*, a collection of four Wilson stories of which the title story is new (Crimetec 1946). Both books have 64 pages and have title and authors on the front covers only, black on a red binding for the former and red on grey for the latter. Each is dated opposite the title-page.

Superintendent Wilson's Holiday has eight Wilson stories; *A Lesson in Crime* has eight with Wilson, one with Mrs Warrender and two non-series items; *Mrs. Warrender's Profession* has five Warrender stories, including 'The Mother of the Detective' from *A Lesson in Crime*; and *Wilson and Some Others* has seven Wilson stories and six non-series.

The Brooklyn Murders has a wrapper by Percy Graves, showing a man at his desk with a revolver in his right hand, prevented from threatening or shooting the woman standing before him by a hand grasping his arm from behind. Elliott's black wrapper for *Burglars in*

Bucks shows the outline of Headingham Manor at night, its windows gleaming silver in the darkness. *A Lesson in Crime* has the plain series wrapper with the black gunman shown repeatedly on a green background. *The Brothers Sackville* is distinguished by a meticulous drawing, brown on cream, of the head of a man lying asleep, or, more probably, dead in a chair. *Mrs. Warrender's Profession* shows a dark figure making for an isolated house lit by a single window on a rainy night. Stead's design for *Murder at the Munition Works* forms the title from the smoke of three factory chimneys. The plain green wrapper of *Toper's End* inaccurately suggests a plurality of topers. The red wrapper of *Birthday Gifts* has Wilson trying to save Percy Seaton's life, while Martha Milliken looks anxiously from below.

Wilson novel by G. D. H. Cole

The Brooklyn Murders Collins 1923, Seltzer 1924

Novels by G. D. H. and M. Cole

(with Wilson, except where stated; others as indicated)

The Death of a Millionaire Collins 1925, Macmillan 1925

The Blatchington Tangle Collins 1926, Macmillan 1926 (Blatchington)

The Murder at Crome House Collins 1927, Macmillan 1927 (non-series)

The Man from the River Collins June 1928, Macmillan 1928

Poison in the Garden Suburb Collins 1929

a.k.a. *Poison in a Garden Suburb* Payson & Clarke 1929

Burglars in Bucks Crime Club June 1930 (Blatchington)

a.k.a. *The Berkshire Mystery* Brewer 1930

Corpse in Canonicals Crime Club November 1930

a.k.a. *Corpse in the Constable's Garden* Morrow 1931, Collins 1933

The Great Southern Mystery Crime Club March 1931

a.k.a. *The Walking Corpse*   Morrow 1931

Dead Man's Watch   Crime Club September 1931, Doubleday 1932 (non-series)

Death of a Star   Crime Club 1932, Doubleday 1933 (Blatchington only)

The Affair at Aliquid   Crime Club September 1933 (non-series)

End of an Ancient Mariner   Crime Club December 1933, Doubleday 1934

Death in the Quarry   Crime Club May 1934, Doubleday 1934 (Blatchington)

Big Business Murder   Crime Club January 1935, Doubleday 1935

Dr. Tancred Begins   Crime Club May 1935, Doubleday 1935 (Tancred)

Scandal at School   Crime Club December 1935 (Blatchington only)

a.k.a. *The Sleeping Death*   Doubleday 1936

Last Will and Testament   Crime Club July 1936, Doubleday 1936 (Tancred)

The Brothers Sackville   Crime Club December 1936, Macmillan 1937 (Fairford)

Disgrace to the College   Hodder & Stoughton June 1937 (Blatchington only)

The Missing Aunt   Crime Club December 1937, Macmillan 1938

Off with her Head!   Crime Club December 1938, Macmillan 1939 (Fairford)

Double Blackmail   Crime Club July 1939, Macmillan 1939

Greek Tragedy   Crime Club November 1939, Macmillan 1940

Murder at the Munition Works   Crime Club August 1940, Macmillan 1940

Counterpoint Murder   Crime Club December 1940, Macmillan 1941

Knife in the Dark   Crime Club 1941, Macmillan 1942 (Warrender)

Toper's End   Crime Club 1942, Macmillan 1942

Story collections

Superintendent Wilson's Holiday   Collins November 1928, Payson & Clarke 1929

A Lesson in Crime   Crime Club June 1933

Mrs. Warrender's Profession   Crime Club July 1938, Macmillan 1939

Wilson and Some Others   Crime Club April 1940

Birthday Gifts Polybooks 1946

Separately published story

Death of a Bride   Vallancey 1945

Uncollected story

'Too Clever by Half' (*Detection Medley*, Hutchinson n.d. (1939))

Novel with other members of the Detection Club (q.v.)

The Floating Admiral   Hodder n.d. (1931), Doubleday 1932

Between 1943 and 1948 nineteen other Cole items were published, single stories, paired stories and collections of three, all reprinted from the major collections.   *BP*

J. J. Connington (1880–1947)

J. J. Connington was the pseudonym of an eminent chemist whose detective novels attain a high degree of technical ingenuity. They show us a time when the leisured classes were anchored in complacent self-esteem, but the codes of conduct were exacting, and even within the charmed circle many hung on precariously. Sir Clinton Driffield is their principal detective, a well-bred tough with innate authority, the status of Chief Constable, and a habit of mind at once forthright and uncompromising: in his dealings with others he is commonly brisk and frequently brusque. In all but four of his cases he is accompanied by his friend Wendover, the squire of Talgarth Grange in Sir Clinton's county, who exemplifies the belief that position entails some responsibility for others less fortunate. Wendover is absent from *Tragedy at Ravensthorpe, The Case with Nine Solutions, Nemesis at Raynham Parva*, and *For Murder Will Speak*. Connington's other detectives are Superintendent Ross, a patient, practical policeman, and Mark Brand, who runs a radio counselling service, broadcasting advice to those who seek his help. They have a mere two cases apiece, as opposed to Sir Clinton's seventeen.

Connington began with two non-series novels, trial runs for the more substantial series that began with Driffield's first case in 1927. He published one more novel without a series detective, the thriller *Tom Tiddler's Island*, set on the Scottish island of Ruffa. The first of his three publishers was Ernest Benn, who published four of his novels in the space of two years. *Death at Swaythling Court* and *The Dangerfield Talisman* are red books, each with black spine lettering and a black border on the front cover. *Murder in the Maze* is a darker red, with black lettering on the spine, which also has a double rule at the head and foot, in which the outer lines are the heavier. The front cover has title and author in black near the top and a double border, graded like the rules on the spine. The contents page gives a series of chapter headings which are not used in the book. *Tragedy at Ravensthorpe* has the black binding with orange lettering and decorations that became standard for

Benn books over the next few years. Besides its printed lettering, the spine has two rules at top and bottom, fringed on the inside, like icicles or the teeth of a comb. The front cover has a border with a similar tasselled effect, with the title printed in the centre and two pistols pointing at each other in the opposing top corners.

The six Gollancz books that followed are all black with orange lettering on their spines. In *Mystery at Lynden Sands* the contents page faces the title-page, and what is usually the copyright page has a map of the approaches to Neptune's Seat. *Nemesis at Raynham Parva* makes acknowledgement to Victor Gollancz for the basic idea of the narrative, and includes a plan of the smoke-room at Fern Lodge. *The Two Tickets Puzzle* has a frontispiece plan of Horston Station.

From *The Sweepstake Murders* in 1931, Connington was published by Hodder & Stoughton, whose books are all blue with black lettering, except for *The Counsellor*, which is dark red and gilt, and *Commonsense Is All You Need*, which is maroon and white.

From *The Sweepstake Murders* to *For Murder Will Speak* the front covers have the title in black; and *The Sweepstake Murders* also has Connington's initials in decorative script. The three books from *The Ha-ha Case* are taller than the rest of the sequence. From *In Whose Dim Shadow* to *For Murder Will Speak* the books have blue endpapers. *The Counsellor, The Four Defences*, and *The Twenty-one Clues* all have their lettering enclosed within a double border towards the top of the spine, gilt for *The Counsellor*, black for the others. *The Ha-ha Case, In Whose Dim Shadow, A Minor Operation*, and *No Past Is Dead* have advertisements at the back. *Commonsense Is All You Need* has the title in white on the front cover.

Tom Tiddler's Island has exquisite front endpapers of the Isle of Ruffa and a fine plan of the subterranean labyrinth at Wester Voe. *The Ha-ha Case, In Whose Dim Shadow*, and *The Counsellor* have frontispieces, of the scene of the crime, of Hernshaw Park, and of Mark Brand at his microphone respectively: that for *The Ha-ha Case* is tipped in and photographic. *Commonsense Is All You Need* has three diagrams by

Professor Dundas, showing his version of the murder method, and Sir Clinton's meticulous sketch-map of the terrain, remarkable for its botanical detail.

The wrapper for *Death at Swaythling Court* has a bright-red panel on which the Lethal Ray Generator shows black, framed by a butterfly and two significant weapons. The spine has a non-slip tyre surmounted by a mudguard. *The Dangerfield Talisman* has an elaborate design with a yellow and white chessboard and selected chessmen. E. McKnight Kauffer designed wrappers in an abstract style for *Mystery at Lynden Sands* and *The Case with Nine Solutions*, so sparing them the lurking yellow plague that was just about to engulf Gollancz fiction and make artists expendable. *In Whose Dim Shadow* has a splendid aerial view of Hernshaw Park. *No Past is Dead* and *Commonsense Is All You Need* have wrappers by Nicolson: the former with a burning city and a skeletal hand reaching towards a clock on which the usual numbers are replaced by specific years; and the latter with a clear view of Friar's Pardon and the 'extension built on to its western end', spoiling the symmetry with its 'square, squat tower surmounted by a dome'.

Connington's books from all three of his publishers are dated, without exception. His American publishers were Little, Brown, who brought out all but the last of his novels.

Three uncollected stories are known, of which 'Beyond Insulin' features Driffield and Wendover.

Novels

(with Driffield and Wendover, except as stated)

Death at Swaythling Court Benn Mar. 1926, Little, Brown 1926 (non-series)

The Dangerfield Talisman Benn Sept. 1926, Little 1927 (non-series)

Murder in the Maze Benn Mar. 1927, Little 1927

Tragedy at Ravensthorpe Benn Sept. 1927, Little 1928 (Driffield only)

Mystery at Lynden Sands Gollancz Apr. 1928, Little 1928

The Case with Nine Solutions Gollancz Sept. 1928, Little 1929 (Driffield only)

Nemesis at Raynham Parva Gollancz Apr. 1929 (Driffield only)

a.k.a. *Grim Venegeance* Little 1929

The Eye in the Museum Gollancz Oct. 1929, Little 1930 (Ross)

The Two Tickets Puzzle Gollancz 1930 (Ross)

a.k.a. *The Two Ticket Puzzle* Little 1930

The Boathouse Riddle Gollancz Apr. 1931, Little 1931

The Sweepstake Murders Hodder & Stoughton Nov. 1931, Little 1932

The Castleford Conundrum Hodder 1932, Little 1932

Tom Tiddler's Island Hodder 1933 (non-series)

a.k.a. *Gold Brick Island* Little 1933

The Ha-ha Case Hodder 1934

a.k.a. *The Brandon Case* Little 1934

In Whose Dim Shadow   Hodder 1935
a.k.a. *The Tau Cross Mystery*   Little 1935
A Minor Operation   Hodder 1937, Little 1937
Truth Comes Limping   Hodder Feb. 1938, Little 1938
For Murder Will Speak   Hodder Oct. 1938 (Driffield only)
a.k.a. *Murder Will Speak*   Little 1938
The Counsellor   Hodder 1939, Little 1939 (Brand)
The Four Defences   Hodder 1940, Little 1940 (Brand)
The Twenty-one Clues   Hodder 1941, Little 1941
No Past Is Dead   Hodder 1942, Little 1942
Jack-in-the-Box   Hodder 1944, Little 1944
Commonsense Is All You Need   Hodder 1947

Uncollected stories

'After Death the Doctor' (*The First Class Omnibus*, Hodder 1934)
'Beyond Insulin' (*Fifty Masterpieces of Mystery*, Odhams 1935)
'The Thinking Machine' (*My Best Mystery Story*, Faber 1939)   *BP*

Patricia D. Cornwell
a.k.a. Patricia Daniels Cornwell

In 1990 *Postmortem* propelled Patricia Daniels Cornwell to the forefront of contemporary crime writing by winning four major awards. Since then the author's detective, Dr Kay Scarpetta, has had three further cases. A divorced, middle-class Italian from Miami, she is Chief Medical Examiner for Virginia, a forensic pathologist whose work always makes fascinating reading, whether she is investigating paper ashes, feathers, residue with DNA, fibres or bones. Her detective activities are assisted by Richmond Police Lieutenant Pete Marino, a large, formidable, untidy man, and by FBI Special Agent Benton Wesley, who is handsome and dapper.

Scribner have published all the American first editions, all quarterbound with black spines and grey boards, except for *Postmortem*, which has orange boards. *Postmortem* has gilt spine lettering; *Body of Evidence* has author and title silver and publisher red; and the others have all-red

lettering. All but the first title have red endpapers. *Cruel and Unusual* has the author's name blind-stamped on the grey front cover.

In Britain, Macdonald issued *Postmortem* in black cloth with gilt spine lettering. The later titles were published by Little, Brown, all with spines lettered silver. *Cruel and Unusual* has dark-blue cloth, the other two black.

The author used her full name for her first book but abridged 'Daniels' to 'D.' for her later work. *All That Remains* was first published in Britain.

The US wrapper for *Postmortem* has a woman's left hand bound with cord and the UK equivalent shows Kay Scarpetta looking on as the dead, bound body of Lori Petersen is photographed. Stanislaw Fernandes illustrated the wrapper (and title-page) of *Body of Evidence* (US) with barbed wire twisted into a heart

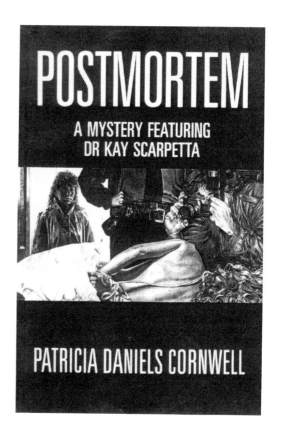

shape, spotted with blood. He also designed *All That Remains* (US), which has a jack of hearts with blood dripping from one heart, towards the bottom of the wrapper. *Cruel and Unusual* shows a white feather in drops of blood. The author is known to prefer her British wrappers, photographed by Adrian Mott: a mysterious gloved hand opening a door for *Body of Evidence*, a leg among fallen leaves for *All That Remains* and a hand lying among feathers for *Cruel and Unusual*.

Scarpetta novels

Postmortem   Scribner 1990, Macdonald 1990
Body of Evidence   Scribner 1991, Little, Brown 1991
All That Remains   Little, Brown 1992, Scribner 1992
Cruel and Unusual   Scribner 1993, Little, Brown 1993   JC

Edmund Crispin (1921–1978)

Edmund Crispin was the pseudonym of Robert Bruce Montgomery who, as Bruce Montgomery, was a composer, particularly of film music. He wrote nine novels and forty-two stories, collected in two volumes. There is also one uncollected story. Crispin's writing exhibits a skill for combining ingenious plotting with a stylish wit. Dialogue flows naturally and often hilariously to provide some of the most memorable light comedy in the field of detective fiction.

Crispin created Gervase Fen, who appears in all the novels and thirty-one of the stories. He is an Oxford Professor of English by profession, an investigator of mysteries by inclination. His articulate speech and frequent use of literary allusions raise him above the level of the average sleuth. Detective-Inspector Humbleby of Scotland Yard assists Fen in his investigations in two of the novels and many of the stories. In two stories he is on his own. The frail, aged don, Wilkes, of Fen's college, St Christopher's, features with comic effect in three novels, although his presence perpetually irritates Fen.

The books were all first published in London by Gollancz, and they are all dated. The first book was issued in green cloth, with gilt lettering on the spine. This is most unusual, as nearly all Gollancz's books were published in blue cloth at this time. The next five books, in fact, have blue cloth, and are lettered gilt on the spine. These early titles were war economy issues. Consequently, the size of the print and the thinness of the books belie the treat in store for lovers of detective fiction. The remaining five books were issued in red cloth, *Frequent Hearses* and *The Long Divorce* with black lettering on the spine, the others with their spines lettered gilt. All the books have yellow dust-wrappers with red or black or magenta lettering. *Swan Song* and *The Case of the Gilded Fly* are two of several books that have American variant titles.

The most difficult first edition to obtain is *Beware of the Trains*.

THE CASE OF THE GILDED FLY

a

detective story

by

A NEW WRITER

who calls himself

EDMUND CRISPIN

Fen novels

The Case of the Gilded Fly   Gollancz 1944
a.k.a. *Obsequies at Oxford*   Lippincott 1945
Holy Disorders   Gollancz 1945, Lippincott 1946
The Moving Toyshop   Gollancz 1946, Lippincott 1946
Swan Song   Gollancz 1947, Walker 1980
a.k.a. *Dead and Dumb*   Lippincott 1947
Loves Lies Bleeding   Gollancz 1948, Lippincott 1948
Buried for Pleasure   Gollancz 1948, Lippincott 1949
Frequent Hearses   Gollancz 1950
a.k.a. *Sudden Vengeance*   Dodd, Mead 1950
The Long Divorce   Gollancz 1951, Dodd 1951
a.k.a. *A Noose for Her*   Spivak 1952
The Glimpses of the Moon   Gollancz 1977, Walker 1978

Story collections

Beware of the Trains   Gollancz 1953, Walker 1962 (16 stories, 2 without Fen)
Fen Country   Gollancz 1979, Walker 1980 (26 stories, 9 without Fen)

Uncollected story

'St. Bartholomew's Day' (*EQMM*, Feb. 1975) (not Fen)   *JC*

Freeman Wills Crofts (1879–1957)

Freeman Wills Crofts wrote thirty-three novels, fifty-two stories, some radio plays, and a junior detective novel, *Young Robin Brand, Detective*. The stories have been collected in three volumes, and there are also two stories published as separate items. Three more stories remain uncollected. At least one juvenile story is known, featuring Robin Brand. Crofts also contributed to four collaborative books written by Detection Club members: the novels *The Floating Admiral*, *Double Death* and *The Scoop*, and the story collection *Six Against the Yard*. He was one of the first writers to use police procedure methodically. His novels are the essence of fair play,

Exhibit 11

since he gives the reader all the necessary clues. They evoke the gentler, slower way of life in England that preceded the Second World War. Several books are 'inverted', showing how a murderer is trapped by his crime.

Crofts created one of the greatest police detectives, Inspector Joseph French, whose forte was cracking the apparently cast-iron alibis of his suspects. There are thirty French novels and fifty-three stories, of which three are uncollected.

The books, with two exceptions, were first published in London either by Collins or by Hodder & Stoughton, and are all clearly dated. The two exceptions are *Silence for the Murderer* and *Dark Journey* (*French Strikes Oil* in the UK), of which the American editions pre-date the British by one year. *Anything to Declare?* and the two collections of stories, *Murderers Make Mistakes* and *Many a Slip*, were not published in the USA. Many books have variant

American titles, among them *The Box Office Murders* and *The End of Andrew Harrison*.

Crofts' first two books were published by Collins in red cloth. *The Cask* has black lettering on the spine and has title and author blind-stamped on the front cover. *The Ponson Case* has black lettering on the spine and on the front cover, which also has a black border. The next five titles all have dark-blue cloth, with red lettering on the spine and front cover. Of these, the first four have a double red border, and *Inspector French and the Starvel Tragedy* has a single red border, on the front cover in each case. There are corresponding rules at the top and base of each spine. If any of these titles has pale-blue cloth with black lettering it must be a later issue. *The Sea Mystery* has black cloth and is lettered gilt on the spine. *The Box Office Murders* is black, with red lettering on the spine and front cover, which also has a red border. The spine has a red line at the head and foot.

From *Sir John Magill's Last Journey* the books from Collins were Crime Club titles, with orange/red cloth and black lettering on the spine and front cover. *Sir John Magill's Last Journey* and *Mystery in the Channel* have a black border on the front cover. *The Loss of the Jane Vosper* and *Man Overboard* have blank front covers. Copies with black cloth and red lettering are later issues. All the Collins titles have advertisements at the back except *Sir John Magill's Last Journey*.

With the exception of *Fatal Venture*, which is bound in red cloth, with the spine lettered gilt, the Hodder & Stoughton titles all have blue cloth lettered in black, until the publication of *Enemy Unseen* in 1945. All the Hodder books before *Fatal Venture* have the title in black on the front cover. *Found Floating* and *Mystery in Southampton Water* are slightly taller than the rest of the Crofts collection. *Enemy Unseen*, *Death of a Train*, and *Murderers Make Mistakes* all have maroon cloth, with the spine lettered in white, and the title in white on the front cover. *Silence for the Murderer* has green cloth, with black spine lettering, and the title in black on the cover. The last four books have a smoking revolver under the author's name, and their front covers are blank. *French Strikes Oil* and *Many A Slip* have maroon cloth, and *The Mystery of the Sleeping Car Express* has green cloth. All three have black lettering. *Anything to Declare?* is dark blue and lettered gilt. Three variant bindings are known: gold for *Golden Ashes*, blue for *Fatal Venture* and red for *Murderers Make Mistakes*. The last has white lettering, the others black.

'The Hunt Ball' is a story published originally in *Detective Stories of Today*, edited by Raymond Postgate for Faber in 1940. It was later published separately as *The Hunt Ball Murder* in the Polybooks series, by Todd in 1943, and is included in *Country House Murders*, O'Mara 1989. A different story with the original title is collected in *Murderers Make Mistakes*. 'The Match' from John Rhode's anthology, *Detection Medley* (Hutchinson 1939), was also published separately, by Vallancey Press in 1944, with a new title, *Mr. Sefton, Murderer*. This slim book, which is bound in red and dated, has a frontispiece by Frank R. Grey, showing the moment after Mr. Sefton has become a murderer. 'The Case of the Old Gun', in *Murderers Make Mistakes*, is a variation on this story, with a new dénouement.

Death on the Way has endpapers showing that section of the Lydmouth to Bournemouth line running along the coast between Redchurch and Whitness; and the front endpaper of *Found Floating* follows the course of the TSS *Patricia* on its Olympic cruise from Glasgow to Athens. Several of the wrappers of Crofts' novels, with their portrayals of early boats and trains, are a source of nostalgic pleasure: those for *Found Floating*, *Death of a Train*, and *Many a Slip*, for example.

Lendon's design for the wrapper of *The Cask* shows a hand protruding from the broken side of a cask as gold sovereigns and sawdust cascade to the floor. M. H.'s grey, white and yellow design for *The Ponson Case* depicts two men carrying the body of a third. C. Morse designed two early wrappers. *Inspector French's Greatest Case* shows a puzzled Inspector French looking down on the body of Mr Gething, lying by an open safe in the office of Duke and Peabody; and *Inspector French and the Cheyne Mystery* has a thoughtful French sitting by a telephone in the foreground, while behind him Joan Merrill, in purple, discovers the injured Maxwell Cheyne lying near the Hopefield Avenue palings. For *The Sea Mystery*, H. Dixon has French looking down on a large crate, washed on a beach with a body sprawling out from it. *The Box Office Murders* shows the bound Molly Moran staring in horror at Mr Style. The scene is lit by a spotlight and overseen by French's head. *Sir John Magill's Last Journey* is dominated by a train painted with a white skull on the front of the engine, and, again, French's head appears over the scene. For *Sudden Death* a mysterious woman in red looks over her shoulder as she tries the handle of a door: in the foreground, Inspector French calmly smokes his pipe. E. P. K.'s brown wrapper for *The Hog's Back Mystery* disposes several figures with spades and a torch around a newly unearthed body. The aeroplane Hengist features dramatically on *The 12.30 from Croydon*, with a smaller, darker view of it at the top of the spine. *Mystery on Southampton Water* has a map of this region, with two figures carrying a body towards a boat on the Solent. *Crime at Guildford* has a man sprawling in a spotlight under an ornate clock showing eight minutes past ten. *The Loss of the 'Jane Vosper'* shows the ship sinking within a circular, nautical framework. C. Leslie's design for *Man Overboard!* has a man struggling in the sea as a liner moves away towards the horizon. The brown wrapper for *The End of Andrew Harrison* has a painting of 'The Thames at Henley', and D. Burroughes' design for *Antidote to Venom* has a viper, upreared against a green background. Morton Sale's design for *Fatal Venture* depicts a stormy scene with a liner looming in the background, while one plane flies overhead and a second rests on the waves. In the lower foreground a group of civilians recoils from officials. *Golden Ashes* shows the paintings at Forde Manor being damaged by the fire. *James Tarrant, Adventurer* shows a man fishing in silhouette against an orange background. *Fear Comes to Chalfont* has a grey stone owl against a green background, and *The Affair of Little Wokeham* shows a man walking along a street (Little Wokeham represents Blackheath, near Guildford, the Surrey village where the author lived for many years).

Stead's design for *Enemy Unseen* features a hand writing the title in chalk on a black background.

Nicolson designed two wrappers for Crofts. The first, for *Death of a Train*, has the driver, Garth, standing by the side of his engine, and a gun with a silencer illustrates the basically green wrapper for *Silence for the Murderer*. A giant accusing finger points at murderer and victim in a striking design by Bip Pares for *Murderers Make Mistakes*. Pauline Selmer is seen holding back an orange curtain from a window on *French Strikes Oil*. *The Mystery of the Sleeping Car Express* has a red fingerprint on black with the designer's initials M. M. Jarvis' design for *Anything to Declare?* shows watches falling out of a night sky towards the boat *Komforta*. The three scarcest first editions seem to be *The Cask*, *The Ponson Case*, and *The Losing Game*.

Novels

The Cask Collins 1920, Seltzer 1924
The Ponson Case Collins 1921, Boni 1927
The Pit-Prop Syndicate Collins 1922, Seltzer 1925
The Groote Park Murder Collins 1923, Seltzer 1925

French novels

Inspector French's Greatest Case Collins 1924, Seltzer 1925
Inspector French and the Cheyne Mystery Collins 1926
a.k.a. *The Cheyne Mystery* Boni 1926
Inspector French and the Starvel Tragedy Collins 1927
a.k.a. *The Starvel Hollow Tragedy* Harper 1927
The Sea Mystery Collins 1928, Harper 1928
The Box Office Murders Collins 1929
a.k.a. *The Purple Sickle Murders* Harper 1929
Sir John Magill's Last Journey Collins Crime Club 1930, Harper 1930
Mystery in the Channel Crime Club 1931
a.k.a. *Mystery in the English Channel* Harper 1931
Sudden Death Crime Club 1932, Harper 1932

Death on the Way Crime Club 1932

a.k.a. *Double Death* Harper 1932

The Hog's Back Mystery Hodder & Stoughton 1933

a.k.a. *The Strange Case of Dr. Earle* Dodd, Mead 1933

The 12.30 from Croydon Hodder 1934

a.k.a. *Wilful and Premeditated* Dodd 1934

Mystery on Southampton Water Hodder 1934

a.k.a. *Crime on the Solent* Dodd 1934

Crime at Guildford Crime Club 1935

a.k.a. *The Crime at Nornes* Dodd 1935

The Loss of the 'Jane Vosper' Crime Club 1936, Dodd 1936

Man Overboard! Crime Club 1936, Dodd 1936

a.k.a. *Cold-Blooded Murder* Avon 1947 (abridged)

Found Floating Hodder 1937, Dodd 1937

The End of Andrew Harrison Hodder 1938

a.k.a. *The Futile Alibi* Dodd 1938

Antidote to Venom Hodder 1938, Dodd 1939

Fatal Venture Hodder 1939

a.k.a. *Tragedy in the Hollow* Dodd 1939

Golden Ashes Hodder 1940, Dodd 1940

James Tarrant, Adventurer Hodder 1941

a.k.a. *Circumstantial Evidence* Dodd 1941

The Losing Game Hodder 1941

a.k.a. *A Losing Game* Dodd 1941

Fear Comes to Chalfont Hodder 1942, Dodd 1942

The Affair at Little Wokeham Hodder 1943

a.k.a. *Double Tragedy* Dodd 1943

Enemy Unseen Hodder 1945, Dodd 1945

Death of a Train Hodder 1946, Dodd 1947

Silence for the Murderer Dodd 1948, Hodder 1949

Dark Journey Dodd 1951

a.k.a. *French Strikes Oil* Hodder 1952

Anything to Declare? Hodder 1957

French juvenile novel

Young Robin Brand, Detective ULP 1947, Dodd 1948

Novels with other members of the Detection Club (q.v.)

The Floating Admiral Hodder n.d. (1931), Doubleday 1932

Double Death Gollancz 1939

The Scoop Gollancz 1983 (with *Behind the Screen*)

Stories and story collections

The Hunt Ball Murder Todd 1943 (French)

Mr. Sefton, Murderer Vallancey Press 1944 (French)

Murderers Make Mistakes Hodder 1947 (23 French stories)

Many a Slip Hodder 1955 (21 stories, 20 with French)

The Mystery of the Sleeping Car Express Hodder 1956 (9 stories, 5 with French)

Uncollected French stories

'Fingerprints' (*ES*, 20 Mar. 1952)

'The Faulty Stroke' (*ES*, 30 Dec. 1952)

'The Target' (*ES*, 14 Oct. 1953)

Robin Brand story

'Danger in Shroude Valley' (*The Golden Book of the Year*, Blandford n.d. (c. 1950)) *JC*

Amanda Cross (b. 1926)

Amanda Cross is the pseudonym of Carolyn Heilbrun, a distinguished literary historian and biographer. Her detective, Kate Fansler, is, like herself, Professor of English at an American university, and the mysteries that engage her are pre-eminently literary and intellectual: the chapter headings of *The James Joyce Murder* are taken from *Dubliners*, and *Poetic Justice* is festooned with quotations from Auden. The author herself has described her books as conversation pieces, and they are notable for studied wit, the avoidance of violence, and an increasingly feminist bias. Their appeal is to the educated mind and mature sympathies, to instincts of civilization and responsibility.

In Britain Amanda Cross was published by Gollancz, until her move to Virago in 1987. The seven Gollancz books are red with gilt spine lettering and yellow wrappers. *The Theban Mysteries* is a darker shade of red than the others. *The Question of Max* has a decorated title-page. *Death in a Tenured Position* became *Death in the Faculty* in Britain. *No Word from Winifred* came from Virago in 1987, with a black binding, gilt spine lettering, and a handsome wrapper by Barbara Kaiser, showing Kate and her niece Leighton. This design is on the front cover of a simultaneous paperback edition. *A Trap for Fools* was published in Britain in paperback only, in the Virago crime series with the publisher's apple motif prominent on the front cover, which also has a woman, perhaps Kate, in profile. *The Players Come Again* is a hardback, black with gilt lettering on the spine. The text reproduces that of the US edition and the wrapper is dark and dismal. All the British editions are dated, the Gollancz titles on the title-page, the Virago on the copyright page.

In America, Amanda Cross was published in turn by Macmillan, Knopf, Dutton and, most recently, Random House. *Poetic Justice* is the first Knopf book, elegantly quarterbound in mustard boards with drab green spine and adjacent cover strips. The spine has gilt lettering and the front cover has the author's initials blind-stamped within a decorative framework. The rear cover has a blind-stamped logo for Borzoi Books. The top edge is mustard and the other edges are roughly trimmed. The title-page is dated and the copyright page states 'First edition'. The white wrapper has a quill pen entangled in leaves, with a drop of blood dripping from it. *No Word from Winifred* is the third of four titles from Dutton, in blue boards with white spine and cover strips and gilt lettering on the spine. Winifred Ashby's school composition book appears on the title-page. The copyright page has 'First edition' and a printer's key starting at 1. *The Players Come Again* was published by Random House in grey-blue boards with off-white spine and cover strips and silver-blue lettering and decoration on the spine. The author's initials appear within a silver-blue framework on

IN THE LAST ANALYSIS

A debut in detection by an academic, comparable to Michael Innes' with *Death at the P's Lodging*

BY AMANDA CROSS

the front cover. The title-page has a decorative border and the copyright page states 'First edition' and has a printer's key starting at 2, which is standard for this house. The white wrapper has a smudgy brown photograph and nothing to recommend it. The latter pair are dated by the copyright notice only.

Stories featuring Kate Fansler began to appear in 1987.

Fansler novels

In the Last Analysis   Macmillan 1964, Gollancz 1964

The James Joyce Murder   Macmillan 1967, Gollancz 1967

Poetic Justice   Knopf 1970, Gollancz 1970

The Theban Mysteries   Knopf 1971, Gollancz 1972

The Question of Max   Knopf 1976, Gollancz 1976

Death in a Tenured Position   Dutton 1981
a.k.a. *A Death in the Faculty*   Gollancz 1981

Sweet Death, Kind Death Dutton 1984, Gollancz 1984

No Word from Winifred Dutton 1986, Virago 1987

A Trap for Fools Dutton 1989, Virago 1990

The Players Come Again Random House 1990, Virago 1990

Fansler stories

'Tania's No Where' (*EQMM*, Mar. 1987; *Distant Danger*, Wynwood 1988)

'Once Upon a Time' (*EQMM*, Aug. 1987; *Ms. Murder*, Xanadu 1989)

'Arrie and Jasper' (*EQMM*, Dec. 1987; *Murder Most Cozy*, Signet 1993)

'The Disappearance of Great-Aunt Flavia' (*Reader, I Murdered Him*, Women's Press 1989)

'Murder Without a Text' (*A Woman's Eye*, Delacorte 1991, Virago 1991)

'Who Shot Mrs. Byron Boyd?' (*Malice Domestic 2*, Pocket Books 1993)   BP

Elizabeth Daly (1878–1967)

Elizabeth Daly's books were highly regarded by Agatha Christie, who must have recognized a fellow craftsman. Blessedly, there are sixteen of them, all involving rich, high-born families, stirred up and set dancing by doubt and apprehension. Each is utterly absorbing, and the outcome is often astonishing. All sixteen books feature the modest but resolute figure of Henry Gamadge, a practical scholar, with high integrity, considerable erudition, and some wit. He is an expert on rare books and literary manuscripts, and will authenticate your Chaucer holograph, if it doesn't go up in flames first.

Miss Daly hit her stride immediately with *Unexpected Night*, which appeared in 1940 from Farrar & Rinehart, and in Britain from Gollancz in the same year. The latter edition is dated and has the black binding and orange lettering of the 1930s books from this firm. In America, the books continued to be published by Farrar (later becoming Rinehart), but in Britain there was a switch to Eyre & Spottiswoode for the second book and to Hammond, Hammond for all the

others. *Deadly Nightshade* is out of sequence in Britain: the second in the series, its British appearance was delayed until 1948. *Murders in Volume 2* came from Eyre in 1943, a red book with black lettering along the spine, the base of the letters towards the front cover. In both known copies, including that in the BL, the edge of a putative half-title page is visible between the front free endpaper and the title-page. The book is dated.

The long Hammond sequence began in 1945 with *The House Without the Door*. All the books are dated, and from *Any Shape or Form* they also have the printer's code on the reverse of the title-page. Three books have no rear endpaper: *Nothing Can Rescue Me*, *Arrow Pointing Nowhere*, and *The Book of the Dead*. From *The House Without the Door* to *Night Walk* the bindings are all blue-green, some with a heavier texture than others. The spine lettering is black or blue up to *The Book of the Dead* and gilt from *Any Shape or Form* to *Night Walk*. *The Book of the Lion* and *And Dangerous to Know* are green with black spine lettering; *Death and Letters* is blue and gilt; and *The Book of the Crime* is maroon and yellow. Printer's codes and BL datings suggest that *The Wrong Way Down* and *Night Walk* may actually have appeared in January of the years after those given in the books themselves. *The Wrong Way Down* is also known in a variant red binding, with black spine lettering, and with the identical printer's code, and a blue *Deadly Nightshade* is recorded.

Unexpected Night has the cheap yellow wrapper inflicted by Victor Gollancz on all his hapless authors. Ellen Edwards' design for *Murders in Volume 2* shows Lydia Wagoneur, the English governess who vanished on 3 May 1840 with volume 2 of a set of Byron's poems. She is wearing her 'cornflower-blue silk dress', and is flanked by volumes 1 and 3. The wrappers from *The House Without the Door* to *Any Shape or Form* are uniform in format, with one pistol on the spine for the first book, two for the second, and so on. Later volumes revert to a single pistol, with the appropriate number of bullets beneath. Each front panel features the principal woman in the case, with a significant detail from the action: a planchette board for *Nothing Can*

Rescue Me, 'Views on the Hudson' for *Arrow Pointing Nowhere*, the Crenshaw Shakespeare for *The Book of the Dead. Somewhere in the House* and *Night Walk* share this format.

The Wrong Way Down includes a vivid impression of Iris Vance with the 'red hair that she wore to her shoulders'. For *The Book of the Lion*, Sax shows Vera Bradlock lying dead, while 'The Boke of the Leoun' flames above her. *And Dangerous to Know* shows Alice Dunbar transforming her appearance just before she leaves home for the last time. *Death and Letters* includes an excellent representation of Grandmother Coldfield's portrait in the dining-room at the Maples, Cliffside (though the text suggests that Gamadge should not be viewing it with his hat on). Zelig's rather crude wrapper for *The Book of the Crime* shows Gray Austen looking fraught.

No short stories are recorded for Elizabeth Daly, and it seems unlikely that she published any.

Gamadge novels

Unexpected Night Farrar & Rinehart 1940, Gollancz 1940

Deadly Nightshade Farrar 1940, Hammond 1948

Murders in Volume 2 Farrar 1941, Eyre & Spottiswoode 1943

The House Without the Door Farrar 1942, Hammond 1945

Nothing Can Rescue Me Farrar 1943, Hammond 1945

Evidence of Things Seen Farrar 1943, Hammond 1946

Arrow Pointing Nowhere Farrar 1944, Hammond 1946

a.k.a. *Murder Listens In* Bantam 1949

The Book of the Dead Farrar 1944, Hammond 1946

Any Shape or Form Farrar 1945, Hammond 1949

Somewhere in the House Rinehart 1946, Hammond 1949

The Wrong Way Down Rinehart 1946, Hammond 1949

a.k.a. *Shroud for a Lady* Bestseller 1956

Night Walk Rinehart 1947, Hammond 1950

The Book of the Lion Rinehart 1948, Hammond 1951

And Dangerous to Know Rinehart 1949, Hammond 1952

Death and Letters Rinehart 1950, Hammond 1953

The Book of the Crime Rinehart 1951, Hammond 1954   *BP*

Clemence Dane (1888–1965) and Helen Simpson (1897–1940)

Clemence Dane and Helen Simpson were versatile writers, each with several strings to her bow. They were members of the Detection Club and joint authors of three elegant detective novels featuring a debonair actor-manager in the du Maurier mould: Sir John Saumarez, formerly Jonathan Simmonds. He walks on in *Author Unknown* but takes the lead in the other two titles. Besides collaborating with each other, each author contributed to novels written in multiple collaboration: Clemence Dane to *The Floating Admiral* and *The Scoop*, and Helen Simpson to *Ask a Policeman* (with a pastiche of Gladys Mitchell's Mrs Bradley). *'Vantage Striker* is a crime novel written by Helen Simpson alone; and she also published at least two pertinent stories. Despite its inclusion in *Great Short Stories of Mystery, Detection and Horror*, however, Clemence Dane's 'The King Waits' is not criminous.

Enter Sir John was published by Cosmopolitan in 1928 in a yellow binding with black lettering on the spine and front cover. On the spine, title and authors are divided by a single black rule and framed top and bottom by double black rules, of which the outer in each case is thicker and in nine segments. This pattern is repeated on the cover with a double dividing line and twenty segments to the outermost rules. The book is dated on the title-page and illustrated by Sydney Seymour Lucas with a frontispiece, a double-page trial scene and a third drawing, full page, all in black and white. The UK edition was published by Hodder & Stoughton in February 1929 (though the book is undated). Like its two successors, it is blue with black lettering and a single black rule on the spine and the title in black at the top of the front cover. Like *Printer's Devil* only, it has a blind-stamped border on the front cover. *Printer's Devil* and *Re-enter Sir John* are dated on the title-page and the former has advertisements at the rear. *Author Unknown* preceded *Printer's Devil* by three months, so the latter is both the later edition and the variant title. It is a yellow book with black lettering on the spine, title and author separated by a double black rule. The front cover has a central panel of green bounded by black rules, single horizontally and double vertically. Within are title and authors in black. The book is dated on the title-page. Primacy between the UK and US editions of *Re-enter Sir John* is not established.

F. E. Warren's mauve wrapper for *Enter Sir John* (US) shows Gordon Druce and the policeman knocking on Miss Mitcham's front door in the small hours. The UK edition has blue and black lettering against a streaky background like melted coffee ice-cream. *Printer's Devil* has

Morton Sale's wispy water-colour of part of a suspension bridge. *Re-enter Sir John* shows the beaming actor at a film studio, raising his topper with a white-gloved hand.

'Vantage Striker is a green book with gilt lettering on the spine and gilt rules, one at each extremity. The front cover has a blind-stamped border and the rear cover the Heinemann windmill, blind-stamped.

Sir John Saumarez novels in collaboration

Enter Sir John   Cosmopolitan 1928, Hodder & Stoughton n.d. (1929)
Author Unknown   Cosmopolitan March 1930
a.k.a. *Printer's Devil*   Hodder June 1930
Re-Enter Sir John   Hodder 1932, Farrar & Rinehart 1932

Novel by Helen Simpson

'Vantage Striker   Heinemann 1931
a.k.a. *The Prime Minister is Dead*   Doubleday 1931

Stories by Helen Simpson

'Death versus Debt' (*Nine O'Clock Stories* Bell 1934)

'A Posteriori' (*EQMM*, Sept. 1954)

Other collaborations (see the Detection Club)

The Floating Admiral Hodder n.d. (1931), Doubleday 1932

Ask a Policeman Barker n.d. (1933), Morrow 1933

The Scoop and *Behind the Screen* Gollancz 1983

(Clemence Dane contributed to *The Floating Admiral* and *The Scoop*; Helen Simpson contributed to *Ask a Policeman*.) *BP*

Glyn Daniel (1914–1986)
a.k.a. Dilwyn Rees

Glyn Daniel was Disney Professor of Archaeology at Cambridge and became a well-known public figure through his appearances on the television programme 'Animal, Vegetable, Mineral?'. He published two detective novels, *Welcome Death* and *The Cambridge Murders*, the latter under the pseudonym of Dilwyn Rees. He decided shortly before his death that a third was not good enough to publish. *The Cambridge Murders* introduced his amateur detective, the gastronome Sir Richard Cherrington, Vice-President of Fisher College in Cambridge, where murder takes place. It is an excellent example of the academic type of detective novel. Cherrington also features in the second book, which has a Welsh setting, and in a Dilwyn Rees story. There is also a non-series story written in the author's real name.

Both books were published by Gollancz and are dated. *The Cambridge Murders* has blue cloth and *Welcome Death* red. Both have gilt spine lettering and the typical yellow Gollancz wrappers. *The Cambridge Murders* was not published in the USA.

THE CAMBRIDGE MURDERS

---

a

detective story

by

DILWYN REES

Cherrington novel by Dilwyn Rees

The Cambridge Murders Gollancz 1945; Penguin 1965 as by Glyn Daniel

Cherrington novel by Glyn Daniel

Welcome Death Gollancz 1954, Dodd, Mead 1955

Cherrington story by Dilwyn Rees

'Six Feet Under the Ground' (*ES*, 23 Nov. 1953)

Story by Glyn Daniel

'Delayed in Transit' (*ES*, 3 Dec. 1954) *JC*

Lillian de la Torre (1902–1993)

Lillian de la Torre specialises in the reconstruction of historical crimes, factual except for the series of stories featuring Dr Samuel Johnson, all but two of which are collected in four volumes. All her work is remarkable for its combination of zestful narrative with truth or verisimilitude. In particular, the Dr Johnson stories are widely and justly esteemed.

The first book is 'Elizabeth is Missing', the story of the Canning Wonder, which owes much of its manner and method to Carr's *The Murder of Sir Edmund Godfrey*. *The Heir of Douglas* is also an eighteenth-century mystery and *The Truth about Belle Gunness* deals with a nineteenth-century serial killer.

'Elizabeth is Missing' was first published by Knopf in 1945 and by Joseph in 1947, in a dark blue-green binding with silver lettering and decoration on the spine, title and author against a dark blue panel near the top. The front cover has a dark-blue picture of Elizabeth Canning within a silver locket-frame. The top edge is dark blue-green and the bottom edge is roughly trimmed. The book is dated on the elaborate title-page, opposite which is a photographic frontispiece of Elizabeth Canning. Further portraits, caricatures and plans punctuate the narrative; and the illustration of 'Elizabeth Canning at the House of Mother Wells at Enfield Wash' (facing page 138) is the centrepiece of the black and yellow wrapper by E. McKnight Kauffer.

The Heir of Douglas was also published by Knopf and Joseph, by the latter in 1953, in a red-brown binding with gilt lettering and decoration on the spine and a dated copyright page. The top edge is red-brown and the title-page is again unusually elaborate. The illustrations include six portraits and a letter. The wrapper shows the portrait of Archibald Douglas attributed to George Willison. *The Truth about Belle Gunness* was published in Britain as a paperback original, by Muller in 1960. The true first was issued by Fawcett in 1955. The Muller edition is dated by the copyright notice only and has a vivid cover drawing by Barye Phillips of Belle, 'the mail-order Circe, the lush, magnetic Amazon', looking appropriately seductive, framed by a window. The rear cover has an extract from one of her letters and a pen and inkpot.

The Knopf edition of *Dr. Sam: Johnson Detector* is a brown book with gilt lettering and decoration on the spine and a gilt vignette of Johnson and Boswell on the front cover. The Borzoi Books logo is blind-stamped on the rear cover. The top edge is orange and the fore-edge roughly trimmed. The full-page frontispiece of Johnson and Boswell is a larger, coloured version of the cover illustration. The elaborate title-page is dated and the copyright page states 'First edition'. Each story is headed by a black-and-white illustration, unattributed, like the frontispiece. The UK first edition from Joseph has a red-brown binding with silver lettering on the spine and dated copyright page.

The second collection appeared only in America at the time of publication. It is a grey-green book with black lettering on the spine. The date appears opposite the title-page and the copyright page states 'First edition'. The British edition is a paperback in black wrappers, delayed until 1989 and with minuscule print. The cover shows Johnson, with Boswell looking over his shoulder, staring down at the supine corpse of a man with a dagger in his chest.

The later Johnson collections were published by International Polygonics in the 1980s as paperback originals. Both are dated on the copyright page, with printer's keys running from 1. They have pictorial covers by Stephen Sweny, *The Return of Dr. Sam: Johnson, Detector* showing Johnson being attacked from behind by a lean, hatchet-faced man who has him by the neck, and *The Exploits of Dr. Sam: Johnson, Detector* showing him reading by candlelight, with a hand twitching aside a curtain behind him. The wrappers for the earlier hardbacks also show the Great Cham in one form or another. The Knopf edition of the first collection has an ornate orange wrapper with a vignette of Johnson and Boswell, reduced from the frontispiece; and the Joseph edition has a yellow wrapper with a black-and-white drawing of the pair within a white disc in the lower right corner. *The Detections* also has a yellow wrapper with a black-and-white bust portrait of Johnson by Edward Gorey.

A limited edition of 'The Stolen Christmas Box' appeared at Christmas 1945, published by *EQMM*, in the January 1946 issue of which, on sale in November, it had first appeared. The edition was limited to two hundred copies and the limitation statement at the end claims that the pamphlet was 'privately printed for the author', despite the publisher's being given as *EQMM* on the title-page. The story appears in the first collection.

Two further Johnson stories and a Sherlock Holmes pastiche have appeared since the last collection was published. The author's other shorter pieces are factual reconstructions and she also edited a book of these, by various authors: *Villainy Detected* (Appleton 1947).

A pastiche Dr Johnson story appeared in *EQMM* in Feb. 1983: 'Abduction from the Seraglio' by the author's brother, Theodore de la Torre Bueno.

Dr. Sam: Johnson collections

Dr. Sam: Johnson, Detector   Knopf 1946, Joseph 1948 (9 stories)

The Detections of Dr. Sam: Johnson   Doubleday 1960, Xanadu 1989 (8 stories)
The Return of Dr. Sam: Johnson, Detector International Polygonics 1985 (7 stories)
The Exploits of Dr. Sam: Johnson, Detector International Polygonics 1987 (7 stories)

Uncollected stories

'The Adventure of the Persistent Marksman' (*The New Adventures of Sherlock Holmes*, Carroll & Graf 1987)
'The Earl's Nightingale' (*EQMM*, May 1989)
'The Highwayman's Hostage' (*EQMM*, Nov. 1990)

Other narratives

'*Elizabeth is Missing*'   Knopf 1945, Joseph 1947
The Heir of Douglas   Knopf 1952, Joseph 1953
The Truth about Belle Gunness   Gold Medal 1955, Muller 1960   *BP*

The Detection Club

The Detection Club was founded in 1928 by Anthony Berkeley Cox, who became its first honorary secretary. The first meetings were held in Kingly Street, London.

There were twenty-six founder members: H. C. Bailey, E. C. Bentley, Anthony Berkeley, G. K. Chesterton, Agatha Christie, G. D. H. and M. Cole, J. J. Connington, Freeman Wills Crofts, Clemence Dane, Robert Eustace, R. Austin Freeman, Lord Gorell, Edgar Jepson, Ianthe Jerrold, Milward Kennedy, Ronald A. Knox, Mrs Marie Belloc Lowndes, A. E. W. Mason, A. A. Milne, Arthur Morrison, Baroness Orczy, John Rhode, Dorothy L. Sayers, Henry Wade, Victor L. Whitechurch. The first President was G. K. Chesterton.

The club existed so that members could meet and enjoy the society of other crime writers. There were occasional guest speakers, usually experts on aspects of criminology. The club had its own library and a specially commissioned bookplate, designed by Ardizzone. To raise funds for permanent premises, members collaborated on works of fiction, and the proceeds enabled the club to establish itself at 31 Gerrard Street. In more recent years, meetings have been held at the Garrick Club. The current president is H. R. F. Keating.

Members of the Detection Club were responsible jointly for three full-length novels, three shorter novels, and four story anthologies. *The Anatomy of Murder* is a non-fiction collection concerned with true crime.

Two short novels appeared as serials in *The Listener – Behind The Screen* in 1930, and *The Scoop* in 1931. They were published together in book form by Gollancz in 1983. The book is dated, and has the red cloth, gilt spine lettering, and yellow dust-wrapper typical of this publisher. *Behind the Screen* was written by Hugh Walpole, Agatha Christie, Dorothy L. Sayers, Anthony Berkeley, E. C. Bentley, and Ronald A. Knox. The authors of *The Scoop* were Dorothy L. Sayers, Agatha Christie, Clemence Dane, E. C. Bentley, Anthony Berkeley, and Freeman Wills Crofts.

A full-scale novel, *The Floating Admiral*, appeared in 1931, with contributions from G. K. Chesterton, Dorothy L. Sayers, V. L. Whitechurch, G. D. H. and M. Cole, Henry Wade, Agatha Christie, John Rhode, Milward Kennedy, Ronald A. Knox, Freeman Wills Crofts, Edgar Jepson, Clemence Dane, and Anthony Berkeley. The book was published by Hodder & Stoughton, in blue cloth, and with black lettering on the spine and front cover. Both on the spine and the front cover, the book is attributed to 'certain members of the Detection Club', and a list of the individual contributors appears in the lower part of the cover, to the right. The book is undated, and it contains a frontispiece map of the villages of Lingham and Whynmouth. Hastain's elegant wrapper sets two masked flunkeys in pink coats at a doorway and invites readers to step in and solve the mystery. All contributors are named on both spine and front panel.

Ask a Policeman, a further novel, was published in 1933 by Arthur Barker. The contributors were Anthony Berkeley, Milward Kennedy, Gladys Mitchell, John Rhode, Dorothy L. Sayers, and Helen Simpson. John Rhode launched the story and Milward Kennedy completed it. In between, four detectives worked on

the case: Mrs Bradley, Sir John Saumarez, Lord Peter Wimsey, and Roger Sheringham, but the authors wrote about each others' characters (Simpson/Bradley, Mitchell/Saumarez, Berkeley/ Wimsey, and Sayers/Sheringham). The book is undated and has blue cloth, with green lettering on the spine and front cover. On the spine, a dagger dripping blood appears below the title. Underneath this are a list of all the authors and the publisher's name. The front cover has just the title on it. A plan of Hursley Lodge and its grounds appears as frontispiece. The wrapper shows a pattern of many revolvers evenly distributed over an orange and cream background. Two copies are known with red lettering and decoration and a 3/6d. dust-wrapper, indicating that this was a later issue.

The third novel, *Double Death*, appeared first as a six-part serial in the *Sunday Chronicle*, beginning in May 1937. Its original title was *Night of Secrets*. The book was published by Gollancz in black cloth, with the contributors listed in red on the spine. It is dated and has the usual yellow dust-wrapper. The authors involved were Dorothy L. Sayers, Freeman Wills Crofts, Valentine Williams, F. Tennyson Jesse, Anthony Armstrong, and David Hume, and John Chancellor wrote the preface and a prologue.

The other short novel, *No Flowers by Request*, first appeared as a serial in the *Daily Sketch* in 1953. It was written by Dorothy L. Sayers, E. C. R. Lorac, Gladys Mitchell, Anthony Gilbert and Christianna Brand. It appeared in book form from Gollancz in 1984, together with *Crime on the Coast*, in red cloth, and with gilt spine lettering and the standard yellow wrapper. *Crime on the Coast* is not attributed to the Detection Club. It first appeared as a serial in the *News Chronicle* in 1954, and the authors were John Dickson Carr, Valerie White, Laurence Meynell, Joan Fleming, Michael Cronin, and Elizabeth Ferrars.

Detection Medley was edited by John Rhode, with an introduction by A. A. Milne. It is a compilation of articles and stories by Detection Club members. Since many stories first appeared in book form in this volume, it has become an important item for collectors. It was published by Hutchinson in 1939 but is undated. It has black cloth, lettered gilt on the spine, and with the publisher's name in gilt across the lower right-hand corner of the front cover. There is a fifty-two-page advertisement section at the back. Grey or blue cloth indicates a later issue.

Verdict of Thirteen is a Detection Club anthology in which all the stories are concerned with a jury. It was published by Faber in 1979, in black cloth, with the spine lettered gilt, and it is dated. A golden skull appears above the publisher's name on the spine. The wrapper illustration by Peter Branfield is of a judge's wig on a red background. The names of the thirteen distinguished contributors appear where the judge's face should be.

The Man Who . . . is an anthology containing stories by thirteen members of the Detection Club, published by Macmillan in 1992 in honour of Julian Symons' eightieth birthday. The book has black cloth with silver spine lettering. The wrapper has a photograph of a skull with a list of the thirteen writers by its side. The book was edited by H. R. F. Keating, who also wrote an introduction. An expensive alternative edition was published in 1992 by Scorpion Press. Its most interesting feature is that it is signed by all contributors: Catherine Aird, Eric Ambler, Simon Brett, Len Deighton, Antonia Fraser, Michael Gilbert, Reginald Hill, P. D. James, H. R. F. Keating, Peter Lovesey, Ruth Rendell, George Sims and Michael Underwood. This edition also has a frontispiece by Gary Short. The spine is of white leather with the title in silver. The marbled board sides have a wave-like pattern in black, white and grey. The book also has grey patterned endpapers and a silver top edge. This edition was limited to 125 numbered copies, the first fifteen of which were produced in a de luxe binding and slipcased.

Six against the Yard contains six stories, each by a different author, and each with a commentary by ex-Superintendent Cornish of the CID. The stories by Margery Allingham, Freeman Wills Crofts, and Dorothy L. Sayers were reprinted in collections by these authors, but Anthony Berkeley's 'The Policeman Only Taps Once' and Ronald A. Knox's 'The Fallen Idol' remain uncollected. The sixth author was Russell Thorndike. The book was published in 1936 by Selwyn & Blount, in salmon-pink cloth with the

spine lettered in black. It is undated except by the publisher's 32-page Spring 1936 catalogue at the back. The wrapper, by P. Youngman Carter, is two-toned, and each half shows a different scene: the left, in blue, has Scotland Yard, and the right, in red, has a scene on the Thames embankment, with a policeman.

Six Against the Yard became *Six Against Scotland Yard* in the USA, and *Detection Medley* was abridged for its American edition and re-titled *Line-up*. *Double Death* was not published in the USA.

Checklist

The Floating Admiral Hodder & Stoughton n.d. (1931), Doubleday 1932

Ask a Policeman Arthur Barker n.d. (1933), Morrow 1933

Six Against the Yard Selwyn & Blount n.d. (1936) (6 stories)

110

a.k.a. *Six Against Scotland Yard* Doubleday 1936
Double Death Gollancz 1939
Detection Medley Hutchinson n.d. (1939) (35 stories and articles)
a.k.a. *Line-up* Dodd, Mead 1940 (abridged)
Verdict of Thirteen Faber 1979, Harper 1979 (13 stories)
The Scoop and *Behind the Screen* Gollancz 1983, Berkley 1987
Crime on the Coast and *No Flowers by Request* Gollancz 1984, Berkley 1987
The Man Who . . . Macmillan 1992, Scorpion 1992 (13 stories)   *JC*

D. M. Devine (1920–1980)
a.k.a. Dominic Devine

David McDonald Devine, who later used the pseudonym Dominic Devine, wrote thirteen detective novels with ingenious plots and good characterization. He should be collected by all

who relish the traditional whodunit. Several of his books are set in his native Scotland. He had no series characters. *The Fifth Cord* and *The Royston Affair* are fine examples of his work.

Devine's books were all first published by Collins Crime Club in red cloth, and they are all dated. The first and second books have black lettering and the others have gilt. From *The Sleeping Tiger* the books are taller, coinciding with the author's name-change.

William Randell's design for *My Brother's Killer* shows Simon Barnett holding a flickering match, against an orange background. The chilling design for *Doctors Also Die* is a skull with a stethoscope hanging from it, and a broken pair of spectacles illustrates *The Royston Affair*. Two striking wrappers were designed by Kenneth Farnhill for *The Fifth Cord* and *The Sleeping Tiger*. The most difficult title to find is *My Brother's Killer*.

Novels by D. M. Devine

My Brother's Killer Collins Crime Club 1961, Dodd, Mead 1962
Doctors Also Die Crime Club 1962, Dodd 1963
The Royston Affair Crime Club 1964, Dodd 1965
His Own Appointed Day Crime Club 1965, Walker 1966
Devil At Your Elbow Crime Club 1966, Walker 1967
The Fifth Cord Crime Club 1967, Walker 1967

Novels by Dominic Devine

The Sleeping Tiger Crime Club 1968, Walker 1968
Death Is My Bridegroom Crime Club 1969, Walker 1969
Illegal Tender Crime Club 1970, Walker 1970
Dead Trouble Crime Club 1971, Doubleday 1971
Three Green Bottles Crime Club 1972, Doubleday 1972
Sunk Without Trace Crime Club 1978, St Martin's 1979
This Is Your Death Crime Club 1981, St Martin's 1982   *JC*

Colin Dexter (b. 1930)

Colin Dexter is a crossword champion and this shows in his writing. Many writers are capable of providing good plots, but few can match the ingenious storylines and breathtaking twists offered by Dexter. The ten novels he has written to date prove that the classical detective story is in safe, clever hands.

Dexter has created two very human characters. Detective Chief Inspector E. Morse and his assistant, Sergeant Lewis, feature in all his titles, as they battle to solve the most difficult crimes facing the Thames Valley police. Logical, introverted, and inspired, Morse is addicted to the delights of Wagner, devilish crosswords, and real ale. All seem to stimulate his thought processes most effectively, and are positive aids, central to his method of criminal detection. Lewis is the perfect foil for Morse, the conventional family man as opposed to the eccentric bachelor, his quiet logic contributing significantly to the success of this amiable partnership.

All Dexter's books were first published in London by Macmillan and are dated. Colours of cloth and spine lettering vary from title to title. In the first edition of *The Wench is Dead*, the date on the headstone on page 38 is incorrect. In the second edition it was changed from 'June 14 1859' to 'June 21 1859'. The first edition of *The Way Through the Woods* must have the printer's key 135798642 on the copyright page. Later editions drop one digit or more. *The Way Through the Woods* has attractive endpapers by Graeme James featuring a map of Wytham Woods. The map recurs in the text, together with a map of Blenheim Park. The map of Wytham Woods is authentic, except for Rejt's Seat, a fictional area named after the author's editor at Macmillan. *Morse's Greatest Mystery* has pale blue end-papers, a ribbon bookmark to match and a printer's key on the copyright page.

Sylvia Kaye's body illustrates the dust-wrapper of *Last Bus to Woodstock*. John Ireland's striking design for *Last Seen Wearing* is of the disembodied clothes of a schoolgirl making their way past a row of houses. *The Silent World of Nicholas Quinn* has a bloodstained paperknife resting on an examination paper, with a bottle and glass of dry sherry beside it. St Frideswide Church at night decorates *Service of All the Dead*. Mark Wilkinson provided the sinister view of the houses in Canal Reach for *The Dead of Jericho*. The grey wrapper for *The Riddle of the Third Mile* depicts a weathered bust in a niche. Martin White's effective design of a faceless postman on a delivery bike appears on *The Secret of Annexe 3*. Matthew Cook's illustration for *The Wench is Dead* shows a body floating face down in the Oxford Canal. The wrapper for *The Jewel that was Ours* shows the entrance to a stairway off a cloister and that for *The Way Through the Woods* offers a segment of Wytham Woods.

Colin Dexter has also written four non-series stories and six Morse stories, all collected in *Morse's Greatest Mystery*, published by Macmillan. One Morse story is uncollected. Two others were separately published before collection and so rate as authentic first editions. *The Inside Story*, which has Morse's red Jaguar on the front cover, was specially commissioned by American Express Travellers' Cheques and published in association with Pan Macmillan. This fifty-nine-page paperback also contains a crossword by Don Manley, based on Morse and Oxford. *Neighbourhood Watch*, published by Hartley Moorhouse and Geir Moe Sorenson, contains illustrations by Suzanne Hammond and was limited to 226 copies, of which seventy-six were signed by the author. Twenty-six copies were issued as hardbacks, in black cloth, with a page of the original manuscript reproduced in facsimile and with the additional signature of the illustrator. The remaining two hundred copies have card covers. 'The Secrets of Morse' is a five-part serial story based on *The Riddle of the Third Mile* but containing considerable new material. It was published in the *Daily Mail* from Fri. 22 Jan. to Wed. 27 Jan. 1993.

Morse novels

(Binding details refer to Macmillan editions.)

Last Bus to Woodstock Macmillan 1975, St Martin's 1975 (brown binding, black lettering)
Last Seen Wearing Macmillan 1976, St Martin's 1976 (pale blue, black)
The Silent World of Nicholas Quinn Macmillan 1977, St Martin's 1977 (dark green, white)
Service of All the Dead Macmillan 1979, St Martin's 1980 (pale blue, silver)
The Dead of Jericho Macmillan 1981, St Martin's 1981 (black, gilt)
The Riddle of the Third Mile Macmillan 1983, St Martin's 1984 (grey, silver)
The Secret of Annexe 3 Macmillan 1986, St Martin's 1987 (blue, silver)
The Wench is Dead Macmillan 1989, St Martin's 1990 (brown, gilt)

The Jewel that was Ours Macmillan 1991, Crown 1992 (black, gilt)
The Way through the Woods Macmillan 1992, Crown 1993 (green, gilt)

Story collection

Morse's Greatest Mystery Macmillan 1993 (10 stories, 6 with Morse) (black, gilt)

Separately published stories

The Inside Story Pan Macmillan 1993 (Morse)
Neighbourhood Watch Moorhouse/Sorenson 1993 (Morse)

Uncollected story

'The Secrets of Morse' (*Daily Mail*, 22–27 Jan. 1993) *JC*

Peter Dickinson (b. 1927)

From reviewing crime fiction for *Punch*, Peter Dickinson turned in 1968 to writing it. His first book won the Crime Writers Association's Gold Dagger, as did his second, uniquely, a year later. The wonder is not that he won the award twice, but that he has not had it since. His fictions are deep and devious, and to negotiate them is an exhilarating experience. The least predictable of writers, he has dazzling powers of invention, and a delight in eccentric communities, for each of which he devises a complex environment of total conviction. He has become a master of indirect narrative, increasingly fascinated by the interaction of past and present.

Even his detective is eccentric, an ageing, insecure policeman called Jimmy Pibble, who features in the five books from *Skin Deep* to *The Lizard in the Cup*, and celebrates his swansong in style, with *One Foot in the Grave*. Though edged into retirement after *The Seals*, his tepid reputation is not borne out by the wary persistence with which he threads his way to enlightenment through successive mazes. Even at the geriatric stage, his mind bemused, his body enfeebled, he still functions, instinctively and effectively, as a detective.

Two especially engaging novels feature an alternative Royal Family: *King and Joker* and *Skeleton-in-Waiting*. Both have preliminary family trees and Princess Louise, daughter of King Victor II, as detective.

Peter Dickinson began with Hodder and Stoughton, who published eleven of his crime novels and *A Summer in the Twenties*, a mainstream novel with a slight mystery element. From 1982 his books have been brought out by the Bodley Head. Eight of the Hodder books are black, but *The Lizard in the Cup* and *Walking Dead* are blue, and *King and Joker* is maroon. The more recent sequence from the Bodley Head is variously coloured. All the books are dated and lettered gilt on the spine. The top edges of *The Seals* and *The Green Gene* are green, and that for *Sleep and His Brother* is blue. From *Sleep and His Brother* to *One Foot in the Grave*, the books are taller than their predecessors and smaller than their successors, so that the series on the shelf looks like two ascending steps.

Three of the Hodder dust-wrappers are notable, especially that for *The Lizard in the Cup*, for which Colin Andrews achieved a memorable image by grafting Pibble's mournful features on to a Greek ikon. *Skin Deep* has Salim Patel's montage of Flagg Terrace and the Ku community, framed by the head of their murdered leader. *Walking Dead* has a vigorous portrait by Terry Oates of David Foxe and his deviant rat, Quentin. The fantastic clock at Snailwood Castle decorates the wrapper of *The Last House-Party*, the figure of Spring to the fore, with the shadows of Death and Time behind her. The artist, Barbara Lofthouse, also provided the stag and the long view of Paddery for the next novel, *Hindsight*.

Two stories by Peter Dickinson are known: 'Who Killed the Cat?', written for the Detection Club collection *Verdict of Thirteen*, and nastier than any of the novels, though no less brilliant, and 'Mink', a ghost story.

Novels

(with Pibble or Princess Louise, as stated. Details of bindings refer to Bodley Head editions.)

Skin Deep Hodder & Stoughton 1968 (Pibble)
a.k.a. *The Glass-Sided Ants' Nest* Harper 1968, Penguin 1981
A Pride of Heroes Hodder 1969 (Pibble)
a.k.a. *The Old English Peep Show* Harper 1969
The Seals Hodder 1970 (Pibble)
a.k.a. *The Sinful Stones* Harper 1970
Sleep and His Brother Hodder 1971, Harper 1971 (Pibble)
The Lizard in the Cup Hodder 1972, Harper 1972 (Pibble)
The Green Gene Hodder 1973, Pantheon 1973
The Poison Oracle Hodder 1974, Pantheon 1974
The Lively Dead Hodder 1975, Pantheon 1975
King and Joker Hodder 1976, Pantheon 1976 (Louise)
Walking Dead Hodder 1977, Pantheon 1978
One Foot in the Grave Hodder 1979, Pantheon 1980 (Pibble)
The Last House-Party Bodley Head 1982, Pantheon 1982 (blue binding)
Hindsight Bodley Head 1983, Pantheon 1983 (orange)
Death of a Unicorn Bodley Head 1984, Pantheon 1984 (red)
Tefuga Bodley Head 1986, Pantheon 1986 (brown)
Perfect Gallows Bodley Head 1988, Pantheon 1988 (light brown)
Skeleton-in-Waiting Bodley Head 1989, Pantheon 1990 (grey) (Louise)
Play Dead Bodley Head 1991, Mysterious Press 1992 (black)
The Yellow Room Conspiracy Little, Brown 1994 (purple)

Stories

'Who Killed the Cat?' (*Verdict of Thirteen*, Faber 1979, Harper 1979)
'Mink' (*The After Midnight Ghost Book*, Hutchinson 1980)

BP

114

Sir Arthur Conan Doyle (1859–1930)

Sir Arthur Conan Doyle became world-famous for his creation of Sherlock Holmes and his evocation of Victorian London. He is appreciated for his memorable dialogue and his ability to write a fascinating story. Sherlock Holmes was based on an Edinburgh surgeon, Dr Joseph Bell, who shared Holmes' belief in the value of observation. Holmes featured in four full-length novels and in fifty-six stories housed in five collections.

Doyle also wrote several other collections of stories, some of which involve mystery and detection; the most noted of these is *Round the Fire Stories*. In addition, he wrote a number of historical novels.

Sherlock Holmes, the world's greatest and most famous detective, ran a detective consultancy from his rooms at 221B Baker Street, Marylebone. He became a household name for his scientific approach and skills of deduction. Part of his attraction is the complexity of his character: he has faults and failings as well as his more positive attributes. Physically, he is a striking figure, tall, thin, strong and athletic, with piercing eyes set above an aquiline nose. Unless in one of his many masterly disguises, he is instantly recognisable by his Inverness cape, deerstalker hat, curved pipe and magnifying glass. At home he relaxes in a dressing gown, perhaps playing the violin or, when life fails to offer sufficient stimulation, injecting himself with cocaine. Though eccentric, he is highly intelligent with a vast store of knowledge and a love of music. The beautiful Irene Adler was the only woman to stir him emotionally.

John H. Watson, MD, a former army doctor, first met Holmes in the laboratory of Bart's Hospital. He later shared the flat in Baker Street, using it as the base for his practice. Watson is gentle, kind and handsome, with brown hair and eyes. Holmes admired his honesty, integrity and courage. All but four of the sixty stories and the four novels are based on Watson's case notes. He acts as Holmes' assistant and as a sounding-board for his ideas. Other series characters include the mathematics professor turned master criminal, James Moriarty, who apparently plunged to his death at the Reichenbach Falls in Switzerland. His intelligence matches that of Holmes but is used only for evil. More benign characters are Mycroft Holmes, Sherlock's older brother, and Mrs Martha Hudson, the housekeeper at 221B, Baker Street.

In the course of his career, Holmes deals with four Scotland Yard inspectors who figure in more than one story: G. Lestrade, in eleven cases; Stanley Hopkins, in four; Tobias Gregson, in three; and Inspector Bradstreet, in three. None can compete with Holmes in intellect, education or imagination.

Eight titles in the Holmes canon were first published in the UK. The exception is *The Valley of Fear*, which appeared first in the USA. Apart from *A Study in Scarlet* and *The Sign of Four*, the Holmes series first appeared in the *Strand Magazine*. *The Sign of Four* was first serialised in the USA in *Lippincott's Magazine* in Feb. 1890 as *The Sign of the Four*.

The *Strand* was first published in Jan. 1891 with pictorial paper wrappers depicting a bustling scene of a crowded Strand looking towards St Clement Dane's Church. Half-yearly volumes of the monthly magazine were published in June and December, bound in light-blue cloth, lettered black and gilt, with the illustration of the Strand street-scene on the front cover. The two volumes for 1891 have the street name near the top on the left as Burleigh Street, whereas later volumes have Southampton Street.

A Study in Scarlet, Ward Lock 1888. Illustration by Charles Doyle, the author's father.

A Study in Scarlet, illustrated by D. H. Friston, had its first publication during November 1887 in *Beeton's Christmas Annual*, published by Ward, Lock. The periodical was priced at one shilling

and sold out before Christmas. It has paper wrappers and contains stories by other writers also.

In 1888 Ward, Lock published *A Study in Scarlet* as a separate book 18.2 cm × 12 cm in size. The white paper front cover has a red border round the edges, broken at the top by the price, 'one shilling'. The title, with 'By Conan Doyle' below at an angle, and the publisher's name at the bottom, 'Ward Lock & Co. London & New York', are all red against a pink mosaic background. The title in red appears on the spine. The rear cover has an advertisement in red for Pears Soap. Inside the front cover is an advertisement for Sir James Murray's Pure Fluid Magnesia. The page opposite has advertisements for Matthews's Fullers Earth, Ridge's Food and Rowland's Kalydor. Facing the title-page are seven press opinions of *A Study in Scarlet*. The book is dated 1888 at the base of the title-page and contains six line-drawings by Charles Doyle, the author's father. There are fourteen pages of advertisements at the back, including seven pages of 'The Select Library of Fiction', the last entry numbered 793. Inside the back wrapper is an advertisement for Barber & Company's French Coffee.

A second impression is easily recognized as it has added at the bottom of the front cover: 'This design, with the exception of the lettering, is composed with the "Patent Kalido Mosaic Type" '.

The Sign of Four was published by Spencer Blackett and issued in dark-red cloth. The book has a double black border enclosing a tooth design, edging the front and back covers and the top and base of the spine. Inside the border at the corners is a floral design. The title and author – A. Conan Doyle – are lettered gilt on the front cover. The spine is also lettered gilt, with title and author and, at the base, 'Spencer Blackett's Standard Library'. The book has black endpapers and is dated 1890 on the title-page. There is a black-and-white frontispiece by Charles Kerr with a tissue guard tipped in. The scene shown is from the chapter 'The Tragedy of Pondicherry Lodge', where, 'In the light of the lantern I read, with a thrill of horror, "The Sign of Four" '. On the contents page, the '8' is missing from 'page 138', which appears as 'page 13'. Some copies of the book have a thirty-two-page catalogue of books for October 1890 at the rear, while others lack this feature.

The next four titles were published by George Newnes, *The Adventures of Sherlock Holmes* and *The Memoirs of Sherlock Holmes* in a similar format. Both are large-sized books measuring 24.5 cm × 16.3 cm and each has title and author – 'By A. Conan Doyle' – gilt on the front cover. Each cover has the Strand street-scene with no name on the street sign for the *Adventures* and Southampton Street named for the *Memoirs*. Both books have bevelled boards, *Adventures* in light-blue cloth, *Memoirs* in darker blue. The spines have the same decoration and style of lettering: a black rule at the top; then a toothed gilt border with a single gilt rule beneath; the title lettered black against a gilt rectangular panel ruled black and gilt above and below; 'By A. Conan Doyle' lettered gilt; 'The Strand Library' lettered black on a gilt rectangular panel enclosed within a black and gilt border; a black rule with curled edges; publisher's name and address gilt within two gilt rules; a thicker gilt rule with a black rule at the base. Both books have gilt page edges.

The endpapers for *Adventures* are grey with a leaf and flower design; the *Memoirs* has either a grey floral or an orange peacock feather design on the endpapers. Each book is dated at the base of the title-page. *Adventures* has eight previous works by the author listed facing the title-page; ten such titles appear on the back of the contents page in *Memoirs*. *Adventures* has 104 illustrations by Sidney Paget (but no frontispiece). *Memoirs* has ninety Paget illustrations and his frontispiece 'The death of Sherlock Holmes' from 'The Final Problem', showing Holmes and Moriarty grappling by the Reichenbach Falls. The two books were issued in blue dustwrappers, lettered in black as on the front covers and with publisher's advertisements on the back panels.

The third Holmes novel, *The Hound of the Baskervilles*, has scarlet cloth lettered gilt and with a design that is also mainly gilt. The title appears at the top of the front cover, with a gilt rule underneath. The Hound appears in black silhouette on the moor against a gilt moon enclosed within a gilt ruled square. On either side of the square a gilt question-mark appears, superimposed on a circle. A very ornate gilt design is drawn below and partly around the square enclosing the Hound and is signed at the bottom right 'A. G. J.' (Alfred Garth Jones). Under this is another gilt rule, with Conan Doyle's name gilt at the bottom of the front cover. Everything on the spine is gilt: the title, with a dot on either side of 'The'; the intricate design under the title, which includes a thistle topped by a rising sun; 'Conan Doyle'; a question-mark on a circle; and the publisher's name with a dot on either side of 'Ltd.'. The rear cover is blank. The book has white endpapers and is dated 1902 on the title-page. Twenty-one previous titles of the author are listed on the back of the title-page. Sidney Paget's sixteen black-and-white illustrations include a frontispiece, 'The Shadow of Sherlock Holmes'. There are no advertisements at the rear.

The Hound of the Baskervilles was issued in a grey dust-wrapper with a similar design to that on the book but lettered in red. The question-mark over the circle on the spine is replaced by the price, 6/-. There are publisher's advertisements on the back panel of the wrapper.

The Return of Sherlock Holmes is generally seen with dark-blue cloth but light-blue copies are known. The title and author appear in gilt towards the top of the front cover and spine. The word 'by' also appears before A. Conan Doyle on the cover. The publisher in gilt appears at the base of the spine. The book has white endpapers and is dated MCMV on the title-page. There are sixteen full-page black-and-white illustrations by Sidney Paget, including a frontispiece depicting a scene from 'The Adventure of the Missing Three-Quarter': 'We were clear of the town and hastening down a country road' (a draghound with Holmes and Watson in tow). Twenty previous works by the author are listed on the back of the half-title. Four pages of advertisements appear at the rear. The book was issued with a grey wrapper lettered blue on the front cover and spine.

The Valley of Fear was published by Smith, Elder in a reddish pink cloth with a blind-stamped border on the front cover. The title and 'A.

Conan Doyle' appear on the front cover and spine, with the publisher additionally on the spine, throughout in gilt lettering. The endpapers are white and the book is dated 1915 on the title-page. A black-and-white frontispiece by Frank Wiles shows Holmes examining a piece of footwear. There are thirty-four previous titles listed on the reverse of the half-title and six pages of advertisements at the back. A white wrapper has Holmes kneeling, with the forearm of Douglas against a yellow background. There are publisher's advertisements on the rear panel. According to Richard Lancelyn Green and John Michael Gibson (*A Bibliography of A. Conan Doyle* OUP 1983), the first edition of *The Valley of Fear* appeared in June 1915 and the Colonial edition a year later, from George Bell. However, a copy of the Colonial edition is reported with a publisher's list dated April 1915 at the rear.

The last two Holmes titles were published by John Murray in the same external format of the Smith, Elder volume, in a pink cloth binding with a blind-stamped border on the front cover. All the lettering is again gilt, with the title near the top and A. Conan Doyle towards the bottom of the front cover and the publisher additionally on the spine. *His Last Bow* is dated 1917 at the base of the title-page, with twenty-six previous works listed on the back of the half-title. There are six pages of advertisements at the rear. *The Case-book of Sherlock Holmes* is dated 1927 on the copyright page with thirty-nine previous works listed on the back of the half-title. There are no advertisements at the back. Both Murray books have white endpapers.

They also have white wrappers with designs by J. Abbey. *His Last Bow* shows Holmes with a cockerel and the tag 'some reminiscences of Sherlock Holmes' supplementing the title. The price, 6/-, also appears on the front panel. *The Case-book* has Holmes holding a revolver at the head of a cowering figure. Both wrappers carry advertisements on the rear panel.

One Sherlock Holmes story, 'The Adventure of the Dying Detective', was published separately by Collier in the USA in December 1913. It was issued as a forty-page booklet as the last of four booklets (Vol. IV) enclosed in a grey cardboard slipcase. It has grey paper boards with square vellum spine. 'Sherlock Holmes' appears gilt on the front cover. There is a white paper label on the spine with 'Sherlock Holmes' in black.

Conan Doyle wrote one play, *The Speckled Band*, 'An Adventure of Sherlock Holmes', published in August 1912 by Samuel French. The light-green paper covers are lettered black, with the title in Gothic script. A floral border appears near the top and bottom of the front cover. The play is priced one shilling and sixpence on the front cover. Later printings have dark-green and light-brown covers. The world première of the play was at the Adelphi Theatre in London on 4 June 1910, two years before publication.

In 1896, Doyle wrote a two-page Holmes parody, which first appeared in the Bazaar number of *The Student* in Edinburgh on 20 November 1896: as 'The Memoirs of Sherlock Holmes: The Field Bazaar', Vol. II, pages 35–6. This was published separately in 1934 by the Athenaeum Press, London, as 'The Field Bazaar', in an edition of one hundred copies.

The most difficult title to locate in first edition form is *A Study in Scarlet* in *Beeton's Christmas Annual* and the next most difficult must be the 1888 Ward Lock edition of the same novel. *The Sign of Four* and *The Return of Sherlock Holmes* are also scarce.

Sherlock Holmes novels

A Study in Scarlet Ward Lock 1887 in *Beeton's Christmas Annual*; Ward Lock 1888; Lippincott 1890
The Sign of Four Blackett 1890, Lippincott 1893
The Hound of the Baskervilles Newnes 1902, McClure 1902
The Valley of Fear Doran 1914, Smith, Elder 1915

Holmes story collections

The Adventures of Sherlock Holmes Newnes 1892, Harper 1892 (12 stories)
The Memoirs of Sherlock Holmes Newnes 1894, Harper 1894 (11 stories)

The Return of Sherlock Holmes   Newnes 1905, McClure 1905 (13 stories)

His Last Bow   Murray 1917, Doran 1917 (8 stories)

The Case-book of Sherlock Holmes   Murray 1927, Doran 1927 (12 stories)

Other story collections

Mysteries and Adventures   Scott 1889

a.k.a. *The Gully of Bluemansdyke*   Scott 1889

The Captain of the Polestar and Other Tales   Longman 1890, Munro 1894

My Friend the Murderer and Other Mysteries and Adventures   Lovell (New York) 1893

Round the Fire Stories   Smith, Elder 1908, McClure 1908

The Black Doctor and Other Tales of Terror and Mystery   Doran 1925   *JC*

'A Scandal in Bohemia', The *Strand Magazine*, Jul. 1891. Illustration by Sidney Paget.

Margaret Erskine (d. 1984)

Margaret Erskine published a single detective novel before the war and a further twenty after it. They are vivacious, crowded narratives, invariably set in picturesque houses, where rich eccentrics brood over dark family secrets and eerie atmospherics are a *sine qua non*. All twenty-one feature Inspector Septimus Finch, a big, burly man with a soft, high voice, 'like a penny whistle out of a steam engine'. However startling the developments, he remains rational and reassuring.

And Being Dead was published by Bles in 1938, in a black binding, with white spine lettering and the title in white on the front cover. The book is dated. After the war, Hammond took over the Finch novels, publishing seven, the last in 1955. The four books from *The Whispering House* are blue-green, the first pair with black lettering, the latter pair with gilt, invariably on the spine. *Death of Our Dear One* is blue and reverts to black lettering. *Dead by Now* and *Fatal Relations* are maroon, with yellow lettering. *The Whispering House* is undated, except for the printer's code, which places it in 1947. All the later books are dated, all except *I Knew Macbean* with the printer's code as well.

From 1956 to 1975, Hodder & Stoughton were Margaret Erskine's publishers. They issued twelve of her novels in a variety of colours, all but one with gilt spine lettering. *Harriet Farewell* is the exception, with silver lettering. All the Hodder books are dated; and *The Woman at Belguardo*, *The Case of Mary Fielding*, *The Brood of Folly*, and *Harriet Farewell* are taller than the rest of the sequence. At least four of the Hodder books appeared first in the USA in their Doubleday editions, and this is also true of the final novel, *The House in Hook Street*, which Hale published in Britain in 1978. It is uncharacteristic of this publisher, with its brown binding and gilt spine lettering. It is also taller than usual for Hale, the same height as *Harriet Farewell*; and it is dated. Eight novels have variant titles in their original US editions and a further four in American reprint form. The DBC edition of *Fatal Relations* appeared in a volume also containing two other novels.

Margaret Erskine was fortunate in her publishers, who used designers to give her books character and individuality. The best of Stein's wrappers for the earlier Hammond books is that for *The Whispering House*, showing the odd spectacle that greets Finch on his arrival at Lorne Abbey. Three designs by Sax are notably impressive: for *Death of Our Dear One*, with Finch and Freddie Dawes approaching the newly dead Gail Heneker; for *Dead By Now*, with the Luxuria Theatre and the ghost with the tilted head; and for *Fatal Relations*, with its view of the gate of Hammerford Hall, its 'massive brick-built piers' each surmounted by 'a strange beast, unknown outside heraldry'. Later wrappers focus on various sinister houses: on Belguardo and Number 9, Belmont Square, on Wallinger's House, where the portrait of the enchantress hangs, and on Glebe Cottage, amid the 'great trees' that threaten to engulf it (in *Take a Dark Journey*). Peter Schaumann's impression of Mary Fielding is especially elegant; and Studio Stead's macabre Gothic design for *The Brood of Folly* includes a vivid reminder of the skull beneath the skin.

Finch novels

(Binding colours refer to Hodder editions.)

And Being Dead   Bles 1938
a.k.a. *The Limping Man*   Doubleday 1939
a.k.a. *The Painted Mask*   Ace 1972
The Whispering House   Hammond n.d. (1947)
a.k.a. *The Voice of the House*   Doubleday 1947
I knew Macbean   Hammond 1948, Doubleday 1948
a.k.a *Caravan of Night*   Ace 1972
Give Up the Ghost   Hammond 1949, Doubleday 1949
The Disappearing Bridegroom   Hammond 1950
a.k.a. *The Silver Ladies*   Doubleday 1951
Death of Our Dear One   Hammond 1952
a.k.a. *Look Behind You, Lady*   Doubleday 1952
a.k.a *Don't Look Behind You*   Ace 1972
Dead By Now   Hammond 1954, Doubleday 1954
Fatal Relations   Hammond 1955

a.k.a. *Old Mrs. Ommanney Is Dead*   Doubleday 1955
a.k.a. *The Dead Don't Speak*   DBC 1955
The Voice of Murder   Hodder & Stoughton 1956, Doubleday 1956 (dark red)
Sleep No More   Hodder 1958, Ace 1969 (dark red)
The House of the Enchantress   Hodder 1959 (green)
a.k.a. *A Graveyard Plot*   Doubleday 1959
The Woman at Belguardo   Hodder 1961, Doubleday 1961 (green)
The House in Belmont Square   Hodder 1963 (dark blue)
a.k.a. *Number 9, Belmont Square*   Doubleday 1963
Take a Dark Journey   Hodder 1965 (green)
a.k.a. *The Family at Tammerton*   Doubleday 1966
Case with Three Husbands   Doubleday 1967, Hodder 1967 (green)

The Ewe Lamb   Doubleday 1969, Hodder 1969 (red)

The Case of Mary Fielding   Doubleday 1970, Hodder 1970 (blue)

The Brood of Folly   Hodder 1971, Doubleday 1971 (green)

Besides the Wench Is Dead   Hodder 1973, Doubleday 1973 (red)

Harriet Farewell   Doubleday 1975, Hodder 1975 (maroon)

The House in Hook Street   Doubleday 1977, Hale 1978   *BP*

Elizabeth Ferrars (b. 1907)
a.k.a. E. X. Ferrars

Elizabeth Ferrars is the pseudonym of Morna Brown, who is known as E. X. Ferrars in the USA. She has written sixty-seven novels and two collections of stories. She also contributed the last two chapters to the collaborative novel *Crime on the Coast* (see under 'Detection Club'), and there are fifteen uncollected stories known.

She is now a veteran, with a marvellous talent for weaving elegant mysteries around middle-class characters in a traditional English setting. Five of her series detectives are amateurs. The young Toby Dyke, who appeared in her first five novels, is 'a journalist of sorts'. Andrew Basnett, a retired professor of botany, first appeared in the excellent *Something Wicked*, and has to date solved six mysteries. Felix and Virginia Freer are a husband and wife who have been separated for several years, but continue to meet. They appear in eight recent novels and are two of the most interesting of modern amateur investigators. Detective-Superintendent Downey and Sergeant Wells encounter the Freers in three novels: *Woman Slaughter, Sleep of the Unjust* and *Beware of the Dog*. Jonas P. Jonas, a garrulous, conceited old codger, features in six stories. At least four books were first published in the USA, three with alternative titles to the British editions. Seven books have not appeared in American editions, and many that have are differently titled.

In Britain, the first six books were published by Hodder & Stoughton. Five appeared in blue cloth, with black lettering on the spine. The sixth, *I, Said the Fly*, has maroon cloth, with white spine lettering. All the remaining titles have been published by Collins Crime Club in red cloth. They are all lettered on the spine in black, until *Ninth Life* in 1965, when the lettering becomes, and remains, gilt. From *The Swaying Pillars*, the books are all taller. The books from both publishers are all dated. From *Beware of the Dog*, the books have printers' keys on their copyright pages.

Thompson's blue and white wrapper for *Remove the Bodies* has a policeman and another figure carrying a long ladder on their right shoulders. The wrapper for *Don't Monkey with Murder* shows the beech wood near East Leat. Morton Sale's design for *Your Neck in a Noose* has the illuminated head of a strange-looking young woman. Winslade's effective design for *Murder Among Friends* cuts the cranium from a large skull, in which three couples sit, while a woman stands on the edge. The skull appears to be floating on water. *With Murder in Mind* has an arm reaching for a pipe against a green and purple background. Stead's design for *The March Hare Murders* is eye-catchingly simple: a white hare on a green background. A pearl necklace and the head of a disapproving tortoise are featured on *Hunt the Tortoise*. *Milk of Human Kindness* depicts the shadow of a man climbing through a window. The head and shoulders of a brunette in large yellow sunglasses shares the wrapper of *Alibi for a Witch* with a witch on a broomstick. An evil, red-haired figure leers at the hands of a clock for *The Clock That Wouldn't Stop*, and *Murder in Time* shows the hands of another clock, which seem to be reaching out for a suspicious-looking man, clutching a briefcase.

Fifteen books in the 1950s and 1960s have wrappers with black front panels and spines and coloured lettering. The later wrappers are photographic, and *The Seven Sleepers* and *Breath of Suspicion* have excellent photographs by Margaret Murray. *Sequence of Events* was published by Eurographica in Nov. 1989 in a limited edition of 350 copies. It has blank white wrappers with a plain brown dust-wrapper, lettered black, and contains four stories, two previously uncollected.

The most difficult first edition to obtain is *Death in Botanist's Bay.*

Novels

(with series characters, as stated)

Give a Corpse a Bad Name Hodder & Stoughton 1940 (Dyke)
Remove the Bodies Hodder 1940 (Dyke)
a.k.a. *Rehearsals for Murder* Doubleday 1941
Death in Botanist's Bay Hodder 1941 (Dyke)
a.k.a. *Murder of a Suicide* Doubleday 1941
Don't Monkey with Murder Hodder 1942 (Dyke)
a.k.a. *The Shape of a Stain* Doubleday 1942
Your Neck in a Noose Hodder 1942 (Dyke)
a.k.a. *Neck in a Noose* Doubleday 1943
I, Said the Fly Hodder 1945, Doubleday 1945
Murder Among Friends Collins Crime Club 1946
a.k.a. *Cheat the Hangman* Doubleday 1946
With Murder in Mind Crime Club 1948
The March Hare Murders Crime Club 1949, Doubleday 1949
Hunt the Tortoise Crime Club 1950, Doubleday 1950
Milk of Human Kindness Crime Club 1950
The Clock that Wouldn't Stop Crime Club 1952, Doubleday 1952
Alibi for a Witch Crime Club 1952, Doubleday 1952
Murder in Time Crime Club 1953
The Lying Voices Crime Club 1954
Enough to Kill a Horse Crime Club 1955, Doubleday 1955
Always Say Die Crime Club 1956
a.k.a. *We Haven't Seen Her Lately* Doubleday 1956
Murder Moves In Crime Club 1956
a.k.a. *Kill or Cure* Doubleday 1956
Furnished for Murder Crime Club 1957
Count the Cost Doubleday 1957
a.k.a. *Unreasonable Doubt* Crime Club 1958
Depart This Life Doubleday 1958
a.k.a. *A Tale of Two Murders* Crime Club 1959
Fear the Light Crime Club 1960, Doubleday 1960

The Sleeping Dogs Crime Club 1960, Doubleday 1960
The Busy Body Crime Club 1962
a.k.a. *Seeing Double* Doubleday 1962
The Wandering Widows Crime Club 1962, Doubleday 1962
The Doubly Dead Crime Club 1963, Doubleday 1963
The Decayed Gentlewoman Doubleday 1963
a.k.a. *A Legal Fiction* Crime Club 1964
Ninth Life Crime Club 1965
No Peace for the Wicked Crime Club 1966, Harper 1966
Zero at the Bone Crime Club 1967, Walker 1968
The Swaying Pillars Crime Club 1968, Walker 1969
Skeleton Staff Crime Club 1969, Walker 1969
The Seven Sleepers Crime Club 1970, Walker 1970
A Stranger and Afraid Crime Club 1971, Walker 1971
Breath of Suspicion Crime Club 1972, Doubleday 1972
Foot in the Grave Doubleday 1972, Crime Club 1973
The Small World of Murder Crime Club 1973, Doubleday 1973
Hanged Man's House Crime Club 1974, Doubleday 1974
Alive and Dead Crime Club 1974, Doubleday 1975
Drowned Rat Crime Club 1975, Doubleday 1975
The Cup and the Lip Crime Club 1975, Doubleday 1976
Blood Flies Upwards Crime Club 1976, Doubleday 1977
The Pretty Pink Shroud Crime Club 1977, Doubleday 1977
Murders Anonymous Crime Club 1977, Doubleday 1978
Last Will and Testament Crime Club 1978, Doubleday 1978 (Freer)
In at the Kill Crime Club 1978, Doubleday 1979
Witness Before the Fact Crime Club 1979, Doubleday 1980

Frog in the Throat Crime Club 1980, Double-day 1980 (Freer)

Experiment with Death Crime Club 1981, Doubleday 1981

Thinner than Water Crime Club 1981, Double-day 1982 (Freer)

Skeleton in Search of a Cupboard Crime Club 1982

a.k.a. *Skeleton in Search of a Closet* Doubleday 1982

Death of a Minor Character Crime Club 1983, Doubleday 1983 (Freer)

Something Wicked Crime Club 1983, Double-day 1984 (Basnett)

Root of All Evil Crime Club 1984, Doubleday 1984 (Basnett)

The Crime and the Crystal Crime Club 1985, Doubleday 1985 (Basnett)

I Met Murder Crime Club 1985, Doubleday 1985 (Freer)

The Other Devil's Name Crime Club 1986, Doubleday 1987 (Basnett)

Come and Be Killed Crime Club 1987, Double-day 1987

A Murder Too Many Crime Club 1988, Doubleday 1989 (Basnett)

Trial by Fury Crime Club 1989, Doubleday 1989

Woman Slaughter Crime Club 1989, Double-day 1990 (Freer)

Smoke Without Fire Crime Club 1990, Double-day 1991 (Basnett)

Sleep of the Unjust Crime Club 1990, Double-day 1991 (Freer)

Danger from the Dead Crime Club 1991, Bantam 1992

Beware of the Dog Crime Club 1992, Bantam 1993 (Freer)

Answer Came There None Crime Club 1992

Thy Brother Death Crime Club 1993

Story collections

Designs on Life Crime Club 1980, Doubleday 1980 (9 stories)

Sequence of Events Eurographica 1989 (4 stories)

Novella with other writers

(See under 'Detection Club')

Crime on the Coast Gollancz 1984 (with *No Flowers by Request*)

Uncollected stories

Jonas stories

'When a Young Girl's Eyes Are Crazy with Worry' (*ES*, 8 Dec. 1958; *EQMM*, Aug. 1959, as 'The Case of the Two Questions')

'No More Milk for Mrs. Toomes' (*ES*, 9 Dec. 1958; *EQMM*, Oct. 1959, as 'The Case of the Blue Bowl')

'The Collector Who Ran Away from Murder' (*ES*, 10 Dec. 1958; *EQMM*, Mar. 1960, as 'The Case of the Auction Catalogue')

'A Lunch Plate Stopped Bardell's Escape' (*ES*, 11 Dec. 1958; *EQMM*, Dec. 1960, as 'The Case of the Left Hand')

'Invitation to Murder – on the Party Line' (*ES*, 12 Dec. 1958)

'A Lipstick Smear Points to the Killer' (*ES*, 13 Dec. 1958)

Other stories

'When a Girl has a Grudge, Look for Trouble' (*ES*, 8 June 1964; *Saint*, June 1965 (UK), as 'Look for Trouble')

'Suicide? In a Car with the Lights On?' (*ES*, 19 Mar. 1963; *Saint*, Dec. 1964 (UK), as 'Suicide?')

'Ashes to Ashes' (*EQMM*, Apr. 1971)

'The Long Way Round' (*Winter's Crimes 4*, Macmillan 1972)

'Instrument of Justice' (*Winter's Crimes 13*, Macmillan 1981, St Martin's 1981; *EQMM* Jan. 1982)

'Fly, Said the Spy' (*Winter's Crimes 15*, Macmillan 1983; St Martin's 1983; *EQMM*, Mar. 1984)

'Custody' (*A Suit of Diamonds*, Crime Club 1990)

'The Cancelling of Mrs. Arbuthnot' (*Julian Symons at 80*, Eurographica 1992)

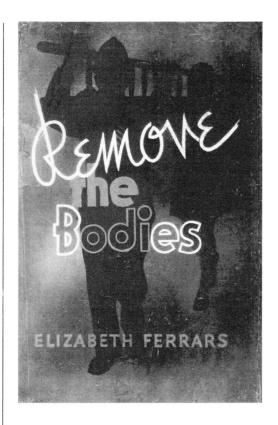

'Stop Thief!' (*EQMM*, Nov. 1992; *Winter's Crimes 24*, Macmillan 1992)   *JC*

Mary Fitt
(Kathleen Freeman (1897–1959))
a.k.a. Stuart Mary Wick

Kathleen Freeman was a distinguished Greek scholar and a multifarious writer under her own name and three pseudonyms. As Kathleen Freeman she published mainstream fiction, works of scholarship, and one crime novel, *Gown and Shroud*. For the bulk of her crime fiction and several juvenile novels, she used the pseudonym Mary Fitt. As Stuart Mary Wick she wrote a crime novel, *And Where's Mr. Bellamy?*, and a romantic melodrama, *The Statue and the Lady*. Her third pseudonym, Caroline Cory, was reserved for a novel of the French Resistance, suggested by the life of her friend and companion, Dr Liliane Clopet, to whom most of her

books are dedicated. Mary Fitt was launched in 1936, with *Three Sisters Flew Home*, the first of twenty-seven novels published under this name. Because she is eccentric, she is somewhat neglected: her intensity sets her rather apart. Her talent was unpredictable, so that her work is uneven, often highly accomplished, but sometimes wayward and implausible. She is very much a novelist of character, with something obsessive about her analysis of human behaviour. Her darkest books have a brooding, fatalistic quality: character is destiny, and emotion has power to destroy.

Her first publishers were Nicholson & Watson, who gave her books distinctive features, like the cover vignettes for *Three Sisters Flew Home* and *The Three Hunting Horns*. Otherwise, the front covers are blank. The bindings and lettering are variously coloured, but there is some uniformity in the format of *Sky-rocket, Death at Dancing Stones*, and *Murder of a Mouse*, which share the same style of lettering, in brown for *Sky-Rocket*, in black for the others. Variant bindings are known for *Sky-rocket* and *Murder of a Mouse*, in red and blue, respectively, with cruder black lettering than that on the true first editions. *Sky-rocket* and *Death at Dancing Stones* have preliminary maps, and the rear endpapers of *Murder Mars the Tour* chart the novel's progress through Germany and Austria. The front endpapers of *The Three Hunting Horns* have a plan of the Château de la Frelonnerie. The top edge of *Expected Death* is green.

The wrapper for *The Three Hunting Horns* has a skeleton dressed for the chase and blowing a horn. That for *Sky-rocket* shows Natasya Gromov lying dead in the summerhouse at Lakeside Grange, with the actor Reynold reclining in his boat, and the eponymous firework exploding in the sky. The predatory cat from *Murder of a Mouse* recurs on the half-title of *Death Starts a Rumour* (and also on the spine of Lowen's wrapper, which features the head and neck of an anxious ostrich). Tributes from Margery Allingham, Freeman Wills Crofts, J. J. Connington, and Dennis Wheatley distinguish the plain brown-and-white wrapper of *Death at Dancing Stones*.

Most of Mary Fitt's series characters begin

their recorded careers in the Nicholson & Watson books. Superintendent Mallett, the shrewd and practical Scot who figures in nineteen of her books, first appears in *Sky-rocket*, together with Dr Jones, who acts as police surgeon until superseded by Dr Fitzbrown. Fitzbrown himself is introduced in *Expected Death*, where he answers to the incongruous nickname of 'Dodo' (his real name is Dudley). Colonel Anderson, from *The Three Hunting Horns*, reappears as Mallett's Chief Constable in *Murder of a Mouse* and others.

In 1941 the author moved to Michael Joseph, who published the five books that followed. Of these, three are black and four have silver lettering on the spine. *Requiem for Robert* has a red binding. *Death on Herons' Mere* is fawn and lettered in green, and is further distinguished by a map of the mere. A. E. Barlow's sombre wrapper for *Clues to Christabel* shows Christabel's headstone.

The long Macdonald series that began in 1947 has the benefit of Broom Lynne's artistry for many of its dust-wrappers. Few designers are as stylish and relevant as he, and his work for Mary Fitt is invariably in his finest vein. From the author's patterns he contrives his own, enhancing each work with a potent image of its theme or its atmosphere. The books in this sequence are all black, with gilt lettering to *The Banquet Ceases* and with yellow thereafter. As a bonus, the wrappers for *Death and the Bright Day* and *The Banquet Ceases* have the entrancing rear panels on which Mr Macdonald offers scenes from his current crime list to potential customers.

Love from Elizabeth records the murder of Lady Elizabeth Carn, whose earlier career is documented in a later book, *Case for the Defence*. *The Man Who Shot Birds* is an attractive collection of twelve stories, variously involving Mallett and Fitzbrown, and Mr Pitt and his Siamese cat, Georgina, whose portrait is the centrepiece of Broom Lynne's dust-wrapper. The title story recounts Fitzbrown's first encounter with crime, as a student. 'A Death in the Blackout' is recast as a radio play in *Butcher's Dozen* (1956). For *Mizmaze*, Mallett's final case, Mary Fitt returned to Michael Joseph, who also published her last novel, '*There Are More Ways of Killing . . .*', the year after her death. Her final detective, Mr Frost, abandoned wife and family to study the Greek classics. Donald Green designed the picturesque wrappers for both books, which are black with gilt lettering. *Mizmaze* also has a white croquet mallet and balls stamped on its spine. *And Where's Mr. Bellamy?* is undated, unlike the rest of Kathleen Freeman's crime fiction, which invariably states the year of publication. It appeared in 1948 from Hutchinson, a brown book, with gilt lettering on the spine and the publisher's name gilt on the front cover. The striking dust-wrapper shows a green hand pouring poison over a plate of tarts on an elegantly appointed tea-tray. The book was reissued in 1976 by Ian Henry, as by Mary Fitt. *Gown and Shroud* is a blue book, with orange lettering on a black spine panel. The dust-wrapper is lamentable, Stein at his crudest.

Only nine of Mary Fitt's novels were published in America, *Pity for Pamela* with an introduction by Anthony Boucher.

At least two of the uncollected Fitt stories feature Mallett and Fitzbrown: 'The Box of Coins' and 'Highlight'. Three stories by Kathleen Freeman appeared in the *LMM* in the early 1950s. They are all concerned with crime in classical Greece (and were, perhaps, offshoots of her work on Greek law, as shown in *The Murder of Herodes and Other Trials from Athenian Law Courts*, Macdonald 1946).

Novels by Mary Fitt

(With Mallett and others, as stated. Details of bindings refer to British editions.)

Three Sisters Flew Home Nicholson & Watson 1936 (blue binding, dark blue lettering on pale blue panel)

Murder Mars the Tour Nicholson 1936 (red, gilt)

Bulls Like Death Nicholson 1937 (red, light blue)

The Three Hunting Horns Nicholson 1937 (pale blue, black)

Sky-rocket Nicholson 1938 (Mallett) (pale blue binding)

Expected Death Nicholson 1938 (Mallett, Fitzbrown) (green, black)

Death at Dancing Stones Nicholson 1939 (Mallett) (orange binding)

Murder of a Mouse Nicholson 1939 (Mallett) (pale brown binding)

Death Starts a Rumour Nicholson 1940 (Mallett, Fitzbrown) (blue, black)

Death and Mary Dazill Joseph 1941 (Mallett, Fitzbrown)

a.k.a. *Aftermath of Murder* Doubleday 1941

Death on Herons' Mere Joseph 1941 (Mallett, Fitzbrown)

a.k.a. *Death Finds a Target* Doubleday 1942

Requiem for Robert Joseph 1942 (Mallett, Fitzbrown)

Clues to Christabel Joseph 1944, Doubleday 1944 (Mallett, Fitzbrown)

Death and the Pleasant Voices Joseph 1946, Putnam 1946 (Mallett, Fitzbrown)

A Fine and Private Place Macdonald 1947, Putnam 1947 (Mallett)

Death and the Bright Day Macdonald 1948 (Mallett, Fitzbrown)

The Banquet Ceases Macdonald 1949 (Mallett, Fitzbrown)

Pity for Pamela Macdonald 1950, Harper 1951

An Ill Wind Macdonald 1951 (Mallett, Fitzbrown)

Death and the Shortest Day Macdonald 1952 (Mallett, Fitzbrown)

The Nightwatchman's Friend Macdonald 1953

Love from Elizabeth Macdonald 1954 (Mallett, Fitzbrown)

Sweet Poison Macdonald 1956 (Mallett, Fitzbrown)

The Late Uncle Max Macdonald 1957

Case for the Defence Macdonald 1958, British Book Centre 1958

Mizmaze Joseph 1959, British Book Centre 1959 (Mallett, Fitzbrown)

'There Are More Ways of Killing...' Joseph 1960, British Book Centre 1960

Story collection by Mary Fitt

The Man Who Shot Birds Macdonald 1954 (Mallett, Fitzbrown)

Novel by Kathleen Freeman

Gown and Shroud Macdonald 1947

Novel by Stuart Mary Wick

And Where's Mr. Bellamy? Hutchinson n.d. (1948); Ian Henry in 1976 as by Mary Fitt

Uncollected stories by Mary Fitt

'The Box of Coins' (*Detective Stories of Today*, Faber 1940)

'The Amethyst Cross' (*The Second Ghost Book*, Barrie 1952)

'The Doctor' (*The Third Ghost Book*, Barrie 1955)

'Highlight' (*Choice of Weapons*, Hodder & Stoughton 1958)

'A Dumb Friend' (*Choice of Weapons*)

'A Death in the Blackout' (radio play) (*Butcher's Dozen*, Heinemann 1956)

'Murder in Athens' (*LMM*, Oct. 1950)
'Mystery in Athens' (*LMM*, June 1951)
'Scandal in Athens' (*LMM*, Oct./Nov. 1951)

BP

Joan Fleming (1908–1980)

Joan Fleming wrote thirty-three novels and seven stories. She is an underrated author, whose great variety of style and content embraces both the traditional detective story and the modern psychological crime novel. She created one series character, the Turkish philosopher Nuri Izkirlak, who features in two books.

Joan Fleming's books were all first published in London. Five titles have not appeared in the USA. *Grim Death and the Barrow Boys* and *You Won't Let Me Finish* have alternative titles in America. Two books, *The Man Who Looked Back* and *The Deeds of Dr. Deadcert*, were republished by Hamish Hamilton with different titles.

The first eight books were published by Hutchinson and, with the exception of the first two in the series, are all dated. *Two Lovers Too Many* has turquoise cloth with the spine lettered in blue. Hutchinson is named in blue across the lower right-hand corner of the front cover. The title-page states that this is Number 134 in the First Novel Library. Ley Kenyon's design for the wrapper shows Dr Alastair Southery in his surgical gown, pulling on his theatre gloves, with the village of Lavister in the background. *A Daisy-chain for Satan* was issued in black cloth, with the spine lettered gilt, and with the publisher's name diagonally across the lower right-hand corner of the front cover, this time gilt. Copies with brown cloth and the spine lettered in yellow or black are later issues. The wrapper is illustrated by a circular daisy chain, in which the lower semicircle of flowers drips blood.

The Gallows in My Garden has green cloth with black lettering on the spine, which also has a black hangman's noose. Barton's clever wrapper design has Startlewood and its grounds seen through a railway tunnel, with a white gallows standing by the track. The brown cloth of *The Man Who Looked Back* is lettered gilt on the spine, again with the hangman's noose, also gilt. *Polly Put the Kettle On* and *The Good and the Bad* are black, with silver spine lettering. The former has a wrapper design by S. Hughes, showing the body of Eli Edge lying on a sofa, with two of his cats for company. *He Ought to Be Shot* has red cloth, with black spine lettering. The noose recurs in black on the spine. *The Deeds of Dr. Deadcert* is black with silver spine lettering. The last three Hutchinson titles have unattractive wrappers designed by Stein.

The bulk of Joan Fleming's remaining novels was published by Collins Crime Club, whose books are all dated. They all have red cloth, with spines lettered black to *Death of a Sardine* and gilt from *The Chill and the Kill*. William Randell's design of blind Mr Totterdell, holding a black Pekingese and carrying a white stick, features on the wrapper of *You Can't Believe Your Eyes*. For *Malice Matrimonial*, the same artist drew the head and shoulders of Pia Paolomi in her wedding veil. John Rose's designs for the two Nuri Izkirlak books are dominated, both on the spine and the front panel, by a skull wearing a Turkish fez. *No Bones About It* and *Kill or Cure* are decorated by two of Kenneth Farnhill's very modern designs. The later Collins wrappers are all of the modern photographic type.

The three books published by Hamish Hamilton all have historical settings. They are all dated and have gilt spine lettering. In sequence, they are grey, red and turquoise. The top edges of *Screams from a Penny Dreadful* and *Dirty Butter for Servants* are mauve and charcoal-grey, respectively. Jillian Willett created two excellent period designs for the wrappers of the first two in this series.

For first edition collectors, the most difficult title to locate is *A Daisy-chain for Satan*.

Novels

(with Izkirlak, as stated)

Two Lovers Too Many   Hutchinson n.d. (1949)
A Daisy-chain for Satan Hutchinson n.d. (1950), Doubleday 1951
The Gallows in My Garden   Hutchinson 1951

The Man Who Looked Back Hutchinson 1951, Doubleday 1952

a.k.a. *A Cup of Cold Poison* Hamish Hamilton 1969

Polly Put the Kettle On Hutchinson 1952

The Good and the Bad Hutchinson 1953, Doubleday 1953

He Ought to Be Shot Hutchinson 1955, Doubleday 1955

The Deeds of Dr. Deadcert Hutchinson 1955, Washburn 1957

a.k.a. *The Merry Widower* Hamish Hamilton 1975

You Can't Believe Your Eyes Collins Crime Club 1957, Washburn 1957

Maiden's Prayer Crime Club 1957, Washburn 1958

Malice Matrimonial Crime Club 1959, Washburn 1959

Miss Bones Crime Club 1959, Washburn 1960

The Man from Nowhere Crime Club 1960, Washburn 1961

In the Red Crime Club 1961, Washburn 1961

When I Grow Rich Crime Club 1962, Washburn 1962 (Izkirlak)

Death of a Sardine Crime Club 1963, Washburn 1964

The Chill and the Kill Crime Club 1964, Washburn 1964

Nothing is the Number When You Die Crime Club 1965, Washburn 1965 (Izkirlak)

Midnight Hag Crime Club 1966, Washburn 1966

No Bones About It Crime Club 1967, Washburn 1967

Kill or Cure Crime Club 1968, Washburn 1968

Hell's Belle Crime Club 1968, Washburn 1969

Young Man, I Think You're Dying Crime Club 1970, Putnam 1970

Screams from a Penny Dreadful Hamish Hamilton 1971

Grim Death and the Barrow Boys Crime Club 1971

a.k.a. *Be a Good Boy* Putnam 1971

Dirty Butter for Servants Hamish Hamilton 1972

Alas, Poor Father Crime Club 1972, Putnam 1973

You Won't Let Me Finish Crime Club 1973

a.k.a. *You Won't Let Me Finnish* Putnam 1974

How to Live Dangerously Crime Club 1974, Putnam 1975

Too Late! Too Late! The Maiden Cried Hamish Hamilton 1975, Putnam 1975

... To Make an Underworld Crime Club 1976, Putnam 1976

Every Inch a Lady Crime Club 1977, Putnam 1977

The Day of the Donkey Derby Crime Club 1978, Putnam 1978

Uncollected stories

'The Graduate' (*LMM*, Oct.–Nov. 1950)

'Writer's Witch' (*LMM*, June 1951)

'Gone is Gone' (*ES*, 23 Apr. 1953; *EQMM*, Apr. 1970, as 'Dead and Gone')

'Boo to a Goose' (*LMM*, Sept. 1955)

'Cat on the Trail of a Wife Killer' (*ES*, 12 Mar. 1963; *Saint*, Aug. 1964 (UK), as 'Cat on the Trail')

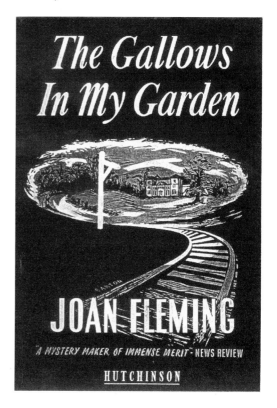

'Still Waters' (*Winter's Crimes 1*, Macmillan 1969, St Martin's 1969)

'The Bore' (*Winter's Crimes 4*, Macmillan 1972)

Novella with other writers (see under 'Detection Club')

Crime on the Coast Gollancz 1984 (with *No Flowers by Request*)   JC

Leslie Ford (1898–1983)
a.k.a. David Frome

Leslie Ford and David Frome were pseudonyms of Mrs Zenith Brown. As Leslie Ford, she wrote a long series of sophisticated whodunits set among American high society, often in Washington. Sixteen novels feature the bachelor Colonel John Primrose and/or the widowed Grace Latham, good friends who might one day marry. Two novels feature Lt Joseph Kelly of the Baltimore Division of Detectives, whose 'Sunday-suited, automobile-mechanic manner and appearance' mask a shrewd and assured competence. Twelve books have no series character and a thirteenth both does and does not: Ellen Nehr names the detective in *The Sound of Footsteps* as Major Heath but in his British incarnation, in *Footsteps on the Stairs*, he is Major Matthew Gregory Lewis, who derives his name from the author of *The Monk* and also appears in three David Frome novels.

David Frome's career began in 1929, two years before Leslie Ford's début. Besides the three Lewis titles and a single non-series novel, there are eleven books about meek Mr Pinkerton and stolid Inspector Bull, set in England, mildly comic in tone and more traditional than the Primrose-Latham series. Altogether, Mrs Brown published forty-six crime novels, now unfairly neglected. She was a skilled professional, who made excellent use of her considerable talents.

Apart from the first and second Frome titles, it appears that all Mrs Brown's books first appeared in America. No detailed description of her US editions is known and what follows touches on the question only. There are many title-changes between America and Britain: also, the second Frome novel was published only in Britain and four Ford titles appeared only in America.

Footsteps on the Stairs was published by Gollancz in 1931 in a black binding with orange lettering on the spine. The book is dated on the title-page and there are two preliminary plans of Monckton Hall. The first Kelly novel was published by Hutchinson in 1933: *Murder in Maryland*, in a pale-blue binding with black lettering on the spine. The book is undated except for an extensive advertisement section at the rear, dated Spring 1933. The second Kelly novel and the first (solo) appearance of Col. Primrose were not published in Britain, but *Burn Forever*, a non-series novel, was published by Hutchinson, as *Mountain Madness*. The binding is black with gilt/yellow lettering on the spine and the book is undated except by an advertisement section dated Autumn 1935 at the end.

For the rest of her British career Leslie Ford was published by Collins' Crime Club (except for *Old Lover's Ghost*, not issued in Britain). All the books have the standard Crime Club features: orange/red binding, black lettering on the spine, the date only on the copyright page (often only in the copyright notice). From *Ill Met by Moonlight* to *A Capital Crime* the books have advertisements at the rear: so do *Crack of Dawn*, *The Philadelphia Murder Story*, *Murder is the Pay-off* and *The Bahamas Murder Case*. *Road to Folly* and *Snow-white Murder* have the Crime Club gunman facing to the right on their title-pages. *Ill Met by Moonlight* has a preliminary double-page map of April Harbor on Chesapeake Bay. *Snow-white Murder* appeared out of sequence in Britain. *Murder Down South* is dated 1942 but *ECB* states that it was published in January 1943. From several known titles it appears likely that most of Leslie Ford's Scribner first editions have the same binding pattern: a neutral base with bold bands and stripes in a single colour, used also for the lettering on both spine and front cover (see checklist for colours where known). *Old Lover's Ghost* and *The Murder of a Fifth Columnist* have matching top edges. The binding and lettering of *Murder Comes to Eden* alternate black and yellow. All known Scribner titles have a dated title-page and a capital *A* under the copyright notice. *All For* the *Love of a Lady* also has a 'wartime book' motif. *The Murder of a Fifth Columnist* is so named internally throughout the book, but the external title is *The Murder of the Fifth Columnist*.

The first Frome book is *In at the Death*, a dark-blue book lettered in black and with double rules in black at each end of the spine. The front cover has title and author in black and a blind-stamped border. The book is undated except by an extended advertisement section at the rear, for Spring 1929. The publisher is Skeffington. Major Lewis appears for the first time here and recurs in two of the three Methuen titles that follow: *The Murder of an Old Man* and *The Murder on the Sixth Hole*. Both have black lettering on the spine and title and author in black on the front cover. Each spine has double rules at top and bottom and each cover has a single black border. Both books are dated on the copyright page and have printer's codes at the end, after advertisement sections: 229 and 331, respectively. The former has a pale-brown binding and front endpapers decorated by Frank Adams with a meticulous map of Ashingdene Manor and its neighbourhood. The latter has a yellow binding. In its American edition, with the variant title *The Strange Death of Martin Green*, it also has a plan of the South River and the South Forest Golf Course, but this does not figure in the Methuen version.

The Hammersmith Murders introduces Evan Pinkerton, the nervous Welsh rabbit. It is dated on the copyright page and also by the printer's code 1229 at the end, after an advertisement section. The binding is red, the lettering black, with title and author on the front cover, which also has a single black border.

From 1932 to 1939, David Frome was published in Britain by Longmans, in a uniform format, though in varying colours (see checklist). Besides the standard spine lettering, each book has the title at the top of the front cover and the author's name in the lower right corner. Except for the dark-red/purple lettering of *The By-pass Murder* all the books have black lettering. The five books to *Arsenic at Richmond* are dated on the title-page, the others on the copyright page. *The Guilt is Plain* has a preliminary plan of the Royal Pavilion at Brighton.

The last Pinkerton novel was published by Hale in 1951 as *Murder on the Square*, in a black binding with green lettering and a silver pistol on the spine and with no indication of the date (BL 16 August 1951, *ECB* September 1951). The American true first, *Homicide House*, has a dark-blue binding with silver lettering on the spine and dated copyright page.

The Strange Death of Martin Green has the standard black binding, orange lettering and red endpapers of the Doubleday Crime Club at the time of publication. The front cover has the title and the Crime Club gunman in orange and each endpaper has the gunman centrally, in white. The book is dated by the copyright notice and states 'First edition'. The plan of the golf course and river appears opposite the title-page. At least three of the original Farrar & Rinehart editions have illustrations by Edward Calman: *Mr. Pinkerton Goes to Scotland Yard/Grows a Beard/Has the Clue*. All three books have neutral bindings somewhere between yellow and grey, lettered on the spine and front cover (red with decoration for *Beard*, plain dark green for the others). Coloured top edges match the lettering and the other edges are roughly trimmed. All are dated by the copyright notice only. In two cases, the opening pages of the novel immediately preceding appear at the end as a lure: *Beard* has two pages of *Mr. Pinkerton Finds a Body* and *Clue* has four pages of *Mr. Pinkerton Grows a Beard*.

The green dust-wrapper for the Scribner *Road to Folly* features a woman, with menacing hands reaching towards her. The British edition has a blue wrapper lettered red and white, with a photograph of the author. *Old Lover's Ghost* has a brownish-purple wrapper showing a woman flitting through trees in Yellowstone Park. *A Capital Crime* illustrates the collision with a telegraph pole of an open red car containing two young men. Barschel's blue wrapper for *Murder in the O.P.M.* shows a boat on the Georgetown Canal, with broken patches of ice and, on the spine, Lawrason Hillyard's hat. Several later Crime Club wrappers have attractive designs, including Stead's newsboy for *The Philadelphia*

Murder Story; Robert Pimlott's black face among green leaves for *Honolulu Murder Story*; the handsome portrait of *The Woman in Black*; and Molly Brent's attempt to defenestrate herself for *The Lying Jade*.

The wrapper for the Doubleday edition of *The Hammersmith Murders* features a skeleton holding a message announcing a murder in Caithness Road. Calman's wrapper for the US edition of *Mr. Pinkerton has the Clue* shows the little man scuttling through Bath. The British edition also features Mr Pinkerton, this time staring in alarm at a figure at the window, while Major Peyton dozes nearby. *The Eel Pie Mystery* shows the stretch of the Thames enclosing Eel Pie Island. *Body in the Turl* offers a stylised view of a prone corpse with an open umbrella beneath a street lamp. *The Body in Bedford Square* puts a supine body beside a car and has a policeman shine his torch on it. *Murder on the Square* has an attractive wrapper by Sax, with Mr Pinkerton on a bench in Godolphin Square with a young woman beside him and Caroline Winship glaring down from an upper window in the house behind them.

Zenith Brown's stories include several that were expanded into novels (or, perhaps, were condensed from novels): 'The Strangled Witness' and 'The Black Envelope' are versions of the novels with the same titles and 'Mr. Pinkerton is Present' and 'Visitor in the Night' correspond to *Mr. Pinkerton has the Clue* and *Mr. Pinkerton at the Old Angel*, respectively. Six other titles appear to exist independently of the full-length works; and of these, 'Passage for One' is listed by Hubin as a separately published item. 'Death Stops at a Tourist Camp' was the leading story in a volume of The Saint Mystery Library. 'The Collapsing Clues' is a true-crime piece and three later titles from 'American Weekly' in 1954 (listed by Reilly) may also be true-crime. *EMD* states that Grace Latham and Colonel Primrose 'had previously appeared in several novelettes published in magazines'. Reilly lists three novels by 'Brenda Conrad' published in the war years by Scribner and two Ford novels serialised in *Collier's Magazine*: 'Story of Jenny Wingate' (Feb.-Mar. 1945) and 'Jealousy' (Apr. 1946). All these are clearly ripe for investigation.

Novels by Leslie Ford

(Colours refer to US editions.)

The Sound of Footsteps   Doubleday 1931
a.k.a. *Footsteps on the Stairs*   Gollancz June 1931 (Lewis)
By the Watchman's Clock   Farrar & Rinehart 1932
Murder in Maryland   Farrar 1932, Hutchinson n.d. (January 1933) (Kelly)
The Clue of the Judas Tree   Farrar 1933 (Kelly)
The Strangled Witness   Farrar 1934 (Primrose)
Burn Forever   Farrar 1935
a.k.a. *Mountain Madness*   Hutchinson n.d. (October 1935)
Ill Met by Moonlight   Farrar 1937, Crime Club July 1937 (Primrose, Latham)
The Simple Way of Poison   Farrar 1937, Crime Club March 1938 (Primrose, Latham)
Three Bright Pebbles   Farrar 1938, Crime Club April 1939 (Latham)
Reno Rendezvous   Farrar 1939 (Primrose, Latham)
a.k.a. *Mr Cromwell is Dead*   Crime Club June 1939
False to Any Man   Scribner July 1939 (Primrose, Latham) (blue)
a.k.a. *Snow-white Murder*   Crime Club June 1940
The Town Cried Murder   Scribner October 1939 (dark red-brown) Crime Club November 1939
Road to Folly   Scribner 1940, Crime Club May 1941 (light green)
Old Lover's Ghost   Scribner 1940 (Primrose, Latham) (maroon)
The Murder of a Fifth Columnist   Scribner 1941 (Primrose, Latham) (orange)
a.k.a. *A Capital Crime*   Crime Club August 1941
Murder with Southern Hospitality   Scribner 1942
a.k.a. *Murder Down South*   Crime Club 1942 (January 1943)
Murder in the O.P.M.   Scribner 1942 (Primrose, Latham) (purple)
a.k.a. *Priority Murder*   Crime Club July 1943

Siren in the Night Scribner 1943, Crime Club March 1944 (dark blue) (Primrose, Latham)

All for the Love of a Lady Scribner 1944 (Primrose, Latham) (red)

a.k.a. *Crack of Dawn* Crime Club February 1945

The Philadelphia Murder Story Scribner 1945, Crime Club August 1945 (dark brown) (Primrose, Latham)

Honolulu Story Scribner 1946 (Primrose, Latham)

a.k.a. *Honolulu Murder Story* Crime Club April 1947

a.k.a. *Honolulu Murder* Popular Library 1967

The Woman in Black Scribner 1947, Crime Club January 1948 (Primrose, Latham)

The Devil's Stronghold Scribner 1948, Crime Club December 1948 (Primrose, Latham)

Date with Death Scribner 1949 (dark red)

a.k.a. *Shot in the Dark* Crime Club September 1949

Murder is the Pay-off Scribner 1951, Crime Club November 1951

The Bahamas Murder Case Scribner 1952, Crime Club November 1952

Washington Whispers Murder Scribner 1953 (Primrose, Latham)

a.k.a. *The Lying Jade* Crime Club August 1953

Invitation to Murder Scribner 1954, Crime Club April 1955

Murder comes to Eden Scribner 1955, Crime Club August 1956

The Girl from the Mimosa Club Scribner 1957, Crime Club November 1957

Trial by Ambush Scribner 1962

a.k.a. *Trial from Ambush* Crime Club June 1962

Novels by David Frome

(with Pinkerton and Bull, except where stated. Binding colours refer to British editions.)

In at the Death Skeffington n.d. (May 1929), Longman (New York) 1930 (Lewis)

The Murder of an Old Man Methuen August 1929 (Lewis)

The Hammersmith Murders Doubleday 1930, Methuen 1930

The Strange Death of Martin Green Doubleday January 1931 (Lewis)

a.k.a. *The Murder on the Sixth Hole* Methuen May 1931

Two Against Scotland Yard Farrar & Rinehart 1931

a.k.a. *The By-pass Murder* Longmans, Green September 1932 (grey)

The Man from Scotland Yard Farrar 1932

a.k.a. *Mr. Simpson finds a Body* Longman February 1933 (orange)

The Eel Pie Murders Farrar 1933

a.k.a. *The Eel Pie Mystery* Longman September 1933 (blue)

Scotland Yard Can Wait! Farrar 1933 (non-series)

a.k.a. *'That's Your Man, Inspector'* Longman February 1934 (orange)

Mr. Pinkerton goes to Scotland Yard Farrar 1934

a.k.a. *Arsenic in Richmond* Longman September 1934 (red)

Mr. Pinkerton finds a Body Farrar 1934

a.k.a. *Body in the Turl* Longman March 1935 (orange)

Mr. Pinkerton Grows a Beard Farrar 1935

a.k.a. *The Body in Bedford Square* Longman September 1935 (red)

Mr. Pinkerton has the Clue Farrar 1936, Longman November 1936 (blue)

The Black Envelope Farrar 1937

a.k.a. *The Guilt is Plain* Longman January 1938 (orange)

Mr. Pinkerton at the Old Angel Farrar 1939

a.k.a. *Mr. Pinkerton and the Old Angel* Longman October 1939 (blue-green)

Homicide House Rinehart 1950

a.k.a. *Murder on the Square* Hale n.d. (September 1951)

Pinkerton story by David Frome

(separately published)

Mr. Pinkerton: Passage for One Royce 1945

Stories by Leslie Ford

'The Strangled Witness' (*American Magazine*, May 1934; *Saint*, Mar. 1954/Mar. 1959) (Primrose)

'The Clock Strikes' (*American Magazine*, May 1935; *The Second Mystery Book* Farrar 1940; *EQMM*, Jun. 1970 & *EQA*, Fall-Winter 1975, Davis 1975 as 'The Supreme Court Murder') (Primrose)

'Death Stops at a Tourist Camp' (*American Magazine*, Apr. 1936; *Story-teller*, Sept. 1936 as 'The Bridge Camp Mystery'; *The Mystery Book*, Farrar 1939; *Saint*, Oct, 1955/Apr. 1956; *The Saint Mystery Library No. 7*, Great American Publishing 1959)

'Farewell Party' (*Pictorial Review*, Feb. 1938; *The Third Mystery Book*, Farrar 1941)

Pinkerton stories by David Frome

'Policeman's Cape' (*ES*, 20 Aug. 1936; *Fifty Famous Detectives of Fiction*, Odhams n.d. (1938); *The Third Mystery Book*, Farrar 1941; *EQMM*, Dec. 1953 & *Masterpieces of Mystery, The Golden Age II*, Davis 1977 as 'The Man on the Iron Palings')

'Mr. Pinkerton is Present' (*American Magazine*, Oct. 1936)

'Mr. Pinkerton Lends a Hand' (1936; *The Second Mystery Book*, Farrar 1940)

'The Black Envelope' (*American Magazine*, July 1937)

'Visitor in the Night' (*American Magazine*, July 1939)   *BP*

Anthea Fraser (b. 1930)

Anthea Fraser is a relative newcomer to crime fiction, who has also written several supernatural novels. With her second crime novel she began a series set in the county of Broadshire, and featuring her two series detectives, the tall, dignified Chief Inspector David Webb and the short, cheeky Sergeant Kenneth Jackson. Together they present an unnerving combination for criminals venturing into the territory of the Shillingham CID.

Home Through the Dark was published by Milton House, in a flecked burgundy cloth with the spine lettered gilt. The dust-wrapper design by Alec Davis shows a red rose and a gold ring on the front cover, while the back cover has a torch with the light shining from it on to the publisher's colophon at the base of the spine. The background for both covers is black. The rest of Anthea Fraser's crime fiction has been published by Collins Crime Club, in red cloth with gilt lettering on the spine, and in unremarkable photographic wrappers.

All eleven books are dated. From *The April Rainers* they became taller. The titles of six books come from the traditional ballad 'Green Grow the Rushes-O'. There are also two stories.

Novels

(with Webb, except as stated)

Home Through the Dark Milton House 1974, Dodd, Mead 1976 (not Webb)

A Shroud for Delilah Collins Crime Club 1984, Doubleday 1986

A Necessary End Crime Club 1985, Walker 1986

Pretty Maids All in a Row Crime Club 1986, Doubleday 1987

Death Speaks Softly Crime Club 1987, Doubleday 1987

The Nine Bright Shiners Crime Club 1987

Six Proud Walkers Crime Club 1988, Doubleday 1989

The April Rainers Crime Club 1989, Doubleday 1990

Symbols at your Door Crime Club 1990, Doubleday 1991

The Lily-white Boys Crime Club 1991
Three, Three, the Rivals Crime Club 1992

Stories

'Nemesis' (*A Suit of Diamonds*, Crime Club 1990)

'Turning Point' (*2nd Culprit*, Chatto and Windus 1993)   *JC*

Antonia Fraser (b. 1932)

Lady Antonia Fraser is one of the Pakenham/Longford family of writers, and she is married to Harold Pinter. Her special achievement as a crime writer is the creation of Jemima Shore, a television journalist with a high degree of control over her own life. Though single, she is far from celibate, using men in the time-honoured tradition of the male sex, for sexual pleasure without commitment. She moves in expensive, modish circles, fastidiously sniffing out privileged killers under threat. The lower orders are little in evidence. After two trial runs, the author found her form with *A Splash of Red*, achieving, as Christopher Wordsworth said, a narrative 'delicious with sinister promise'.

Her earlier books were published by Weidenfeld & Nicolson in Britain and are all dated, with gilt lettering on the spine. *Quiet as a Nun* and *The Wild Island* are blue-green; *A Splash of Red* is red; *Cool Repentance* is blue; *Oxford Blood* and *Jemima Shore's First Case* are orange-brown; and *Your Royal Hostage* is dark red. All except the last have wrappers by Mary French, who tends to focus on the victims: Filly Lennox floating face downwards in the sea off Larmouth; Bim Marcus dead at the foot of Staircase 13 at Rochester College; Sybilla lying in the central aisle of the chapel at Blessed Eleanor's Convent. *Quiet as a Nun* has a nun from the convent clutching a rosary and looking distraught; but *The Wild Island* is more cheerful, with a commanding view of Castle Beauregard and the Red Rose of the Scottish freedom fighters. For *Your Royal Hostage*, Judith Lawton displays the scene at Covent Garden after *Otello*, with Princess Amy and Prince Ferdinand in the royal box and an ominous cloud over the stalls.

The more recent books have appeared from Bloomsbury. Both *The Cavalier Case* and *Jemima Shore at the Sunny Grave* are excessively large blue books, lettered gilt on the spine. Each front cover has the author's initials and four stars, all in gilt. The endpapers are dark blue and the books are dated on the copyright page. Both books have blue ribbon page-markers attached to the top of the spine. The novel has a black wrapper with a distorted image of the portrait of Decimus Meredith at Lackland Court. The collection has a large illuminated house, in spacious grounds with palm trees, under a stormy sky.

Inspector Portsmouth appears with Jemima on occasion and also, solo, in the story 'Dead Leaves' (in *Sunny Grave*). *Jemima Shore Investigates* is an earlier collection of stories, a paperback original deriving from the Thames TV series in which Patricia Hodge was Jemima to the life. The seven stories are written by Frances Heasman and John Burke, from original scripts by Simon Brett and others. Lady Antonia contributes an introduction, 'Investigating Jemima'.

Shore novels

Quiet as a Nun   Weidenfeld & Nicolson 1977, Viking 1977
The Wild Island   Weidenfeld 1978, Norton 1978
A Splash of Red   Weidenfeld 1981, Norton 1982
Cool Repentance   Weidenfeld 1982, Norton 1983
Oxford Blood   Weidenfeld 1985, Norton 1985
Your Royal Hostage   Weidenfeld 1987, Atheneum 1988
The Cavalier Case   Bloomsbury 1990, Bantam 1991

Story collections

Jemima Shore Investigates   Thames Methuen 1983 (7 stories), by Frances Heasman and John Burke from the TV series of the same name, with an introduction by Antonia Fraser
Jemima Shore's First Case   Weidenfeld 1986, Norton 1987 (13 stories, 5 with Shore)
Jemima Shore at the Sunny Grave   Bloomsbury 1991, (9 stories, 4 with Shore) Bantam 1993

Uncollected stories

'The Man Who Wiped the Smile Off Her Face' (*The Man Who . . .* , Macmillan 1992) (non-series)
'The Bottle Dungeon' (*Midwinter Mysteries 2*, Little, Brown 1992)
'Jemima Shore and the Frightened Girl' (*2nd Culprit*, Chatto & Windus 1993)   *BP*

James Fraser (b. 1924)

The James Fraser novels are idiosyncratic village mysteries written by Alan White, whose primary reputation is as a tough adventure novelist. He is an arresting writer, with a vivid, distinctive style, sturdy narrative gifts, and exceptional powers of contrivance. Though set in close-knit rural communities, his books are a long way from St Mary Mead. Much of their content arises from erotic tensions, and the author's exploration of sexual personality gives his work a special intensity. The detective throughout is Bill Aveyard, a high-flying young bachelor policeman, whose career undergoes two setbacks in the course of the series, both, of course, properly surmounted.

The books were published initially by Herbert Jenkins alone and by Barrie and Jenkins from *Death in a Pheasant's Eye* in 1971. They are very attractive, and take the eye when ranged on the shelf. *The Evergreen Death* has a sage-green binding, and the rest are maroon or black: after *A Cockpit of Roses*, which is maroon, and *Deadly Nightshade*, which is black, there are three maroon books in succession and three black. All the spines are lettered in gilt and the entire series is dated. From *The Evergreen Death* to *A Wreath of Lords and Ladies*, the books have meticulous maps of the various villages,

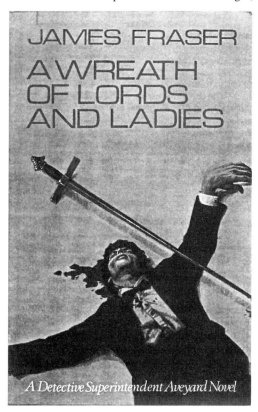

JAMES FRASER
A WREATH OF LORDS AND LADIES

A Detective Superintendent Aveyard Novel

generally on the rear panels of the wrappers, but as preliminaries for the two at the end of the sequence.

The wrappers are an enticing feature of the books and vividly enhance their appeal. Those for *The Evergreen Death* and *A Cockpit of Roses* show Linda Bugbrooke and Betty McClune lying dead, Linda beneath Colonel Innes' shrubbery, Betty amid Peter Marchmont's roses. *Death in a Pheasant's Eye* has a vigorous representation of the Guy Fawkes bonfire at Ulton, with the body burning upon it. Later wrappers are attributed to Barbara Walton, who illustrates the works concerned most eloquently. For *The Five-leafed Clover* she shows Sarah Howe's body floating in the pond at Morton Waterville, with the crows circling overhead. Her designs for *A Wreath of Lords and Ladies* and *Who Steals My Name* are especially fine and extend over both covers. On the front panel of the former, Rupert Samuel lies dead, with the sword which killed him by his side; and the rear panel gives a spacious view of Bushden Hall, with the lords and ladies growing in the grounds. The latter has the scene in the club room at Mawsley Hall, with Cedric Mawsley slumped in one chair and Constable Baron dead in the other, with the blood still running down his neck. The final design in the sequence, which is unattributed, features an austere grey effigy from the Inigo Jones mausoleum at Bollaston Grange.

Aveyard novels

The Evergreen Death Jenkins 1968, Harcourt 1969

A Cockpit of Roses Jenkins 1969, Harcourt 1970

Deadly Nightshade Jenkins 1970, Harcourt 1970

Death in a Pheasant's Eye Barrie & Jenkins 1971, Walker 1972

Blood on a Widow's Cross Barrie & Jenkins 1972

The Five-leafed Clover Barrie & Jenkins 1973

A Wreath of Lords and Ladies Barrie & Jenkins 1974, Doubleday 1975

Who Steals My Name Barrie & Jenkins 1976, Doubleday 1976

Hearts Ease in Death Barrie & Jenkins 1977, Doubleday 1977 *BP*

R. Austin Freeman (1862–1943)
a.k.a. Clifford Ashdown (jointly with J. J. Pitcairn)

R. Austin Freeman's innovative approach to crime fiction ensures his classic status. He devised the format of the inverted story, where the interest arises from the detection of a criminal already known; and he created a credible forensic detective, whose methods and results still bear expert scrutiny. Dr John Thorndyke is a commanding, even awesome, figure with expert knowledge in many fields. He appears in twenty-one novels and forty stories, collected in six volumes of which one, *The Great Portrait Mystery*, is a mixed collection with two Thorndyke items. Outside the Thorndyke canon, four episodic novels are generally included in Freeman's crime fiction, though only *The Uttermost Farthing*, rejected by Hodder & Stoughton as 'a horrible book', is wholeheartedly criminous. Each of the other three titles involves a dubious central figure in a series of raffish adventures: *The Exploits of Danby Croker, The Surprising Experiences of Mr. Shuttlebury Cobb* and *Flighty Phyllis*. It seems a moot point whether these are regarded as novels or collections of stories. *The Mystery of 31, New Inn* and *The Shadow of the Wolf*, both Thorndyke novels, first appeared as novellas, the latter in two parts in *Pearson's* for Oct. and Nov. 1912 as 'The Dead Hand'. The uncollected stories include a further adventure for Professor Humphrey Challoner of *The Uttermost Farthing*: 'The Mystery of Hoo Marsh'.

Before launching the Thorndyke series, Freeman collaborated with a medical colleague, John James Pitcairn, on three series of stories, published in *Cassell's Family Magazine* between 1902 and 1905. The first and second of these involve a rogue named Romney Pringle and the third has a medical protagonist. Only *The Adventures of Romney Pringle* became a book, published by Ward Lock in 1902. The others were forgotten until the 1970s when Oswald Train published *The Further Adventures of Romney Pringle* and George Locke issued *From*

A Surgeon's Diary. Train also published the first US editions of the other two collections (and the first edition of an Ashdown adventure novel, *The Queen's Treasure*). It seems established that Freeman paid to have *The Red Thumbmark* published and an obscure firm named Collingwood Bros. had the distinction of launching Dr Thorndyke on his career. The book has a black binding with white lettering on the spine and title and author in white on the front cover, which also has a large red thumbmark and two white leaves as decoration. According to the Freeman collector, P. M. Stone, part of the edition was bound in black wrappers, also with the thumbmark motif. The book is undated and has a black-and-white frontispiece by T. E. Francis of Drs Thorndyke and Jervis startled by the sound of breaking glass in John Street. The Collingwoods did Freeman proud.

Chatto & Windus published the first Thorndyke collection in 1909. *John Thorndyke's Cases* is a light brown book with gilt lettering on the spine, dated on the title-page. The front cover has the title in pinkish lettering edged with black and the author's name in black. In between is H. M. Brock's illustration for 'The Blue Sequin' of Edith Grant lying dead in the railway carriage at Woldhurst with two officials looking on. The drawing recurs opposite page 125 in black and white; on the cover it is pink on the pale brown. The artist also provided a frontispiece ('Professor Poppelbaum is enlightened') and four other full-page black-and-white illustrations; and there are a further nine illustrations 'from photographs etc.'. At the end is an extensive advertisement section with the printer's code 908.

The Eye of Osiris marks the beginning of Freeman's association with Hodder & Stoughton, who published this and all subsequent Thorndyke books, a sequence of twenty-five all told. Most of the books are blue but *The Singing Bone, A Silent Witness, The Mystery of Angelina Frood* and *The Shadow of the Wolf* are red, *Osiris* is brown and *The Mystery of 31, New Inn* and *The Cat's Eye* are green, the former dark, the latter light. Three novels are set apart by decorative features. *The Eye of Osiris* has the title in white and the author in black on the spine and front cover, in stylised lettering with the *E*s like *W*s laid sideways. The spine has a green border with a green rule crossing beneath the author's name. Within the larger lower segment so formed is an elegant, elongated green vase with brown decorative tracery and black horizontal bands, double at top and bottom, triple between the 'head' and the longer 'body'. Under this, within the border, is the publisher in green. The cover has a stylised representation of Osiris' wicked-looking eye. There is an undated advertisement section at the rear. According to the bookseller Frank Hollings, this binding was used for only 150 copies, retailing at 6/-. A more conventional binding is also known, brown with gilt lettering on the spine and title and author in black on the front cover (and also with advertisements at the end). This is described by Norman Donaldson in *In Search of Dr. Thorndyke* (Popular Press 1971) and is perhaps the 2/- edition issued in Feb. 1912.

The Mystery of 31, New Inn is dark green with gilt lettering on the spine and title and author in white on the front cover, which also has a blind-stamped border and a drawing in black of the entry to New Inn. Another version of this appears as a preliminary with Freeman's signature. *A Silent Witness* has gilt lettering on the spine and title and author in gilt on the front cover, which also has the reliquary found by Dr Jardine on its chain, stamped, like the lettering, in gilt.

The Hodder books before *A Silent Witness* also have gilt lettering on the spine, as do *A Certain Dr. Thorndyke* and *The Stoneware Monkey*. All the other Thorndyke books in the Hodder series have black lettering on the spine, *The Shadow of the Wolf* with blind-stamped rules at top and bottom, *The D'Arblay Mystery* and *Mr. Pottermack's Oversight* with slight black decoration, *Mr. Polton Explains* with all the lettering enclosed within a double black border towards the top of the spine.

Helen Vardon's Confession has a blind-stamped border on the front cover and so do the eight titles from *Angelina Frood* to *Mr. Pottermack's Oversight*. The front cover of *A Certain Dr. Thorndyke* is blank except for the border and the three titles from *The Stoneware Monkey*

have wholly blank covers. Otherwise all the Hodder titles have lettering on the front cover: as described for *The Eye of Osiris, 31, New Inn* and *A Silent Witness*; title and author in black on *The Singing Bone, The Great Portrait Mystery, Helen Vardon's Confession, Angelina Frood, The Puzzle Lock* and *The Shadow of the Wolf*; the title alone in black for all titles between *The D'Arblay Mystery* and *Felo De Se?*, except *A Certain Dr. Thorndyke*. Five books have Freeman's initials, in black with the F at the centre, in the lower right corner of the front cover: *The D'Arblay Mystery, The Magic Casket, As a Thief in the Night, Mr. Pottermack's Oversight* and *Pontifex, Son and Thorndyke*. *Dr. Thorndyke's Case-Book* and *The Cat's Eye* have title and author with a short rule between showing with the colour of the binding through a stamped black rectangle enclosed within a double black border. *The Great Portrait Mystery* has a black oval containing an X between title and author. The top edges of *The Penrose Mystery* and *Felo De Se?* are blue and these titles and *The Stoneware Monkey* have blue endpapers.

The Mystery of 31, New Inn is dated on the copyright page and *A Silent Witness* on the title-page. Otherwise all the Hodder titles to and including *Mr. Pottermack's Oversight* are undated (*Shuttlebury Cobb* and *Flighty Phyllis* as well as the Thorndyke series). *Pontifex, Son and Thorndyke* is dated on the title-page as are the three titles that follow it. The rest of the run, from *The Penrose Mystery*, have dated copyright pages. Like *The Eye of Osiris, The D'Arblay Mystery, The Magic Casket, A Certain Dr. Thorndyke, The Penrose Mystery, Felo De Se?* and *The Jacob Street Mystery* have advertisements at the end. Norman Donaldson also describes, besides the variant *Osiris*, alternative issues of *A Silent Witness, The Mystery of Angelina Frood, Mr. Pottermack's Oversight* and *Mr. Polton Explains*, all surely later than the true firsts. He cites a green binding for *Mr. Polton Explains* but Paul Moy records that green copies have inferior paper to the blue and the blank leaf before the rear endpaper present in the blue edition is lacking in the green. *The Cat's Eye* has opposite the title-page an illustration of Mr

Halliburton's mascot and other items. *The Puzzle Lock* has Mr Luttrell's seal as frontispiece and *The Stoneware Monkey* has the pottery figure aptly described by Thorndyke as 'particularly hideous'.

According to Allen Hubin, the Dodd, Mead edition of *The Shadow of the Wolf* appeared in September 1925, thus preceding the British edition which came out in October. Norman Donaldson describes this edition as black with a red top edge, red lettering on the spine and front cover and dated title-page. The front cover also has a blind-stamped device (unspecified). Two of the four non-series titles are also Hodder books. *The Surprising Experiences of Mr. Shuttlebury Cobb* is a brown book with black lettering on the spine, the author's name dividing the curves of a yellow oval. The front cover has title and author in black over a representation of a mermaid with a looking-glass, within a decorative framework. Beneath this is the publisher within a black rectangular block. The mermaid recurs opposite the title-page, where she is signed by the author. The copyright page shows previous publications and the book is undated. Advertisements at the rear include one for *Shuttlebury Cobb* at 3/6d (the correct price according to *ECB*). *Flighty Phyllis* has a blue binding with black lettering on the spine and black decoration at either end. The front cover has title and author in black over a black silhouette of a woman, presumably Phyllis, entering a taxi. Beneath this the publisher shows blue through a black rectangular block. This book, too, is undated.

The Uttermost Farthing appeared in America in 1914, having been rejected by Hodder & Stoughton. It is a most striking book with a red binding, gilt lettering on the spine and title and author in gilt on the front cover. The spine is decorated with a pattern of four squares framing a fifth containing a smiling face, all in gilt. This recurs on the front cover as the centrepiece of an expanded pattern of twenty-four squares containing the shrunken heads of Humphrey Challoner's victims. The effect is altogether remarkable. The book has a frontispiece by H. Weston Taylor showing the moment where Professor Challoner finds his wife dead on the hearth-

rug. There are three further illustrations. The book is dated on the copyright page. A British edition, described by Donaldson and in the BL, appeared six years later: a small red book with black lettering and a column of blind-stamped decoration on the spine. The front cover has a border enclosing an elaborate framework within which nestle title and author, all blind-stamped. The title-page is decorated and the copyright page states 'First cheap edition 1920': despite this, the book has gained some acceptance as the true British first. At the end are pages of advertisement for Pelmanism.

The Exploits of Danby Croker was published by Duckworth in 1916 in a red binding with gilt lettering on the spine and blind-stamped lettering and a blind-stamped border on the front cover. It is dated on the copyright page and has advertisements at the rear. The back cover has the publisher's device blind-stamped. Donaldson omits both the border and the device at the rear.

The wrapper of *The Eye of Osiris* has the stylised eye and ornate lettering of the decorated cover and that for *The Mystery of 31, New Inn* likewise reflects the cover of the book. *Shuttlebury Cobb* shows an elegant mermaid with flowing hair holding up an ornamental box. *The Great Portrait Mystery* has an artist at his easel within the outline of a palette. *Helen Vardon's Confession* has Ellen Edwards' elegant period portrait of Helen Vardon looking cowed. *Pontifex, Son and Thorndyke* shows Dr Thorndyke reading a document, with a boy pushing a barrow and a hansom cab in the background. *When Rogues Fall Out* presents a thoughtful-looking judge, both on the spine and the front panel, and *Dr. Thorndyke Intervenes* has a cross-looking barrister about to read a book with the aid of a magnifying lens. *For the Defence: Dr. Thorndyke* depicts the scene where the body from the foot of the cliff is transferred from the seaweed cart to the police stretcher. *The Stoneware Monkey* has a blue wrapper with the figure from the frontispiece seen from a different angle. *Mr. Polton Explains* has a wrapper design by Freeman himself, depicting an elaborately ornamental clock with a swinging pendulum. *The Penrose Mystery* and *Felo De Se?* have plain lettered wrappers.

The Adventures of Romney Pringle is a blue book with gilt lettering on the spine and title and author in gilt on the front cover, above and below a drawing in white relief of Romney Pringle at work with a lens and mirror on the blotter used by Julius Schillinghammer, in 'The Chicago Heiress'. This recurs in expanded form and in black and white opposite page 79. The artist Fred Pegram also provided a frontispiece and two further illustrations. The book is dated on the title-page and there are advertisements at the rear. Norman Donaldson also records a red binding, confirmed by Robert Adey. The Further Adventures of Romney Pringle has a red binding with gilt lettering on the spine, attributing the book to Freeman and Pitcairn, though Clifford Ashdown gets his due on the title-page. The book is dated 1969 but did not appear until 1970. The preliminaries are an introduction by August Derleth and a 'retrospect' by Norman Donaldson.

From a Surgeon's Diary is a tall blue paperback of 56 pages, unlettered on the spine and dated on the title-page. It was issued in a limited edition of 500 copies, reproducing the original text from Cassell's and illustrated by P. B. Hickling with a cover illustration, a frontispiece, a title-page vignette and ten illustrations in the text.

Freeman also published in magazines some twenty stories that remain uncollected. Most of these appear to be other than criminous: some are emotional melodramas, others deal with Thames watermen, perhaps in imitation of W. W. Jacobs. 'A Suburban Autolycus' (Cassell's Family Magazine, Nov. 1904) is a neat story about an incompetent burglar but not a mystery. 'By the Black Deep' (Windsor Magazine, Apr. 1903) was written with 'Ashdown Piers', probably, though not necessarily, John J. Pitcairn.

Thorndyke novels

The Red Thumbmark   Collingwood n.d. (1907), Newton 1911
The Eye of Osiris   Hodder & Stoughton n.d. (1911).
a.k.a. The Vanishing Man   Dodd, Mead 1912

The Mystery of 31, New Inn   Hodder Sept. 1912, Winston 1913
A Silent Witness   Hodder 1914, Winston 1915
Helen Vardon's Confession   Hodder n.d. (1922)
The Cat's Eye   Hodder n.d. (Sept. 1923), Dodd 1927
The Mystery of Angelina Frood   Hodder n.d. (1924), Dodd 1925
The Shadow of the Wolf   Dodd Sept. 1925, Hodder n.d. (Oct. 1925)
The D'Arblay Mystery   Hodder n.d. (1926), Dodd 1926
A Certain Dr. Thorndyke   Hodder n.d. (Oct. 1927), Dodd 1928
As a Thief in the Night   Hodder n.d. (Oct. 1928), Dodd 1928
Mr. Pottermack's Oversight   Hodder n.d. (1930), Dodd 1930
Pontifex, Son and Thorndyke   Hodder 1931, Dodd 1931
When Rogues Fall Out   Hodder 1932
a.k.a. Dr. Thorndyke's Discovery   Dodd 1932
Dr. Thorndyke Intervenes   Hodder 1933, Dodd 1933
For the Defence: Dr. Thorndyke   Hodder 1934, Dodd 1934
The Penrose Mystery   Hodder 1936, Dodd 1936
Felo De Se?   Hodder   1937
a.k.a. Death at the Inn   Dodd 1937
The Stoneware Monkey   Hodder 1938, Dodd 1939
Mr. Polton Explains   Hodder 1940, Dodd 1940
The Jacob Street Mystery   Hodder 1942
a.k.a. The Unconscious Witness   Dodd 1942

Story collections

John Thorndyke's Cases   Chatto & Windus 1909 (8 stories)
a.k.a. Dr. Thorndyke's Cases   Dodd 1931
The Singing Bone   Hodder n.d. (Feb. 1912), Dodd 1923 (5 stories)
a.k.a. The Adventures of Dr. Thorndyke   Popular Library 1947
The Great Portrait Mystery   Hodder n.d. (1918) (7 stories, 2 with Thorndyke)
Dr. Thorndyke's Case-book   Hodder n.d. (Apr. 1923) (7 stories)
a.k.a. The Blue Scarab   Dodd 1924

The Puzzle Lock Hodder n.d. (Jun. 1925), Dodd 1926 (9 stories)

The Magic Casket Hodder n.d. (Mar. 1927), Dodd 1927 (9 stories)

Other books

The Uttermost Farthing Winston 1914 (Challoner)

a.k.a. *A Savant's Vendetta* Pearson 1920

The Exploits of Danby Croker Duckworth 1916

The Surprising Experiences of Mr. Shuttlebury Cobb Hodder n.d. (Apr. 1927)

Flighty Phyllis Hodder n.d. (Jan. 1928)

Uncollected stories

'The Sign of the Ram' (*Everybody's Weekly*, 20 May 1911)

'The Mystery of Hoo Marsh' (*Pearson's*, Mar. 1917) (Challoner)

'The Mystery of the Seven Banana Skins' (*Everyman*, Dec. 1 & 8 1933)

Story collections by Clifford Ashdown (written with J. J. Pitcairn)

The Adventures of Romney Pringle Ward, Lock 1902, Train 1968 (6 stories)

The Further Adventures of Romney Pringle Train 1969 (1970) (6 stories)

From a Surgeon's Diary Ferret 1975, Train 1977 (6 stories)   *BP*

Elizabeth George (b. 1949)

Although an American, Elizabeth George sets her books in Britain and writes in the style of the very best of traditional British detective writers. Her affection for England comes through in her writing and all her books are cleverly plotted. An abiding interest of the series is the fascinating web of relationships among the characters. Inspector Thomas Lynley of Scotland Yard, who is also the eighth Earl of Asherton, is tall, blond, handsome and well groomed, was educated at Eton, drives a silver Bentley and has a valet called Denton. Lynley and his assistant, Sergeant Barbara Havers, are the antithesis of each other, as she is short, unattractive and frumpy and comes from a working-class background. Lynley's girlfriend, Lady Helen Clyde, who has rejected his offer of marriage, works part time with Simon Allcourt St James in his forensic laboratory. St James is an old school friend of Lynley and also a former lover of Lady Helen. St James is married to Deborah, a photographer, who has had a previous affair with Lynley. Joseph Cotter plays the unusual dual role of manservant and father-in-law to St James. There is one story featuring Lynley and Lady Helen. *A Suitable Vengeance* deals with events preceding the three earlier titles.

Four titles were first published in the USA but *For the Sake of Elena* and *Missing Joseph* had their first publication in the UK. All books are dated. The US edition of *Well-Schooled in Murder* has a plan of the independent school, Bredgar Chambers, on the front endpapers. All Elizabeth George's books have been published by Bantam, with different colours for binding and spine lettering.

Tom Hollman designed the wrappers of the

first three US titles, an axe among a bunch of cereals for *A Great Deliverance*, Joy Sinclair's black hair coiled around a dagger for *Payment in Blood* and the padlocked gates to Bredgar Chambers for *Well-schooled in Murder*. A photograph of Elena Weaver's outstretched hand among dead leaves on Robinson Crusoe's Island appears on *For the Sake of Elena* (UK) and the sun sets over a cottage in the lonely, darkened, wintry Lancashire countryside for *Missing Joseph* (UK).

Lynley novels

A Great Deliverance Bantam US 1988 (red boards, red spine, gilt lettering) Bantam UK 1989 (brown, gilt)
Payment in Blood Bantam US 1989 (blue, mauve, silver), Bantam UK 1989 (grey, gilt)
Well-schooled in Murder Bantam US 1990 (black, black, gilt) Bantam UK 1990 (red, gilt)
A Suitable Vengeance Bantam US 1991 (black, black, gilt) Bantam UK 1991 (blue, gilt)

For the Sake of Elena Bantam UK 1992 (green, gilt), Bantam US 1992 (dark blue, dark blue, silver)
Missing Joseph Bantam UK 1993 (maroon, gilt), Bantam US 1993 (grey, red, silver)

Lynley story

'The Evidence Exposed' (*Sisters in Crime 2*, Berkley 1990) *JC*

Val Gielgud (1900–1981)

Val Gielgud was a member of the Terry family, a great-nephew of Ellen Terry, and a brother of Sir John Gielgud. He was Head of BBC Radio Drama for many years, and appeared as Julian Caird in the film of his early novel, *Death at Broadcasting House* (a collaboration with Holt Marvell). He wrote twenty-seven novels and a collection of three stories, as well as six uncollected stories. Sixteen of his novels are detective stories: the others are either mainstream novels or thrillers, including four about Antony Havilland. He collaborated on five detective novels with Eric Maschwitz, who used the pseudonym Holt Marvell for four of the series. Detective-Inspector Simon Spears appears in four of these books. Val Gielgud later wrote an enjoyable series of eleven detective novels featuring Gregory Pellew, who is nobly assisted in ten of them by Humphrey, Viscount Clymping. Together they form an inquiry agency called Prinvest-London, when Pellew retires from the CID. *And Died So?* is a classic English village whodunit, and *A Necessary End*, involving a murderer lurking among a shipboard community, is another good example of Gielgud's work.

Only two of his sixteen titles have been published in the USA, both with alternative titles.

The Gielgud-Marvell collaborations were published by Rich & Cowan and are all dated. Each has the authors' initials in a double monogram at the top right-hand corner of the front cover, in the same colour as the spine lettering. *Under London* has green cloth, with the spine lettered in red, and *Death at Broadcasting House* is turquoise with orange lettering. These two titles have red top edges. *London Calling* lacks the casting sheet for *The Scarlet Highwayman* present in the UK edition. *Death as an Extra* and *Death in Budapest* both have black cloth, lettered in blue. The fifth collaboration, for which Maschwitz dropped the pseudonym, was published by Hutchinson and is undated. It has green cloth, with black lettering on the spine and the publisher, also in black, in the lower corner of the front cover. There are thirty-two pages of advertisements at the back of the book. Copies with blue cloth and no advertisements are later issues. For the wrapper of *Under London*, Barbara Brady created a collage in shades of green, burgundy and white with stylized heads of an oriental, a monocled gentleman and two women. The dust-wrapper for *Death as an Extra* is by Youngman Carter, and shows the body of Jerome B. Cole lying on the studio floor, with a microphone and cameras ranged all around him.

The first seven in the Gregory Pellew series were published by Collins Crime Club, in red cloth, and they are all dated. The spine lettering on the first four is black and on the last three it is gilt. Kenneth Farnhill produced a very striking wrapper design for *A Necessary End*, but the rest have wrappers with uniform coloured lettering on a black background. The last four titles were published by Macmillan, and are also dated. The first three have spines lettered in black, and *A Fearful Thing* has white lettering on the spine. In order of publication, they have red, brown, red, and green cloth. The wrappers for the Macmillan books are all photographic.

The story collection, *Beyond Dover*, was published by Hutchinson and is undated. It is bound in black cloth and lettered in yellow on the spine. The publisher is named in yellow across the lower corner of the front cover.

Two plays, *Inspector Silence Takes the Air* and *Thirteen to the Gallows*, were written with John Dickson Carr but remain unpublished.

Novels with Holt Marvell/Eric Maschwitz

(with Spears, except as stated)

Under London   Rich & Cowan 1933 (not Spears)

Death at Broadcasting House   Rich 1934
a.k.a. *London Calling*   Doubleday 1934
Death as an Extra   Rich 1935
Death in Budapest   Rich 1937
The First Television Murder   Hutchinson n.d. (1940)

Pellew novels

(also with Clymping, except as stated)

Gallows Foot   Collins Crime Club 1958 (not Clymping)
To Bed at Noon   Crime Club 1960
And Died So?   Crime Club 1961
The Goggle-Box Affair   Crime Club 1963
a.k.a. *Through a Glass Darkly*   Scribner 1963
Prinvest-London   Crime Club 1965
Conduct of a Member   Crime Club 1967
A Necessary End   Crime Club 1969
The Candle-Holders   Macmillan 1970
The Black Sambo Affair   Macmillan 1972
In Such a Night . . .   Macmillan 1974
A Fearful Thing   Macmillan 1975

Story collection

Beyond Dover Hutchinson n.d. (1940) (3 stories)

Uncollected stories

'Hot Water' (*The Great Book of Thrillers*, Odhams n.d. (1935))

'Life is Like That' (*Best Stories of the Underworld*, Faber 1942)

'Who Killed the Drama Critic?' (*ES*, 11 Mar. 1963; *Saint*, Jan./May 1964) (Pellew)

'The Man Who Forgot His Blind Spot' (*ES*, 9 June 1964)

'To Make a Holiday' (*Winter's Crimes 2*, Macmillan 1970) (Pellew)

'A Policeman's Lot' (*Winter's Crimes 6*, Macmillan 1974, St Martin's 1974) (Pellew)　　*JC*

Anthony Gilbert (1899–1973)
a.k.a. J. Kilmeny Keith
a.k.a. Anne Meredith

Lucy Beatrice Malleson, niece of the actor Miles Malleson, wrote sixty-five detective novels and some sixty known stories under the pseudonym Anthony Gilbert. She also used two other pseudonyms: J. Kilmeny Keith for her first two books (one of which, *The Sword of Harlequin*, is less a detective novel than a psychological study); and Anne Meredith, of whose twenty-two novels two only contain elements of crime (but little detection). She contributed two chapters to the collaborative novel *No Flowers by Request* (see under 'Detection Club').

Anthony Gilbert was a reliable and very popular writer right through the Golden Age into the early 1970s. She is noted for vigorous characterisation and adroit plotting. The first of her several series characters is Scott Egerton, a member of Parliament, fair-haired, good-looking, flawlessly dressed and painfully precise. He appears in ten novels. Three more feature a French detective, M. Dupuy of the Sureté, a dapper, bow-legged little man, bursting with vitality. The author's most famous detective was Arthur Crook, known as 'The Criminal's Hope', who became a more likable character as time

went on. This slow-speaking, beer-swilling, pot-bellied, middle-aged lawyer, with a great circular face and a crafty eye, figures in fifty-one novels and four stories. He wears 'snuff-coloured' clothes, suffers from gout and loves his cars. He is outrageously cheeky rather than vulgar and rushes in where angels fear to tread, going to unprofessional lengths to clear his clients. He uses an unofficial enquiry agent, Bill Parsons, in many of his cases, an ex-professional crook whose criminal career was cut short when he was shot in the heel by an official bullet that gave him a permanent limp.

Inspector Field of Scotland Yard is assisted by all three detectives on different occasions, and solves at least seven shorter cases on his own.

Apart from *A Spy for Mr. Crook*, which seems to have appeared only in the USA (unless it is a later printing of an earlier UK title), and *A Question of Murder* (US)/*Is She Dead Too?* (UK), which was first published in America, all the books were first published in London and are dated. Thirteen titles, including the Kilmeny Keith books, have been published only in the UK. Many books have alternative titles in America, including *Courtier to Death* and *Death Wears a Mask*

Except for *The Mystery of the Open Window* and *The Night of the Fog*, which were published by Gollancz with black cloth and red spine lettering, all Anthony Gilbert's books were published by Collins. The two Kilmeny Keith books were also published by Collins and have dark-blue cloth with the title and author's name lettered red on the spine and front cover. There is a double red border on each front cover and there are corresponding red rules at the top and bottom of each spine. The first two Gilbert titles are similarly bound, but have only a single red border on the front cover and single rules on the spine. *Death at Four Corners* has black cloth with title and author in red on the spine and front cover, the former with single red rules at each end, the latter with a single red border.

The rest of the long series of Anthony Gilbert's books were published by Collins' Crime Club and all have red cloth. *The Case Against Andrew Fane* has author and title in black on the spine and front cover, the latter with a single black border. The next six books have title and author black on the spine and front cover, but no border. All subsequent books have black lettering on the spine only, until *Knock, Knock, Who's There?* in 1964, when the lettering becomes gilt, remaining so to the end. With the publication of *Night Encounter*, the books become taller. Except for *The Man Who Was London* and *Death at Four Corners*, all the Collins books to 1941 contain advertisements at the rear. After this, only four titles – *Lift up the Lid, Lady Killer, Miss Pinnegar Disappears* and *Out for the Kill* – contain advertisements. The two Anne Meredith titles came from different publishers, *Portrait of a Murderer* from Gollancz, in black cloth with red spine lettering, *There's Always Tomorrow* from Faber, with green cloth and a gilt-lettered spine.

Some of the Collins wrappers for Anthony Gilbert are particularly attractive. Elizabeth Pyke's stylish study in red and black for *Tragedy at Freyne* surrounds the head and shoulders of a startled Lady Catherine Chandos with six accusing fingers. *The Body on the Beam* has Ellen Edwards' design of a young woman sitting up in bed, staring in horror at a man opening the window from outside. Both front panel and spine of *Murder by Experts* have a stern oriental gentleman in traditional dress, on a blue background. Three hands try to grasp a revolver on *The Man who was Too Clever*. *The Scarlet Button* has the end of a stick, from which drops of blood fall on to a red seahorse. H. W.'s blue and yellow wrapper for *Don't Open the Door* depicts the nurse, Nora Deane, looking round the bedroom door at the body of Adele Newstead, lying in bed. *A Nice Cup of Tea* has a woman with a blue face, an overturned teacup and a medicine bottle. *Lady Killer* has a classic lounge-lizard with a narrow moustache and blue bow-tie. A pattern of fingerprints, cigarettes and bloodstains appears on *The Fingerprint* and a snake coils against a green background for *The Looking Glass Murder*. Bernard Allum's striking face mask shows effectively on the wrapper of *Death Wears a Mask*.

The uncollected stories include a series for Inspector Field and another two with Sebastian Sanjoy, the Cavalier of Fleet Street (with something of Robin Hood about him and something, too, of Raffles, since he is more concerned with jewels than corpses). 'The Following Feet', a Sanjoy story, appears to have been revised for Inspector Field; and variants of two further Sanjoy titles occur in both his series.

Novels

(with Crook, except where stated)

The Tragedy at Freyne   Collins 1927, Dial 1927 (Egerton)
The Murder of Mrs. Davenport   Collins 1928, Dial 1928 (Egerton)
The Mystery of the Open Window   Gollancz 1929, Dodd, Mead 1930 (Egerton)
Death at Four Corners   Collins 1929, Dial 1929 (Egerton)
The Night of the Fog   Gollancz 1930, Dodd 1930 (Egerton)
The Case Against Andrew Fane   Collins Crime Club 1931, Dodd 1931 (non-series)
The Body on the Beam   Crime Club 1932, Dodd 1932 (Egerton)
The Long Shadow   Crime Club 1932 (Egerton)
The Musical Comedy Crime   Crime Club 1933 (Egerton)
Death in Fancy Dress   Crime Club 1933 (non-series)
The Man in Button Boots   Crime Club 1934, Holt 1935 (Dupuy)
An Old Lady Dies   Crime Club 1934 (Egerton)
The Man Who Was Too Clever   Crime Club 1935 (Egerton, Dupuy)
Murder by Experts   Crime Club 1936, Dial 1937
Courtier to Death   Crime Club 1936 (Dupuy)
a.k.a. *The Dover Train Mystery*   Dial 1936
The Man Who Wasn't There   Crime Club 1937
Murder Has No Tongue   Crime Club 1937
Treason In My Breast   Crime Club 1938
The Clock in the Hat Box   Crime Club 1939, Arcadia House 1943
The Bell of Death   Crime Club 1939
Dear Dead Woman   Crime Club 1940, Arcadia House 1942

a.k.a. *Death Takes a Redhead* Arrow (New York) 1944

The Vanishing Corpse Crime Club 1941

a.k.a. *She Vanished in the Dawn* Arcadia House 1941

The Woman in Red Crime Club 1941, Smith & Durrell 1943

a.k.a. *The Mystery of the Woman in Red* Quin 1944

Something Nasty in the Woodshed Crime Club 1942

a.k.a. *Mystery in the Woodshed* Smith & Durrell 1942

The Case of the Tea-Cosy's Aunt Crime Club 1942

a.k.a. *Death in the Blackout* Smith & Durrell 1943

The Mouse Who Wouldn't Play Ball Crime Club 1943

a.k.a. *Thirty Days to Live* Smith & Durrell 1944

A Spy for Mr. Crook Barnes (New York) 1944

He Came By Night Crime Club 1944

a.k.a. *Death at the Door* Smith & Durrell 1945

The Scarlet Button Crime Club 1944, Smith & Durrell 1945

a.k.a. *Murder is Cheap* Bantam 1949

The Black Stage Crime Club 1945, Barnes 1946

a.k.a. *Murder Cheats the Bride* Bantam 1948

Don't Open the Door Crime Club 1945

a.k.a. *Death Lifts the Latch* Barnes 1946

The Spinster's Secret Crime Club 1946

a.k.a. *By Hook or Crook* Barnes 1947

Death in the Wrong Room Crime Club 1947, Barnes 1947

Die in the Dark Crime Club 1947

a.k.a. *The Missing Widow* Barnes 1948

Lift up the Lid Crime Club 1948

a.k.a. *The Innocent Bottle* Barnes 1949

Death Knocks Three Times Crime Club 1949, Random House 1950

Murder Comes Home Crime Club 1950, Random 1951

A Nice Cup of Tea Crime Club 1950

a.k.a. *The Wrong Body* Random 1951

Lady Killer Crime Club 1951

Miss Pinnegar Disappears Crime Club 1952

a.k.a. *A Case for Mr. Crook* Random 1952

Footsteps Behind Me Crime Club 1953

a.k.a. *Black Death* Random 1953

a.k.a. *Dark Death* Pyramid 1963

Snake in the Grass Crime Club 1954

a.k.a. *Death Won't Wait* Random 1954

A Question of Murder Random 1955

a.k.a. *Is She Dead Too?* Crime Club 1956

And Death Came Too Crime Club 1956, Random 1956

Riddle of a Lady Crime Club 1956, Random 1957

Give Death a Name Crime Club 1957

Death Against the Clock Crime Club 1958, Random 1958

Death Takes a Wife Crime Club 1959

a.k.a. *Death Casts a Long Shadow* Random 1959

Third Crime Lucky Crime Club 1959

a.k.a. *Prelude to Murder* Random 1959

Out for the Kill Crime Club 1960, Random 1960

She Shall Die Crime Club 1961

a.k.a. *After the Verdict* Random 1961

Uncertain Death Crime Club 1961, Random 1962

No Dust in the Attic Crime Club 1962, Random 1963

Ring for a Noose Crime Club 1963, Random 1964

The Fingerprint Crime Club 1964, Random 1964

Knock, Knock, Who's There? Crime Club 1964

a.k.a. *The Voice* Random 1965

Passenger to Nowhere Crime Club 1965, Random 1966

The Looking Glass Murder Crime Club 1966, Random 1967

The Visitor Crime Club 1967, Random 1967

Night Encounter Crime Club 1968

a.k.a. *Murder Anonymous* Random 1968

Missing From Her Home Crime Club 1969, Random 1969

Death Wears a Mask Crime Club 1970

a.k.a. *Mr. Crook Lifts the Mask* Random 1970

Tenant for the Tomb Crime Club 1971, Random 1971

Murder's a Waiting Game Crime Club 1972, Random 1972

A Nice Little Killing Crime Club 1974, Random 1974

Novels as J. Kilmeny Keith

The Man Who Was London Collins 1925
The Sword of Harlequin Collins 1927

Novels as Anne Meredith

Portrait of a Murderer Gollancz 1933, Reynal 1934
There's Always Tomorrow Faber 1941
a.k.a. *Home is the Heart* Howell Soskin 1942

Collaborative novel (see under Detection Club)

Crime on the Coast and *No Flowers by Request* Gollancz 1984 (Anthony Gilbert contributed to *No Flowers by Request*)

Uncollected stories

(with Sanjoy, Field or Crook, as stated)

A Seeker after Romance (*Sketch* 1927) (Sanjoy)
 'The Adventure at the Cat in the Kitchen' (16. Mar.)
 'The Affair of the Duchess of Kewe' (23 Mar.)
 'The Following Feet' (30 Mar.)
 'The Saga of the Plain Woman' (6 Apr.)
 'The Honest Man' (13 Apr.)
 'A Cavalier of Lost Causes' (20 Apr.)
'The Confessional' (*Graphic*, 18 Jun. 1927)
'The Murder at Heath Court' (*Eve*, 3 Aug. 1927)
'The Mayfair Murder' (*Eve*, 10 Aug. 1927)
'The Man with the Chestnut Beard' (*Eve*, 17 Aug. 1927)
'The Reading of the Will' (*Eve*, 24 Aug. 1927)
The Cavalier of Fleet Street (*20-Story Magazine* 1928–9) (Sanjoy)
 'The Lady of Hanging Sword Alley' (Sept.)
 'The Plain Woman of Bond Street' (Oct.)
 'The Game and the Candle' (Nov.)
 'A Fool Among Ladies' (Dec.)
 'The Adventure of the Honest Man' (Jan.)
 'The Crooked House' (Feb.)

Meet Inspector Field (*Daily Express* 1935)
 'The Man in Bond Street' (15 Apr.)
 'Murderer at the Bar' (16 Apr.)
 'Dark Horse' (17 Apr.)
 'Woman in the Park' (18 Apr.)
 'Following Feet' (22 Apr.)
'The Cockroach and the Tortoise'
'Horseshoes for Luck' } *Detection Medley*, Hutchinson n.d. (1939) (Field)
'The Black Hat' (*Best Stories of the Underworld*, Faber 1942; *The Armchair Detective Reader*, Boardman 1948) (Crook)
'You Can't Hang Twice' (*EQMM*, Nov. 1946; *The Queen's Awards 1946*, Little, Brown 1946, Gollancz 1948) (Crook)
'Black for Innocence' (*ES*, 16 Jan. 1950; *The Evening Standard Detective Book*, Gollancz 1950)
'What Would You Have Done?' (*The Evening Standard Detective Book, Series 2*, Gollancz 1951)
'Here Comes a Candle' (*ES*, 13 June 1951)
'Over My Dead Body' (*ES*, 19 June 1951; *EQMM*, Jul. 1952; *MacKill's*, Sept. 1952; *Ellery Queen's Minimysteries*, World 1969)
'Curtains for Me' (*ES*, 3 Oct. 1951; *JCMM*, Feb. 1958; *The Mystery Bedside Book*, Hodder & Stoughton 1960)
'Cul-de-sac' (*ES*, 17 June 1952)
'Madame Clementine' (*ES*, 21 Jan. 1953; *EQMM*, Oct. 1955 as 'Remember Madame Clementine')
'Three Living and One Dead' (*ES*, 13 Jul. 1955)
'Give me a Ring' (*Illustrated London News*, 11 Nov. 1955)
'Once is Once Too Many' (*EQMM*, Dec. 1955) (Crook)
'Sequel to Murder' (*Eat, Drink and Be Buried*, Viking 1956/*For Tomorrow We Die* Macdonald 1958)
'Blood Will Tell' (*A Choice of Murders*, Scribner 1958, Macdonald 1960)
'The Goldfish Button' (*EQMM*, Feb. 1958; *The Lethal Sex*, Dell 1959, Crime Club 1962 as 'You'll be the Death of Me'; *Some Like Them Dead*, Hodder 1960)
'A Nice Little Mare Called Murder' (*Crime Writers' Choice*, Hodder 1964) (Crook)

'He Found Out Too Late' (*ES*, 2 June 1964; *Saint*, May 1966/June 1966)

'Even a Woman' (*Saint* (US) Jul. 1964)

'Christmas Spirit' (*Illustrated London News*, 16 Nov. 1964)

'The Eternal Chase' (*EQMM*, Aug. 1965; *Ellery Queen's Crime Carousel*, NAL 1966, Gollancz 1967)

'The Dove and the Hawk' (*EQMM*, June 1966; *EQA*, Spring-Summer 1971, Davis 1971; *Stories of Crime and Detection*, McGraw-Hill 1974)

'Cat Among the Pigeons' (*EQMM*, Oct. 1966; *EQA*, Fall-Winter 1972, Davis 1972)

'Sleep is the Enemy' (*EQMM*, Feb. 1966; *Ellery Queen's All-Star Line-up*, NAL 1967, Gollancz 1968)

'The Intruders' (*EQMM*, Dec. 1967; *Ellery Queen's Mystery Parade*, NAL 1968, Gollancz 1969)

'Point of No Return' (*EQMM*, May 1968; *EQA*, Spring-Summer 1973, Davis 1973)

'Who Cares About an Old Woman?' (*EQMM*, Oct. 1968; *Ellery Queen's Murder Menu*, World 1969, Gollancz 1969)

'The Puzzled Heart' (*EQMM*, Mar. 1969; *EQA*, Fall-Winter 1974, Davis 1974)

'The Mills of God' (*EQMM*, Apr. 1969)

'The Quiet Man' (*EQMM*, June 1969; *Ellery Queen's Grand Slam*, World 1970, Gollancz 1971)

'Tiger on the Premises' (*EQMM*, Sep. 1969)

'The Funeral of Dendy Watt' (*EQMM*, Jan. 1970)

'Door to a Different World' (*EQMM* Mar. 1970; *Ellery Queen's Headliners*, World 1971, Gollancz 1972)

'When Suns Collide' (*EQMM*, Apr. 1971; *Ellery Queen's Mystery Bag*, World 1972, Gollancz 1973)

'A Day of Encounters' (*EQMM* Feb. 1972; *Ellery Queen's Crookbook*, Davis 1974, Gollancz 1974)

'Fifty Years After' (*EQMM*, Mar. 1973; *Ellery Queen's Murdercade*, Random House, 1975, Gollancz 1976)

'The Invisible Witness' (*EQMM*, Jan. 1974; *Ellery Queen's Crime Wave*, Putnam 1976)

JC

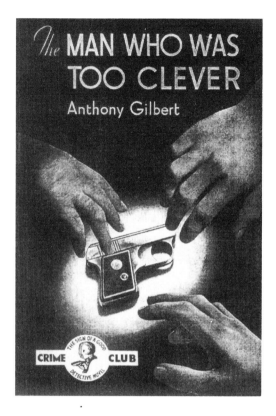

Michael Gilbert (b. 1912)

Michael Gilbert is a master of story-telling, author of some of the most entertaining novels and stories in the genre. His books vary from police procedural and espionage to straight-forward detection. His legal career has helped to bring witty, authentic detail to many of his books and stories. He has written twenty-seven novels, four plays, and 164 stories, 79 of which are collected in seven volumes. He has also written one criminous poem and contributed a 'recollection' of Dorothy Rigby to a multiple collaboration, *The Rigby File*.

Michael Gilbert has created many series characters. Patrick Petrella is the son of a Spanish policeman father and an upper-middle-class English mother. He appears in two novels, *Blood and Judgement* and *Roller Coaster*, and fifty-one stories, thirty-two of which are collected in five volumes. On his first appearance he was called

Peter. He started his career in the police force as a constable, based at Highside Police Station, pounding the beat in Highside and Pound End, districts in South London. His superiors in these early days are Sergeant Gwilliam, Superintendent Haxtell, and Chief Superintendent Barstow. He gradually makes his way up through the ranks, becoming a sergeant in the story 'Breach of the Peace'. While an inspector he works with Superintendent Benjamin on several cases. Eventually, he becomes a chief inspector at Patton Street in Q Division, in the story 'Rough Justice', and by the time of 'The Spoilers' (from *Game without Rules*) he is a superintendent.

Chief Inspector (later Superintendent) Hazlerigg of Scotland Yard, who began his career on the beat in Whitechapel, plays an important role in six novels and nineteen stories, six of which are collected. The original version of 'Back in Five Years' makes it clear that Hazlerigg is the narrator, but this story has also appeared without his name attached to it.

Daniel John Calder and Samuel Behrens are seemingly mild retired gentlemen who are, in fact, ruthless and efficient counter-intelligence agents. Calder's Persian deerhound, Rasselas, assists in some of their investigations. They feature in twenty-four stories, all but one of which are collected in two volumes. In the collected version of the story 'A Prince of Abyssinia', in *Game Without Rules*, Rasselas dies, but when it first appeared, in *Argosy* for March 1962, he survived. Mr Calder also features in the first Jonas Pickett story, 'Anything for a Quiet Life'.

The wily solicitor Mr Rumbold, senior partner in the firm of Wragg and Rumbold, appears in the novel *Death Has Deep Roots* and in five stories, three of which are collected. Another lawyer, Henry Bohun, of Horniman, Birley, and Craine, features in *Smallbone Deceased* and eight stories, including three that are collected. The unsmiling, monocled Hargest Macrea, QC, makes significant contributions to *Death Has Deep Roots* and three collected stories. Jonas Pickett, solicitor and commissioner for oaths, of Highgate, appears briefly in *The Long Journey Home* and plays a larger part in the nine stories collected in *Anything for a Quiet Life*. Some of the stories in this collection have additions and deletions since their first publication in *EQMM*.

Detective Chief Inspector William Mercer is in charge of the CID at Stoneferry-on-Thames during the investigations in *The Body of a Girl*. He later operates as an ex-policeman in three linked stories, all uncollected. Major Angus McCann, ex-Commando, ably assists the police in the course of *Death Has Deep Roots, They Never Looked Inside*, and *The Doors Open*.

Michael Gilbert's books were first published in London by Hodder & Stoughton, except for *Game Without Rules, End Game, The Long Journey Home*, and *Amateur in Violence*, a story collection which has not appeared in Britain. *Stay of Execution*, another collection, was not published in the USA. Some books have alternative American titles, including *They Never Looked Inside* and *Sky High*. For the American edition of *Death in Captivity*, retitled *The Danger Within*, the author rewrote the final sequence, so that the dénouement took place inside the prison camp. *They Never Looked Inside* has 'First printed 1947' on the copyright page but it was not published until July 1948.

The first book, *Close Quarters*, has grey cloth, with the spine lettered in red. The title also appears in red on the front cover. The book contains three plans of Melchester Cathedral and its close. *They Never Looked Inside* has maroon cloth, with white lettering, including the title on the front cover. The blue cloth of *The Doors Open* has black lettering on the spine and the title in black on the cover. After this the front covers are blank. The wrappers for these three books were designed by Bip Pares. *Close Quarters* shows an elderly man leaning on a walking-stick, standing on a ledge under an arch, with two white cathedral spires looming to his left on a flame-coloured background. *They Never Looked Inside* has a room with a desk being rifled by an intruder, while a young accomplice holding a cosh sits on the staircase outside. Double doors open to reveal a strange-looking man in spectacles, writing at a desk, with a giant spider's web behind him, on the wrapper of *The Doors Open*.

The following six titles all have maroon cloth. *Smallbone Deceased* and *Be Shot for Sixpence* have their spines lettered gilt, and a smoking golden revolver appears on the spine of the latter. *Death Has Deep Roots, Fear to Tread, Death in Captivity*, and *Sky High* have black spine lettering, and a black revolver also appears on the latter pair. *Blood and Judgement* was issued in green cloth, with the spine lettered gilt. A man leaning against a lamp-post is also shown in gilt on the spine. This title marks the end of any uniformity in the physical appearance of the books produced by Hodder & Stoughton, until a pattern was reestablished in 1980.

From *After the Fine Weather*, all the books have the spine lettered gilt, but the colour of cloth varies from one title to another. Four titles have coloured top edges: in yellow for *The Etruscan Net*, in lime-green for *Stay of Execution*, in blue for *The Body of a Girl*, and in dark green for *The Ninety-second Tiger*. The title of *Game Without Rules* is lettered gilt on a green rectangle.

A short section from *Paint, Gold and Blood* first appeared in a free sampler from the publisher. There is one uncollected poem, 'a ruthless rhyme': 'Arnold, or the Uses of Electricity', in *Julian Symons at 80*, published in 1992 and limited to one thousand numbered copies.

Smallbone Deceased has a most attractive wrapper showing the front of the office of Horniman, Birley, and Craine, with a cat eating a dove in the foreground. The design is based on Michael Gilbert's own office in London at that time. Victoria Lamartine, standing in the dock against a green background of various Parisian scenes, is shown on Jarvis' wrapper for *Death Has Deep Roots*. Two prisoners creeping from the prison camp are caught in a spotlight on the wrapper of *Death in Captivity*. Antony Lake's design for *Sky High* shows a motor cycle being driven at great speed past a large house. Eileen Walton's design for *After the Fine Weather* has a close-up of Laura Hart's horror-stricken face. Mick and Ging created a very stylish wrapper for *Game Without Rules*, showing Calder, Behrens, and Rasselas. The majority of the later wrappers are photographic.

Amateur in Violence is a paperback, published in New York by Davis, with a short introduction by Ellery Queen, who edited the volume. *The*

Road to Damascus (Eurographica 1990) contains four reprinted Calder and Behrens stories.

The most difficult titles for first-edition collectors to find seem to be *The Doors Open, Smallbone Deceased*, and *Flash Point*.

Novels

(With series characters, as stated. Binding details refer to British editions.)

Close Quarters Hodder & Stoughton 1947, Walker 1963 (Hazlerigg)
They Never Looked Inside Hodder 1947 (1948) (Hazlerigg)
a.k.a. *He Didn't Mind Danger* Harper 1949
The Doors Open Hodder 1949, Walker 1962 (Hazlerigg)
Smallbone Deceased Hodder 1950, Harper 1950 (Hazlerigg, Bohun)
Death Has Deep Roots Hodder 1951, Harper 1951 (Hazlerigg, Rumbold)
Death in Captivity Hodder 1952
revised as *The Danger Within* Harper 1952
Fear to Tread Hodder 1953, Harper 1953 (Hazlerigg)
Sky High Hodder 1955
a.k.a. *The Country-House Burglar* Harper 1955
Be Shot for Sixpence Hodder 1956, Harper 1956
Blood and Judgement Hodder 1959, Harper 1959 (Petrella)
After the Fine Weather Hodder 1963, Harper 1963 (blue binding)
The Crack in the Teacup Hodder 1966, Harper 1966 (dark blue)
The Dust and the Heat Hodder 1967 (blue)
a.k.a. *Overdrive* Harper 1968
The Etruscan Net Hodder 1969 (red)
a.k.a. *The Family Tomb* Harper 1969
The Body of a Girl Hodder 1972, Harper 1972 (Mercer) (blue)
The Ninety-second Tiger Hodder 1973, Harper 1973 (green)
Flash Point Hodder 1974, Harper 1974 (green)
The Night of the Twelfth Hodder 1976, Harper 1976 (blue)

The Empty House Hodder 1978, Harper 1978 (black)

Death of a Favourite Girl Hodder 1980 (maroon)

a.k.a. *The Killing of Katie Steelstock* Harper 1980

End-Game Harper 1982

a.k.a. *The Final Throw* Hodder 1982 (burgundy)

The Black Seraphim Hodder 1983, Harper 1984 (black)

The Long Journey Home Harper 1985, Hodder 1985 (black)

Trouble Hodder 1987, Harper 1987 (green)

Paint, Gold and Blood Hodder 1989, Harper 1989 (black)

The Queen Against Karl Mullen Hodder 1991, Carroll & Graf 1991 (grey)

Roller-Coaster Hodder 1993 (black) (Petrella)

Story collections

Game Without Rules Harper 1967, Hodder 1968 (11 Calder and Behrens stories, 1 with Petrella) (mottled red binding)

Stay of Execution Hodder 1971 (13 stories, 2 with Hazlerigg, 1 with Petrella, 3 with Bohun, 3 with Rumbold) (green)

Amateur in Violence Davis 1973 (11 stories, 3 with Hazlerigg, 4 with Petrella)

Petrella at Q Hodder 1977, Harper 1977 (12 Petrella stories) (blue-grey)

Mr. Calder and Mr. Behrens Hodder 1982, Harper 1982 (12 Calder & Behrens stories) (blue)

Young Petrella Hodder 1988, Harper 1988 (16 Petrella stories, 2 also with Hazlerigg) (black)

Anything for a Quiet Life Hodder 1990, Carroll & Graf 1990 (9 Pickett stories) (black)

Uncollected Petrella stories

'One-tenth Man' (*EQMM*, Oct. 1956; *Ellery Queen's Awards*, 11th series, Collins Crime Club 1958) (Peter Petrell)

'The Girl who Moved' (*Argosy*, Jan. 1957)

'Counter-attack' (*Argosy*, Dec. 1957)

'Deep and Crisp and Even' (*Argosy*, Jan. 1958)

'Freedom of the Press' (*Argosy*, Feb. 1958)

'Amateur Detective' (*Argosy*, Mar. 1958)

'Somebody' (*Argosy*, May 1958)

'Miss Bell's Stocking' (*Argosy*, June 1958)

'Kendrew's Private War' (*Argosy*, Apr. 1959; *Daily Herald*, as 'The Young Policeman')

'The White Slaves' (*Argosy*, June 1959)

'The Terrible Mrs. Barker' (*Argosy*, July 1959)

'Petrella's Holiday' (*Argosy*, Sept. 1959)

'A Real Born Killer' (*Argosy*, Oct. 1959; *EQMM*, Apr. 1960 and *John Creasey's Mystery Bedside Book*, Hodder 1967, as 'The Terror of Pardoe Street')

'Old Mr. Martin' (*Argosy*, Apr. 1960)

'The Facts of Life' (*Argosy*, May 1960)

'The Battle of Bank Street' (*Argosy*, July 1960; *EQMM*, May 1961, as 'London Manhunt')

'The Man Who Hated Banks' (*Argosy*, Sept./Oct. 1964; *EQMM*, Jan. 1966, as 'C.12: Department of Bank Robberies')

'It Never Pays To Be Too Clever' (*EQMM*, Apr. 1973)

'Decoy' (*EQMM*, Sept. 1990)

Uncollected Hazlerigg stories

'Back in Five Years' (*John Bull*, 18 Dec. 1948; *EQMM*, Oct. 1953; *Ellery Queen's More Lost Ladies and Men*, Davis 1985)

'A Nose in a Million' (*John Bull*, 1 Oct. 1949; a.k.a. 'A Matter of Confidence')

'A Neat, Cold Killing' (*Reveille*, 27–9 Jan. 1950; a.k.a. 'On the Foreigners')

'Something Like Hard Work' (*ES*, 11 July 1950; *EQMM*, July 1953, as 'The Automobile Game')

'Balloons Will Be Released' (*John Bull*, 12 May 1951)

'Death Duties' (*ES*, 31 May 1951)

'Death Money' (*ES*, 21 Oct. 1952)

'Snuffy' (*ES*, 8 April 1953)

'The Awkward Customer' (*ES*, 9 Apr. 1953; *EQMM*, Sept. 1954, as 'The Customer Is Not Always Right')

'Friends of the Groom' (*ES*, 11 Apr. 1953)

'Follow My Leader' (*Reveille*, 1 Mar. 1955; *Weekend*, vol. 5, no. 14 (1955), as 'Follow the Leader')

'Ticker Batson's Last Job' (*Best Underworld Stories*, Faber 1969)

Uncollected Bohun stories

'A Long Time Ago' (*ES*, 10 July 1954; *EQMM*, Apr. 1956 and *Eat, Drink and Be Buried*, Viking 1956/*For Tomorrow We Die*, Macdonald 1958, as 'After All These Years')

'The Dogs of War' (*ES*, 1 Nov. 1954; *EQMM*, Feb. 1956, as 'Every Monday a New Letter')

'An Appealing Pair of Legs' (*ES*, 22 Sept. 1955; *EQMM*, Apr. 1957, as 'If You Know How') (also Hazlerigg)

'Money is Honey' (*Butcher's Dozen*, Heinemann 1956)

'Bird of Dawning' (*National and English Review*)

Uncollected Mercer stories

'The Man at the Bottom' (*EQMM*, Apr. 1979)

'The Man in the Middle' (*EQMM*, May 1979)

'The Man at the Top' (*EQMM*, June 1979)

Other stories

(with series characters, as stated)

'Blackmail Is so Difficult' (*John Bull*, 24 June 1950; *EQMM*, Sept. 1953 and *The Second Mystery Bedside Book*, Hodder 1961, as 'The Blackmailer'; *Suspense*, Dec. 1958, as 'Did You Say Blackmail?')

'Even Murderers Take Holidays' (*ES*, 9 Oct. 1950; *MSMM*, Mar. 1961)

'The Indifferent Shot' (*ES*, 23 Oct. 1950; *The Evening Standard Detective Book*, series 2, Gollancz 1951)

'Drop Shot' (*ES*, 27 Nov. 1950)

'The Squeeze' (*ES*, 29 Jan. 1951; *EQMM*, Mar. 1953, as 'Squeeze Play')

'The Brave Don't Talk' (*John Bull*, 1 Dec. 1951)

'The Smiler' (*John Bull*, 9 Aug. 1952; a.k.a. 'Bird of Passage' and 'Bird of Prey')

'Mrs. Haslet's Gone' (*John Bull*, 27 Dec. 1952; *This Week*, as 'The Great Tulip Mystery'; a.k.a. 'Tulips Are Such Greedy Feeders')

'Cumberland v. Cumberland' (*ES*, 12 Feb. 1953)

'Hangover' (*ES*, 6 Apr. 1953)

'Five on the Gun' (*ES*, 7 Apr. 1953)

'The Seventh Musket' (*Argosy*, Aug. 1954)

'Twm Carney' (*ES*, 15 Sept. 1954; *EQMM*, May 1957, as 'Three Times Loser')

'A Corner of the Cellar' (*Argosy*, Mar. 1955; *EQMM*, Sept. 1956, as 'Under the Last Scuttleful')

'Scream from a Soundproof Room' (*This Week*; *Reveille*, 26 Apr. 1955, as 'The Cabinet Maker'; *This Week's Stories of Mystery and Suspense*, Random House 1957; *Alfred Hitchcock Presents: The Master's Choice*, Random House 1979, as 'Scream in a Soundproof Room')

'The Man Who Sold Out' (*Adventure*, June 1955; *Argosy*, Feb. 1956, as 'Dead Reckoning')

'Trust Little Al' (*Argosy*, Oct. 1955; *Choice of Weapons*, Hodder 1958).

'Prize of Santenac' (*John Bull*, 22 Oct. 1955; a.k.a. 'The Santenac Treasure') (Rumbold)

'Safe!' ('*Woman's Weekly*, 1956; *Suspense*, Aug. 1958)

'What Happened at Castelbonato', (*Good Housekeeping*, Jul./Aug. 1956)

'No Place Like Home' (*ES*, 3 Aug. 1957)

'The Great German Spy-hunt' (*Lilliput*, Mar. 1958)

'The Craven Case' (*Suspense*, June 1959)

'Villa Almirante' (*Argosy*, Dec. 1959)

'When a Girl Moves Among Diplomats' (*ES*, 10 June 1964; *Saint*, May 1965/Dec. 1965)

'Double-double' (*Argosy*, Apr. 1967; *EQMM*, Oct. 1967, as 'The Terrorists') (Calder and Behrens)

'The Revenge of Martin Lucas Field on Colonel Cristobal Ocampos' (*Argosy*, Apr. 1968; *EQMM*, Oct. 1969 and *EQA*, Spring-Summer 1975, Davis 1975/*Ellery Queen's Christmas Hamper*, Gollancz 1975, as 'The Cork in the Bottle')

'Basilio' (*Winter's Crimes I*, Macmillan 1969, St Martin's 1969; *EQMM*, June 1971, as 'The Wrong Fox')

'Grandmother Clatterwick and Mr. McGuffog' (*Accent on Good Living*, May/June 1970; *EQMM*, Mar. 1972 and *Ellery Queen's Faces of Mystery*, Davis 1977, as 'The Curious Conspiracy')

'Blood Match' (*Metropolis*, autumn 1970; *Crime Waves 1*, Gollancz 1991) (Rumbold)

'Verdict of Three' (*Verdict of Thirteen*, Faber 1979, Harper 1979)

'Audited and Found Correct' (*Winter's Crimes 12*, Macmillan 1980, St Martin's 1980)

'Camford Cottage' (*The After Midnight Ghost Book*, Hutchinson 1980)

'Coronation Year' (*Who Done It?*, Houghton 1980)

'Who Killed Karl Carver?' (*TV Times*, 1981)

'The Inside Pocket' (*Crime Wave*, Collins 1981)

'A Very Special Relationship' (*Winter's Crimes 16*, Macmillan 1984, St Martin's 1985)

'A Pity About the Girl' (*New Black Mask Number 3*, Harcourt 1985)

'The Two Footmen' (*The New Adventures of Sherlock Holmes*, Carroll & Graf 1987)

'The Jackal and the Tiger' (*Winter's Crimes 20*, Macmillan 1988)

'Good Old Monty' (*Midwinter Mysteries*, Scribner 1991)

'The Man Who Was Reconstituted' (*The Man Who . . .* , Macmillan 1992)

'Judith' (*EQMM*, Apr. 1993; *Midwinter Mysteries 3*, Little, Brown 1993)

'Clos Carmine, 1945' (*Sunday Dispatch*)

'The Klagenfurt Tote' (*Lilliput*)

'The Sheik Goes Shopping' (*Lilliput*)

Collaborative novel

The Rigby File Hodder 1989

Poem

'Arnold, or The Uses of Electricity' (*Julian Symons at 80*, Eurographica 1992)   JC

B. M. Gill (b. 1921)

Barbara Gill is a deep, impassioned writer, at her best with the darker tensions that arise from human affairs. Four novels in particular demonstrate her considerable powers: *Death Drop, Victims, The Twelfth Juror* and *The Fifth Rapunzel*. She won the CWA Gold Dagger for *The Twelfth Juror* and might equally have won it for any of these. She adopted a more relaxed approach for *Seminar for Murder*, a stylish whodunit set at a crime-writers' convention, and with *Nursery Crimes* made an unexpected attempt to use an instinctive killer as a pivot for farce.

Her early thriller, *Target Westminster*, was published by Hale in 1977, in the standard late-Hale format, a black binding with silver spine lettering. The wrapper shows the woman terrorist, Briony, against a background of Big Ben. Two years later, *Death Drop* appeared from Hodder & Stoughton, who have continued to publish her work. A black book, with gilt spine lettering, it has a poignant wrapper by Alan Hood, showing David Fleming's blindfolded body and the open hatch through which he fell to his death. *Victims* is a maroon book with gilt spine lettering, taller than its predecessors.

The Twelfth Juror and *Seminar for Murder* are black with gilt spine lettering. The former has a subtle wrapper by Steve Ridgway, who ranges his jurors like ninepins, crowning the twelfth with a judge's wig, to remind us of Robert Quinn's tragic assumption of power. *Nursery*

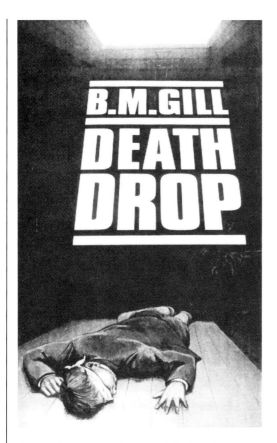

The Twelfth Juror   Hodder 1984, Scribner 1984
Seminar for Murder   Hodder 1985, Scribner 1986
Nursery Crimes   Hodder 1986, Scribner 1987
Dying to Meet You   Hodder 1988, Doubleday 1990
Time and Time Again   Hodder 1989, Scribner 1990
The Fifth Rapunzel   Hodder 1991, Scribner 1991

Stories

'A Certain Kind of Skill' (*Winter's Crimes 18*, Macmillan 1986, St Martin's 1987)
'Murder Most Kind' (*Good Housekeeping*, Nov. 1987)
'Forty-two Headmasters are Missing' (*Winter's Crimes 23*, Macmillan 1991)   *BP*

Sue Grafton (b. 1940)

Sue Grafton, like Margery Allingham, is a chip off the old block: her father, C. W. Grafton, was also a crime writer. After two earlier novels, she launched her own detective series in 1982 with *'A' is for Alibi*. Each subsequent title has taken her further down the alphabet; and by the turn of the century she should be more than half-way to 'Z'. Her series character is a professional detective, Kinsey Millhone, now firmly established and widely admired as a prototype of the modern female private eye. She narrates her own cases, revealing much about herself in the process: she is independent and good at her job, with humour, candour, courage and an unambitious dress code. Though tough, she is humanly vulnerable and gets hurt.

The books are published in America by Holt and in Britain by Macmillan. The Holt editions vary in colour and style of binding and in colour of spine lettering. They have blank covers, the date on the copyright page and printer's keys to establish primacy. All except *'C' is for Corpse* also state 'First edition' on the copyright page. From *'D' is for Deadbeat* the rear covers show the publisher's logo, blind-stamped for *'D'* and *'E'*, in the colour of the lettering for the others. From *'G' is for Gumshoe* the books are taller.

Crimes is green, with silver lettering. The wrapper has a fetching photo of the juvenile killer at the time of her first murder, 'all yellow curls and sweetness'. *Dying to Meet You, Time and Time Again* and *The Fifth Rapunzel* are taller books, black, blue and red, respectively, all with gilt spine lettering and photographic wrappers. All B. M. Gill's books have the date on the copyright page. Detective Chief Inspector Tom Maybridge of the Avon Police appears in *Seminar for Murder, The Fifth Rapunzel* and 'Murder Most Kind'.

Novels

Target Westminster   Hale 1977
Death Drop   Hodder & Stoughton 1979, Scribner 1980
Victims   Hodder 1981
a.k.a. *Suspect*   Scribner 1981

The wrappers are routine photographic, lacking, unlike Kinsey, in appeal.

The Macmillan editions have gilt spine lettering and dated copyright pages. *'G' is for Gumshoe* is the first of a taller run and the last in the standard Macmillan format, with author's surname and title lying along the spine, separated by a single rule. *'J' is for Judgment* has a printer's key, 9–1. The bindings are, in order, green, grey, red, dark green, yellow, purple, sage green, black, maroon tinged with blue, maroon. At least since 1992, the books have had pictorial wrappers by Tom Adams, with flowers to the fore: but the spines have stayed plain.

Kinsey and Me is a collection of stories published in a limited edition of three hundred copies numbered and signed by the author and twenty-six lettered and signed by her. 'Part One: Kinsey' has eight stories; the eight stories in Part Two are not criminous. 'She Didn't Come Home' (*Redbook*, Apr. 1986) is collected as 'Long Gone'. The book measures 9″ × 6″ and is slip-cased. It has grey boards, a burgundy spine with a label in the same colour lettered gilt, and burgundy marbled endpapers.

The early novels – *Keziah Dane* (1968) and *The Lolly Madonna War* (1969) – deal with poor rural families and, despite the high incidence of violent crime in the latter, neither is properly a crime novel. The brutish community of *The Lolly Madonna War* resembles the Starkadders of *Cold Comfort Farm*, but in grim earnest.

Millhone novels

(Binding details refer to US editions.)

'A' is for Alibi   Holt, Rinehart & Winston 1982, Macmillan 1986 (grey binding, red lettering)
'B' is for Burglar   Holt 1985, Macmillan 1986 (grey boards, red spine, silver lettering)
'C' is for Corpse   Holt 1986, Macmillan 1987 (grey, silver)
'D' is for Deadbeat   Holt 1987, Macmillan 1987 (black, gilt)
'E' is for Evidence   Holt 1988, Macmillan 1988 (grey, black, silver)
'F' is for Fugitive   Holt 1989, Macmillan 1989 (pink, black, gilt)

'G' is for Gumshoe   Holt 1990, Macmillan 1990 (mauve-grey, black, red)
'H' is for Homicide   Holt 1991, Macmillan 1991 (dark grey, black, green)
'I' is for Innocent   Holt 1992, Macmillan 1992 (dark pink, black, dark pink)
'J' is for Judgment   Holt 1993, Macmillan 1993 (blue, black, copper/gilt)

Story collection

Kinsey and Me   Bench Press (Santa Barbara) 1991 (16 stories)   *BP*

Caroline Graham (b. 1931)

With her first detective novel *The Killings at Badger's Drift* Caroline Graham produced one of the best post-war whodunits. Since then she has written two other fine traditional detective stories and the disappointing *Murder at Madingley Grange*, which is more comic than criminous.

The Envy of the Stranger is a murder story rather than detective.

The firm and dependable Chief Inspector Tom Barnaby and the aggressive Sergeant Gavin Troy of the Causton CID are featured in three of the novels.

Caroline Graham's books were first published in the UK and are all dated. Her first two crime novels were published by Century, both with gilt lettering on the spine. *The Envy of the Stranger* has red cloth and *The Killings at Badger's Drift*, which is shorter in height, has black cloth. *Death of a Hollow Man* and *Murder at Madingley Grange* were published by Mysterious Press and *Death in Disguise*, a taller book, appeared from Headline. All three later titles have black cloth with gilt spine lettering. The Mysterious Press books have red endpapers with the Press logo in black, repeated many times. *Death in Dis-*

guise has a printer's key, 10–1, on the copyright page.

All Caroline Graham's detective novels have attractive wrappers. Graham Potts' design for *Badger's Drift* shows the spurred coral root orchid, its position marked by Miss Simpson's stick with a red ribbon tied to it. A cut-throat razor and various articles of make-up appear on *Death of a Hollow Man*. *Murder at Madingley Grange* illustrates the Grange and part of its gardens, with an ornamental figure holding a joker. Fred Preston's design for *Death in Disguise* has the Elizabethan manor house, The Golden Windhorse, in the background, and a bloodied kitchen-knife among the ox-eye daisies in the foreground.

The most difficult first edition to find is *The Killings at Badger's Drift*.

Novels

(with Barnaby, except as stated)

The Envy of the Stranger Century 1984 (not Barnaby)
The Killings at Badger's Drift Century 1987, Adler & Adler 1988
Death of a Hollow Man Mysterious Press 1989, Morrow 1990
Murder at Madingley Grange Mysterious Press 1990, Morrow 1991 (not Barnaby)
Death in Disguise Headline 1992, Morrow 1993
JC

Dashiell Hammett (1894–1961)
a.k.a. Peter Collinson
a.k.a. Samuel Dashiell
a.k.a. Mary Jane Hammett

Dashiell Hammett is the author of five novels, one unfinished novel, two linked novellas, fifty-five collected stories, one uncollected story and adventures for a cartoon strip. He was a trail-blazer of the American detective novel, breaking new ground with his abrasive style and blunt, earthy language. He drew much of the inspiration for his work from his experiences while working for the Pinkerton Detective Agency in Baltimore and San Francisco. His books are

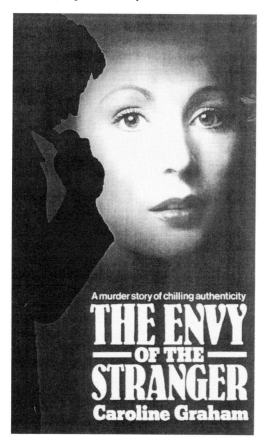

A murder story of chilling authenticity
THE ENVY OF THE STRANGER
Caroline Graham

populated with realistic characters using down-to-earth, terse language and their violence is often spectacular. Underlying all the gunfire and flying fists is an implacable hatred of corruption. The books are genuine detective puzzles narrated in a lean, mean style, devoid of unnecessary description and with the emotional impact of a clinical report.

The pseudonym Peter Collinson was used for the author's earliest *Black Mask* stories: 'The Road Home' (Dec. 1922), 'The Vicious Circle' (June 1923), 'Arson Plus' (1 Oct. 1923) and 'Slippery Fingers' (15 Oct. 1923), the latter pair with the Continental Op as protagonist. 'The Diamond Wager' appeared in *Detective Fiction Weekly* for 19 Oct. 1929 as by Samuel Dashiell. Fewer than ten copies of this story were privately printed on unbound sheets at Portage, Indiana in 1977. The pseudonym Mary Jane Hammett was used for 'The Crusader' in *The Smart Set* magazine for Aug. 1923. This, too, was privately printed much later: in 1980, at Sherman Oaks, California, in an edition of eighty-five numbered copies, bound in buckram with black spine lettering and a slipcase. Dashiell Hammett has three important series characters: the Continental Op, Sam Spade and Secret Agent X–9. The Op derives his unromantic but intriguing name from the continental detective agency for which he was an operative: it reflects his tough, no-nonsense nature. He is a loner, fat, short and in his forties; and though he is physically unattractive and not averse to shooting a villain or beating someone up in a fist fight, he has sterling qualities, too. He is honest, totally loyal to his employers and compassionate towards his clients. He has a highly developed sense of justice and a desire for order in society. Hammett based the character on an assistant superintendent of the Baltimore branch of Pinkerton's, James Wright.

The Op appeared originally in thirty-six stories written mainly for the pulp magazine *Black Mask*. Four stories published between Nov. 1927 and Feb. 1928 were revised to form the novel *Red Harvest*. Four further stories published from Nov. 1928 to Feb. 1929 were revised similarly for the novel *The Dain Curse*. The two linked Op novellas published in 1943 by Spivak as *$106,000 Blood Money* first appeared in *Black Mask* in Feb. and May 1927. The Spivak book is a digest-magazine-sized paperback with orange covers printed black and white. The remaining twenty-six Op stories from the pulps were collected in book form in eight further digest-sized paperbacks, published between 1945 and 1962. These have variously coloured covers and printing. Collectors should be aware that *The Continental Op* (Spivak 1945) has blue covers and black-and-white lettering in its true first edition. Green covers, multicoloured lettering and a price of 35c indicate a reissue. Likewise, *Dead Yellow Women* was reprinted, with identical covers, but again with a price increase from 25c to 35c.

Sam Spade, Hammett's most famous detective, is revered as the virtual prototype of the tough-guy private investigator. He appears in one novel, *The Maltese Falcon*, and three stories. He, too, is a solitary man, hard-drinking and chain-smoking. He works from an office on Sutter Street, near Kearney, San Francisco. He walks a tightrope between the legal and the illegal, but when he bends the law it is generally to bring a criminal to book. He is tall, with pale green eyes and light-brown hair. Though tough and ready to fight, he prefers to use his brain to trap a villain rather than a gun. In appearance and manner he could be mistaken for one of the criminals he tracks, but he is, in fact, an idealist. He also has a liking for wisecracks. The three Spade stories are collected in *The Adventures of Sam Spade*, published in 1944 by Spivak as a digest-sized paperback with brown covers printed black and white.

The violent adventures of Secret Agent X–9 were written for a newspaper cartoon strip drawn by Alex Raymond. Hammett supplied the text for the FBI man's investigations from Jan. 1934 to Apr. 1935. The strips continued to appear but were written by other writers. Two oblong paperbacks with pictorial covers featuring the newspaper strips were published by McKay in 1934. *Secret Agent X–9* has a red cloth spine. Both covers show an elderly man being shot in a library, while Agent X–9 wheels round to aim a gun at the attacker and a horrified woman looks on. *Secret Agent X–9, Book 2* has a blue cloth spine and covers showing Agent X–9 seizing an elderly man who appears to be trying to escape, while a smartly-dressed woman holds, in turn, the agent's arm. The scene is played against an inferno of smoke and flame. Later editions from Nostalgia Press in 1976 and International Polygonics in 1983 reprinted the contents of the original books and added different additional comic strips.

The novel *The Glass Key* was first published in book form in the UK. Otherwise, the books made their first appearance in the USA. Knopf published all the novels in America and all except *The Thin Man* in Britain. The UK edition of *The Thin Man* came from Barker. All Hammett's first editions are dated.

The US edition of *Red Harvest* has red cloth with a single black border on the front cover, which also has a yellow skull and crossbones (repeated in red on the title-page). The rear cover has the Borzoi Books logo, with a dog between the two words, within a black rectangle in the lower right corner. The spine is amazingly complicated, with a single black rule at the top; a red rectangle within a black border under it; then title and author in red against a black rectangle within a red border that is itself contained in a yellow border; then a single black rule, a split yellow rule and a pattern of six black and six red diamonds, each with a yellow vertical rule; then the publisher's name in yellow within a red rectangle surrounded by a black border; and finally a third black rule.

The US *Dain Curse* has yellow cloth with a dark-brown single border on the front cover, which also has a red skull and crossbones. The rear cover has the publisher's logo in brown. The spine is printed in red and brown. The British edition has orange cloth with black lettering on the spine, which also has two black rules at either end. The rear cover has the publisher's logo in orange within a small black rectangle. The title-page has a brown skull and crossbones and is dated 1930.

The Maltese Falcon first appeared in *Black Mask* from Sept. 1929 to Jan. 1930 and was then revised for book publication. The US edition has grey cloth with a single black border on the front cover, which also has a falcon in blue at the centre. The rear cover has the publisher's logo in black. The spine is printed in blue and black. The top edge is grey and the spine reproduces the design of US *Red Harvest*, but in black, grey and blue. The title-page also has the falcon.

The Glass Key also appeared first in *Black Mask*, between Mar. and June 1930. There was some slight revision for book publication. The US edition has pale-green cloth and a single red border on the front cover, which also has a broken green key. The rear cover has the publisher's logo in dark green. The spine is printed in red and dark green. Copies with 'First and second printings before publication' on the copyright page are clearly not true first editions. The Knopf UK edition has blue cloth with a white key in the top right corner of the front cover. The publisher's dog motif appears blue within a red rectangle on the rear cover. The spine has red lettering, with a white key in the middle and a red fringed design at either end. The title-page has a green key. The top edge is blue.

The Thin Man was first published in *Redbook Magazine* in Dec. 1933 and the abridged version was included in *Six Redbook Novels*, issued in 1934. The first book edition was published in Jan. 1934 in green cloth, with a single red border on the front cover, which also has a blue mask. The back cover has the publisher's logo in red and the spine is printed red and blue. The UK edition from Barker has orange cloth with the spine lettered black. Title and author appear on the front cover, separated by a lined drawing of a thin man. This design recurs on the title-page. The book is dated 1934 on the copyright page

The US wrapper for Hammett's first novel has 'Red Harvest A Thrilling Detective Story by Dashiell Hammett' on a plain panel, with a vertical pattern of alternate diamonds and double stars on either side of the lettering. The spine has no decoration. The wrapper for both US and UK editions of *The Dain Curse* has a stylized figure in a clinging gown, with crossed arms displaying a claw-like hand. A bird-like image appears in the lower right corner. The American wrapper for *The Maltese Falcon* has the model of the falcon clinging to its plinth, beside a further claw-like hand, dripping, this time, with jewels. The falcon's head appears in the middle

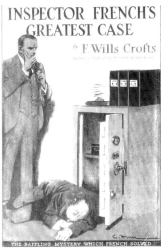

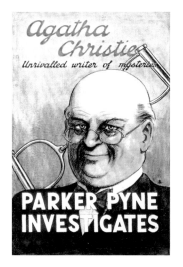

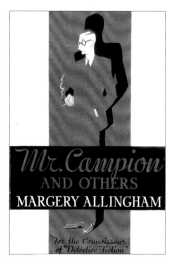

Detective Portraits

Three major series

Into the Golden Age: 1887-1930

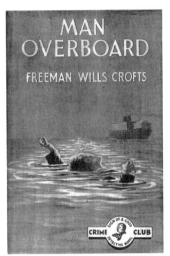

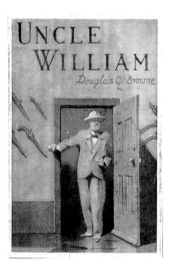

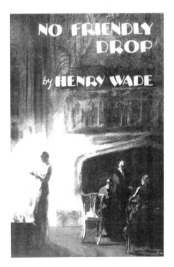

From the 1930s: I

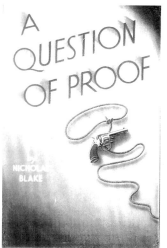

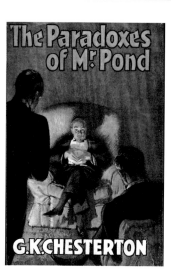

From the 1930s: II

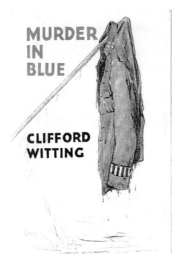

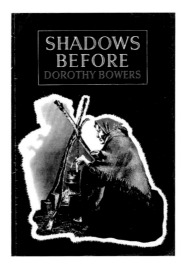

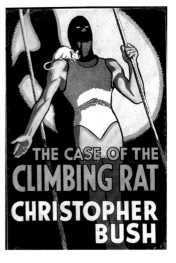

From the 1930s: III

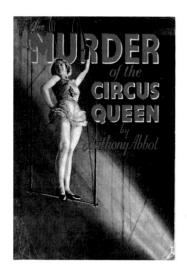
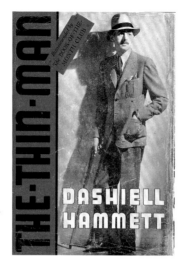

The Golden Age in America

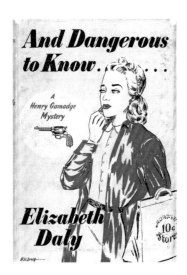

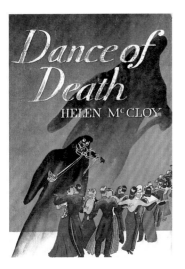

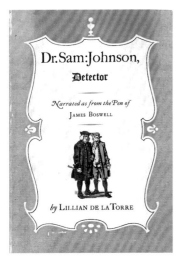

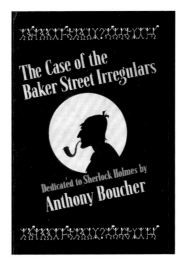

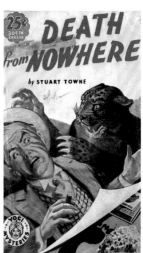

More American writers

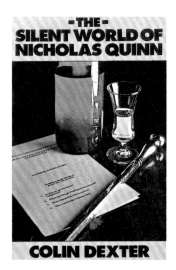

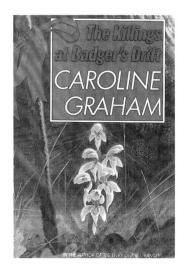

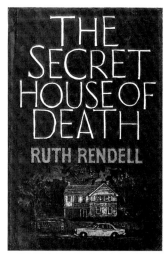

After 1940:   Britain

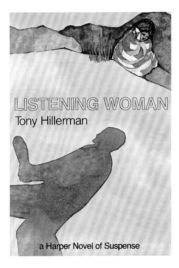

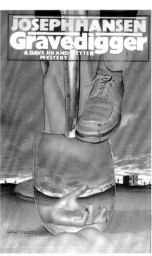

After 1940: America

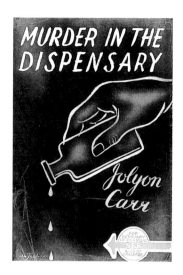

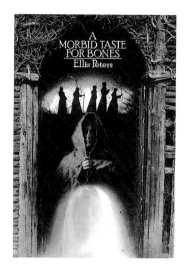

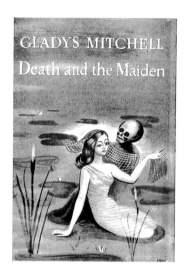

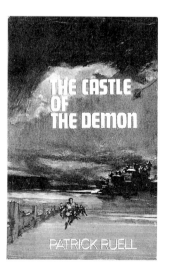

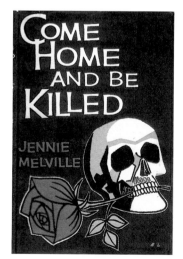

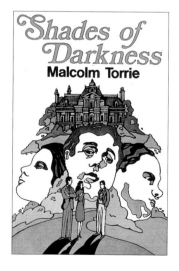

Split personalities

of the spine. *The Glass Key* (US) shows the face of a terrified woman, framed by the head of a key. The design is photographic, with the title above and the author's name, angled, below. The spine has a latchkey obliterated towards the top by title and author. *The Thin Man* (US) has a full-length black-and-white photograph of Dashiell Hammett, wearing a trilby and standing with one hand in his pocket and the other holding a walking stick at his side. He casts a shadow on the wall behind him. The title, unusually, appears in a red or green panel adjacent to the spine, with the words arranged vertically, sideways on. The photograph recurs on the spine, which can be red or green. No priority is established for the red or the green wrapper. Later wrappers for *Red Harvest* include notes about *The Dain Curse* and those for *The Maltese Falcon* have reviews of the book.

The unfinished novel, *Tulip*, was first published in *The Big Knockover* (Random House 1966). This has black cloth with the spine lettered gilt. The green wrapper has a burial casket at the bottom of the front panel and a disembodied eye over an elongated chequer-board above.

The single uncollected story, 'The Road Home', was first published as by Peter Collinson.

Novels

(with series characters, as stated)

Red Harvest Knopf US & UK 1929 (Continental Op)

The Dain Curse Knopf US 1929, Knopf UK 1930 (Continental Op)

The Maltese Falcon Knopf US & UK 1930 (Spade)

The Glass Key Cassell and Knopf UK 1931, Knopf US 1931

The Thin Man Knopf US 1934, Barker 1934

Novella

$106,000 Blood Money Spivak 1943 (Continental Op)

Story collections

The Adventures of Sam Spade Spivak 1944 (3 Spade stories, 4 others) (brown covers; black and white printing)

The Continental Op Spivak 1945 (4 Op stories)

The Return of the Continental Op Spivak 1945 (5 Op stories) (red; white, black and blue)

Hammett Homicides Spivak 1946 (4 Op stories and 2 others) (green; black and white)

Dead Yellow Women Spivak 1947 (4 Op stories and 2 others) (green; white, black, red, blue and brown)

Nightmare Town Mercury 1948 (2 Op stories and 2 others) (brown; black, white and blue)

The Creeping Siamese Spivak 1950 (3 Op stories and 3 others) (red; black, white, yellow, blue, green, brown, grey)

Woman in the Dark Spivak 1951 (3 Op stories and 4 others) (blue; black, white, green and yellow)

A Man Named Thin Ferman 1962 (1 Op story and 7 others) (blue; black, white, yellow and green)

The Big Knockover Random House 1966 (9 reprinted Op stories and *Tulip*)

Separately published stories

The Diamond Wager privately printed, Portage 1977

The Crusader privately printed, Sherman Oaks 1980

Cartoon strip

Secret Agent X–9 McKay 1934 (2 volumes) strip drawn by Alex Raymond

Uncollected story by Peter Collinson

'The Road Home' (*Black Mask*, Dec. 1922; as by Dashiell Hammett in *The Hard-Boiled Detective Stories from 'Black Mask' Magazine*, Random House 1977) *JC*

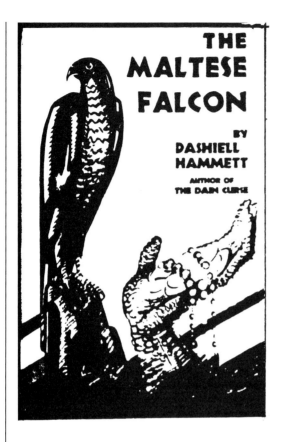

THE
MALTESE
FALCON

BY
DASHIELL
HAMMETT

AUTHOR OF
THE DAIN CURSE

Joseph Hansen (b. 1923)
a.k.a. Joseph Colton

Joseph Hansen's principal contribution to crime fiction has been the creation of a credible homosexual detective, an insurance claims investigator, well clear of stereotype. Dave Brandstetter is blessedly masculine, as many gay men are, and he is more concerned with sexual stability than promiscuity. He has two lovers during the series (and a third has died before it opens). In the course of Dave's investigations, Hansen explores the homosexual life of California, with authentic insights into gay people and their slant on the world (though this is by no means his exclusive brief). His powers are considerable, and he handles human tensions with acute perception and humane concern. His grasp of deviant motivation never fails him, and in

Gravedigger in particular it proves astonishingly powerful.

Brandstetter figures in twelve novels and two of the five stories in the collection *Brandstetter and Others*. *A Country of Old Men* ends his career. A second detective, Hack Bohannon, appears in 'The Tango Bear', originally in *Brandstetter and Others*, but also in *Bohannon's Book*, with four other Bohannon stories. He is also in three of the stories in *Bohannon's Country* and in the uncollected story 'A Woman's Voice'. A former sheriff's deputy, he loves horses and runs a boarding stable in California.

There are two non-series novels, *Backtrack* and *Steps Going Down*. Enthusiasts may even wish to investigate Hansen's earlier pseudonymous titles: a group by Joseph Colton and two Gothic novels by Rose Brock. At least one of the Colton books has been reissued in Joseph Hansen's name: *Known Homosexual*, retitled *Pretty Boy Dead*.

In Britain, the Brandstetter novels were published successively by Harrap, Faber and Peter Owen. *Steps Going Down* was brought out by Arlington Books in 1986, and *Backtrack* made a belated appearance from GMP in 1987 (having been published in the USA in 1982). The three Harrap books are handsomely individual: *Fadeout* in grey binding, with white spine lettering; *Death Claims* in maroon, with silver lettering; and *Trouble Maker* in green, with gilt lettering. All three have the publisher's circular logo on the front cover. Faber gave *The Man Everybody Was Afraid Of* a blue-green binding and gilt spine lettering, and *Skinflick* a black binding, lettered in silver. The two Owen books are also individual, red with gilt lettering and black with silver, respectively. They are also taller than the preceding volumes. *Steps Going Down* is taller still, a substantial green book with gilt spine lettering. The books are all dated.

Since 1986, Hansen's books have appeared only in America. Holt published *The Little Dog Laughed* in a pale-blue binding with darker blue lettering along the spine. *Early Graves* and *Obedience* appeared from Mysterious Press, both quarterbound, the former with cream boards and fawn spine, lettered purple, the latter red with black spine, lettered gilt. *Early Graves* has cream endpapers, *Obedience* red. Viking published the final pair of Brandstetter novels. *The Boy Who Was Buried This Morning* has pale-grey board and red endpapers. The spine and cover strips are navy blue with silver lettering running along the spine. *A Country of Old Men* has mauve boards with a yellow spine lettered purple.

Foul Play Press published the two non-series novels and two story collections. *Backtrack* and *Brandstetter and Others* are dark blue, *Steps Going Down* is cream and *Bohannon's Book* has oatmeal boards and brown spinal area. All four have gilt lettering along the spine. All the books are dated, all except the Viking books with 'First edition' or 'First printing' on the copyright page. All except the Foul Play books have a printer's key running from 1 on the copyright page. *The Little Dog Laughed* and *Bohannon's Book* are less tall than the others. *Gravedigger* preceded *Backtrack*, *Nightwork*, *Brandstetter and Others* and *Bohannon's Book*, *Obedience*.

With two exceptions, the UK dust-wrappers enhance the texts to which they relate. *Fadeout* and *Death Claims* have stylized designs, making patterns from themes, with a dream-like effect. *Trouble Maker* is more explicit: Rick Wendell lies dead and Larry Johns wipes the gun that shot him. For *The Man Everybody Was Afraid Of* Police Chief Ben Orton is represented as a poster torn across the face, with the people who feared him ranged behind. The powerful design for *Gravedigger* matches the intensity of this narrative: Kathy Staico Schorr shows the killer's feet as he buries one of his victims in the desert, beneath a glaring red sky. This design was used for both the US and UK editions. Sue Dray's stylish wrapper for *Steps Going Down* shows Chick Pelletier, Darryl Cutler and Stewart Moody, arranged in such a way as to illustrate the title.

The British *Backtrack* is a paperback, with a pictorial cover by Gwyn Rowlands, showing the Los Angeles skyline, with tracks running out across a wide highway.

The wrapper for *The Little Dog Laughed* is by Kathy Staico Schorr and shows a young soldier smiling as he discharges a machine-gun. *Early Graves* has a sensitive portrait of Brandstetter by John Jinks. He holds a cigarette and looks sombre, as well he might in a novel with AIDS as its theme. He wears a wide-brimmed hat and a private-eye trench-coat with the collar pulled up at the back. *Obedience*, also by Jinks, shows the gang boss Don Pham with two thugs. *A Country of Old Men* has a vivid design centred on a guitar and an epicene figure who might be Cricket Shales, who played it. *Steps Going Down* shows a deserted beach with a skull at the water's edge and a sad-looking man in the foreground.

The title story of *The Dog and Other Stories* (Momentum Press 1979) appeared in the MWA anthology *Killers of the Mind* (Random House 1974, Gollancz 1975), but the collection as a whole is not criminous.

Novels

(with Brandstetter, except as stated)

Fadeout   Harper 1970, Harrap 1972
Death Claims   Harper 1973, Harrap 1973
Trouble Maker   Harper 1975, Harrap 1975
The Man Everybody Was Afraid Of   Holt 1978, Faber 1978
Skinflick   Holt 1979, Faber 1980
Gravedigger   Holt 1982, Owen 1982
Backtrack   Foul Play Press 1982, GMP 1987 (not Brandstetter)
Nightwork   Holt 1984, Owen 1984
Steps Going Down   Foul Play Press 1985, Arlington 1986 (not Brandstetter)
The Little Dog Laughed   Holt 1986
Early Graves   Mysterious Press 1987
Obedience   Mysterious Press 1988
The Boy Who Was Buried This Morning   Viking 1990
A Country of Old Men   Viking 1991

Story collections

Brandstetter and Others   Foul Play Press 1984 (5 stories)
Bohannon's Book   Foul Play Press 1988 (5 stories)
Bohannon's Country   Viking 1993 (5 stories)

Joseph Hansen

DEATH CLAIMS

Uncollected stories

'Mourner' (*EQMM*, Oct. 1983)
'Storm Damage' (*AHMM* Nov. 1992)
'A Woman's Voice' (*AHMM*, Sep. 1993)

Novel by Joseph Colton

Known Homosexual Brandon House 1968
a.k.a. *Stranger to Himself* Major 1978
a.k.a. *Pretty Boy Dead* Gay Sunshine Press
    1984, as by Joseph Hansen   *BP*

Cyril Hare (1900–1958)
a.k.a. T. G. Clark

Cyril Hare is the principal pseudonym of Alfred
Gordon Clark. T. G. Clark is an early pen-name,
the 'T' representing 'Taffy', a family nickname
deriving from 'Affy' for 'Alfred'. Six stories are

known in this name: three are confirmed as criminous.

This much-admired writer has yet, however,
to be discovered by many current readers of
detective fiction. A barrister who became a
judge and often drew on his legal experience for
his writing, he published nine witty novels, one
collection of thirty stories, and eleven uncollected stories. His stories are some of the best
examples of the genre.

An elderly, unsuccessful lawyer, Francis Pettigrew, is introduced in the excellent *Tragedy at
Law*. He later marries the younger Eleanor
Brown, whom he meets in the course of his
investigations in *With a Bare Bodkin*. Pettigrew
features in three other novels and two of the
collected stories. Inspector John Mallett of Scotland Yard is tall and solid, with a military bearing. He appears in the author's first three books
and three of the Pettigrew novels, as well as in
two collected stories.

Cyril Hare's books were all first published in
London by Faber. They are lettered only on the
spine and are dated. Two titles have not been
published in the US, where some of the books
have alternative titles.

Tenant for Death was issued in black cloth,
lettered gilt. The wrapper design by Victor Reinganum continues from the front panel on to the
spine. It shows Jack Roach passing 27 Dayles-
ford Gardens in the dusk, just as a bearded
silhouetted figure is coming out. *Death Is No
Sportsman* has grey cloth lettered in red.
Barbosa's wrapper shows Jimmy Rendel coming
up the bank of the Didder, rod in hand, towards
the stockinged legs of Sir Peter Parker, which
are projecting from the reeds round the tump.
For *Suicide Excepted*, Faber reverted to black
cloth and gilt lettering. The front of the wrapper
by Reinganum shows the hand of Mr Dickinson
reaching from his bed to the pill bottles on the
bedside table, and the spine has pills dropping
out of a bottle.

Tragedy at Law has beige cloth lettered in
red, with the scales of Justice below the author's
name. The grey wrapper is lettered in black, with
four red horizontal lines. *With a Bare Bodkin* is
salmon-pink with gilt lettering, and its cream
wrapper has a red bodkin on the front panel.

The brown cloth of *When the Wind Blows* is lettered gilt. Reinganum's wrapper shows the dead body of Lucy Carless, in a long yellow dress, sprawled in an armchair. Her violin in its open case lies nearby on a table. *An English Murder* has red cloth lettered gilt. Edward Ardizzone's outstanding design for the wrapper shows the drawing-room at Warbeck Hall, where the butler, Briggs, holds a tray of champagne glasses, with the dead body of Robert Warbeck at his feet. This book was adapted from a radio play called *The Murder at Warbeck Hall*.

That Yew Tree's Shade was issued in brown cloth with green lettering. Miss Pink is seen walking over Yew Hill on Ardizzone's dustwrapper. This design is based on a sketch made by the artist from an upper window of the author's home, Berry's Croft, West Humble, near Dorking, which has a view of Box Hill. The last novel, *He Should Have Died Hereafter*, has claret-coloured cloth, lettered gilt. A later issue has blue cloth, lettered in yellow. The wrapper by Felix Kelly shows a figure on the roof of the outhouse at Swallowcombe.

The story collection, *Best Detective Stories of Cyril Hare*, has an introduction by Michael Gilbert. It, too, has claret-coloured cloth and gilt lettering. The wrapper is plainly lettered in yellow and red on black. Many of the stories have alternative titles, especially in *EQMM* (where 'Death of a Blackmailer' becomes 'The Homing Wasp' and 'The Old Flame' becomes 'The Boldest Course'). 'Miss Burnside's Dilemma' appeared originally in *Pearson's* in Nov. 1939, in a radically different version as 'Miss Burnside's Mistake'.

The most difficult first edition to locate is *Suicide Excepted*.

Novels

(with Mallett and/or Pettigrew, as stated)

Tenant for Death Faber 1937, Dodd, Mead 1937 (Mallett)
Death Is No Sportsman Faber 1938 (Mallett)
Suicide Excepted Faber 1939, Macmillan 1954 (Mallett)

Tragedy at Law Faber 1942, Harcourt 1943 (Mallett, Pettigrew)
With a Bare Bodkin Faber 1946 (Mallett, Pettigrew)
When the Wind Blows Faber 1949 (Pettigrew)
a.k.a. *The Wind Blows Death* Little, Brown 1950
An English Murder Faber 1951, Little 1951
a.k.a. *The Christmas Murder* Spivak 1953
That Yew Tree's Shade Faber 1954 (Pettigrew)
a.k.a. *Death Walks the Woods* Little 1954
He Should Have Died Hereafter Faber 1958 (Mallett, Pettigrew)
a.k.a. *Untimely Death* Macmillan 1958, Hogarth 1987

Story collection

Best Detective Stories of Cyril Hare Faber 1959, Walker 1961 (30 stories)
a.k.a. *Death Among Friends* Perennial 1984

Uncollected stories

'Spare the Rod and Spoil the Crime' (*ES*, 24 Jan. 1951)
'The Will' (*ES*, 6 Dec. 1951)
'Accident' (*ES*, 21 June 1952)
'This Side Up With Care' (*ES* 8 July 1954)
'The Man from Pannonia' (*ES* 30 Sept. 1955)
'The Magnifying Glass' (*ES* 10 Mar. 1956; *Planned Departures*, Hodder & Stoughton 1958)
'The Euthanasia of Hilary's Aunt' (*Some Like Them Dead*, Hodder 1960)
'Punctuality Grant' (publication details unknown)

Uncollected stories by T. G. Clark

'The Alsatian' (*Pearson's Weekly*, 27 Oct. 1928)
'The Blackmailers' (*Bystander*, 2 Jan. 1929)
'Lady Felicia's Pearls' (*Bystander*, 13 Feb. 1929). *JC*

Roy Hart (b. 1930)

Roy Hart should be read and collected by anyone who enjoys the traditional British whodunit, since he successfully combines convincing characterization with clever plotting. *A Pretty Place for a Murder* and *Blood Kin* are fine examples of his writing. Superintendent Douglas Roper is shrewd, smartly dressed and close to retirement. He features in nine books and is ably assisted in six investigations by Inspector David Price, later promoted to Chief Inspector. Three books – *Remains To Be Seen*, *Blood Kin* and *Deadly Schedule* – describe earlier cases, when Roper himself was a Chief Inspector. *The Gadfly Summer* is an Edwardian romance with murder thrown in and *A Position of Trust* is an excellent spy story.

All the books are dated and were first published in the UK. *The Gadfly Summer* is the only title with no US publication. It was published by Hale in 1978 and issued in dark-blue cloth with gilt spine lettering. Hale also published *A Position of Trust* in black cloth with silver lettering on the spine.

The first six Roper titles were published by Macmillan, all with silver spine lettering but in various coloured bindings. *Blood Kin* appeared from Scribner and *Final Appointment* and *A Deadly Schedule* came from Little, Brown, all three with maroon cloth, gilt-lettered spines and pink endpapers patterned with the publisher's name.

Martin White's illustration for *Seascape with Dead Figures* depicts the body of George Winterton on the rocks at Monk's Cave. The rest of the wrappers for the Roper series are, sadly, photographic.

Novels

(with Roper, except where stated)
(Binding colours refer to Macmillan editions.)

The Gadfly Summer   Hale 1978 (not Roper)
A Position of Trust   Hale 1985, St Martin's 1985 (not Roper)

Seascape with Dead Figures   Macmillan 1987, St Martin's 1987 (maroon)

A Pretty Place for a Murder   Macmillan 1987, St Martin's 1988 (light tan)

A Fox in the Night   Macmillan 1988, St Martin's 1988 (green)

Remains To Be Seen   Macmillan 1989, St Martin's 1989 (brown)

Robbed Blind   Macmillan 1990, St Martin's 1990 (red)

Breach of Promise   Macmillan 1990, St Martin's 1991 (grey)

Blood Kin   Scribner 1991, St Martin's 1992

Final Appointment   Little, Brown 1993, St Martin's 1993

A Deadly Schedule   Little, Brown 1993   *JC*

John Harvey (b. 1938)

John Harvey's complex and highly satisfying police procedural novels combine the best of the American and British schools of crime writing. His convincing characters convey the stresses and strains of modern police work within a sharply drawn inner-city environment. Nottingham provides the setting for clever plots and subplots, presented with realistic insights into modern city life with its vitality but also its ever-present underlying menace. The books also crackle with wit and sharp dialogue.

Detective Inspector Charlie Resnick and his DS Graham Millington, are part of a team of five officers who feature in five books. They are based at an inner-city police station in Nottingham. A divorcee of Polish descent, Resnick has an appealing vulnerability and a liking for sandwiches, stray cats and jazz.

Six other books, all paperback first editions in Harvey's own name, are thrillers rather than novels of detection, as is *Endgame*, published in hardback under the pseudonym James Mann. *Hard Cases* is also a paperback first, but it is not a detective novel: it is based on a TV series about inner-city probation officers.

John Harvey's Resnick stories were all first published in the UK by Viking; they are all dated and have printer's keys, 1–10, on the copyright page. *Lonely Hearts* was issued in blue cloth with black spine lettering. All other titles

have black cloth with silver lettering. *Off Minor* and *Wasted Years* had simultaneous hardback and paperback editions, the paperbacks with front cover designs reproducing those on the hardbacks' wrappers. Apart from *Off Minor*, all the books have attractive wrappers featuring collages of scenes from the stories.

Lonely Hearts is the most difficult first edition to find.

Resnick novels

Lonely Hearts   Viking 1989, Holt, 1989
Rough Treatment   Viking 1990, Holt 1990
Cutting Edge   Viking 1991, Holt 1991
Off Minor   Viking 1992, Holt 1992
Wasted Years   Viking 1993, Holt 1993
NB The simultaneous paperback editions of *Off Minor* and *Wasted Years* have different ISBNs from the hardback editions.   *JC*

Keith Heller
a.k.a. Allan Lloyd

Keith Heller's historical detective novels began to appear in 1984, from Collins Crime Club. His first book is set in 1722 and records an investigation undertaken in middle life by George Man, a London parish watchman. His second case harks back to his young manhood in 1703, and his third moves ahead to 1727. Heller's narratives are enriched by recorded history – the Great Plague, the devastating storm of November 1703, an actual eighteenth-century murder. Man also encounters the celebrities of his time: Jonathan Wild, Thomas Coram, Daniel Defoe, Henry Fielding. The author reveals considerable knowledge of the period, and achieves a convincing pastiche of seventeenth-century style for a diary of the Plague.

All three books are red, with gilt lettering on the spine. They are all dated and have wrapper drawings by Geoff Taylor, which exercise a far more potent appeal than the usual photographs. Two Man stories have appeared since the latest novel was published.

In *Mystery Readers' Journal*, Fall 1993, Heller reveals that he is also Allan Lloyd, in which name two stories have appeared in *EQMM*, both featuring the real-life Chinese magistrate Ti Jen-Chieh, on whom Robert van Gulik based his Judge Dee.

Man novels

Man's Illegal Life Collins Crime Club 1984, Scribner 1985
Man's Storm Crime Club 1985, Scribner 1986
Man's Loving Family Crime Club 1986

Man stories

'Man's Inherited Death' (*EQMM*, Mar. 1987)
'Man's Noble Art of Self-Defence' (*EQMM* Apr. 1988).

Ti Jen-Chieh stories

'The Man Who Wiped Away Footprints' (*EQMM* Sept. 1988)
'Under a Plum Tree' (*EQMM* Nov. 1989) *BP*

Georgette Heyer (1902–1974)

Although she is probably better known for her many historical romances, Georgette Heyer also wrote twelve detective novels, which alone would have given her literary fame. There is also one story. Sergeant (later Inspector) Hemingway appears in eight novels serving in the first four under Superintendent Hannasyde. As his career progresses, Hemingway's special interests in psychology and the theatre are developed.

Georgette Heyer's books were all first published in London, and they are all dated. *Death in the Stocks* has the alternative American title *Merely Murder*.

The first four books were published by Longmans, Green, with the title and author's name on the front cover as well as on the spine. *Footsteps in the Dark* has black cloth with silver lettering. *Why Shoot a Butler?* has orange cloth,

The Unfinished Clue has red, and Death in the Stocks has fawn. All three are lettered in black.

The next four titles were published by Hodder & Stoughton in blue cloth, with seventeen horizontal black lines, which run from below the author's name on the spine right across the front cover. In all four books, the publisher's name and colophon appear in black at the base of the spine. For *Behold Here's Poison*, the title and author's name are lettered in black on a gilt background. The other three books have the title and author's name in gilt. The last Hodder title, *Envious Casca*, has blue cloth, lettered in black on the spine. *They Found Him Dead* has blue and white pictorial endpapers designed by Chesterman. Clement Kane lies 'crumpled across his desk, one arm hanging limply at his side', while various suspects occupy the background, all in the spotlight from a torch. This design recurs on the wrapper. The wrapper for *Behold, Here's Poison* has the silhouette of a wind-blown poplar tree in the foreground, with the house, Poplars, set against a blue and green background. *A Blunt Instrument* has a green bush with pink bows on it. Stead's wrapper for *No Wind of Blame* shows the green gardens of the Dower House as background for his drawing of the wooden bridge that provides the setting for a shooting. Stead also drew the two brown doors sealed by white tape and sealing wax for *Envious Casca*.

The final three books were published by Heinemann, *Penhallow* in khaki cloth, with the spine lettered in white. The others have black cloth. All three have the author's initials blind-stamped at the lower right-hand corner of the front cover. *Duplicate Death* and *Detection Unlimited* are lettered gilt on the spine, and the latter also has a prone figure in black on a gilt background.

The mystery story 'Night at the Inn' is collected in *Pistols for Two*, with other non-mystery stories with historical settings. This book has red cloth lettered gilt on the spine and the usual blind-stamped initials on the front cover. The first publication of 'Night at the Inn' was in *John Bull* for 11 Mar. 1950.

The plain lettered wrapper for *Penhallow* is in red and cream. A bridge set by C. W. Bacon illustrates the wrapper of *Duplicate Death*.

Stein's design for *Detection Unlimited* is in red, white, and green on a largely black background. An assortment of people from the novel point accusingly at each other.

The author's first two books are the most difficult first editions to find.

Regarding *Penhallow*, the author wrote: 'Although it was listed by Heinemann as a thriller, *Penhallow* really is *not* one'.

Novels

(with Hannasyde and/or Hemingway, as stated)

Footsteps in the Dark   Longmans, Green 1932, Berkley 1986
Why Shoot a Butler?   Longman 1933, Doubleday 1936
The Unfinished Clue   Longman 1934, Doubleday 1937
Death in the Stocks Longman 1935 (Hannasyde, Hemingway)
a.k.a. *Merely Murder*   Doubleday 1935

NO WIND OF BLAME
GEORGETTE HEYER

Behold, Here's Poison Hodder & Stoughton, 1936, Doubleday 1936 (Hannasyde, Hemingway)

They Found Him Dead Hodder 1937, Doubleday 1937 (Hannasyde, Hemingway)

A Blunt Instrument Hodder 1938, Doubleday 1938 (Hannasyde, Hemingway)

No Wind of Blame Hodder 1939, Doubleday 1939 (Hemingway)

Envious Casca Hodder 1941, Doubleday 1941 (Hemingway)

Penhallow Heinemann 1942, Doubleday 1943

Duplicate Death Heinemann 1951, Dutton 1969 (Hemingway)

Detection Unlimited Heinemann 1953, Dutton 1969 (Hemingway)

Story

'Night at the Inn' (*Pistols for Two*, Heinemann 1960, Dutton 1964) JC

Reginald Hill (b. 1936)
a.k.a. Patrick Ruell

Reginald Hill is the author of seventeen detective novels, one novella, three collections of stories and eleven uncollected stories in his own name. There are also eight crime novels as Patrick Ruell and three thrillers as Reginald Hill. In twelve novels, one novella and three stories the detectives are Superintendent Andrew Dalziel and Sergeant Peter Pascoe, later an inspector. They work in Yorkshire and, since their personalities complement each other and each is gifted in his way, they make a very effective team. Dalziel is gross, outspoken and coarse-grained, Pascoe more personable, better educated, less prejudiced. Several of their investigations also feature the ugly Sergeant Wield. Despite the style and wit of this series, some of it may prove too harsh and uncomfortable for those who read for relaxation and reassurance. Hill has recently created a new series character, Joe Sixsmith, a balding, middle-aged West Indian, who sets up as a private eye when made redundant as a lathe operator. He has featured to date in one novel and two stories.

All the Reginald Hill books have appeared from Collins, the series and other detective novels from the Crime Club, the thrillers under the firm's general imprint. The Crime Club books all have gilt lettering on the spine and, apart from four titles, are all bound in red cloth. The four exceptions are *Bones and Silence, Recalled to Life, An April Shroud* and the novella *One Small Step*, the former pair with blue cloth, the latter pair with black. All the books are dated, with a printer's key on the copyright page from *Recalled to Life*. With two exceptions, they have the standard photographic wrappers. *There Are No Ghosts in the Soviet Union* has an illustration by Val Hill of the open lift at the Gorodok Building and *One Small Step* has Dalziel and Pascoe meeting Colonel Ed Druson in the lunar village on the moon. This novella is illustrated with seven line drawings. It was revised and abridged for publication in *EQMM* in Oct. 1993.

Under World was reprinted during 1988 but this fact was not indicated in the reprint, which resembles the first edition except that the red cloth is smoother and the gilt lettering much brighter. The reprint wrapper is priced £10.95, whereas the first edition was priced £9.95, and the orange lettering of the title is in a darker shade.

Brother's Keeper collects four stories, two previously uncollected, including the title story, specially written. The book has plain white wrappers and is lettered black on both spine and front cover of the brown dust-wrapper. The edges are roughly trimmed and there is a limitation notice (of 350 copies) at the end.

The Patrick Ruell books eschew the patterns of formal detection, opting instead for odd goings-on set in, and dependent on, a particular landscape: *Death Takes the Low Road*, for instance, entails a 'crazy chase all over Scotland'. Despite their free-wheeling air, they are meticulously shaped, with an edge of intellectual excitement to give an added distinction. Eccentric male and female protagonists meet the hazards resourcefully and pair romantically. After an interval of several years, *The Long Kill* proved less exuberant and larky than its predecessors. Bleak and bitter, and sexually over-explicit, it leaves its moral position in doubt until the end.

The first and second Ruell books were published by John Long, the third and fourth by Hutchinson. All four are black, with gilt spine lettering, and they are dated. Colin Andrews' wrapper for *Red Christmas* shows a Christmas stocking, with a hand holding a gun protruding from the top of it.

The Long Kill, Death of a Dormouse and *Dream of Darkness* were published by Methuen and are dated. The cloth colours are green, red and black, respectively, and all have gilt spine lettering. The latest Ruell title, *The Only Game*, was published by Collins, is dated and has grey cloth with the spine lettered silver. Paul Finn's dust-wrapper for *The Long Kill* shows Jaysmith lying on Wanthwaite Crags aiming his M21 rifle through his adjustable ranging telescope at the head of Steven Bryant, in the garden of Naddle Foot across the valley. The design covers the whole wrapper, front and back.

The most elusive titles are the earliest: *A Clubbable Woman, Fell of Dark* and *The Castle of the Demon*.

Novels by Reginald Hill

(with Dalziel and Pascoe, except as stated)

A Clubbable Woman   Collins Crime Club 1970, Countryman 1984

Fell of Dark   Crime Club 1971, NAL 1986 (non-series)

An Advancement of Learning   Crime Club 1971, Countryman 1985

A Fairly Dangerous Thing   Crime Club 1972, Countryman 1983 (non-series)

Ruling Passion   Crime Club 1973, Harper 1977

A Very Good Hater   Crime Club 1974, Countryman 1982 (non-series)

An April Shroud   Crime Club 1975, Countryman 1986

Another Death in Venice   Crime Club 1976, NAL 1987 (non-series)

A Pinch of Snuff   Crime Club 1978, Harper 1978

The Spy's Wife   Collins 1980, Pantheon 1980 (non-series)

A Killing Kindness   Crime Club 1980, Pantheon 1981

Who Guards a Prince?   Collins 1982 (non-series)

a.k.a. *Who Guards the Prince?*   Pantheon 1982

Traitor's Blood   Collins 1983, Countryman 1986 (non-series)

Deadheads   Crime Club 1983, Macmillan 1984

Exit Lines   Crime Club 1984, Macmillan 1985

Child's Play   Crime Club 1987, Macmillan 1987

Under World   Crime Club 1988, Scribner 1988

Bones and Silence   Crime Club 1990, Delacorte 1990

Recalled to Life   Crime Club 1992, Delacorte 1992

Blood Sympathy   Crime Club 1993 (Sixsmith)

Novella by Reginald Hill

One Small Step   Crime Club 1990

Story collections by Reginald Hill

Pascoe's Ghost   Crime Club 1979 (7 stories, 2 with Dalziel and Pascoe)

There Are No Ghosts in the Soviet Union   Crime Club 1987 (6 stories, 1 with Dalziel and Pascoe, 1 with Sixsmith)

Brother's Keeper   Eurographica 1992 (4 stories)

Novels by Patrick Ruell

The Castle of the Demon   John Long 1971, Hawthorn 1973

Red Christmas   Long 1972, Hawthorn 1974

Death Takes the Low Road   Hutchinson 1974, Mysterious Press 1987

Urn Burial   Hutchinson 1975, Countryman 1987

The Long Kill   Methuen 1986, Countryman 1988

Death of a Dormouse   Methuen 1987, Mysterious Press 1987

Dream of Darkness   Methuen 1989, Countryman 1990

The Only Game   Collins 1991, Countryman 1993

169

Uncollected stories by Reginald Hill

'The Thaw' (*Winter's Crimes 5*, Macmillan 1973)

'Urban Legend' (*EQMM*, March 1989, *Crime Waves 1*, Gollancz 1991)

'A Shameful Eating' (*A Suit of Diamonds*, Crime Club 1990)

'Proxime Accessit' (*TAD*, Summer 1990, *New Crimes 2*, Robinson 1990)

'The Running of the Deer' (*Christmas Stalkings*, Mysterious Press 1991, HarperCollins 1992) (Sixsmith)

'Realpolitik' (*Julian Symons at 80*, Eurographica 1992)

'The Man Who Defenestrated His Sister' (*The Man Who...*, Macmillan 1992)

'Stonestar' (*1st Culprit*, Chatto & Windus 1992)

'Strangers on a Bus' (*Midwinter Mysteries 2*, Little, Brown 1992)

'Market Forces' (*Northern Blood*, Didsbury Press 1992)

'True Thomas' (*2nd Culprit*, Chatto & Windus 1993)   *JC/BP*

Tony Hillerman (b. 1925)

Tony Hillerman's mysteries are set in the American west, where Utah, Arizona, Colorado and New Mexico meet. He is deeply concerned with American Indian lore, specifically of the Navajo tribe, to which his two series detectives belong. Joe Leaphorn is the senior: in rank, in years and in having appeared first. He is shorter and broader than Jim Chee, the junior, who looks 'destined to be a skinny old man'. Each has three cases of his own and from *Skinwalkers* they work together, with complementary personalities and skills. Leaphorn has adapted more to the white man's world; Chee is immersed in his native culture, studying to be a yataalii, or shaman, seeking to keep 'the People in harmony with their universe'. The books draw strongly on the desert landscape and the Navajo culture: they are shaped and driven by the ways of this particular world, precisely defined and imaginatively applied. The standard lusts of the western world are also much in evidence, threatening, as always, stability and tradition.

All the books were published by Harper in America but *The Ghostway* was first published by Dennis Macmillan in a limited edition, preceding that from Harper. Its priority, regrettably, makes it significant for many collectors, though the strong-minded may choose to consider it irrelevant. With one exception, the Harper firsts are quarterbound in a range of colours. *A Thief of Time* has an undivided off-white binding with dark red-brown lettering on the spine. In the other books the spine lettering, too, varies from one title to another.

Five books are identified as 'Joan Kahn' books and have coloured endpapers with 'A Harper Novel of Suspense' repeated many times in white lettering: with a purple background for *The Blessing Way*, a blue for *Fly on the Wall* and *Dance Hall of the Dead* and a black for *Listening*

Woman and *People of Darkness*. *Talking God* has dark blue endpapers, *Coyote Waits* has purple and *Sacred Clowns* has orange-brown. The endpapers for *A Thief of Time* are brown and feature an enticing map of the Anasazi country. The front covers of several books have the publisher's logo of a torch within a square over '1817'. This is dark blue for *Fly on the Wall* and blind-stamped for *Listening Woman, People of Darkness, The Dark Wind* and *A Thief of Time. Skinwalkers, Talking God, Coyote Waits* and *Sacred Clowns* have thematic devices on their front covers, blind-stamped, pinkish gilt, gilt and gilt, respectively. The books are all dated by the copyright notice and have printer's keys: at the end of the book for the three to *Dance Hall of the Dead* and on the copyright page for the others. All state 'First edition' on the copyright page. *Dance Hall of the Dead, Listening Woman, Talking God* and *Sacred Clowns* have roughly trimmed fore-edges. *Talking God* and *Coyote Waits* have decorated title-pages. From *Skinwalkers*, the books are taller, too large for many shelves.

The wrappers for the series are invariably vivid and arresting, drawing on themes and images from the culture defined in the novels. *The Blessing Way* has a man wearing a wolf-skin, its head in profile over his own. *Dance Hall of the Dead* features a desert landscape with a boy holding a bow and a grotesque icon in a feathered head-dress behind him. *Listening Woman* has a lemon-yellow wrapper with the shadow of a man wielding a club and Listening Woman hunched in the upper right corner. From *Skinwalkers* the books have wrappers by Peter Thorpe: a skull in the desert for *Skinwalkers*; a black-and-white pot and a piper for *A Thief of Time*; and a picturesque god with some resemblance to Mr Chad for *Talking God*.

The Ghostway is a blue book with silver lettering on the spine and a silver device on the front cover. It has blue endpapers and a dated title-page and the copyright page has 'First edition' and the date of publication, Oct. 1984 (the Harper edition came out in 1985). The complex scene on the wrapper, in vibrant primary colours, extends over the spine and both covers.

The British editions are markedly inferior to the American, since neither Macmillan nor Gollancz made much attempt to individualize their crime fiction. From *Skinwalkers* the books have been published by Joseph and, like the US series, they are taller from this title on. *Dance Hall of the Dead* was published in Britain by Pluto Press, simultaneously in hardback and paperback. *Fly on the Wall*, a non-series novel, has not appeared in Britain. Despite the prevalence of witches and Jim Chee's participation, it appears that 'The Witch, Yazzie and the Nine of Clubs' and 'Chee's Witch' are different stories. There is also a 'non-fiction story', published in *EQMM*.

Tony Hillerman contributed to Jack Hitt's *The Perfect Murder*, published in 1991.

Novels

(with Leaphorn and/or Chee, as stated)
(Binding details refer to Harper editions.)

The Blessing Way Harper & Row 1970, Macmillan 1970 (Leaphorn) (blue boards, purple spine, red lettering)

Fly on the Wall Harper 1971 (blue, blue, dark blue and white)

Dance Hall of the Dead Harper 1973, Pluto 1985 (Leaphorn) (blue, dark pink, blue)

Listening Woman Harper 1978, Macmillan 1979 (Leaphorn) (fawn, pale yellow, black)

People of Darkness Harper 1980, Gollancz 1982 (Chee) (grey, red, silver)

The Dark Wind Harper 1982, Gollancz 1983 (Chee) (blue, blue, silver)

The Ghostway Dennis Macmillan Oct. 1984 (Harper 1985), Gollancz 1985 (Chee)

Skinwalkers Harper 1987, Joseph 1988 (Leaphorn, Chee) (mushroom, dark red, gilt)

A Thief of Time Harper 1988, Joseph 1989 (Leaphorn, Chee)

Talking God Harper 1989, Joseph 1990 (Leaphorn, Chee) (sand, dark blue, pinkish gilt)

Coyote Waits Harper 1990, Joseph 1991 (Leaphorn, Chee) (orange, purple, gilt)

Sacred Clowns HarperCollins 1993 (Leaphorn, Chee) (orange-brown, off-white, gilt)

Stories

'The Replacement' (*New Mexico Quarterly*, Autumn 1967; revised and expanded for *Tierra: Contemporary Short Fiction of New Mexico*, 1989)

'The Witch, Yazzie and the Nine of Clubs' (*Crime Wave*, Collins 1981) (Chee)

'Chee's Witch' (*The New Black Mask 7*, Harcourt, Brace 1986) (Chee)

Non-fiction story

'First Lead Gasser' (*EQMM*, Apr. 1993; *2nd Culprit*, Chatto & Windus 1993)

Collaboration

The Perfect Murder HarperCollins 1991 *BP*

John Buxton Hilton (1921–1986) a.k.a. John Greenwood

John Buxton Hilton was the primary pseudonym of a voluminous crime writer who launched a second byline, John Greenwood, late in his career. His work is very uneven, largely because he wrote too much and too quickly: sometimes two books a year, often three. At his best, he is a deeply satisfying writer, vigorous and various, and richly inventive. Much of his work is set in the Peak District, and the Greenwood books inhabit the hill country of the Lancashire/Yorkshire border.

He has three series detectives, all men of character, emphatically themselves. Simon Kenworthy appears most frequently, in the first novel, *Death of an Alderman*, and in sixteen later titles. He is wily and persistent, exacting and unpredictable; yet a genuine personality, for all his waywardness. Had he been a criminal, he would have given the police a run for their money. Tom Brunt is a Victorian detective, born around 1850 and active into George V's reign. He is unhurried and tenacious, waiting and watching until he has sounded out both crime and criminal. He appears in *Rescue from the Rose* and five others. The six Greenwood novels feature Inspector Jack Mosley, a subtle comic figure in the classic tradition of those whose success confounds expectation. It is cause for regret that he came so late on to the scene.

Hilton's first publisher was Cassell, who brought out *Death of an Alderman* in 1968 and *Death in Midwinter* the following year. Both books are black, with white lettering along the spine. After an interval of six years, *Hangman's Tide* appeared from Macmillan, who issued five more books, the last in 1978. In sequence, the six books are black, green, blue, light brown, dark blue, and maroon. They have the standard Macmillan lettering: the author's surname and the title printed along the spine, with a dividing line between. *Hangman's Tide* has white lettering and *Some Run Crooked* silver: on the other four it is black. The Macmillan books are taller than their predecessors. From 1980, the Hilton books were published by Collins Crime Club, in red bindings, with gilt spine lettering. *The Anathema Stone* has advertisements at the back. The Greenwood books are published by Quartet and are taller than average, with a uniform format: black binding and white lettering along the spine. All the books in both names are dated.

The wrapper for *Death of an Alderman* is black and white, with a representation of bullet holes in glass. *Death in Midwinter*'s is much more satisfactory, with its realization of the scene described on the last page of the book. The Macmillan wrappers vary from the usual photographs to such vivid designs as Paul Goodfellow's mirror view of the gamekeeper's gallows, and Patricia Ludlow's portrait of Julie Wimpole, for *Some Run Crooked*. The Crime Club run is almost exclusively photographic, with the honourable exception of Paddy Eckersley's inspired design for *Playground of Death*, which represents the murder as a child's drawing on a wall.

The Greenwood series has handsome photographic wrappers, more appealing than most because of their framing and uniform presentation. Stephen Baxter's photo of Upper Marldale's church clock under a full moon intensifies the lure of *Mists Over Mosley*.

Six uncollected stories are known, all except 'The Kitchen' and 'Taken at the Ebb' with Kenworthy as detective.

Berkley Diamond reissued several Hilton novels with new titles. Those matched to the originals are listed. *The Fatal Curtain, Dead Man's Path* and *Twice Dead* are further new titles.

Novels

(with Kenworthy, except as stated)

Death of an Alderman   Cassell 1968, Walker 1968

Death in Midwinter   Cassell 1969, Walker 1969

Hangman's Tide   Macmillan 1975, St Martin's 1975

No Birds Sang   Macmillan 1975, St Martin's 1976

Rescue from the Rose   Macmillan 1976, St Martin's 1976 (Brunt)

Gamekeeper's Gallows   Macmillan 1976, St Martin's 1977 (Brunt)

Dead-Nettle   Macmillan 1977, St Martin's 1977 (Brunt)

Some Run Crooked   Macmillan 1978, St Martin's 1978

The Anathema Stone   Collins Crime Club 1980, St Martin's 1980

Playground of Death   Crime Club 1981, St Martin's 1983

Surrender Value   Crime Club 1981, St Martin's 1981

The Green Frontier   Crime Club 1982, St Martin's 1982

The Sunset Law   Crime Club 1982, St Martin's 1982

Mr. Fred   Crime Club 1983, St Martin's 1983 (Brunt)

The Asking Price   Crime Club 1983, St Martin's 1983

a.k.a. *Ransom Game*   Berkley Diamond 1992

Corridors of Guilt   Crime Club 1984, St Martin's 1984

The Hobbema Prospect   Crime Club 1984, St Martin's 1984

a.k.a. *Cradle of Crime*   Berkley Diamond 1991

The Quiet Stranger   Crime Club 1985, St Martin's 1985 (Brunt)

Passion in the Peak   Crime Club 1985, St Martin's 1985

a.k.a. *Holiday for Murder*   Berkley Diamond 1991

Moondrop to Murder   Crime Club 1986, St Martin's 1986

The Innocents at Home   Crime Club 1986, St Martin's 1987

a.k.a. *Lesson in Murder*   Berkley Diamond 1991
Slickensides   Crime Club 1987, St Martin's 1987
   (Brunt)
Displaced Person   Crime Club 1987, St Martin's
   1988

Mosley novels by John Greenwood

Murder, Mr. Mosley   Quartet 1983, Walker 1983
Mosley by Moonlight   Quartet 1984, Walker
   1985
Mosley Went to Mow   Quartet 1985
a.k.a. *The Missing Mr. Mosley*   Walker 1985
Mists Over Mosley   Quartet 1986, Walker 1986
The Mind of Mr. Mosley   Quartet 1987, Walker
   1987
What, Me, Mr. Mosley? Quartet 1987

Uncollected stories

'The Kitchen' (*Magpie*, Feb. 1952)
'Taken at the Ebb' (*Winter's Crimes 7*, Macmillan 1975, St Martin's 1975)
'Bellamy's Bus' (*Winter's Crimes 8*, Macmillan 1976, St Martin's 1976)
'Saskja' (*Winter's Crimes 10*, Macmillan 1978, St Martin's 1978)
'The Wedding Party' (*AHMM*, 27 Oct. 1980)
'Four Ways' (*John Creasey's Crime Collection 1980*, Gollancz 1980)   *BP*

Michael Innes (b. 1906)

Michael Innes is the pseudonym of the retired Oxford don J. I. M. Stewart, who has written forty-five crime novels and seventy-four stories, eighteen of which remain to be collected. He is also a well-known novelist under his own name.

It is through his main series character, the urbane, articulate John Appleby, that the author's considerable learning and wit make themselves felt. This unusual policeman uses literary quotations to great effect. Readers must be grateful for the long series of novels tracing his career from the rank of inspector to his appointment as Commissioner of London's Metropolitan Police, with a knighthood bestowed before his retirement (during which he happily goes on solving crimes). He meets his future wife, the sculptor, Judith Raven, in *Appleby's End*, and she plays an important part in several novels and many stories. Their youngest son, Bobby, undergraduate and author, assists his father in three novels and one story: 'A Question of Confidence', collected in *The Appleby File*. In all, Appleby appears in thirty-two novels and seventy-three stories, including all the uncollected stories, except 'The Man Who Collected Satchels'. Other series characters are Inspector Cadover, who has three cases, including one with Appleby; Charles Honeybath, RA, who also shares one of his four cases with Appleby; and Hildebert Braunkopf, the art dealer and proprietor of the Da Vinci Gallery, who is in three novels and two stories.

Many of the books have alternative titles in the USA, including the first, *Death at the President's Lodging*, which became *Seven Suspects*. *The Weight of the Evidence* and *A Night of Errors* were first published in the USA.

In Britain, all Michael Innes' books have been published by Gollancz. They are all dated and have the usual yellow dust-wrappers. The first five titles have black cloth, lettered in red on the spine. *Stop Press* is a little taller than the rest. There is a pull-out plan of St Anthony's College opposite page 318 of *Death at the President's Lodging*. *Hamlet, Revenge!* has a fine preliminary drawing of the setting for *Hamlet* at Scamnum Court.

The Secret Vanguard and *Appleby on Ararat* have blue cloth with the spine lettered in blue. The latter is the most elusive title to find in first edition. The following six titles are thin, war-economy books, in blue cloth with gilt lettering on the spine. All the remaining titles have red cloth with gilt spine lettering, except *The Journeying Boy*, *Operation Pax*, and *The New Sonia Wayward*, which have the spine lettered in black. *Operation Pax* is a darker red, shading into mauve.

Novels

(with Appleby, except as stated; with Cadover, Honeybath, Braunkopf, and Bobby Appleby, as stated)

Death at the President's Lodging   Gollancz 1936
a.k.a. *Seven Suspects*   Dodd, Mead 1937
Hamlet, Revenge!   Gollancz 1937, Dodd 1937
Lament for a Maker   Gollancz 1938, Dodd 1938
Stop Press   Gollancz 1939
a.k.a. *The Spider Strikes*   Dodd 1939
There Came Both Mist and Snow   Gollancz 1940
a.k.a. *A Comedy of Terrors*   Dodd 1940
The Secret Vanguard   Gollancz 1940, Dodd 1941
Appleby on Ararat   Gollancz 1941, Dodd 1941
The Daffodil Affair   Gollancz 1942, Dodd 1942
The Weight of the Evidence   Dodd 1943, Gollancz 1944

Appleby's End   Gollancz 1945, Dodd 1945
From London Far   Gollancz 1946 (not Appleby)
a.k.a. *The Unsuspected Chasm*   Dodd 1946
What Happened at Hazelwood   Gollancz 1946, Dodd 1946 (Cadover)
A Night of Errors   Dodd 1947, Gollancz 1948
The Journeying Boy   Gollancz 1949 (Cadover)
a.k.a. *The Case of the Journeying Boy*   Dodd 1949
Operation Pax   Gollancz 1951
a.k.a. *The Paper Thunderbolt*   Dodd 1951
A Private View   Gollancz 1952 (also Cadover, Braunkopf)
a.k.a. *One-Man Show*   Dodd 1952
a.k.a. *Murder Is an Art*   Avon 1959
Christmas at Candleshoe   Gollancz 1953, Dodd 1953 (not Appleby)
a.k.a. *Candleshoe*   Penguin 1978
The Man from the Sea   Gollancz 1955, Dodd 1955 (not Appleby)
a.k.a. *Death by Moonlight*   Avon 1957
Old Hall, New Hall   Gollancz 1956 (not Appleby)
a.k.a. *A Question of Queens*   Dodd 1956
Appleby Plays Chicken   Gollancz 1956
a.k.a. *Death on a Quiet Day*   Dodd 1957
The Long Farewell   Gollancz 1958, Dodd 1958
Hare Sitting Up   Gollancz 1959, Dodd 1959
The New Sonia Wayward   Gollancz 1960 (not Appleby)
a.k.a. *The Case of Sonia Wayward*   Dodd 1960
Silence Observed   Gollancz 1961, Dodd 1961
A Connoisseur's Case   Gollancz 1962
a.k.a. *The Crabtree Affair*   Dodd 1962
Money From Holme   Gollancz 1964, Dodd 1965 (Braunkopf)
The Bloody Wood   Gollancz 1966, Dodd 1966
A Change of Heir   Gollancz 1966, Dodd 1966 (not Appleby)
Appleby at Allington   Gollancz 1968
a.k.a. *Death by Water*   Dodd 1968
A Family Affair   Gollancz 1969 (also Braunkopf, Bobby Appleby)
a.k.a. *Picture of Guilt*   Dodd 1969
Death at the Chase   Gollancz 1970, Dodd 1970 (also Bobby Appleby)
An Awkward Lie   Gollancz 1971, Dodd 1971 (also Bobby Appleby)

The Open House   Gollancz 1972, Dodd 1972
Appleby's Answer   Gollancz 1973, Dodd 1973
Appleby's Other Story   Gollancz 1974, Dodd 1974
The Mysterious Commission   Gollancz 1974, Dodd 1975 (Honeybath)
The Gay Phoenix   Gollancz 1976, Dodd 1977
Honeybath's Haven   Gollancz 1977, Dodd 1978 (Honeybath)
The Ampersand Papers   Gollancz 1978, Dodd 1979
Going It Alone   Gollancz 1980, Dodd 1980 (not Appleby)
Lord Mullion's Secret   Gollancz 1981, Dodd 1981 (Honeybath)
Sheiks and Adders   Gollancz 1982, Dodd 1982
Appleby and Honeybath   Gollancz 1983, Dodd 1983 (also Honeybath)
Carson's Conspiracy   Gollancz 1984, Dodd 1984
Appleby and the Ospreys   Gollancz 1986, Dodd 1987

Appleby story collections

Appleby Talking   Gollancz 1954 (23 stories)
a.k.a. *Dead Man's Shoes*   Dodd 1954
Appleby Talks Again   Gollancz 1956, Dodd 1957 (18 stories)
The Appleby File   Gollancz 1975, Dodd 1976 (15 stories)

Uncollected stories

'The Scattergood Emeralds' (*ES*, 10 Aug. 1954; *EQMM*, May 1955, as 'True or False?')
'A Small Peter Pry' (*ES*, 12 Aug. 1954)
'The Impressionist' (*ES* 23 July 1955)
'The Perfect Murder' (*ES*, 5 Aug. 1955)
'The General's Wife is Blackmailed' (*ES*, 22 Apr. 1957)
'The Left-handed Barber' (*ES*, 23 Apr. 1957)
'A Change of Face' (*ES*, 24 Apr. 1957)
'The Theft of the Downing Street Letter' (*ES*, 25 Apr. 1957)
'The Man Who Collected Satchels' (*ES*, 26 Apr. 1957)
'The Tinted Diamonds' (*ES*, 27 Apr. 1957).

'Jerry Does a Good Turn for the DJAM' (*ES*, 7 Apr. 1958)
'The Mystery of Paul's "Posthumous" Portrait' (*ES*, 8 Apr. 1958)
'Who Suspects the Postman?' (*ES*, 9 Apr. 1958; *Saint*, July 1960 (UK), as 'In the Bag')
'The Inspector Feels the Draught' (*ES*, 10 Apr. 1958)
'The Author Changes His Style' (*ES*, 10 Apr. 1958; *Saint*, July 1960 (UK), as 'News Out of Persia')
'The Party That Never Got Going' (*ES*, 19 Feb. 1959)
'The Secret in the Woodpile' (*EQMM*, Oct. 1975; *Ellery Queen's Searches and Seizures*, Dial 1975)
'Pelly and Cullis' (*Verdict of Thirteen*, Faber 1979, Harper 1979)   *JC*

the second detective story of

MICHAEL INNES

whose first

"Death at the President's Lodging"

was called by " Torquemada "

"A new detective classic"

and was generally received with the

utmost enthusiasm

P. D. James (b. 1920)

P. D. James has brought lustre to crime fiction and may be said to have ennobled the form. After years of neglect, she is now widely celebrated, even revered. Few writers are as scrupulous as she in preserving the traditional patterns and disciplines of the detective novel. At the same time, her work has many of the qualities commonly regarded as the preserves of mainstream fiction: amplitude, depth, and resonance. She has two series detectives, a young private investigator, Cordelia Gray, and a senior policeman, Adam Dalgliesh (whose name undergoes a change of spelling after *Cover Her Face*, where he is Dalgleish). Dalgliesh has had nine cases to date, including one short story. He also features briefly in the first of Cordelia Gray's two cases. Two books, *Innocent Blood*, a bleak psychological novel, and *The Children of Men*, a grim thriller set in 2021, are different in kind from the rest of the books.

Cover Her Face appeared in 1962, from Faber, still P. D. James' publisher. It is a green book with gilt lettering, and with a wrapper by Charles Mozley, showing the enigmatic face and 'heavy red-gold hair' of Sally Jupp. The same artist designed the pink wrapper for *A Mind to Murder*, where Enid Bolam, 'afloat on a tide of paper', holds in death 'a heavy and grotesque image carved in wood'. No spectacles hanging askew are in evidence, however, as they should be. The book is red and lettered gilt. *Unnatural Causes* is also red, but with silver lettering, and a photographic wrapper featuring a map of the Suffolk coast in front and a coastal view behind.

Shroud for a Nightingale is the first of the taller books that put paid to any hope of formal unity. It is red, with gilt lettering, and with a skull in a nurse's cap on the wrapper. *An Unsuitable Job for a Woman* introduces Cordelia Gray, who investigates a complex case in Cambridge. The book is green with gilt lettering, and the pale green wrapper shows a belt tied like a noose, with King's College Chapel in the background. *The Black Tower*, which returns to Dalgliesh, has an arresting wrapper by Errol Le Cain, with a cowled and faceless figure set against the sweep of the cliff under the tower. It is a grey book, lettered gilt.

Death of an Expert Witness and *Innocent Blood* have routine photographic wrappers of scant appeal. Both books are red with gilt lettering. *The Skull Beneath the Skin* is Cordelia Gray's second case, and, in keeping with the density of the text, it is an imposing tome, black with silver lettering. The eccentric purple wrapper, by Pentagram, features the title in small, slim letters, mainly lower case, while the author's name looms disproportionately large in hefty capitals, over which a hand drips blood. The obsessive collector will want the American edition of this book, which preceded the British by several months. It is slightly smaller than the Faber volume, with a black binding and vivid red lettering that sometimes looks purple, depending on the light.

A Taste for Death was properly called by H. R. F. Keating 'magisterial'. It is magisterial in appearance, too, as tall as its immediate predecessor, but even broader, to allow for seventy more pages of text. The binding is again black and the lettering silver. The wrapper is an eloquent enhancement of the narrative, with images both of St Matthew's Church and of the appalling deaths that occurred within it.

Devices and Desires and *The Children of Men* are bigger still: indeed, the former would make a good doorstop. Both are black with white lettering along the spine. The wrappers have, respectively, a nocturnal scene of church ruins and a sunlit wood, with, by contrast, a doll lying on paving stones and two staring glass eyes.

All the Faber books are dated on the copyright page. The Scribner *Skull Beneath the Skin* is also so dated, but with the addition of a printer's key from 1–20, the odd numbers divided from the even by the letters F/C. A later issue is known that lacks this feature.

In December 1983 *The Mail on Sunday* published a Christmas serial by P. D. James, as the basis of a competition. *The Murder of Santa Claus* appeared in three episodes, on 4, 11, and 18 December. The issue of 22 Jan. 1984 revealed the murderer's identity, and the author's final episode was circulated to those who had entered the competition or had applied for a copy. The story appeared in book form in *Great Detectives* (Pantheon 1984).

The single Dalgliesh story is 'Great-Aunt Allie's Fly-papers', first published in the Detection Club anthology, *Verdict of Thirteen*. Seven other stories have appeared.

The Maul and the Pear-tree is a true-crime work written with T. A. Critchley and published by Constable in 1971. The author's only play to date, *A Private Treason*, was performed at Watford in March 1985, with Susannah York and Robert Eddison in leading parts. Sheila Mitchell, Mrs H. R. F. Keating, played a supporting role. A dense and thoughtful work, the play examines the extraordinary circumstances in which a risky marriage is destroyed. Because it is in no sense a whodunit, it perhaps disappointed the expectations of its audiences.

Novels

(with Dalgliesh except as stated)

Cover Her Face   Faber 1962, Scribner 1966
A Mind to Murder   Faber 1963, Scribner 1967
Unnatural Causes   Faber 1967, Scribner 1967
Shroud for a Nightingale   Faber 1971, Scribner 1971
An Unsuitable Job for a Woman   Faber 1972, Scribner 1973 (Gray; Dalgliesh only briefly)
The Black Tower   Faber 1975, Scribner 1975
Death of an Expert Witness   Faber 1977, Scribner 1977
Innocent Blood   Faber 1980, Scribner 1980 (non-series)
The Skull Beneath the Skin   Scribner 1982, Faber 1982 (Gray)
A Taste for Death   Faber 1986, Scribner 1986
Devices and Desires   Faber 1989, Knopf 1990
The Children of Men   Faber 1992, Knopf 1993 (non-series)

Newspaper serial

The Murder of Santa Claus (*The Mail on Sunday*, Dec. 1983; also in *Great Detectives*, Pantheon 1984)

Uncollected stories

'Moment of Power' (*EQMM*, July 1968; *Ellery Queen's Murder Menu*, World 1969, Gollancz 1969; *John Creasey's Crime Collection 1981*, Gollancz 1981, as 'A Very Commonplace Murder')

'Murder 1986' (*EQMM*, Oct. 1970; *Ellery Queen's Masters of Mystery*, Davis 1975, Gollancz 1977)

'The Victim' (*Winter's Crimes 5*, Macmillan 1973, St Martin's 1973)

'A Very Undesirable Residence' (*Winter's Crimes 8*, Macmillan 1976, St Martin's 1976)

'Great-Aunt Allie's Fly-papers' (*Verdict of Thirteen*, Faber 1979, Harper 1979; *Woman's Realm*, 2 Mar. 1985, as 'The Boxdale Inheritance')

'The Girl Who Loved Graveyards' (*Winter's Crimes 15*, Macmillan 1983, St Martin's 1983)

'The Mistletoe Murder' (*Spectator*, 21/28 Dec. 1991 & 4 Jan. 1992)

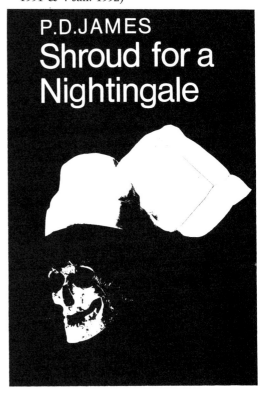

'The Man Who Was Eighty' (*The Man Who ...*,
  Macmillan 1992)   *BP*

Lucille Kallen

Maggie Rome, like Archie Goodwin, is that rare
phenomenon, a first-person narrator with class.
She figures in the novels of Lucille Kallen,
together with her employer, C. B. Greenfield,
the proprietor and editor of *The Sloan's Ford
Reporter*. Again like Archie, she regards her
employer with a critical eye, exploring for the
diversion of the reader every aspect of his eccentric personality. Operating jointly, they make a
formidable team, confronting local murders in
particular and modern barbarism in general. For
all its exhilarating wit, the series is fuelled by
anger and even by despair.

Introducing C. B. Greenfield was published by
Crown in 1979. *The Tanglewood Murder* and *No
Lady in the House* came from Wyndham, the
former in a blue-green binding, the latter quarterbound with pale-green boards and the spine
and cover strips in a brighter green. Both have
gilt lettering on the spine and the former has
the Wyndham logo of a bird in flight blind-stamped on the front cover. Both are dated by the
copyright notice only and have printer's keys
running from 1 on their copyright pages. *The
Piano Bird* and *A Little Madness* were published
by Random House, both quarterbound with
silver lettering on the spine. The former has
mauve boards and black spine and cover strips
and the author's initials, silver within a matching
rectangular frame, on the front board. The latter
has pale-blue boards, with the spine and cover
strips in a deeper blue and with double silver
rules framing the title on the spine. Both books
are dated on the copyright page, which states
'First edition' and has a printer's key running,
correctly, from 2 in each case.

The wrapper for *The Tanglewood Murder* has
a map of the Tanglewood area with a musical
clef in blood at the centre. *No Lady in the House*
has the open front door of a wooden house and
The Piano Bird has a bird in flight set against a
tropical landscape, with a dead hand protruding
from the greenery. *A Little Madness* shows two
women, one of whom is shining a torch on the
legs and skirt of a woman lying dead outside a
missile base.

All five novels were published in Britain by
Collins Crime Club in red bindings with gilt
spine lettering and dated copyright pages. The
titles all include Greenfield's name, and his
glasses are a feature of all the dust-wrappers,
giving them an individual stamp and fostering
an agreeable sense of continuity.

Greenfield novels

(also with Rome)

Introducing C. B. Greenfield Crown 1979, Col-
  lins Crime Club 1979
C. B. Greenfield: The Tanglewood Murder
  Wyndham 1980, Crime Club 1980
C. B. Greenfield: No Lady in the House Wynd-
  ham 1982, Crime Club 1982
C. B. Greenfield: The Piano Bird Random
  House 1984, Crime Club 1984

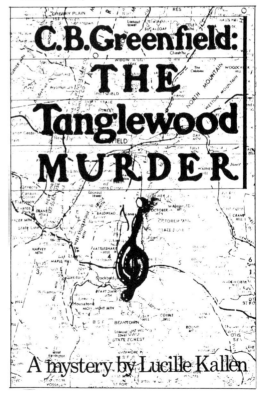

C. B. Greenfield: A Little Madness Random House 1986, Crime Club 1986   *BP*

H. R. F. Keating (b. 1926)
a.k.a. Evelyn Hervey

H. R. F. Keating has to date published thirty-two novels, including three under the pseudonym Evelyn Hervey. Thirty-four of his stories are collected and a further forty or so await collection.

He was first published by Gollancz, who brought out four books between 1959 and 1962. They are exuberant, explosive diversions, almost too bizarre and idiosyncratic. Narrative is fired at the reader in unnerving staccato bursts, with sentences split and adverbs adrift. A move to Collins Crime Club in 1963 brought a less frenetic manner and two endearing series detectives: Emma Craggs, an acute, resourceful char, in *Death of a Fat God*; and Inspector Ganesh Ghote, of the Bombay CID, in *The Perfect Murder*. Mrs Craggs has since appeared only in stories, most of which are collected in *Mrs. Craggs: Crimes Cleaned Up*. Ghote figures in a further nineteen novels, two story collections and four uncollected stories. Both are essentially comic characters, with unexpected features: the char never misses a trick, and the policeman repeatedly wins through in the teeth of widespread corruption and his own fallibility.

In 1986, Keating moved to Hutchinson, who published five more Ghote novels and the Ghote collection, with an invaluable introduction by the author. The Craggs collection was published by Buchan & Enright.

Inspector Ghote and Some Others is a limited edition collection of three stories, two with Ghote ('Nil by Mouth, Inspector Ghote' and 'The Evidence I Shall Give') and one without ('Gup'). 'Nil by Mouth' is from *Inspector Ghote, His Life and Crimes* but the others are previously uncollected. The edition, in wrappers, is limited to 350 copies.

A Remarkable Case of Burglary is a Victorian novel, set in 1871 (and so a forerunner of the Evelyn Hervey series). *The Murder of the Maharajah* takes place in 1930, in the Summer Palace of Bhopore. It deservedly won the CWA Gold Dagger, and it is and is not a Ghote novel. *Is Skin-Deep, Is Fatal* and *Murder by Death* are also non-series. The latter is a narrative version of Neil Simon's film of the same name. He holds the copyright and gets the star billing on cover and spine. In 1993, Macmillan launched a new series featuring separate detectives, each distinguished by a particular quality, beginning with Bill Sylvester, *The Rich Detective*.

The four Gollancz books have red bindings, generally with gilt spine lettering, except for *Zen There Was Murder*, which has black. *The Dog It Was That Died* and the Crime Club books to *Inspector Ghote Caught in Meshes* are less tall than the books on either side of them. *The Murder of the Maharajah* is taller than its neighbours, and *Mrs Craggs* and the Evelyn Hervey novels are taller still. *Death of a Fat God* is red and *Inspector Ghote Caught in Meshes* is red threaded with black; and the three books between them partake of the two, their spines and the adjacent strips of each cover in red, and the rest of the covers in red-black. From *Inspector Ghote Hunts the Peacock* to *The Sheriff of Bombay* the books are red. Except for *Death of a Fat God*, which has black spine lettering, the Crime Club books are lettered gilt. *Mrs. Craggs* is a black book with gilt spine lettering. Four of the Hutchinson books are also black: the earlier novels and the collection. These are uniform in size with *Mrs. Craggs* and the Hervey novels. The final pair from Hutchinson are taller and have brighter bindings: yellow for *The Iciest Sin* and red for *Cheating Death*. The latter title and the collection have gilt lettering on the spine but the others have silver. *The Rich Detective* is cream with gilt lettering and a printer's key from 1 on the copyright page. All Keating's books are dated on the copyright page.

The three Hervey novels were published by Weidenfeld & Nicolson, who gave the first and second an attractive uniform format, only to disrupt it with the third. They feature a Victorian governess named Harriet Unwin. H. R. F. Keating was not identified as their author until the third volume, and then only on the dust-wrapper. He acknowledges a debt to Philip MacDonald in *Into the Valley of Death*. *The Governess* is green, *The Man of Gold* black, and *Into the*

Valley of Death red. All three are dated and have gilt spine lettering. *Into the Valley of Death* also has crossed swords within a noose at the head of the spine.

Murder by Death first appeared in the USA in 1976, published by Warner, and the British edition is a Star paperback, issued by Wyndham in the same year. The cover has a still from the film, showing the assembled company at dinner, at 22 Lola Lane, San Francisco. Prominent among them are Sidney Wang, Jessica Marbles, and Dick and Dora Charleston, who are seated, and Milo Perrier and Sam Diamond, who are on their feet.

The Gollancz wrappers are the usual affronts to the sensibilities, and the Crime Club series began ill with the standard format of lettering on a black background that obsessed this house in the 1950s and 1960s. But some of the later wrappers for the Ghote novels have wit and charm, largely because the Indian settings demand creative design rather than the pedestrian photography that obtains elsewhere. For *Inspector Ghote Draws a Line*, Johnny Pau elegantly combines a typewriter, a hookah, and a bundle of explosive; and for *Go West, Inspector Ghote*, Peter Sojke shows an exotic green figure with four arms, balanced on a Coke bottle, against a background of stars and stripes. Andrew Key shows Miss Unwin and a headless sugar-mouse on the wrapper of *The Governess*, and George Smith, for *The Man of Gold*, depicts her with the Partington twins.

Mrs. Craggs has a linking commentary from Mrs Craggs' colleague and friend, Florrie Milhorne, elicited in the course of an interview. The book is decorated with a mop and bucket at the head of each story and with two recurrent silhouettes of Mrs Milhorne in the linking sections. 'Mrs. Craggs Sings a Different Tune' is an extract from *Death of a Fat God* adapted as a story. 'Mrs. Craggs and the Pale Ella' was originally entitled 'A Paperback, a Deckchair and Murder'.

The uncollected stories include two Sherlock Holmes pastiches, 'The Adventure of the Suffering Ruler' and 'A Trifling Affair'. 'Jack Fell Down' is a Sven Hjerson story after Ariadne Oliver. 'The Locked Bathroom' and 'The Case

of Seven Santas' feature Mrs Craggs, and 'Miss Unwin Goes a-Hunting' and 'A Common Error' are Harriet Unwin stories, the former antedating the novels.

Inspector Ghote appears in 'Death Hath Also This', 'Softly, Softly, Catchee Monkey', 'Shaky' and 'Murder Again on the Orient Express', which was published in three parts as a competition story in *Radio Times*. 'You Haven't Got a Clue', in which Bill Sylvester, the Rich Detective, features as a raw detective constable, was also a competition story. 'Fonsy Noonan's Story', in *Ellery Queen's Prime Crimes 3*, Davis 1985, is an extract from the mainstream novel *The Lucky Alphonse* (Enigma 1982).

H. R. F. Keating also contributed to an episodic novel written in multiple collaboration, *The Rigby File*.

Novels

(with Ghote, except as stated)

Death and the Visiting Firemen   Gollancz 1959, Doubleday 1973 (not Ghote)

Zen There Was Murder   Gollancz 1960 (not Ghote)

A Rush on the Ultimate   Gollancz 1961 (not Ghote)

The Dog It Was That Died   Gollancz 1962 (not Ghote)

Death of a Fat God   Collins Crime Club 1963, Dutton 1966 (Craggs)

The Perfect Murder   Crime Club 1964, Dutton 1965

Is Skin-Deep, Is Fatal   Crime Club 1965, Dutton 1965 (not Ghote)

Inspector Ghote's Good Crusade   Crime Club 1966, Dutton 1966

Inspector Ghote Caught in Meshes   Crime Club 1967, Dutton 1968

Inspector Ghote Hunts the Peacock   Crime Club 1968, Dutton 1968

Inspector Ghote Plays a Joker   Crime Club 1969, Dutton 1969

Inspector Ghote Breaks an Egg   Crime Club 1970, Doubleday 1971

Inspector Ghote Goes by Train   Crime Club 1971, Doubleday 1972

Inspector Ghote Trusts the Heart   Crime Club 1972, Doubleday 1973
Bats Fly Up for Inspector Ghote   Crime Club 1974, Doubleday 1974
A Remarkable Case of Burglary   Crime Club 1975, Doubleday 1976 (not Ghote)
Murder by Death   Warner 1976, Wyndham 1976 (not Ghote), from a screenplay by Neil Simon
Filmi, Filmi, Inspector Ghote   Crime Club 1976, Doubleday 1977
Inspector Ghote Draws a Line   Crime Club 1979, Doubleday 1979
The Murder of the Maharajah   Crime Club 1980, Doubleday 1980 (not Ghote)
Go West, Inspector Ghote   Crime Club 1981, Doubleday 1981
The Sheriff of Bombay   Crime Club 1984, Doubleday 1984
Under a Monsoon Cloud   Hutchinson 1986, Viking 1986
The Body in the Billiard Room   Hutchinson 1987, Viking 1987
Dead on Time   Hutchinson 1988, Mysterious Press 1989
The Iciest Sin   Hutchinson 1990, Mysterious Press 1990
Cheating Death   Hutchinson 1992
The Rich Detective   Macmillan 1993, Mysterious Press 1993 (not Ghote)
Doing Wrong   Macmillan 1994

Story collections

Mrs. Craggs: Crimes Cleaned Up   Buchan & Enright 1985, St Martin's 1985 (18 Craggs stories)
Inspector Ghote, His Life and Crimes   Hutchinson 1989 (14 Ghote stories)
Inspector Ghote and Some Others   Eurographica 1991 (3 stories, 2 with Ghote)

Unwin novels by Evelyn Hervey

The Governess   Weidenfeld & Nicolson 1984, Doubleday 1984
The Man of Gold   Weidenfeld 1985, Doubleday 1985
Into the Valley of Death   Weidenfeld 1986, Doubleday 1986

Collaborative novel

The Rigby File   Hodder & Stoughton 1989

Uncollected stories

'The Justice Boy' (*EQMM*, Aug. 1967; *Ellery Queen's Mystery Parade*, NAL 1986)
'The Old Shell Collector' (*EQMM*, July 1970; *Ellery Queen's Headliners*, World 1971, Gollancz 1972)
'An Upright Woman' (*Winter's Crimes 2*, Macmillan 1970)
'The Old Haddock' (*EQMM*, June 1971)
'A Little Rain in a Few Places' (*EQMM*, Sept. 1972)
'Memorial to Speke' (*EQMM*, Nov. 1972)
'The Butler Did It' (*EQMM*, May 1973)
'Torture Chamber' (*EQMM*, Sept. 1974)
'Liar, Liar, Pants on Fire' (*EQMM*, Apr. 1976)
'Mr. Saul' (*The 13th Ghost Book*, Barrie & Jenkins 1977)
'The Spirit of Service' (*The Midnight Ghost Book*, Barrie & Jenkins 1978)
'The Adventure of the Suffering Ruler' (*Blackwood's*, May 1979; *John Creasey's Crime Collection 1983*, Gollancz 1983)
'The Locked Bathroom' (*EQMM*, June 1980)
'A Trifling Affair' (*John Creasey's Crime Collection 1980*, Gollancz 1980)
'Miss Unwin Goes a-Hunting' (*EQMM*, 24 Mar. 1982)
'A Hell of a Story' (*EQMM*, June 1982; *John Creasey's Crime Collection 1984*, Gollancz 1984)
'Dead Letter Drop' (*EQMM*, mid-July 1982)
'A Crime Child' (in *EQMM*, mid-July 1983)
'And We in Dreams' (*Winters Crimes 15*, Macmillan 1983, St Martin's 1983)
'Two Grave Robbers' (*Woman's Own*, Jul. 1983)
'The Hand' (*Ellery Queen's Prime Crimes 3*, Davis 1985)
'Old P' (*Ellery Queen's Prime Crimes 4*, Davis 1986)
'A Common Error' (*EQMM*, Feb. 1987)
'Murder Again on the Orient Express' (*Radio Times*, 11, 18, 25 Mar. 1989)
'A Snaking Suspicion' (*EQMM*, mid-Dec. 1989)

'Death Hath Also This' (*Catholic Herald*, Lent 1990; *The Seven Deadly Sins*, Spire 1990)

'Jack Fell Down' (*A Classic English Crime*, Pavilion 1990; *EQMM*, Aug. 1991)

'Softly, Softly, Catchee Monkey' (*New Crimes 2*, Robinson 1990)

'The Case of Seven Santas' (*EQMM*, mid-Dec. 1990)

'Shaky' (*Winter's Crimes 23*, Macmillan 1991)

'There's an Explanation for Everything' (*Midwinter Mysteries 1*, Scribner 1991)

'That's Frank' (*Constable New Crimes 1*, Constable 1992)

'The Man Who Killed for Pleasure' (*The Man Who . . .* , Macmillan 1992)

'You Haven't Got a Clue' (*Weekend Telegraph*, 19 Dec. 1992)

'Fog of Doubt' (*EQMM*, June 1993)

'Incident at Millionaires' Row' (*2nd Culprit*, Chatto & Windus 1993)

'A Carpet of Snow' (*Midwinter Mysteries 3*, Little, Brown 1993)

'A Sort of Miss Marple' (*Royal Crimes*, Penguin (US) 1994)   *BP*

Harry Kemelman (b. 1908)

Harry Kemelman's novels offer an absorbing account of life in a suburban Jewish community, with a young Rabbi exercising the traditional function of his office, that of judge and 'interpreter of the law'. The author's avowed aim was to make murder 'provide only one thread, albeit an important one, of a larger narrative' and, from the opening paragraph of the first book, the Jewish faith and its rituals create the context for the mysteries. Even the Rabbi's intricate reasoning derives from the Talmud. Though confined by most of the series to local concerns, he twice escapes to Israel and becomes involved in a wider scene.

A collection of eight stories features Nicky Welt, the Snowdon Professor of English Language and Literature at a New England university. The book is named after its most celebrated component 'The Nine Mile Walk', in which Nicky Welt builds from a single sentence a chain of inference that points to a crime which then proves to have happened in precisely that way.

Harry Kemelman has had five American publishers but in Britain he remained with Hutchinson (or Century Hutchinson) for ten of his eleven books. His most recent novel was published by Severn House. Except for *Friday the Rabbi Slept Late*, which is dark blue, all the Hutchinson books are black. *Friday the Rabbi Slept Late* and *Saturday the Rabbi Went Hungry* have white lettering on the spine and *Someday the Rabbi Will Leave* has silver. All the others have gilt spine lettering. The six titles to *Tuesday the Rabbi Saw Red* (including *The Nine Mile Walk*) have grey endpapers. *One Fine Day the Rabbi Bought a Cross* has red endpapers with the Mysterious Press logo in black massed ranks. From *Monday the Rabbi Took Off* to *Someday the Rabbi Will Leave* the books are taller. *The Day the Rabbi Resigned* was published in Britain by Severn House in a red binding with gilt spine lettering and a dated copyright page.

The wrappers for the 'daily' series feature parts of a calendar, each corresponding to the day featured in the title. *One Fine Day* has a striking illustration of an archaeological dig, with a man's foot protruding from the rubble. *The Nine Mile Walk* shows two male legs in boots walking in rain.

Two American editions are known, one from Fields, the other from Morrow. *Tuesday the Rabbi Saw Red* is a black book with silver spine lettering and the author's facsimile signature in silver on the front cover. The fore-edge is roughly trimmed and the title-page has a vignette of a classical male bust broken into three pieces (also on the wrapper). The book is dated by the copyright notice and the copyright page states 'First edition', with a printer's key, 10–1. *Wednesday the Rabbi Got Wet* is quarterbound, with orange boards and gilt and orange lettering on a blue spine. The endpapers are black and the book is dated on the title-page. The copyright page has a printer's key running forward from 1 and backwards from 76. Despite their being from different publishers, these two books have wrappers in uniform style.

Rabbi Small novels

Friday the Rabbi Slept Late Crown 1964, Hutchinson 1965
Saturday the Rabbi Went Hungry Crown 1966, Hutchinson 1967
Sunday the Rabbi Stayed Home Putnam 1969, Hutchinson 1969
Monday the Rabbi Took Off Putnam 1972, Hutchinson 1972
Tuesday the Rabbi Saw Red Fields 1973, Hutchinson 1974
Wednesday the Rabbi Got Wet Morrow 1976, Hutchinson 1976
Thursday the Rabbi Walked Out Morrow 1978, Hutchinson 1979
Someday the Rabbi Will Leave Morrow 1985, Hutchinson 1985
One Fine Day the Rabbi Bought a Cross Morrow 1987, Century Hutchinson 1988
The Day the Rabbi Resigned Fawcett Columbine 1992, Severn House 1992

Story collection

The Nine Mile Walk Putnam 1967, Hutchinson 1968
                                              BP

C. Daly King (1895–1963)

The novels of C. Daly King are less celebrated than his single book of stories, *The Curious Mr. Tarrant*, the most valuable of all Collins Crime Club books, according to a recent listing. In 1959 Ellery Queen remarked on the 'immense scarcity of this book', as if this were phenomenal, and repeated expressions of wonder over the years have inflated its value as an infinitely desirable prize. It was the third of Daly King's books to be published by Collins and appeared in October 1935, in the usual orange binding, with black lettering on the spine only. The eponymous investigator is Trevis Tarrant, who is curious in both senses, though perhaps more

184

inquisitive than strange. He has eight cases here and three in *EQMM*. In his preamble to 'The Episode of the Sinister Invention', Ellery Queen refers to a Tarrant novel, *The Episode of the Demoiselle d'Ys*, but this seems not to have been heard of since. A fourth uncollected Tarrant story was published as by his usual narrator, Jeremiah Phelan.

The published novels have a rather uncertain classic status: though cunning and intricate, they are also arid and portentous. They play with ideas, but in a rather ponderous way; and the eccentric promise of outlandish names is largely unfulfilled. They carry, too, an awesome amount of paraphernalia: narrative inversions, clue-finders, time tables, and a plethora of plans and diagrams, not all of them relevant. There are five plans of the SS *Meganaut*, seven of the *Transcontinental*, and three of the plane in *Obelists Fly High*. *Careless Corpse* includes a deck plan of the *Varlet* and two floor-plans of Careless Castle; and *Arrogant Alibi* includes three floor-plans of Perkette, Victoria Timothy's house in West Hartford. *Obelists En Route* and *Obelists Fly High* have clue-finders at the end, with which the reader may trace through the narrative the hints and nudges pointing to the murderer. The latter novel begins with the epilogue and ends with the prologue. Inscrutably, two definitions of the word 'obelist' are given: 'a person who has little or no value' in *Obelists at Sea*, and 'one who harbours suspicions' in *Obelists En Route*. The fourth novel, *Careless Corpse*, is designated a Thanatophony, Daly King's Opus 4, Number 4: its narrative stages are named as musical divisions, and the characters are listed as instrumentalists. *Bermuda Burial* carries the lightest freight: 'a note on the setting' appears as an appendix.

All Daly King's novels feature a young New York policeman named Michael Lord, who adopts the nom-de-guerre 'Younghusband' in his first case, *Obelists at Sea*. He is invariably assisted by Dr L. Rees Pons, an integrative psychologist, whose professional disciplines colour Lord's investigations.

Obelists at Sea was published in November 1932 by John Heritage. The book is black with green spine lettering and is undated. The later books were published by the Crime Club and are all dated. They have the standard orange bindings and black spine lettering of this publisher. *Obelists En Route* and *Obelists Fly High* also have title and author in black on the front cover. The title-page of *Bermuda Burial* has the Crime Club gunman facing to the right. The dust-wrapper of *Obelists En Route* is by Asta, who shows the killer toting his gun. On the spine is a frontal view of the Trans-continental's engine. *Careless Corpse* has a steaming cup of coffee on its saucer, repeated in reduced form on the spine. *Arrogant Alibi* has a frowning man hearing bad news on the telephone. *Obelists En Route* and *Careless Corpse* are still unpublished in America, and even *The Curious Mr. Tarrant* had no US edition until Dover issued it in 1977.

Lord Novels

Obelists at Sea Heritage n.d. (1932), Knopf 1933

ARROGANT ALIBI

C. DALY KING

Obelists En Route   Collins Crime Club 1934

Obelists Fly High   Crime Club Feb. 1935, Smith 1935

Careless Corpse   Crime Club 1937

Arrogant Alibi   Crime Club 1938, Appleton 1939

Bermuda Burial   Crime Club 1940, Funk 1941

Tarrant story collection

The Curious Mr. Tarrant   Crime Club October 1935, Dover 1977 (8 stories)

Uncollected Tarrant stories

'Lost Star' (*EQMM*, Sept. 1944)

'The Episode of the Sinister Invention' (*EQMM*, Dec. 1946)

'The Episode of the Absent Fish' (*EQMM*, Apr. 1979)

Uncollected Tarrant story by Jeremiah Phelan

'The Episode of the Perilous Talisman' (*Fantasy and Science Fiction*, Feb. 1951)   *BP*

Ronald A. Knox (1888–1957)

Ronald A Knox was a Monsignor of the Roman Catholic Church, a brother of the editor of *Punch*, and a voluminous writer in various fields, one of which was detective fiction. He was never a very committed crime writer, and he largely abandoned the form after his sixth novel appeared in 1937. He contributed chapters to two of the Detective Club's collaborative novels, and wrote four short crime stories, one of which is a Sherlockian pastiche. He also published a celebrated study of Sherlock Holmes (in *Essays in Satire* (Sheed & Ward 1928)), and formulated rules for detective writers (in his introduction to *The Best Detective Stories of 1928* (Faber 1929)). Twenty years after his death, his niece, Penelope Fitzgerald, wrote a distinctive crime novel of her own: *The Golden Child* (Duckworth 1977) (and two years later she won the Booker Prize). Knox's novels are ruminative and digressive,

avoiding sensational developments and proceeding at an unhurried pace, in keeping with an age when the leisured classes had all the time in the world. All but the first involve Miles and Angela Bredon, a genial claims investigator for the Indescribable Assurance Co. and his accommodating wife. *Still Dead* is remarkable for its scrupulous assemblage of clues, each identified by a page reference as it contributes to the unravelling. *The Three Taps*, especially, is still very charming.

The Viaduct Murder appeared from Methuen on 23 April 1925, with a red binding and a printer's code at the end reading 1124, which suggests that the book was ready five months ahead of publication. Like its two successors, it is dated, lettered gilt on the spine, and blind-stamped with title and author on the front cover. Reissues have black lettering and a later printer's code. The second edition of 1926 is named as such, but subsequent issues are not identified and can be mistaken for the true first edition: as late as 1929 Methuen still claimed that reissues were 'first published in 1925'.

The Three Taps is unusual among Methuen books of this period for having no advertisement section at the end and no printer's code. The binding is a dull orange. *The Footsteps at the Lock* is blue and is dated 1027 at the end. Frank Marston's wrapper shows Nigel Burtell, 'dressed up very carefully as a "river-man"', while, beyond him, his cousin Derek's Homburg floats on the Thames.

In 1933 Hodder & Stoughton published *The Body in the Silo*, a blue book, undated. The title page has a drawing of the Lastbury silo by Bip Pares, who must also have designed the dust-wrapper. *Still Dead* and *Double Cross Purposes* had the same publisher. *Still Dead* is black, with a dust-wrapper and title-page by Bip Pares, both showing Dorn House, looking grim. *Double Cross Purposes* has the standard blue binding of Hodder books at this time. Both books are dated. *The Body in the Silo* and *Double Cross Purposes* are lettered in black on the spine and *Still Dead* in red. All three books have the title on the front cover, in the corresponding colour.

All but one of Knox's books have a map or a plan to heighten interest for the reader. *The Viaduct Murder* has a preliminary drawing of the railway line between Paston Whitchurch and Paston Oatvile, with the viaduct over the River Gudgeon. The front endpapers of *The Footsteps at the Lock*, by A. E. Taylor, show that stretch of the Thames between the Gudgeon Inn and Millington Bridge, with Shipcote Lock in the middle. Bip Pares drew Lastbury Hall and its environs for *The Body in the Silo* and provided handsome red endpapers of the Dorn Estate for the front of *Still Dead*. *Double Cross Purposes* has a map of the Isle of Erran and an impression of 'Henderson's photograph of the chart'.

Knox contributed chapter 6, 'Mr. Parsons on the Case', to *Behind the Screen*, and chapter 8, 'Thirty-nine Articles of Doubt', to *The Floating Admiral*. The former appeared in *The Listener* for 23 July 1930. Three stories appeared in the 1930s, one – 'Solved by Inspection' – with Bredon as detective. The Conan Doyle pastiche was published in 1947 and represents the author's criminous swan-song.

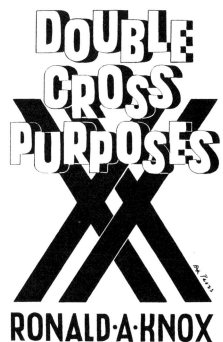

Non-series novel

The Viaduct Murder Methuen 1925, Simon & Schuster 1926

Bredon novels

The Three Taps Methuen 1927, Simon 1927
The Footsteps at the Lock Methuen 1928, Dover 1983
The Body in the Silo Hodder & Stoughton n.d. (1933)
a.k.a. *Settled Out of Court* Dutton 1934
Still Dead Hodder 1934, Dutton 1934
Double Cross Purposes Hodder 1937, Dover 1986

Novels with other members of the Detection Club (q.v.)

The Floating Admiral Hodder n.d. (1931)
Behind the Screen Gollancz 1983 (with *The Scoop*)

Uncollected stories

'Solved by Inspection' (*My Best Detective Story*, Faber 1931; *Tales of Detection*, Dent 1936; *Thirteen Ways to Kill a Man*, Faber 1966)
'The Fallen Idol' (*Six Against the Yard*, Selwyn & Blount n.d. (1936))
'The Motive' (*Illustrated London News*, 17 Nov. 1937; *The Second Century of Detective Stories*, Hutchinson n.d. (1938); *EQMM*, Nov. 1948; *MacKill's*, Jan. 1954)
'The Adventure of the First-class Carriage' (*Strand*, Feb. 1947; *The Sherlock Holmes Scrapbook*, NEL 1973; *The Further Adventures of Sherlock Holmes*, Penguin 1985) *BP*

Jane Langton (b. 1922)

Jane Langton's novels are hand-made pieces, each individually crafted at a high inventive level. They are vivacious, busy narratives, complex and elegant, with authentic settings, impeccably realized. The reader comes to share the author's enthusiasms for music, literature, history, architecture and the natural world; and she wears her learning lightly – it is never just for show. *Natural Enemy*, a chilling inverted story, extends her range. Her constant detective is Homer Kelly, an exuberant and unpredictable professor of American Literature. Though no textbook detective, he is resourceful and imaginative and always excellent company.

All the books except *The Transcendental Murder* have illustrations by the author. This and the two that followed were published by Harper & Row, all quarterbound, with roughly trimmed fore-edges, the date in the copyright notice and 'First edition' on the copyright page. *Dark Nantucket Noon* has a printer's key at the end of the book and *The Memorial Hall Murder* has one on the copyright page. All three books have endpapers decorated by the author: with maps of Concord, Nantucket Island and Harvard University, the sun in total eclipse and Harvard's Memorial Hall. *Dark Nantucket Noon* has the Harper logo in blue on the front cover and the eclipsed sun on the spine. *The Memorial Hall Murder* has a musical vignette, also in blue, on its front cover and a frontispiece drawing of the Memorial Hall. *The Transcendental Murder* has a double title-page and *Dark Nantucket Noon* a decorated one. *Natural Enemy* was published by Ticknor & Fields in grey marbled boards with gilt lettering on the spine and dated title-page. A frontispiece drawing of the Heron house extends on to the title-page. The copyright page has a printer's key.

Three titles came from St Martin's, all with black bindings, two with gilt spine lettering, *Good and Dead* with silver. All three are dated on the copyright page, state 'First edition' and have printer's keys. *Emily Dickinson is Dead* has a putative photograph of the poet as frontispiece and this recurs with an authentic image at the rear. The half-title and title-pages of *Murder at the Gardner* are decorated.

The Dante Game, God in Concord and *Divine Inspiration* were published by Viking, all quarterbound and dated on the copyright page. Each also has a printer's key on the copyright page.

The Dante Game has decorations on the half-title and the title-page; *God in Concord* has a drawing of a gnarled but leafy tree extending onto the title-page from the page opposite; *Divine Inspiration* has five organ-stops. *God in Concord* has a preliminary double-page map of Concord. *Divine Inspiration* follows the Christian calendar through the year, each stage introduced by a preliminary page with an appropriate illustration and musical quotation from Bach.

The dust-wrappers are largely by the author, in a variety of styles. *The Transcendental Murder* shows the falling of the bust of Louisa M. Alcott, which also features on the spine. She shares the front panel with Homer Kelly, looking grim and with fingers splayed against his arms, and a dark-haired woman on to whom she is falling. *Dark Nantucket Noon* features the eclipse of the sun, a vast black disc with fiery yellow edges. Beneath, Kitty Clark races towards the Nantucket Observatory. *Good and Dead* has a blue, white and grey wrapper of gravestones in the churchyard of Old West Church at Nashoba, Massachusetts. *Murder at the Gardner* sets Isabella Stewart Gardner on an ornamental balcony and flanks her with two round green shrubs in pots. *The Dante Game* has Nan Parsons' muted impression of the skyline of Florence with mountains beyond; and *God in Concord* features Robert Crawford's picture of a small red-roofed house among trees, with a sprawling male corpse before it.

Only four of Jane Langton's novels have appeared in Britain. Three were published by Gollancz: *Emily Dickinson is Dead, The Memorial Hall Murder* and *The Dante Game*. All three are black with gilt lettering on the spine, dated title pages and yellow wrappers. *Emily Dickinson is Dead* has the photographs of the poet, authentic and putative, and *The Dante Game* has a title-page with one of the author's illustrations. Otherwise, the Gollancz editions are unillustrated. *Dark Nantucket Noon* was published by Chivers in 1992 with the author's illustrations and the endpaper map reproduced as preliminary. This, too is a black book with gilt spine lettering. It is dated on the copyright page and has the standard typographical wrapper of the Black Dagger series.

Homer Kelly novels

(Binding details refer to US editions)

The Transcendental Murder Harper & Row 1964 (orange boards, black spine, orange & blue lettering)
a.k.a. *The Minuteman Murder* Dell 1976
Dark Nantucket Noon Harper 1975, Chivers 1992 (slate-blue, fawn, blue)
The Memorial Hall Murder Harper 1978, Gollancz 1990 (light blue, dark blue, silver)
Natural Enemy Ticknor & Fields 1982
Emily Dickinson is Dead St Martin's 1984, Gollancz 1989
Good and Dead St Martin's 1986
Murder at the Gardner St Martin's 1988
The Dante Game Viking 1991, Gollancz 1991 (pearl-grey, navy blue, silver)
God in Concord Viking 1992 (pale yellow, maroon, gilt)
Divine Inspiration Viking 1993 (pale grey, lightly flecked; blue, gilt) *BP*

BANKING ON DEATH

We particularly like this whodunit for three reasons:

I.

The banking and business background is delightfully authentic and "new"

2.

The writing is greatly superior to what we're used to in a thriller

3.

The characterisation is exceptional

EMMA LATHEN

Emma Lathen
a.k.a. R. B. Dominic

Emma Lathen is the primary pseudonym of two American businesswomen, who also wrote as R. B. Dominic. Their knowledge of the corridors of power on Wall Street and in Washington is formidably exact, and their books provide innumerable insights into these high-flying worlds. They are also richly diverting as narratives and deft and satisfying as mysteries.

Throughout the Lathen books the detective is John Putnam Thatcher, Senior Vice President of the Sloan International Bank. In the usual absence of his feckless president, he performs a dual role; as the ultimate authority for all decisions affecting the bank's welfare, and as nemesis for a long succession of killers whose greed or folly involve them with the Sloan's affairs. Several supporting members of the bank-

189

ing community are also established through the series, both acutely and affectionately. Miss Corsa, Thatcher's secretary, is especially endearing. The Dominic books are recognizably from the same expert hands: they show the same shrewd wit and insight into the more public of human affairs. They revolve around a Democratic congressman named Benton Safford, or Ben to his familiars; and again the most remarkable of the tributary personnel is a woman, the Republican congresswoman Elsie Hollenbach, who contrives to be both stately and tough. Both series include a devastating attack on American doctors.

All but one of the Lathen novels were published in Britain by Gollancz, all with gilt lettering on the spine. Except for *Right on the Money*, which is black and dated only on the copyright page, they have red bindings and dated title-pages. *A Place for Murder* is not as tall as the others and *East is East* and *Right on the Money* are taller than the main run. The wrappers are standard yellow to *Green Grow the Dollars* and standard photographic thereafter. *Come to Dust* was published out of sequence in Britain.

Something in the Air was published both in America and Britain by Simon & Schuster, Emma Lathen's US publisher from *Come to Dust*. The book is quarterbound with blue boards and black spinal section, lettered silver on the spine and with 'Emma Lathen' blind-stamped on the front cover. The endpapers are blue and the title-page has a plane in flight over the title. The date appears on the copyright page only. The UK wrapper is plain but the US has bloodstained hundred-dollar bills floating on a blue background.

The true, American, firsts are elusive in Britain and there has been no published account of them. Five titles only are known. *Pick up Sticks* is a green book with dark-blue lettering on the spine. It is dated by the copyright notice only and states 'First printing' on the copyright page. The top edge is charcoal and the white wrapper has a tree growing from the needle of a compass. On the spine another tree grows from a knife. *Going for the Gold* and *Double, Double, Oil and Trouble* are taller books, dated by the copyright notice only and with printers' keys 1–10 on the

copyright page. The former is red with a blue spine and gilt lettering, the latter grey with a black spine, lettered and with rules in silver, and grey endpapers. *East is East* has mauve boards, a purple spine with gilt lettering, mauve endpapers and the date and a printer's key on the copyright page. *Right on the Money* has pale green 'eggshell' boards with a blue-green spine, which has gilt lettering. The book is dated on the copyright page, which also has a printer's key ascending from 1 and descending to 2.

The first Dominic novel was published by Abelard-Schuman, and to locate it is a tall order. It is not in the BL, which perhaps indicates that it did not appear in Britain. The rest of the Safford series came from Macmillan and have the standard lettering of this house, with the author's surname and the title printed along the spine, on either side of a dividing line. From *Murder in High Place* to *Murder Out of Commission* the lettering is black. For *The Attending Physician* it is gilt, and for *A Flaw in the System* it is silver. In sequence, the six bindings are pale green, blue, red, light brown, black, and green. The copyright pages establish the precedence of the US editions of *Epitaph for a Lobbyist* and *The Attending Physician*, but three of the others first appeared in Britain, and *Murder Out of Commission* may also have done so. From *Murder Out of Commission*, the authors' cover is blown by the publisher, presumably in the hope of improving sales. A note, '(pseudonym of Emma Lathen)', appears on its wrapper, and the subsequent titles were announced as by Emma Lathen writing as R. B. Dominic. The Dominic wrappers are generally run-of-the-mill photographic, but *Murder in High Place* has a rather wild design in a Hockneyish, op-art style, with lots of blood.

Thatcher novels by Emma Lathen

Banking on Death   Macmillan 1961, Gollancz 1962

A Place for Murder   Macmillan 1963, Gollancz 1963

Accounting for Murder   Macmillan 1964, Gollancz 1965

Murder Makes the Wheels Go Round Macmillan 1966, Gollancz 1966

Death Shall Overcome Macmillan 1966, Gollancz 1967

Murder Against the Grain Macmillan 1967, Gollancz 1967

A Stitch in Time Macmillan 1968, Gollancz 1968

Come to Dust Simon & Schuster 1968, Gollancz 1969

When in Greece Simon 1969, Gollancz 1969

Murder to Go Simon 1969, Gollancz 1970

Pick Up Sticks Simon 1970, Gollancz 1971

Ashes to Ashes Simon 1971, Gollancz 1971

The Longer the Thread Simon 1971, Gollancz 1972

Murder Without Icing Simon 1972, Gollancz 1973

Sweet and Low Simon 1974, Gollancz 1974

By Hook or By Crook Simon 1975, Gollancz 1975

Double, Double, Oil and Trouble Simon 1978, Gollancz 1979

Going for the Gold Simon 1981

a.k.a. *Going for Gold* Gollancz 1981

Green Grow the Dollars Simon 1982, Gollancz 1982

Something in the Air Simon 1988

East is East Simon 1991, Gollancz 1991

Right on the Money Simon 1993, Gollancz 1993

Safford novels by R. B. Dominic

Murder, Sunny Side Up Abelard-Schuman 1968

Murder in High Place Macmillan 1969, Doubleday 1970

Murder Out of Court Macmillan 1971

a.k.a. *There Is No Justice* Doubleday 1971

Epitaph for a Lobbyist Doubleday 1974, Macmillan 1974

Murder Out of Commission Macmillan 1976, Doubleday 1976

The Attending Physician Harper 1980, Macmillan 1980

A Flaw in the System Macmillan 1983

a.k.a. *Unexpected Developments* St Martin's1984   *BP*

Elizabeth Lemarchand (b. 1906)

Those who do not wish to read quiet rural mysteries solved by the mildest of policemen will do well to avoid the work of Elizabeth Lemarchand; but for those who like the gentle tradition, she is heaven-sent. Her Scotland Yard team, Tom Pollard and Gregory Toye, are incredibly nice, but they work in welcome harmony and spend most of their time detecting, unlike much of the competition. They have seventeen cases all told, beginning with *Death of an Old Girl*, set in a smart girls' school, with an insider's knowledge of how such institutions work (the author was assistant head at the Godolphin School, where Dorothy L. Sayers and Josephine Bell were educated). The publisher was Rupert Hart-Davis, whose firm underwent various identity crises while the Pollard books were appearing. He was eventually swallowed by Granada, whose regrettably small printing of the tenth

book, *Suddenly While Gardening*, perhaps precipitated a parting of the ways. Thereafter, Miss Lemarchand was with Judy Piatkus.

Except for the final title, the books are, blessedly, of uniform size, so that a switchback effect on the shelf is avoided. The Hart-Davis books are bound in various colours, with spines lettered gilt or silver. The Piatkus books are more uniform, with mauve or dark red bindings and gilt spine lettering. All the books are dated.

Death of an Old Girl has a striking dust-wrapper by Colin Andrews, showing Beatrice Baynes as a woeful puppet, bleeding from her forehead. The same designer provided the toy-town view of Affacombe for the second book, *The Affacombe Affair*. From *Let or Hindrance* to *Suddenly While Gardening*, the wrappers adopt a uniform style of lettering over photographs of relevant details. Ken Leeder took the photographs for most of the Piatkus series, four of which, from *Troubled Waters*, are also lettered in a similar style.

The Affacombe Affair and *Cyanide with Compliments* both feature Olivia Strode, a local historian, whose son and daughter-in-law play small but crucial roles in *Change for the Worse*. Many of the books have a map of the terrain, whether Affacombe, Loxford, or Minstow and Twister Down. In some cases, a plan of the central building is more appropriate: Meldon School, the Ramsden Athenaeum, or the stately home, Brent.

The nine known stories are uncollected. They ante-date the novels and, though certainly mysterious, are not detective stories.

Pollard novels

(Details of bindings refer to British editions.)

Death of an Old Girl   Hart-Davis 1967, Award 1970 (mauve binding, gilt lettering)

The Affacombe Affair Hart-Davis 1968, Walker 1985 (blue, gilt)

Alibi for a Corpse Hart-Davis 1969, Walker 1986 (red, gilt)

Death on Doomsday Hart-Davis 1971, Walker 1975 (dark red, gilt)

Cyanide with Compliments   MacGibbon & Kee 1972, Walker 1973 (dark red, gilt)

Let or Hindrance   Hart-Davis MacGibbon 1973 (blue, silver)

a.k.a. *No Vacation from Murder*   Walker 1974

Buried in the Past Hart-Davis MacGibbon 1974, Walker 1975 (black, silver)

Step in the Dark   Hart-Davis MacGibbon 1976, Walker 1977 (maroon, silver)

Unhappy Returns Hart-Davis MacGibbon 1977, Walker 1978 (red, gilt)

Suddenly While Gardening   Hart-Davis MacGibbon 1978, Walker 1979 (green, silver)

Change for the Worse   Piatkus 1980, Walker 1981

Nothing to Do with the Case   Piatkus 1981, Walker 1981

Troubled Waters   Piatkus 1982, Walker 1982

The Wheel Turns   Piatkus 1983, Walker 1984

Light Through Glass   Piatkus 1984, Walker 1986

Who Goes Home?   Piatkus 1986, Walker 1987

The Glade Manor Murder   Piatkus 1988, Walker 1989

Uncollected stories

'Black Bartholomew' (*Argosy*, Oct. 1963; *John Creasey's Mystery Bedside Book 1974*, Hodder & Stoughton 1973)

'The Comeback' (*Argosy*, Nov. 1963; *John Creasey's Mystery Bedside Book 1976*, Hodder 1975)

'The Stone of Witness' (*Argosy*, Dec. 1963; *John Creasey's Mystery Bedside Book 1970*, Hodder 1969)

'Pussycats and Owls' (*Argosy*, Jan. 1964)

'The Beckoning Beeches' (*Argosy*, Feb. 1964; *John Creasey's Mystery Bedside Book 1969*, Hodder 1968)

'The Quiet Pupil' (*Argosy*, Mar. 1964)

'Time to be Going' (*Argosy*, May 1964; *More Tales of Unease*, Pan 1969)

'Comfort from Capricorn' (*Argosy*, July 1964)

'The Long House' (*Argosy*, Dec. 1964)   *BP*

E. C. R. Lorac (1894–1958)
a.k.a. Carol Carnac

E. C. R. Lorac and Carol Carnac are pseudonyms of Edith Caroline Rivett. There are twenty-three Carnac books and forty-eight as by Lorac. Two chapters of the collaborative novel *No Flowers by Request* (see under 'Detection Club') and the five known uncollected stories were also written under the Lorac name.

Because they are very scarce, the books by this writer are always among the most sought-after items on second-hand book lists. Writing as Carol Carnac, the author created three series characters: the neat, pleasant Inspector Ryvet, in five novels; the quiet and polite Chief Inspector Julian Rivers of Scotland Yard in fifteen books; and his assistant, the more physically active Inspector Lancing, in fourteen cases. Lancing also features in four titles with Ryvet, as a detective-sergeant. For the Lorac novels, the main series detectives are the energetic Chief Inspector Robert Macdonald, in forty-six books, and his able assistant, the Cockney Detective-Inspector Reeves, in twenty-eight. Macdonald also features in an uncollected story. The beautiful fell country of Lunesdale in Lancashire is the setting for five novels. In four of these we meet the owners of Netherbeck Farm, Giles and Kate Haggett, whose neighbour, John Staple, is also present on three occasions.

All the books in both names were first published in London. Fourteen Carnac and twenty-four Lorac titles have not been published in the USA. Many books have alternative titles in America, including *The Double Turn* and *Policemen in the Precinct*.

Carol Carnac's first book was published by Thornton Butterworth in yellow cloth, with the publisher's colophon blind-stamped on both covers. The spine is lettered in black and the front cover has title and author, also in black. The book is undated. The author's next two novels were published by Skeffington and are undated. *Murder at Mornington* was issued in fawn cloth with the spine lettered in blue. Two blue rules appear at the top and base of the spine. *The Missing Rope* has blue cloth lettered in black on the spine. Peter Davies published the three titles that followed, all of which are dated. *The Case of the First Class Carriage* and *When the Devil Was Sick* have yellow cloth, while *Death in the Diving Pool* has blue cloth. All are lettered in black on the spine. A skull and crossbones also appear on each spine, between the title and the author's name.

Macdonald were the publishers of the next six titles. With the exception of *A Double for Detection*, all are dated. This book usually has blue cloth, lettered on the spine in black, but an orange variant is known. Collectors should note that it generally appears without a front free endpaper (though the BL copy does have one). The red wrapper shows twin mirror images in eccentric profile. *The Striped Suitcase* has a beige-green cloth and the spine is lettered gilt. Stein's wrapper shows a figure carrying a striped suitcase, under the watchful eye of a policeman. *Clue Sinister* was issued in blue cloth, with title and author in red on a black band on the spine. *Upstairs, Downstairs* has blue cloth with gilt spine lettering and Stein's striking wrapper of Mr Chindle carrying some pearls. *Over the Garden Wall* has green cloth and gilt spine lettering, and the wrapper, again by Stein, shows one man pursuing another, who scales a garden wall, putting a cat to flight. *Copy for Crime* also has green cloth, but the spine lettering is yellow.

Carol Carnac's last eleven titles were published by Collins Crime Club. All have red cloth lettered in black on the spine and, with one exception, are dated. *A Policeman at the Door* is the undated title, most unusually for Collins, who are generally careful to date their first editions. The wrappers for this series are noteworthy: *Murder as a Fine Art*, for example, shows the crushed body of Edwin Pomfret in the hall of Medici House. The final four books have wrappers designed by William Randell.

The first nine books by E. C. R. Lorac were published by Sampson Low in black cloth with gilt lettering on the spine. The publisher's colophon is blind-stamped on the back cover in each case, and all the books are undated. Collectors should beware of red or brown cloth editions, since these are all reprints. The frontispiece of *The Organ Speaks* is a diagram of the console of the four-manual organ in the Waldstein Hall, drawn by the author herself. With the exception of *Murder in Chelsea* and *Death of an Author*, all the Low books have advertisement sections at the rear. Morton Sale's wrapper for *The Murder on the Burrows* shows a gaunt, sinister man in a black hat gripping a steering-wheel, while the face of a vamp looks over his left shoulder. Youngman Carter's dust-wrapper for *The Case of Colonel Marchand* shows the colonel's butler holding a circular tray, and looking towards a bell ringing over his head. To his left a wide bell-pull bears the words 'Ring the bell – the Colonel is dead!'. Evans' design for *Murder in Chelsea* shows a woman in blue dwarfed by her own shadow as she climbs a staircase clutching a pink hot-water bottle.

The rest of the Lorac books were published by Collins Crime Club, in red cloth, with black spine lettering. These are all dated. The Crime Club gunman looks to the right in *Tryst for a Tragedy*. Many of the wrappers for this series are very effective. A woman's body drifts in water on both the front panel and spine of *Crime Counter Crime*. *A Pall for a Painter* has a bearded artist holding a brush and palette in the foreground, with a draped, armless statue beyond him. The body of a wide-eyed brunette lies in bed on *Post After Post-mortem*. *Bats in the Belfry* shows the ruined Belfry studio, encircled by bats. An elderly woman's body lies at the foot of a flight of stairs on the apricot wrapper for *Slippery Staircase*. *John Brown's Body* has two goose-stepping men in black carrying a coffin. The grey, yellow and black wrapper of *Black Beadle* has a bald beadle in a black cassock holding his symbol of office in one hand and an open book surmounted by a skull in the other. He reappears on the spine. The simple but striking design for *Death at Dyke's Corner* sets a signpost against a dark green background.

Stead provided an eerie blue, black and white wrapper for *Tryst for a Tragedy*, showing two black birds perched on wooden gateposts, with windblown trees and a hump-backed bridge in the background. His design for *Death Came Softly* has a figure in silhouette against the entrance of a cave. *The Theft of the Iron Dogs* has a corpse in a sack, weighted and chained to the roots of a tree in the River Lune. Desperate

hands reach out from the mill-race in the design for *Murder in the Millrace*. A body slumped behind a luggage trolley on a foggy Paddington Station illustrates *Shroud of Darkness*. A red shepherd's crook dominates a view of the fells of Lunesdale, while a man sits on a rock in the foreground of *Crook o' Lune*.

For *Case in the Clinic* Stead depicts the wrought-iron gates and the drive leading up to White Gables; and his design of two men with a torch discovering a body in a barn distinguishes the wrapper of *Still Waters*.

J. Z. Atkinson drew Garthmere Hall for *Fell Murder* and his stylized design for *Checkmate to Murder* features a man shining a torch on the entrance of a house set on a chessboard. William Randell created some effective designs for several of the later books. His sombre blue, black and white design for *Murder in Vienna* shows ornamental palace walls reflected in a pool; *Picture of Death* has a startled woman turning away from a period portrait of a man on horseback; a policeman blows a whistle as a man is attacked in front of a town house on *Dangerous Domicile*; a man running away from the Victor Emmanuel monument in Rome appears on *Murder on a Monument*; and *Dishonour Among Thieves* has Rory Macshane emerging from a Dartmoor mist. Stein's wrapper for *Fire in the Thatch* attributes the book to F. C. R. Lorac.

Novels by E. C. R. Lorac

(with Macdonald, except as stated)

The Murder on the Burrows Sampson Low 1931, Macaulay 1932
The Affair on Thor's Head Low 1932
The Greenwell Mystery Low 1932, Macaulay 1934
Death on the Oxford Road Low 1933
The Case of Colonel Marchand Low 1933, Macaulay 1933
Murder in St. John's Wood Low 1934, Macaulay 1934
Murder in Chelsea Low 1934, Macaulay 1935
The Organ Speaks Low 1935

Death of an Author   Low 1935, Macaulay 1937 (not Macdonald)

Crime Counter Crime   Collins Crime Club 1936

Post After Post-mortem   Crime Club 1936

A Pall for a Painter   Crime Club 1936

Bats in the Belfry   Crime Club 1937, Macaulay 1937

These Names Make Clues   Crime Club 1937

The Devil and the CID   Crime Club 1938

Slippery Staircase   Crime Club 1938

John Brown's Body   Crime Club 1938

Black Beadle   Crime Club 1939

Death at Dyke's Corner   Crime Club 1940

Tryst for a Tragedy   Crime Club 1940

Case in the Clinic   Crime Club 1941

Rope's End, Rogue's End   Crime Club 1942

The Sixteenth Stair   Crime Club 1942

Death Came Softly   Crime Club 1943, Mystery House 1943

Checkmate to Murder   Crime Club 1944, Mystery House 1944

Fell Murder   Crime Club 1944

Murder by Matchlight   Crime Club 1945, Mystery House 1946

Fire in the Thatch   Crime Club 1946, Mystery House 1946

The Theft of the Iron Dogs   Crime Club 1946

a.k.a. *Murderer's Mistake*   Mystery House 1947

Relative to Poison   Crime Club 1947, Doubleday 1948

Death Before Dinner   Crime Club 1948

a.k.a. *A Screen for Murder*   Doubleday 1948

Part for a Poisoner   Crime Club 1948

a.k.a. *Place for a Poisoner*   Doubleday 1949

Still Waters   Crime Club 1949

Policemen in the Precinct   Crime Club 1949

a.k.a. *And Then Put Out the Light*   Doubleday 1950

Accident by Design   Crime Club 1950, Doubleday 1951

Murder of a Martinet   Crime Club 1951

a.k.a. *I Could Murder Her*   Doubleday 1951

The Dog It Was That Died   Crime Club 1952, Doubleday 1952

Murder in the Millrace   Crime Club 1952

a.k.a. *Speak Justly of the Dead*   Doubleday 1953

Crook o' Lune   Crime Club 1953

a.k.a. *Shepherd's Crook*   Doubleday 1953

Shroud of Darkness   Crime Club 1954, Doubleday 1954

Let Well Alone   Crime Club 1954

Ask a Policeman   Crime Club 1955

Murder in Vienna   Crime Club 1956

Picture of Death   Crime Club 1957

Dangerous Domicile   Crime Club 1957

Death in Triplicate   Crime Club 1958 (not Macdonald)

a.k.a. *People Will Talk*   Doubleday 1958

Murder on a Monument   Crime Club 1958

Dishonour Among Thieves   Crime Club 1959

a.k.a. *The Last Escape*   Doubleday 1959

Novels by Carol Carnac

(with Rivers, except as stated)

Triple Death   Thornton Butterworth 1936 (Ryvet)

Murder at Mornington   Skeffington 1937 (non-series)

The Missing Rope   Skeffington 1937 (Ryvet)

When the Devil Was Sick   Davies 1939 (Ryvet)

The Case of the First-class Carriage   Davies 1939 (Ryvet)

Death in the Diving-pool   Davies 1940 (Ryvet)

A Double for Detection   Macdonald n.d. (1945)

The Striped Suitcase   Macdonald 1946, Doubleday 1947

Clue Sinister   Macdonald 1947

Over the Garden Wall   Macdonald 1948, Doubleday 1949

Upstairs, Downstairs   Macdonald 1950

a.k.a. *Upstairs and Downstairs*   Doubleday 1950

Copy for Crime   Macdonald 1950, Doubleday 1951

It's Her Own Funeral   Collins Crime Club 1951, Doubleday 1952

Crossed Skis   Crime Club 1952

Murder as a Fine Art   Crime Club 1953

A Policeman at the Door   Crime Club n.d. (1953), Doubleday 1954

Impact of Evidence   Crime Club 1954, Doubleday 1954

Murder Among Members   Crime Club 1955

Rigging the Evidence   Crime Club 1955

The Double Turn   Crime Club 1956

a.k.a. *The Late Miss Trimming*   Doubleday 1957
The Burning Question   Crime Club 1957 (non-series)
Long Shadows   Crime Club 1958
a.k.a. *Affair at Helen's Court*   Doubleday 1958
Death of a Lady Killer   Crime Club 1959 (non-series)

Novel with other members of the Detection Club (q.v.), as E. C. R. Lorac

No Flowers By Request   Gollancz 1984 (with *Crime on the Coast*)

Uncollected stories by E. C. R. Lorac

'The Live Wire' (*Detection Medley*, Hutchinson n.d. 1939)
'Remember to Ring Twice' (Macdonald) (*ES*, 7 June 1950; *Mackill's*, Sept. 1952)

'Chance is a Great Thing' (*ES*, 8 Aug. 1950; *MacKill's*, Jan. 1953)
'Death at the Bridge Table' (*ES*, 11 Oct. 1950; *The Evening Standard Detective Book*, Series 2, Gollancz 1951, as 'A Bit of Wire-pulling')
'Permanent Policeman' (*ES*, 18 June 1951; *MacKill's*, Mar. 1953)

JC

Peter Lovesey (b. 1936)

Peter Lovesey made his name as a historical crime novelist, but some of his more recent work has brought him closer to the present. He won a competition with his first book, *Wobble to Death*, which introduces Sergeant Cribb and Constable Thackeray, Victorian policemen, overworked and undervalued. They had a further seven cases before their author abandoned them – regrettably, since their world is deeply fascinating and they explore some of its choicest areas. Later novels are set at various times in the twentieth century, and *Rough Cider* moves forward to the 1960s, besides harking back to the Second World War. *Bertie and the Tinman* returns to the Victorian era founding a new series that draws on 'the detective memoirs of King Edward VII'. *On the Edge* is a non-series thriller set in the 1940s and *The Last Detective* introduces Peter Diamond, a traditional policeman at odds with technology in Bristol. *Butchers* is a collection of sixteen 'stories of crime' with minimal detection.

This collection and the novels to *Keystone* were published by Macmillan, in various colours and in general with the author's surname and the title running along the spine, in the standard house fashion. *The False Inspector Dew* and *Butchers* are taller than the rest and do not have the uniform lettering. *Rough Cider* and *Bertie and the Tinman* were published by the Bodley Head, both in black bindings and with gilt spine lettering. They and their various successors are the same height as the taller Macmillan volumes. *On the Edge* and *Bertie and the Seven Bodies* are Mysterious Press books, both black with gilt lettering on the spine and red endpapers decorated with multiple repetitions of the publisher's logo in black. *The Last Detective* was published by Scribner shortly before the firm's demise (with that of Robert Maxwell). Little, Brown took over and is currently Lovesey's publisher. *The Last Detective* has a maroon binding with gilt lettering on the spine and pink endpapers on which the publisher's name recurs many times. The Little, Brown books are also maroon and gilt. All Peter Lovesey's books are dated on their copyright pages.

The wrappers for the Macmillan series are often admirable: would that the designs had been allowed to extend on to the spines, which make the usual deadening effect on the shelf. *Abracadaver* has a flamboyant conjuror by Peter Brookes, impaling with a sword his woman assistant, who is imprisoned in a cabinet. *Mad Hatter's Holiday* shows Carol Lawson's portrait of Albert Moscrop with his binoculars, and Brighton Pier beyond. For *Swing, Swing Together* Joseph Wright gives a jaunty view of Messrs Humberstone, Gold, and Lucifer in their boat, with Towser balanced on their luggage. *Waxwork* benefits greatly from Patricia Ludlow's handsome portrait of Miriam Cromer. Tom Scobie's macabre design for *Rough Cider* centres on a skull that is also a nightmarish apple; and a portrait of the royal narrator is featured on the wrappers of at least the earlier Bertie books. *The Last Detective* has a photograph of Peter Diamond as we first meet him, asleep on his back on a mortuary trolley.

Besides his solo novels, Peter Lovesey has written two books in multiple collaboration: *The Rigby File* and *The Perfect Murder*. He also collaborated on a story published in *The Bell House Book* (1979): 'A Slight Case of Scotch'. His uncollected stories include a Sherlock Holmes pastiche and competition stories. In November/December 1986, *The Observer* based a competition on five brief Lovesey stories. With the help of clues hidden elsewhere in the paper, readers were invited to solve the crimes and name the murderers. 'Murder by Christmas Tree' is also a competition story. A collection from Eurographica, *The Staring Man* (1990), contains four stories reprinted from *Butchers*.

Peter Lovesey has also written three thrillers under the name Peter Lear.

Cribb and Thackeray novels

(Details of bindings refer to Macmillan editions.)

Wobble to Death   Macmillan 1970, Dodd, Mead 1970 (red binding, black lettering)

The Detective Wore Silk Drawers   Macmillan 1971, Dodd 1971 (red, black)

Abracadaver   Macmillan 1972, Dodd 1972 (red, black)

Mad Hatter's Holiday   Macmillan 1973, Dodd 1973 (green, black)

Invitation to a Dynamite Party   Macmillan 1974 (black, white)

a.k.a. *The Tick of Death*   Dodd 1974

A Case of Spirits   Macmillan 1975, Dodd 1975 (maroon, white)

Swing, Swing Together   Macmillan 1976, Dodd 1976 (blue-green, black)

Waxwork   Macmillan 1978, Pantheon 1978 (dark green, silver)

Other novels

The False Inspector Dew   Macmillan 1982, Pantheon 1982 (red, silver)

Keystone   Macmillan 1983, Pantheon 1983 (maroon, silver)

Rough Cider   Bodley Head 1986, Mysterious Press 1987

Bertie and the Tinman   Bodley Head 1987, Mysterious Press 1988

On the Edge   Century/Mysterious Press 1989, Mysterious Press 1989

Bertie and the Seven Bodies   Century/Mysterious Press 1990, Mysterious Press 1990

The Last Detective   Scribner 1991, Doubleday 1991

Diamond Solitaire   Little, Brown 1992, Mysterious Press 1993

Bertie and the Crime of Passion   Little, Brown 1993, Mysterious Press 1994

Story collection

Butchers   Macmillan 1985, Mysterious Press 1987 (16 stories) (grey, gilt)

Collaborations

The Rigby File Hodder & Stoughton 1989
The Perfect Murder HarperCollins (New York) 1991

Uncollected stories

'Murder in Store' (*Woman's Own*, 21 Dec. 1985; *New Black Mask* 8, 1987; *Crime at Christmas*, Equation 1988)
'Curl Up and Dye' (*EQMM*, July 1986; *John Creasey's Crime Collection 1987*, Gollancz 1987)
'Photographer Slain: Unusual Development'; 'Peer's Grisly Find: Butler Dead in Bath'; 'Brighton Line Murder'; 'The Poisoned Mince Pie'; 'The Royal Plot' (*Observer*, 30 Nov.–28 Dec. 1986)
'Friendly Yachtsman, 39' (*Woman's Own*, 18 July 1987)
'The Curious Computer' (*The New Adventures of Sherlock Holmes*, Carroll & Graf 1987)
'The Pomeranian Poisoning' (*Winter's Crimes 19*, Macmillan 1987; as 'The Zenobia Hatt Prize', *EQMM*, Aug. 1988)
'Where is thy Sting?' (*Winter's Crimes 20*, Macmillan 1988; *EQMM*, Nov. 1988 as 'The Wasp')
'Oracle of the Dead' (*EQMM*, mid-Dec. 1988)
'A Case of Butterflies' (*Winter's Crimes 21*, Macmillan 1989; *EQMM*, Dec. 1989)
'The Haunted Crescent' (*Mistletoe Mysteries*, Mysterious Press 1989)
'Youdunnit' (*New Crimes*, Robinson 1989; *EQMM*, mid-Dec. 1989)
'The Valuation' (*EQMM*, Feb. 1990; *Winter's Crimes 22*, Macmillan 1990 as 'Shock Visit')
'The Christmas Present' (*Woman's Own*, 24 Dec. 1990; *EQMM*, mid-Dec. 1991 as 'Supper with Miss Shivers')
'Ginger's Waterloo' (*Cat Crimes 1*, Fine 1991)
'The Lady in the Trunk' (*A Classic English Crime*, Pavilion 1990)
'Being of Sound Mind' (*EQMM*, Jul. 1991; *Winter's Crimes 23*, Macmillan 1991)
'The Crime of Miss Oyster Brown' (*EQMM*, May 1991; *Midwinter Mysteries 1*, Scribner 1991)

'The Man Who Ate People' (*The Man Who . . .*, Macmillan 1992)
'You May See a Strangler' (*Midwinter Mysteries 2*, Little, Brown 1992)
'The Mighty Hunter' (*Cat Crimes 3*, Fine 1992)
'Murder by Christmas Tree' (*Observer*, 20 Dec. 1992)
'Pass the Parcel' (*Midwinter Mysteries 3*, Little, Brown 1993)
'Bertie and the Fire Brigade' (*Royal Crimes*, Penguin (US) 1994)

Collaborative story

'A Slight Case of Scotch' (*The Bell House Book*, Hodder & Stoughton 1979) *BP*

Philip MacDonald (1900–1981)
a.k.a. Martin Porlock
a.k.a. Anthony Lawless

Philip MacDonald was the grandson of George MacDonald, and his earliest works were collaborations with his father, also a novelist. The bulk of his mystery writing was done in the early 1930s, before he became a Hollywood scriptwriter: between May 1930 and April 1933 he was averaging five crime novels a year. Inevitably, he was uneven: but despite excesses and absurdities he remains an exciting writer, and on top form he is masterly. Twelve novels and one story feature Colonel Anthony Ruthven Gethryn, an energetic toff, with whimsical humour and some style. He personifies all the manly virtues of his time, and repeatedly earns the gratitude of Assistant Commissioner Egbert Lucas. He is hero-worshipped by Superintendent Arnold Pike, who, in *Murder Gone Mad*, is allowed to go it alone.

For the earlier, more productive phase of his career, MacDonald was published by Collins, under his own name and as Martin Porlock. His third Gethryn novel was one of the first titles issued by the Crime Club, in May 1930. *The Rasp* and *The White Crow* preceded it, and a further fifteen titles appeared before the war. Collins issued a collaboration (with A. Boyd Correll) and a book of stories in the post-war years, and Herbert Jenkins published the later books, two novels and two story collections.

Philip MacDonald's bibliography is bedevilled by revisions, pseudonyms, title-changes, and a different order of publication in America from that adopted in Britain. Four of the pre-war novels were first published by Doubleday, including *Harbour*, as by Anthony Lawless. All three of the story collections and two late novels are also known to have appeared first in America.

There are some textual differences between *Rynox* and *The Rynox Murder Mystery* and *Persons Unknown* and *The Maze*. As one instance, the letter from Lucas that launches *The Maze* is not included in *Persons Unknown*. The *Rynox Murder* (Avon 1965) has more drastic revisions. *The Choice* and *X v. Rex* have three titles apiece,

and *Rynox* has four, two in Britain and two in America.

Martin Porlock is the important pseudonym: the others can largely be disregarded. W. J. Stuart was used for a science-fiction paperback, *Forbidden Planet*, and Anthony Lawless for *Harbour* in America (but not, as Reilly claims, for the British edition as well). Oliver Fleming was the joint pseudonym of MacDonald and his father, Ronald, adopted for *Ambrotox and Limping Dick* and *The Spandau Quid*, picturesque thrillers with more action than detection. The former involves a wonder drug and the abduction and complicated rescue of a fetching young woman. The latter is even more intricate, with horses, smugglers, anarchists, and the titular sovereign contributing to the final design. Contrary to expectation, Limping Dick is the hero of the first book, and his name recurs in the second, with the power to open doors and command men. According to Hubin, the Porlock novels were published in America as by Philip MacDonald (and *Mystery in Kensington Gore* and *X v. Rex* were eventually issued in this name in Britain). All MacDonald's British editions are dated, and those from Doubleday must be, too.

The Collins edition of *The Rasp* is a brown book, with orange capital lettering on the spine. The front cover has the title near the top, within a border running close to the edges. *The White Crow* has a black binding, orange lettering, and a border. Both title and author are given on the cover, and the lettering is in lower case, except for the initial letters of each word. *The Noose, The Link, Murder Gone Mad*, and *The Choice* have orange bindings, borders, and black capital lettering, including title and author on the front covers. From *The Wraith* to *R.I.P.* this format is retained, except that there are no borders on the covers. The three Martin Porlock novels share this later format. *Rynox* and *Harbour* are Collins rather than Crime Club books, and they resemble *The White Crow*, except that their lettering is in capitals, and *Harbour* has no border. From *The Nursemaid Who Disappeared*, the Crime Club books are orange with black spine lettering.

M. Elliott's dramatic wrapper for *Rynox* has a man's body spreadeagled over the ledge of an open window. *The Link* has a silhouetted gunman and *The Noose* has a prison yard, with the rope hanging grimly. J. L. Carstairs' design for *R.I.P.* is bold and brilliant: in vivid shades of orange and purple, it centres on a coffin being opened from within. The wrapper for *Death on My Left* is of a type used for several books of its time, with the Crime Club gunman recurring against a plain green background. The uniformed nursemaid of *The Nursemaid Who Disappeared* looks back into a room, her hand on the door and an anxious expression on her face. The lurid pink wrapper for *The Dark Wheel* has Lawrence Bradford in his wheelchair, confronting a conflagration. *Fingers of Fear* shows a red-haired woman with varnished nails holding her fingers against her face.

The four Jenkins books are not uniform, and *The List of Adrian Messenger* is taller than the others. The first pair is red with black lettering, the second, black and lettered gilt. Tansley's wrapper for *The Man Out of the Rain* shows Jack Zakka, still engulfed by the downpour. Cole's design for *The List of Adrian Messenger* has Gwendolynne LaDoll going to her death under a bus in the Fulham Road, framed by the names from Messenger's list. *Death and Chicanery* has a gloved hand holding the ace of spades, devised by Bill Payne.

The Doubleday books of the early 1930s are very handsome, bound in black and lettered in orange on spine and cover. Their endpapers show the white American Crime Club gunman against a red background. *Persons Unknown* is dated 1931 but was published in November 1930. It has plans of the study and second floor at 44 Rajah Gardens. *The Crime Conductor* has a plan of Sigsbee's house and the title and publisher in red on the title-page. It and *The Polferry Riddle* are dated on the copyright page only, but *Persons Unknown* is also dated on the title-page. After the war, Doubleday's books lost weight, becoming taller but slimmer. *Something to Hide, Guest in the House* and *The Man Out of the Rain* are all black books, the first with green spine lettering, the others with white. All three are dated on the title-page and state 'First edition' on the copyright page. Joan Cummings' wrapper for *Guest in the House* has Ivor St

George framed in Mary Gould's french window. Consuelo Joerns, like Tansley, shows Jack Zakka before he escapes from the rain.

Three of the collected stories feature a new series character, Dr Alcazar, a dubious seer, living by his wits. He appears in 'Something to Hide' and 'The Green-and-gold String' in the first collection and in 'The Elephant's Head' in the second. The sole Gethryn story is 'The-Wood-for-the-Trees' from *Something to Hide* (or *Fingers of Fear*). The uncollected stories include two brief 'Exploits of Harry the Hat', who figures in 'The Go Between' from *The Man Out of the Rain*. An untitled story was used as the basis of a competition in *EQMM*, for October 1949. Later it acquired not one but two titles.

Novels

(with Gethryn, except as stated)

The Rasp   Collins 1924, Dial 1925
The White Crow   Collins 1928, Dial 1928
The Noose   Collins Crime Club May 1930, Dial 1930
The Link   Crime Club July 1930, Doubleday 25 July 1930
Rynox   Collins Oct. 1930 (not Gethryn)
a.k.a. *The Rynox Murder Mystery*   Doubleday 1931
a.k.a *The Rynox Mystery*   Collins 1933
revised as *The Rynox Murder*   Avon 1965
Persons Unknown   Doubleday 1931 (Nov. 1930)
revised as *The Maze*   Crime Club Apr. 1932
Murder Gone Mad   Crime Club Feb. 1931, Doubleday July 1931 (Pike)
The Wraith   Doubleday Feb. 1931, Crime Club Sept. 1931
The Choice   Crime Club Mar. 1931
a.k.a. *The Polferry Riddle*   Doubleday June 1931
a.k.a. *The Polferry Mystery*   Collins 1932
The Crime Conductor   Doubleday Aug. 1931, Crime Club Feb. 1932
Rope to Spare   Crime Club Sept. 1932, Doubleday Oct. 1932
Death on My Left   Crime Club Jan. 1933, Doubleday Mar. 1933
R.I.P.   Crime Club Apr. 1933 (not Gethryn)

a.k.a. *Menace* Doubleday Oct. 1933

The Nursemaid Who Disappeared Crime Club
7 Feb. 1938

a.k.a. *Warrant for X* Doubleday 11 Feb. 1938

The Dark Wheel (with A. Boyd Correll) Crime
Club 1948, Morrow 1948 (not Gethryn)

a.k.a. *Sweet and Deadly* Zenith 1959

Guest in the House Doubleday 1955, Jenkins
1956 (not Gethryn)

a.k.a. *No Time for Terror* Spivak 1956

The List of Adrian Messenger Doubleday 1959,
Jenkins 1960

Novel by Anthony Lawless

Harbour Doubleday Apr. 1931; Collins Oct.
1931 as by Philip MacDonald

Novels by Martin Porlock (Philip MacDonald in US)

Mystery at Friar's Pardon Crime Club Oct.
1931, Doubleday Feb. 1932

Mystery in Kensington Gore Crime Club Mar.
1932

a.k.a. *Escape* Doubleday May 1932

X v. Rex Crime Club Mar. 1933

a.k.a. *The Mystery of the Dead Police* Doubleday July 1933

a.k.a. *The Mystery of Mr. X* Collins Detective
Story Club n.d. (1934)

Story collections

Something to Hide Doubleday 1952 (6 stories)

a.k.a. *Fingers of Fear* Crime Club 1953

The Man Out of the Rain Doubleday 1955, Jenkins 1957 (6 stories)

Death and Chicanery Doubleday 1962, Jenkins
1963 (4 stories)

Uncollected stories

'Our Feathered Friends' (1931; *Best Ghost
Stories*, Faber 1945; *The Saint's Choice of
Hollywood Crime*, Saint, 1946; *Saint*, Nov.
1963 (UK))

'Two Exploits of Harry the Hat' ('The Absence

of Tonathal' and 'Sheep's Clothing') (*EQMM*,
Feb. 1949)

Untitled story (published as '?') (*EQMM*, Oct.
1949; *Ellery Queen's Minimysteries*, World
1969 as 'Robbie Always Pays'; a.k.a. 'Long
Shot')

'The Star of Starz' (*EQMM*, Oct. 1973; *Ellery
Queen's Murdercade*, Random House 1975,
Gollancz 1976) *BP*

Charlotte Macleod (b. 1922)
a.k.a. Alisa Craig

Charlotte Macleod is an adroit exponent of the
criminous comedy, with several strings to her
bow, including two buoyant series in her own
name and a pseudonym for her various sidelines.
She is a graceful, fluent writer, with two series
detectives, both operating from New England:
Peter Shandy at Balaclava Agricultural College,
and Sarah Kelling in and around Boston. The

Shandy novels tend to be more rustic and exuberant, the Kellings more urban and elegant. The former approach farce on occasion, stepping up the action with hordes of eager students or faculty wives on horseback. The latter draw felicitously on the eccentric tribal customs of the upper-crust family to which Sarah belongs.

Eleven novels by Alisa Craig are set in Canada and comprise two series and a singleton. Five books involve a Mountie named Madoc Rhys and five more the members of the Grub and Stake Gardening and Roving Club. *The Terrible Tide*, the non-series novel, is set, like the Rhys series, in New Brunswick. *Grab Bag* is a collection of seventeen stories, of which two involve Sarah Kelling and her second husband, Max Bittersohn. Peter Shandy figures in 'Rest You Merry', an early version of the novel of the same name. Other characters recur: James Charter-Harrison and Bill Williams in two stories and Augustus Fox in two more.

Most of Charlotte Macleod's novels are published in Britain by Collins Crime Club, but one Shandy novel has not had a British edition: *The Curse of the Giant Hogweed*, a bizarre fantasy set in a medieval dream-world. The Crime Club books have the standard red bindings and gilt spine lettering. They have the date on the copyright page and *The Resurrection Man* also has a printer's key, 9–1, US-style. From *Vane Pursuit* the books are taller. *The Corpse in Oozak's Pond, The Recycled Citizen* and *The Silver Ghost* were first published in Britain and the three titles from *The Gladstone Bag* appeared 'virtually at the same time in both countries', according to the author herself. All the Crime Club books have photographic wrappers, some worse than others. That for *The Bilbao Looking-Glass* is especially awful. One Alisa Craig title has also appeared from a British publisher: *The Terrible Tide*, which Hale brought out in 1985. It is a black book with silver spine lettering and dated copyright page.

In America, both the Macleod series and the Craig books were published till 1986 by the Doubleday Crime Club. Since 1987, Charlotte Macleod has been with the Mysterious Press, except for *Grab Bag*, published in that year by Avon as a paperback original. Alisa Craig was taken up by Avon, who followed *Grab Bag* with three further paperback originals. In 1992, Morrow restored Madoc Rhys to hardback form, doing likewise for the Grub-and-stakers in 1993. *The Case of the Giant Hogweed* is a tall red book with blue lettering along the spine and the date on the title-page. The copyright page states 'First edition', which is standard for Doubleday: copies without this assurance may be identical otherwise but that does not make them first editions. Margot Herr's appealing wrapper displays the hogweed.

The Avon paperbacks have bright pictorial covers and printer's keys running from 1 on the copyright page. *Grab Bag* has a bag decorated with a black skull, with murderous implements protruding from it. This book, like most Craigs, is not published in Britain. The two Morrow books are quarterbound, the earlier with cream boards and light-green spinal section, the later white and dark green. Both have gilt lettering along the spine and state 'First edition' on the copyright page, which also has a printer's key, 1–10. *The Grub-and-stakers House a Haunt* has light-brown endpapers.

The uncollected stories include one with Peter Shandy ('Counterfeit Christmas'), one with Sarah Kelling ('A Cozy for Christmas') and a Kelling family story ('A Sticky Business'). The three *Cold Blood* stories feature the Rev. Strongitharm Goodheart.

Charlotte Macleod has also written a number of juvenile mysteries and two romantic suspense novels for older girls, under the name Matilda Hughes.

Novels

(with Shandy or Kelling, as stated)

Rest You Merry Doubleday 1978, Collins Crime Club 1979 (Shandy)

The Family Vault Doubleday 1979, Crime Club 1980 (Kelling)

The Luck Runs Out Doubleday 1979, Crime Club 1981 (Shandy)

The Withdrawing Room Doubleday 1980, Crime Club 1981 (Kelling)

The Palace Guard Doubleday 1981, Crime Club 1982 (Kelling)

Wrack and Rune Doubleday 1982, Crime Club 1982 (Shandy)

The Bilbao Looking-Glass Doubleday 1983, Crime Club 1983 (Kelling)

Something the Cat Dragged In Doubleday 1983, Crime Club 1984 (Shandy)

The Convivial Codfish Doubleday 1984, Crime Club 1984 (Kelling)

The Curse of the Giant Hogweed Doubleday 1985 (Shandy)

The Plain Old Man Doubleday 1985, Crime Club 1985 (Kelling)

The Corpse in Oozak's Pond Crime Club 1986, Mysterious Press 1987 (Shandy)

The Recycled Citizen Crime Club 1987, Mysterious Press 1988 (Kelling)

The Silver Ghost Crime Club 1987, Mysterious Press 1988 (Kelling)

Vane Pursuit Mysterious Press 1989, Crime Club 1989 (Shandy)

The Gladstone Bag Crime Club 1989, Mysterious Press 1989 (Kelling)

An Owl Too Many Crime Club 1991, Mysterious Press 1991 (Shandy)

The Resurrection Man Crime Club 1992, Mysterious Press 1992 (Kelling)

Something in the Water Crime Club 1994, Mysterious Press 1994 (Shandy)

Story collection

Grab Bag Avon 1987 (17 stories)

Novels by Alisa Craig

(with Rhys, as stated)

A Pint of Murder Doubleday 1980 (Rhys)

The Grub-and-stakers Move a Mountain Doubleday 1981

Murder Goes Mumming Doubleday 1981 (Rhys)

The Terrible Tide Doubleday 1983, Hale 1985

The Grub-and-stakers Quilt a Bee Doubleday 1985

A Dismal Thing to Do Doubleday 1986 (Rhys)

The Grub-and-stakers Pinch a Poke Avon 1988

Trouble in the Brasses Avon 1989 (Rhys)

The Grub-and-stakers Spin a Yarn Avon 1990

The Wrong Rite Morrow 1992 (Rhys)

The Grub-and-stakers House a Haunt Morrow 1993

Uncollected stories

'A Tale of a Tub' (*Cold Blood II*, Mosaic 1989)

'A Cozy for Christmas' (*Mistletoe Mysteries*, Mysterious Press 1989)

'A Sticky Business' (*A Suit of Diamonds*, Crime Club 1990)

'Button in the Bag' (*Cold Blood III*, Mosaic 1990)

'Counterfeit Christmas' (*Christmas Stalkings*, Mysterious Press 1991)

'Why the C Was Boiling Hot' (*Cold Blood IV*, Mosaic 1992)

'A Long Time Sitting' (*Cat Crimes II*, Fine 1992)

The Curse of the Giant Hogweed

Charlotte MacLeod

A Crime Club Selection

'The Perplexing Puzzle of the Perfidious Pigeon Poisoner' (*Malice Domestic I*, Pocketbooks 1992)   BP

Jessica Mann (b. 1937)

Jessica Mann is a distinctive writer, resisting classification. She has her own ideas as to the possibilities of crime fiction, touching on significant themes in the course of her narratives. Her most interesting protagonists are women, and her principal series characters are female: Thea Crawford, a professor of archaeology, elegant, assured, and liberated; and Tamara Hoyland, her sometime pupil, an intelligence agent of awesome all-round competence. The former has two books of her own, besides appearing briefly in the Hoyland novels (as an off-stage force, even if not actually in person). Tamara has had six cases to date.

Jessica Mann's first novel came from Collins Crime Club in 1971, with the standard red binding and gilt spine lettering, and a grey Kenneth Farnhill dust-wrapper, enlivened by the vivid pink of a bottle of nail varnish. Subsequent books were published by Macmillan, generally with the standard lettering of this house, showing the author's surname and the title along the spine. The lettering is different on *The Sting of Death*, and the author is named in full. The bindings are in various colours, with silver lettering from *The Sting of Death*, except for *Death Beyond the Nile*. *Faith, Hope and Homicide* is taller than the rest. *Telling Only Lies* is a non-series novel, published by Chatto & Windus in 1992 in a black binding with gilt lettering on the spine. All Jessica Mann's books have the date on the copyright page.

Some of the Macmillan books have attractive designs (limited to the front panels of the wrappers and not permitted to overflow on to the spines, which would benefit from colour and variety). Yves Simard's bold design for *Captive Audience* shows a student demo at Buriton, with the registry building on fire and Thea's husband Sylvester looking on. For *The Eighth Deadly Sin*, the same artist sets 'Jane Shore', looking cool and contained in black, against a scene of erotic abandon. *No Man's Island* has Tony Masero's

impression of the granite cliffs of Forway, with a fire raging above and the Atlantic crashing below. Martin White's design for *A Kind of Healthy Grave* selects the war memorial from Rex's drawing, with the mongrel dog lifting its leg, and wearing on its head 'the little crown with which Rex signed his work'.

Novels

(With Crawford or Hoyland, as stated. Binding details refer to British editions.)

A Charitable End   Collins Crime Club 1971, McKay 1971
Mrs. Knox's Profession   Macmillan 1972, McKay 1972 (black binding, grey-blue lettering)
The Only Security   Macmillan 1973 (Crawford) (brown, black)
a.k.a. *Troublecross*   McKay 1973

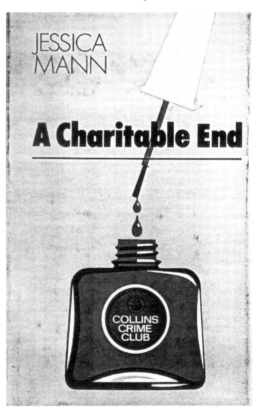

The Sticking Place Macmillan 1974, McKay 1974 (black, white)

Captive Audience Macmillan 1975, McKay 1975 (Crawford) (brown, black)

The Eighth Deady Sin Macmillan 1976 (black, white)

The Sting of Death Macmillan 1978, Doubleday 1983 (purple binding)

Funeral Sites Macmillan 1981, Doubleday 1982 (Hoyland) (black)

No Man's Island Macmillan 1983, Doubleday 1983 (Hoyland) (brown)

Grave Goods Macmillan 1984, Doubleday 1985 (Hoyland) (red)

A Kind of Healthy Grave Macmillan 1986, St Martin's 1987 (Hoyland) (grey)

Death Beyond the Nile Macmillan 1988, St Martin's 1989 (Hoyland) (blue, gilt)

Faith, Hope and Homicide Macmillan 1991 (Hoyland) (maroon)

Telling Only Lies Chatto & Windus 1992, Carroll & Graf 1993   *BP*

Dame Ngaio Marsh (1895–1982)

Ngaio Marsh wrote thirty-two novels, collaborating on one with Dr H. Jellett. She also wrote three plays and eight collected stories. She was born in New Zealand and became one of the 'Queens of Crime'. Her many excellent novels all feature Roderick Alleyn, one of the most famous policemen in detective fiction, who also has three shorter cases to solve. He is staunchly assisted by Inspector Fox in twenty-four of his cases. In the early days, he also had his Watson, the journalist Nigel Bathgate, who helps in nine investigations. Alleyn's wife, Agatha Troy, a famous painter, plays an important role in twelve of the books. Dame Ngaio's abiding interest in the theatre is borne out by the settings of many of her books. Notable examples are *Enter a Murderer* and *Opening Night* – and her last book, *Light Thickens*, about a production of *Macbeth*.

For most of her books, the British editions are the true firsts, but there are thirteen exceptions, including *Death of a Peer, Death and the Dancing Footman, Singing in the Shrouds*, and *Killer Dolphin*. All the American firsts were published by Little, Brown of Boston, with the exception of the short fiction collection, which has no UK edition. The US editions are all dated. Many have variant titles.

In London the first seven books were published by Geoffrey Bles. The first two have red cloth, lettered in black on the spine. The title also appears on the front cover, together with a black border. Blue, purple, or brown cloth with black lettering signify a later issue. The following five titles have red cloth with white lettering on the spine and the title in white on the front cover. Copies with red or blue cloth and black lettering are later issues.

All the Bles books are dated, as are the author's remaining books, published by Collins Crime Club, generally in orange or red cloth. *False Scent, Black as He's Painted* and *Last Ditch* have black bindings. The books with orange/red covers all have black spine lettering until the publication of *Dead Water*, when it becomes gilt. Collectors should be warned of two later issues: an undated *Overture to Death*, which is otherwise identical to the first edition, and a red cloth *Death at the Dolphin* with black lettering. *Scales of Justice, Clutch of Constables*, and *Death at the Dolphin* have pictorial endpapers, and *Black as He's Painted* has a map of the Capricorns. *Overture to Death* is slightly taller than the others before and after it.

The dust-wrappers for the Bles books were of the black-and-white photographic type. *A Man Lay Dead* has a pocket watch showing the time 7.55, and the stage door at the Unicorn Theatre appears on *Enter a Murderer*. Two syringes in a dish feature on *The Nursing-home Murder*; a fallen goblet with spilled contents on *Death in Ecstasy*; a wine bottle on *Vintage Murder*; and a man in evening dress on *Death in a White Tie*. The orange/red wrapper for *Overture to Death* is lettered in white. The green wrapper of *Death at the Bar* has a dartboard on the front panel, with a hand and arm superimposed across it, and a yellow dart appears on the spine below the author's name. Stead's very stylish design for *Surfeit of Lampreys* has a lamprey with a skewer through its head, and this is reproduced on the spine. His design for *Death and the Dancing Footman*, however, simply puts coloured letters on a dark blue background, although the word 'Death' is formed by bones.

Ironically, *Colour Scheme* must have one of the world's drabbest wrappers, with white lettering on olive-green. Russ designed the split bale of wool for *Died in the Wool*, in yellow, brown and black. Dark-red theatre curtains decorate *Final Curtain* with the lettering in yellow, and a swinging noose against a blue background is found on *Swing, Brother, Swing*. The first-night audience is shown arriving at the Vulcan Theatre for *Opening Night*. Several of the later wrappers were designed by Kenneth Farnhill, but are generally uninspired.

In 1989, the stories of Ngaio Marsh were collected by Douglas G. Greene and published by International Polygonics. The book is quarterbound, with salmon-pink boards and black spine, with silver lettering. It is dated on the copyright page, which also has a 10–1 printer's key. A paperbound edition followed in 1991 with an additional story, newly discovered. The augmented edition has an updated copyright notice.

Enter a Murderer and *Overture to Death* seem to be the most difficult first editions to find.

Alleyn novels

A Man Lay Dead   Bles 1934, Sheridan 1942
Enter a Murderer   Bles 1935, Pocket Books 1941
The Nursing-home Murder   Bles 1935, Sheridan 1941, with Henry Jellett
Death in Ecstasy   Bles 1936, Sheridan 1941
Vintage Murder   Bles 1937, Sheridan 1940
Artists in Crime   Bles 1938, Furman 1938
Death in a White Tie   Bles 1938, Furman 1938
Overture to Death   Collins Crime Club 1939, Furman 1939
Death at the Bar   Crime Club 1940, Little, Brown 1940
Death of a Peer   Little 1940
a.k.a. *Surfeit of Lampreys*   Crime Club 1941
Death and the Dancing Footman   Little 1941, Crime Club 1942
Colour Scheme   Little 1943, Crime Club 1943
Died in the Wool   Crime Club 1945, Little 1945
Final Curtain   Crime Club 1947, Little 1947
A Wreath for Rivera   Little 1949

a.k.a. *Swing, Brother, Swing*   Crime Club 1949
Opening Night   Crime Club 1951
a.k.a. *Night at the Vulcan*   Little 1951
Spinsters in Jeopardy   Little 1953, Crime Club 1954
a.k.a. *The Bride of Death*   Spivak 1955
Scales of Justice   Crime Club 1955, Little 1955
Death of a Fool   Little 1956
a.k.a. *Off with His Head*   Crime Club 1957
Singing in the Shrouds   Little 1958, Crime Club 1959
False Scent   Little 1959, Crime Club 1960
Hand in Glove   Little 1962, Crime Club 1962
Dead Water   Little 1963, Crime Club 1964
Killer Dolphin   Little 1966
a.k.a. *Death at the Dolphin*   Crime Club 1967
Clutch of Constables   Crime Club 1968, Little 1969
When in Rome   Crime Club 1970, Little 1971
Tied up in Tinsel   Crime Club 1972, Little 1972

NGAIO MARSH'S Mystery Novel
ENTER A MURDERER
STAGE DOOR

Black as He's Painted   Crime Club 1974, Little 1974
Last Ditch   Crime Club 1977, Little 1977
Grave Mistake   Crime Club 1978, Little 1978
Photo-Finish   Crime Club 1980, Little 1980
Light Thickens   Little 1982, Crime Club 1982

Story collection

The Collected Short Fiction of Ngaio Marsh, International Polygonics 1989; augmented edition 1991.   *JC*

A. E. W. Mason (1865–1948)

A. E. W. Mason was a great romancer, and so much of his fiction has elements of crime and mystery that dividing lines are sometimes difficult to draw. While bearing in mind that this might not be the whole story, collectors could reasonably focus on the famous series involving Inspector Gabriel Hanaud and his incongruous friend, Mr Julius Ricardo. They figure in five novels and two stories, and are oddly, but rewardingly, matched: Hanaud a confident veteran of the Sûreté in Paris, an ebullient bourgeois, disconcerting and unpredictable; Ricardo a fastidious dilettante, correct and inhibited, outlandish only in his passion for criminal investigation.

Surprisingly, for books published over thirty-six years, the Hanaud novels are uniform in format, bound in blue, with gilt spine lettering, and title and author in black on the front cover. *At the Villa Rose* also exists in two variant forms, differing only externally from what might be called the standard edition. One is dark red with title and author stamped white on the front cover, the former at the top, the latter at the bottom. The spine has stamped gilt lettering. Two pairs of vertical yellow bands decorate the front cover and a further pair decorate the spine. These are broken by title and author on the cover and by title, author and publisher on the spine. This format is known for other titles from Hodder at this time (by Jacques Futrelle and Gaston Leroux, for instance.) The other binding is red with gilt lettering on the spine and a pictorial front cover showing a man in cap and overcoat – perhaps Perrichet – peering in through french windows at the Villa Rose. Except for *The House of the Arrow* and *The Prisoner in the Opal*, the books are dated. *At the Villa Rose*, *They Wouldn't Be Chessmen*, and *The House in Lordship Lane* are Hanaud's other major investigations: he and Ricardo also figure briefly in *The Sapphire*, in the chapter called 'The Man from Limoges', set in a Savile Row gambling-den. Hanaud's flamboyance embarrasses Mr Ricardo, and his bravura demonstration of how 'the 705 formula' works is sufficient to enforce the closure of the house. The thriller *No Other Tiger* was originally intended as a further Hanaud novel, but only Mr Ricardo survives into the published version. This book, too, is blue, lettered gilt on the spine and black on the front cover. Like the other 1920s books, it is undated. Mr. Ricardo does not appear in *The House of the Arrow*, the wrapper for which shows Ann Upcott cowering. For *No Other Tiger*, Leo Bates presents Lady Ariadne Ferne, in splendid procession with a tiger. S. S. (perhaps Stephen Spurrier) has, for *The Prisoner in the Opal*, Joyce Whipple, at the house of the Widow Chicholle, holding out her handcuffed wrists, in 'the extremity of her distress'. Spurrier's vivid design for *They Wouldn't be Chessmen* shows Prince Ali Ibrahim, 'his balancing-pole waist high in his hands', negotiating his tight-rope, over the heads of Mr Ricardo and others of the fashionable company at Guy Stallard's party. Stead's view of *The House in Lordship Lane* records the 'plain, unbedizened beauty' of White Barn at night, with a light burning in the Horburys' bedroom window.

Two stories complete the Hanaud canon, 'The Ginger King' and 'The Affair at the Semiramis Hotel' (scene of the Choral Benevolent Society banquet in *No Other Tiger*). The latter appeared first in Britain in *Pearson's*, Christmas 1916 and was collected in October of the next year, in *The Four Corners of the World*. It was published in America, also in 1917, as a separate booklet (of seventy-seven pages according to Hubin); and was reprinted in *EQMM* for January 1950 (where Ellery Queen mentions an unpublished Hanaud story called 'The Healer', on which *They Wouldn't be Chessmen* came to be based).

'The Clock' and 'The Secret Fear' also had separate American publication, so that Mason has the distinction of having three of his stories preserved in individual editions. Besides the Hanaud story, *The Four Corners of the World* contains eleven stories and a short play, 'Under Bignor Hill'. 'The Clock' is a mystery, and 'The House of Terror' is a suspense story with a strong supernatural element. The book is dated and has the same format as the Hanaud novels.

Seven other books are listed as crime fiction by Hubin and Reilly: the novels *The Watchers* (1899), *Running Water* (1907), *The Witness for the Defence* (1913), *The Summons* (1920), and *The Winding Stair* (1923); and the story collections *Ensign Knightley* (1901) and *Dilemmas* (1934). 'The Italian', collected in *Dilemmas*, appeared in *EQMM* for April 1949.

An uncollected story called 'The Sapphire' was published in *Pall Mall* in May 1927. It is narrated by Colonel Strickland, from *No Other Tiger*, and was later expanded into the novel of the same name. Mason's last short detective story was 'The Secret Fear' featured in *The Strand* for April 1940 and serving eventually as the basis for *The House in Lordship Lane*. Reilly's list of the uncollected stories virtually reproduces Roger Lancelyn Green's in his biography of Mason. In its new context, it is misleading, since it is by no means limited to crime and mystery stories.

Novels

(with Hanaud and Ricardo, except as stated)

At the Villa Rose Hodder & Stoughton 1910, Scribner 1910
a.k.a. *Murder at the Villa Rose* Chivers 1992
The House of the Arrow Hodder n.d. (1924), Doran 1924 (Hanaud only)
No Other Tiger Hodder n.d. (1927), Doran 1927 (Ricardo only)
The Prisoner in the Opal Hodder n.d. (1928), Doubleday 1928
The Sapphire Hodder 1933, Doubleday 1933
They Wouldn't be Chessmen Hodder 1935, Doubleday 1935

The House in Lordship Lane Hodder 1946, Dodd, Mead 1946

Story collection

The Four Corners of the World Hodder 1917 (includes 'The Affair at the Semiramis Hotel')

Separately published stories

'The Clock' Paget 1910
'The Affair at the Semiramis Hotel' Scribner 1917
'The Secret Fear' Doubleday 1940

Uncollected stories

'The Sapphire' (*Pall Mall*, May 1927)
'The Ginger King' (*Strand*, Aug. 1940; *EQMM*, Aug. 1950; *Great Stories of Detection*, Barker 1960)   *BP*

Helen McCloy (1904–1993)

Because she experimented continually and fought shy of formula, Helen McCloy's work is very varied, but also very uneven. She is a daring, unpredictable writer, handling original concepts boldly, and adapting them to the mystery with varying degrees of conviction. At her best, she is remarkable, highly imaginative and fiercely intelligent. Her principal detective, Basil Willing, is a distinguished psychiatrist who first appears in 1938 in *Dance of Death*. He has twelve other full-length cases, in one of which his involvement is not apparent until the end. With the author's own extensive knowledge of psychology to give him stature, he carries complete conviction. He is also tougher than he looks. The author's other detective is the Captain of Police at Puerta Vieja in the Caribbean. His name is Miguel Urizar and he has two recorded cases.

Two novels and a novella remain unpublished in Britain, and other books had to wait years for their British editions, so that the order of publication is different in the two countries. Three books have variant British titles, including the first, *Dance of Death*. As *Design for Dying*, this appeared from Heinemann in 1938, a black book, with gilt spine lettering, red endpapers, and the publisher's windmill blind-stamped on the rear cover. The second and third books came from Hamish Hamilton, *The Man in the Moonlight* in a pale-brown binding, and *The Deadly Truth* in pale yellow. Both have green spine lettering, and the former also had the title in green on its front cover. All three books are dated.

The later wartime books had more varied fortunes in Britain. *Who's Calling?* came out from Nicholson & Watson in 1948, as an undated one-shilling paperback with minuscule print. *Cue for Murder* was also announced for the same series but is not listed by the BL catalogue nor by *ECB*, which does list *Who's Calling?*. *Do Not Disturb* was published only in America (and is more likely to surface in Britain as a Tower Book reissue than a Morrow first edition.). *The Goblin Market* was published by Hale in 1951, in a black binding, with green lettering and the silver Hale pistol on the spine. *Panic*, which appeared in the US in 1944, had to wait nearly thirty years for its 'specially revised' British edition, issued by Gollancz in 1972. This is the standard late Gollancz product, red with gilt spine lettering and the usual featureless wrapper. *The One That Got Away* is also a Gollancz book, red and gilt, but in the smaller format of the 1950s. *She Walks Alone*, a post-war book, appeared from Coker in 1950, in a blue binding and with black spine lettering. Except for *Who's Calling?* all these books are dated. The novella *Better Off Dead* was published in 1951, in the USA only, as an undated Dell paperback costing ten cents.

From 1951 Helen McCloy was published in Britain by Gollancz. She found a settled publisher, but her books lost their visual interest and individuality. All the Gollancz books are dated. *Through a Glass Darkly* is a dark-red book and *Alias Basil Willing* is green. Both have black spine lettering. *Unfinished Crime* became *He Never Came Back* in its Gollancz edition. Like all its successors except *The Long Body*, it is red with gilt spine lettering. *The Long Body* is lettered in gilt with a brown binding. From *Surprise, Surprise!*, the story collection, the books are taller. *Burn This*, the last, appeared in 1980.

Surprise, Surprise! contains eight stories, two of which feature Basil Willing: 'Through a Glass Darkly', a version of the novel, and 'The Singing Diamonds', after which the US edition is named. 'Windless', the last story, was originally published as 'The Last Day' by Helen Clarkson. Brett Halliday's introduction to the US edition states that the novel of the same name is an expanded version of this story. It was published in 1959 by Torquil, a division of Dodd, Mead, as by Helen Clarkson, but it is more SF than crime fiction. *The Early McCloy* is an omnibus published by Gollancz in 1973, and containing *Dance of Death*, *The Deadly Truth*, and *Who's Calling?* The British title of *Dance of Death* was discarded on this occasion.

Who's Calling? has a pictorial cover with Frieda Frey in black lace, her pink telephone unnervingly to hand. *The Goblin Market* shows the newspaperman known as Philip Stark at his desk, with one of the novel's glamorous women standing by. *She Walks Alone* has a vivid wrapper by G. P. Micklewright, showing the body of 'Livia Crespi', on board the *Santa Cristina*, with the bushmaster snake 'coiled around her neck, like a collar'. The American editions, by and large, are more varied and interesting than the British, too many of which form a yellow slab on the shelf. *Dance of Death* is a black book with blue lettering on the spine. The front cover has the title in a blue border and a blue disc enclosing a dancing couple in black silhouette. The dated title-page is decorated with more dancers. *The Man in the Moonlight* is blue with black lettering on the spine, which also has a running man blue within a black disc. *The Deadly Truth* is green with dark-green spine lettering. A dark-green necklace coils from the spine on to the front cover. The top edge is green. *Who's Calling?* is a purple book with yellow lettering on the spine, which also has a yellow question mark enclosing an unknown caller in the curl at the top and a woman below. The dated title-page is decorated with a double border, containing four question marks, one at each corner. *Cue for Murder* has an orange binding with black lettering on the spine and a housefly and a canary in flight. *Do Not Disturb* is blue-grey with red lettering on the spine, which also has a red male figure pushing open a door with 'Do Not Disturb' on it.

From 1948, Helen McCloy was published by Random House, often (and perhaps always) in a uniform binding format. *Through a Glass Darkly, Unfinished Crime, The Long Body* and *Two-Thirds of a Ghost* have similar spines with gilt lettering set within a pattern of gilt and black rules and bands, the title showing gilt against a central black block. The front covers have the publisher's circular logo of a house among trees. *Through a Glass Darkly* has a grainy pale-brown binding, blue-grey end-papers with the logo in white, a green top edge and a roughly trimmed fore-edge. The others are grey with charcoal top edges, smooth fore-edges and blank white endpapers. All four books are dated by the copyright notice only and state 'First printing' on the copyright page. All except *Through a Glass Darkly* have title-pages with the title within a

tilted rectangle laid across and partly obscuring the Random House logo.

Better Off Dead is a small paperback, Dell 10c. Book no. 34. The only date is that of the copyright notice (1949) but it was published in 1951. On the cover Robert Stanley shows the attempted murder of Frank Bly.

The later McCloys were published by Dodd, Mead. *The Singing Diamonds* has a blue binding with yellow spine lettering and the Red Badge logo yellow on the front cover. *The Sleepwalker* is light blue with black spine lettering and *Burn This* is quarterbound, with black boards, orange spine and black spine lettering. The copyright page has a printer's key 1–10. All three are dated by the copyright notice only.

Dance of Death has a splendidly macabre wrapper showing skeletons in evening dress dancing among an elegant company. *The Deadly Truth* shows Liebermann's necklace from the spine and cover, this time with bright-green stones. *Who's Calling?* also has the decoration from the spine of the book on the wrapper: a large yellow question mark with the two telephone speakers. *Cue for Murder* has a black wrapper with an elaborate pattern composed of elements from the narrative, of which the canary and fly recur on the spine. Carl Becker's stylish wrapper for *Panic* shows large trees through which a small house on a hill can be seen. *The One That Got Away* has a black wrapper with Hoffman's drawing of a man running through leafless trees. *Through a Glass Darkly* gives a distorted view of the face of a frightened woman. *The Sleepwalker* has a striking design by Doug Anderson, with a woman casting a long shadow amid swirling coils of blue. *Burn This* has a white wrapper with a hand holding a flaring match.

Eight of the known uncollected stories feature Basil Willing: all those from 'Thy Brother Death' onwards. A second collection is long overdue. 'Of Time and Murder' in *EQMM*, July 1968 is the same as *Better Off Dead*, which is also known as 'Murder is a Brutal Business' (and may also have 'Return of a Dead Man' (*MSMM*, June 1961) as a further variant title).

Novels

(with Willing and/or Urizar, as stated)

Dance of Death Morrow 1938 (Willing)
a.k.a. *Design for Dying* Heinemann 1938
The Man in the Moonlight Morrow 1940, Hamilton 1940 (Willing)
The Deadly Truth Morrow 1941, Hamilton 1942 (Willing)
Who's Calling? Morrow 1942, Nicholson & Watson n.d. (1948) (Willing)
Cue for Murder Morrow 1942 (Willing)
Do Not Disturb Morrow 1943
The Goblin Market Morrow 1943, Hale 1951 (Willing, Urizar)
Panic Morrow 1944, revised edition Gollancz 1972
The One That Got Away Morrow 1945, Gollancz 1954 (Willing)
She Walks Alone Random House 1948, Coker 1950 (Urizar)
a.k.a. *Wish You Were Dead* Bestseller 1958
Through a Glass Darkly Random House 1950, Gollancz 1951 (Willing)
Alias Basil Willing Random House 1951, Gollancz 1951 (Willing)
Better Off Dead Dell n.d. (1951) (novella)
Unfinished Crime Random House 1954
a.k.a. *He Never Came Back* Gollancz 1954
The Long Body Random House 1955, Gollancz 1955 (Willing)
Two-Thirds of a Ghost Random House 1956, Gollancz 1957 (Willing)
The Slayer and the Slain Random House 1957, Gollancz 1958
Before I Die Dodd, Mead 1963, Gollancz 1963
The Further Side of Fear Dodd 1967, Gollancz 1967
Mr. Splitfoot Dodd 1968, Gollancz 1969 (Willing)
A Question of Time Dodd 1971, Gollancz 1971
A Change of Heart Dodd 1973, Gollancz 1973
The Sleepwalker Dodd 1974, Gollancz 1974
Minotaur Country Dodd 1975, Gollancz 1975
The Changeling Conspiracy Dodd 1976
a.k.a. *Cruel as the Grave* Gollancz 1977
The Imposter Dodd 1977
a.k.a. *The Impostor* Gollancz 1978

The Smoking Mirror Dodd 1979, Gollancz 1979
Burn This Dodd 1980, Gollancz 1980 (Willing)

Story collection

The Singing Diamonds Dodd 1965 (8 stories)
a.k.a. *Surprise, Surprise!* Gollancz 1965

Uncollected stories

'The Nameless Clue' (*Five-Novel Monthly*, Nov. 1941; *Murder Cavalcade*, Duell 1946, Macdonald 1953; *EQMM*, Apr. 1961, as 'The Black Disk')
'Shake Hands with Death' (*American Magazine*, Apr. 1950; *EQMM*, Apr. 1959, as 'The Outer Darkness')
'The Man Who Talked' (*American Magazine*, Jul. 1951)
'The Waiting Shadow' (*American Magazine*, June, 1952; *EQMM*, June 1962, as 'The Shadows Outside')

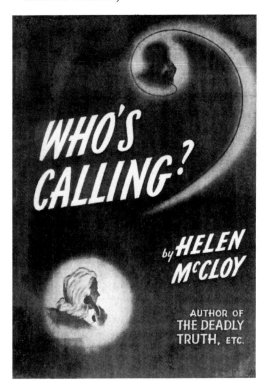

'Murder is Everybody's Business' (*EQMM*, Feb. 1953; *EQA*, vol. 1, Davis 1959, May Fair 1959)

'Thy Brother Death' (1955; *EQMM*, Jul. 1957 and *EQA* 1964, Davis 1964 as 'Shock Tactics')

'Murder Stops the Music' (*This Week*, 1957; *EQMM*, Jul. 1958, as 'The Silent Informer')

'Murder Ad Lib' (*EQMM*, Nov. 1964; *Ellery Queen's Twentieth Anniversary Annual*, Random House 1965, Gollancz 1966; *Miniature Mysteries*, Taplinger 1981 as 'The Quick and the Dead')

'Into Thin Air' (*EQMM*, Feb. 1965)

'The Pleasant Assassin' (*EQMM*, Dec. 1970; *EQA*, Spring-Summer 1975, Davis 1975/*Ellery Queen's Christmas Hamper*, Gollancz 1975)

'A Case of Innocent Eavesdropping' (*EQMM*, Mar. 1978)

'Murphy's Law' (*EQMM*, May 1979)

'That Bug that's Going Around' (*EQMM*, Aug. 1979)   *BP*

Jill McGown (b. 1947)
a.k.a. Elizabeth Chaplin

Although she is still less widely celebrated than she should be, Jill McGown, a gifted writer in the ingenious classic tradition, has written ten intricately plotted novels and a single story. She has also published a psychological thriller under the name Elizabeth Chaplin. Her talent is major and she deserves a wider audience.

All the McGown novels were first published in London by Macmillan and they are all dated. The cloth and spine lettering colours vary from title to title. *Murder... Now and Then* has a printer's key on the copyright page. Two books have variant titles in the USA. The Elizabeth Chaplin title was published by Scribner: it is dated and has maroon cloth with the spine lettered gilt. The pink endpapers have a pattern made up of the publisher's name repeated over and over again.

Two series characters, Detective-Inspector Lloyd and Detective-Sergeant Judy Hill, appear in six books. Both gain promotion in the course of the series and their relationship, personal and professional, is a source of continual interest.

Most of Jill McGown's wrappers are photographic, in Macmillan's worst vein. The unsigned black-and-white wrapper for *Record of Sin* shows the village of Upper Caswell with a plane flying overhead, casting its shadow over the whole scene.

Novels

(with Lloyd and Hill, except as stated)

(Binding details refer to Macmillan editions)

A Perfect Match Macmillan 1983, St Martin's 1983 (blue binding, silver lettering)

Record of Sin Macmillan 1985, Curley 1986 (grey, gilt) (non-series)

An Evil Hour Macmillan 1986, St Martin's 1987 (green, silver) (non-series)

The Stalking Horse Macmillan 1987, St Martin's 1988 (blue, silver) (non-series)

Redemption Macmillan 1988 (red, silver)

a.k.a. *Murder at the Old Vicarage* St Martin's 1989
Death of a Dancer Macmillan 1989 (red, silver)
a.k.a. *Gone To Her Death* St Martin's 1990
Murder Movie Macmillan 1990, St Martin's 1990 (beige, gilt) (non-series)
The Murders of Mrs. Austin and Mrs. Beale Macmillan 1991, St Martin's 1991 (red, gilt)
The Other Woman Macmillan 1992, St Martin's 1993 (light brown, gilt)
Murder . . . Now and Then Macmillan 1993, St Martin's 1993 (green, gilt)

Novel by Elizabeth Chaplin

Hostage to Fortune Scribner 1992, Mysterious Press 1993

Story

'A Fine Art' (*Winter's Crimes 20*, Macmillan 1988)   *JC*

James Melville (b. 1933)
a.k.a. Hampton Charles

James Melville was for many years a cultural diplomat in Japan, and the revelation of Japanese life in his novels gives them a rare fascination. A particular aspect of Japanese culture is absorbed into each narrative: Zen Buddhism, netsuke, the tea ceremony. The mysteries are neatly contrived, and our affection for the policemen who solve them makes it a pleasure to renew their acquaintance. Happily, they are continually on call: the superintendent, Otani, and his two inspectors, Kimura and Noguchi, each making a distinctive contribution.

Nine books appeared from Secker & Warburg, the first, *The Wages of Zen*, in 1979. Their wrappers give most of them an agreeable uniformity, but they are bound and lettered in a range of colours.

In 1988, James Melville moved to Headline, whose books are black with gilt lettering, in line with the last Secker title. They also have Otani's own motif, representing the impression of his personal seal, gilt on each spine (and this also features on all the Headline wrappers). The

latest Otani is *The Body Wore Brocade*, published by Little, Brown in 1992, in a maroon binding with gilt lettering on the spine. It is 'by Tetsuo Otani as told to James Melville'. All the books are dated on the copyright page and have as preliminary the title written as closely as possible in Japanese. *A Haiku for Hanae* has a preliminary map showing the position of Awaji Island in relation to the Japanese mainland.

The uniform style of the wrappers was preserved until *Kimono for a Corpse* appeared in 1987 in a new format. Items from the V & A's Japanese collection figure on some: an exquisite piece of netsuke, a warlord's accoutrements, an Utamaro painting of a kiss between lovers. *Sayonara, Sweet Amaryllis* has a photo of a fugu fish, and *The Death Ceremony* a chaste Japanese interior by Eric Rose, with Otani's motif on one of the walls. Despite later changes in the wrappers, the elegance of the series is preserved, as sinister shadows are thrown across a sequence of graceful interiors. The Headline wrappers also feature the title in Japanese.

In 1990, Berkley revived Heron Carvic's Miss Seeton, the endearing protagonist of five gentle thrillers published between 1968 and 1975. As 'Hampton Charles', James Melville wrote three sequels, all paperback originals with pictorial covers of Miss Seeton and her umbrella at significant moments. The famous umbrella, open, features on each spine. The books have yellow edges and are dated on the copyright page, also with a printer's key, 10–1.

Besides the novels, there are four stories, two with Otani.

Otani novels

(Binding details refer to Secker editions.)

The Wages of Zen Secker & Warburg 1979, Fawcett 1985 (yellow binding, blue lettering)
The Chrysanthemum Chain Secker 1980, St Martin's 1982 (black gilt)
A Sort of Samurai Secker 1981, St Martin's 1982 (orange-brown, black)
The Ninth Netsuke Secker 1982, St Martin's 1982 (cream, black)

213

Sayonara, Sweet Amaryllis Secker 1983, St Martin's 1984 (black, gilt)

Death of a Daimyo Secker 1984, St Martin's 1985 (red, gilt)

The Death Ceremony Secker 1985, St Martin's 1985 (black, gilt)

Go Gently, Gaijin Secker 1986, St Martin's 1986 (black, silver)

Kimono for a Corpse Secker 1987, St Martin's 1988

The Reluctant Ronin Headline 1988, Scribner 1988

A Haiku for Hanae Headline 1989, Scribner 1989

The Bogus Buddha Headline 1990, Scribner 1991

The Body Wore Brocade Little, Brown 1992, Macmillan 1992

Miss Seeton novels by Hampton Charles

Miss Seeton, By Appointment Berkley Apr. 1990

Advantage, Miss Seeton Berkley June 1990

Miss Seeton at the Helm Berkley Sept. 1990

Otani stories

'Santa-san Solves It' (*Crime at Christmas*, Equation 1988)

'Otani Has a Haircut' (*New Crimes 2*, Robinson 1990)

Other Stories

'Programmed for Murder' (*1st Culprit*, Chatto & Windus 1992)

'Gambling on Ganymede' (*Midwinter Mysteries 2*, Little, Brown 1992)   *BP*

Gladys Mitchell (1901–1983)
a.k.a. Malcolm Torrie

Gladys Mitchell was a compulsive writer of amazing energy and industry, who can never have wasted a moment. She taught in schools for most of her life, and yet contrived to write well over eighty novels of one kind or another. Though her work is very uneven, she has properly been called a fantasist of genius. Her principal achievement is the long series of novels featuring Beatrice Adela Lestrange Bradley, consultant psychiatrist to the Home Office and a vivid eccentric of enduring appeal. She was already elderly in 1929 when, most memorably, her extraordinary career began, and her last recorded case appeared in 1984, fifty-five years later. Much ado is made of Poirot's longevity, but Dame Beatrice must be at least as old, and, unlike him, she remains active to the end (when, according to the evidence, she could be as old as 125). She performs idiosyncratically in all sixty-six of the author's detective novels and at least seven stories. She is Dame Beatrice from *Twelve Horses and the Hangman's Noose. Laurels Are Poison*, the fourteenth book, introduces Laura Menzies, the gifted and resourceful student teacher who eventually becomes Mrs Bradley's secretary and a participant in most of her later cases. She is hefty and handsome, a natural athlete, with uninhibited confidence and good humour. Years later, Philip Larkin wrote wistfully of the days before Laura arrived to muddle Mrs Bradley's wits. Numerous members of Mrs Bradley's family also participate, from her son, Ferdinand Lestrange KC, to younger, remoter connections.

In her sixties, Miss Mitchell launched a second detective, a young architect called Timothy Herring, with a brief to preserve historic buildings. He appears in six novels published under the pseudonym Malcolm Torrie. The author's other pseudonym, Stephen Hockaby, was reserved for her mainstream historical fiction.

Her first publisher was Victor Gollancz, who issued *Speedy Death* and its immediate successors in the black binding with orange spine lettering that distinguished his books before the war (and with his characteristic yellow dustwrappers). *The Longer Bodies* features Matilda Puddequet's family tree and a plan of her sports ground. Between the four Gollancz books and the long series from Michael Joseph are two from Grayson and Grayson, a short-lived 1930s firm. *Death at the Opera* is a red book, lettered in gilt on the spine. A variant with black lettering, though identical internally, is perhaps the reissue of March 1935. In America, the book was called *Death in the Wet*. *The Devil at Saxon Wall* is a black book, with gilt spine lettering and a red top edge.

Michael Joseph's association with Gladys Mitchell endured for nearly fifty years, from the firm's inception in 1936 to her death in 1983. The series of sixty novels began with *Dead Man's Morris*, the first of four ample brown books, lettered in silver on the spine. The endpapers show the shields of the dancers and a jingle to accompany their dance, and the frontispiece is a map of the country east of Oxford.

The first war-time book, *Brazen Tongue*, breaks the brown and silver pattern; it is blue, with silver lettering (but a variant in a lighter blue, with dark-blue lettering, is also known). It is also a less substantial book than its predecessors; and the next title, *Hangman's Curfew*, was the last to benefit from 1930s solidity. *When*

Last I Died is drastically scaled down by wartime economy, and the publisher apologises for its meagre appearance. The American edition still has a pre-war opulence.

Apart from the initial group of four, the Joseph bindings vary considerably, though black with silver lettering obtains from *Death and the Maiden* to *The Devil's Elbow*, and, later, from *The Whispering Knights* to *Death of a Burrowing Mole*. Except for *A Hearse on Mayday*, which has silver lettering, all the books from *The Echoing Strangers* to *Convent on Styx* have gilt lettering on the spine. All the books from *Merlin's Furlong* to *Adders on the Heath* have black bindings. From *The Croaking Raven*, the books are taller. *Hangman's Curfew* has a noose on the spine and *Tom Brown's Body*, the victim, supine, contrary to the text.

All Gladys Mitchell's books are dated, and later impressions of the Gollancz books, at least, are properly identified. Twenty-two books have had American editions, a number in recent years. For *When Last I Died* Miss Mitchell wrote a special dedicatory letter to her American readers from the London of the Blitz.

She was fortunate in many of her dust-wrapper designers, who include some of the best in the field: Youngman Carter, C. W. Bacon, Kenneth Farnhill, and Broom Lynne. The wrapper for *The Devil at Saxon Wall* is by G. W. Goss and illustrates the nocturnal confrontation between Mrs Passion, naked under a raincoat, and Hannibal Jones, in red and white pyjamas. For *Printer's Error* Youngman Carter shows the printing press of Saxant and Senss, with a gun, a sheaf of printed paper, and a crocodile, to remind us of Mrs Bradley's more saurian attributes. C. W. Bacon's wrapper for *Brazen Tongue* has a rare portrait of Mrs Bradley, sitting erect in a basket chair, looking alert and quizzical, beneath a wide red hat. *When Last I Died* features a green wreath, with pink roses, a purple sash, and a card inscribed 'in loving and affectionate memory'. *The Worsted Viper* shows the playing cards designed by Amos Bleriot on the cover, and Alice Boorman's handwritten letter on the front flap. *Sunset Over Soho* has a large hand, with the index finger pointing at the coffin found at the Maidenhead Close Rest

Centre. Stein's elegant design for *Death and the Maiden* features a fey girl with a death's-head, and is genuinely eerie. Freda Nichols' work for *Tom Brown's Body* and *Groaning Spinney* is appealing but inaccurate, since she fails to show the bodies in the positions indicated by the text.

Some of Kenneth Farnhill's finest work was done for Gladys Mitchell, and the seven books from *The Twenty-third Man* are a tribute to his artistry. *My Bones Will Keep* and *Adders on the Heath* bring the series to a fine conclusion, the one with its fabulous beast rearing its mocking head, the other with its bravura pattern of New Forest ponies, hooves flying as they trample a man to death. Farnhill was succeeded by Broom Lynne, whose designs for Gladys Mitchell are less memorable than those he did for Mary Fitt, largely because his style was more directly illustrative at this time. His image of *The Croaking Raven* is striking, however. *Wraiths and Changelings* has a composed and chilling drawing of the Black Monk of Ranworth and his dog, by Nigel Mynheer. *Here Lies Gloria Mundy* has a vivid impression of the dead witch by Mark Wilkinson. Otherwise, all the books from *Mingled with Venom* have wrappers by Graham Rogers, who provides a series of arresting images: the skeletal scarecrow of *Uncoffin'd Clay*; the looming toadstool of *The Death-cap Dancers;* the bird-haunted ruin of *Death of a Burrowing Mole*; the skull-like landscape of *Cold, Lone and Still*; and the noble heads of the Rant sisters' dogs for *The Crozier Pharaohs*.

The Malcolm Torrie books were published at the rate of one a year between 1966 and 1971. *Heavy as Lead* is lettered in silver, the others in gilt; the bindings are of various colours. All the wrappers are effective, that by John Storey for *Bismarck Herrings* especially so.

Gladys Mitchell contributed to two collaborative works, the substantial *Ask a Policeman*, and the more ephemeral *No Flowers By Request*. The special savour of *Ask a Policeman* derives from the address of the four writers who parody each other's styles. Miss Mitchell wrote 'Sir John Takes His Cue', the chapter in imitation of Helen Simpson and Clemence Dane, whose detective is the soigné actor-manager, Sir John Saumarez. This episode follows Miss Simpson's

own pastiche of Gladys Mitchell, 'Mrs. Bradley's Dilemma'. Miss Mitchell's contributions to the novella were two chapters, entitled 'Murder by Poison' and 'But I Didn't Poison My Wife' in the *Daily Sketch* of 27 and 28 Nov. 1953, but simply numbered v and vi for the book publication in 1984.

Thirty-one stories are known, all uncollected. 'Daisy Bell', 'The Case of the Hundred Cats', 'Strangers' Hall', 'A Light on Murder', 'Rushy Glen', 'Juniper Gammon', and 'The Spell' are Mrs Bradley stories. Two versions of 'Manor Park' exist. *Full Fathom Five* is an unpublished two-part radio play, featuring Mrs Bradley, and broadcast on 28 Sept. and 1 Oct. 1940.

Bradley novels

(Details of bindings refer to British editions.)

Speedy Death   Gollancz 1929, Dial 1929
The Mystery of a Butcher's Shop   Gollancz 1929, Dial 1930
The Longer Bodies   Gollancz 1930
The Saltmarsh Murders   Gollancz 1932, Macrae Smith 1933
Death at the Opera   Grayson 1934
a.k.a. *Death in the Wet*   Macrae Smith 1934
The Devil at Saxon Wall   Grayson 1935
Dead Man's Morris   Joseph 1936
Come Away, Death   Joseph 1937
St. Peter's Finger   Joseph 1938, St. Martin's 1987
Printer's Error   Joseph 1939
Brazen Tongue   Joseph 1940
Hangman's Curfew   Joseph 1941 (yellow binding, purple lettering)
When Last I Died   Joseph 1941, Knopf 1942 (pale yellow, blue)
Laurels Are Poison   Joseph 1942 (pale yellow, dark blue)
The Worsted Viper   Joseph 1943 (grey, red)
Sunset Over Soho   Joseph 1943 (blue-green, black)
My Father Sleeps   Joseph 1944 (yellow, blue)
The Rising of the Moon   Joseph 1945, St Martin's 1985 (black, gilt)
Here Comes a Chopper   Joseph 1946 (red, silver)
Death and the Maiden   Joseph 1947

The Dancing Druids   Joseph 1948, St Martin's 1986

Tom Brown's Body   Joseph 1949

Groaning Spinney   Joseph 1950

The Devil's Elbow   Joseph 1951

The Echoing Strangers   Joseph 1952 (red binding)

Merlin's Furlong   Joseph 1953

Faintley Speaking   Joseph 1954, St Martin's 1986

Watson's Choice   Joseph 1955, McKay 1976

Twelve Horses and the Hangman's Noose   Joseph 1956, British Book Centre 1958

a.k.a. *Hangman's Noose*   Severn House 1983

The Twenty-third Man   Joseph 1957

Spotted Hemlock   Joseph 1958, British Book Centre 1958

The Man Who Grew Tomatoes   Joseph 1959, London House 1959

Say It with Flowers   Joseph 1960, London House 1960

The Nodding Canaries   Joseph 1961

My Bones Will Keep   Joseph 1962, British Book Centre 1962

Adders on the Heath   Joseph 1963, London House 1963

Death of a Delft Blue   Joseph 1964, London House 1964 (blue)

a.k.a. *Death in Amsterdam*   Severn House 1990

Pageant of Murder   Joseph 1965, London House 1965 (red)

The Croaking Raven   Joseph 1966 (black)

Skeleton Island   Joseph 1967 (dark blue)

Three Quick and Five Dead   Joseph 1968 (red)

Dance to Your Daddy   Joseph 1969 (blue)

Gory Dew   Joseph 1970 (red)

Lament for Leto   Joseph 1971 (orange-brown)

A Hearse on Mayday   Joseph 1972 (black, silver)

The Murder of Busy Lizzie   Joseph 1973 (black binding)

A Javelin for Jonah   Joseph 1974 (red)

Winking at the Brim   Joseph 1974, McKay 1977 (dark red)

Convent on Styx   Joseph 1975 (mauve)

Late, Late in the Evening   Joseph 1976 (black, silver)

Noonday and Night   Joseph 1977 (maroon, gilt)

Fault in the Structure   Joseph 1977 (black, silver)

Wraiths and Changelings   Joseph 1978 (blue-green, gilt)

Mingled with Venom   Joseph 1978 (black, gilt)

Nest of Vipers   Joseph 1979 (blue, gilt)

The Mudflats of the Dead   Joseph 1979 (dark blue, silver)

Uncoffin'd Clay   Joseph 1980, St Martins 1982 (blue, gilt)

The Whispering Knights   Joseph 1980

The Death-cap Dancers   Joseph 1981, St Martin's 1981

Lovers Make Moan   Joseph 1981

Here Lies Gloria Mundy   Joseph 1982, St Martin's 1983

Death of a Burrowing Mole   Joseph 1982

The Greenstone Griffins   Joseph 1983 (green, gilt)

Cold, Lone and Still   Joseph 1983 (sage, gilt)

No Winding Sheet   Joseph 1984 (black, silver)

The Crozier Pharaohs   Joseph 1984 (black, silver)

Herring novels by Malcolm Torrie

Heavy as Lead   Joseph 1966 (dark blue)
Late and Cold   Joseph 1967 (red)
My Secret Friend   Joseph 1968 (black)
Churchyard Salad   Joseph 1969 (brown)
Shades of Darkness   Joseph 1970 (black)
Bismarck Herrings   Joseph 1971 (black)

Collaborations with other members of the Detection Club (q.v.)

Ask a Policeman   Barker n.d. (1933), Morrow 1933

No Flowers By Request   Gollancz 1984 (with *Crime on the Coast*)

Uncollected stories

'The Case of the Hundred Cats' (*ES*, 17 Aug. 1936; *Fifty Famous Detectives of Fiction*, Odhams n.d. (1938); *Ladies in Crime*, Faber 1947)

'Daisy Bell' (*Detective Stories of Today*, Faber 1940; *Crime on Her Mind*, Joseph 1976)

'Strangers' Hall' (*ES*, 17 Jan. 1950; *The Evening Standard Detective Book*, Gollancz 1950)

'A Light on Murder' (*ES*, 15 Feb. 1950; *The Evening Standard Detective Book*, Gollancz 1950)

'Rushy Glen' (*ES*, 5 June 1950)

'Juniper Gammon' (*ES*, 14 June 1950)

'Manor Park' (*ES*, 18 Aug. 1950; *The Evening Standard Detective Book*, series 2, Gollancz 1951; variant text in *The Third Bedside Book of Great Detective Stories*, Barker 1978)

'The Jar of Ginger' (*ES*, 28 Sept. 1950; *The Evening Standard Detective Book*, series 2, Gollancz 1951)

'The Knife' (*ES*, 11 Jan. 1951)

'Practical Joke' (*ES*, 19 Jan. 1951)

'Our Pageant' (*ES*, 19 Sept. 1951)

'The Tree' (*ES*, 21 Sept. 1951)

'Sammy' (*ES*, 29 Sept. 1951)

'Peach Jam' (*ES*, 6 Nov. 1951)

'The Plumb-line' (*ES*, 13 Nov. 1951)

'Haunted House' (*ES*, 9 Feb. 1952)

'The Falling Petals' (*ES*, 6 Mar. 1952)

'The Price of Lead' (*ES* 6 June 1952)

'The Spell' (*ES*, 14 June 1952)

'A Bit of Garden' (*ES*, 18 June 1952)

'The Swimming Gala' (*ES*, 25 July 1952)

'The Tooth-pick' (*ES*, 3 Oct. 1952)

'The Bodkin' (*ES*, 11 Oct. 1952)

'The Boxer' (*ES*, 17 Jan. 1953)

'The Visitor' (*ES*, 4 Feb. 1953)

'Oversight' (*ES*, 13 Feb. 1953)

'The Manuscript' (*ES*, 11 May 1953)

'The Fish Pond' (*ES*, 19 May 1953)

'Alibi' (*ES*, 23 May 1953)

'The Vacuum Cleaner' (*ES*, 2 July 1953)

'Arsenic in the House' (*ES*, 6 June 1956)   *BP*

Gwen Moffat (b. 1924)

Gwen Moffat's detective novels are distinguished by their open-air ambience and, frequently, a background of mountains. Her premier detective is a tough, self-sufficient spinster named Melinda Pink, a seasoned naturalist and climber, like her creator. Assiduously she quarters each terrain, from Snowdonia to the Rockies and the Arizona desert. Corpses are found in the open and investigation draws on the logic of the natural environment. Eight books have preliminary maps to assist the reader, often invaluably. All but four involve Miss Pink and they, too, define a landscape as well as resolving a mystery. *Pit Bull* and *The Outside Edge* feature Jack Pharaoh, a former member of the RAF Mountain Rescue team, invalided out because of a fall. Ten novels were published by Gollancz, generally in red bindings, though the first of the series, *Lady with a Cool Eye*, is maroon. The lettering throughout is gilt and the title-pages are dated. They all have yellow wrappers with minimal decorative features, though *Over the Sea to Death* has the music to 'The Skye Boat Song' and the 'Y' of *Last Chance Country* burgeons into a cactus. From *Snare* in 1987, the books have been published by Macmillan: to *Pit Bull* in the standard format of this publisher, with the author's surname above and the title below a single rule on the spine, the lettering to appear upright when

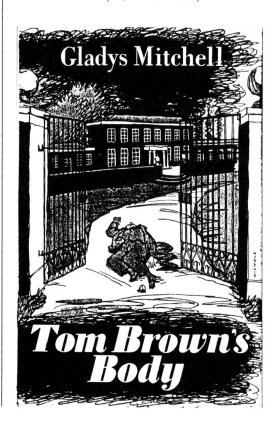

Gladys Mitchell

Tom Brown's Body

the book is laid face up. From *The Stone Hawk* to *The Raptor Zone* the lettering is silver, but for *Snare, Pit Bull* and *Veronica's Sisters* it is gilt. Binding colours vary but the date appears consistently on the copyright page (which also has a printer's key, 9–1, in the case of *The Outside Edge*). From *The Raptor Zone* the books are taller.

The most interesting wrappers have drawings by Martin White: of eagles soaring over pinnacles of pink rock for *The Stone Hawk* and a jeep hurtling through the air into an abyss for *Rage*. All the spines are red and white, graceless and glaring.

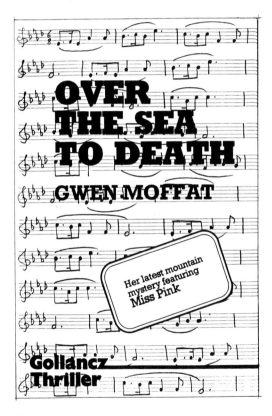

Novels

(with Pink, except where stated)
(Binding colours refer to Macmillan editions.)

Lady with a Cool Eye   Gollancz 1973
Deviant Death   Gollancz 1973 (not Pink)
The Corpse Road   Gollancz 1974 (not Pink)
Miss Pink at the Edge of the World   Gollancz 1975, Scribner 1975
Over the Sea to Death   Gollancz 1976, Scribner 1976
A Short Time to Live   Gollancz 1976
Persons Unknown   Gollancz 1978
Die Like a Dog   Gollancz 1982
Last Chance Country   Gollancz 1983
Grizzly Trail   Gollancz 1984
Snare   Macmillan 1987, St Martin's 1988 (black)
The Stone Hawk   Macmillan 1989, St Martin's 1989 (blue)
Rage   Macmillan 1990, St Martin's 1990 (red)
The Raptor Zone   Macmillan 1990 (grey)
Pit Bull   Macmillan 1991 (brown) (Pharaoh)
Veronica's Sisters   Macmillan 1992 (black)
The Outside Edge   Macmillan 1993 (blue) (Pharaoh)   *BP*

Anne Morice (1918–1989)

Anne Morice was a daughter of Frederick Lonsdale and something of his wit and lightness of touch is apparent in the vivacious series of detective novels she published betwen 1970 and 1990. All but two involve Tessa Crichton, an actress with a husband in the CID at Scotland Yard and a cousin who is, like the author's father, a successful light dramatist. Two late novels feature a rural superintendent called Tubby Wiseman, who lives up to his surname. Two non-series stories appeared in *Winter's Crimes* and three others have Group Captain Dick Stevenson and his wife Pamela, of Hurst Lodge, Maresfield.

All but one of the books were published in the standard format of Macmillan's crime series, with the author's surname above and the title below a single rule on the spine, the letters set along the spine with their tops towards the front cover. *Murder by Proxy* has variant lettering. The binding colours vary considerably. The lettering is white for *Death and the Dutiful Daughter*, *Death of a Wedding Guest* and *Scared To Death*; black for the other eight titles to *Murder in Mimicry*; and silver from *Murder by Proxy*. All the books are dated on the copyright page.

219

Murder by Proxy has a preliminary plan of part of Roakes Common.

Anne Morice was ill served by Macmillan's design department. The wrappers for her books offer a succession of charmless photographs and their spines are either drab (when white) or harsh (when red and white). A few books have attractive designs, including *Death of a Heavenly Twin*, for which Jennifer Eachus provided a graceful drawing of the Benson-Jones twins; and *Nursery Tea and Poison*, with Ken Laidlaw's skull and crossbones ominous among the cosy trappings of a tea-table. *Hollow Vengeance* has Martin White's arresting image of a bleeding oak; and two colourful designs by John Ireland enliven *Murder in Mimicry* and *Murder by Proxy*: gloved hands pushing aside a pot of geraniums to retrieve a key; and an overturned wheelchair in a vivid garden. Of the others, *The Men in Her Death, Murder Post-dated* and *Dead on Cue* are particularly dreadful.

Novels

(with Tessa Crichton except where stated)

Death in the Grand Manor Macmillan 1970 (pale green)

Death in Married Life Macmillan 1970 (green)

Death of a Gay Dog Macmillan 1971 (blue-green)

Murder on French Leave Macmillan 1972 (yellow)

Death and the Dutiful Daughter Macmillan 1973, St Martin's 1974 (black)

Death of a Heavenly Twin Macmillan 1974, St Martin's 1974 (orange-brown)

Killing with Kindness Macmillan 1974, St Martin's 1975 (blue)

Nursery Tea and Poison Macmillan 1975, St Martin's 1975 (blue)

Death of a Wedding Guest Macmillan 1976, St Martin's 1976 (black)

Murder in Mimicry Macmillan 1977, St Martin's 1977 (orange-brown)

Scared to Death Macmillan 1977, St Martin's 1978 (dark green)

Murder by Proxy Macmillan 1978, St Martin's 1978 (dark green)

Murder in Outline Macmillan 1979, St Martin's 1979 (red)

Death in the Round Macmillan 1980, St Martin's 1980 (navy blue)

The Men in Her Death Macmillan 1981, St Martin's 1981 (red)

Hollow Vengeance Macmillan 1982, St Martin's 1982 (brown)

Sleep of Death Macmillan 1982, St Martin's 1983 (pale brown)

Murder Post-dated Macmillan 1983, St Martin's 1984 (red)

Getting Away with Murder? Macmillan 1984, St Martin's 1985 (puce)

Dead on Cue Macmillan 1985, St Martin's 1985 (blue)

Publish and be Killed Macmillan 1986, St Martin's 1987 (mustard)

Treble Exposure Macmillan 1987, St Martin's 1988 (dark green)

Death of a Heavenly Twin
Anne Morice

Design for Dying   Macmillan 1988, St Martin's 1988 (grey) (Wiseman)

Fatal Charm   Macmillan 1988, St Martin's 1988 (dark green)

Planning for Murder   Macmillan 1990, St Martin's 1991 (dark blue) (Wiseman)

Stories

'False Alarm' (*AHMM*, Aug. 1979; *Alfred Hitchcock's A Mystery by the Tale*, Davis 1986)

'The Rise and Fall of Sarah Merrion' (*AHMM*, 30 Jan. 1980)

'The Extra Man' (*AHMM*, 27 Oct. 1980)

A Good Night's Sleep' (*Winter's Crimes 12* Macmillan 1980)

'Young Man on a Train' (*Winter's Crimes 18*, Macmillan 1986)   *BP*

Arthur Morrison (1863–1945)

Arthur Morrison wrote one episodic detective novel – *The Red Triangle* – and nineteen stories collected in three volumes, all involving Martin Hewitt, a plump, friendly man with a round face and a frequent, ready smile. The stories are narrated by Hewitt's journalist friend Brett and are in the same mould as the Sherlock Holmes stories, though Martin Hewitt lacks the eccentricities that so distinguish Holmes. The first series of seven stories appeared in the *Strand Magazine* between March and December 1894 and the rest were published in the *Windsor Magazine*.

Morrison's other detective, Horace Dorrington, features in the six stories that make up *The Dorrington Deed-box*. A criminal turned private detective for the Dorrington & Hicks Inquiry Agency, he cuts a handsome figure: approaching forty, he is tall and erect, with a round face, penetrating eyes and a debonair military moustache. The books were first published in the UK and two, *Adventures of Martin Hewitt* and *The Dorrington Deed-Box*, have not had American editions.

Martin Hewitt, Investigator and *Chronicles of Martin Hewitt* were published by Ward, Lock & Bowden and are bound in red cloth (although blue and green bindings are also known for the former). Both are lettered gilt on spine and front cover. In addition, each front cover has an illustration. For *Martin Hewitt, Investigator* this consists of six pieces of a torn letter, with a magnifying glass in black and gilt laid over one of the torn pieces; and for *Chronicles of Martin Hewitt* a man kneeling by a fire and burning a human hand appears in gilt in the lower right corner. The former cover illustrates 'The Loss of Sammy Throckett' and the latter 'The Case of the Missing Hand'. The spine of *Martin Hewitt, Investigator* has an illustration for 'The Case of the Dixon Torpedo' showing Mirsky kneeling and speaking through a keyhole; it also states 'illustrated by Sydney Paget'. This book also has the author's name on the front cover but *Chronicles of Martin Hewitt* has only the title, together with 'Being the second series of Martin Hewitt, Investigator'. Both rear covers are blank. Each book has the date at the base of the title-page and pages of advertisements at the rear, four in *Investigator* and six in *Chronicles*. The endpapers of the former are light brown and patterned, with the publisher's colophon regularly repeated, but those for the latter are plain white.

Martin Hewitt, Investigator has black-and-white illustrations by Sidney Paget, whose name is incorrectly spelt on the spine of the book. A frontispiece depicts a scene from 'The Case of the Dixon Torpedo' and there are fifteen further full-page drawings and thirty-five smaller illustrations in the text. *Chronicles* is illustrated in black and white by D. Murray Smith, whose frontispiece, covered by a tissue guard, illustrates 'The Case of the Lost Foreigner', showing Hewitt placing his hand on the shoulder of the person in question. There are twenty more full-page illustrations and seven smaller ones set in the text. Ward, Lock (without Bowden) published *Adventures of Martin Hewitt* and *The Dorrington Deed-box*, the former in a light-blue cloth, lettered gilt on the spine and front cover. The front cover has the title and 'Third Series' in brackets, together with a gilt illustration for 'The Case of the Late Mr. Rewse', showing Hewitt levering up a hearthstone with coal-tongs. The spine has another illustration for the same story, depicting Mrs Hurley holding a letter. The endpapers are plain, the title-page is dated, there are ten pages of advertisements at the back and the rear cover is blank. T. S. C. Crowther is the illustrator for *Adventures of Martin Hewitt*. Twenty full-page illustrations include the frontispiece, which has a tissue guard. Fifteen smaller drawings punctuate the text. *The Dorrington Deed-box* has maroon cloth, lettered gilt on spine and front cover. The latter has title and author, with twenty-three gilt dots under 'Dorrington'. The spine has a gilt illustration of an earnest-looking woman facing left and eighteen gilt dots under 'Dorrington'. The book is undated, with plain endpapers and four advertisement pages at the end. Stanley J. Wood is the first of the book's three illustrators. He provided the frontispiece (which has a tissue guard) and eight further illustrations. The frontispiece illustrates 'The Case of Mr. Loftus Deacon' and shows Beard, the porter, looking down on Deacon's body, lying in blood. The other Wood illustrations are for three further stories. 'The Case of the Mirror of Portugal' has four drawings by Sydney Cowell and 'Old Cater's Money' has three by Paul R. Hardy. All the illustrations are full page. These four books are among the most attractive in detective fiction.

Eveleigh Nash published *The Red Triangle* in blue cloth with gilt spine lettering. The front cover has the title in white at the top with 'Being some further Chronicles of Martin Hewitt: Investigator' underneath. Below this is a red triangle enclosing three men, two of whom observe the third, who is poring over papers with a magnifying glass. Under the triangle is the author's name in white. The title-page is dated and also has 'Red Triangle' and the publisher's colophon in red. The endpapers are plain, there are no illustrations and there are no advertisements. Two variant bindings are known, one blue, the other red, both with gilt spine lettering and blank front covers.

Neither *The Hole in the Wall*, nor *The Green Eye of Goona* is a detective story. The former has theft and murder but is a study of life in London's slums; the latter is an adventure story involving a quest for a gem that is smuggled out of India. A story, 'A Professional Episode', appears in *Detection Medley* (Hutchinson n.d.

(1939)) and is collected in the mixed volume *Fiddle O'Dreams and More* (Hutchinson 1933).

'As Far As They Had Got' is a collaborative story launched by E. Phillips Oppenheim, continued, in succession, by W. Pett Ridge, Arthur Morrison, Horace Annesley Vachell, Barry Pain and Charles Garvice, and completed by Richard Marsh (with a feeble conclusion that dodges the issue entirely).

All five of Arthur Morrison's detective titles are extremely scarce in first edition.

Episodic novel
(with Hewitt)

The Red Triangle Nash 1903, Page 1903

'The Case of the Lost Foreigner' from Chronicles of Martin Hewitt, 1895. Frontispiece by D. Murray-Smith

Story collections

Martin Hewitt, Investigator Ward, Lock & Bowden 1894, Harper 1894 (7 stories)
Chronicles of Martin Hewitt Ward, Lock & Bowden 1895, Appleton 1896 (6 stories)
Adventures of Martin Hewitt Ward, Lock 1896 (6 stories)
The Dorrington Deed-Box Ward, Lock 1897

Collaborative story

'As Far As They Had Got' (*Strand*, Aug. 1911) Arthur Morrison wrote Chapter 3.   *JC*

Patricia Moyes (b. 1923)

Patricia Moyes is the justifiably popular author of nineteen novels and over twenty stories. Many readers and collectors already know her work, but those who do not should try *Falling Star* or *Who Saw Her Die?* Her series characters are Henry Tibbett and his wife Emmy, who feature in all the novels, but in none of the stories. Henry is a sympathetic policeman, with a nose for seeking out criminals. In the first book, he is a Chief Inspector at Scotland Yard, and he eventually reaches the rank of Detective Chief Superintendent. The Tibbetts are portrayed realistically, as characters whose private joys and sorrows, as well as their professional successes, are to be savoured and shared. The indefatigable Lucy Pontefract-Deacon features in three of the books with a Caribbean setting.

The books have all been published in Britain by Collins Crime Club, and they are all dated. *Black Widower* has black cloth, and the rest have red. The first four titles all have black lettering on the spine, and the rest have gilt. *Season of Snows and Sins* was reissued in first edition format with black lettering. With *Death of a Dutch Uncle* the books become taller. *Black Widower* is taller than the rest. There are some differences in the texts of the US and UK editions of *Night Ferry to Death*. Several books have alternative American titles.

Twice in a Blue Moon has a printer's key on the copyright page. At least two books, *Night Ferry to Death* and *Black Girl, White Girl*, are known to have been first published in the USA. Publication details are not known for two stories: 'The Representative' and 'Fairy Goddaughter'.

The wrapper for *Dead Men Don't Ski* has crossed skis on a blue background, and a white sailing boat dominates the pale-blue wrapper for *The Sunken Sailor*. The highly effective design for *Falling Star* has a skeleton set in a director's chair, against the brown background of a film studio; and part of this is reproduced on the spine. A black fighter plane with a white body in the cockpit flies through a midnight-blue sky in the illustration for *Johnny Under Ground*. Kenneth Farnhill's modern pink and grey design for *Murder Fantastical* shows a white revolver with black thread wrapped around the trigger and snaking across the lower half of the wrapper. Other earlier wrappers are black with coloured lettering, but from 1970 they are mainly of the photographic type.

The most difficult first edition to locate seems to be *Death on the Agenda*.

Tibbett novels

Dead Men Don't Ski Collins Crime Club 1959, Rinehart 1960
The Sunken Sailor Crime Club 1961
a.k.a. *Down Among the Dead Men* Holt Rinehart 1961
Death on the Agenda Crime Club 1962, Holt 1962
Murder a la Mode Crime Club 1963, Holt 1963
Falling Star Crime Club 1964, Holt 1964
Johnny Under Ground Crime Club 1965, Holt 1966
Murder Fantastical Crime Club 1967, Holt 1967
Death and the Dutch Uncle Crime Club 1968, Holt 1968
Who Saw Her Die? Crime Club 1970
a.k.a. *Many Deadly Returns* Holt 1970
Season of Snows and Sins Crime Club 1971, Holt 1971
The Curious Affair of the Third Dog Crime Club 1973, Holt 1973
Black Widower Crime Club 1975, Holt 1975
To Kill a Coconut Crime Club 1977

a.k.a. *The Coconut Killings*   Holt 1977, Penguin (UK) 1978

Who Is Simon Warwick?   Crime Club 1978, Holt 1979

Angel Death   Crime Club 1980, Holt 1981

A Six-Letter Word for Death   Crime Club 1983, Holt 1983

Night Ferry to Death   Holt 1985, Crime Club 1985

Black Girl, White Girl   Holt 1989, Crime Club 1990

Twice in a Blue Moon   Holt 1993, Crime Club 1993

Uncollected stories

'The Treasure' (*EN*, 30 Aug. 1961)

'Murder! for Five Bob's Worth of Human Misery' (*ES*, 16 Mar. 1963; *EQMM*, 10 Mar. 1980 as 'The Most Hated Man in London'; a.k.a. 'A Question of Timing')

'The Holly Wreath' (*Woman's Mirror* (1965); *Ellery Queen's Prime Crimes*, Davis 1984)

'Deadlock' (*EQMM*, Dec. 1979; a.k.a. 'The Judgment of Solomon')

'A Suitable Revenge' (*EQMM*, 14 Jan. 1980; a.k.a 'The Revenge')

'A Man without Papers' (*EQMM*, 5 May 1980)

'Who Killed Father Christmas?' (*Who Done It?*, Houghton 1980; *EQMM*, 1 Jan. 1982)

'Beyond the Reef' (*EQMM*, 24 Feb. 1982)

'A Whispering in the Reeds' (*EQMM*, 24 Mar. 1982)

'A Matter of Succession' (*EQMM*, May 1982)

'Hit and Run' (*EQMM*, July 1982)

'The Honest Blackmailer' (*EQMM*, Sept. 1982)

'The Small Train Robbery' (*EQMM*, Nov. 1982)

'A Lonely Profession' (*EQMM*, Mar. 1983)

'Faces of Betrayal' (*EQMM*, June 1983)

'The Faithful Cat' (*EQMM*, July 1983)

'Flowers of the Dead' (*EQMM*, Apr. 1984)

'A Young Man Called Smith' (*AHMM*, mid-Dec. 1986)

'Love at Second Sight' (*AHMM*, Mar. 1987; a.k.a. 'A Dream of a Girl')

'The Extra Mile' (*EQMM*, Mar. 1989)

'The Man Who Had Everything' (*A Suit of Diamonds*, Crime Club 1990)

'Family Christmas' (*Christmas Stalkings*, Mysterious Press 1991, HarperCollins 1992)   *JC*

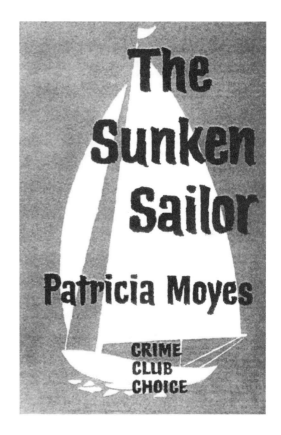

Magdalen Nabb (b. 1947)

Magdalen Nabb was admired by Georges Simenon, whose praise was used to promote her early in her career. Like him, she has few illusions and broad sympathies. Her books are set in Florence, which she knows intimately and brings vividly alive. Her invariable detective is a Sicilian Marshal, based at the Carabinieri Station at the Pitti Palace: Salvatore Guarnaccia. He is 'large and fat', with a voluble wife and eyes that weep in the sunlight. He doesn't look like a hero but his modesty, humanity and dogged shrewdness make him one. He has true stature and commands affection and respect.

The books were all first published by the Crime Club in Britain, in red bindings with gilt lettering on the spine and dated copyright page. From *The Marshal's Own Case* they are taller and from *The Marshal Makes His Report* they

The Marshal and the Murderer Crime Club 1987, Scribner 1987

The Marshal and the Madwoman Crime Club 1988, Scribner 1988

The Marshal's Own Case Crime Club 1990, Scribner 1990

The Marshal Makes His Report Crime Club 1991, HarperCollins 1992

The Marshal at the Villa Torrini Crime Club 1993

Non-series collaboration

The Prosecutor Collins 1986, Scribner 1987
with Paolo Vagheggi   *BP*

Beverley Nichols (1898–1983)

Beverley Nichols wrote many books, but unfortunately only five are detective novels. These are little known by readers and collectors in general, who have a considerable treat in store when they discover them. Their series detective is a small,

have a printer's key with the copyright notice. Most of the wrappers have the usual dreary photographs (not unpleasing for *Death of an Englishman* and *The Marshal and the Murderer*). *The Marshal Makes His Report* has a handsome marbled design by Joe Partridge, with the author's name incised in gilt over a red family crest, split diagonally.

With Paolo Vagheggi, Magdalen Nabb has also written a non-series thriller, *The Prosecutor*.

Salvatore Guarnaccia novels

Death of an Englishman Crime Club 1981, Scribner 1982

Death of a Dutchman Crime Club 1982, Scribner 1983

Death in Springtime Crime Club 1983, Scribner 1984

Death in Autumn Crime Club 1985, Scribner 1985

rotund, almost Pickwickian private investigator named Horatio Green, now retired. Not only is he the author of *First Principles in Detection*, but he has a passionate love for gardening. Like all great detectives, he has his peculiarities – blinking while deep in thought, making cryptic comments, and using his acute sense of smell as an aid to solving his cases.

All Beverley Nichols' detective novels were published by Hutchinson, and they are all dated. There is one variant title; *The Moonflower* which becomes *The Moonflower Murder* in the USA.

No Man's Street was issued in blue cloth in a dust-wrapper of which the designer has the initials J. E. V. It features an old-fashioned street lamp, both on the front panel and the spine. This lamp reappears in gilt on the spine and front cover of the book. The spine also has gilt lettering. *The Moonflower* has black cloth lettered in gilt on the spine. Green cloth lettered in black indicates a later issue. G. W. Anderson's design of the flower of the title is on the front panel and spine of the wrapper. The third book, *Death to Slow Music*, was first issued in blue cloth with gilt lettering on the spine. The later issue has blue cloth lettered in black. Seabourne Pier is shown attractively illuminated at night on G. W. Anderson's wrapper. *The Rich Die Hard* has black cloth lettered in gilt on the spine. Trevor Denning's design for the wrapper shows a ticker-tape machine on a grey background. The main characters in this novel are based on Dorothy and Geoffrey Hart and the setting is their Sussex mansion, Wych Cross Place. The last novel, *Murder by Request*, was issued in black cloth with red spine lettering. The author's name and the title appear within a white border. The black wrapper, designed by William Randell, features 'a humble bunch of white chrysanthemums'.

Green novels

No Man's Street   Hutchinson 1954, Dutton 1954
The Moonflower   Hutchinson 1955
a.k.a. *The Moonflower Murder*   Dutton 1955
Death to Slow Music   Hutchinson 1956, Dutton 1956
The Rich Die Hard   Hutchinson 1957, Dutton 1958

Murder By Request   Hutchinson 1960, Dutton 1960
                                                    JC

Gil North (b. 1916)

Gil North is the mainstream novelist Geoffrey Horne, who launched a sequence of idiosyncratic crime novels in 1960 with *Sergeant Cluff Stands Firm*. Ten further books completed the series, which culminated in *Sergeant Cluff Rings True* in 1972. *Sergeant Cluff and the Madmen* contains the novellas 'The Blindness of Sergeant Cluff' and 'Sergeant Cluff Laughs Last'. Apart from the Cluff books, Gil North's only other novel is *A Corpse for Kofi Katt*, set in Africa, with a half-caste police superintendent as a protagonist. Sergeant Cluff – Caleb to those few who know him best – is the CID man in Gunnarshaw, a small Yorkshire market town. He is fiercely independent, with his own integrity and his own ideas of how best to serve his unsophisticated community. His contempt for official rules and procedures puts him continually under threat

from more orthodox elements in the force. Leslie Sands played him memorably in a far-off television series.

Despite changes in the constitution of their publishers, the Cluff books are all black with silver spine lettering: and they are all dated. Even the black and white photographic dust-wrappers preserve a kind of uniformity, so that the series looks handsome on the shelf, all of a piece, yet individually appealing. The earlier wrappers feature photos of Cluff by Frank Hermann. *Sergeant Cluff Stands Firm* gives us our best view of him, looking both wary and formidable, as he stands outside Gunnarshaw's police station in his 'ancient and disreputable Burberry' and 'shapeless tweed hat, with the grouse feather in its band'. He is seen from behind for *Sergeant Cluff Goes Fishing* and through a grille for *Sergeant Cluff and the Madmen*. From *Sergeant Cluff and the Price of Pity*, the wrappers focus on significant features of the investigations; and Cluff's hat appears at the head of each spine.

Like the Cluff series, *A Corpse for Kofi Katt* is also black with silver spine lettering, in the standard late-Hale format. It too is dated.

Novels

(with Cluff, except were stated)

Sergeant Cluff Stands Firm   Chapman & Hall 1960
The Methods of Sergeant Cluff   Chapman 1961
Sergeant Cluff Goes Fishing   Chapman 1962
More Deaths for Sergeant Cluff   Chapman 1963
Sergeant Cluff and the Madmen   Chapman 1964 (2 novellas)
Sergeant Cluff and the Price of Pity   Chapman 1965
The Confounding of Sergeant Cluff   Chapman 1966
Sergeant Cluff and the Day of Reckoning   Chapman 1967
The Procrastination of Sergeant Cluff   Eyre & Spottiswoode 1969
No Choice for Sergeant Cluff   Eyre & Spottiswoode 1971
Sergeant Cluff Rings True   Eyre Methuen 1972
A Corpse for Kofi Katt   Hale 1978 (not Cluff)

BP

Anthony Oliver (b. 1923)

With a spell as Detective-Sergeant Trotter in *The Mousetrap* to his credit, Anthony Oliver shares with Dulcie Gray the distinction, unusual for a crime writer, of having played an Agatha Christie character on the London stage. His acute and accomplished novels are set in the world of antiques, with a particular emphasis on collectors' china, on which he is an authority. They are intelligent, alluring diversions, with an alert wit and something of the relaxed charm of V. C. Clinton-Baddeley (though wider in scope and more robustly rewarding). The author shows great affection for his detectives, a shrewd but modest ex-policeman and a restless Welsh widow with troublesome legs and a taste for vivid clothes: the developing relations of John Webber and Lizzie Thomas constitute one of the series' most attractive features.

Four books have appeared to date, all from Heinemann, who know a good thing when they see it. *The Pew Group* is a brown book, with gilt spine lettering. The wrapper by Mary Cartwright gives a view of Flaxfield, including St Paul's Church and the late Rupert Corder's antique shop. *The Property of a Lady* is also brown and gilt, with a particularly fetching wrapper by Fiona Bell Currie, showing the controversial antique shop established by Mark Carter and Margaret Garland. *The Elberg Collection* is a black book, with silver spine lettering. Robin Rout's wrapper shows a connoisseur, perhaps Elberg, examining a Staffordshire double figure. *Cover-up* is grey and gilt, with a wrapper by Claudia Zeff of cottages by the Flaxfield grave-yard, under an oppressively pink sky. All four books are dated.

Novels

(with Webber and Thomas)

The Pew Group Heinemann 1980, Doubleday 1981
The Property of a Lady Heinemann 1983, Doubleday 1983
The Elberg Collection Heinemann 1985, Double-day 1985
Cover-up Heinemann 1987, Doubleday 1987

BP

Baroness Orczy (1865–1947)

Baroness Orczy is best known for her Scarlet Pimpernel novels but she also wrote about several interesting detectives. Her spirited stories are nostalgically attractive. She is noted for having created the first armchair detective, the Old Man in the Corner, who features in thirty-seven stories, collected in three volumes. All his cases are narrated by Polly Burton, a young journalist on 'The Evening Observer'. The thin, pale old man, timid-looking and bespectacled, sits in a corner of an ABC teashop in Norfolk Street, off the Strand, consuming milk and cheesecake and incessantly tying knots in pieces

of string. Mainly by using newspaper cuttings, he solves cases which have baffled the police. 'The Mysterious Death in Percy Street', the last story in *The Old Man in the Corner*, has a sur-prising revelation at the end.

Lady Molly Robertson-Kirk is in charge of the 'Female Department of Scotland Yard' and is assisted in her eleven collected cases by Mary Grenard. Like the Scarlet Pimpernel, she is skil-ful at disguise. She is respected by the rest of the police force and the real reason for her taking up her position at Scotland Yard is eventually revealed. Lady Molly also appears in an uncol-lected story.

Patrick Mulligan, an unscrupulous lawyer, nicknamed 'Skin o' my Tooth', appears in twelve clever stories, all narrated by his confidential clerk, Alexander Stanislaus Mullins, invariably addressed as 'Muggins' by his employer. The stories are collected in *Skin o' my Tooth*.

The Case of Miss Elliott is the first of the Old Man in the Corner collections. It was published by T. Fisher Unwin in red cloth with title and author on the front cover, each gilt within a double green border. Between them, also framed by a double green border, is an illustration in red, green, black and white by P. B. Hickling. It illustrates the title story and shows Polly and the Old Man, she with a cup of tea and a set of photographs on the table before her, he tying a knot in a piece of string and with an empty glass and plate in front of him. The spine is lettered gilt, with the title punctuated by small gilt tri-angles and 'author of The Scarlet Pimpernel' as designation of the author. The rear cover is blank. The title-page is dated and has author and publisher in red. The twelve stories are illus-trated by sixteen full-page black-and-white plates by P. B. Hickling. The frontispiece, which has a tissue guard, illustrates 'The Ayrsham Mystery' and depicts two labourers looking down at the corpse of Old Mat Newton, while Samuel Holder arrives on the scene. *The Case of Miss Elliott* has not been published in the USA.

The Old Man in the Corner originally appeared in the *Royal Magazine* in 1901 in a series of twelve stories. These were collected by Greening in 1909 as *The Old Man in the Corner*.

The book has blue cloth lettered gilt on the spine. The front cover has title and author in gilt with a circular head and shoulders portrait of the Old Man between them. The portrait has a red background. In the centre of the rear cover, in black, is the publisher's colophon. The book is dated on the title-page and there are eight full-page black-and-white illustrations by H. M. Brock.

Ten more stories about the Old Man were published in six slim volumes by Doran in the USA from 1923 to 1925. With three further stories these were collected as *Unravelled Knots* and published by Hutchinson in 1925. The book has grey-green cloth and the spine is lettered black. The front cover has a double blind-stamped border, with title and author in black. The book is undated and there are forty-eight pages of advertisements at the rear. Absurd though it seems, one of the Doran six is listed by both Hubin and Reilly as *The Mystery of the Fulton Gardens Mystery and the Moorland Tragedy* (and is so listed here).

Lady Molly of Scotland Yard was published by Cassell and bound in red cloth. The front cover has a single blind-stamped border with title and author in black towards the top. The spine is lettered gilt and the rear cover is blank. The title-page is dated 1910 and there is a sixteen-page advertisement section at the end. There are sixteen full-page black-and-white illustrations by Cyrus Cuneo. The frontispiece has a tissue guard and shows a scene from 'Sir Jeremiah's Will', with Captain Hubert holding out his wrists for the irons to be put on them by Detective Inspector Etty, while Lady Molly looks on. *Skin o' my Tooth* was issued in blue cloth by Hodder & Stoughton in 1928. The lettering on spine and front cover is black. Title and author are separated by a black rule on the spine. The front cover has a single blind-stamped border with the title at the top and the author's name in the lower right corner. The book is undated and contains eight pages of advertisements at the back.

The later of the two known uncollected stories was written as a sequel to another by 'Q' and appeared in the *Premier Magazine* for 15 Jul. 1915. 'Q' wrote the opening section, 'The Troop

Train Mirror' and Baroness Orczy supplied the sequel, 'Lady Molly and the Tressider Affair'.

The two collections *The Man in Grey* and *Castles in the Air* contain adventure rather than detective stories. The novel *The Celestial City* is also an adventure story and the uncollected novel, *Jasper Tarkington's Wife* (*New Magazine*, Sept. 1924) is more truly romantic than criminous.

Story collections

The Case of Miss Elliott Unwin 1905
The Old Man in the Corner Greening 1909
a.k.a. *The Man in the Corner* Dodd, Mead 1909
Lady Molly of Scotland Yard Cassell 1910, Arno 1976
Unravelled Knots Hutchinson n.d. (1925), Doran 1926

'The Irish Tweed Coat' from Lady Molly of Scotland Yard, 1910. Illustration by Cyrus Cuneo.

Skin o' my Tooth Hodder & Stoughton n.d. (1928), Doubleday 1928

Stories published by Doran, singly or in pairs

The Old Man in the Corner unravels the Mystery of the Khaki Tunic (1923)
The Old Man in the Corner unravels the Mystery of the Pearl Necklace and the Tragedy in Bishop's Road (1924)
The Old Man in the Corner unravels the Mystery of the Russian Prince and of Dog's Tooth Cliff (1924)
The Old Man in the Corner unravels the Mystery of the White Carnation and the Montmartre Hat (1925)
The Old Man in the Corner unravels the Mystery of the Fulton Gardens Mystery and the Moorland Tragedy (1925)
The Miser of Maida Vale (1925)

Uncollected stories

'The Case of Mrs. Cridlan' (*Queen*, 4 Jan. 1908)
'Lady Molly and the Tressider Affair' (*Premier*, 15 Jul. 1915)   *JC*

Emma Page
a.k.a. Honoria Tirbutt

Emma Page is the pseudonym of Honoria Tirbutt, who has written thirteen novels, but remains a comparatively little-known writer. Since she works very capably in the tradition of Agatha Christie, however, she deserves wider recognition.

Detective Chief Inspector Kelsey and Detective-Sergeant Lambert have to date appeared in all the books from *Missing Woman*. This title was published by Hale, in black cloth, with silver lettering on the spine. Laurence Cutting's wrapper shows part of the faces of two women superimposed on each other. All the other titles were issued by Collins Crime Club, bound in red, with gilt lettering on the spine. *Mortal Remains* has a printer's key on the copyright page.

With the exception of Alan Burton's design for *Family and Friends* – of a dead black cat and a spilt glass of milk on a green background – all the wrappers are of the modern photographic type.

All Emma Page's books were first published in London, and they are all dated. Four have never been published in the USA. *A Fortnight By the Sea* has the alternative American title *Add a Pinch of Cyanide*. *Missing Woman* is the most elusive title for collectors.

Two stories are known, published in the author's real name.

Novels

(with Kelsey and Lambert from Missing Woman)

In Loving Memory Collins Crime Club 1970
Family and Friends Crime Club 1972

A Fortnight by the Sea Crime Club 1973
a.k.a. *Add a Pinch of Cyanide* Walker 1973
Element of Chance Crime Club 1975
Missing Woman Hale 1980
Every Second Thursday Crime Club 1981, Walker 1981
Last Walk Home Crime Club 1982, Walker 1983
Cold Light of Day Crime Club 1983, Walker 1984
Scent of Death Crime Club 1985, Doubleday 1986
Final Moments Crime Club 1987, Doubleday 1987
A Violent End Crime Club 1988, Doubleday 1990
Deadlock Crime Club 1991
Mortal Remains Crime Club 1992

Stories by Honoria Tirbutt

'Rendezvous' (*LMM*, Mar. 1975)
'Daybreak' (*LMM*, June 1975)   *JC*

Stuart Palmer (1905–1968)
a.k.a. Jay Stewart

Stuart Palmer's enduring fame rests with Hildegarde Withers, his brisk, bossy schoolmarm detective. He sets the comic stereotype of the nosy old maid in a context that allows it to blossom. Her classroom authority carries into her investigations, and energy, imagination, and courage supplement her curiosity. With her ex-fiancé, Inspector Oscar Piper of the New York Police Department, she enjoys a working friendship founded on mutual exasperation and regard. He is involved in all her full-length cases except *The Puzzle of the Silver Persian*, in which she visits Britain and crosses swords with Chief Inspector Cannon of Scotland Yard. There are fourteen novels in the Withers series, from the first in 1931 to the last, a collaboration with Fletcher Flora, in 1969. Three story collections were also published, in the last of which Miss Withers works in tandem with John J. Malone, the Chicago lawyer from Craig Rice's novels. Late in his career, Stuart Palmer launched a second detective, an ursine journalist turned private eye named Howie Rook, who figures in two novels and at least one story.

Two earlier novels have no series character: *Ace of Jades*, written before Hildegarde Withers was invented, and *Omit Flowers*, about a family gathering for Christmas at the home of their rich, eccentric uncle. A third non-series novel was published in America only, under the pseudonym Jay Stewart. One more volume completes the canon: *The Adventure of the Marked Man*, a late, posthumous publication from the Aspen Press, bringing together the author's two Sherlock Holmes stories from the 1940s.

Ace of Jades was published in the USA by Mohawk Press in 1931. A British edition appeared in 1940 from Wells Gardner, in paperback. The covers are plain, decoration being reserved for the wrapper, which has a vivid portrait of Bubbles Deegan, living up to her name. An alternative wrapper is plain green with white lettering and a white spine with the title in green. The book is dated and described on the copyright page as the first cheap edition. Also in 1931, Brentano's brought out *The Penguin Pool Murder*, which introduced Hildegarde Withers. It was published in Britain in February 1932 by John Long, who also published *Murder on Wheels*, the second Withers novel, later that year. *The Penguin Pool Murder* is a red book with black lettering on the spine. It is not dated, but an advertisement section at the rear is headed 'Spring 1932'. *Murder on Wheels* is also undated but has no advertisement section. A sand-coloured book with black spine lettering, it was published in October 1932.

Stuart Palmer had two more British publishers before joining the Crime Club in 1935; Eldon, who published *Murder on the Blackboard* in February 1934, and Jarrolds, who issued *The Puzzle of the Pepper Tree* in April of the same year. The Eldon book is red, with black spine lettering, and the title and the author's initials on the front cover, in red against a black background. A black line is ruled at the head of the spine and another at the foot, and both are continued on to and across the front cover. The book is dedicated to Edna May Oliver, who played Miss Withers in films, with great success. It is dated and has two pages of advertisements at the rear. On page 31 is Miss Withers' plan of Jefferson School, her place of work. The Jarrolds book is red with black spine lettering, and it is undated, with an advertisement section at the back headed 'Spring 1934'.

The Puzzle of the Silver Persian is the first of the Crime Club series, which persisted to *Death in Greasepaint* in 1956. All the Crime Club books are orange, shading into red in the later volumes. All are dated and have black spine lettering. *The Puzzle of the Silver Persian* also has title and author in black on the front cover and, at the back, an introduction of the author to Crime Club readers, with a puff from Margery Allingham. From *The Puzzle of the Happy Hooligan* the books are thinner and carry no advertisements. Five books were retitled for the British market.

The wrapper of *The Puzzle of the Briar Pipe* has a splendid portrait of Hildegarde Withers examining the pipe. *Miss Withers Regrets* shows Pat Montague and Joe Searles about to remove the drowned body of Huntley Cairns from his swimming pool. *At One Fell Swoop* features an expensive-looking woman, with a green hand clutching at her shoulder. *Nipped in the Bud* has Tony Fagan's legs showing through the open doorway of his flat, and a menacing shadow thrown on the door. *Exit Laughing* shows Joyce Reed with her ex-husband's photograph album and, on the spine, one of the anonymous messages bedevilling the cartoon unit of the Miracle-Paradox Studios. *Death in Greasepaint* has a vivid circus clown (perhaps by William Randell).

In the USA, Stuart Palmer's novels were published by six firms altogether, Doubleday, Mill, Harper, and Random House following on Mohawk and Brentano's.

The Penguin Pool Murder has a blue-grey binding with black lettering on the spine and a black penguin on the front cover. It has a roughly trimmed fore-edge and is dated on the title-page. *Murder on the Blackboard* is a pale-blue book with black spine lettering and a black insect escaping from a circle up on the right of the front cover. The fore-edge is rough and the title-page is dated. William Siegel's wrapper shows a blackboard ledge with board-rubber and chalk and the title written across the board. *The Puzzle of the Silver Persian* is black with red lettering on the spine, except for the title, which shows black through a red rectangular block. A red Persian cat also appears on the spine and the book's top edge is red. The fore-edge is roughly trimmed and the front cover and endpapers are blank. A preliminary page has the blurb; the half-title has a black-and-white drawing of a cat, framed by a porthole, with a rectangular frame on either side, enclosing a ship at sea to the left and open sea to the right; and the dated title-page shows a corpse on a slab with a white-coated pathologist to the left and a helmeted policeman to the right. The copyright page states 'First edition'. There are further illustrations on the dedication page and on a further leaf before the text begins. *The Puzzle of the Blue Banderilla* is black with red spine lettering and a red banderilla overlapping from the spine on to the front cover. The top edge is red, the fore-edge roughly trimmed, the title-page dated and the copyright page with 'First edition'. The vivid wrapper has the blue banderilla with a red shadow dripping blood.

The Random House books – the second Rook novel and the last of the Withers series – were not published in Britain. Both have what is presumably a standard Random House binding, with an assortment of black vertical lines on a brown background. The publisher's 'house' motif recurs in a vertical sequence on the front cover. On the spine the publisher's name is lettered in silver and the title and author show up in brown against a silver cylinder with rounded ends. Both books are dated and state that they are first editions. The wrapper of *Hildegarde Withers Makes the Scene* has Robert Dale's portrait of Miss Withers, together with the corpse of Captain Westering.

None of the story collections has been published in Britain. The two paperbacks were issued by Spivak, with introductions by Ellery Queen. *The Riddles of Hildegarde Withers* is number J26 of the Jonathan Mysteries, a tall green paperback, with a cover by George Salter, showing the gift-wrapped brick used to smash the window of Vandercook *et Cie* in 'The Riddle of the Green Ice'. It is dated 1947 by the copyright notice. Oscar Piper is featured in all eight of the stories. *The Monkey Murder* appeared in 1950 from the same publisher and collects a further eight Withers stories. It is a blue book decorated with a mask and gun by Salter on the front cover and dated by the copyright notice only. There is an introduction by Ellery Queen and there are penguin drawings by Stuart Palmer. *People vs. Withers and Malone* was published by Simon & Schuster in 1963. It contains six stories written with Craig Rice and an introduction by Ellery Queen. It also has a foreword by Stuart Palmer, in which he states that Craig Rice supplied ideas and situations for the stories, and he did most of the writing. The book is quarterbound with orange boards flecked with brown and grey spine and wide cover strips. The spine has black lettering and orange decoration and the front cover has 'W & M' black within a black rectangle, the letters arranged vertically. Orange asterisks above and below complete the decoration. The top edge is red and the fore-edge is roughly trimmed. The title-page is dated and the copyright page states 'First printing'. The bright orange-red wrapper features a green floral hat and a bottle.

The Sherlockian pastiches were published as *The Adventure of the Marked Man and One Other* by the Aspen Press in October 1973, in an edition of 500 copies. The book has light-blue card covers with green lettering. The cover shows Holmes stepping down from a hansom cab on to a road leading down to the sea, with distant boats in the harbour. There is a note on the author by Tom Schantz, and there are a frontispiece and six illustrations by Enid Schantz. The frontispiece illustrates that moment in 'The Adventure of the Marked Man' when 'the door was suddenly opened from within'. Besides the title story, the book contains 'The Adventure of the Remarkable Worm' and a preliminary essay by Stuart Palmer, 'The IOU of Hildegarde Withers', in which he acknowledges his debt to Conan Doyle in the invention of his own series detective.

The uncollected stories are legion and need detailed study and research. As early as 1928 Palmer was working on a magazine called *Ghost Stories* and an improbable tale set in Baraboo and involving the ghosts of ten-ton elephants is, by implication, by him (though attributed in 1931 to 'Theodore Orchards'). Other stories, published in 1928, are signed by him. Cook & Miller list a number of hard-boiled stories for pulp magazines, preceding the creation of Hildegarde Withers. In 1952, in *Maiden Murders*, Palmer described 'The Riddle of the Dangling Pearl' as 'the first of some fifty short stories about Miss Withers'. Allowing for the two collections, this means that over thirty Withers stories remain uncollected from the 1930s and 1940s, in addition to the later stories. Reilly dodges the difficulty by listing none at all. Listed here are all titles not known to have been collected (and including new titles from Cook and Cook & Miller). Apart from stories with her name as part of the title, Hildegarde Withers features in all the 'Riddle' stories and in 'Where Angels Fear to Tread', 'The Jinx Man', 'You Bet Your Life' and 'Who is Sylvia?'. Thus, she is in twenty of the listed items. 'The Stripteaser and the Private Eye' features Howie Rook. Four items are listed by Cook for *Mystery Digest*: 'Be My Dead Valentine' (Sept. 1957); 'Murder is my Business' (Jan. 1958); 'The Murder Mask' (Mar. 1958); and 'The Sweet Trap' (Jan. 1959). 'The Murder Mask' appeared first in *American Magazine* and was expanded into the novel *Unhappy Hooligan*. 'Be My Dead Valentine' is presumably the same as 'A Valentine for the Victim', which also appeared originally in *American Magazine* and became a novel, *Cold Poison*.

Novels

(with Withers, except as stated)

Ace of Jades Mohawk 1931, Wells Gardner 1940 (not Withers)

The Penguin Pool Murder Brentano's 1931, John Long n.d. (1932)

Murder on Wheels Brentano's 1932, Long n.d. (1932)

Murder on the Blackboard Brentano's 1932, Eldon 1934

The Puzzle of the Pepper Tree Doubleday 1933, Jarrolds n.d. (1934)

The Puzzle of the Silver Persian Doubleday 1934, Collins Crime Club 1935

The Puzzle of the Red Stallion Doubleday 1936

a.k.a. *The Puzzle of the Briar Pipe* Crime Club 1936

Omit Flowers Doubleday 1937 (not Withers)

a.k.a. *No Flowers by Request* Crime Club 1937

The Puzzle of the Blue Banderilla Doubleday 1937, Crime Club 1937

The Puzzle of the Happy Hooligan Doubleday 1941, Crime Club 1941

Miss Withers Regrets Doubleday 1947, Crime Club 1948

Four Lost Ladies Mill 1949, Crime Club 1950

The Green Ace Mill 1950

a.k.a. *At One Fell Swoop* Crime Club 1951

Nipped in the Bud Mill 1951, Crime Club 1952

a.k.a. *Trap for a Redhead* Spivak 1955

Cold Poison Mill 1954

a.k.a. *Exit Laughing* Crime Club 1954

Unhappy Hooligan Harper 1956 (Rook)

a.k.a. *Death in Greasepaint* Crime Club 1956

Rook Takes Knight Random House 1968 (Rook)

Hildegarde Withers Makes the Scene Random 1969, with Fletcher Flora

Story collections

(with Withers, except as stated)

The Riddles of Hildegarde Withers Spivak 1947 (8 stories)

The Monkey Murder Spivak 1950 (8 stories)

People vs. Withers and Malone Simon & Schuster 1963 (6 stories) with Craig Rice

The Adventure of the Marked Man and One Other Aspen 1973 (not Withers)

Novel by Jay Stewart

Before It's Too Late Mill 1950; Dell n.d. as by Stuart Palmer

Uncollected stories

'Exit the Big Shot' (*Gun Molls*, Oct. 1930)

'O'Sullivan's Heels' (*Gun Molls*, May 1931)

'Satan's Sister' (*Gun Molls*, Sept.-Dec. 1931)

'The Smiling Killer' (*Complete Gang Novel*, Nov. 1931)

'Hell on High Heels' (*Gun Molls*, Jan. 1932)

'The Defense Rests' (*Courtroom Stories*, Feb. 1932)

'The Make and the Take' (*Gun Molls*, Feb. 1932)

'Mirrors of a Moll' (*Gun Molls*, Mar.-Apr. 1932)

'Even a Worm' (*Five-cent Detective*, 18 June 1932)

'The Riddle of the Dangling Pearl' (*Mystery*, Nov. 1933; *Maiden Murders*, Harper 1952, Hammond 1953)

'The Riddle of the Flea Circus' (*Mystery*, Dec. 1933)

'The Riddle of the Forty Costumes' (*Mystery*, Jan. 1934)

'The Riddle of the Brass Band' (*Mystery*, Mar. 1934)

'The Riddle of the Blueblood Murders' (*Mystery*, Jun. 1934; *Third Mystery Companion*, Gold Label 1945; *Saint* (UK) Apr. 1963)

'The Riddle of the Forty Naughty Girls' (*Mystery*, Jul. 1934)

'The Riddle of the Hanging Men' (*Mystery*, Sep. 1934; *Saint* (UK), May 1965)

'The Riddle of the Black Spade' (*Mystery*, Oct. 1934; *Saint* (UK), May 1964)

'The Riddle of the Marble Blade' (*Mystery*, Nov. 1934; *Saint* (UK), Nov. 1962)

'The Riddle of the Whirling Lights' (*Mystery*, Jan. 1935; *Second Mystery Companion*, Gold Label 1944)

'The Riddle of the Jack of Diamonds' (*Fifty Famous Detectives of Fiction*, Odhams n.d. (1938))

'The Riddle of the Tired Bullet' (*EQMM*, Mar. 1948; *Four and Twenty Bloodhounds*, Simon & Schuster 1950, Hammond 1951)

'Where Angels Fear to Tread' (*EQMM*, Feb. 1951; *Crime for Two*, Lippincott 1955, Macdonald 1957)

'The Jinx Man' (*EQMM*, Dec. 1952)

'She Never Lets You Go' (*LMM*, Feb. 1955)

'The Mirror' (*LMM*, June 1955)

'Hildegarde and the Spanish Cavalier' (*EQMM*, Dec. 1955)

'Once Aboard the Lugger' (*Mercury Mystery Book Magazine*, Sept. 1956)

'You Bet Your Life' (*EQMM*, May 1957; *Ellery Queen's Choice 13*, Random House 1958; Crime Club 1960)

'Future Imperfect' (*A Choice of Murders*, Scribner 1958, Macdonald 1960)

'Who is Sylvia?' (*EQMM*, July 1961)

'Cure for a Headache' (Ed McBain's Mystery Book, No. 3, 1961)

'The Return of Hildegarde Withers' (*EQMM*, July 1964)

'Hildegarde Withers is Back' (*EQMM*, Apr. 1968)

'The Stripteaser and the Private Eye' (*EQMM*, Nov. 1968)

'Hildegarde Plays it Calm' (*EQMM*, Apr. 1969)

BP

Sara Paretsky (b. 1947)

Sara Paretsky's novels feature a private investigator named Vic Warshawski who, despite her name, is a woman, tough and compassionate and an unremitting feminist. She works in Chicago, fighting corruption in public institutions and seeking redress for its victims. She usually has a personal stake in her investigations and her private life is intrinsic to her first-person narratives. Her first case was published in 1982, the year in which Sue Grafton's detective made her initial appearance: clearly, there was something in the air. In the ten years since then, Sara Paretsky has become an acknowledged leader in this particular, popular field. She has changed publishers frequently: from Dial to Morrow to Delacorte in America and from Gollancz to Chatto to Hamish Hamilton in Britain. All her books except *Toxic Shock* were first published in America: *Blood Shot* appeared with its variant title in Sept. 1988, a month after its UK equivalent.

The American first editions are discussed in *Firsts* for June 1992 by Robin H. Smiley, who illustrates all the wrappers and gives details of the copyright statements that determine first edition status. The two Dial books state 'First printing'; the two Morrow books state 'First edition' and have a printer's key running 1–10; and the Delacorte books give the month of publication and have a reverse printer's key, 10–1.

The Gollancz editions have red bindings, except for *Toxic Shock*, which is black. Their spine lettering is gilt and they have dated title-pages. *Indemnity Only* and *Deadlock* have pistols as chapter headings and *Bitter Medicine* has a line of decoration on the title-page. The Chatto *Burn Marks* is a hefty blue book with gilt spine lettering, except for 'Paretsky', which shows blue through a gilt rectangular block. The book is dated on the copyright page. The Hamilton *Guardian Angel* is likewise a doorstop: black with silver lettering on the spine, a dated copyright page and a printer's key ascending from 1 and descending to 2.

The US wrappers are striking in the modern manner. *Indemnity Only* has a lipstick, a powder compact, a cracked mirror and a gun. Vic herself appears for *Blood Shot* and *Guardian Angel*, cut off below the eyes for the former and in partial silhouette from behind for the latter. The Gollancz wrappers are standard yellow but Chatto has a fetching photograph of Vic for *Burn Marks*, together with part of a street map of Chicago.

Robin Smiley states that there are textual differences between the US and UK editions of *Killing Orders* and that 'the British edition is reported to be the original'.

Sara Paretsky's stories are as yet uncollected. 'The Pietro Andromache' features Vic Warshawski in a rare third-person narrative. 'Dealer's Choice' is a Chandler pastiche.

Warshawski novels

Indemnity Only   Dial 1982, Gollancz 1982
Deadlock   Dial 1984, Gollancz 1984
Killing Orders   Morrow 1985, Gollancz 1986
Bitter Medicine   Morrow 1987, Gollancz 1987
Toxic Shock   Gollancz Aug. 1988
a.ka. *Blood Shot*   Delacorte Sept. 1988
Burn Marks   Delacorte 1990, Chatto & Windus 1990
Guardian Angel   Delacorte 1992, Hamilton 1992

Stories

'The Takamoku Joseki' (*AHMM*, Nov. 1983) (Warshawski)
'Three-Dot Po' (*The Eyes Have It*, Mysterious Press 1984) (Warshawski)
'At the Old Swimming-hole' (*Mean Streets*, Mysterious Press 1986) (Warshawski)
'Skin Deep' (*Black Mask Quarterly*, Oct. 1986; *The New Black Mask 8*, Harcourt, Brace 1987) (Warshawski)
'The Case of the Pietro Andromache'(*AHMM*, Dec. 1988; *The Year's Best Mystery and Suspense Stories 1989*, Walker 1989; *New Crimes*, Robinson 1989 as 'The Pietro Andromache') (Warshawski)
'Dealer's Choice' (*Raymond Chandler's Philip Marlowe*, Knopf 1988)
'A Taste of Life' (*Reader, I Murdered Him*, Women's Press 1989, St Martin's 1989)
'The Maltese Cat' (*Sisters in Crime 3*, Berkley 1990) (Warshawski)
'Settled Score' (*A Woman's Eye*, Delacorte 1991, Virago 1991) (Warshawski)

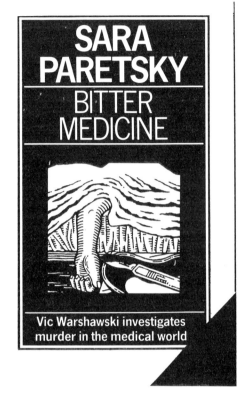

SARA PARETSKY BITTER MEDICINE

Vic Warshawski investigates murder in the medical world

'Freud at Thirty Paces' (*1st Culprit*, Chatto & Windus 1992)   *BP*

Ellis Peters
(Edith Pargeter (b. 1913))
a.k.a. Jolyon Carr
a.k.a. John Redfern

Edith Pargeter was established as a mainstream novelist when she published a detective story, without resort to a pseudonym. Her readers' indignant reactions surprised her, and she learnt what Ruth Rendell and others might with advantage learn today: that 'the reading public likes to know just what to expect from an author and resents being disconcerted'. From this lesson arose the pseudonym Ellis Peters, and a new reputation which has now overtaken the author's primary identity.

She had, in fact, already published crime fiction under two earlier pseudonyms, both male: four novels as Jolyon Carr and one as John

Redfern, all between 1938 and 1940. Of the four Carr novels, one only – *Death Comes By Post* – is more than incidentally a detective story: it has a properly inquisitive young constable, who solves a murder and traces a spate of anonymous letters to its source. *Murder in the Dispensary* is an intense, inverted novel, where the killer's act and his identity are no secret from the reader; *Freedom for Two* is a romantic thriller about a woman married to a successful criminal; and *Masters of the Parachute Mail* is a traditional adventure thriller involving drugs and impersonation. The mystery in *The Victim Needs a Nurse*, the John Redfern novel, has Gothic elements, and the threat to the safety of a spirited young woman is an important issue.

The Pargeter novel which 'approached the detective story almost inadvertently' is *Fallen Into the Pit*, published in 1951 and introducing the Felse family, the policeman George, his wife Bunty, and their schoolboy son, Dominic. The Peters pseudonym was launched with *Death Mask*, the first of only five in the sequence without any of the author's series characters. The Felse family recurs in *Death and the Joyful Woman*, the third Peters novel, and is represented by one or more of its number in a further eleven novels, the last of which, *Rainbow's End*, appeared in 1978. Most of the Felse novels involve George, with or without his family; but Bunty is the protagonist of *The Grass Widow's Tale*, and the adult Dominic features in *Mourning Raga* and *Death to the Landlords!*, which are set in India. *Flight of a Witch* has not been published in America. Two other novels have variant US titles, both feebler than their British originals.

In 1977 Ellis Peters introduced a new detective, the twelfth-century monk Brother Cadfael. He has since nudged aside all opposition, dislodging the Felses and clearly taking over both mind and heart of his author. Ellis Peters was always a romantic, with a ready emotionalism that sometimes seems over-generous (though in the best of the Felse novels she achieves a relative austerity that greatly enhances their appeal: *The Knocker on Death's Door*, for example, is the more powerful for its sober restraint). But in the Cadfael novels, she manipulates romantic cliché with delicacy and skill. The narratives have an extraordinary and engaging immediacy, set within a medieval world that is lovingly observed, with a scholar's eye and a romantic's imaginative sympathy. Cadfael has true stature in all his different roles, and he reveals that utter dependability which marks the greatest of fictional detectives.

The Assize of the Dying by Edith Pargeter is also usually regarded as crime fiction, reasonably, since two of its three stories have murder as their mainspring: the title story and 'Aunt Helen'.

From 1959 to 1969, the Peters series was published by Collins Crime Club. The four books to *Funeral of Figaro* are red with black spine lettering. From *Flight of a Witch* to *Black Is the Colour of My True Love's Heart*, the bindings are red, threaded closely with black; but the spines of *Flight of a Witch* and *A Nice Derangement of Epitaphs* are clear red, and an area extending on either side to a vertical dividing line is also clear of the black. *The Grass Widow's Tale* and *The House of Green Turf* are taller books which revert to clear red covers. The spine lettering on all the Crime Club books from *Flight of a Witch* is gilt.

In 1969, Ellis Peters moved to Macmillan, who issued all her books to *An Excellent Mystery* with uniform spine lettering, mainly in lower case, with capitals as appropriate. The author's surname and the title run sideways, with the base of the letters towards the back cover, and the colours of the bindings and the lettering vary considerably. *The Raven in the Foregate* and *The Rose Rent* break this pattern. They are taller books, lettered along the spine in gilt in a more elaborate style than that adopted for the earlier run. The former is black, the latter green.

Since 1987, Ellis Peters has been published by Headline, who, on the 'big is beautiful' principle, have increased the size of the books, so that they are now like tombstones. *A Rare Benedictine*, a collection of three Cadfael stories, is big enough to serve as a cheeseboard. The books are bound in various colours but have 'medieval' gilt lettering on the spine in common. The novels have decorated title-pages and chapter headings, as well as endpaper maps by D. J. C. *A Rare Ben-*

edictine is lavishly illustrated by Clifford Harper and the first word of each story starts with a decorated initial. All the Ellis Peters books are dated, from *The Summer of the Danes* also with a printer's key on the copyright page.

Fallen Into the Pit is bound in turquoise, with gilt spine lettering, and *The Assize of the Dying* is red, with silver lettering. Both are from Heinemann and are dated. Both have been reissued as by Ellis Peters, the latter with the third story omitted (as in the Doubleday first edition). A second Pargeter novel, the mildly criminous *Holiday with Violence*, has also recently appeared under the Peters byline. The four Jolyon Carr books are typical Herbert Jenkins products, with orange bindings and black lettering on the spines, which are all ruled at the head and the foot. On each front cover title and author are printed in black, and *Murder in the Dispensary* also has a black border. The publisher's logo occurs on all the rear covers as well as on the spines. All four books are dated and have advertisements at the rear. The single John Redfern book is deep red with black spine lettering. It is undated and came out in the autumn of 1940 (the BL copy is dated 2 October 1940). At the end is an eight-page advertisement section, which is absent from the otherwise identical later issue.

City of Gold and Shadows has endpapers of the Roman city of Aurae Phiala, on the banks of the Comer. *The Horn of Roland* has a preliminary map of Himmelhof and Gries-am-See in the Swiss Alps. Many of the Cadfael series have maps of Shrewsbury Abbey and its environs; and *The Virgin in the Ice* and *Dead Man's Ransom* move further afield with maps of Ludlow and the Welsh border.

For the wrapper of *Fallen Into the Pit*, Broom Lynne gives a vigorous impression of Comerford, the mining village where George Felse is the police sergeant. William Randell transcends his usual level of routine competence with his fine design for *Death Mask*: against a rich blue background a noble Greek mask encloses Bruce Almond's sprawled body. He reverts to form for *The Will and the Deed*, with its overturned glass (the bottle of champagne for *Death and the Joyful Woman* is surely his, too). *Funeral of*

Figaro has a distinctive wrapper suggesting from two musical notes the face of someone mourning the dead baritone. The venerable tomb on *A Nice Derangement of Epitaphs* has its slab removed (or deranged). Kenneth Farnhill drew the man caught in a monocular lens for *The Piper on the Mountain* and the guitar with a frightened face within it for *Black Is the Colour of My True Love's Heart*.

The Macmillan wrappers suffer from featureless spines, with uniform black lettering on a white foundation or, from *Rainbow's End*, with an upper red segment, slanted diagonally at the bottom, against which the author's name is given in black and the title in white. The latter group is equally unattractive and rather more aggressive. Had the publisher had the wit to extend the front panel designs on to the spines, a brave display would have resulted, since much of the work is appealing. Holmes Kitley's representation of *The Knocker on Death's Door* exactly displays the 'beast's head' at St Eata's Church in Mottisham, with its 'patently amiable jaws' holding 'a large twisted ring of iron'. *City of Gold and Shadows* shows Charlotte Rossignol running through the wood, with a ghostly Roman helmet in the background. *The Horn of Roland* has a horn-player, presumably playing Lucas Corinth's composition of the same name. A suggested headstone for Arthur Rainbow by Linnet Gotch appropriately figures on *Rainbow's End*. Both Indian novels feature swarthy Asian faces, that on *Mourning Raga* with frightened eyes and someone else's black hand held over the mouth.

Apart from the spines, the Cadfael series is generally appealing. *A Morbid Taste for Bones* has St Winifred and a group of monks (of whom the central figure is too young to be Cadfael). *One Corpse Too Many* shows Cadfael in profile, in a portrait by Chris Yates, and Bill Richmond's striking photo of Gervase Bonel's 'livid head' at the point of death decorates *Monk's Hood*. Geoff Taylor, whose work so notably enchances Keith Heller's books, provided the picturesque encounter between quick and dead for *Saint Peter's Fair*. The elaborate drawing of Liliwin, clutching at the chapel altarcloth, for *The Sanctuary Sparrow* is by Robert Adams. *The Devil's*

Novice has a handsome silhouette of an archer, and *Dead Man's Ransom* a vivid picture by Martin White of Elis' head in the river. From *Monk's Hood* to *An Excellent Mystery* the lettering on the front panels is uniform; and from *The Devil's Novice* to *An Excellent Mystery* the rear panels include an oval photograph of Cadfael (actually the author's late brother, Ellis Pargeter). *The Raven in the Foregate* and *The Rose Rent* attempted to establish a new visual series but were thwarted by the author's change of publisher. They have bolder lettering than formerly and attractive stained glass vignettes on their front panels. The Headline books have ornate wrappers in medieval pastiche by Clifford Harper, each with a stylized scene from the novel and a decorated initial in the title.

Alex Jardine's wrapper for *Murder in the Dispensary* shows the hand of the murderer measuring out the three drachms of syrup of chloral that kill Walter Gyfford. *The Victim Needs a Nurse* has a grey wrapper by Nina Mallinson, with the fatal glass of medicine set against a black leaf (perhaps from the aconite that makes the draught lethal).

Five uncollected stories by Ellis Peters are listed by Reilly and five more have appeared in *Winter's Crimes* and elsewhere. At least five stories by Edith Pargeter are also criminous. Sue Feder, founder of the Ellis Peters Appreciation Society, is working on a comprehensive bibliography. *The Benediction of Brother Cadfael* (Mysterious Press 1992) brings together the first and second Cadfael novels and selections from *Cadfael Country*, a topographical survey published in Britain in 1990.

Novels by Jolyon Carr

Murder in the Dispensary   Jenkins 1938
Freedom for Two   Jenkins 1939
Death Comes by Post   Jenkins 1940
Masters of the Parachute Mail   Jenkins 1940

Novel by John Redfern

The Victim Needs a Nurse   Jarrolds n.d. (1940)

Novels by Edith Pargeter

Fallen Into the Pit   Heinemann 1951 (Felse); Futura 1990 as by Ellis Peters
Holiday with Violence   Heinemann 1952; Headline 1992 as by Ellis Peters

Novels by Ellis Peters

(With at least one Felse, as stated. Binding details refer to Macmillan editions.)

Death Mask   Collins Crime Club 1959, Doubleday 1960
The Will and the Deed   Crime Club 1960
a.k.a. *Where There's a Will*   Doubleday 1960
Death and the Joyful Woman   Crime Club 1961, Doubleday 1961 (Felse)
Funeral of Figaro   Crime Club 1962, Morrow 1964
Flight of a Witch   Crime Club 1964 (Felse)
A Nice Derangement of Epitaphs   Crime Club 1965 (Felse)
a.k.a. *Who Lies Here?*   Morrow 1965
The Piper on the Mountain   Crime Club 1966, Morrow 1966 (Felse)
Black Is the Colour of My True Love's Heart   Crime Club 1967, Morrow 1967 (Felse)
The Grass Widow's Tale   Crime Club 1968, Morrow 1968 (Felse)
The House of Green Turf   Crime Club 1969, Morrow 1969 (Felse)
Mourning Raga   Macmillan 1969, Morrow 1970 (Felse) (red binding, black lettering)
The Knocker on Death's Door   Macmillan 1970, Morrow 1971 (Felse) (green, black)
Death to the Landlords!   Macmillan 1972, Morrow 1972 (Felse) (red, black)
City of Gold and Shadows   Macmillan 1973, Morrow 1974 (Felse) (dark blue, white)
The Horn of Roland   Macmillan 1974, Morrow 1974 (light blue, black)
Never Pick Up Hitch-hikers!   Macmillan 1976, Morrow 1976 (red, black)
Rainbow's End   Macmillan 1978, Morrow 1979 (Felse) (green, gilt)

Cadfael novels by Ellis Peters

A Morbid Taste for Bones Macmillan 1977, Morrow 1978 (orange-brown, black)

One Corpse Too Many Macmillan 1979, Morrow 1980 (green, silver)

Monk's Hood Macmillan 1980, Morrow 1981 (yellow, gilt)

Saint Peter's Fair Macmillan 1981, Morrow 1981 (green, gilt)

The Leper of Saint Giles Macmillan 1981, Morrow 1982 (mauve, silver)

The Virgin in the Ice Macmillan 1982, Morrow 1983 (brown, silver)

The Sanctuary Sparrow Macmillan 1983, Morrow 1983 (brown, silver)

The Devil's Novice Macmillan 1983, Morrow 1984 (orange-brown, silver)

Dead Man's Ransom Macmillan 1984, Morrow 1984 (green, silver)

The Pilgrim of Hate Macmillan 1984, Morrow 1985 (fawn, gilt)

An Excellent Mystery Macmillan 1985, Morrow 1986 (red, gilt)

The Raven in the Foregate Macmillan 1986, Morrow 1986

The Rose Rent Macmillan 1986, Morrow 1987

The Hermit of Eyton Forest Headline 1987, Mysterious Press 1988 (blue)

The Confession of Brother Haluin Headline 1988, Mysterious Press 1988 (purple)

The Heretic's Apprentice Headline 1989, Mysterious Press 1990 (dark blue)

The Potter's Field Headline 1989, Mysterious Press 1990 (blue)

The Summer of the Danes Headline 1991, Mysterious Press 1991 (black)

The Holy Thief Headline 1992, Mysterious Press 1993 (green)

Cadfael story collection by Ellis Peters

A Rare Benedictine Headline 1988, Mysterious Press 1989 (dark blue) (3 stories)

Story collection by Edith Pargeter

The Assize of the Dying Heinemann 1958, Doubleday 1958; Headline 1991 as by Ellis Peters

Uncollected stories by Edith Pargeter

'A Question of Faith' (*Argosy*, Feb. 1958)

'The Man who Met Himself' (*Argosy*, Nov. 1958)

'Change of Heart' (*Argosy*, Jan. 1959)

'O Gold, O Girl!' (*Argosy*, Jan. 1965; *Alfred Hitchcock Presents: Stories Not for the Nervous*, Random House 1965, as 'The Golden Girl')

'Hostile Witness' (*Argosy*, May 1965)

Uncollected stories by Ellis Peters

'Guide to Doom' (*This Week*, 10 Nov. 1963; *Alfred Hitchcock Presents: Stories That Scared Even Me*, Random House 1967)

'The Chestnut Calf' (*This Week*, 29 Dec. 1963)

'With Regrets' (*This Week*, 30 May 1965)

'Villa for Sale' (*This Week*, 12 Dec. 1965)

'A Grain of Mustard Seed' (*This Week*, 30 Jan. 1966)

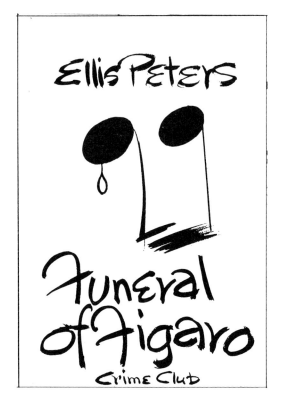

'Maiden Garland' (*Winter's Crimes 1*, Macmillan 1969, St Martin's 1969)

'The Trinity Cat' (*Winter's Crimes 8*, Macmillan 1976, St Martin's 1976)

'Come to Dust' (*Winter's Crimes 16*, Macmillan 1984, St Martin's 1985)

'Let Nothing You Dismay!' (*Winter's Crimes 21*, Macmillan 1989)

'The Frustration Dream' (*2nd Culprit*, Chatto & Windus 1993)   *BP*

Joyce Porter (1924–1990)

Joyce Porter is a vigorous and consistently entertaining writer, whose novels derive their comic momentum from the ineptitude of their investigators, all of whom tend to crack their cases in spite of themselves. In addition, her books are wrought with sufficient cunning to be satisfying as mysteries: they develop logically within the comic framework. She began in 1964 with Inspector Wilfred Dover, a gross slob who is, quite literally, disgustingly funny. In 1966, after three Dover books, she rang the first of two changes on the formula with Eddie Brown, an inept, craven spy; and in 1970 she introduced the Hon. Constance Morrison-Burke, a hefty, forceful maiden lady in need of occupation. Both Dover and the Hon. Con have sidekicks to pick up the pieces: the fastidious Sergeant MacGregor, whose career ambitions are at a perpetual standstill from his association with Dover, and the stoic Miss Jones, who sighs a lot. Every detail of life at Shangrila, 14 Upper Waxwing Drive, Totterbridge, is especially to be relished, not least the Hon. Con's sock drawer. There are ten novels with Dover, four with Eddie Brown, and five with the Hon. Con. Of the seventeen uncollected stories, eleven feature Dover, and the rest are Hon. Con stories.

Seven books were published by Cape and twelve by Weidenfeld & Nicolson, beginning with *Neither a Candle Nor a Pitchfork*, the third Eddie Brown novel. Both series are bound in a variety of colours, with spine lettering in black, silver, or gilt. The Weidenfeld books are taller than the Cape sequence, and from *Who the Heck Is Sylvia?* they are taller still. All the books, from both publishers, are dated.

Joyce Porter was fortunate in her publishers, who not only bound her books individually but also gave them distinctive dust-wrappers. *Dover One* has a green wrapper, with a large white fingerprint serving as a background for a portrait of Dover. This motif recurs on the spine, and also on the spines of the three Dover books that follow in sequence. A splendid late portrait of Dover by Michael Davidson glowers at the reader of *Dover and the Claret Tappers*: he is locked in a lavatory, with one of his kidnappers glimpsed through a keyhole. A full-length puppet of Dover by the Strimbans forms part of Tom Simmonds' design for *Dover Strikes Again*. Keith Jones' wrapper for *Dover Beats the Band* gives an intimate insight into the Dovers' home life, with Mrs Dover on her knees, removing the boot and sock from her husband's right foot, with a dazed expression on her face.

Only with a Bargepole has Craig Dodd's impression of Eddie Brown, looking like a stereotyped bookmaker, with a flower springing from his gun, and Muriel Drom peering nervously over his shoulder. The earlier portraits of the Hon. Con are by Michael Trevithick, who presents her in caricature (with her chest-expanders for *Rather a Common Sort of Crime*). Michael Davidson has her peering under a block of Russian buildings for *The Package Included Murder*, and Offa Jones shows her in Whoopee-land at Girlstone-on-Sea for *Who the Heck is Sylvia?* Keith Jones provides our final view of her, struggling with two policemen during the royal visit to Totterbridge, for *The Cart Before the Crime*.

Novels

(With Dover, except as stated. Details of bindings refer to British editions.)

Dover One   Cape 1964, Scribner 1964 (green binding, black lettering)

Dover Two   Cape 1965, Scribner 1965 (black, silver)

Dover Three   Cape 1965, Scribner 1966 (red, gilt)

Sour Cream with Everything   Cape 1966, Scribner 1966 (Brown) (blue-green, black)

Dover and the Unkindest Cut of All   Cape 1967, Scribner 1967 (pink, black)

The Chinks in the Curtain   Cape 1967, Scribner 1968 (Brown) (sage, black)

Dover Goes to Pott   Cape 1968, Scribner 1968 (maroon, gilt)

Neither a Candle nor a Pitchfork   Weidenfeld & Nicolson 1969, McCall 1970 (Brown) (black, gilt)

Rather a Common Sort of Crime   Weidenfeld 1970, McCall 1970 (Hon. Con) (maroon, gilt)

Dover Strikes Again   Weidenfeld 1970, McKay 1973 (green, gilt)

Only with a Bargepole   Weidenfeld 1971, McKay 1974 (Brown) (pale brown, gilt)

A Meddler and Her Murder   Weidenfeld 1972, McKay 1973 (Hon. Con) (pale blue, gilt)

It's Murder with Dover   Weidenfeld 1973, McKay 1973 (red, gilt)

The Package Included Murder   Weidenfeld 1975, Bobbs-Merrill 1976 (Hon. Con) (dark red, black)

Dover and the Claret Tappers   Weidenfeld 1976, Countryman 1989 (blue-green, gilt)

Who the Heck Is Sylvia?   Weidenfeld 1977 (Hon. Con) (blue, silver)

Dead Easy for Dover   Weidenfeld 1978, St Martin's 1979 (blue, silver)

The Cart Before the Crime   Weidenfeld 1979 (Hon. Con) (red, gilt)

Dover Beats the Band   Weidenfeld 1980 (brown, gilt)

Uncollected stories

'Dover Pulls a Rabbit' (*EQMM*, Feb. 1969)

'Dover Tangles with High Finance' (*EQMM*, Dec. 1970; *Ellery Queen's Masters of Mystery*, Davis 1975, Gollancz 1977)

'Dover and the Dark Lady' (*EQMM*, May 1972; *Ellery Queen's Masks of Mystery*, Davis 1978, Gollancz 1979)

'Dover Does Some Spadework' (*EQMM*, Oct. 1976; *Best Detective Stories of the Year 1977*, Dutton 1977)

'Dover Goes to School' (*EQMM*, Feb. 1978; *Ellery Queen's Circumstantial Evidence*, Davis 1980)

'A Gross Miscarriage of Justice' (*AHMM*, July 1978)

'Dover Without Perks' (*EQMM*, Nov. 1978; *Ellery Queen's Eyewitnesses*, Davis 1982)

'A Case of Malicious Mischief' (*AHMM*, May 1979)

'Dover and the Smallest Room' (*EQMM*, Nov. 1979)

'The Mystery of the White Elephant' (*AHMM*, June 1980)

'Sweating It Out with Dover' (*EQMM*, 18 Aug. 1980; *John Creasey's Crime Collection 1981*, Gollancz 1981)

'The Stuff of Crime' (*AHMM*, Feb. 1982)

'Dover Weighs the Evidence' (*EQMM*, 24 Mar. 1982)

'Dover Sees the Trees' (*EQMM*, Sept. 1982)

'Stamping on Crime' (*AHMM*, mid-Sept. 1982)

'A Souvenir for Dover' (*EQMM*, Dec. 1985)

'But once a year – Thank God!' (*EQMM*, mid-

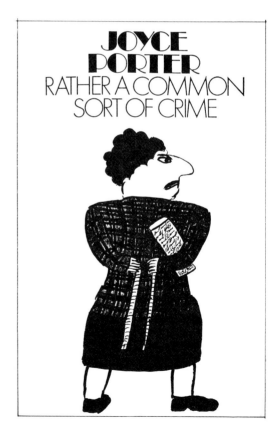

Dec. 1991; *Murder Under the Mistletoe*, Signet 1992) *BP*

E. R. Punshon (1872–1956)
a.k.a. Robertson Halkett

E. R. Punshon was writing popular fiction in the late Victorian era, but his career as a true detective novelist began in 1929, with the first of the Carter and Bell series. He was lavishly praised by Dorothy L. Sayers in the 1930s, but his reputation has since declined. He is perhaps more of a romancer than other Golden Age figures, more picturesque and fanciful, less sober and doggedly reliable. His narrative tone is often heightened by melodrama, and he reveals a rather manic imagination, fired by powerful emotions and driven personalities.

Five novels feature Inspector Carter and Sergeant Bell, whose working relations have something of the tortoise and the hare about them, the slow, melancholy sergeant being altogether more astute and imaginative than his showy, shallow superior. The series comes to a startling end, effectively ensuring that it could not continue; but Bell recurs years later in *Music Tells All*, as a rural superintendent. The rest of Punshon's novels document the varied career of Bobby Owen, a cheerful sprig of the nobility who rises through the ranks and ends as a deputy commander. He appears in thirty-five titles and in at least five uncollected stories.: 'A Study in the Obvious', 'Making Sure', 'Good Beginning', 'Three Sovereigns', and 'Find the Lady'. Two earlier stories feature a fourth policeman, Sergeant Boys: 'The Secret of the Chessboard' and 'The Double Six Domino'.

The Carter and Bell series came from Ernest Benn, as did the first and second of Bobby Owen's adventures. All seven books are black, with orange lettering on the spines, which also have rules at the head and foot, each with a fringe, like stalactites at the top and stalagmites at the bottom. The Carter and Bell books also have the title in orange on the front cover, with two pistols facing each other in the top corners, all within a border, fringed like the rules on the spine. The front covers of the two Owen titles

are blank. The top edge of *Genius in Murder* is orange.

Gollancz published the rest of the Owen series, from *Crossword Mystery* in 1934. The twelve books to *Four Strange Women* in 1940 are black with orange lettering. *Ten Star Clues*, *The Dark Garden*, and *Diabolic Candelabra* are blue, with dark blue lettering. *The Conqueror Inn* initiates a run of blue books with gilt lettering, the last of which is *The House of Godwinsson*. The rest of the sequence are red, with black lettering to *The Golden Dagger* and with gilt from *The Attending Truth*. Five of the wartime books from *Diabolic Candelabra* suffer from the minuscule print Gollancz employed at this time. All the Gollancz books are lettered on the spine only. The books from both publishers are all dated. *Crossword Mystery* features a plan of Suffby Cove and George Winterton's homemade crossword, which readers may solve and interpret for themselves, in advance of Bobby.

Neither of his publishers gave Punshon attractive dust-wrappers. Those for the Benn books are off-white or buff, lettered in black in the style of the cover and spine lettering. That for *Genius in Murder* identifies the book as 'a Benn's thin paper novel', oddly, as it now seems, since the paper does not seem at all flimsy. The Gollancz series has the inevitable yellow jackets, enlivened only by a resounding quotation from Miss Sayers, which first appeared in the 1930s and continued to surface intermittently until its last appearance in 1955. Fifteen only of Punshon's novels appeared in the USA, two with title-changes.

On page 12 of her catalogue for February 1986, Camille Wolff established that E. R. Punshon also wrote under the pseudonym Robertson Halkett, for whom two titles are listed in Hubin. *Where Every Prospect Pleases* is a Benn book, dated 1933 and in the same format as *Information Received* and *Death Among the Sunbathers*. It deals with Philip Hargreaves' investigation into his brother's death in Monte Carlo. The second Halkett book, *Documentary Evidence*, is not listed in the BL catalogue.

Besides the forty-two novels and fifteen stories listed here, Hubin records ten titles from Punshon's earlier phase. Of these, seven were classified by Gollancz as 'thrillers' and one, *The Woman's Footprint*, as 'adventure'. The others were published in America, *The Bittermeads Mystery* by Knopf in 1922 and *The Blue John Diamond* by Clode in 1929. The latter had a belated British edition in abridged form as a Cherry Tree paperback in 1946. Hubin does not list *The Ruby Bracelet*, a novella in nine chapters and thirty-two pages, published as No. 27 in Newnes' Princess Library. Though undated, it is thought (by Jack Adrian) to date from January 1920. It is an elegant little booklet with a pictorial cover, with the price – 2d – prominently displayed. The rear cover has an advertisement for Fry's Cocoa.

Punshon was also a prolific writer of stories, not necessarily criminous, for such magazines as *Black and White, London, Grand, Red* and *Twenty-Story*. Like his work in general, these await a full investigation.

Carter and Bell novels

The Unexpected Legacy   Benn 1929
Proof, Counter Proof   Benn 1931
The Cottage Murder   Benn 1931, Houghton 1932
Genius in Murder   Benn 1932, Houghton 1933
Truth Came Out   Benn 1932, Houghton 1934

Owen novels

Information Received   Benn 1933, Houghton 1934
Death Among the Sunbathers   Benn 1934
Crossword Mystery   Gollancz 1934
a.k.a. *The Crossword Murder*   Knopf 1934
Mystery Villa   Gollancz 1934
Death of a Beauty Queen   Gollancz 1935
Death Comes to Cambers   Gollancz 1935
The Bath Mysteries   Gollancz 1936, Hillman 1938
Mystery of Mr. Jessop   Gollancz 1937, Hillman 1937
The Dusky Hour   Gollancz 1937, Hillman 1938
Dictator's Way   Gollancz 1938
a.k.a. *Death of a Tyrant*   Hillman 1938
Comes a Stranger   Gollancz 1938
Suspects – Nine   Gollancz 1939

Murder Abroad   Gollancz 1939
Four Strange Women   Gollancz 1940
Ten Star Clues   Gollancz 1941
The Dark Garden   Gollancz 1941
Diabolic Candelabra   Gollancz 1942
The Conqueror Inn   Gollancz 1943, Macmillan 1944
Night's Cloak   Gollancz 1944, Macmillan 1944
Secrets Can't be Kept   Gollancz 1944, Macmillan 1946
There's a Reason for Everything   Gollancz 1945, Macmillan 1946
It Might Lead Anywhere   Gollancz 1946, Macmillan 1947
Helen Passes By   Gollancz 1947
Music Tells All   Gollancz 1948 (also with Bell)
The House of Godwinsson   Gollancz 1948
So Many Doors   Gollancz 1949, Macmillan 1950
Everybody Always Tells   Gollancz 1950
The Secret Search   Gollancz 1951
The Golden Dagger   Gollancz 1951
The Attending Truth   Gollancz 1952
Strange Ending   Gollancz 1953
Brought to Light   Gollancz 1954
Dark Is the Clue   Gollancz 1955
Triple Quest   Gollancz 1955
Six Were Present   Gollancz 1956

Novels by Robertson Halkett

Where Every Prospect Pleases   Benn 1933
Documentary Evidence   Nicholson & Watson 1936

Novella

The Ruby Bracelet   Newnes n.d. (c.1920)

Uncollected stories

'Too Late for his Hat and Coat' (*Detective Story Magazine*, 31 Jan. (1925)
'The Last Ascent'
'The Unknown Quantity'   (all in *Ghost Stories and Other Queer Tales*, Pearson 1931)
'The Haunted Chessmen'
'A Study in the Obvious' (*ES*, 26 Aug. 1936; *Fifty*

Famous Detectives of Fiction, Odhams n.d. (1938), as 'A Study of the Obvious')

'Who Was it?' | (both in *Detection*
'The Secret of the | *Medley*, Hutchinson
Chessboard' | n.d. (1939)

'The Double Six Domino' (*Detective Stories of Today*, Faber 1940)

'Making Sure' (*ES*, 16 Feb. 1950; *The Evening Standard Detective Book*, Gollancz 1950)

'Good Beginning' (*ES*, 1 Aug. 1950)

'Three Sovereigns' (*ES*, 17 Oct. 1950; *The Evening Standard Detective Book*, series 2, Gollancz 1951, as 'Where There's a Coffin There's a Way'; *Saint*, Feb. 1957 (UK), as 'Three Sovereigns for a Corpse')

'Find the Lady' (*ES*, 21 Dec. 1950)

'Dead Man's Hand' (*ES*, 16 Feb. 1951)

'The Tide Runs Strongly (*ES*, 26 May 1952)

'A Dead Man Laughs' (*ES*, 22 Jan. 1953)

'The Four Liars' (*ES*, 21 July 1955)   *BP*

Ellery Queen (b. 1905)
a.k.a. Barnaby Ross

It now seems established that the Ellery Queen canon was achieved in three distinct stages; the main body of work from 1929 to 1958, written by the two men who founded the pseudonym, Manfred Lee (1905–71) and Frederic Dannay (1905–82); a second sequence of novels from 1963 to 1971, in which Dannay only collaborated with ghost writers; and a third series, overseen by Manfred Lee, but written entirely by other hands. Collectors interested in the first and second groups will perhaps prefer to disregard the third. Even if the second group was not written by the founders of the pseudonym, one at least was actively involved in its creation, and some at least of the ghost-written works are worthy of the Queen name.

Most of them also share the same series detective, himself a detective novelist called Ellery Queen. He first appears in *The Roman Hat Mystery*, published both in America and Britain in 1929, and is involved in a further thirty-one novels, four novellas, and seventy-three stories, usually with his father, Inspector Richard Queen of the New York Police (whose one solo investigation is emphatically identified as *Inspector Queen's Own Case*). Ellery also features in five books and three stories written by other hands but published in the Queen name. These all appeared between 1940 and 1942 and were derived from films and radio plays. Three authentic radio plays featuring Ellery were collected with reprinted stories in *The Case Book of Ellery Queen* in 1945, and a number of Queen plays were also featured in *EQMM* and elsewhere.

The collaboration of Manfred Lee and Frederic Dannay ended with *The Finishing Stroke*, an elegant, intricate harking-back to their early fantastical vein. Of the nine novels in which Dannay alone was involved, three are known to have been written by Avram Davidson and one by Theodore Sturgeon: *And On the Eighth Day*, *The Fourth Side of the Triangle* and *The House of Brass* by Davidson and *The Player on the Other Side* by Sturgeon. *A Study in Terror* is a marginal novel of Sherlock Holmes pastiche, within a sketchy Queen framework, and *Cop*

Out is a tough private-eye novel more in keeping with the ersatz Lee series than the official Queen canon. *The Last Woman in His Life* is a frenetic exercise in deviant psychology.

In 1961 a series of twenty-eight paperback novels using the Queen name but written by ghost-writers began to appear in the USA. Five of these were published in Britain by Gollancz as continuations of the primary and secondary series. Readers and reviewers appear to have been successfully hoodwinked, since no outcry is recorded: but one wonders if five only appeared because someone at Gollancz eventually took fright. The NEL issued more of these novels in British paperback editions. In *Mystery and Detective Monthly* for October 1986, Edward D. Hoch reported that Manfred Lee needed in his later years to maintain his income but found himself barren of ideas for further books. The series of ghosted paperbacks provided the answer and became his special province: he 'chose the writers from those suggested by Scott Meredith [the literary agent], approved their outlines, and edited or rewrote their books'. Dannay had 'no part in the operation' but both men shared the income from the enterprise. The ghost-writers include Richard Deming, Edward D. Hoch, Stephen Marlowe, Charles Runyon, Talmage Powell, and Jack Vance. The series ended when Manfred Lee died.

The authentic canon opened with an exhilarating sequence of nine novels named from specific locations: a city, Rome, and eight countries. They established Ellery as an intellectual detective, sensitive and intuitive, but also acutely, meticulously logical. They embody the fair-play principle and each issues a challenge to the reader at an appropriate point in the narrative. Later books relied less on intricate artifice and gained in depth and intensity. Three novels only exclude Ellery: the Richard Queen novel, *The Glass Village*, and the appropriately named *Cop Out* (which, incredibly, is celebrated as the authors' fortieth anniversary novel and dedicated to 'our readers').

Six primary collections of stories admirably supplement the novels. Of these, *The New Adventures of Ellery Queen* contains eight stories and a novella, *The Lamp of God*, which appeared separately as a Dell paperback in 1951; *Calendar of Crime* includes a story for each month of the year; *Queens Full* includes three stories and two novellas, *The Death of Don Juan* and *The Case Against Carroll*; and *Q.E.D.* includes fifteen stories and a novella, *Mum's the Word*. *The Best of Ellery Queen* is a seventh, posthumous collection, edited by Francis M. Nevins, Jr and Martin H. Greenberg, and including fourteen reprinted stories and, for the first time, 'Wedding Anniversary'. Six uncollected stories exist, all with Ellery, except 'Terror Town'. The last Queen story, 'The Reindeer Clue', was ghosted by Edward D. Hoch. Three secondary collections contain largely familiar material. The exception is the US version of *The Case Book of Ellery Queen*, which includes three radio plays uncollected elsewhere: 'The Invisible Clock', 'The Honeymoon House', and 'The Double Triangle'. The British *Case Book* is an omnibus volume containing *The Adventures* and *The New Adventures*. *More Adventures of Ellery Queen* contains reprinted stories only.

In America Ellery Queen was published by a multiplicity of publishers from Stokes in 1929 to World in 1969. In Britain, Gollancz issued the entire series, all except *The Spanish Cape Mystery* in unadorned yellow dust-wrappers. The exception has handsome black-and-white endpapers of Spanish Cape and Walter Godfrey's house and grounds; and the stylish wrapper design shows John Marco sitting 'very dead, in a chair . . . a black stick still in his right hand . . . his black crisp curls covered by a black fedora hat a trifle askew, a theatrical-looking black opera cloak draped about his shoulders . . . and otherwise naked'. Most of the other books in the 'geographical' sequence have maps or plans of the terrain: the Roman Theatre, the Dutch Memorial Hospital, Georg Khalkis' 'drooping brownstone at 11 East Fifty-fourth Street'. *The American Gun Mystery* has a view of New York's Colosseum, and *The Chinese Orange Mystery* a plan of the twenty-second floor of the Hotel Chancellor. The late novel, *The Finishing Stroke*, has the title-page of John Sebastian's first book of poems, with the type in black and the decoration in red.

From *The Roman Hat Mystery* to *The New*

Adventures of Ellery Queen, all the books are black with orange spine lettering, with the exception of *The Devil to Pay*, which is known only in a blue binding, with dark blue spine lettering. *The Door Between* is also known in a blue variant binding, with black spine lettering. *Calamity Town* is a blue book with dark blue lettering on the spine. In *Royal Bloodline* (Popular Press 1974) Francis M. Nevins Jr states that owing to 'a scheduling error the English is the true first edition, preceding the US edition by six or seven weeks'. The two later wartime books are thinner than their predecessors, with blue bindings, gilt spine lettering, and tiny print. The first of the post-war books, *Ten Days' Wonder*, is also blue and gilt, but the print is mercifully larger. Most of the subsequent books are red with gilt spine lettering, but *Cat of Many Tails, Double, Double*, and *The Origin of Evil* have black lettering, and *The Last Woman in His Life* is bound in maroon. *And On the Eighth Day, The Fourth Side of the Triangle*, and *Queens Full* are taller than the general run, and so is the final sequence of four from *Q.E.D.* All the books are dated.

A Study in Terror, a Lancer paperback original in America, was retitled *Sherlock Holmes Versus Jack the Ripper* for British publication. Other variant titles were used for American paperback editions.

Frederic Dannay and Manfred Lee also published four novels under a second pseudonym, Barnaby Ross, two in 1932 and two in 1933. All four came from Viking in the USA and from Cassell in Britain, and have since been reissued as by Ellery Queen. The detective throughout is Drury Lane, an eccentric classical actor with remarkable histrionic gifts, retired from the stage because of increasing deafness. The Ross pseudonym was also used by other writers, for *The Scrolls of Lysis* and other historical novels in the 1960s.

The Tragedy of X has the uniform Cassell appearance of its time, with lines ruled at the top and bottom of the spine. It has a brown binding, with black spine lettering and rules, and a blind-stamped border on the front cover. The three later books have their own uniformity, with grey bindings, blank covers, and similar spines.

All three have the author's name set between two sets of six close lines, increasing in thickness from top to bottom above and from bottom to top below. In the titles, the *Y* and *Z* are very large, occupying about a third of the spine area, and the word 'last' is in italics, with the others in capitals. For *The Tragedy of Y* and *Drury Lane's Last Case* the lettering and rules are dark blue, and for *The Tragedy of Z* they are red. All four books are dated and have confirmatory printers' codes, at the end in the earlier pair and on the copyright page in the latter pair.

A few US firsts are known, scratchings on the surface of the full-scale bibliography that is long overdue. *Double, Double* has a shiny blue-green binding with black lettering on the spine and title and author black on the front cover, which also shows a man on an upper window ledge, also in black. The endpapers have a plan of the area round The Square at High Village, Wrightsville. The title-page is dated and the copyright page states 'First edition' and 'Published June 1950'. *The Origin of Evil* has a red binding with black lettering on the spine and title and author black on the front cover. Two wavy rules cross the spine and one the front cover. The book is dated on the title-page and states 'First edition' and 'Published April 1951' on the copyright page. *Calendar of Crime* is also red with black spine lettering and two wavy black rules. It is dated on the title-page and states 'First edition' on the copyright page. The contents are presented in the form of a calendar, with a story for each month. *The Glass Village* is a pale green book with dark-blue lettering and a token simulation of the village on the spine. The endpapers have a map of Shinn Corners. The copyright page has the date in the copyright notice and the statement 'First edition'. *And on the Eighth Day* has a blue binding with gilt lettering running along and two wide vertical rules on the spine. The covers have a pattern of black lines, most of which are indented twice. The front cover also has the Random House logo, gilt within a circle, matching its appearance on the spine. The top edge is dark blue and the fore-edge is roughly trimmed. *Queens Full* is blue with gilt lettering and a pattern of ten red rules, seven thick, three thin, on the spine. The front cover has 'EQ' within a rectangular framework, all gilt. The top edge is red and the fore-edge is roughly trimmed. In both Random books the copyright page states 'First printing' and the date appears only in the copyright notice.

The Tragedy of X, The Tragedy of Y and *Drury Lane's Last Case* are black books with similar lettering and decoration on their spines, though in different colours, red for *X*, gilt for *Y* and yellow for the *Last Case*. All three have coloured top edges corresponding to their lettering, roughly trimmed fore-edges and dated and decorated title-pages. The two earlier titles have, respectively, a red *X* and a gilt *Y* on the front cover and *Drury Lane's Last Case* has author and title in yellow. *The Tragedy of Y* has a preliminary plan of two floors of the Hatter house.

The queen of diamonds features on several of the early wrappers: on *The Egyptian Cross Mystery*, with a large capital *T* superimposed; on *The Dutch Shoe Mystery*, with a large feminine shoe; and on *The Siamese Twin Mystery*, with the twins in silhouette. *The Spanish Cape Mystery* has the grim portrait of John Marco that so distinguishes the British edition. *The Adventures of Ellery Queen* shows Ellery as gumshoe, rounding the edge of a door, gun in hand. *The Four of Hearts* has a plane in flight and *The Door Between* a front door with four panels. *Double, Double* has John O'Hara Cosgrave II's picturesque view of the house with the man on the ledge, from the cover. *Calendar of Crime* reproduces the calendar of stories from the contents page, here attributed to Samuel Bryant. *The King Is Dead* shows twin globes with a crown and a large right hand, a revolver against the palm and a watch on the inside wrist. For *The Glass Village* Cosgrave lines up the villagers of Shinn Corners as for a lynching party, with the church beyond them. *And on the Eighth Day* has a dark desert landscape with a single star in a lurid sky. *Queens Full* has a playing card with a standard queen at the top and her skull below.

Ellery Queen also founded the long-running mystery magazine that bears his name, and edited numerous anthologies. It seems established that Frederic Dannay was more actively involved in these than his partner, and he edited *EQMM* until his death.

Novels by Ellery Queen

(with Queen, except as stated)

The Roman Hat Mystery Stokes 1929, Gollancz 1929

The French Powder Mystery Stokes 1930, Gollancz 1930

The Dutch Shoe Mystery Stokes 1931, Gollancz 1931

The Greek Coffin Mystery Stokes 1932, Gollancz 1932

The Egyptian Cross Mystery Stokes 1932, Gollancz 1933

The American Gun Mystery Stokes 1933, Gollancz 1933

a.k.a *Death at the Rodeo* Mercury 1951

The Siamese Twin Mystery Stokes 1933, Gollancz 1934

The Chinese Orange Mystery Stokes 1934, Gollancz 1934

The Spanish Cape Mystery Stokes 1935, Gollancz 1935

Halfway House Stokes 1936, Gollancz 1936

The Door Between Stokes 1937, Gollancz 1937

The Devil to Pay Stokes 1938, Gollancz 1938

The Four of Hearts Stokes 1938, Gollancz 1939

The Dragon's Teeth Stokes 1939, Gollancz 1939

a.k.a. *The Virgin Heiresses* Pocket Books 1954

Calamity Town Gollancz 1942, Little, Brown 1942

There Was an Old Woman Little 1943, Gollancz 1944

a.k.a. *The Quick and the Dead* Pocket, 1956

The Murderer Is a Fox Little 1945, Gollancz 1945

Ten Days' Wonder Little 1948, Gollancz 1948

Cat of Many Tails Little 1949, Gollancz 1949

Double, Double Little 1950, Gollancz 1950

a.k.a. *The Case of the Seven Murders* Pocket, 1958

The Origin of Evil Little 1951, Gollancz 1951

The King is Dead Little 1952, Gollancz 1952

The Scarlet Letters Little 1953, Gollancz 1953

The Glass Village   Little 1954, Gollancz 1954 (not Queen)

Inspector Queen's Own Case   Simon & Schuster 1956, Gollancz 1956 (Richard Queen)

The Finishing Stroke   Simon 1958, Gollancz 1958

The Player on the Other Side   Random House 1963, Gollancz 1963

And on the Eighth Day   Random 1964, Gollancz 1964

The Fourth Side of the Triangle   Random 1965, Gollancz 1965

A Study in Terror   Lancer 1966

a.k.a. *Sherlock Holmes Versus Jack the Ripper* Gollancz 1967

Face to Face   NAL 1967, Gollancz 1967

The House of Brass   NAL 1968, Gollancz 1968

Cop Out   World 1969, Gollancz 1969 (not Queen)

The Last Woman in His Life   World 1970, Gollancz 1970

A Fine and Private Place   World 1971, Gollancz 1971

Story collections by and with Ellery Queen

The Adventures of Ellery Queen   Stokes 1934, Gollancz 1935 (11 stories)

The New Adventures of Ellery Queen   Stokes 1940, Gollancz 1940 (8 stories and a novella)

Calendar of Crime   Little 1952, Gollancz 1952 (12 stories)

Q.B.I.: Queen's Bureau of Investigation   Little 1955, Gollancz 1955 (18 stories)

Queens Full   Random 1965, Gollancz 1966 (3 stories, and 2 novellas)

Q.E.D.   NAL 1968, Gollancz 1969 (15 stories and a novella)

The Best of Ellery Queen   Beaufort 1985 (15 stories, including one newly collected)

The Case Book of Ellery Queen   Spivak 1945 (Bestseller Book No. B59) (includes 3 radio plays)

Uncollected stories

'Terror Town' (*Argosy*, Aug. 1956; *Best Detective Stories of the Year*, Dutton 1957/*Best American*

Detective Stories of the Year 8, Boardman 1958; *EQMM*, Aug. and Sept. 1958, as 'The Motive')

'Uncle from Australia' (*Diner's Club Magazine*, June 1965; *EQMM*, Nov. 1967)

'The Three Students' (*Playboy*, Mar. 1971; *EQMM*, Nov. 1973)

'The Odd Man' (*Playboy*, June 1971; *EQMM*, Oct. 1975)

'The Honest Swindler' (*Saturday Evening Post*, summer 1971; *EQMM*, Nov. 1979, as 'The Adventure of the Honest Swindler')

'The Reindeer Clue' (*National Enquirer*, 23 Dec. 1975)

Lane novels by Barnaby Ross

The Tragedy of X   Viking 1932, Cassell 1932; Stokes 1940, as by Ellery Queen

The Tragedy of Y   Viking 1932, Cassell 1932; Stokes 1941, as by Ellery Queen

The Tragedy of Z Viking 1933, Cassell 1933; Little 1942, as by Ellery Queen

Drury Lane's Last Case Viking 1933, Cassell 1933; Little 1946, as by Ellery Queen

Novels and stories by other writers featuring Ellery Queen

The Last Man Club Whitman 1940

Ellery Queen, Master Detective Grosset & Dunlap 1941

The Penthouse Mystery Grosset 1941

The Perfect Crime Grosset 1942

The Murdered Millionaire Whitman 1942

'Here is a Mystery' ('The Cellini cup') (*Radio Guide*, 26 Jan. 1940)

'The Man Who Wanted to be Murdered' (*Radio and Television Mirror*, Aug. 1940)

'The Scorpion's Thumb' (*Radio and Television Mirror*, Dec. 1940)

The ghost-written paperback novels issued in the Queen name are not listed.   *BP*

Sheila Radley (b. 1928)

Sheila Radley is the pseudonym of Sheila M. Robinson, who has published eight novels, all evocatively set in East Anglia, where she lives. Although she is yet relatively unknown, she is a most dependable writer, and her subtle modern mysteries will greatly reward those who seek her out. Her series characters are Chief-Inspector Douglas Quantrill and Detective-Sergeant Martin Tait, both of the Breckham Market police force. Quantrill's family sometimes becomes involved with the narrative.

Sheila Radley's first book was published by Hamish Hamilton, in black cloth with gilt lettering on the spine. Ken Reilly's impressionistic design for the wrapper, in black and white within a red framework, shows the dead body of Mary Gedge in the river. The later titles have all been published by Constable, generally in black cloth with silver spine lettering. *The Chief Inspector's Daughter* is the exception, with blue cloth and silver lettering. The later wrappers are all photo-graphic. Two by Nick Yates, for *Fate Worse than Death* and *Blood on the Happy Highway*, are very atmospheric. All Sheila Radley's books are dated. The Constable books are taller than the Hamilton title.

Two books have variant American titles. *The Chief Inspector's Daughter* was first published by Scribner.

Quantrill novels

Death and the Maiden Hamish Hamilton 1978 a.k.a. *Death in the Morning* Scribner 1979

The Chief Inspector's Daughter Scribner 1980, Constable 1981

A Talent For Destruction Constable 1982, Scribner 1982

Blood on the Happy Highway Constable 1983 a.k.a. *The Quiet Road to Death* Scribner 1984

Fate Worse than Death Constable 1985, Scribner 1986

Who Saw Him Die? Constable 1987, Scribner 1988

This Way Out Constable 1989, Scribner 1989

Cross my Heart and Hope to Die Constable 1992, Scribner 1992

Non-series story

'All in the Family' (*Reader, I Murdered Him,* Women's Press 1989) *JC*

Ian Rankin (b. 1960)
a.k.a. Jack Harvey

Ian Rankin's John Rebus novels and stories are particularly enjoyable examples of the police procedural story. Rebus is a detective-sergeant in the Edinburgh CID, a former SAS man, untidy but formidable. Later, he becomes an inspector. The author pulls no punches in his vivid portrayal of contemporary city life. Rebus figures in five novels and seventeen stories, five of which are uncollected. There are also two non-series stories.

Knots and Crosses appeared from the Bodley Head in 1987, in a red binding with gilt spine lettering. *Hide and Seek*, from Barrie & Jenkins, is also red with gilt lettering. *Wolfman* and *Strip Jack* both have a violet binding, the former with silver spine lettering, the latter with gilt. The latter appeared in a simultaneous paperback edition with a different ISBN from the hardback. *The Black Book* is black with silver lettering. All the books are dated and were first published in the UK.

The wrapper for *Knots and Crosses* is streaky grey and features a noughts and crosses diagram with the noughts in knotted rope and the crosses in matchsticks. For *Hide and Seek*, James Hutcheson sets the Edinburgh skyline against a blood-red sky, with, below, a five-pointed star encompassed by two concentric circles. Nick Hardcastle designed the wrappers for *A Good Hanging* and *Wolfman*. The former has a hangman's noose and gallows before a view of Edinburgh Castle; and the latter shows the figure of Justice over the Old Bailey with blood trickling down from a blindfolded eye and with the London skyline, including St Paul's, in the background.

Three novels, *The Flood, Watchman* and *Westwind* are not detective stories. One thriller, *Witch Hunt* was written under the pseudonym Jack Harvey.

Rebus novels

Knots and Crosses, Bodley Head 1987, Doubleday 1987

Hide and Seek Barrie & Jenkins 1991

Wolfman Century 1992

Strip Jack Orion 1992

The Black Book Orion 1993

Rebus story collection

A Good Hanging Century 1992 (12 stories)

Uncollected Rebus stories

'Talk Show' (*Winter's Crimes 23*, Macmillan 1991)
'Trip Trap' (*1st Culprit*, Chatto & Windus 1992)
'In the Frame' (*Winter's Crimes 24*, Macmillan 1992)
'Castle Dangerous' (*EQMM*, Oct. 1993)
'Well Shot' (*2nd Culprit*, Chatto 1993)

Other stories

'Marked for Death' (*Constable New Crimes 1*, Constable 1992)
'Video, Nasty' (*Constable New Crimes 2*, Constable 1993) JC

Clayton Rawson (1906–1971)
a.k.a. Stuart Towne

Clayton Rawson's crime fiction is rightly esteemed for its fantastic ingenuity but is deficient in human qualities: the people are diminished by the tricks. Four novels and a collection of twelve stories feature The Great Merlini, a retired conjuror with a magic shop. Two books by 'Stuart Towne' collect four novellas about Don Diavolo, also a magician: two in each. All but the last of the Merlini novels were published by Putnam in America and the Crime Club in Britain.

The American series is more elegant. *Death from a Top Hat* is a blue book with black lettering on the spine. The front cover has 'A Merlini Mystery' with a skull in a top hat and a stick laid underneath, all in black. The top edge is red. The book is dated on the title-page, which also has the slogan and motifs from the front cover. There is a photographic frontispiece of 'Dr Cesare Sabbat's apartment as the police found it' and a further photograph occurs opposite page 122, of 'Duvallo's apartment as it appeared just after Grimm and Jones broke in'. Page 70 has a woodcut of the demon Surgat.

The Footprints on the Ceiling has a green binding and a matching top edge, with black lettering on the spine. The front cover has the same features as its predecessor, as does the title-page, which is dated. There is a preliminary plan of

Skelton Island and page 104 has a drawing of ' "Aimee" the Human Fly'. *The Headless Lady* has a dark-pink binding with black lettering on the spine and a charcoal top edge. Otto Penzler (in *TAD* 15, 3, 1982) records a blue top edge and also a variant blue binding with a plain top edge. The fore-edge is roughly trimmed and the front cover has the same features as its predecessors, repeated on the title-page. The book is dated by the copyright notice only. There is a frontispiece photograph of Rawson with the headless lady linked to apparatus by tubes leading from where her head should be. Page 25 has 'The Mighty Harmon Shows', drawn by the author.

The British editions are all orange with black lettering on the spine, the date in the copyright notice and advertisements at the rear. *The Headless Lady* is dated 1940 but appeared in February 1941 according to *ECB*. This book lacks the American frontispiece but all other illustrations in the series are present.

Otto Penzler describes the US edition of *No Coffin for the Corpse* as having a black binding with orange lettering on the spine and further lettering and a vignette, also in orange, on the front cover. The book is dated 1942 and has 'First edition' on the copyright page. The publisher is Little, Brown. The British edition appeared thirty years later in Tom Stacey's crime series, under the enlightened editorship of Anthony Lejeune. It is a large green book with gilt lettering on the spine, a dated copyright page and advertisements at the rear.

The Great Merlini collects all twelve Merlini stories and appeared from Gregg Press in 1979 with an introduction by Eleanor Sullivan. It is white with dark-red lettering on the spine and the four playing card symbols arranged on the front cover in their appropriate colours. The endpapers are black and the text is decorated with hearts, clubs, diamonds and spades. There are three full-page illustrations: of a nine of clubs, a three-toed footprint and a photograph of a street scene. One of the stories – here retitled 'Merlini and the Photographic Clues' – was issued separately *c*. 1950 as an undated 16-page pamphlet to accompany a jigsaw puzzle. As 'Pictures Don't Lie' it was published by Pearl Publishing with a cover design of a camera with a flash bulb and a skull on the lens (also on the box containing the puzzle and the story).

Death out of Thin Air was published in America in 1941 by Coward-McCann and in the UK by Cassell in March 1948, according to *ECB*. The American edition is black with orange lettering on the spine, a red top edge and a roughly trimmed fore-edge. The front cover has Don Diavolo in orange, with flames rising from his top hat. The book is dated by the copyright notice. The Cassell edition is a deep-blue book with black lettering on the spine. Despite *ECB*'s claim it is dated 1947 on the copyright page, which also has a printer's code F.447. The second Towne book is an undated paperback with a lurid cover showing a terrified man recoiling from the embrace of Naga the Leopard Man. It was published by Wiegers Publishing Co. and is dated by Otto Penzler *c.* 1943. All Clayton Rawson's US dust-wrappers are illustrated in Penzler's *TAD* article, from the skull grinning within a topper for *Death from a Top Hat* to the hat, stick and gloves of *The Great Merlini*. The most striking of the series are the designs for *The Headless Lady* (by Rawson himself) and *Death out of Thin Air*. The former has a headless woman in a swimsuit with a circus big top, an elephant and a barker in his booth; and the latter shows Don Diavolo in evening dress against a backdrop of skyscrapers. The British series begins with a red wrapper for *Death from a Top Hat* featuring Merlini's hat and stick with a skull (and effectively reproducing the vignette from the American edition). *The Headless Lady* has a green wrapper with a girl in a green patterned swimsuit, cut off at the neck and just below the knees. *No Coffin for the Corpse* shows a naked man heaving himself clear of a grave. The blue wrapper for *Death out of Thin Air* shows Don Diavolo pulling a young blonde woman out of his hat by her hair, surrounded by multiple images of a dark woman wearing only a bra and a flimsy skirt.

Besides the four collected Towne items, Cook and Miller list five others, given here as uncollected. Whether any of them features Don Diavolo is unknown.

Merlini novels

Death from a Top Hat   Putnam 1938, Crime Club 1938

The Footprints on the Ceiling   Putnam 1939, Crime Club 1939

The Headless Lady   Putnam 1940, Crime Club 1940 (February 1941)

No Coffin for the Corpse   Little, Brown 1942, Stacey 1972

Merlini story collection

The Great Merlini   Gregg Press 1979

Paired novellas by Stuart Towne, with Don Diavolo

Death out of Thin Air Coward-McCann 1941, Cassell 1947 (March 1948)
Death from Nowhere Wiegers n.d. (*c*. 1943)

Uncollected stories by Stuart Towne

'Stand-in for a Kill' (*Detective Fiction Weekly*, 8 June 1940)
'Mr. Mystery' (*Detective Fiction Weekly*, 3 Aug. 1940)
'The Man with the Radio Mind' (*Detective Fiction Weekly*, 2 Aug. 1941)
'The Ace of Death' (*Detective Fiction Weekly*, 24 Jan. 1942)
'The Man with X-Ray eyes' (*New Detective Magazine* Mar. 1944)   *BP*

Ruth Rendell (b. 1930)
a.k.a. Barbara Vine

Ruth Rendell has to date written thirty-eight novels, including six as Barbara Vine. She has also published two novellas and forty-seven stories, collected in five volumes, and there are ten uncollected stories. She has some outstanding mysteries to her credit, especially those in her series about Detective Chief Inspector Reginald Wexford. Her particular strengths are plotting and characterization, and her Wexford books understandably caught the imagination of the reading public. The author now openly prefers her novels of abnormal psychology, but this sentiment is not altogether shared by her readers. Her earlier psychological novels include some that were highly successful, and *The Lake of Darkness*, for instance, reached breathtaking heights in its plot development. Regrettably, however, this level has not been sustained, and some of her later books have simply ceased to entertain. *Live Flesh* and *Talking to Strange Men* are particular disappointments in that respect.

Chief Inspector Wexford appears in fifteen novels and seven stories, usually with Inspector Michael Burden, who is absent from two of the stories and the novel *Murder Being Once Done*. Both are based at Kingsmarkham police station

in Sussex. They are not static characters, but develop and change, with their families, as the series goes on. Often the emotional situation within their personal lives provides a fascinating subplot which complements the primary action.

Ruth Rendell's books were all first published in London, and they are all dated. Several have alternative titles in the USA. John Long published the first seven books. *From Doon With Death* has green cloth, with the title in white on the spine and the author and publisher in yellow. The other six have black cloth. *To Fear a Painted Devil* has the title in red on the spine, and the author and publisher in blue, and *Vanity Dies Hard* has these features in blue and yellow, respectively. The four remaining Long titles have the spine lettered gilt. The dust-wrappers for the Long books were all designed by William Randell. Those for *To Fear a Painted Devil* and *Vanity Dies Hard* are very crudely drawn. *The Secret House of Death* shows the green Ford Zephyr parked at night outside Braeside in Orchard Drive. *Wolf to the Slaughter* has a daffodil, a knife, and spots of blood, and *The Best Man to Die*, a white rose buttonhole, also surrounded by blood-spots.

The rest of Ruth Rendell's books have been published by Hutchinson, usually with black cloth and gilt spine lettering. *The Tree of Hands*, *An Unkindness of Ravens*, and *Live Flesh*, however, have silver lettering on black cloth, and *Put On By Cunning* and *Talking to Strange Men* have blue cloth with silver lettering. *A Sleeping Life* is maroon and is lettered gilt. *Going Wrong* is white with gilt lettering and *Kissing the Gunner's Daughter* has black cloth with white spine lettering. *The Crocodile Bird* is black with gilt lettering. The endpapers for the early Hutchinson books to *Some Lie and Some Die* are grey. The end-papers are cream for *Going Wrong*, brown for *The Copper Peacock*, red for *Kissing the Gunner's Daughter* and black for *The Crocodile Bird*.

The wrappers for most of the Hutchinson books are of the standard modern photographic type. However, Terry Pastor provided four attractive designs for the books published from 1980 to 1982, the most effective being that for *The Lake of Darkness*, which shows a Tarot card, numbered thirteen, and dominated by a skeleton draped in a red robe and holding a scythe – the symbol of death. Below this a blue van is being driven along a snow-covered road. Tim Gill's fine design for *The Speaker of Mandarin* has Thatto Hall Farm, backed by woods, and overlooked by a fierce-looking Chinese dragon, in orange. A raven's head towers menacingly over a country road outside Kingsmarkham in Mark Harrison's design for *An Unkindness of Ravens*.

The Barbara Vine books are intended to be closer to mainstream fiction. They are published by Viking, in black cloth, except for *The House of Stairs*, which is brown. *A Dark-adapted Eye* has the spine lettered red, *A Fatal Inversion* has silver and *King Solomon's Carpet* has white. The other three titles have gilt spine lettering. All the Vine books are dated. *A Fatal Inversion* has red endpapers and *Asta's Book* has cream endpapers showing extracts in Danish from Asta's diary. David Kearney's wrapper for *A Fatal Inversion* shows Wyvis Hall surrounded by trees on a summer day. Robert Mason illustrates *The House of Stairs* with an attractive collage of images from the text, carried over on to the back of the wrapper. Graham Bence depicts for *Gallowglass* the gateway to Jared's drive.

There is no printer's key on the copyright page of the first edition of either *The House of Stairs* or *Gallowglass*. Later editions do have a printer's key on the copyright page: 3579108642 for the second impression, for instance. Both *King Solomon's Carpet* and *Asta's Book* have a printer's key in their first editions, running from 1 and on the copyright page. Later editions have a higher digit as the lowest component of the key, even where, as in *Asta's Book*, the statement 'First edition' remains underneath. W. H. Smith issued free booklets containing sample chapters from *The Bridesmaid* and *Gallowglass* before publication.

Ruth Rendell's novella, *Heartstones*, was published by Hutchinson, in black quarter-binding, with the author's signature in gilt on the front of the light-brown cover. The spine is lettered gilt, and the book has brown endpapers. Five unexceptional illustrations by George Underwood illustrate the text, and he also designed the wrapper. The reverse of the title-page states

that a limited edition of *Heartstones* was also published, but, in fact, no such edition exists. The novella *The Strawberry Tree* was published with Helen Simpson's *Flesh and Grass* in *Unguarded Hours*, by Pandora in 1990. The book has green cloth with the spine lettered gilt. The author of the second novella should not be confused with Clemence Dane's collaborator: she is a much younger writer. Ruth Rendell wrote the third part of a collaborative story, 'Death in the Square', co-written with Roald Dahl, Ted Willis and Peter Levi and published in the *Daily Telegraph Weekend Magazine* of 24 Dec. 1988. *Matters of Suspense* (Eurographica 1986) and *Three Cases for Inspector Wexford* (Eurographica 1990) contain reprinted stories only. The story 'Trebuchet', published in *The Listener* on 18 July 1985, is an anti-nuclear story and not conventional crime fiction. For first-edition collectors, the two most difficult titles are probably *Vanity Dies Hard* and *Wolf to the Slaughter*.

Novels

(with Wexford, as stated)

From Doon with Death John Long 1964, Doubleday 1965 (Wexford)
To Fear a Painted Devil Long 1965, Doubleday 1965
Vanity Dies Hard Long 1965, Beagle 1970
a.k.a. *In Sickness and in Health* Doubleday 1966
A New Lease of Death Long 1967, Doubleday 1967 (Wexford)
a.k.a. *Sins of the Fathers* Ballantine 1970
Wolf to the Slaughter Long 1967, Doubleday 1968 (Wexford)
The Secret House of Death Long 1968, Doubleday 1969
The Best Man to Die Long 1969, Doubleday 1970 (Wexford)
A Guilty Thing Surprised Hutchinson 1970, Doubleday 1970 (Wexford)
One Across, Two Down Hutchinson 1971, Doubleday 1971
No More Dying Then Hutchinson 1971, Doubleday 1972 (Wexford)

Murder Being Once Done Hutchinson 1972, Doubleday 1972 (Wexford)

Some Lie and Some Die Hutchinson 1973, Doubleday 1973 (Wexford)

The Face of Trespass Hutchinson 1974, Doubleday 1974

Shake Hands for Ever Hutchinson 1975, Doubleday 1975 (Wexford)

A Demon in My View Hutchinson 1976, Doubleday 1977

A Judgement in Stone Hutchinson 1977, Doubleday 1978

A Sleeping Life Hutchinson 1978, Doubleday 1978 (Wexford)

Make Death Love Me Hutchinson 1979, Doubleday 1979

The Lake of Darkness Hutchinson 1980, Doubleday 1980

Put On By Cunning Hutchinson 1981 (Wexford)

a.k.a. *Death Notes* Pantheon 1981

Master of the Moor Hutchinson 1982, Pantheon 1982

The Speaker of Mandarin Hutchinson 1983, Pantheon 1983 (Wexford)

The Killing Doll Hutchinson 1984, Pantheon 1984

The Tree of Hands Hutchinson 1984, Pantheon 1985

An Unkindness of Ravens Hutchinson 1985, Pantheon 1985 (Wexford)

Live Flesh Hutchinson 1986, Pantheon 1986

Talking to Strange Men Hutchinson 1987, Pantheon 1987

The Veiled One Hutchinson 1988, Pantheon 1988 (Wexford)

The Bridesmaid Hutchinson 1989, Mysterious Press 1989

Going Wrong Hutchinson 1990, Mysterious Press 1990

Kissing the Gunner's Daughter Hutchinson 1992, Mysterious Press 1992 (Wexford)

The Crocodile Bird Hutchinson 1993, Crown 1993.

Novellas

Heartstones Hutchinson 1987, Harper 1987

The Strawberry Tree (in *Unguarded Hours*, with Helen Simpson's *Flesh and Grass*, Pandora 1990)

Novels by Barbara Vine

A Dark-adapted Eye Viking 1986, Bantam 1986

A Fatal Inversion Viking 1987, Bantam 1987

The House of Stairs Viking 1988, Crown 1989

Gallowglass Viking 1990, Harmony/Crown 1990

King Solomon's Carpet Viking 1991, Harmony 1992

Asta's Book Viking 1993

a.k.a. *Anna's Book* Harmony 1993

Story collections

The Fallen Curtain Hutchinson 1976, Doubleday 1976 (11 stories)

Means of Evil Hutchinson 1979, Doubleday 1980 (5 Wexford stories)

The Fever Tree Hutchinson 1982 Pantheon 1983 (11 stories)

The New Girl Friend Hutchinson 1985, Pantheon 1986 (11 stories)

The Copper Peacock Hutchinson 1991, Mysterious Press 1991 (9 stories, 1 with Wexford)

Uncollected stories

'The Long Corridor of Time' (*EQMM*, Feb. 1974; *Ladies of the Gothics*, Lothrop 1975; *Ellery Queen's Napoleons of Mystery*, Davis 1978, Gollancz 1981)

'A Spot of Folly' (*EQMM*, Nov. 1974)

'A Drop Too Much' (*Winter's Crimes 7*, Macmillan 1975, St Martin's 1975; *EQMM*, Aug. 1976)

'The Price of Joy' (*EQMM*, Apr. 1977)

'The Irony of Hate' (*Winter's Crimes 9*, Macmillan 1977; *EQMM*, Sept. 1978, as 'Born Victim')

'The Haunting of Shawley Rectory' (*EQMM*, mid-Dec. 1979)

'Digby's Wives' (*Woman's Own*, 12 Jan. 1985)

'Mother's Help' (*Daily Telegraph*, 28 Dec. 1987–1 Jan. 1988)

'Mouse in the Corner' (*Esquire*, Winter 1991–2; *1st Culprit*, Chatto & Windus 1992) (Wexford)
'The Man Who Was the God of Love' (*The Man Who . . .* , Macmillan 1992; *EQMM*, Mar. 1993)

Collaborative story

'Death in the Square' (*Daily Telegraph Weekend Magazine*, 24 Dec. 1988)   *JC*

Louisa Revell

Louisa Revell is an entertaining writer in the crisp American tradition, a specialist in the detective novel as intelligent diversion. Her seven novels all feature a retired Latin teacher from Virginia, a spirited Southern lady, fixed in her time and class but far from inflexible. Though shrewd and sensible, with a lively interest in all that comes her way, she has a tendency to misread the signs and reach the wrong conclusion.

The books were all published in America by Macmillan. In Britain, four titles became atypical Boardman Bloodhounds and a fifth was brought out by Gollancz. The other two have not appeared in Britain, which is Britain's loss. *The Bus Station Murders* has a plum-coloured binding with gilt lettering on the spine; and *No Pockets in Shrouds* is red with silver lettering. *A Silver Spade* and *The Kindest use a Knife* are orange with black lettering on the spine and the Boardman bloodhound in black on both front cover and spine. All four are dated on the copyright page and have pictorial wrappers by Denis McLoughlin, highlighting dramatic moments in the text. Miss Julia herself appears for *The Bus Station Murders*, waving beside the yellow Annapolis bus, towards which a policeman is running. *A Silver Spade* and *The Kindest Use a Knife* have anxious people up to something: a man with a spade on a beach and a woman about to push a knife into the ground, respectively. The single Gollancz title is *See Rome and Die*, issued in a red binding with gilt lettering on the spine, a dated title-page and the standard yellow wrapper.

The Men with Three Eyes has a grey binding with red lettering on the spine and *A Party for the Shooting* is light brown with yellow spine lettering. Both books have the Cock Robin motif on the front cover in the colour of the lettering. They have the date on the title-page and 'First printing' on the copyright page. Vera Bock's wrapper for *A Party for the Shooting* shows a vast room in Colburn Hall, with a suit of armour in the left foreground and, beyond it, a supine male corpse and assorted visitors.

Julia Tyler novels

The Bus Station Murders Macmillan 1947, Boardman 1949
No Pockets in Shrouds Macmillan 1948, Boardman 1949
A Silver Spade Macmillan 1950, Boardman 1950

NO POCKETS IN SHROUDS

a Mystery Novel by
LOUISA REVELL

d.mcloughlin.

The Kindest use a Knife Macmillan 1952,
  Boardman 1953
The Men with Three Eyes Macmillan 1955
See Rome and Die Macmillan 1957, Gollancz
  1958
A Party for the Shooting Macmillan 1960. *BP*

John Rhode (1884–1964)
a.k.a. Miles Burton

Major Cecil Street was one of the most prolific
of true detective novelists, an accomplished puz-
zle-maker, with 140 titles to his credit under two
pseudonyms, seventy-seven as John Rhode and
sixty-three as Miles Burton. He established a
rhythm of four books a year, maintaining it, with
extraordinary consistency, over three decades.

In Dr Lancelot Priestley he achieved one of
the enduring figures of detective fiction, an awesome old party with a passion for truth and a
restless, analytic brain that forbids compromise
and marshals evidence with mathematical pre-

cision. Through him, in seventy-two novels,
Rhode exploits the perennial appeal of the
oracle, the infallible fount of wisdom, to whom
ritual application is made: he enlightens lesser
men and directs them in the way that they
should go. In comparison Desmond Merrion, in
the Burton books, lacks charisma. A breezy ex-
naval spy, with the endless leisure conferred by
substantial private means, he is more relaxed
and worldly, less godlike than the sage of
Westbourne Terrace. Both he and Priestley have
their attendant policemen. Hanslet and Waghorn
in the Rhode books, Arnold in the Burtons.
Arnold operates on his own on occasion, but
Hanslet and Jimmy Waghorn, in the books at
least, do not. (In the radio play, *Death Travels
First*, broadcast in two parts on 2 and 3 July
1940, Jimmy does not have Dr Priestley's help.)

Dr Priestley first appears in *The Paddington
Mystery* in 1925, and he recurs in all subsequent
books except *Night Exercise* and *Drop to His
Death*, a collaboration with Carter Dickson. He
is also featured in two of the uncollected stories,
so that the final tally of his cases is seventy-four.
(Inspector Purley investigates in 'The Purple
Line'). *The Telephone Call* is based on the 1931
Wallace Case. Three non-series novels ante-date
Priestley's first appearance.

The first Burton book has Dick Penhampton
in pursuit of the Funny Toff with the mad laugh,
and the sixth is investigated by Superintendent
Yardley and Inspector Caldwell. Otherwise,
every Burton title features Merrion or Arnold
or, more probably, Merrion and Arnold. Both
men are involved in *The Three Crimes*, working
with Inspector Young, but independently of each
other. They join forces in *Death of Mr. Gantley*,
the first of the fifty-four books in which they
actively share an investigation. Each man has
cases not involving the other: *The Secret of High
Eldersham* and *Murder Unrecognised* are exclusive to Merrion; and Arnold is on his own in
*The Menace on the Downs, Death Leaves No
Card, Death of Two Brothers*, and *This Undesirable Residence*.

Bibliographically, the Burton books are easier
to document than the Rhodes, since they were
all published in Britain by Collins Crime Club.
This means that they are all dated and have

orange or red bindings with black lettering on the spine. *The Hardway Diamonds Mystery, The Secret of High Eldersham* and *The Three Crimes* also have title and author and a black border on the front cover; and the nine books from *The Menace on the Downs* to *The Devereux Court Mystery* have title and author on the cover but no border. From *The Milk Churn Mystery*, Burton's books have black lettering on the spine only. On the title-pages of *Murder in the Coal-hole* and *Dead Stop* the Crime Club gunman faces to the right.

The Rhode books started with Geoffrey Bles in 1924, moved to the Crime Club in 1931, and returned to Bles in 1946. Like the Burton titles, the thirty-two Crime Club items are easier to define, since they are all dated, bound in orange, and with black spine lettering. Each of the eleven titles from *Tragedy on the Line* to *Hendon's First Case* also has title and author in black on the front cover. *Dead Men at the Folly* has an endpaper map of the area between East Hensley and Pucklebury. The gunman faces to the right on the title-page of *Dead on the Track*.

The pre-war Bles books favour red bindings, but *The Paddington Mystery, Dr. Priestley's Quest*, and *Peril at Cranbury Hall* are orange, and *The Alarm* is green. All have black lettering on the spine, and title and author in black on the front cover, which also has a border (single for the Priestley novels, double for the others). *The Double Florin, The Paddington Mystery*, and *Dr. Priestley's Quest* have advertisements at the rear. Nine of the books are dated, but *The Murders in Praed Street, Tragedy at the Unicorn*, and *The Davidson Case* are not. The Bles eagle is in profile on all the spines of these books and on the title-page of *A. S. F.* On the other title-pages, it is seen from the front, with its wings spread.

By an entrancing quirk of Geoffrey Bles in his salad days, five of the early Rhode books have additional printings of their dust-wrappers bound in at the front, the black and white rear panel covering the pastedown, and the coloured front panel forming a pictorial endpaper. The main design for *A. S. F.* shows a hand with a pen ringing these letters as they occur in sequence in successive newspaper adverts (a feature preserved on the post-war reissue of this novel).

The Double Florin has a specimen of the eponymous coin dated 1882, with a gunman advancing from the left and another man retreating on the right. *The Alarm* focuses a strong searchlight on to the body of a soldier, lying on rocks. Abbey's design for *The Ellerby Case* has Sir Noel Ellerby lying dead by his open, empty safe; and Philip Simmonds for *The Murders in Praed Street* shows a 27 bus advancing after dark through a brightly lit Paddington. The most interesting of the rear panels is that for *The Double Florin*, which has a rabble-rouser in a truck, haranguing workers outside their factory.

The post-war Bles series divides, broadly, into three groups, six with yellow bindings, fifteen with red, and a final sequence of ten where there is no colour consistency. For *The Lake House* to *The Telephone Call* the books are yellow, with red lettering on the spine. On the front covers, the title appears in yellow lettering against a red background, contained within two close borders, one yellow, one red. From *Blackthorn House* to *An Artist Dies*, the bindings are in various shades of red with black lettering on the spine. The front covers of *Blackthorn House* and *Up the Garden Path* show the title red against a black background within a red and black border. Later covers are blank. From *Open Verdict* the books have variously coloured bindings with lettering in equally varied colours. At least four are known in variant bindings: *Robbery With Violence* in red or blue; *Death of a Bridegroom* and *Licenced For Murder* in red or brown; and *Twice Dead*, either black with yellow lettering or light blue with black. The lettering for *Three Cousins Die* can be either red or blue, on a green binding. There is also a considerable variation in the publisher's logo at the base of the spine, ranging from the later Bles eagle, enclosed in a circle, through a sequence labelled 'Eagle Detective', to the final run, which tends to favour 'Bles Detective'. It is probably not possible to establish priority between a book with 'Eagle Detective' on its spine and another copy without this legend. All the post-war Bles books are dated. The year of *By Registered Post* is usually given as 1953, but the book is dated 1952.

The Venner Crime is advertised as one of 'the six books which comprise the "Passing Show"'s wonderful library of new fiction', issued by Odhams Press in enormous editions, and available only through the magazine. It is a mauve book with gilt spine lettering and is dated 1933. A reference on the wrapper to *The Claverton Mystery*, which came out in May 1933, confirms its place in the sequence.

Drop to His Death is a non-series collaboration with Carter Dickson, published by Heinemann, Dickson's publisher, in a black binding with gilt spine lettering and mauve endpapers. The book is undated, but the BL copy indicates that publication was in January 1939. The American edition, known as *Fatal Descent*, came from Dodd, Mead in the same year. It is a yellow book, doubly dated, and with the typical endpapers of the Dodd, Mead Red Badge mystery series. The title is printed vertically on the title-page, in imitation of the lift-shaft in the story. The front cover and spine list title and authors in black, and the cover also has a representation of a lift floor-indicator. Youngman Carter's dustwrapper for *Drop to His Death* shows a crowded London street, with newsboys proclaiming the death of Sir Ernest Tallant.

Philip Simmonds designed the wrapper for *Dr. Priestley's Quest*, the spine of which features a portrait of the Professor himself, in a skull cap. His secretary, Harold, appears twice, on the front panel, where he lurks by the side of a road, while a lorry disappears into the distance; and on the rear, where he climbs down into the dene-hole, while Dr Priestley watches from the top. *The Claverton Mystery* has a man leaning forward in his armchair and looking round towards an advancing shadow. *The Venner Crime* has Asta's design, with a sinister, dark figure tiptoeing menacingly towards a sleeping victim. *The Robthorne Mystery* confronts one bowler-hatted man with his twin and sets a noose hanging between them. A nightmarish figure in a greenery-yallery gas mask haunts both cover and spine of Youngman Carter's wrapper for *Poison for One*. *Shot at Dawn* has Hastain's view of a sinister male face within a yellow diving sphere, with a mooring post beside a river. *Death at Breakfast* shows a man clutching his throat with his left hand and his coffee cup in his right, while his bacon and eggs lie neglected before him. Four

fishermen in oilskins inspect by the light of a storm-lantern the body of Major Walter Bedworthy on Asta's wrapper for *In Face of the Evidence*. For *Death in the Hopfields*, Collins used a photograph of the oast-houses at Beltring Hop Farm, at Paddock Wood in Kent. *Death on the Board* shows a skeleton standing before a board table, holding a document. *Death on Sunday* has a white-haired clergyman with a stick, sitting in a garden beneath a tree, of which a large branch is breaking over his head. *Night Exercise* features a collage of Home Guard impedimenta and *Vegetable Duck* shows Mrs Fransham lying dead and the plate containing the remains of her fatal meal.

The long post-war series from Bles has exclusively photographic dustwrappers, in black and white to begin with, but taking on more colour as the sequence advances. The earlier designs in the series focus on objects relevant to each investigation: an AA box for *Nothing But the Truth*, a typewriter for *Death of an Author*, a chemist's shelves for *Dr. Goodwood's Locum*, cheque-stubs and a bank statement for *Death in Wellington Road*. *Death on the Lawn* has an archery target and arrows, and *Licenced for Murder* the signboard of the Knappers' Arms; and *Family Affairs* affords a glimpse of Dr Priestley's hand making notes on the case. As the sequence drew to a close, the front-panel photograph came to be reproduced on the front flap of the wrapper, and, increasingly, people began to feature in the shots. *Murder at Derivale* has a hurricane lamp, but also a man with a cigar, and *Three Cousins Die* embraces a motor-cycle accident and its victim. Peter Pitt's photo of a secretary dead at her desk adorns *The Vanishing Diary*, and, most spectacular of all, *The Fatal Pool* shows Yvonne Bardwell, drowned in the pool at Framby Hall, in a striped bathing-suit and a cap of the kind associated with Elizabeth Taylor.

To Catch a Thief has a green series wrapper with the gunman's image repeated several times. *Death Takes a Flat* encloses within the outline of a large key a white-haired man, lying with a knife in his back. An earlier secretary, also dead at her desk, features on Sheilds' wrapper for *Situation Vacant*, and a frightened man peers round a large tombstone in Stead's design for *Death Takes the Living*. The wrapper for *Dead Stop* shows a car moving through a twilit landscape, with an owl looming in a corner. *Murder Out of School* has the grim figure of a schoolmaster in gown and mortarboard, by Alex Jardine. Several of Burton's 1950s wrappers were designed by William Randell: *Bones in the Brickfield* shows Jeremiah Reeve being stalked by a man with a gun, and *Death in a Duffle Coat* has an anonymous figure, wielding a knife and appropriately shrouded.

Most of John Rhode's books appeared in the USA, but fewer than half of the Miles Burton series. There are many title-changes, usually to make a title more obviously criminous. According to Hubin, *In the Face of the Verdict* came out in the USA four years after its British edition, but in general the American editions followed closely on the British. Two books have the same title, *Up the Garden Path*, one by Rhode and one by Burton. *The Button on the Plate* is listed as a Burton novel in some of his 1940s titles, but Hubin attributes it to Vernon Loder.

Rhode also contributed to two of the Detection Club novels, providing chapter 5, 'Inspector Rudge Begins to Form a Theory', for *The Floating Admiral*, and part 1, 'Death at Hursley Lodge', for *Ask a Policeman*.

Novels by John Rhode

(With Priestley, except as stated. Details of bindings refer to British editions.)

A.S.F.   Bles 1924 (not Priestley)
a.k.a. *The White Menace*   McBride 1926
The Double Florin   Bles 1924 (not Priestley)
The Alarm   Bles 1925 (not Priestley)
The Paddington Mystery   Bles 1925
Dr. Priestley's Quest   Bles 1926
The Ellerby Case   Bles 1927, Dodd, Mead 1927
The Murders in Praed Street   Bles n.d. (1928), Dodd 1928
Tragedy at the Unicorn   Bles n.d. (1928), Dodd 1928
The House on Tollard Ridge   Bles 1929, Dodd 1929

The Davidson Case   Bles n.d. (1929)
a.k.a. *Murder at Bratton Grange*   Dodd 1929
Peril at Cranbury Hall   Bles 1930, Dodd 1930
Pinehurst   Bles 1930
a.k.a. *Dr Priestley Investigates*   Dodd 1930
Tragedy on the Line   Collins Crime Club 1931, Dodd 1931
The Hanging Woman   Crime Club 1931, Dodd 1931
Mystery at Greycombe Farm   Crime Club 1932
a.k.a. *The Fire at Greycombe Farm*   Dodd 1932
Dead Men at the Folly   Crime Club 1932, Dodd 1932
The Motor Rally Mystery   Crime Club 1933
a.k.a. *Dr. Priestley Lays a Trap*   Dodd 1933
The Claverton Mystery   Crime Club 1933
a.k.a. *The Claverton Affair*   Dodd 1933
The Venner Crime   Odhams 1933, Dodd 1934
The Robthorne Mystery   Crime Club 1934, Dodd 1934
Poison for One   Crime Club 1934, Dodd 1934
Shot at Dawn   Crime Club 1934, Dodd 1934
The Corpse in the Car   Crime Club 1935, Dodd 1935
Hendon's First Case   Crime Club 1935, Dodd 1935
Mystery at Olympia   Crime Club 1935
a.k.a. *Murder at the Motor Show*   Dodd 1936
Death at Breakfast   Crime Club 1936, Dodd 1936
In Face of the Verdict   Crime Club 1936
a.k.a. *In the Face of the Verdict*   Dodd 1940
Death in the Hopfields   Crime Club 1937
a.k.a. *The Harvest Murder*   Dodd 1937
Death on the Board   Crime Club 1937
a.k.a. *Death Sits on the Board*   Dodd 1937
Proceed with Caution   Crime Club 1937
a.k.a. *Body Unidentified*   Dodd 1938
Invisible Weapons   Crime Club 1938, Dodd 1938
The Bloody Tower   Crime Club 1938
a.k.a. *The Tower of Evil*   Dodd 1938
Drop to His Death   Heinemann n.d. (1939) (not Priestley)
a.k.a. *Fatal Descent*   Dodd 1939; with Carter Dickson
Death Pays a Dividend   Crime Club 1939, Dodd 1939

Death on Sunday   Crime Club 1939
a.k.a. *The Elm Tree Murder*   Dodd 1939
Death on the Boat Train   Crime Club 1940, Dodd 1940
Murder at Lilac Cottage   Crime Club 1940, Dodd 1940
Death at the Helm   Crime Club 1941, Dodd 1941
They Watched by Night   Crime Club 1941
a.k.a. *Signal for Death*   Dodd 1941
The Fourth Bomb   Crime Club 1942, Dodd 1942
Night Exercise   Crime Club 1942 (not Priestley)
a.k.a. *Dead of the Night*   Dodd 1942
Dead on the Track   Crime Club 1943, Dodd 1943
Men Die at Cyprus Lodge   Crime Club 1943, Dodd 1944
Death Invades the Meeting   Crime Club 1944, Dodd 1944
Vegetable Duck   Crime Club 1944
a.k.a. *Too Many Suspects*   Dodd 1945
Bricklayer's Arms   Crime Club 1945
a.k.a. *Shadow of a Crime*   Dodd 1945
The Lake House   Bles 1946
a.k.a. *The Secret of the Lake House*   Dodd 1946
Death in Harley Street   Bles 1946, Dodd 1946
Nothing But the Truth   Bles 1947
a.k.a. *Experiment in Crime*   Dodd 1947
Death of an Author   Bles 1947, Dodd 1948
The Paper Bag   Bles 1948
a.k.a. *The Links in the Chain*   Dodd 1948
The Telephone Call   Bles 1948
a.k.a. *Shadow of an Alibi*   Dodd 1949
Blackthorn House   Bles 1949, Dodd 1949
Up the Garden Path   Bles 1949
a.k.a. *The Fatal Garden*   Dodd 1949
The Two Graphs   Bles 1950
a.k.a. *Double Identities*   Dodd 1950
Family Affairs   Bles 1950
a.k.a. *The Last Suspect*   Dodd 1951
Dr. Goodwood's Locum   Bles 1951
a.k.a. *The Affair of the Substitute Doctor*   Dodd 1951
The Secret Meeting   Bles 1951, Dodd 1952
Death in Wellington Road   Bles 1952, Dodd 1952
Death at the Dance   Bles 1952, Dodd 1953

By Registered Post   Bles 1952
a.k.a. *The Mysterious Suspect*   Dodd 1953
Death at the Inn   Bles 1953
a.k.a. *The Case of the Forty Thieves*   Dodd 1954
The Dovebury Murders   Bles 1954, Dodd 1954
Death on the Lawn   Bles 1954, Dodd 1955
The Domestic Agency   Bles 1955
a.k.a. *Grave Matters*   Dodd 1955
Death of a Godmother   Bles 1955
a.k.a. *Delayed Payment*   Dodd 1956
An Artist Dies   Bles 1956
a.k.a. *Death of an Artist*   Dodd 1956
Open Verdict   Bles 1956, Dodd 1957 (purple binding, yellow lettering)
Robbery with Violence   Bles 1957, Dodd 1957 (black lettering)
Death of a Bridegroom   Bles 1957, Dodd 1958 (green lettering)
Murder at Derivale   Bles 1958, Dodd 1958 (green, red)
Death Takes a Partner   Bles 1958, Dodd 1959 (grey, gilt)
Licenced for Murder   Bles 1958, Dodd 1959 (silver lettering)
Three Cousins Die   Bles 1959, Dodd 1960
Twice Dead   Bles 1960, Dodd 1960 (black, yellow)
The Fatal Pool   Bles 1960, Dodd 1961 (green, yellow)
The Vanishing Diary   Bles 1961, Dodd 1961 (dark blue, white)

Novels by Miles Burton

(with Merrion and Arnold, except as stated)

The Hardway Diamonds Mystery   Collins Crime Club 1930, Mystery League 1930 (non-series)
The Secret of High Eldersham   Crime Club 1930, Mystery League 1931
a.k.a. *The Mystery of High Eldersham*   Collins 1933 (Merrion only)
The Three Crimes   Crime Club 1931
The Menace on the Downs   Crime Club 1931 (Arnold only)
Death of Mr. Gantley   Crime Club 1932
Murder at the Moorings   Crime Club 1932 (non-series)

262

Fate at the Fair   Crime Club 1933

Tragedy at the Thirteenth Hole   Crime Club 1933

Death at the Cross Roads   Crime Club 1933

The Charabanc Mystery   Crime Club 1934

To Catch a Thief   Crime Club 1934

The Devereux Court Mystery   Crime Club 1935

The Milk Churn Murder   Crime Club 1935

a.k.a. *The Clue of the Silver Brush*   Doubleday 1936

Death in the Tunnel   Crime Club 1936

a.k.a. *Dark Is the Tunnel*   Doubleday 1936

Murder of a Chemist   Crime Club 1936

Where is Barbara Prentice?   Crime Club 1936

a.k.a. *The Clue of the Silver Cellar*   Doubleday 1937

Death at the Club   Crime Club 1937

a.k.a. *The Clue of the Fourteen Keys*   Doubleday 1937

Murder in Crown Passage   Crime Club 1937

a.k.a. *The Man with the Tattooed Face*   Doubleday 1937

Death at Low Tide   Crime Club 1938

The Platinum Cat   Crime Club 1938, Doubleday 1938

Death Leaves No Card   Crime Club 1939 (Arnold only)

Mr. Babbacombe Dies   Crime Club 1939

Murder in the Coalhole   Crime Club 1940

a.k.a. *Written in Dust*   Doubleday 1940

Mr. Westerby Missing   Crime Club 1940, Doubleday 1940

Death Takes a Flat   Crime Club 1940

a.k.a. *Vacancy with Corpse*   Doubleday 1941

Death of Two Brothers   Crime Club 1941 (Arnold only)

Up the Garden Path   Crime Club 1941

a.k.a. *Death Visits Downspring*   Doubleday 1941

This Undesirable Residence   Crime Club 1942 (Arnold only)

a.k.a *Death at Ash House*   Doubleday 1942

Dead Stop   Crime Club 1943

Murder M. D.   Crime Club 1943

a.k.a. *Who Killed the Doctor?*   Doubleday 1943

Four-ply Yarn   Crime Club 1944

a.k.a. *The Shadow on the Cliff*   Doubleday 1944

The Three Corpse Trick   Crime Club 1944

Not a Leg to Stand On   Crime Club 1945, Doubleday 1945

Early Morning Murder   Crime Club 1945

a.k.a. *Accidents Do Happen*   Doubleday 1946

The Cat Jumps   Crime Club 1946

Situation Vacant   Crime Club 1946

Heir to Lucifer   Crime Club 1947

A Will in the Way   Crime Club 1947, Doubleday 1947

Death in Shallow Water   Crime Club 1948

Devil's Reckoning   Crime Club 1948, Doubleday 1949

Death Takes the Living   Crime Club 1949

a.k.a. *The Disappearing Parson*   Doubleday 1949

Look Alive   Crime Club 1949, Doubleday 1950

Ground for Suspicion   Crime Club 1950

A Village Afraid   Crime Club 1950

Beware Your Neighbour   Crime Club 1951

Murder Out of School   Crime Club 1951

Murder on Duty   Crime Club 1952

Something to Hide   Crime Club 1953

Heir to Murder   Crime Club 1953

Murder in Absence   Crime Club 1954

Unwanted Corpse   Crime Club 1954

Murder Unrecognised   Crime Club 1955 (Merrion only)

A Crime in Time   Crime Club 1955

Found Drowned   Crime Club 1956

Death in a Duffle Coat   Crime Club 1956

Chinese Puzzle   Crime Club 1957

The Moth Watch Murder   Crime Club 1957

Bones in the Brickfield   Crime Club 1958

Death Takes a Detour   Crime Club 1958

Return from the Dead   Crime Club 1959

A Smell of Smoke   Crime Club 1959

Legacy of Death   Crime Club 1960

Death Paints a Picture   Crime Club 1960

Novels with other members of the Detection Club (q.v.), as John Rhode

The Floating Admiral   Hodder & Stoughton n.d. (1931), Doubleday 1932

Ask a Policeman   Barker n.d. (1933), Morrow 1933

263

DEATH TAKES THE LIVING

MILES BURTON

CRIME CLUB

Uncollected stories by John Rhode

'The Elusive Bullet' (*Great Short Stories of Detection, Mystery and Horror*, series 2, Gollancz 1931/*The Second Omnibus of Crime*, Coward 1932; *Tales of Detection*, Dent 1936; *Fifty Famous Detectives of Fiction*, Odhams n.d. (1938))

'The Vanishing Diamond' (*The Great Book of Thrillers*, Odhams 1935)

'The Purple Line' (*ES*, 20 Jan. 1950; *The Evening Standard Detective Book*, Gollancz 1950) *BP*

Craig Rice (1908–1957)
a.k.a. Michael Venning
a.k.a. Daphne Sanders

Craig Rice was an ebullient and entertaining writer, whose accomplished fusion of the crimin-

ous and the comic became her trademark. Her narratives tend to be intricate and eventful, with much chasing around and some stretching of the law by her investigators. Action centres on a hard-drinking Chicago lawyer named John J. Malone, who is tough on top but sentimental underneath, like the novels in which he performs. His chief associates are Jake and Helene Justus, free spirits like himself. They share all his full-length cases and are sometimes the cause of his involvement. A secondary series features Bingo Riggs and Handsome Kusak, a complementary pair of struggling street photographers, with ambitions to better themselves. Handsome's photographic memory is a feature of their investigations, the last of which was completed by Ed McBain.

Besides the twelve Malone novels and the three about Bingo and Handsome, Craig Rice wrote a wide range of other fiction in five different names. As Craig Rice she wrote three non-series novels, one of which, *Home Sweet Homicide*, is a criminous domestic comedy, involving the three children of a woman mystery writer in a neighbour's murder. The other two deviate even more markedly from her breezy, humorous norm: *Innocent Bystander*, a harsh, bleak book in a tough, laconic mode, and *Telefair*, an atmospheric novel of unexpected intensity, written in a mannered, heightened style wholly different from anything else in her *oeuvre*. The three novels written as Michael Venning are also more sober than the mainline sequence, and feature an unobtrusive private detective named Melville Fairr, who merges with his background. One novel, *To Catch a Thief*, appeared in the name of Daphne Sanders, and three were ghost-written for celebrities, two for Gypsy Rose Lee and one, with Cleve Cartmill, for George Sanders.

Most of Craig Rice's books were published initially by Simon & Schuster in the USA. British publication was more erratic: eight books were not published in Britain, and the appearance of three others was delayed for several years, so that the order of publication is different in the two countries. Eyre & Spottiswoode published *8 Faces at 3* and the three books that followed it, though by the time *The Right Murder* appeared in 1948, two other novels had been published by Nicholson & Watson (and a third appeared from this second publisher later in the same year). There is no uniformity of binding or lettering from either publisher, but all seven books are dated. *8 Faces at 3* has the title in letters only on the spine, but everywhere else the *8* and *3* are given as numbers. *The Wrong Murder* features a character called Daphne Sanders, and *The Right Murder* involves a Michael Venning. *Having Wonderful Crime* records the action of the later novel, *The Fourth Postman*, as having already taken place.

Hammond took over in 1950, with the belated British edition of *Trial By Fury*. They published five more novels and the story collection, *The Name Is Malone*, which had previously appeared as a Pyramid paperback in America. *Innocent Bystander* is maroon with yellow spine lettering, as are all later books from Hammond. Both earlier titles from this publisher have green bindings with gilt spine lettering (blue-green for *Trial by Fury*). *The Double Frame* also exists in a black-lettered red binding. All seven Hammond books have the printer's date code on the reverse of the title-page. Apart from the US copyright date, which is misleading, *Innocent Bystander* is dated only in this way, but the others also have the publisher's dating. *Telefair* was published only in America, by Bobbs-Merrill in 1942. It is a large, pale-green book with gilt lettering on the spine and title and author on the front cover, also gilt. The title is lettered in script in both places. The book is dated and states that it is the first edition. *The Big Midget Murders* and *The Lucky Stiff* are black with gilt spine lettering and dated title-pages. The wrapper for the former shows a skeleton in red dangling a midget man in evening dress from a string before a large placard containing title and author; and that for the latter has the title over a large blue four-leaved clover, with a yellow horseshoe substituting for the U of 'Lucky'. *Knocked for a Loop* has blue boards and a red spine, with white lettering and a vertical white curve. The title-page is dated and the copyright page states 'First printing'. The fore-edge is roughly trimmed. Paul Bacon's wrapper shows the interior of Joe the Angel's City Bar, perhaps with Malone on the left, facing Joe, who is

behind the bar. *But the Doctor Died* is a paperback original, announced as a posthumous discovery but apparently of dubious authenticity.

The Name Is Malone collects ten stories, all of which feature Malone, almost entirely without the Justuses, though Helene makes a late entry in the last item, 'The End of Fear'. The other Rice collection is *People vs. Withers and Malone*, published only in the USA, and bringing together six stories written with Stuart Palmer, in which Malone and Hildegarde Withers work together. Palmer implies that he did most of the actual writing: 'Craig's real contribution . . . apart from the unique character of Malone . . . was in the gimmicks, the gadgets, the slant – a beginning or an ending or a line or two of dialogue.'

Malone's admirers should also be aware of a Craig Rice pastiche, in which he, Jake, and Helene are featured. *The Pickled Poodles* by Larry M. Harris was published by Random House in 1960 and by Boardman a year later, as American Bloodhound No. 342.

The wrapper for the Eyre edition of *The Right Murder* shows the first Gerald Tuesday, with his murderer just behind him, knife at the ready. Both men are bathed in a lurid green light. Crisp's design for the Nicholson *Having Wonderful Crime* shows the decapitated woman at the St Jacques Hotel in New York. For the Hammond series, Sax designed several wrappers matching the Craig Rice manner. *The Fourth Postman* shows Malone at the bar in Lew Browne's 'stinky saloon', with Helene renewing her make-up and the 'homeless mutt', with its paws on the counter. *The Double Frame* has Malone and Helen (or, perhaps, 'Tommy' Storm) at the top, and the chauffeur Tony's body below. Delora Deanne figures on *My Kingdom for a Hearse*, appropriately for the story, in segments. For *The Name Is Malone*, the lawyer is seated at his desk, looking apprehensive, with a gun and a bottle of rye to hand, and a blonde advancing purposefully towards him. *Innocent Bystander* is suitably grimmer: Jerry McGurn, with a knife in his back, is set against a garish fairground scene.

Two Michael Venning books appeared in Britain, both from Nicholson & Watson in 1947. *Murder Through the Looking Glass* is a slim, fawn book, and *Jethro Hammer* is dark red and rather more substantial. Both books have gilt spine lettering and are dated; and both look to have been produced rather cheaply. The latter has a wrapper by Bruce Roberts showing a stylish company in a smart interior.

The Gypsy Rose Lee novels were published in Britain by the Bodley Head and the George Sanders by Walter Edwards. *Mother Finds a Body*, dated 1943, is a red book with black spine lettering and a frontispiece by Vertes of 'the author at work' (Gypsy Rose Lee – at her typewriter, in case you were wondering). 'Mother' is the Ethel Merman character from *Gypsy*. She figures on the wrapper, looking horrified at the sight of a nude male corpse. The Sanders book is black with blue spine lettering, and is undated. The wrapper by Griff has a photo of the actor's head attached to a Holmesian figure with pipe and magnifying glass.

Reilly lists sixty-five uncollected Craig Rice stories, including one as Michael Venning and three in a sixth, posthumous pseudonym, Ruth Malone. Many of these are fact-crime pieces, and several others are variant titles for late reprints. In addition, it seems, there is a considerable problem of authenticity. Writing of Craig Rice in *TAD* for Oct. 1971, David A. Jasen refers to 'short stories written under her byline but not by her'. Mr Jasen is sceptical of a number of stories published after 1953, including the three Ruth Malone titles. Detailed research is evidently needed.

With many deletions and a few additions, Reilly's list reduces to thirty-five 'Craig Rice' stories and the single Michael Venning. 'Dead Men's Shoes', listed in the first edition of this guide, is equated with the collected story 'The Bad Luck Murders' (by Francis M. Nevins Jr in *TAD*, Jan. 1972). 'The Headless Hatbox' was expanded into the novel *My Kingdom for a Hearse* but ends differently. At least twenty titles are believed to feature John J. Malone, who is probably also in some of the others. Melville Fairr figures in the Venning story and one of the Rices, 'Death in the Moonlight'. David Jasen lists one other story, 'The Green Menace', for which no details are known. It is certain that Malone is not in 'A Quiet Day in the County

Jail', 'The Last Man Alive', and 'Mrs Schultz is Dead'. No stories are recorded for Bingo and Handsome.

Novels by Craig Rice

(With Malone and the Justuses, except as stated. Details of bindings and lettering refer to British editions.)

8 faces at 3 Simon & Schuster 1939, Eyre & Spottiswoode 1939 (black binding, red lettering)
a.k.a. *Death at Three* Withy Grove n.d. (1941) (Cherry Tree Book no. 141)
The Corpse Steps Out Simon Mar. 1940, Eyre 1940 (orange, black)
The Wrong Murder Simon Nov. 1940, Eyre 1942 (blue-green, black)
The Right Murder Simon Mar. 1941, Eyre 1948 (green, black)
Trial By Fury Simon Nov. 1941, Hammond 1950
Telefair Bobbs-Merrill Feb. 1942 (not Malone)
a.k.a. *Yesterday's Murder* Popular Library 1950
The Big Midget Murders Simon June 1942
The Sunday Pigeon Murders Simon Nov. 1942, Nicholson & Watson 1948 (Riggs and Kusak) (deep red, yellow)
Having Wonderful Crime Simon 17 Apr. 1943, Nicholson 1944 (red-brown, gilt)
The Thursday Turkey Murders Simon Nov. 1943, Nicholson 1946 (Riggs and Kusak) (light brown, black)
Home Sweet Homicide Simon 1944 (not Malone)
The Lucky Stiff Simon 1945
The Fourth Postman Simon 1948, Hammond 1951
Innocent Bystander Simon 1949, Hammond n.d. (1958) (not Malone)
My Kingdom for a Hearse Simon Jan. 1957, Hammond 1959
Knocked for a Loop Simon Sept. 1957
a.k.a. *The Double Frame* Hammond 1958
The April Robin Murders Random House 1958, Hammond 1959 (Riggs and Kusak); with Ed McBain.
But the Doctor Died Lancer 1967

Story collections by Craig Rice

The Name Is Malone   Pyramid 1958, Hammond 1960 (10 stories)
People vs. Withers and Malone   Simon 1963 (6 stories), with Stuart Palmer

Fairr novels by Michael Venning

The Man Who Slept All Day   Coward July 1942
Murder Through the Looking Glass   Coward Jan. 1943, Nicholson 1947
Jethro Hammer   Coward July 1944, Nicholson 1947

Novel by Daphne Sanders

To Catch a Thief   Dial 26 Apr. 1943

Novels ghost-written for Gypsy Rose Lee

The G-String Murders   Simon Oct. 1941
a.k.a. *Lady of Burlesque*   Tower 1942
a.k.a. *The Strip-Tease Murders*   Bodley Head 1943
Mothers Finds a Body   Simon Oct. 1942, Bodley Head 1943

Novel ghost-written for George Sanders

Crime on My Hands   Simon Oct. 1944, Edwards n.d. (1948); with Cleve Cartmill

Uncollected stories 'by Craig Rice'

'Death in the Moonlight' (*Popular Detective*, Mar. 1953)
'Don't Go Near' (*Manhunt*, May 1953)
'Hanged Him in the Mornin'' (*Verdict*, June 1953)
'A Quiet Day in the County Jail' (*Manhunt*, July 1953; *Cream of the Crime*, Holt 1962, Harrap 1964)
'The Dead Mr. Duck' (*Verdict*, Aug. 1953; *EQMM*, Jan. 1959, as 'The Man Who Swallowed a Horse')
'Motive' (*Verdict*, Sept. 1953; *EQMM*, Aug. 1959, as 'Smoke Rings')
'The Bells are Ringing' (*Manhunt*, Nov. 1953)

'Murder Marches On' (*Manhunt*, Dec. 1953; *Manhunt*, Apr./May 1967, as 'The Dead Undertaker')
'The Last Man Alive' (1953; *My Best Murder Story*, Merlini 1955, Boardman 1957)
'. . . And Be Merry' (*Manhunt*, Jan. 1954)
'I'm a Stranger Here Myself' (*Manhunt*, Feb. 1954; *Manhunt*, July 1965, as 'Alias: Trouble')
'The Little Knife that Wasn't There' (*Malcolm's*, May 1954; *EQMM*, Aug. 1961, as 'Malone and the Missing Weapon')
'I'll See You in My Dreams' (*Nero Wolfe Mystery Magazine*, June 1954)
'No Vacancies' (*Manhunt*, June 1954)
'Murder in the Family' (*Saint*, Nov. 1954/Mar. 1955)
'Flowers to the Fair' (*Manhunt*, 25 Dec. 1954; *Manhunt*, Aug-Sept. 1966, as 'A Weakness for Women')
'Beyond the Shadow of a Dream' (*EQMM*, Feb., 1955; *Best Detective Stories of the Year 1956*, Dutton 1956/*Best American Detective Stories of the Year 1956*, Boardman 1956)
'Mrs Schultz is Dead' (*Saint*, Mar. 1955/Aug. 1955)
'No Motive for Murder' (*Saint*, July 1955 (US))
'Shot in the Dark' (*Manhunt*, Aug. 1955)
'The Headless Hatbox' (*Double-Action Detective 3*, 1955)
'The Frightened Millionaire' (*Saint*, Apr. 1956/ Aug. 1956; *Women Write Murder*, Academy Chicago 1987)
'Dead Men Spend No Cash' (*Suspect*, Aug. 1956)
'The Quiet Life' (*MSMM* Sept. 1956)
'The Deadly Deceiver' (*Pursuit*, Nov. 1956)
'No, Not Like Yesterday' (*Saint*, Nov. 1956/Dec. 1957; *Best Detective Stories of the Year, 12*, Dutton 1957/*Best American Detective Stories of the Year 8*, Boardman 1958)
'And Do Write Often' (*Caper*, May 1957)
'Say It with Flowers (*Manhunt*, Sept. 1957; *Best Detective Stories of the Year 13*, Dutton 1958/ *Best American Detective Stories of the Year 9*, Boardman 1959)
'Cheese It, the Corpse!' (*Manhunt*, Nov. 1957)
'One More Clue' (*Manhunt*, Apr. 1958; *Best Detective Stories of the year 14*, Dutton 1959/ *Best American Detective Stories of the Year 10*, Boardman 1960)

'The Very Groovy Corpse, (*Saint*, Nov. 1958/ June 1959)

'They're Trying to Kill Me' (*Saint*, Feb. 1959/ Dec. 1959)

'Wry Highball' (*EQMM*, Mar. 1959; *Ellery Queen's Choice 14*, Random House 1959, Crime Club 1961)

'Hard Sell' (*Ed McBain Mystery Magazine 1*, 1960; *Best Detective Stories of the Year 17*, Dutton 1972/*Best American Detective Stories of the Year 12*, Boardman 1963)

'The Butler Who Didn't Do It' (*AHMM*, June 1960)

Uncollected story by Michael Venning

'How Now, Ophelia' (*EQMM*, June 1947)　　*BP*

Peter Robinson (b. 1950)

Peter Robinson's six very readable whodunits are all set in Eastvale and charmingly evoke his native Yorkshire. Five series characters appear in all the books: Chief Inspector Alan Banks, Superintendent Gristhorpe, Sergeant Jim Hatchley, Constable (later Sergeant) Philip Richmond and Home Office Pathologist Dr Glendenning. Banks, a solid family man and a sensitive, dependable policeman, has moved to Yorkshire to escape the stresses of London. Gristhorpe is a kind and compassionate dalesman, near retirement and fond of reading, gardening and the building of dry-stone walls. Banks has a good working relationship with Hatchley, who is transferred to nearby Saltby Bay to allow for the promotion of Philip Richmond, a computer expert and potential high-flyer. Susan Gay replaces him as Detective Constable and plays an important part in the solution of Banks' two most recent cases. Banks and Glendenning also appear in the story 'Anna Said . . .'. *Caedmon's Song* is extra-series, an impressive psychological thriller.

All the books are dated and were first published by Viking in Canada. *Wednesday's Child* is a paperback original. The rest are hardbacks, bound (or quarterbound) and lettered in various colours. These are all most attractively produced. Several contain maps, two of the town of Eastvale in *Gallows View* and a map of Swainsdale in both *A Dedicated Man* and *A Necessary End*. *Caedmon's Song* has two maps by Brian Lehan, one of Whitby and one of the Yorkshire coast. The books are unpublished in Britain.

The wrappers for the Banks novels feature a scene from the story, framed in an arched window on the front and back panels, with a small detail from the illustration on the spine. Simon Ng illustrates the wrapper of *Gallows View* and the cover of *Wednesday's Child*, the former with the silhouette of a peeping tom watching Coral Ellins undressing, the latter with the doll of kidnapped Gemma Scupham. For *A Dedicated Man*, George Sauvé shows the farmer Tavistock and his dog looking down at Harry Steadman's body lying by a dry-stone wall, the

Yorkshire Dales rolling behind. *Past Reason Hated* has Richard Waldrep's illustration of Caroline Harvey's stabbed, nude body, lying before a blazing fire with Christmas stockings on the mantelpiece and a Vivaldi record cover propped against a wall.

Novels

(With Banks, except as stated. Binding details refer to Viking editions.)

Gallows View Viking (Canada) 1987, Scribner 1990 (cream boards, green spine, cream lettering)

A Dedicated Man Viking (Canada) 1988, Scribner 1991 (cream, green, cream)

A Necessary End Viking (Canada) 1989, Scribner 1992 (maroon, silver)

The Hanging Valley Viking (Canada) 1989, Scribner 1992 (blue, silver)

Caedmon's Song Viking (Canada) 1990 (grey, red, grey) (non-series)

Past Reason Hated Viking (Canada) 1991, Scribner 1993 (black, gilt)

Wednesday's Child Viking (Canada) 1992

Stories

'Fan Mail' (*Cold Blood II*, Mosaic (Canada) 1989)

'Innocence' (*Cold Blood III*, Mosaic 1990)

'Anna Said . . .' (*Cold Blood IV*, Mosaic 1992) (Banks)

'Not Safe After Dark' (*Criminal Shorts*, Macmillan (Canada) 1992)

'Just My Luck' (*Bouchercon XXII*, Souvenir Programme Book, Toronto 1992)   *JC*

Jonathan Ross
(John Rossiter (b. 1916))

Jonathan Ross is the pseudonym of John Rossiter, an ex-detective chief superintendent of police. Under the Ross pseudonym he has written eighteen books, which are probably the best examples of the British police procedural novel. All but three of the books written in his own name are thrillers rather than novels of detection, and they are therefore disregarded here. There is also one story.

Jonathan Ross's most important series character, who features in all his books, is Detective Chief Inspector George Rogers, later a detective-superintendent. He receives his well-deserved promotion in the sixth book of the series. He is a tough, realistic policeman, demonstrating a range of human feelings – most notably a weakness for the opposite sex. He is assisted in sixteen investigations by Detective-Inspector David Lingard, who later becomes a detective chief inspector. The elegant Lingard is a natty dresser, who takes snuff and drives a Bentley. Two lesser policemen, the tank-like Coltart and the small, dapper Hagbourne, make welcome appearances in several of the cases. Rogers finds the copper-haired pathologist, Dr Bridget Hunter, very desirable. She plays havoc with his blood-pressure on social occasions and causes turmoil to his stomach when he has to attend the post-mortems she conducts. Unhappily, after nine books, the author replaces her in the pathology department with the slapdash dissector, Dr Wilfred Twite.

The Jonathan Ross books were all first published in London, and they are all dated. The first three were not published in the USA. Cassell published the first four titles, issuing them in black cloth with white lettering on the spine. The remaining books have all come from Constable and have their spines lettered in silver. They all have black cloth, except for *A Rattling of Old Bones*, which is charcoal grey. The books twice became taller, from *Here Lies Nancy Frail* and from *Dark Blue and Dangerous*. The first printing of *I Know What It's Like to Die* was issued with the name of Richard Clapperton on the spine, instead of Jonathan Ross. Once the mistake was realized the print run was supposed to have been recalled by the publisher, but some incorrect copies have escaped the net. A corrected edition is believed to have been issued.

Two uniformed policemen discover the body of Michael Clancy hanging from a tree in Tadpole Lane, on the wrapper of *The Deadest Thing You Ever Saw*. The token black-and-white 'design' by Graham Bishop for *Here Lies Nancy Frail* and *The Burning of Billy Toober* is hardly worth mentioning, whereas Harold George's wrapper for *A Rattling of Old Bones* features a clever collage, in black and white, of characters and events from the text. The later books all have the modern photographic type of wrapper. The author himself took the photograph for *Sudden Departures*.

John Rossiter has also written three police novels under his own name, all published by Cassell, and all dated.

The two most elusive titles for collectors are *Dead at First Hand* and *I Know What It's Like to Die*.

Rogers novels by Jonathan Ross

(also with Lingard, except as stated)

The Blood Running Cold Cassell 1968 (not Lingard)

Diminished By Death Cassell 1968

Dead at First Hand Cassell 1969 (not Lingard)

The Deadest Thing You Ever Saw Cassell 1969, McCall 1970

Here Lies Nancy Frail Constable 1972, Saturday Review 1972

The Burning of Billy Toober Constable 1974, Walker 1976

I Know What It's Like to Die Constable 1976, Walker 1978

A Rattling of Old Bones Constable 1979, Scribner 1982

Dark Blue and Dangerous Constable 1981, Scribner 1981

Death's Head Constable 1982, St Martin's 1983

Dead Eye Constable 1983, St Martin's 1984

Dropped Dead Constable 1984, St Martin's 1985

Burial Deferred Constable 1985, St Martin's 1986

Fate Accomplished Constable 1987, St. Martin's 1987

Sudden Departures Constable 1988, St Martin's 1988.

A Time for Dying Constable 1989, St Martin's 1989

Daphne Dead and Done For Constable 1990, St Martin's 1991

Murder be Hanged Constable 1992, St Martin's 1993

Police novels by John Rossiter

(Binding details refer to British editions.)

The Victims Cassell 1971 (red binding, gilt lettering)

The Manipulators Cassell 1973, Simon & Schuster 1974 (orange, black)

The Villains Cassell 1974, Walker 1976 (black, silver)

Story by John Rossiter

'Yes, Sir, No, Sir' (*John Creasey's Crime Collection 1978*, Gollancz 1978)

N.B. John Rossiter has also published four thrillers. *JC*

Dorothy L. Sayers (1893–1957)

Dorothy L. Sayers is a doyenne of the detective story, with a well-deserved reputation for dazzling her readers. She created one of the most distinguished of all fictional detectives, that erudite, stylish amateur Lord Peter Wimsey. He appears in eleven novels and the twenty-one stories collected in the American volume *Lord Peter*. M. R. Ridley, sometime Chaplain of Balliol, is thought to be the original inspiration for the character. The detective novelist Harriet Vane appears in four novels and becomes Lady Peter after a long courtship. Montague Egg, a cheerful traveller in wines, is the detective in eleven stories. One novel, *The Documents in the Case*, a collaboration with Robert Eustace, does not feature Wimsey. *Busman's Honeymoon* was a play written with Muriel St Clare Byrne before it became a novel. Twelve of the forty-four stories are non-series, and all the stories are collected. Miss Sayers also contributed to seven of the collections and collaborations of the Detection Club (q.v.), including *Six Against the Yard*.

In the UK, the first two books were published by Fisher Unwin and are clearly dated, like all the rest of the British first editions. *Whose Body?* was published in 1923, with two states of binding and no priority determined for the first edition. One has blue cloth, with black spine lettering, and the title in black and a blind-stamped border on the front cover. The other has red cloth, again with black spine lettering and the title in black on the cover, but this time with a black border. *Clouds of Witness* has the same features as the blue-cloth edition of *Whose Body?*

The next three novels were published by Ernest Benn, *Unnatural Death* in yellow cloth, lettered in black on the spine, and with the title in black on the front cover. There are also two guns on the cover, in black, facing each other and pointing towards the centre, and there is a border of black icicles, also pointing inwards. The spine has a row of icicles projecting downwards at the top, and another row pointing upwards at the bottom. *The Unpleasantness at The Bellona Club* and *The Documents in the Case* have exactly the same features, except that they have black bindings and orange lettering and decoration. *The Documents in the Case* has an additional orange star towards the centre of the front cover.

The remaining UK first editions were all published by Gollancz, generally in black cloth with red lettering on the spine (though some call it orange). Red cloth with black lettering indicates a later issue. *Gaudy Night* and *Busman's Honeymoon* are taller volumes, bound in black, but with gilt lettering on the spine.

With the exception of *Whose Body?* and *Busman's Honeymoon*, all the UK editions were the

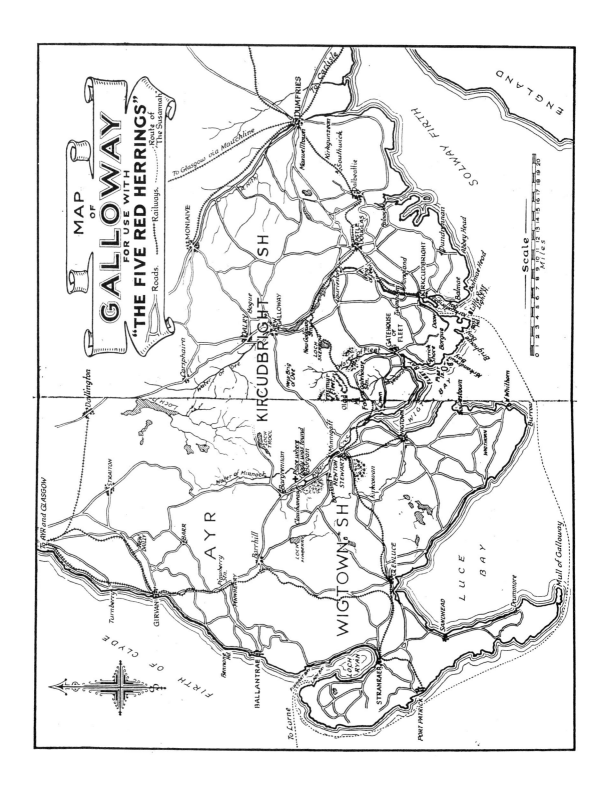

MAP
OF
GALLOWAY
FOR USE WITH
"THE FIVE RED HERRINGS"

Roads.————
Railways. ··········
Route of
The Susannah. ··········

Scale
0 1 2 3 4 5 6 7 8 9 10 11 12 13 14 15 16 17 18 19 20
Miles

first publications. Three books have variant American titles.

Three final Wimsey stories were not collected in the original collections published by Gollancz. 'Striding Folly' and 'The Haunted Policeman' first appeared in book form in *Detection Medley*, edited by John Rhode in 1939. They had previously been published in *The Strand Magazine*, in July 1935 and March 1938 respectively. The latter story first appeared in *Harper's Bazaar* in February 1938. 'Talboys' was written in 1942 but not discovered until 1961. It was first printed as a 32-page unbound pamphlet, issued by Harper & Row in 1972. The pages were numbered 431–53, so that owners of *Lord Peter*, which came out in January 1972, could add the pamphlet to the book, so making it truly complete. The first time all three stories were collected in a Sayers volume was in the second edition of *Lord Peter* in May 1972. The UK first publication was in volume 15 of the Collected Edition, *In the Teeth of the Evidence*, which Gollancz published in October 1972. A paperback containing all three stories, entitled *Striding Folly*, was published by NEL in the same year.

A biographical notice for Wimsey was included in July 1935 in the Gollancz editions of *Clouds of Witness, Unnatural Death, Whose Body?* and *The Unpleasantness at the Bellona Club*. This had previously appeared in slightly different form in *Sleuths*, edited by K. Macgown in 1931 for Harcourt, Brace.

Clouds of Witness has a frontispiece showing the sheet of blotting paper from the library at Riddlesdale Lodge. *The Five Red Herrings* has illustrated endpapers, showing a map of Galloway, but copies are also known without this feature. *The Nine Tailors* has a noble frontispiece of the Church of Fenchurch St Paul by W. J. Redhead. E. McKnight Kauffer designed the wrapper for *Lord Peter Views the Body*, which shows a stylized representation of a hotel porter, with his right hand raised in alarm, as another, larger right hand confronts him. The design is in cream, orange and brown. The other Gollancz wrappers are the standard yellow.

There is an unfinished sequel to *Busman's Honeymoon* called *Thrones, Dominations*. It is still unpublished. *Where Do We Go from Here?*

is an original radio play, broadcast on 24 February 1948.

The most difficult first editions to acquire are the first two.

Novels

(with Wimsey, except as stated)

Whose Body? Boni & Liveright 1923, Unwin 1923

Clouds of Witness Unwin 1926
a.k.a. *Clouds of Witnesses* Dial 1927

Unnatural Death Benn 1927
a.k.a. *The Dawson Pedigree* Dial 1928

The Unpleasantness at the Bellona Club Benn July 1928, Payson & Clarke 1928

The Documents in the Case Benn July 1930, Brewer & Warren 1930; with Robert Eustace (not Wimsey)

Strong Poison Gollancz Sept. 1930, Brewer 1930

The Five Red Herrings Gollancz 1931
a.k.a. *Suspicious Characters* Brewer 1931

Have His Carcase Gollancz 1932, Brewer 1932

Murder Must Advertise Gollancz Feb. 1933, Harcourt Brace 1933

The Nine Tailors Gollancz 1934, Harcourt 1934

Gaudy Night Gollancz 1935, Harcourt 1936

Busman's Honeymoon Harcourt 1937, Gollancz 1937

Story collections

Lord Peter Views the Body Gollancz Nov. 1928, Payson 1929 (12 Wimsey stories)

Hangman's Holiday Gollancz May 1933, Harcourt 1933 (12 stories, 4 with Wimsey, 6 with Egg)

In the Teeth of the Evidence Gollancz 1939, Harcourt 1940 (17 stories, 2 with Wimsey, 5 with Egg)

In the Teeth of the Evidence Gollancz Oct. 1972 (with 3 additional Wimsey stories)

Lord Peter Harper Jan. 1972 (20 Wimsey stories) 2nd edn. Harper May 1972 (21 Wimsey stories)

Striding Folly NEL 1972 (3 Wimsey stories)

Collaborations with other members of the Detection Club (q.v.)

The Floating Admiral Hodder & Stoughton n.d. (1931), Doubleday 1932
Ask a Policeman Arthur Barker n.d. (1933), Morrow 1933
Double Death Gollancz 1939
The Scoop and *Behind the Screen* Gollancz 1983
No Flowers By Request Gollancz 1984 (with *Crime on the Coast*)   *JC*

Anthony and Peter Shaffer (b. 1926) a.k.a. Peter Antony

Peter Antony is the pseudonym of the twin brothers Anthony and Peter Shaffer. Both are better known for their several plays, notably *Sleuth* for Anthony and *Amadeus* for Peter. For the two books they wrote as Peter Antony their detective is Mr Verity, but for some unfathomable reason he undergoes a name change to Mr Fathom for the third book, written under their own names. Mr Verity is a larger-than-life character of immense size, who sports a Vandyke beard, wears a cloak, and smokes black Cuban cigars. Detective-Inspector Rambler, 'a great, sad-faced hulk with a heavy, pink jowl and a fierce, cold brain' assists Verity in his cases.

The books are noted for other eccentric characters, much humour, and brilliant plotting. They were all first published in London, the first two, both dated, by Evans. *The Woman in the Wardrobe* was issued in brown cloth, with the spine lettered in black. The word 'Crime' also appears on the spine. The book contains a front-ispiece of Mr Verity and seven illustrations of various characters by Nicolas Bentley, who also provided the drawing for the red dust-wrapper (of Mr Verity admiring a statuette, which he holds out towards Inspector Rambler). The book was not published in America. *How Doth the Little Crocodile?* has green cloth and gilt lettering on the spine. The wrapper is illustrated with another Bentley drawing of Mr Verity. *Withered Murder* was published by Gollancz in red cloth, with the spine lettered gilt, and it is dated. The wrapper is plain yellow.

Absolution is Anthony Shaffer's novelization of his screenplay for the film of the same name. It was first published as a Corgi paperback. The first hardback edition was brought out later the same year by Severn House. The wrapper is illustrated by a scene from the film.

Mr Verity also appears in the uncollected story, 'Before and After'.

Verity novels by Peter Antony

The Woman in the Wardrobe Evans 1951
How Doth the Little Crocodile? Evans 1952, Macmillan 1957, as by Anthony and Peter Shaffer, with Mr Fathom

Fathom novel by A. and P. Shaffer

Withered Murder Gollancz 1955, Macmillan 1956

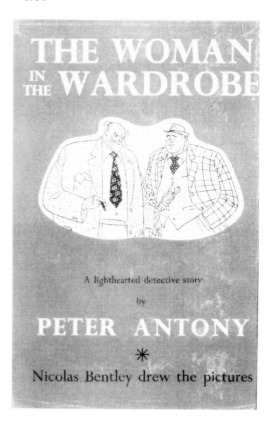

THE WOMAN IN THE WARDROBE

A lighthearted detective story

by

PETER ANTONY

✳

Nicolas Bentley drew the pictures

Novel by Anthony Shaffer

Absolution   Corgi 1979

Uncollected stories

By Peter Antony

'Before and After' (*LMM*, 16, June 1953, illustrated by Nicolas Bentley)
By Anthony Shaffer
'Larger than Life' (*LMM*, 18 (1953))
By Peter Shaffer
'Suffer a Witch' (*LMM*, 20 (1954), illustrated by Peter Kneebone)   *JC*

Dorothy Simpson (b. 1933)

Dorothy Simpson is one of the more promising recent writers, who has to date written thirteen novels and five stories. Apart from the first book, all titles are set in Kent, in the town of Sturrenden, where Detective-Inspector Luke Thanet and Sergeant Mike Lineham uphold law and order. Perhaps more than any other current writer of detective fiction, Dorothy Simpson involves us in the family life of her series detectives. Wives, mothers, and daughters colour the moods of both Thanet and Lineham. Far from being shadowy figures in the background, they all have a significant and continuing influence on the storylines.

Dorothy Simpson's first book was published by Macdonald and Jane's in brown cloth, with the spine lettered gilt. A very worried-looking Sarah Royal is featured on the wrapper designed by Eric Earnshaw. This book was not published in the USA. The Thanet series has been published in Britain by Michael Joseph, with cloth and lettering colours varying from title to title. The five books from *Six Feet Under* to *Dead on Arrival* have gilt spine lettering and the two after them have lettering in two colours. The wrappers of the first six have striking modern designs by Graham Rogers. Why the publisher felt the need to change the format for the seventh is beyond comprehension. All the books, from both publishers, are dated. *Suspicious Death* has most

attractive pictorial endpapers of the village of Telford Green drawn by Peter McClure.

The stories are all non-series and are crime rather than detective stories.

Novels

(With Thanet from **The Night She Died.** *Details of bindings refer to British editions.)*

Harbingers of Fear   Macdonald & Jane's 1977
The Night She Died   Joseph 1981, Scribner 1981 (blue binding, silver lettering)
Six Feet Under   Joseph 1982, Scribner 1982 (black)
Puppet for a Corpse   Joseph 1983, Scribner 1983 (black)
Close Her Eyes   Joseph 1984, Scribner 1984 (dark blue)
Last Seen Alive   Joseph 1985, Scribner 1985 (green)
Dead on Arrival   Joseph 1986, Scribner 1986 (black)
Element of Doubt   Joseph 1987, Scribner 1987 (blue, red and silver)
Suspicious Death   Joseph 1988, Scribner 1988 (green, red and silver)
Dead by Morning   Joseph 1989, Scribner 1989 (blue, silver)
Doomed to Die   Joseph 1991, Scribner 1991 (blue, white)
Wake the Dead   Joseph 1992, Scribner 1992 (burgundy, gilt)
No Laughing Matter   Joseph 1993, Scribner 1993 (green, silver)

Stories

'The Wisp of Sound' (*EQMM*, Nov. 1977)
'The Sanctuary' (*AHMM*, Apr. 1978)
'Boxes Within Boxes' (*EQMM*, Mar. 1980)
'Two's Company' (*John Creasey's Crime Collection 1984*, Gollancz 1984)
'The Person Inside' (*EQMM*, Apr. 1987)   *JC*

ann in 1932. It was Snow's first novel and is a black book with red lettering on the spine and a small vignette of the *Siren* in red on the front cover. There is also a plan of the sleeping arrangements on board. *A Coat of Varnish* is Snow's last novel, and it appeared from Macmillan in 1979. It is a substantial green book, with title and author in gilt enclosed within a border on the spine. The handsome dust-wrapper by David Eastbury shows a stylized view of Aylstone Square. Both books are dated.

Novels

Death Under Sail   Heinemann 1932, Doubleday 1932

A Coat of Varnish   Macmillan 1979, Scribner 1979   *BP*

C. P. Snow (1905–1980)

C. P. Snow was a celebrated mainstream novelist, married to Pamela Hansford Johnson, who herself wrote occasional crime fiction. His detective novels are *Death Under Sail* and *A Coat of Varnish*: the former a classical closed circle whodunit, set on a yacht on the Norfolk Broads; and the latter a profound and powerful novel, absorbing as a mystery and acute and disturbing as a comment on our civilization. It was adapted for the stage by Ronald Miller, and memorably performed by Peter Barkworth as Frank Briers, the senior policeman in charge of the investigation. The murder victim was played by Dulcie Gray, doubly distinguished as actor and crime novelist.

Death Under Sail was published by Heinem-

Rex Stout (1886–1975)

As a crime-writer Rex Stout performed at a consistently high level for over forty years, and in Nero Wolfe he established one of the legendary figures in detective fiction. Everything about Wolfe sets him apart; his phenomenal brain, his formidable bulk, his attitudes, habits, and tastes. Our view of him is determined exclusively from the relaxed and subtle narratives of Archie Goodwin, the indispensable aide whose remarkable gifts perfectly complement his own. Archie's continuous commentary on his employer is, in its way, no less dazzling than the prodigious courses of Wolfe himself. The decision to reveal Wolfe's eccentric power through the medium of Archie's flippant, dismissive wit provided Rex Stout with a formula that served him magnificently throughout the long series. Their combination is irresistible.

There are thirty-three novels and forty-one novellas about Wolfe (and narrated by Archie). All the novellas are collected in fourteen volumes, of which the last, *Death Times Three*, is a recent American paperback original. Two also appeared separately; *Door to Death* as a Dell ten-cent paperback, and *Bitter End* in a limited edition volume called *Corsage*.

Seven other novels, two uncollected stories, and a posthumous collection of early crime stories complete the Stout canon. Three novels feature a private investigator named Tecumseh Fox, another eccentric, but in a less spectacular mode than Nero Wolfe; and three others feature recurring detectives: Dol Bonner, Alphabet Hicks, and Inspector Fergus Cramer, who also contributes richly to the Wolfe series. Miss Bonner encounters Fox in *Bad for Business* and Wolfe in 'Too Many Detectives' from *Three for the Chair*; and Alphabet Hicks recurs in the uncollected story 'His Own Hand'. *Mountain Cat* and the other uncollected story, 'Tough Cop's Gift', do not contain series characters. *Red Threads*, the Cramer novel, and *Bad for Business*, the second Fox novel, first appeared in mixed collections in the USA. The Rex Stout Bibliography lists separate editions of *Red Threads* from OUP in Toronto in 1939 and Collins Crime Club in 1941. *Bad for Business* was published separately by the Crime Club in 1945.

The posthumous collection, *Justice Ends at Home*, contains sixteen stories assembled by John McAleer from the author's early magazine fiction. *Corsage* was published by James Rock in 1977 in a limited edition of 1,750 copies, of which 250 were hardbacks. It was edited with a preface by Michael Bourne, and has a frontispiece by Marvin Morrison and illustrations by Sid Wright. It includes the previously uncollected novella *Bitter End*, adapted from the Fox novel *Bad for Business*, together with *Why Nero Wolfe Likes Orchids*, attributed to Archie Goodwin, and a Rex Stout interview and checklist. *Death Times Three* is a Bantam paperback containing *Bitter End* and two previously uncollected novellas, *Frame-up for Murder* and *Assault on a Brownstone*. The latter is a variation on *Counterfeit for Murder*, collected in *Homicide Trinity*, with a substantially different plot development. The former is an expanded version of *Murder is no Joke*, from *And Four to Go*, and is not included in John McAleer's tally of forty for the Wolfe novellas. The book has an introduction by McAleer.

Six titles were changed for British publication. The three posthumous volumes have not been published in Britain; nor has *Not Quite Dead Enough*, which, according to *CC*, was first published as a Dell paperback, in advance of the Farrar hardback in the same year. (John McAleer, however, does not accept this and the published list of Dell paperbacks for the relevant period does not include an edition of this book preceding the hardback.)

There are eleven omnibus volumes, which are not important, since they contain no new material. *Triple Zeck*, however, does bring together the three novels in which Wolfe is in conflict with a powerful criminal called Arnold Zeck: *And Be a Villain*, *The Second Confession*, and *In the Best Families*. It was published by Viking in 1974. *The President Vanishes* is sometimes included among Rex Stout's crime fiction, but it was classified as a mainstream novel by his publishers. It was issued anonymously by Farrar & Rinehart in September 1934, shortly before *Fer-de-Lance*, and has been described as a fusion of thriller and pacifist propaganda.

Rex Stout's American first editions are fully described by John McAleer and others in *Rex Stout: an annotated primary and secondary bibliography* (Garland 1980) and also by Otto Penzler in *TAD*, Summer and Fall 1990 and Winter 1991. The latter also illustrates most of the dust-wrappers.

In his long career Stout had two publishers only in the USA and two only in Britain: Farrar & Rinehart and Viking, and Cassell and Collins Crime Club. He stayed with Farrar until the end of the war, but left Cassell after only four books. They published *Fer-de-Lance* in February 1935, four months after its American publication. It is a black book, lettered in mauve on the spine, which is also ruled at the top and the bottom, like Bush and Wentworth titles of this era. The subtitle – 'a Nero Wolfe mystery' – confirms that a new series is getting under way. *The League of Frightened Men* also came out in 1935, in the same format, though in different colours: dark-green binding and lettering and ruling in orange. *The Rubber Band* has the same colours but the spine is not ruled, and *The Red Box* is red with ornate yellow lettering on the spine. All four books are dated and have the printer's code on the reverse of the title-page.

The British edition of the next book in the sequence was delayed for two years (and underwent a title-change when it did finally appear – from *Crime on Her Hands* to *The Hand in the Glove*). *Too Many Cooks*, its immediate successor, became the first of the Crime Club series, published in September 1938. The earlier Crime Club books have orange bindings, which gave way to redder shades in the post-war sequence. *Trio for Blunt Instruments*, *A Right to Die*, and *The Doorbell Rang* have two-colour bindings, with a larger section of red seamed with black on each cover, divided vertically from the spine and its adjacent areas, which are clear red. *Death of a Doxy* is entirely red threaded with black. From *Too Many Cooks* to *Where There's a Will*, the books are thicker and have advertisement sections at the back. The entire series to *The Mother Hunt* has black spine lettering, and from *Trio for Blunt Instruments* is lettered gilt. The

final run from *The Father Hunt* is taller than the rest. All the books are dated, *Three for the Chair* and *If Death Ever Slept* on the title-page, unusually for this house, which tends to date its books only with the copyright notice. According to the Stout Bibliography, the British first edition of *More Deaths than One* is a White Circle paperback published in 1948, the year preceding the hardback. This claim is otherwise unconfirmed. The US edition of *Where There's a Will* includes six of Sara Dunn's snapshots, reproduced at the point where they feature in the narrative, but these are not present in the Collins edition. British collectors may find the photos in the Stacey reissue of 1971.

Justice Ends at Home is a Viking book with a two-colour binding. The larger vertical areas are grey, and the spine areas black. The title appears in silver lettering and the author and publisher in mauve, on the spine only. *Death Times Three* is a Bantam paperback dated December 1985. The cover shows a knife piercing a pile of hundred-dollar bills.

The wrapper of *Fer-de-Lance* shows an opulent pink orchid with a silhouette of Nero Wolfe. *Too Many Cooks* features a group of chefs, of whom the foremost holds a tray with a knife on it. *Some Buried Caesar* has a plain brown wrapper with a small head of the bull Caesar, repeated on the spine. Thompson's design for *Red Threads* shows the killer's gloves with a single strand of red thread. *Black Orchids* has a spray of black orchids with a medicine bottle and spoon. *Bad for Business* presents a crudely drawn urban scene in falling rain and *The Silent Speaker* has Pollack's portrait of a tough-looking man with the monkey wrench that killed Cheney Boone. *Too Many Women* shows a man and woman in a classic pre-pick-up situation, he lighting up, she with her legs crossed. *More Deaths Than One* has a city scene with a concentration of lighted skyscrapers. *Trouble in Triplicate* also has skyscrapers, with three sinister figures advancing towards them. *Murder By the Book* shows Leonard Dykes going to his death in the East River. *Out Goes She* has Priscilla Eades with the hands and cord that strangled her.

William Randell took over Rex Stout's Crime

Club wrappers in the 1950s and John Rose and Kenneth Farnhill in the 1960s. Randell twice provided portraits of Nero Wolfe, with Archie for *The Black Mountain*, on his own, full-length, for *Crime and Again*. Otherwise his most striking design is that for *If Death Ever Slept*, which shows Mrs Wyman Jarrell, with a snake coiling round her. John Rose signed the wrapper for *The Mother Hunt* and looks also to have provided those for *Gambit* and *Trio for Blunt Instruments* and the skeletal hand at the typewriter for *The Final Deduction*. Kenneth Farnhill provided the designs for *A Right to Die, Death of a Doxy* and *Death of a Dude*. All three are characteristically stylish and individual. Margaret Murray's photograph for *A Family Affair* is notable for the view it affords of Nero Wolfe's right hand, handcuffed to a policeman, holding an orchid, and with a gold ring on the little finger.

Novels

(with Wolfe and Goodwin, except as stated)

Fer-de-Lance Farrar & Rinehart Oct. 1934, Cassell Feb. 1935
a.k.a. *Meet Nero Wolfe* Mercury n.d. (abridged)
The League of Frightened Men Farrar Aug. 1935, Cassell Nov. 1935
The Rubber Band Farrar Apr. 1936, Cassell July 1936
a.k.a. *To Kill Again* Hillman-Curl 1960
The Red Box Farrar Apr. 1937, Cassell Aug. 1937
The Hand in the Glove Farrar Sept. 1937, Hogarth 1984 (Bonner)
a.k.a. *Crime on Her Hands* Collins Crime Club Dec. 1939
Too Many Cooks Farrar Aug. 1938, Crime Club Sept. 1938
Some Buried Caesar Farrar Feb. 1939, Crime Club July 1939
a.k.a. *The Red Bull* Dell 1945
Mountain Cat Farrar July 1939, Crime Club Mar. 1940 (not Wolfe)
a.k.a. *The Mountain Cat Murders* Pyramid 1971
Double for Death Farrar Oct. 1939, Crime Club July 1940 (Fox)

Red Threads Farrar Dec. 1939 in *The Mystery Book*, Crime Club July 1941 (Cramer)
Over My Dead Body Farrar 1939 (Jan. 1940), Crime Club Oct. 1940
Where There's a Will Farrar June 1940, Crime Club Mar. 1941
Bad for Business Farrar Nov. 1940 in *The Second Mystery Book*, Crime Club July 1945 (Fox, Bonner)
The Broken Vase Farrar Jan. 1941, Crime Club Mar. 1942 (Fox)
Alphabet Hicks Farrar Dec. 1941, Crime Club Sept. 1942 (Hicks)
a.k.a. *The Sound of Murder* Pyramid 1965
The Silent Speaker Viking Oct. 1946, Crime Club Mar. 1947
Too Many Women Viking Oct. 1947, Crime Club Apr. 1948
And Be a Villain Viking Sept. 1948, Panther 1964
a.k.a. *More Deaths than One* Crime Club Feb. 1949
The Second Confession Viking Sept. 1949, Crime Club Apr. 1950
In the Best Families Viking Sept. 1950
a.k.a. *Even in the Best Families* Crime Club Apr. 1951
Murder By the Book Viking Oct. 1951, Crime Club Apr. 1952
Prisoner's Base Viking Oct. 1952
a.k.a. *Out Goes She* Crime Club June 1953
The Golden Spiders Viking Oct. 1953, Crime Club May 1954
The Black Mountain Viking Oct. 1954, Crime Club Aug. 1955
Before Midnight Viking Oct. 1955, Crime Club May 1956
Might as Well Be Dead Viking Oct. 1956, Crime Club Aug. 1957
If Death Ever Slept Viking Oct. 1957, Crime Club Sept. 1958
Champagne for One Viking Nov. 1958, Crime Club Sept. 1959
Plot it Yourself Viking Oct. 1959
a.k.a. *Murder in Style* Crime Club Aug. 1960
Too Many Clients Viking Oct. 1960, Crime Club Aug. 1961
The Final Deduction Viking Oct. 1961, Crime Club Apr. 1962

Gambit Viking Oct 1962, Crime Club Apr. 1963

The Mother Hunt Viking July 1963, Crime Club Jan. 1964

A Right to Die Viking Oct. 1964, Crime Club Apr. 1965

The Doorbell Rang Viking Oct. 1965, Crime Club Jan. 1966

Death of a Doxy Viking Aug 1966, Crime Club June 1967

The Father Hunt Viking May 1968, Crime Club Mar. 1969

Death of a Dude Viking Aug. 1969, Crime Club Apr. 1970

Please Pass the Guilt Viking Sept. 1973, Crime Club Apr. 1974

A Family Affair Viking May 1975, Crime Club June 1976

Wolfe novella collections

(with three novellas, except as stated)

Black Orchids Farrar & Rinehart May 1942, Crime Club July 1943 (2 novellas)

Not Quite Dead Enough Farrar Sept. 1944 (2 novellas)

Trouble in Triplicate Viking Feb. 1949, Crime Club Aug. 1949

Three Doors to Death Viking Apr. 1950, Crime Club Sept. 1950

Curtains for Three Viking Feb. 1951, Crime Club Oct. 1951

Door to Death Dell 1951 (novella)

Triple Jeopardy Viking Mar. 1952, Crime Club Oct. 1952

Three Men Out Viking Mar. 1954, Crime Club Jan. 1955

Three Witnesses Viking Mar. 1956, Crime Club Oct. 1956

Three for the Chair Viking May 1957, Crime Club Apr. 1958 (also with Bonner)

And Four to Go Viking Feb. 1958 (4 novellas) a.k.a. *Crime and Again* Crime Club May 1959

Three at Wolfe's Door Viking Apr. 1960, Crime Club Jan. 1961

Homicide Trinity Viking Apr. 1962, Crime Club Feb. 1963

Trio for Blunt Instruments Viking Apr. 1964, Crime Club Jan. 1965

Death Times Three Bantam 1985

Story collection

Justice Ends at Home Viking 1977 (16 stories)

Miscellany

Corsage Rock 1977 (includes 'Bitter End')

Uncollected stories

'His Own Hand' (*Manhunt*, Apr. 1955; *Eat, Drink and Be Buried*, Viking 1956/*For Tomorrow We Die*, Macdonald 1958, as 'By His Own Hand'; *EQMM*, May 1964 and *Ellery Queen's Twentieth Century Detective Stories*, World 1964, as 'Curtain Line') (Hicks)

'Tough Cop's Gift' (*What's New* (Christmas Annual, Abbott Laboratories), Dec. 1953; *Butcher Baker, Murder-maker*, Knopf 1954, Macdonald 1956, and *Cream of the Crime*, Holt 1962, Harrap 1964, as 'Cop's Gift'; *EQMM*, Jan. 1956, as 'Santa Claus Beat'; *Saint*, Aug. 1959 (US), as 'Nobody Deserved Justice'; *Scholastic Scope*, 1978, as 'Christmas Beat')   *BP*

Julian Symons (b. 1912)

Julian Symons has to date written twenty-seven novels and fifty-four stories spread over four collections. There are also many uncollected stories, seventy of which can be identified, and there is one separately published story, *Did Sherlock Holmes Meet Hercule...? The Great Detectives* contains seven original investigations of such important figures as Sherlock Holmes, Miss Marple, and Ellery Queen. Symons is one of the masters of the genre and has written some outstanding crime novels, like *The Man Who Killed Himself.* He has also written detective novels, like his first three books, which chronicle the investigations of Inspector Bland. His other series characters are the highly efficient private detective Francis Quarles and the actor Sheridan Haynes. Quarles, whose past is as inscrutable as the Orient in which he is rumoured to have spent part of his youth, appears in thirty-seven collected stories and fifty-one of the known uncollected ones. Sheridan Haynes is an actor who features in two Sherlockian novels and one story.

With two exceptions the British editions are the true firsts, and they are all dated. Three books have not appeared in the USA: *A Man Called Jones* and two paperback collections of stories, *Murder! Murder!* and *Francis Quarles Investigates.* Some books have alternative US titles, including *The Paper Chase* and *The Gigantic Shadow.* The first six books were published by Gollancz: the first two in blue cloth with gilt spine lettering, the next two in red cloth with black spine lettering, and the last two in red cloth with gilt spine lettering. All six were issued in the usual yellow dust-wrappers. The fifteen novels that followed were all published by Col-

lins Crime Club, generally in red cloth; but *The Man Whose Dreams Came True* is blue and *A Three-pipe Problem* is black. The first five Collins books have black lettering on the spine and the remaining ten have gilt. George Coral's designs for *The Man Who Killed HImself* and *The Man Whose Dreams Came True* are especially notable. The six most recent books have been published by Macmillan in bindings of various colours. The first and second have silver lettering, the next three gilt and the latest black. *Did Sherlock Holmes Meet Hercule...* ? was published in the USA in 1988 by the Yellow Barn Press and limited to two hundred copies. The book has a red cloth spine with grey and white patterned boards and was issued without a wrapper. There are five wood engravings by John de Pol, who also designed the pattern on the boards. The story appeared in *The Illustrated London News* for Apr. 1987 as 'Sherlock Holmes and the Poirot Connexion' and was reprinted in *EQMM* for mid-Dec. 1987 with the new title.

'Sherlock's Christmas', a competition story with Sheridan Haynes, appeared in three issues of *Punch* in Dec. 1990. Once published, it was forgotten: no solution or list of winners appeared.

Somebody Else (Eurographica 1990) reprints four stories from *The Tigers of Subtopia.*

The first three story collections are paperback first editions and hence very difficult to find in fine condition. The most elusive first edition seems to be *The Narrowing Circle.*

Bloody Murder (Faber 1972) is a history of mystery fiction 'from the detective story to the crime novel'.

Novels

(with Bland or Haynes, as stated. Details of bindings refer to British editions.)

The Immaterial Murder Case Gollancz 1945, Macmillan 1957 (Bland)
A Man Called Jones Gollancz 1947 (Bland)
Bland Beginning Gollancz 1949, Harper 1949 (Bland)

281

The Thirty-First of February Gollancz 1950, Harper 1951

The Broken Penny Gollancz 1953, Harper 1953

The Narrowing Circle Gollancz 1954, Harper 1955

The Paper Chase Collins Crime Club 1956

a.k.a. *Bogue's Fortune* Harper 1957

The Colour of Murder Crime Club 1957, Harper 1958

The Gigantic Shadow Crime Club 1958

a.k.a. *The Pipe Dream* Harper 1959

The Progress of a Crime Crime Club 1960, Harper 1960

The Killing of Francie Lake Crime Club 1962

a.k.a. *The Plain Man* Harper 1962

The End of Solomon Grundy Crime Club 1964, Harper 1964

The Belting Inheritance Crime Club 1965, Harper 1965

The Man Who Killed Himself Crime Club 1967, Harper 1967

The Man Whose Dreams Came True Crime Club 1968, Harper 1969

The Man Who Lost His Wife Crime Club 1970, Harper 1971

The Players and the Game Crime Club 1972, Harper 1972

The Plot Against Roger Rider Crime Club 1973, Harper 1973

A Three-pipe Problem Crime Club 1975, Harper 1975 (Haynes)

The Blackheath Poisonings Crime Club 1978, Harper 1978

Sweet Adelaide Crime Club 1980, Harper 1980

The Detling Murders Macmillan 1982 (grey binding)

a.k.a. *The Detling Secret* Viking 1983

The Name of Annabel Lee Macmillan 1983, Viking 1983 (blue)

The Criminal Comedy of the Contented Couple Macmillan 1985 (black)

a.k.a. *A Criminal Comedy* Viking 1986

The Kentish Manor Murders Macmillan 1988, Viking 1988 (tan) (Haynes)

Death's Darkest Face Macmillan 1990, Viking 1990 (maroon)

Something Like a Love Affair Macmillan 1992, Mysterious Press 1993 (cream)

Separately published story

Did Sherlock Holmes Meet Hercule . . .? Yellow Barn Press 1988

Story collections

Murder! Murder! Fontana 1961 (21 Quarles stories)

Francis Quarles Investigates Panther 1965 (15 Quarles stories)

How to Trap a Crook Davis 1977 (13 stories, 4 with Quarles)

The Great Detectives Orbis 1981, Abrams 1981 (7 'Investigations')

The Tigers of Subtopia Macmillan 1982, Viking 1983 (11 stories) (maroon binding)

Uncollected stories with Quarles

'Affection Unlimited' (*ES*, 10 July 1950)

'Mrs. Rolleston's Diamonds' (*ES*, 10 Aug. 1950)

'A Cup of Tea' (*ES*, 12 Sept. 1950)

'Happy Hexing' (*ES*, 19 Sept. 1950)

'The Desk' (*ES*, 29 Sept. 1950; *The Evening Standard Detective Book*, series 2, Gollancz 1951)

'Who Killed Harrington?' (*ES*, 28 Nov. 1950)

'Death in the Scillies' (*ES*, 13 Mar.1951; *EQMM*, Mar. 1954, as 'Life and Death in the Scillies')

'Ghost from the Past' (*ES*, 1 Oct. 1951)

'The Pepoli Case' (*ES*, 2 Feb. 1952)

'The Clue in the Book' (*ES*, 5 May 1952)

'Red Rum Means Murder' (*ES*, 15 May 1952)

'The Whistling Man' (*ES*, 9 July 1952)

'The Vanishing Trick' (*ES*, 28 July 1952)

'An Exercise in Logic' (*ES*, 8 Sept. 1952)

'Poison Pen' (*ES*, 15 Sept. 1952)

'Preserving the Evidence' (*ES*, 18 Sept. 1952; *John Creasey's Mystery Bedside Book 1970*, Hodder & Stoughton 1969)

'Nothing Up His Sleeve' (*ES*, 23 Sept. 1952)

'Double Double Cross' (*ES*, 25 Sept. 1952)

'Death for Mr. Golightly' (*ES*, 22 Dec. 1952)

'The Duke of York' (*ES*, 27 Jan. 1953)

'The Conjuring Trick' (*ES*, 28 Jan. 1953)

'No Deception' (*ES*, 29 Jan. 1953)

'The Link' (*ES*, 30 Jan. 1953; *JCMM*, Aug. 1957)

'A Man with Blue Hair' (*ES*, 31 Jan. 1953)

'The Swedish Nightingale' (*ES*, 14 Sept. 1953)

'The Two Suitors' (*ES*, 15 Sept. 1953)

'Tattoo' (*ES*, 16 Sept. 1953)

'The Collector' (*ES*, 18 Sept. 1953)

'Jack and Jill' (*ES*, 19 Sept. 1953)

'Iced Champagne' (*ES*, 19 Oct. 1953)

'Ten Thousand Dollars a Dance' (*Nero Wolfe Mystery Magazine*, Mar. 1954)

'The Barton Hall Dwarf' (*ES*, 16 Aug. 1954)

'Little Boy Blue' (*ES*, 20 Aug. 1954)

'Summer Show' (*ES*, 21 Aug. 1954; *Saint*, Nov. 1957 (UK))

'A Present from Santa Claus' (*ES*, 24 Dec. 1954)

'Murder Too Perfect' (*ES*, 19 July 1955)

'Death of an M.P.' (*ES*, 29 Aug. 1955)

'Dial 999' (*ES*, 30 Aug. 1955)

'The Claimant' (*ES*, 31 Aug. 1955)

'Mr. Longden Had a Diary' (*ES*, 1 Sept. 1955)

'The Briefcase' (*ES*, 2 Sept. 1955)

'Final Night Extra' (*ES*, 3 Sept. 1955)

'Airborne with a Borgia' (*ES*, 28 Sept. 1955)

'Murder – But How Was It Done?' (*ES*, 29 Oct. 1956)

'Party Line' (*ES*, 30 Oct. 1956)

'The Second Bullet' (*ES*, 31 Oct. 1956)

'Murder in Reverse' (*ES*, 2 Nov. 1956)

'Ancestor Worship' (*ES*, 3 Nov. 1956)

'No Use Turning a Deaf Ear to Murder' (*ES*, 1 June 1964)

'Art-loving Mr. Lister Lands a Fake . . .' (*ES*, 13 Mar. 1963; *Saint*, June 1964 (UK), as 'A Taste for Art')

'The Impossible Theft' (*EQMM*, Jan. 1966)

Other uncollected stories

'The Accident' (*ES*, 17 Sept. 1953; *With Malice Toward All*, Putnam 1968, Macmillan 1969)

'The Crime of Mr. Bonny' (*ES*, 15 May 1954)

'The Cupboard Was Bare' (*ES*, 6 July 1955)

'The What's My Line Murder' (*ES*, 27 Feb. – 8 Mar. 1956, in 10 parts)

'James Mason Investigates' (*ES*, 18–27 Mar. 1957, in 8 parts)

'Cup Final Kidnap' (*ES*, 28 Apr. – 3 May 1958, in 6 parts)

'Murder on Tour' (*ES*, 25 July – 3 Aug. 1960, in 9 parts; *Some Like Them Dead*, Hodder 1960,

as 'The Summer Holiday Murders'; *EQMM*, Apr. 1967, as 'The Crimson Coach Murders')

'Father Christmas Comes to Orbins' (*Illustrated London News*, 7 Nov. 1963, Christmas number)

'Castle in Spain' (*Crimes Across the Sea*, Harper 1964, Harrap 1965)

'Waiting for Mr. McGregor' (*Verdict of Thirteen*, Faber 1979, Harper 1979)

'The Dream Is Better' (*EQMM*, Aug. 1982; *Winter's Crimes 14*, Macmillan 1982)

'The Birthmark' (*Winter's Crimes 17*, Macmillan 1985; *EQMM*, mid-Dec. 1985)

'Has Anybody Seen Me?' (*EQMM*, Sept. 1987; *Winter's Crimes 19*, Macmillan 1987, as 'Has Anybody Here Seen Me?')

'The Borgia Heirloom; (*EQMM*, Nov. 1987)

'The Affair of the Vanishing Diamonds' (*Daily Mail*, 24 Dec. 1987)

'I, Too, Lived in Arcadia' (*EQMM*, Sept. 1989;

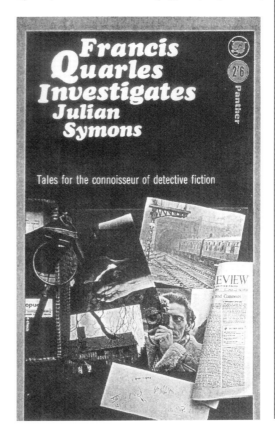

Winter's Crimes 21, Macmillan 1989 as 'Et in
   Arcadia Ego')
'The Conjuring Trick' (*EQMM*, Mar. 1990)
'Holocaust at Mayhem Parva' (*A Classic English
   Crime*, Pavilion 1990)
'Sherlock's Christmas' (*Punch*, 12, 18 Dec.,
   Almanac 1990)   *JC*

Phoebe Atwood Taylor (1909–1976)
a.k.a. Alice Tilton
a.k.a. Freeman Dana

In her twenty years as a writer, Phoebe Atwood
Taylor wrote thirty-one novels under three
names. Most of her work appeared in her own
name, but she also established a secondary reputation as Alice Tilton, and in 1938 she published
a single novel as Freeman Dana. She is one of
the leading exponents of comic crime, a high-
grade formula writer who brought a buoyant
gaiety to the mystery. All her Taylor books are
elaborate whodunits, narrated in a sprightly,
salty style and maintaining a cracking pace. She
is also a devoted regional novelist, with a familiar's fervent affection for the life and customs
of Cape Cod. The Cape and its culture are a
constant, enlivening theme. Her detective is the
unpretentious Asey Mayo, the 'Hayseed Sherlock', who picks his way through each maze with
wily persistence and native wit. He figures in all
twenty-two of the novels, in the six novellas that
make up the other two volumes, and in the two
uncollected novellas.

The Cape Cod Mystery appeared in 1931 from
Bobbs-Merrill, but was not published in Britain.
Nor was *Death Lights a Candle*, which came out
the following year. Both books are dated and
state that they are first editions. Each has endpapers by Charles K. Stevens, showing the terrain
of the narrative. *The Cape Cod Mystery* is blue
and is lettered in green on the spine. The front
cover has title and author stamped in green,
with a framework of green lines enclosing the
author's name. It also has a blind-stamped
border. *Death Lights a Candle* is a green book
lettered gilt. The front cover features title and
author, with the former underlined. On the spine
the title and author are separated by three ruled
lines, the topmost of which is thicker than the

others. In both books Prudence Whitsby is the
narrator.

In 1933 Norton took over the Mayo series,
continuing to publish it until the end of the war,
when *Proof of the Pudding* appeared. Several
of the Norton editions have the same format,
suggesting that the entire run from this publisher
may be uniform. Those known have four horizontal blocks of a single colour laid across the
spine and both covers. The second from the top
is much thicker than the other three and contains the title, showing through in the colour of
the binding (except on the back cover, where it
is blank). On the front cover 'An Asey Mayo
Mystery' also appears within the largest block in
this manner, under the title. On the spine,
'Taylor' and 'Norton' appear in the colour of the
blocks, the one above and the other below (see
checklist for details of titles known). Asey's head
appears on the title-page of *Three Plots for Asey
Mayo*, drawn from the photograph that appears
on the wrappers of certain 1930s titles.

All known Norton editions are dated by their
copyright notice only. In *Firsts*, November 1991,
Katherine Kominis confirms that all the Norton
series have 'First edition' on the copyright page
– and this also applies to Norton's Tilton titles.
(She also gives some account of the later books,
which came from three new publishers: *The Asey
Mayo Trio* from Messner, with no 'statement of
printing'; *Punch with Care* and *The Iron Clew*
from Farrar, Straus, with 'colophon on copyright
page'; and *Diplomatic Corpse* from Little,
Brown, with 'First edition' and 'Published March
1951'.) In 1934 Eyre & Spottiswoode introduced
Asey to Britain with *The Mystery of the Cape
Cod Players*. *The Mystery of the Cape Cod
Tavern* followed in 1935. The former is red and
the latter green: both have black spine lettering
and dated title-pages. *The Mystery of the Cape
Cod Players* has a plan of the cottage at Weesit.
Five books were published by Gollancz between
1935 and 1937, in a different order from their
American editions. All except *The Crimson
Patch* are known to have the black bindings and
orange spine lettering standard for Gollancz at
this time. *The Crimson Patch* is known only from
the BL copy, which is mauve with dark-blue
lettering. *Sandbar Sinister* also exists in a mauve

binding, with black lettering. All the Gollancz books are dated. From *Octagon House* in March 1938 to her final novel in 1951, Phoebe Atwood Taylor was published by Collins Crime Club. Again the first book appeared out of sequence: *Figure Away* predated it in America. All the Crime Club books are orange with black spine lettering, and are dated. The earlier books are thicker, with advertisement sections at the back. From *The Six Iron Spiders* they are thinner, with no advertisement sections. A purple variant of *The Asey Mayo Trio* is known.

Two volumes contain three each of the author's novellas: *Three Plots for Asey Mayo* and *The Asey Mayo Trio*. The former appeared after *The Six Iron Spiders* and remains unpublished in Britain. *The Swan-boat Plot* is available to British readers in the MWA anthology *Murder Calvalcade* (Hammond 1953) (as *The Swan-boat Murder*).

The wrapper of *The Mystery of the Cape Cod Tavern* shows Asey in front of Prence's Tavern with Cape Cod beyond. The author's middle name is misspelt on the spine. *Figure Away* has three elegant male dummies strung up on a wooden frame. *Spring Harrowing* has an orange wrapper with a black drawing of a man on a motor-bike being pursued by a car along a winding country road. *Criminal C.O.D.* has a plain red wrapper with a puff from Dorothy L. Sayers. *The Perennial Boarder* shows a man with a lighted triple candelabrum and an alarmed expression. *The Six Iron Spiders* has the eponymous frying pans caught in a spider's web. The design for *The Asey Mayo Trio* illustrates *Murder Rides the Gale* and centres on Jinx Granville dashing out into the storm with Asey in hot pursuit. *Punch with Care* shows the warning notice by the mud meadow that figures in the novel, and *Diplomatic Corpse* has an animated scene in the Quanomet graveyard. The Norton wrappers focus on scenes and objects from the narratives: *Figure Away* on three wooden figures, two female, one male, with other items from an antique shop; *The Annulet of Gilt* on the annulet and a blue elephant; *Spring Harrowing* on a signboard with a skull beside it; *The Perennial Boarder* on an overturned rocking-chair; *The Deadly Sunshade* on the opened sunshade; and

Going, Going, Gone on an auction room with its trappings.

The eight Tilton novels feature Leonidas Witherall, a teacher and sensational novelist, with a close resemblance to Shakespeare. Alice Tilton was promoted as 'the detective writer with the Wodehouse touch', and her books lean more towards farce. The series is properly deft and inventive, as this exacting mode demands. They were all published in Britain by the Crime Club, with orange bindings and black spine lettering. The entire series is dated. *The Hollow Chest* is the first of the slimmer wartime books, with no advertisement sections. There is one British title-change. Norton was the American publisher throughout but did not issue *Beginning with a Bash* until 1972, as part of a uniform set. The Norton edition of *The Hollow Chest* is a grey book elegantly decorated with purple bands of colour running up the spine and across the front cover. The lettering is also purple and includes 'A Leonidas Witherall Mystery' framing a tiny head of the detective. The wrapper has a much larger portrait of Witherall, in top hat and tails, clutching the troublesome chest and wielding a makeshift weapon. The British edition also has a portrait of Witherall in formal dress, again with the chest but also with the horse George.

The yellow wrapper for *Beginning with a Bash* shows a hand wielding a hammer, both on the spine and the front panel. *The Cut Direct* puts six bats to flight across a full moon and *The Left Leg* matches a trousered right leg with sock and shoe with an empty left leg. *The Iron Hand* has Leonidas trudging through snow with a violin case in his left hand and a package under his right arm. *Dead Ernest* shows Matt and Shorty in transit, with the deep freeze harbouring the body of Ernest Finger.

The single Freeman Dana book is *Murder at the New York World's Fair*, published by Random House in 1938. It is bound in segments of orange and blue, with the orange on top: it seems these are the colours not only of the Fair but of New York State. Title and author are shown in blue lettering on the spine; and on the front cover the publisher's initials occur, together with an impression of the Fair, also in blue on the orange background. The lower blue segment is blank on both spine and covers. The World Fair motif recurs on the title-page and the book is copyrighted 1938. The wrapper also has the Fair motif with a plane leaving a trail of smoke that runs into the tail-end of the title. Ellen Nehr first attributed this book to Phoebe Attwood Taylor and later established that only nine hundred copies were printed.

'The Riddle of Volume Four' is an early version of *Beginning with a Bash*, published in *Mystery League* as by Phoebe Atwood Taylor. Two Asey Mayo novellas remain uncollected: both appeared originally in *American Magazine* in the 1940s and are anthologized in Jon and Rita Breen's *American Murders* (Garland 1986).

Mayo novels by Phoebe Atwood Taylor

(Binding colours refer to Norton editions.)

The Cape Cod Mystery   Bobbs-Merrill 1931
Death Lights a Candle   Bobbs 1932
The Mystery of the Cape Cod Players   Norton 1933, Eyre & Spottiswoode 1934
The Mystery of the Cape Cod Tavern   Norton 1934, Eyre 1935
Sandbar Sinister   Norton 1934, Gollancz Feb. 1936
The Tinkling Symbol   Norton 1935, Gollancz Sep. 1935
Deathblow Hill   Norton 1935, Gollancz Oct. 1936
The Crimson Patch   Norton 1936, Gollancz June 1936
Out of Order   Norton 1936, Gollancz 1937 (black, white)
Figure Away   Norton 1937, Collins Crime Club July 1938 (dark blue, yellow)
Octagon House   Norton 1937, Crime Club March 1938
The Annulet of Gilt   Norton 1938, Crime Club Feb. 1939 (grey, red)
Banbury Bog   Norton 1938, Crime Club June 1939 (maroon, blue)
Spring Harrowing   Norton 1939, Crime Club Oct. 1939 (green, purple)
The Criminal C.O.D.   Norton 1940
a.k.a. *Criminal C.O.D.*   Crime Club 1940

The Deadly Sunshade   Norton 1940, Crime Club 1941 (red, black)
The Perennial Boarder   Norton 1941, Crime Club 1942
The Six Iron Spiders   Norton 1942, Crime Club 1943
Going, Going, Gone!   Norton 1943, Crime Club 1944
Proof of the Pudding   Norton 1945, Crime Club 1945
Punch with Care   Farrar Straus 1946, Crime Club 1947
Diplomatic Corpse,   Little, Brown 1951, Crime Club 1951

Mayo novella collections by Phoebe Atwood Taylor

Three Plots for Asey Mayo   Norton 1942 (3 novellas) (black, yellow)
The Asey Mayo Trio   Messner 1946, Crime Club 1946 (3 novellas)

Witherall novels by Alice Tilton

Beginning with a Bash   Crime Club 1937, Norton 1972
The Cut Direct   Norton 1938, Crime Club 1938
Cold Steal   Norton 1939, Crime Club 1940
The Left Leg   Norton 1940, Crime Club 1941
The Hollow Chest   Norton 1941, Crime Club 1942
File for Record   Norton 1943, Crime Club 1944
Dead Ernest   Norton 1944, Crime Club 1945
The Iron Clew   Farrar Straus 1947
a.k.a. *The Iron Hand*   Crime Club 1947

Novel by Freeman Dana

Murder at the New York World's Fair   Random House 1938

Uncollected novellas by Phoebe Atwood Taylor

The Disappearing Hermit (*American Magazine*, Apr. 1946)
Deadly Festival (*American Magazine*, Mar. 1948) (both also in *American Murders*, Garland 1986)

BP

PHOEBE ATWOOD TAYLOR

SPRING HARROWING

Josephine Tey (1897–1952)
a.k.a. Gordon Daviot

Elizabeth Mackintosh was a novelist and dramatist whose work appeared only under pseudonyms, in keeping with her very private life. She became famous twice, first as Gordon Daviot, author of *Richard of Bordeaux* and other historical plays, and then as Josephine Tey, a popular mystery writer. Her third pseudonym, Craigie Howe, was used only once, for a modern comedy, *Cornelia*.

Six of her eight crime novels feature Alan Grant, a sophisticated, sensitive policeman, who fights against claustrophobia in his last recorded investigation. He first appears in *The Man in the Queue*, written under the Daviot byline for a competition (which was won by N. A. Temple-Ellis's *The Inconsistent Villains*). The book is brown with black lettering on the spine and, within a border, on the front cover. The half-

title announces it as one of Methuen's Clue Stories, and a gun-and-dagger motif on the front cover further suggests a crime fiction series. Though the book is dated 1929, the printer's code at the end must be 1128 for a true first edition. 129 at this point indicates a later issue.

A Shilling for Candles introduces the Tey pseudonym and absorbs Grant from his Daviot debut. The book, which is yellow, with bold blue lettering on cover and spine, is dated 1936. The remaining six novels were published by Peter Davies, who also reissued *The Man in the Queue* under the Tey pseudonym in 1953. All six Davies books are dated, and all except *The Franchise Affair* have his initials blind-stamped on the rear cover: *The Franchise Affair* has them in white on the spine, over the publisher's name. *Miss Pym Disposes* is a purple book with pink lettering along the spine. The dust-wrapper shows a group of students from the Leys Physical Training College for women. Miss Lucy Pym detects and plays God. Grant is in, but not really of, *The Franchise Affair*, which is more sympathetically investigated by a young solicitor, Robert Blair. The book is red with white lettering and a circular motif on the spine, representing the window in the attic at The Franchise. This window is central to Ray Russell's wrapper design, which shows the cracked pane and the view of the drive from the attic.

Brat Farrar also excludes Grant. The book is brown, with gilt spine lettering; and the wrapper, which spreads over both covers and the spine, shows the picturesque landscape of the novel, very green under a pinkish sky, with Latchetts in the foreground and Clare House prominent across the valley. *To Love and Be Wise* is green, with red lettering, and with the figure of the dancer Serge Ratoff stamped in red on the front cover. The figure of Ratoff is central also to the stylized dustwrapper, which represents him dancing by the light of the moon. The designer's initials are J. E. V.

The Daughter of Time is a red book with black lettering on the spine and a black vignette on the front cover. This is the famous novel in which Grant inquires from a hospital bed into the murder of the Princes in the Tower. The reference in the title is to truth, which Grant brings to light after nearly 500 years. The cover vignette shows two figures descending stairs beneath an arch (perhaps the princes): and they recur on J. E. V.'s blue and yellow wrapper, which is largely taken up by a broad heraldic banner. The endpapers display the family tree of Richard III and his nephews. *The Singing Sands* was published after the author's premature death in 1952. The fawn book has brown lettering, and the wrapper design is an impressionistic swirl of sand, sea, and dark sky, with an unconfirmed look of J. E. V. about it.

Josephine Tey's death was especially cruel, since it occurred at a time when she was entering on a period of personal freedom. For her readers it meant a very great loss, since she had remarkable gifts and might have achieved much more than her time allowed. Each of her eight novels has its memorable features and each represents a departure: no writer wrote less to formula than she. Relatively few detective novels have hidden depths, but Josephine Tey's do.

Grant novel by Gordon Daviot

The Man in the Queue Methuen 1929, Dutton 1929; Davies 1953 as by Josephine Tey
a.k.a. *Killer in the Crowd* Spivak 1954

Novels by Josephine Tey

(with Grant except as stated)

A Shilling for Candles Methuen 1936, Macmillan 1954
Miss Pym Disposes Davies 1946, Macmillan 1948 (not Grant)
The Franchise Affair Davies 1948, Macmillan 1949
Brat Farrar Davies 1949, Macmillan 1950 (not Grant)
a.k.a. *Come and Kill Me* Pocket Books 1951
To Love and Be Wise Davies 1950, Macmillan 1951
The Daughter of Time Davies 1951, Macmillan 1952
The Singing Sands Davies 1952, Macmillan 1953. *BP*

June Thomson (b. 1930)

June Thomson has published seventeen detective novels and thirty-six stories, all collected except one, her first. Twenty-one of the stories are Sherlockian pastiches, collected in three volumes. The quiet, thoughtful, persistent, and perceptive Detective-Inspector Finch appears in all the novels, but in none of the stories. Finch's understanding of country folk helps him to solve rural mysteries set in Essex. He is assisted in all his cases, except *The Long Revenge*, by the burly, deep-voiced Detective-Sergeant Tom Boyce. In the USA Finch was renamed Rudd when the author moved to Doubleday, because this publisher already had an Inspector Finch, in the books of Margaret Erskine.

Two titles, *Not One of Us* and *A Question of Identity*, first appeared in the USA. Others, like *Deadly Relations* have alternative American titles. The British first editions were all published by Constable, in black cloth with silver lettering, except for *Deadly Relations*, which has charcoal grey cloth. From *Alibi in Time*, the books are taller. The whole series is dated.

With one exception, the wrappers up to and including *Deadly Relations* are white, with black and red designs, three by Graham Bishop. Rene Eyre's design for *Deadly Relations* shows the heads of a man, woman, and child enmeshed together by the long blonde hair of the woman, all set against a background of the Essex countryside. Stanislaw Fernandes' design for *The Long Revenge* has a single white rose casting a shadow, when the head of the rose becomes a swastika. The later wrappers are all photographic.

The most difficult first edition to find is *A Question of Identity*.

Finch novels

Not One of Us   Harper 1971, Constable 1972
Death Cap   Constable 1973, Doubleday 1977
The Long Revenge   Constable 1974, Doubleday 1975
Case Closed   Constable 1977, Doubleday 1977
A Question of Identity   Doubleday 1977, Constable 1978
Deadly Relations   Constable 1979
a.k.a. *The Habit of Loving*   Doubleday 1979
Alibi in Time   Constable 1980, Doubleday 1980
Shadow of a Doubt   Constable 1981, Doubleday 1982
To Make a Killing   Constable 1982
a.k.a. *Portrait of Lilith*   Doubleday 1983
Sound Evidence   Constable 1984, Doubleday 1985
A Dying Fall   Constable 1985, Doubleday 1986
The Dark Stream   Constable 1986, Doubleday 1986
No Flowers, By Request   Constable 1987, Doubleday 1987
Rosemary for Remembrance   Constable 1988, Doubleday 1988
The Spoils of Time   Constable 1989, Doubleday 1989
Past Reckoning   Constable 1990, Doubleday 1990

Foul Play   Constable 1991

Story collections

The Secret Files of Sherlock Holmes   Constable 1990 (7 stories)
The Secret Chronicles of Sherlock Holmes   Constable 1992 (7 stories)
Flowers for the Dead   Constable 1992 (14 stories)
The Secret Journals of Sherlock Holmes   Constable 1993 (7 stories)

Uncollected story

'The Girl with the Red-gold Hair' (*The Third Bedside Book of Great Detective Stories*, Barker 1978)   JC

John Trench (b. 1920)

John Trench is less celebrated than he deserves to be, probably because he wrote three detective stories thirty years ago, and then stopped. What makes him permanently interesting is the exceptional quality of his three novels, which still make exhilarating reading. They have zest and wit, and offer puzzles of substance and complexity. All three involve Martin Cotterell, a youthful archaeologist with only one hand. He is erudite and mischievous, and moves about the country from the fells of northern England to the cliffs and caves of Dorset and a beleaguered cathedral city. His last case is particularly distinguished by its 'underlying purpose', to which the blurb draws attention: the author's deep concern adds weight and force to a wholly persuasive narrative.

All three novels were published in Britain by Macdonald and in America by Macmillan. The Macdonald books are black, with yellow lettering and the publisher's dagger on the spine. All three are dated. Broom Lynne provided the wrappers for *Docken Dead* and *Dishonoured Bones*, both in his most felicitous manner. The former records an explosive moment in the siege of Aske Place. The latter is attractively layered and exhibits the subterranean world that is such a feature of the novel, with the body of Lord Garnish near the surface and questionable doings in the labyrinth below. Furtive figures hump a body towards the cathedral at Cunningsbury on the wrapper for *What Rough Beast*. Although this is unattributed, a comparison with *The Crystal Gazers* by Helen Robertson confirms Harry Toothill as the artist.

Cotterell novels

Docken Dead Macdonald 1953, Macmillan 1954

Dishonoured Bones Macdonald 1954, Macmillan 1955

What Rough Beast Macdonald 1957, Macmillan 1957   *BP*

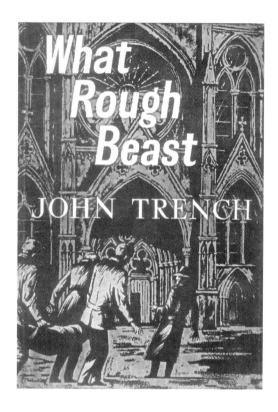

S. S. Van Dine (1888–1939)

S. S. Van Dine was enormously popular between the wars, but tends now to be more lowly regarded. He wrote an imposing series of opulent, doom-laden melodramas, elaborate, intense, and portentous. Their detective is a languid nonpareil known as Philo Vance, whose immeasurable superiority to the rest of mankind is exhaustively demonstrated. Their appeal is almost wholly intellectual, both in the complexity of their challenge to the reader and in the elaborate trappings designed to establish Vance as a dilettante polymath of unmatched erudition. Even in his heyday Vance alienated many readers, but his finest cases continue, nevertheless, to exercise a bizarre fascination. They are monuments of ingenuity and artifice, and some, at least, of their extraordinary power remains.

Twelve Vance novels appeared from Scribner between 1926 and 1939, the last posthumously.

In Britain, three were published by Ernest Benn and the others by Cassell. In general, their titles vary only with the six-letter name of each case, from *The Benson Murder Case* in 1926 to *The Winter Murder Case* in 1939; but *The Gracie Allen Murder Case* disturbs the symmetry in two ways: by having two key words and by having a variant paperback title. It is also lighter in tone than the rest. In Britain, at least, *The Winter Murder Case* has an editor's preface and, as an appendix, Van Dine's 'Twelve Rules for Writing Detective Stories.'

The American first editions have a high degree of uniformity, but this is not true of the British. *The Benson Murder Case* is bound in red ribbed cloth, with black lettering on the spine and a black border on the front cover. *The Canary Murder Case* is yellow, with black spine lettering, and title and author on the front cover, also in black. Each left-hand page of the text is headed with the title, including the word 'Canary' in inverted commas, but it is not so distinguished on the spine, cover, or title-page. *The Greene Murder Case* has the standard Benn binding that was also used for books by J. J. Connington, E. R. Punshon, and others: it is black, with printed orange lettering on the spine and the title in capitals on the front cover. The spine has fringed rules at top and bottom, and the cover a fringed border, in each case with the fringes on the inside. A late Benn reissue of this book has a fine drawing by Abbey of Vance at the bedside of Ada Greene. This has a decidedly 1920s look about it and may perhaps be reproduced from the first edition.

The Cassell books are all blue, with blank front covers and gilt lettering, except for *The Winter Murder Case* which has yellow lettering. *The Kennel Murder Case* and *The Dragon Murder Case* have rules at top and bottom of the spine, to bring them into line with other Cassell books of the time. The others have 'a Philo Vance story' on the spine, in addition to the standard lettering. All twelve books are dated, the Cassell books with the printer's code as well, at the rear for *The Bishop Murder Case* and *The Scarab Murder Case*, on the copyright page for the others. The text of *The Gracie Allen Murder Case* begins on page thirteen, despite there being only eight preliminary pages.

The American series is bound in uniform black, except, again, for *Gracie Allen*, which is yellow. The lettering varies in colour from one title to another, though always in the same style. The books are all dated on the title-page and from *The Scarab Murder Case* must show the letter 'A' on the copyright page, the mark of the true first editions. *The Greene Murder Case* is seen with variant copyright notices for which priority is not established (according to Otto Penzler in *TAD* 15, 4, 1982). In one the copyright is for '1927, 1928' and in the other for '1928' only. Penzler favours the latter. From *The Benson Murder Case* to *The Dragon Murder Case*, the books have maps and plans, some relatively simple, others fascinatingly complex. Most of these are present in both US and UK editions, but the Benn edition of *The Greene Murder Case* lacks the sombre Scribner frontispiece of the Greene mansion by Lowell L. Balcom (or, at least, the BL copy does). *The Bishop Murder Case* has two exquisite fold-out plans, the first a 'three-dimensional' drawing of the archery range and the neighbourhood of Professor Dillard's house, the second a map of the Riverside Drive setting. The fold-out plan for *The Scarab Murder Case* shows the Egyptology museum of Dr Mindrum Bliss on 20th Street, in meticulous detail; and the book also has a message in 'middle kingdom Egyptian' (which Vance, of course, though a little rusty, is able to translate). *The Dragon Murder Case* has a fine view of the Stamm Estate, which looks a little cramped on its single Cassell page (though more happily spread over the endpapers of the Scribner edition).

The Scribner wrappers are largely uniform and feature a file card of the case in the colour of the book's lettering. The wrapper of *The Dragon Murder Case* has the file card only on the rear panel, its front panel being pictorial. *The Casino Murder Case* also has a roulette wheel. Eight of the Scribner wrappers are illustrated in Otto Penzler's article. At least two of the Cassell editions have 'file card' wrappers: *The Kidnap Murder Case* and *The Gracie Allen Murder Case*. The latter also features a small portrait of Gracie

Allen, absent from the US original. *The Garden Murder Case* has three rampant horses with, beneath, a man approaching a long, low building, casting his shadow before him.

S. S. Van Dine also wrote part of *The President's Mystery Story*, a collaborative novel 'propounded' by President Roosevelt and 'solved' also by Rupert Hughes, Samuel Hopkins Adams, Anthony Abbot, Rita Weimann, and John Erskine. His contribution, the fifth of six chapters, brings into the narrative District Attorney Markham from the Vance novels, though not, alas, the great Philo himself. The book has a preface by Fulton Oursler (Anthony Abbot in his true name), explaining its gestation. It also has a frontispiece portrait of the President. The US edition came from Farrar & Rinehart in 1935, the British from the Bodley Head a year later. The latter has a grainy blue-on-white binding, with the title only on a spine decorated with stars and curving lines, all in blue. The book is dated and the publisher is named in blue lettering on the rear cover.

The John Riddell Murder Case is a parodic Van Dine novel, published by Scribner in 1930. Vance and Markham seek to establish which of a succession of real-life writers bored Riddell to death. The copyright notice confirms Corey Ford as the author and the book is wittily illustrated by Covarrubias. Jon L. Breen published three shorter Vance parodies.

Vance novels

(Details of lettering refer to US editions.)

The Benson Murder Case   Scribner 1926, Benn 1926 (orange lettering)

The Canary Murder Case   Scribner 1927, Benn 1927 (green)

The Greene Murder Case   Scribner 1928, Benn 1928 (white)

The Bishop Murder Case   Scribner 1929, Cassell 1929 (blue)

The Scarab Murder Case   Scribner 1930, Cassell 1930 (yellow)

The Kennel Murder Case   Scribner 1933, Cassell 1933 (purple)

The Dragon Murder Case   Scribner 1933, Cassell 1934 (red)

The Casino Murder Case   Scribner 1934, Cassell 1934 (green)

The Garden Murder Case   Scribner 1935, Cassell 1935 (gilt)

The Kidnap Murder Case   Scribner 1936, Cassell 1936 (silver)

The Gracie Allen Murder Case   Scribner 1938, Cassell 1938 (black)

a.k.a. *The Smell of Murder*   Bantam 1950

The Winter Murder Case   Scribner 1939, Cassell 1939 (red)

Collaborative novel

The President's Mystery Story   Farrar & Rinehart 1935, Bodley Head 1936   *BP*

Robert van Gulik (1910–1967)

Robert van Gulik was a diplomat in the Dutch Foreign Service, who became Ambassador Extraordinary in Kuala Lumpur, Malaysia. The first of his sixteen mystery novels was a translation from the Chinese. He also published a collection of eight stories, and one volume of two novellas. Apart from the novel *The Given Day*, all his books and stories feature Judge Dee Jendjieh, who is based on Ti Jen-chieh, a magistrate from the T'ang dynasty. After serving as a magistrate in various cities, Dee becomes President of the Metropolitan Court. He has three wives and several sons, and he is assisted in his investigations by his trusted adviser, Hoong Liang (Sergeant Hoong), and his three lieutenants, Ma Joong, Chiao Tai, and Tao Gan. The novels follow a regular pattern in which three apparently separate cases come before Judge Dee, who, in resolving them, discovers common threads. They also provide a convincing description of life in ancient China.

Several books were first published in Holland and had foreign translations before their first English-language editions. This account is restricted to the first English-language editions, all of which are dated. *The Chinese Bell Murders, The Red Pavilion* and *The Haunted Monastery* have variations in text in their different editions.

Dee Goong An was translated from Chinese into English by van Gulik and privately printed by the Toppan Printing Company in Tokyo. Van Gulik designed the cover, in the form of a woodblock print of nine colours. It shows two bearded Chinamen overseeing the suffering of an apparently naked female, whose hands are trapped by vices. The tan-coloured wrapper is plain, with no printing. There are six illustrations by the author in the book. The edition was limited to 1,200 copies, all signed and numbered by the author, but a few unnumbered copies are known.

The Chinese Maze Murders was published by W. van Hoeve in The Hague and Bandung, Indonesia. It was issued in black cloth, lettered in orange on the spine and front cover. The orange wrapper is printed in black and white, and shows two Chinamen studying a scroll, which is resting on a table. The book has a black wrap-around band with a complimentary testimonial from Agatha Christie printed on it. Michael Joseph published the first London edition six years later.

The following four books, *The Chinese Bell Murders, The Chinese Gold Murders, The Chinese Lake Murders*, and *The Chinese Nail Murders*, were all published in London by Joseph. Cloth colour varies from title to title, but they are all lettered gilt on the spine. *The Chinese Gold Murders* has a salmon pink cloth, but a black cloth variant is known. The author designed the illustrations for the books, as well as the pictorial endpapers. The front panel and spine of each wrapper have one basic colour, printed with a Chinese design in two or three other colours.

The next four titles, *The Red Pavilion, The Haunted Monastery, The Lacquer Screen*, and *The Given Day* are all paperbacks published in editions of 2,000 copies by the Art Printing Works in Kuala Lumpur. The author designed the front covers, which again have a basic colour for the background, with the design in two or three other colours. All except *The Given Day* were published by Heinemann in 1963–4. Dennis McMillan issued a limited American edition of *The Given Day* in 1984.

The remaining eight titles were published in London by Heinemann, all lettered gilt on the spine, but in varying cloth colours. The wrappers again have single-colour backgrounds, with Chinese designs in two or three other colours. The illustrations and pictorial endpapers are again the work of the author. *The Monkey and the Tiger* contains two novellas, *The Morning of the Monkey* and *The Night of the Tiger. Judge Dee at Work* contains eight Dee stories, including 'Murder on New Year's Eve', which was first published as 'New Year's Eve in Lan-Fang', in a limited edition of 200 copies, in Beirut in 1958 (to be given by the author to his friends.) It was issued with ivory-coloured wrappers and lettered on the front cover in brown.

Apart from 'New Year's Eve in Lan-Fang', the most difficult titles for first-edition collectors are *Dee Goong An, The Given Day*, and *The Red Pavilion*.

293

Novels

(with Dee, except as stated)

Dee Goong An Toppan (Tokyo) 1949 (translated by Robert van Gulik)
a.k.a. *Celebrated Cases of Judge Dee* Dover 1976
The Chinese Maze Murders W. van Hoeve (The Hague) 1956
The Chinese Bell Murders Joseph 1958 (maroon binding)
The Chinese Gold Murders Joseph 1959 (salmon-pink)
The Chinese Lake Murders Joseph 1960 (blue)
The Chinese Nail Murders Joseph 1961 (orange)
The Red Pavilion Art Printing Works (Kuala Lumpur) 1961
The Haunted Monastery Art Printing Works 1961

The Lacquer Screen Art Printing Works 1962
The Emperor's Pearl Heinemann 1963 (blue)
The Given Day Art Printing Works 1964 (not Dee)
The Willow Pattern Heinemann 1965 (purple)
The Phantom of the Temple Heinemann 1966 (blue)
Murder in Canton Heinemann 1966 (mauve)
Necklace and Calabash Heinemann 1967 (orange)
Poets and Murder Heinemann 1968 (black)
a.k.a. *The Fox-Magic Murders* Panther 1973

Stories and novellas

(all with Judge Dee)

'New Year's Eve in Lan-Fang' privately published (Beirut) 1958
The Monkey and the Tiger Heinemann 1965 (2 novellas) (dark brown)
Judge Dee at Work Heinemann 1967 (8 stories) (black)   *JC*

Roy Vickers (d. 1965) a.k.a. David Durham a.k.a. Sefton Kyle a.k.a. John Spencer

Roy Vickers was a multifarious crime writer, some of whose stories date from before the First World War. His career as a novelist began in 1922, with *The Mystery of the Scented Death*, the first of over sixty novels in his own name and under three pseudonyms (David Durham, Sefton Kyle, and John Spencer). He has six series detectives, chief of whom is the ubiquitous Inspector Rason (more plausibly two men than one). He appears – or they appear – in both Vickers and Sefton Kyle novels. However, no Vickers novel has established a reputation comparable to that achieved by his stories.

For this reason, collectors' interest centres on the stories, particularly those concerned with the Department of Dead Ends (which happily absorbs everything the other Scotland Yard departments reject). The Dead End stories began to appear in the 1930s, and chart the continuous success of this eccentric department in convicting of their crimes those who are confident of having got away with them. A number of earlier stories are known, including 'The Exploits of Sefton Kyle', published in *Magpie* from 1912 to 1914, and a further series called 'Humbugs, Ltd.', in the *Novel Magazine* in 1914. Credit for unearthing these is due, respectively, to Jack Adrian and Paul McCarthy. However, the work preserved in the Vickers collections is all from the high achievement of his later period.

There are nine collections, including one in the name of David Durham. An additional volume contains two novellas. The Durham collection is *The Exploits of Fidelity Dove*, which appeared from Hodder & Stoughton in 1924, and collects twelve extraordinary stories about 'the smartest crook in London, in the world, in history' (according to Inspector Rason, who tries to bring her to book). This collection was reissued by Newnes in 1935 in the author's true name. The first Dead Ends collection is *The Department of Dead Ends*, a Spivak paperback original, published only in the USA in 1947. No. B91 in the Bestseller Mystery series, it contains seven stories and has an introduction by Ellery Queen. In 1949, Faber issued a hardback *Department of Dead Ends*, with a revised introduction by Ellery Queen and ten stories, seven of which were new; and a third collection with the same title appeared in paperback from Dover in 1978, with an introduction by E. F. Bleiler. This contains thirteen reprinted stories and one new one, 'The Parrot's Beak'.

Five more collections appeared, the last, from Faber, just after the author's death in 1965. *Murder Will Out*, also from Faber, includes nine stories, two of which are reprinted; and *Best Detective Stories of Roy Vickers* contains one new story, 'Murderer's Duty', with nine reprinted items. It also has an introduction by the author. The other three volumes contain new stories only: *Seven Chose Murder* is a Faber book and the other two came from Herbert Jenkins. The novellas are 'The Sole Survivor' and 'The Kynsard Affair', the latter in the manner of the Dead Ends stories. They were published together as part of a DBC compendium in America in 1951, and as a separate volume by Gollancz in 1952.

Forty-three stories by Roy Vickers are collected and twelve by David Durham. Not all the collected Vickers items are Dead Ends stories. Paul McCarthy has established that there are thirty-seven Dead Ends stories and eleven others in a similar vein. Five Dead Ends stories are uncollected. Two other late stories, 'Murder Through the Looking Glass' and 'Murder at Bishops Runt', feature Colonel Crisp (who recurs in a late novel, *Murder of a Snob* (Jenkins 1949))

All Roy Vickers' collections include at least one story that is collected nowhere else. The two reprint anthologies have one each; *The Department of Dead Ends* has two in the US version and two in the UK; *Eight Murders in the Suburbs* has two; *Murder Will Out* has three; *Double Image* has four; and *Seven Chose Murder* has five.

The Spivak *Department of Dead Ends* has blue-green wrappers and a cover by George Salter, decorated with a mask and a gun. It is dated on the copyright page. The Faber *Department of Dead Ends* is a red book, with gilt spine lettering, including three rules above and three below the author's name. *Murder Will Out* is salmon-pink and is lettered gilt on the spine, again with six rules, this time framing the title. An inferior brown binding with black lettering is also known.

The Sole Survivor and the Kynsard Affair is a thin red book with gilt spine lettering. *Eight Murders in the Suburbs* and *Double Image* share the same format: red binding and black spine lettering, with advertisement sections at the back. Each spine also features a black Klan-style mask and the word 'crime'. *Seven Chose Murder* is red with yellow spine lettering, and *Best Detective Stories of Roy Vickers* is blue with silver lettering. All the British collections in Vickers' name are dated.

The Exploits of Fidelity Dove, however, is not dated, and it lacks a printer's code or advertisement section to determine its year. The BL copy is stamped 25 March 1924, which accords with the general view (of which it could, of course, be the source). It is a red book, with black lettering on the spine, and title and author in black on the front cover. The spine also has two blind-stamped rules at the top and bottom, and the front cover has a blind-stamped border. Gordon

Robinson's wrapper shows Fidelity, ready for fencing.

The wrapper for the Faber *Department of Dead Ends* is red, with white and black lettering. The cover photo for the Dover edition shows detectives at work, against a pale yellow background. A later issue has a brown background. *Best Detective Stories of Roy Vickers* features an uncompleted jigsaw of parts of page 11 of the author's introduction. The text is printed in black, and the name of the department in white. The jigsaw background is red.

Meade's bleak wrapper for *Murder Will Out* has Dennis Stretton, gun in hand, looking aghast at the sight of Arthur Crouch's mastiff lying across its master's grave. For *Eight Murders in the Suburbs*, Sax shows a stealthy figure lit by a street lamp as he approaches suburban houses under a mauve sky. *Double Image* has a yellow wrapper with a grey gunman about to enter a doorway. Charles Mozley's macabre wrapper for *Seven Chose Murder* clothes a grey skeleton with lank black hair in a pink hat and dress.

Roy Vickers also published thirty novels in his own name, besides three by David Durham and two by John Spencer later issued as by Vickers. As Sefton Kyle he wrote a further twenty-one novels (excluding *The Hawk*, which was published in the USA as by Vickers). Seven other novels are romances rather than crime novels, despite criminous elements.

Story and novella collections by Roy Vickers

The Department of Dead Ends Spivak 1947 (7 Dead Ends stories)

The Department of Dead Ends Faber 1949 (10 Dead Ends stories)

Murder Will Out Faber 1950 (9 Dead Ends stories)

The Sole Survivor and the Kynsard Affair DBC 1951, Gollancz 1952 (2 novellas)

Eight Murders in the Suburbs Jenkins 1954 (6 Dead Ends stories and 2 others)

Double Image Jenkins 1955, Black 1955 (5 stories)

Seven Chose Murder Faber 1959 (3 Dead Ends stories and 4 others)

Best Detective Stories of Roy Vickers Faber 1965 (9 Dead Ends stories and 1 other)

The Department of Dead Ends Dover 1978 (13 Dead Ends stories and 1 other)

Story collection by David Durham

The Exploits of Fidelity Dove Hodder & Stoughton n.d. (1924); Newnes 1935 as by Roy Vickers (12 stories)

Uncollected stories

(excluding stories written before the 1930s)

'The Starting-handle Murder' (*Pearson's*, Oct. 1934; *Fiction Parade*, Dec. 1935, as 'An Edwardian Gentleman'; *EQMM*, May 1949, as 'Wit's End')

'The Three-foot Grave', (*Pearson's*, Nov. 1934; *Fiction Parade* Jan. 1936; *EQMM*, Oct. 1950, as 'The Impromptu Murder')

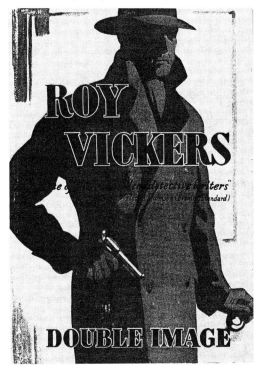

'Dinner for Two' (*EQMM*, Jan. 1949; *MacKill's*, Feb. 1953; *Butcher's Dozen* Heinemann 1956)

'Molly the Marchioness' *Fiction Parade*, Feb. 1936; *EQMM* Oct. 1948, as 'The Man Who Married Too Often')

'The Holborn Murder' (*Fiction Parade*, Apr. 1936; *EQMM*, Feb. 1952, as 'The Pluperfect Murder')

'Murder Through the Looking Glass' (*Mystery Book Magazine*, summer 1948)

'Murder at Bishops Runt' (*Mackill's Choice*, Todd 1953; *The Fifth Mystery Bedside Book*, Hodder 1964)   *BP*

Henry Wade (1887–1969)

Henry Wade was the pseudonym of Sir Henry Aubrey-Fletcher, 6th Baronet, who was at different times High Sheriff and Lord Lieutenant of Buckinghamshire. He wrote twenty crime novels and two collections of stories, besides contributing the chapter 'Bright Thoughts on Tides' to *The Floating Admiral* (see under 'Detection Club').

Seven of Wade's books were not published in the USA. Henry Wade was one of the better writers of the Golden Age. His work is quintessentially English, whether he is writing in the classic form (as in *The Duke of York's Steps*), in the inverted style (as in *Heir Presumptive*), or in the tradition of the police procedural (as in *Bury Him Darkly*). *A Dying Fall* is justly famous for revealing the solution only in the last line. Inspector John Poole serves with great distinction in seven novels and seven of the stories in *Policeman's Lot*. The ambitious young PC John Bragg appears in the thirteen stories collected in *Here Comes the Copper* and in the novel *Released for Death*.

The books were published by Constable and are all dated, but there is no consistency in cloth colours. The four books from *The Verdict of You All* are lettered on the front cover as well as on the spine. *The Verdict of You All* also has a red telephone on the front cover. From *No Friendly Drop*, the books are lettered on the spine only. *No Friendly Drop* and *The Hanging Captain* have their top edges coloured green; those for *Mist on the Saltings* and *Bury Him Darkly* are red and blue, respectively. A helmeted policeman, the same colour as the lettering in each case, features on the cover of the nine books from *The Hanging Captain*, including the two story collections. From *Lonely Magdalen*, the front covers are blank, and from *Be Kind to the Killer*, the spine lettering is silver. Black lettering on a red binding, decorated with black vertical lines, indicates a later issue. A later issue of *Heir Presumptive* is known, in orange cloth with black lettering. It is dated 1935 and has the publisher's name in cursive lettering at the foot of the spine.

Revised editions of *No Friendly Drop* and *Lonely Magdalen* were published in 1932 and 1946, respectively. *The Duke of York's Steps* has two pages of advertisements at the rear. In the first edition the reviews for the two books being advertised were inadvertently reversed, but this was corrected later. Six other books have advertisement sections at the back: *The Missing Partners, The Duke of York's Steps, The Hanging Captain, Policeman's Lot, Mist on the Saltings,* and *Here Comes the Copper.* A later edition of *Constable, Guard Thyself!* has advertisements at the back containing reviews of the book.

Many books contain maps and plans, including folding maps in *Lonely Magdalen, Bury Him Darkly* and *Heir Presumptive*, which also has a folding genealogical table.

Morton Sale's design for the wrapper of *The Duke of York's Steps* shows Leopold Hessel steadying Sir Garth Fratton as he is jostled by a stranger on the steps leading to the Mall. *The Dying Alderman* has two known wrappers, the latter presumably later: one, priced at 7/6d, has mauve question-marks in diagonal rows, separated by alternating rows of black daggers and black pistols; the other, at 3/6d, shows Basil Trant's stabbed body slumped across his desk at Quenborough Town Hall. A scene in the baronial hall at Tassort, with elegant figures in evening dress relaxing over cocktails, illustrates *No Friendly Drop*. Gladys Hynes' wrapper for *Policeman's Lot* has a row of policemen shining their lamps on a skeleton lying at their feet, with a reporter making notes at the feet of the skeleton. Below is a row of criminals carrying various weapons: a knife, a rope, and a bottle of poison. *Constable, Guard Thyself!* shows all the documents in the case laid out, with a heavy pistol laid on top of them, like a paperweight. Part of the Hendel family tree is shown on the wrapper of *Heir Presumptive*, with a skeletal hand pointing at the name Eustace. John Bragg is depicted walking down a street on his beat on *Here Comes the Copper*. *Bury Him Darkly* features a car parked in a lonely lane at night, while a mysterious figure kneels on a hillside. A black-and-white photograph of the lady of the title illustrates *Lonely Magdalen*; and a priest watches a lurking figure in a graveyard on the wrapper of *New Graves at Great Norne*. *Be Kind to the Killer* has the wrists of a policeman and a criminal handcuffed together and *Too Soon to Die* shows the capsized *Tern* on a turquoise sea. The gold and black wrapper of *Gold Was Our Grave* features the prospectus of the San Podino Gold Company. Major John Board's attractive design for *A Dying Fall* shows two jockeys on horseback clearing a jump. *The Litmore Snatch* shows West Way in the rain, with the two schoolboys, Ben and Jack, accepting a lift in a car. Probably the three most difficult Wade titles to find in first edition are *Constable, Guard Thyself!*, *The Duke of York's Steps*, and *Here Comes the Copper*.

Novels

(With Poole or Bragg, as stated. Binding details refer to British editions.)

The Verdict of You All Constable 1926, Payson & Clarke 1927 (blue binding, red lettering)

The Missing Partners Constable 1928, Payson 1928 (fawn, orange)

The Duke of York's Steps Constable 1929, Payson 1929 (light green, black) (Poole)

The Dying Alderman Constable 1930, Brewer & Warren 1930 (blue, red or orange, blue)

No Friendly Drop Constable 1931, Brewer 1932 (dark green, green) (Poole)

The Hanging Captain Constable 1932, Harcourt Brace 1933 (orange, black)

Mist on the Saltings Constable 1933 Harper 1985 (blue, dark blue)

Constable, Guard Thyself! Constable 1934, Houghton 1935 (black, white) (Poole)

Heir Presumptive Constable 1935, Macmillan 1953 (emerald green, blue)

Bury Him Darkly Constable 1936 (dark grey, dark blue) (Poole)

The High Sheriff Constable 1937 (fawn, purple)

Released for Death Constable 1938 (fawn, purple) (Bragg)

Lonely Magdalen Constable 1940 (red, blue) (Poole)

New Graves at Great Norne Constable 1947, Harper 1986 (blue, black)

Diplomat's Folly Constable 1951, Macmillan 1952 (blue, black)

Be Kind to the Killer Constable 1952 (red binding)

Too Soon to Die Constable 1953, Macmillan 1954 (blue) (Poole)

Gold Was Our Grave Constable 1954, Macmillan 1954 (red) (Poole)

A Dying Fall Constable 1955, Macmillan 1955 (red)

The Litmore Snatch Constable 1957, Macmillan 1957 (blue)

Story collections

Policeman's Lot Constable 1933 (black binding, red lettering) (13 stories, 7 with Poole)

Here Comes the Copper Constable 1938 (red, black) (13 Bragg stories)

Collaboration

The Floating Admiral Hodder and Stoughton n.d. (1931), Doubleday 1932   *JC*

R. A. J. Walling   (1869–1949)

R. A. J. Walling's twenty-eight detective novels are firmly rooted in the Golden Age, with a courtly quality long vanished from human affairs. They observe the conventions and exploit the opportunities of the traditional form and are replete with mystery, suspense, cross-purposes and strained relations: in the words of a blurb, 'drama and excitement seethe below the surface'.

Twenty-two of the novels feature Philip Tolefree, a deep, secretive man who broods a lot but also acts decisively, even to the extent of playing God. Benign but tenacious, he sorts out the problems of the well-heeled, though officially an insurance investigator. His police associate is Inspector Pierce, 'a sombre and somewhat sardonic officer', who appears in the second Walling novel, three years before Tolefree's debut. Besides his solo appearance, he features in nine of Tolefree's cases. Another policeman, the vigorous, red-headed Garstang, has two solo investigations and contributes to two of Tolefree's. He, Pierce and Tolefree convene for Walling's last novel. Tolefree's frequent Watson, Mr Farrar, does not appear on his own. *By Hook or Crook* was rewritten for publication in Britain. Two non-series stories are known: more may await discovery.

Walling's bibliography is bedevilled by a high percentage of title-changes and uncertainty in many cases as to whether the UK or the US edition is the earlier. All UK editions are described here and those few US editions known. The evidence suggests that the British editions are the true firsts until early 1932 but that the Americans take precedence thereafter (and the checklist is arranged accordingly). The first book had no American edition, the last no British.

The Strong Room and *The Dinner-Party at Bardolph's* were published by Jarrolds and have the same format. Each spine has a single orange rule between title and author in orange, together with decorative orange bands at either extreme. The front covers have title and author in orange and decorative orange borders, matching the spinal bands. *The Strong Room* also has a masked man within an orange rectangle with rounded corners, down on the right, inside the border. Both books are undated except for advertisement sections at the rear that place them in Spring and Autumn 1927, respectively. *The Strong Room* has a purple binding, *Bardolph's* a black.

Three novels were published by Methuen, two non-series, the third with Garstang. *The Man with the Squeaky Voice* and *The Stroke of One* are blue and red, respectively, and have the same format: black lettering on the spine with double black rules at either end and title and author and a single border all in black on the front cover. They have advertisements at the back and even share a printer's code: 630. *The Stroke of One* has a plan of Dunscombe Church on the front pastedown. *Murder at the Keyhole* is a black book with orange lettering on the spine and double orange rules at either end. The front cover has a black keyhole within a large orange area shaped like a cotton reel. Inside the keyhole are title and author in orange. The fore- and bottom edges are roughly trimmed. All three Methuen books are dated on the copyright page.

The rest of Walling's novels were published by Hodder & Stoughton, who promoted him as 'The Ingenious Mr. R. A. J. Walling'. All but three have blue bindings: *Mr. Tolefree's Reluctant Witnesses* is navy blue, *Dust in the Vault* is dark red and *The Late Unlamented* is maroon. Most of the series have black lettering on the spine but for *Dust in the Vault* it is gilt, for *By Hook or by Crook* it is dark blue and for *The Late Unlamented* it is white. *Mr. Tolefree's Reluctant Witnesses* has all its lettering within a single black border on a yellow panel towards the top of the spine. The four titles from *Dust in the Vault* to *By Hook or by Crook* have theirs within double borders matching the lettering, also within the upper half of the spine. *The Fatal Five Minutes* and *Behind the Crimson Blind* have the title and author's monogram in black on their front covers. *Follow the Blue Car, The Tolliver Case, The Five Suspects* and *The Cat and the Corpse* have the title in black on the front cover: so do the six titles from *The Corpse in the Crimson Slippers* to *More Than One Serpent*. *The Late Unlamented* has the title in white on the

front cover. The other nine titles have blank front covers.

To *The Five Suspects* the books have dated title-pages: thereafter the date is on the copyright page. *A Corpse without a Clue* was 'First printed in December 1944' according to the copyright page, but was not published till March 1945. *The Tolliver Case* has a triple border on the title-page and the sequence from *VIII to IX* to *Dust in the Vault* all have drawings on the title-page: a hat in water for *The Five Suspects*, a padlock and key for *Mr. Tolefree's Reluctant Witnesses* and an elegant vignette for *Dust in the Vault*, with a policeman on the half-title. From *The Five Suspects* to *The Corpse in the Crimson Slippers* the books have advertisements at the rear: so do *The Mystery of Mr. Mock, Bury Him Deeper, The Doodled Asterisk* and *The Late Unlamented*. The front endpapers of *Mr. Tolefree's Reluctant Witnesses* have two plans by F. M. W. (perhaps the author's daughter) of The Coppice and its environs, but the rear endpapers are blank.

The American editions, all from Morrow, are, by and large, more attractive than their British equivalents. The binding colours vary considerably, but at least eleven titles are black: the seven from *-In Time for Murder*, the three from *Marooned with Murder* and *The Corpse without a Clue*. Each known title from *-In Time for Murder* to *The Corpse with the Eerie Eye* has a top edge coloured to match the book's lettering, except for *Murder at Midnight* and *The Corpse with the Blue Cravat*, which have plain top edges. From *The Fatal Five Minutes* to *The Corpse with the Eerie Eye* they also have roughly trimmed fore-edges. The nine books from *The Fatal Five Minutes* have title, author and publisher on both spine and front cover, but the covers of the four titles from *Marooned with Murder* have the title only, and from *The Corpse with the Red-headed Friend* all known titles have blank front covers. Some books have decoration on the front cover: blind-stamped rules closing in towards the bottom for *Murder at Midnight*; an orange disc framing two men in silhouette, one standing, one kneeling, for *Prove It, Mr. Tolefree*; a man lying dead with a gun at hand and a woman looking down at him for *The Bachelor Flat Mystery*; a framework of legal documents and a red rosette enclosing the publisher's circular logo for *Legacy of Death*; and a green segment of Wolborough Castle for *The Corpse in the Green Pyjamas*.

Other books have spinal decoration only: a green hand for *The Corpse with the Grimy Glove*; a yellow nail for *Dust in the Vault*; the head of a woman framed in red for *The Corpse With the Redheaded Friend*; a green fish for *By Hook or Crook*. *The Corpse without a Clue* has three vertical yellow rules separating title from author and author from publisher; and *The Corpse with the Missing Watch* has fragmented purple rules on the spine. *The Corpse with the Eerie Eye* has green spine lettering, except for the title which shows grey through a rounded rectangular panel, surmounted by a supine male corpse, all in green. A few titles have decoration on both spine and front cover: the eponymous slippers for *The Corpse in the Crimson Slippers*; circular red ripples for *Marooned with Murder*; and double blue horizontal rules for *The Corpse with the Blue Cravat*. *The Fatal Five Minutes* has the 'Five' as a numeral on spine and front cover. *Murder at Midnight* has the blurb on the front endpapers and *The Corpse in the Coppice* has F. V. W.'s preliminary plans, one opposite the title-page. *The Corpse without a Clue* has 'Wartime Book' and an accompanying motif on the copyright page. Several titles have decorated or ruled title-pages. All known Morrow books are dated on the title-page.

The Hodder edition of *Behind the Yellow Blind* has a plain blue wrapper with a yellow window divided centrally by blue lines, one horizontal, one vertical. *Follow the Blue Car* has Bip Pares' view of the blue car with its driver at the wheel and *The Tolliver Case* has another car hurtling through space. *VIII to IX* has the white hands of a clock marking the appropriate time on a blue background, and *The Five Suspects* shows circular ripples and reeds by the water. *The Cat and the Corpse* has a blue wrapper with the irregular outline of a castle wall over which a rope is hanging. There are also three black pawprints, well ahead of Lilian Jackson Braun. *Mr. Tolefree's Reluctant Witnesses* has a striking design by Stead, with disembodied hands pointing towards a path running from a house to its front gate. *The Corpse with the Dirty Face* has a body wrapped in a shroud and *The Mystery of Mr. Mock* highlights a man's foot floating above the water of a mill-race. *The Coroner Doubts* shows an overturned teacup with tea spilt in the saucer and over documents. *More than One Serpent* has a blue wrapper with Stead's drawing of a white shark accompanied by the accoutrements of a city man. *Dust in the Vault*, also by Stead, shows a man entering the vault at Albury Chantry with the 'cryptical diagram' superimposed. *Why did Trethewy Die?* has a maidservant approaching a bedroom door left unexpectedly ajar. *A Corpse without a Clue* has a man in a telephone box and *The Late Unlamented* presents the harbour at Porthgover with mauve and yellow cliffs and jetties under a clear blue sky.

Murder at Midnight shows Henry Case lying dead in his dining chair with a lamp and charged wineglass, all seen in silhouette through a yellow window blind. *Prove it, Mr. Tolefree* has a black wrapper with the two figures from the book's cover showing red within a white disc. *Legacy of Death* shows a skeletal hand reaching in through a window towards documents on a table and *The Corpse in the Green Pyjamas* frames a green-clad corpse within a white castle gateway. *The Corpse in the Crimson Slippers* shows the eponymous victim lying on his bedroom floor and *Marooned with Murder* has a dramatic scene on Eilean Rona, with Tolefree being lowered over a cliff. *The Late Unlamented* has a yellow wrapper with a woman happening on a body in a library, its hand and a telephone visible on a desk before her. *The Corpse with the Missing Watch* shows a dark waterside building with a magnified blue watch-face.

Novels

(with Philip Tolefree, except where stated)

The Strong Room   Jarrolds Feb. 1927 (non-series)
The Dinner-Party at Bardolph's   Jarrolds Nov. 1927 (Pierce only)
a.k.a. *That Dinner at Bardolph's*   Morrow 1928
Murder at the Keyhole   Methuen 1929, Morrow 1929 (non-series)

The Man with the Squeaky Voice Methuen 1930, Morrow 1930 (non-series)

The Stroke of One Methuen 1931, Morrow 1931 (Garstang only)

The Fatal Five Minutes Hodder & Stoughton Feb. 1932, Morrow 1932 (Pierce)

Murder at Midnight Morrow 1932 (Garstang only)

a.k.a. *Behind the Yellow Blind* Hodder 1932 (Jan. 1933)

-In Time for Murder Morrow 1933

a.k.a. *Follow the Blue Car* Hodder July 1933

Prove it, Mr. Tolefree Morrow 1933

a.k.a. *The Tolliver Case* Hodder Apr. 1934

The Bachelor Flat Mystery Morrow 1934

a.k.a. *VIII to IX* Hodder Aug. 1934

Legacy of Death Morrow 1934

a.k.a. *The Five Suspects* Hodder Jan. 1935

The Corpse in the Green Pyjamas Morrow 1935

a.k.a. *The Cat and the Corpse* Hodder July 1935

The Corpse in the Coppice Morrow 1935 (Pierce)

a.k.a. *Mr. Tolefree's Reluctant Witnesses* Hodder Jan. 1936

The Corpse in the Crimson Slippers Morrow 1936, Hodder June 1936

The Corpse with the Dirty Face Morrow 1936, Hodder Oct. 1936 (Pierce)

a.k.a. *The Crime in Cumberland Court* Hodder 1938

The Corpse with the Floating Foot Morrow 1936

a.k.a. *The Mystery of Mr. Mock* Hodder Feb. 1937

Marooned with Murder Morrow 1937

a.k.a. *Bury Him Deeper* Hodder Oct. 1937

The Corpse with the Blue Cravat Morrow 1938

a.k.a. *The Coroner Doubts* Hodder June 1938

The Corpse with the Grimy Glove Morrow 1938

a.k.a. *More than One Serpent* Hodder Sept. 1938

The Corpse with the Blistered Hand Morrow 1939

a.k.a. *Dust in the Vault* Hodder Mar. 1939

The Corpse with the Redheaded Friend Morrow 1939

a.k.a. *They Liked Entwhistle* Hodder Nov. 1939

The Spider and the Fly Morrow 1940 (Pierce)

a.k.a. *Why Did Trethewy Die?* Hodder June 1940

By Hook or Crook Morrow Mar. 1941

revised as *By Hook or by Crook* Hodder Jun. 1941

The Corpse with the Eerie Eye Morrow 1942 (Pierce)

a.k.a. *Castle-Dinas* Hodder June 1942

A Corpse by Any Other Name Morrow 1943

a.k.a. *The Doodled Asterisk* Hodder June 1943

The Corpse without a Clue Morrow 1944 (Pierce, Garstang)

a.k.a. *A Corpse Without a Clue* Hodder Mar. 1945

The Late Unlamented Morrow 1948, Hodder 1948

The Corpse with the Missing Watch Morrow 1949 (Pierce, Garstang)

Stories

'The Resurrection of Mr. Benison' (*Windsor*, June 1939)

'The Red Carnation' (*Windsor*, July 1939)   *BP*

Thurman Warriner
a.k.a. Simon Troy
a.k.a. John Kersey

Thurman Warriner's twenty-one crime novels were published between 1950 and 1970, in his own name and under two pseudonyms. As Thurman Warriner he wrote a distinctive series of detective novels with a curious, potent charm and an unusual combination of detectives. A second series, attributed to Simon Troy, tends to sacrifice detection to morbid psychology, although the reassuring presence of a ruminative Cornish policeman is an inducement to persevere. One novel appeared under the name John Kersey: a political thriller set in Communist Europe.

In six of the eight Warriner novels, the detectives are two elderly amateurs and a young, aggressive professional: Charles Ambo and

Archdeacon Toft of Tonchester, and John Scotter of Great Froissart Street in London. Despite their differences they make a formidable team, dedicated to saving innocence from destruction by evil. There are no half measures in the Warriner novels: the evil are beyond redemption, and their victims suffer the more for their goodness. Mr Ambo appears briefly in *She Died, of Course*, but it is otherwise Scotter's case. *The Golden Lantern* is outside the sequence. Scotter's collaborator in *She Died, of Course* is Inspector Hector Smith, whose recorded career had already begun in *Road to Rhuine*, the first of the twelve Simon Troy novels. He recurs in seven more of the Troy books, a benign but watchful presence, whom little escapes. He goes to Guernsey in *Cease Upon the Midnight* and to Provence in *Blind Man's Garden*.

All the Warriner books were published by Hodder & Stoughton, with colour variations both in the bindings and the lettering. *Method*

in His Murder is red, with black spine lettering and the title in black on the front cover. *Death's Dateless Night* and *The Doors of Sleep* also have black lettering on the spine: the former is dark red, the latter green. *Death's Bright Angel* and *She Died, of Course* are dark red books with gilt spine lettering. *The Golden Lantern* and *Heavenly Bodies* are also lettered in gilt, but are bound in green. *Ducats in Her Coffin* is also green, and the lettering, on the spine only, is red. All eight books are dated, *Method in His Murder* with the month as well as the year. *Ducats in Her Coffin* has a map of Shearstone Square in Urmsbury.

Three wrappers focus on the woman in the case: Rhoda Wainfleet, yoked with the Devil, for *Method in His Murder*: a sad-looking member of the Shearstone family for *Ducats in Her Coffin*; and Lucia Calvin, with the Château of Pont du Vendom looming beyond her, for *Death's Dateless Night*. *The Doors of Sleep* features the fair field at Slumber St Mary's, with Amen Sleep's caravan and roundabout, and Charlesworth Vinery's body being tidied away. *She Died, of Course* has a car moving along the coast road towards Meveenah Cottage, high on its cliff overlooking the Atlantic. George Chrichard shows the sands of time running out for the protagonist of *Death's Bright Angel*. *Heavenly Bodies* is perhaps the most appealing of the sequence, with its tranquil view of Ambo and Toft outside Ross Quinton's church at Old Heddle.

Road to Rhuine was published by Collins Crime Club in 1952. It is a red book with black spine lettering, and it is dated. The wrapper shows the torch-bearers passing the house called Edward's Bounty on Mischief Night in Rhuine. The rest of Troy books came from Gollancz and have the standard yellow wrappers of this firm. They are bound in red, usually with gilt lettering on the spine: *Drunkard's End*, exceptionally, is lettered in black. The entire Gollancz series is dated. *Swift to Its Close* and *Blind Man's Garden* are taller than the rest.

The Night of the Wolf, the John Kersey novel, was published by Cassell in 1968 and is dated. It is a maroon book, with silver lettering along the spine.

Thurman Warriner was evidently a prolific story writer, since reference is made in his Penguin biography to fifty stories published before the war, and in *Argosy* for January 1970 to the fact that 'he has written several hundred in the past quarter century'. Research has revealed only eight crime stories in his own name and two by Simon Troy, but there must be many more, even if much of his shorter fiction is not criminous. No series detectives are involved in the ten known stories. A North-country policeman, Inspector Bracegirdle of Holtgill, features in stories published in *John Bull* in the 1950s, but all known stories show him tackling social crises rather than crime.

Novels by Thurman Warriner

(with Ambo, Toft, and Scotter, except as stated)

Method in His Murder   Hodder & Stoughton 1950, Macmillan 1951
Ducats in Her Coffin   Hodder 1951
Death's Dateless Night   Hodder 1952
The Doors of Sleep   Hodder 1955
Death's Bright Angel   Hodder 1956
She Died, of Course   Hodder 1958 (Scotter, Smith, Ambo)
The Golden Lantern   Hodder 1958 (non-series)
Heavenly Bodies   Hodder 1960

Novels by Simon Troy

(with Smith, except as stated)

Road to Rhuine   Collins Crime Club 1952, Dodd, Mead 1952
Halfway to Murder   Gollancz 1955 (not Smith)
Tonight and Tomorrow   Gollancz 1957 (not Smith)
Drunkard's End   Gollancz 1960, Walker 1961 (not Smith)
Second Cousin Removed   Gollancz 1961, Macmillan 1962
Waiting for Oliver   Gollancz 1962, Macmillan 1963 (not Smith)
Don't Play with the Rough Boys   Gollancz 1963, Macmillan 1964

Cease Upon the Midnight   Gollancz 1964, Macmillan 1965
No More a-Roving   Gollancz 1965
Sup with the Devil   Gollancz 1967
Swift to Its Close   Gollancz 1969, Stein & Day 1969
Blind Man's Garden   Gollancz 1970

Novel by John Kersey

The Night of the Wolf   Cassell 1968

Uncollected stories by Thurman Warriner

'The Miracle of Hell Nick' (*John Bull*, 30 June 1951)
'No Police Action' (*John Bull*, 8 Mar. 1952)
'Wanted' (*ES*, 27 July 1953)
'Hour of Darkness' (*John Bull*, 25 Oct. 1958)
'Edge of Terror' (*Suspense*, Apr. 1961)
'Moment of Error' (*Argosy*, Mar. 1965)
'Pursuit' (*Argosy*, Dec. 1967)
'VIP' (*Argosy*, Oct. 1968)

Uncollected stories by Simon Troy

'Once a Policeman' (*EQMM*, Oct. 1969)
'The Liquidation File' (*EQMM*, Aug. 1970; *Ellery Queen's Giants of Mystery*, Davis 1976)
BP

Colin Watson (1920–1983)

Colin Watson's Flaxborough novels derive much of their impact from an entrancing combination of formality and absurdity. The author's voice is wholly distinctive – his style marvellously precise and pointed. His relish for human pretension and hypocrisy is everywhere apparent, and he could on occasion summon an uproarious erotic gusto, at once in mockery and celebration of the sexual impulse. The mysteries are subtle and oblique, founded on hints and discrepancies that nudge the narratives enticingly forward. All twelve novels are set in Flaxborough, a market town on the Lincolnshire coast, of which a detailed and delightful plan is shown in Salim Patell's endpapers for *The Flaxborough Chronicle*. The investigator throughout is Inspector Purbright, a large, amiable man who proves himself an alert and quizzical match for the more devious of Flaxborough's deplorable citizenry. Also on hand, from *Lonelyheart 4122*, is Lucilla Teatime, a genteel adventuress who takes to Flaxborough like a duck to water. She is absent from *Blue Murder* only of the later novels.

The series was published by Eyre & Spottiswoode, becoming Eyre Methuen halfway and Methuen for the final title. All the books are dated, and all except *Bump in the Night, Hopjoy Was Here*, and *Broomsticks Over Flaxborough* are lettered in gilt on the spine. *Hopjoy Was Here* has blue lettering and *Broomsticks Over Flaxborough* has black. *Bump in the Night* is an oddity, with a laminated pictorial cover and no dust-wrapper in its first-edition state. The spine has the title in black on a yellow background and the author's name in white on black. For the second impression the cover design was issued as a conventional dust-wrapper. The other books in the series are bound in various colours; and they grow taller at two points in the sequence, with *The Flaxborough Crab* and, again, with *Blue Murder*. *One Man's Meat* first appeared in the USA as *It Shouldn't Happen to a Dog*, in 1976, according to the author, though the copyright notice has 1977.

Three wrapper designs draw richly on the various vitality of life in Flaxborough: *Charity Ends at Home, The Flaxborough Crab*, and *The Naked Nuns*. All three extend over the spine on to the rear cover and are the work of Salim Patell, whose designs also enhance the appeal of *The Flaxborough Chronicle*, the omnibus which appeared in 1969, with the first, second, and third novels and an introduction by Julian Symons. He depicts for *Charity Ends at Home* a cross-section of Flaxborough society, disposed around the 'little woolly dog' of the novel; for *The Flaxborough Crab* the outing of the Trent Street Darby and Joan Club, at which Alderman Winge chases Bertha Pollock over the skyline; and for *The Naked Nuns* an uninhibited scene at the Floradora Country Club. In comparison, his cat for *Broomsticks Over Flaxborough*, despite original features, is unexpectedly restrained. No other designer approaches Pat-

ell's inventive sympathy with the author's creation; but J. Faczynski's work for *Coffin Scarcely Used* has a sinister resonance that sorts well with this particular novel, which is less larky than some of its successors. The photographic cover of *Bump in the Night* shows a Chalmsbury voyeur with the object of his pleasure. *Plaster Sinners* and *'Whatever's Been Going On at Mumblesby?'* have uniform wrappers with relevant items neatly framed: a 'moulded relief of a cottage' for the former and a fisherman's fly for the latter.

Four uncollected stories are known, all non-series. A fifth story was written in collaboration with seven other writers.

Flaxborough novels

(With Purbright. Details of bindings refer to British editions.)

Coffin Scarcely Used Eyre & Spottiswoode 1958, Putnam 1967 (blue binding)

Bump in the Night Eyre 1960, Walker 1962

Hopjoy Was Here Eyre 1962, Walker 1963 (black)

Lonelyheart 4122 Eyre 1967, Putnam 1967 (sage)

Charity Ends at Home Eyre 1968, Putnam 1968 (blue)

The Flaxborough Crab Eyre 1969 (sage)

a.k.a. *Just What the Doctor Ordered* Putnam 1969

Broomsticks Over Flaxborough Eyre Methuen 1972 (red)

a.k.a. *Kissing Covens* Putnam 1972

The Naked Nuns Eyre Methuen 1975 (dark green)

a.k.a. *Six Nuns and a Shotgun* Putnam 1975

It Shouldn't Happen to a Dog Putnam 1977

a.k.a. *One Man's Meat* Eyre Methuen 1977 (orange-brown)

Blue Murder Eyre Methuen 1979 (brown)

Plaster Sinners Eyre Methuen 1980, Doubleday 1981 (green)

'Whatever's Been Going On at Mumblesby?' Methuen 1982, Doubleday 1983 (red)

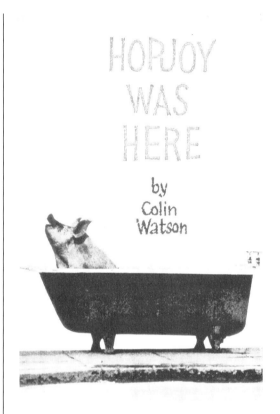

HORJOY
WAS
HERE

by
Colin
Watson

Uncollected stories

'Return to Base' (*EQMM*, June 1967)

'The Infallible Clock' (*EQMM*, Nov. 1967)

'The Harrowing of Henry Pygole' (*Winter's Crimes 6*, Macmillan 1974, St Martin's 1974)

'The Date' (*John Creasey's Crime Collection 1981*, Gollancz 1981)

Collaborative story

'A Slight Case of Scotch' (*The Bell House Book*, Hodder & Stoughton 1979)   *BP*

Patricia Wentworth (1878–1961)

Patricia Wentworth was essentially a romantic novelist, redeemed by a taste for adventure. Though patently destined for the hero's arms, each spirited heroine has first to negotiate some sort of mystery. As the years passed, the early fantastication gave way to a more decorous maturity. Gradually, Miss Silver took over, exerting a benign and steadying influence. A governess turned genteel private eye, Maud Silver first appeared in 1928, in *Grey Mask*, but did not surface again until *The Case Is Closed* in 1937, sixteen books later. By the war years, however, she had either ousted or absorbed the opposition, and her last case, in 1961, marks her thirty-second appearance.

In 1929 Miss Wentworth introduced a second series detective, an eccentric *éminence grise* named Benbow Smith, with a string of nautical forenames and a parrot called Ananias. He first appears in *Fool Errant* and recurs on three later occasions, twice in collaboration with Colonel Frank Garratt, the Head of Intelligence for the Foreign Office (whose name is given as 'Garrett' in three of the five novels that feature him). Garratt becomes a point of reference in two other novels, and in his last case he collaborates with Inspector Ernest Lamb and his high-born sergeant, Frank Abbott, who are later drawn into Miss Silver's orbit. *The Blind Side* is the first of two cases where these two investigate on their own: they make Miss Silver's acquaintance in *Miss Silver Intervenes*. Lamb features in sixteen novels, Frank Abbott in twenty-four. Randal March, who becomes Chief Constable of Ledshire, works with Miss Silver in *Danger Point* and eight other cases (one of which – *The Catherine Wheel* – also features Lamb and Abbott). Garratt, Lamb, and Abbott are together in *Pursuit of a Parcel*. From *The Traveller Returns* all the novels feature Miss Silver, who is on her own in *The Benevent Treasure*, but is otherwise attended by one or more of her menfolk. Of the sixty-five novels, forty-one include at least one of the six series characters.

Patricia Wentworth's first publisher was Andrew Melrose, who brought out her early historical fiction. She remained with him for three more books when she switched to mysteries in 1923. All three Melrose books are dated, with gilt spine lettering, and title and author blind-stamped on the front cover, which also has a blind-stamped triple border. *The Astonishing Adventure of Jane Smith* is bound in deep red cloth. *The Red Lacquer Case* and *The Annam Jewel* are green and red, respectively; and both have a narrow strip of material attached to the top of the spine as a book-mark.

In 1925, Miss Wentworth moved to Hodder & Stoughton, who issued twelve books before she changed publishers again. This series began with *The Dower House Mystery*, issued in June 1925. This and its immediate successor are more distinctive in appearance than the later books, with decorative panels as a feature of their design. *The Dower House Mystery* is a red book, with black spine lettering. Towards the top of the front cover, title and author stand out in red against a black rectangle, framed by two red and two black borders, the innermost of which is narrower than the others. A slim red line divides title from author. *The Black Cabinet* has a blue-green binding, with the author's name in black on spine and front cover, in each case beneath a box containing the title, the lettering of which stands out in blue-green relief against a stamped black rectangle, enclosed within two borders, a raised blue-green one and a stamped black one.

From *The Amazing Chance* the books take on what came to be the standard Hodder look, with blue bindings and black spine lettering. All the front covers to *Danger Calling* have the title and the author's initials in black, and from *The Amazing Chance* to *The Coldstone* they also have a blind-stamped border. Only *Kingdom Lost* of this sequence is dated, and even the occasional advertisement section is undated.

Four books were issued by Cassell between 1932 and 1933, *Red Danger* in maroon, *Walk with Care* in green, and the others in red bindings. *Nothing Venture* and *Walk With Care* have black spine lettering, *Red Danger* has gilt, and *Seven Green Stones* has green. The spines of all except *Seven Green Stones* are ruled at top and bottom, like some of the Christopher Bush books of this era. All four are dated, and all except *Nothing Venture* have the printer's code on the reverse of the title-page. Both *Red Danger* and *Nothing Venture* have a blind-stamped border on the front cover. *Seven Green Stones* has the figure 7 in the title on the spine, but this is spelt out as a word on the title-page. A later edition of this title has black lettering

and inferior red boards but is otherwise identical.

With *Fear By Night*, in April 1934, Patricia Wentworth returned to Hodder, remaining with them to the end of her life. All forty-six books in this later sequence are dated, from January 1942 (*Danger Point*) to February 1949 (*Latter End*) with the month as well as the year. (*Eternity Ring* also gives the month of publication.) With one exception, the run from *Fear By Night* to *Mr. Zero* is bound in blue, with black spine lettering and the title in black on the front cover. *Dead or Alive*, the exception, is a navy-blue book with a blank front cover, and with the spine lettering, including the publisher, shown against a yellow rectangle, within a blind-stamped border. The front cover of *Mr. Zero* also has the motif that became the author's trademark, her entwined initials beneath a black mask. The title-page of *Blindfold* encloses the title within a drawing of a blindfold. Again except for *Dead or Alive*, the sequence from *Red Stefan* to *Lonesome Road* has blue endpapers. The six books from *Devil-in-the-dark* to *The Case Is Closed* are taller than the rest.

Lonesome Road and *The Blind Side* also have distinctive features. The former is blue with gilt spine lettering; the latter is red, with all its lettering, in gilt, in a double border, high on the spine. Both front covers are blank. The five books from *Rolling Stone* to *Pursuit of a Parcel* are blue, with black lettering within a double border in the upper half of the spine. The PW trademark features in black on all five covers. *The Chinese Shawl*, *Miss Silver Intervenes*, and *The Clock Strikes Twelve* dispense with the double border but otherwise have the same features.

The Key is a maroon book and *Silence in Court* is red; both have white lettering on the spine and the PW motif on the front cover, in white. *Silence in Court* also has the title on the front cover. From *The Traveller Returns* to *The Case of William Smith* the books have only the title on the front cover, and from *Miss Silver Comes to Stay* to *The Ivory Dagger* they have the author's trademark (which recurs briefly on *The Watersplash* and *Ladies' Bane*). *Out of the Past* has a blank front cover and *Vanishing Point* has the author's initials but not the mask. From

The Silent Pool the front covers are blank and the spine lettering is gilt. The four books from *The Catherine Wheel* to *The Ivory Dagger* are dark red with black lettering, as are the four from *The Watersplash* to *Vanishing Point. Anna, Where Are you?* is eccentric, bound in maroon, with gilt spine lettering and a blank front cover, and looking unlike a Hodder product. *The Girl in the Cellar* is slightly taller than the others, and the title is set against a black rectangle, with gilt rules at the top and bottom of it.

Where the British and US editions of a novel came out in the same year, it is possible that the British edition may not be the true first, since the dates establish that one pre-war book and twenty-eight published in or after the war first appeared in America. Of the twelve variant titles, four take precedence over their British counterparts: *In the Balance, Miss Silver Deals with Death, She Came Back*, and *Wicked Uncle*. Three others are later paperback variants. *The Girl in the Cellar*, the last novel, was not published in the USA.

The blonde on the wrapper of *Nothing Venture* is probably Rosamund Carew, looking, in her yellow dress, 'as if she knew how beautiful she was'. For *Red Stefan* Stead has provided a head-and-shoulders portrait of Stefan. *Blindfold* has a flight of stairs with a startled maid at the top and a boy beginning his ascent below. The title appears red against a white blindfold and the design of the latter recurs on the spine. Nicholson designed the wrappers for *The Chinese Shawl* and *Lonesome Road*: a black-fringed decorated shawl on a pale-green background for the former and an empty road winding into a grey distance for the latter. Miss Silver's floral wallpaper decorates *Miss Silver Intervenes*, together with a Landseer stag and half a flower-piece. Nicholson designed several of the wrappers of the immediate post-war years, including the decorative box for *Latter End* and the four gilt figures, representing the seasons, for *Miss Silver Comes to Stay*. Jarvis took over in the 1950s, producing a series of bold impressions of highlights from the novels: Lila Dryden sleepwalking at Vineyards, Clarice Dean's hand in the watersplash at Greenings, Pippa Maybury ascending the stairs at Cliff Edge in her bloodstained dress.

He shows us Anna Ball and her suitcase, the Great Prospero in his Inverness cape, and an exotic impression of the gazebo at Grove Hill House. Unattributed designs show Ina Felton crouching behind the balustrade at Cove House, on the night of Helen Adrian's murder, and Mabel Preston falling fatally into the pool at Ford House. At least from *The Chinese Shawl* all the wrappers feature the PW trademark, and several also show Miss Silver's hands knitting on the rear panel (reproducing the original wrapper design for *Pilgrim's Rest*). *Lonesome Road* also has the trademark.

A single story, dating from 1933, is known.

Earlier novels

(some with Silver, and with other series characters, as stated)

The Astonishing Adventure of Jane Smith Melrose 1923, Small Maynard 1923
The Red Lacquer Case Melrose 1924, Small 1925
The Annam Jewel Melrose 1924, Small 1925
The Dower House Mystery Hodder & Stoughton n.d. (1925), Small 1926
The Black Cabinet Hodder n.d. (1925), Small 1926
The Amazing Chance Hodder n.d. (1926), Lippincott 1927
Hue and Cry Hodder n.d. (1927), Lippincott 1927
Anne Belinda Hodder n.d. (1927), Lippincott 1928
Will O'the Wisp Hodder n.d. (1928), Lippincott 1928
Grey Mask Hodder n.d. (1928), Lippincott 1929 (Silver)
Fool Errant Hodder n.d. (1929), Lippincott 1929 (Smith)
The Coldstone Hodder n.d. (1930), Lippincott 1930
Beggar's Choice Hodder n.d. (1930), Lippincott 1931
Kingdom Lost Lippincott 1930, Hodder 1931
Danger Calling Hodder n.d. (1931), Lippincott 1931 (Smith, Garratt)
Nothing Venture Cassell 1932, Lippincott 1932

Red Danger Cassell 1932
a.k.a. *Red Shadow* Lippincott 1932
Seven Green Stones Cassell 1933
a.k.a. *Outrageous Fortune* Lippincott 1933
Walk With Care Cassell 1933, Lippincott 1933 (Smith, Garrett)
Fear By Night Hodder 1934, Lippincott 1934
Devil-in-the-dark Hodder 1934
a.k.a. *Touch and Go* Lippincott 1934
Red Stefan Hodder 1935, Lippincott 1935
Blindfold Hodder 1935, Lippincott 1935
Dead or Alive Hodder 1936 Lippincott 1936 (Garratt)
Hole and Corner Hodder 1936, Lippincott 1936
The Case Is Closed Hodder 1937, Lippincott 1937 (Silver)
Down Under Hodder 1937, Lippincott 1937 (Smith)
Run! Hodder 1938, Lippincott 1938
Mr. Zero Hodder 1938, Lippincott 1938
Lonesome Road Hodder 1939, Lippincott 1939 (Silver)
The Blind Side Hodder 1939, Lippincott 1939 (Lamb, Abbott)
Rolling Stone Hodder 1940, Lippincott 1940 (Garrett)
Who Pays the Piper? Hodder 1940 (Lamb, Abbott)
a.k.a. *Account Rendered* Lippincott 1940
Unlawful Occasions Hodder 1941
a.k.a. *Weekend with Death* Lippincott 1941
In the Balance Lippincott 1941 (Silver, March)
a.k.a. *Danger Point* Hodder 1942
Pursuit of a Parcel Hodder 1942, Lippincott 1942 (Garrett, Lamb, Abbott)
The Chinese Shawl Hodder 1943, Lippincott 1943 (Silver, March)
Miss Silver Deals with Death Lippincott 1943, (Silver, Lamb, Abbott)
a.k.a. *Miss Silver Intervenes* Hodder 1944
The Clock Strikes Twelve Lippincott 1944, Hodder 1945 (Silver)
The Key Lippincott 1944, Hodder 1946 (Silver, Lamb, Abbot)
Silence in Court Lippincott 1945, Hodder 1946

Later novels

(All with Silver, and with other series characters, as stated. Details of bindings refer to British editions.)

She Came Back Lippincott 1945 (Lamb, Abbott)
a.k.a. *The Traveller Returns* Hodder 1948 (blue binding, black lettering)
Pilgrim's Rest Lippincott 1946, Hodder 1948 (March, Abbott) (maroon, white)
a.k.a. *Dark Threat* Popular Library 1951
Latter End Lippincott 1947, Hodder 1949 (Lamb, Abbott) (blue, black)
Wicked Uncle Lippincott 1947 (Lamb, Abbott)
a.k.a. *Spotlight* Hodder 1949 (blue, black)
Eternity Ring Lipppincott 1948, Hodder 1950 (Lamb, Abbott) (maroon, silver)
The Case of William Smith Lippincott 1948, Hodder 1950 (Lamb, Abbott) (green, black)
Miss Silver comes to Stay Lippincott 1949, Hodder 1951 (March) (green, black)
The Catherine Wheel Lippincott 1949, Hodder 1951 (March, Lamb, Abbott)
The Brading Collection Lippincott 1950, Hodder 1952 (March)
a.k.a. *Mr. Brading's Collection* Severn House 1987
Through the Wall Lippincott 1950, Hodder 1952 (March)
The Ivory Dagger Lippincott 1951, Hodder 1953 (Lamb, Abbott)
Anna, Where Are you? Lippincott 1951, Hodder 1953 (Abbott)
a.k.a. *Death at Deep End* Pyramid 1963
The Watersplash Lippincott 1951, Hodder 1953 (Lamb, Abbott)
Ladies' Bane Lippincott 1952, Hodder 1954 (Abbott)
Out of the Past Lippincott 1953, Hodder 1955 (Lamb, Abbott)
Vanishing Point Lippincott 1953, Hodder 1955 (Lamb, Abbott)
The Silent Pool Lippincott 1954, Hodder 1956 (March) (maroon binding)
The Benevent Treasure Lippincott 1954, Hodder 1956 (red)

MISS SILVER INTERVENES

PATRICIA WENTWORTH

Poison in the Pen Lippincott 1955, Hodder 1957 (March, Abbott) (maroon)

The Listening Eye Lippincott 1955, Hodder 1957 (Lamb, Abbott) (navy blue)

The Gazebo Lippincott 1956, Hodder 1958 (Abbott) (dark blue)

a.k.a. *The Summerhouse* Pyramid 1967

The Fingerprint Lippincott 1956, Hodder 1959 (Abbott) (dark blue)

The Alington Inheritance Lippincott 1958, Hodder 1960 (Abbott) (dark blue)

The Girl in the Cellar Hodder 1961 (Abbott) (red)

Story

'Adventure for Two' (*Woman's Magazine Annual*, 1933)   BP

David Williams (b. 1926)

David Williams has written seventeen novels and ten stories. He arrived late on the literary scene from a career in advertising, but quickly became a recognized leader of modern writers in the classic style. His series detective is the elegant, astute merchant banker Mark Treasure, who figures in all the novels and one of the stories. His actress wife Molly often appears, adding to the humour of these witty novels. Anyone who has not yet discovered this hoard of 'treasure' should sample *Murder in Advent* and become addicted.

David Williams' books are all dated. The first seven titles were published in Britain by Collins Crime Club, in red cloth with gilt spine lettering. For the next eight titles, from Macmillan, the cloth colour varies from title to title. Except for the first, *Wedding Treasure*, the books have silver lettering on the spine: *Wedding Treasure* has gilt. In 1992 David Williams returned to the Crime Club and his books from *Planning on Murder* have the usual red cloth and gilt lettering on the spine. They also have printers' keys on the copyright pages.

Treasure novels

(Binding details refer to Macmillan editions.)

Unholy Writ Collins Crime Club 1976, St Martin's 1977

Treasure by Degrees Crime Club 1977, St Martin's 1977

Treasure Up in Smoke Crime Club 1978, St Martin's 1978

Murder for Treasure Crime Club 1980, St Martin's 1980

Copper, Gold and Treasure Crime Club 1982, St Martin's 1982

Treasure Preserved Crime Club 1983, St Martin's 1983

Advertise for Treasure Crime Club 1984, St Martin's 1984

Wedding Treasure Macmillan 1985, St Martin's 1985 (green binding, gilt lettering)

Murder in Advent Macmillan 1985, St Martin's 1986 (maroon, silver)

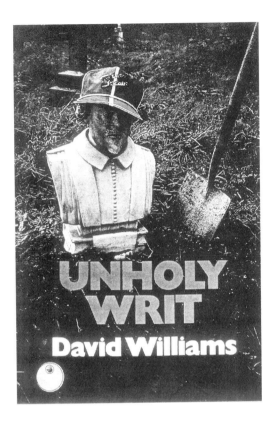

UNHOLY WRIT
David Williams

Treasure in Roubles Macmillan 1986, St Martin's 1987 (green, silver)

Divided Treasure Macmillan 1987, St Martin's 1988 (red, silver)

Treasure in Oxford Macmillan 1988, St Martin's 1989 (olive-green)

Holy Treasure! Macmillan 1989, St Martin's 1989 (brown)

Prescription for Murder Macmillan 1990, St Martin's 1990 (beige)

Treasure by Post Macmillan 1991, St Martin's 1992 (red)

Planning on Murder Crime Club 1992

Banking on Murder Crime Club 1993

Uncollected stories

'Treasure Finds a Mistress' (*Winter's Crimes 12*, Macmillan 1980, St Martin's 1980)

'Uncle's Girl' (*Winter's Crimes 15*, Macmillan 1983, St Martin's 1983)

'The Bully' (*Winter's Crimes 16*, Macmillan 1984, St Martin's 1985)

'Mr Oliver' (*Ellery Queen's Prime Crimes 4*, Davis 1985; *John Creasey's Crime Collection 1988*, Gollancz 1988)

'Three's a Crowd' (*Winter's Crimes 18*, Macmillan 1986, St Martin's 1987)

'Something to Declare' (*EQMM*, Sept. 1988: *Crime Waves 1*, Gollancz 1991)

'The Other Woman' (*Winter's Crimes 20*, Macmillan 1988)

'Freeze Everybody' (*Winter's Crimes 21*, Macmillan 1989; *EQMM*, Aug. 1992)

'Smoke Gets In . . .' (*A Classic English Crime*, Pavilion 1990)

'Take Two Husbands' (*Winter's Crimes 24*, Macmillan 1992; *EQMM*, Dec. 1992)   *JC*

R. D. Wingfield
a.k.a. Rodney Wingfield

R. D. Wingfield writes superbly and his absorbing, witty detective novels of contemporary life never disappoint. The diverse strands of each story are skilfully woven together to produce narratives that are by turn chilling and warmly humorous. Vibrant characters interact convincingly as Detective-Inspector Jack Frost soldiers on despite political infighting and mounting bureaucracy. Frost is, in many respects, the antithesis of the Golden Age detectives. His appearance is unprepossessing, as sloppy as the paper-work that is never up to date. With little respect for the hierarchy, he can be crude, insubordinate and unconventional; and he is a constant thorn in the side of Police Superintendent Mullett, Commander of Denton Division. He succeeds as a detective because he is shrewd, fearless and dedicated to the pursuit of truth. He is also intelligent, warm-hearted and absolutely honest.

There are three Frost novels, all dated. *Night Frost* has not been published in the USA. *Frost at Christmas* was first published by Paperjacks of Canada in October 1984, as a paperpback with yellow page edges. A manacled, skeletal hand poking out of a snow-covered grave and grasping at a holly leaf illustrates the front cover. In November 1987, Paperjacks USA published

the second Frost title, *A Touch of Frost*, also as a paperback. On this occasion, the author was shown as 'Rodney Wingfield' on the cover and spine and 'R. D. Wingfield' on the title-page. The front cover shows a man peering through a window with two bullet holes in it.

In the UK, Constable published the first hardback editions of both books, as well as the first edition of *Night Frost*. All three have black cloth with spines lettered silver. The wrapper of *Night Frost* has a cracked gravestone with blood trickling down the front of it and a jet of flame leaping up behind it. The background is dark blue.

Frost novels

Frost at Christmas Paperjacks Canada 1984, Paperjacks USA 1987, Constable 1989

A Touch of Frost Paperjacks USA 1987, Constable 1990

Night Frost Constable 1992   *JC*

Clifford Witting (1907–1968)

The last of Clifford Witting's sixteen novels appeared in 1964, and he is now relatively unknown on both sides of the Atlantic. He also published one story. He should be read and collected by anyone who enjoys a well-made, old-fashioned English detective novel. *Catt Out of the Bag* and *Measure for Murder* are among his best works. Witting's novels are usually set in rural Downshire, where Inspector Harry Charlton has ten cases to solve, often assisted by his sergeant, Peter Bradfield, who eventually takes over from him. Charlton appears briefly in the first of Bradfield's own investigations, *Silence After Dinner*. Bradfield is involved in thirteen cases altogether, as a detective-constable at the start and a detective-inspector at the close. He and Charlton both appear in the single story. John Rutherford, owner of the Paulsfield bookshop Voslivres, features in two early novels.

The books were all first published in London by Hodder & Stoughton, and they are all dated. Only three titles have appeared in the USA.

The first three of Witting's books were issued in blue cloth, with black lettering on the spine, and the title in black on the front cover. *Catt Out of the Bag* has red cloth, with gilt spine lettering. *Measure for Murder* has blue cloth, with black spine lettering and the masks of comedy and tragedy in black on the front cover. With the later books, the cloth colour varies from one title to another. *Let X Be the Murderer* and *Dead on Time* have the title lettered in white on the front cover. *Silence After Dinner* has the author's initials stamped in black in the lower-right hand corner of the front cover. All the other covers are blank. From *Mischief in the Offing* the books have gilt lettering. A smoking revolver appears on the spines of *The Case of the Busy Bees* and *Mischief in the Offing*. The first and third books are taller than the rest.

There are many maps and drawings through the series. *Catt Out of the Bag* has pictorial endpapers showing a map of Paulsfield by Dick

Kelly, and *Midsummer Murder* has a plan of the Square at Paulsfield by the same artist on its front free endpaper. *Subject: Murder* has front endpapers showing details of Cowfold Camp. *The Case of the Michaelmas Goose* has a very attractive frontispiece of Etchworth Tower, which is also featured in colour on the wrapper by Dick Kelly.

A policeman's jacket being hauled out of the water by a long pole illustrates the wrapper of *Murder in Blue*. The wrapper of *Midsummer Murder* shows the left thigh of Lord Shawford's horse in the statue in Paulsfield Square; two workmen's buckets are balanced by its side. Nicolson's design for *Catt Out of the Bag* shows a collecting box against a background of musical notes. Morton Sale's illlustration for *Measure for Murder* depicts a worried-looking Elizabeth Faggott, in purple for her role as Isabella. Behind her is a bird's nest with a vulture sitting on it. A yellow army badge attached to rope is Stead's design for *Subject: Murder*, and a pair of crossed electric wires is shown on *Let X Be the Murderer*. Wardill was responsible for Witting's next two wrappers: two white rabbits and a clock for *Dead on Time*, and two hands and a revolver superimposed on the quadrangle of Mereworth School for *A Bullet for Rhino*. On the wrapper for *The Case of the Busy Bees*, Miss Kennedy leaves the Monk Jewel museum in some haste, and *Silence After Dinner* has Janet Micheldever and Dick Farrington walking by the millpond at Dark Hollow. *Mischief in the Offing* has a similar design, showing a young girl in a garden with a young man leaning out of an open window. *There Was a Crooked Man* has a blue wrapper with a Bentley parked on Painswick Hill and Martin Keldrick's torch shining on it. The last three books have very striking wrappers by Barbara Walton.

Midsummer Murder was reissued by Hodder in 1953 in a much revised version. The first edition of this book seems to be the most difficult to locate.

Novels

(With Charlton and Bradfield, except as stated. Binding details refer to British editions.)

Murder in Blue Hodder & Stoughton 1937, Scribner 1937

Midsummer Murder Hodder 1937

The Case of the Michaelmas Goose Hodder 1938

Catt Out of the Bag Hodder 1939

Measure for Murder Hodder 1941, Garland 1976

Subject: Murder Hodder 1945 (blue binding, black lettering)

Let X Be the Murderer Hodder 1947 (maroon, white)

Dead on Time Hodder 1948 (maroon, white)

A Bullet for Rhino Hodder 1950 (not Bradfield) (red, black)

313

The Case of the Busy Bees Hodder 1952, (maroon, black)

Silence After Dinner Hodder 1953 (maroon, black)

Mischief in the Offing Hodder 1958 (non-series) (green)

There Was a Crooked Man Hodder 1960, British Book Centre 1962 (not Charlton) (red)

Driven to Kill Hodder 1961 (not Charlton) (green)

Villainous Saltpetre Hodder 1962 (non-series) (maroon)

Crime in Whispers Hodder 1964 (not Charlton) (burgundy)

Story

(with Charlton and Bradfield)

'Hanging by a Hair' (*ES*, 19 Apr. 1950)   *JC*

Sara Woods (1922–1985)
a.k.a. Anne Burton
a.k.a. Mary Challis
a.k.a. Margaret Leek

Sara Bowen-Judd wrote under four pseudonyms. She is chiefly noted for her long series of Sara Woods novels, with their authentic legal background. She wrote only two books each in her other three names: Anne Burton, Mary Challis and Margaret Leek. These six titles are paperback originals, published in Canada by Raven House. Sara Woods' most memorable creation is the barrister Antony Maitland, who uses sound detection and skilful courtroom procedures to win his cases. He prefers to appear for the defence. He figures in all forty-eight Sara Woods novels and in one story. Tall, with dark, untidy hair and a thin, intelligent face, he is a gifted mimic with a good sense of humour. He is troubled by an injured shoulder, a legacy of the war, when he worked in Military Intelligence. He shares a London house and chambers in Inner Temple with his uncle, Sir Nicholas Harding QC, who contributes richly to the series. Antony married Jenny Conway in 1943 and their domestic life features in the books. Roger and Meg Farrell are their closest friends and the former has been helpful in solving several cases. Detective Chief Inspector Sykes of the CID has a lasting friendship with Antony.

Each of the pairs of books written under other pseudonyms has its series character: Richard Trenton for Anne Burton, Jeremy Locke for Mary Challis and Stephen Marryat for Margaret Leek. Besides the Maitland story, 'Every Tale Condemns Me', there is another Sara Woods story.

All the Sara Woods books appeared first in London and are dated. Four titles have not been published in the USA. The titles for the entire series are taken from Shakespeare (but *The Taste of Fears* was re-titled *The Third Encounter* for its American publication). The first eighteen titles were published by Collins Crime Club. They all have red cloth, with black lettering for the initial five titles and gilt for the remaining thirteen. The rest were published by Macmillan in a variety of colours, both of cloth and spine lettering. From *Exit Murderer* the lettering is silver, except for four books with gilt lettering: *This Fatal Writ, Proceed to Judgment, Villains by Necessity* and *Call Back Yesterday. They Love Not Poison* has pictorial endpapers of a map of a Yorkshire village. The last book contains a biography of Antony Maitland. Several of the Crime Club wrappers have individual designs, among them John Rose's composite face made up of three converging facial images for *Malice Domestic*; Alan Burton's stylish depiction of a gun and three playing cards for *An Improbable Fiction*; and the effective design for *This Little Measure*, with its skeletal hand holding a phial of pills labelled 'Crime Club', appearing on both spine and front panel. *Bloody Instructions* and *Past Praying For*, among others, have plain black wrappers with coloured lettering.

The Macmillan wrappers, unfortunately, are mostly photographic, but a few are sufficiently striking to be worth recording, like the mushroom poison bottle and inkblot shaped like a witch and her cat on a broomstick for *They Love Not Poison*; the strangled girl lying prone within a green border for *Yet She Must Die*; and the apprehensive child with the shadow of a man holding an upraised stick for *A Show of Violence*.

Maitland novels by Sara Woods

(Binding details refer to Macmillan editions.)

Bloody Instructions   Collins Crime Club 1962, Harper 1962

Malice Domestic   Crime Club 1962

The Taste of Fears   Crime Club 1963

a.k.a. *The Third Encounter*   Harper 1963

Error of the Moon   Crime Club 1963

Trusted like the Fox   Crime Club 1964, Harper 1965

This Little Measure   Crime Club 1964

The Windy Side of the Law   Crime Club 1965, Harper 1965

Though I Know She Lies   Crime Club 1965, Holt, Rinehart 1972

Enter Certain Murderers   Crime Club 1966, Harper 1966

Let's Choose Executors   Crime Club 1966, Harper 1967

The Case is Altered   Crime Club 1967, Harper 1967

And Shame the Devil   Crime Club 1967, Holt 1972

Knives Have Edges   Crime Club 1968, Holt 1970

Past Praying For   Crime Club 1968, Harper 1968

Tarry and be Hanged   Crime Club 1969, Holt 1971

An Improbable Fiction   Crime Club 1970, Holt 1971

Serpent's Tooth   Crime Club 1971, Holt 1973

The Knavish Crows   Crime Club 1971

They Love Not Poison   Macmillan 1972, Holt 1972 (black, white)

Yet She Must Die   Macmillan 1973, Holt 1974 (maroon, white)

Enter the Corpse   Macmillan 1973, Holt 1974 (red, black)

Done to Death   Macmillan 1974, Holt 1975 (beige, black)

A Show of Violence   Macmillan 1975, McKay 1975 (brown, black)

My Life Is Done   Macmillan 1976, St Martin's 1976 (black, white)

The Law's Delay   Macmillan 1977, St Martin's 1977 (black, white)

A Thief or Two   Macmillan 1977, St Martin's 1977 (green, black)

Exit Murderer   Macmillan 1978, St Martin's 1978 (maroon binding)

This Fatal Writ   Macmillan 1979, St Martin's 1979 (red)

Proceed to Judgment   Macmillan 1979, St Martin's 1979 (brown)

They Stay for Death   Macmillan 1980, St Martin's 1980 (green)

Weep for Her   Macmillan 1980, St Martin's 1981 (turquoise)

Cry Guilty   Macmillan 1981, St Martin's 1981 (green)

Dearest Enemy   Macmillan 1981, St Martin's 1981 (brown)

Enter a Gentlewoman   Macmillan 1982, St Martin's 1982 (green)

Villains by Necessity   Macmillan 1982, St Martin's 1982 (yellow)

Most Grievous Murder   Macmillan 1982, St Martin's 1982 (red)

Call Back Yesterday   Macmillan 1983, St Martin's 1983 (yellow)

The Lie Direct   Macmillan 1983, St Martin's 1983 (grey)

Where Should He Die?   Macmillan 1983, St Martin's 1983 (red)

The Bloody Book of Law   Macmillan 1984, St Martin's 1984 (red)

Murder's Out Of Tune   Macmillan 1984, St. Martin's 1984 (blue)

Defy the Devil   Macmillan 1984, St Martin's 1985 (brown)

An Obscure Grave   Macmillan 1985, St Martin's 1985 (maroon)

Away With Them To Prison   Macmillan 1985, St Martin's 1985 (black)

Put Out the Light   Macmillan 1985, St Martin's 1986 (red)

Most Deadly Hate   Macmillan 1986, St Martin's 1986 (red)

Nor Live so Long   Macmillan 1986, St Martin's 1986 (red)

Naked Villainy   Macmillan 1987, St Martin's 1987 (red)

Trenton novels by Anne Burton

The Dear Departed   Raven House 1980
Where There's a Will   Raven 1980

Locke novels by Mary Challis

Burden of Proof   Raven 1980
Crimes Past   Raven 1980

Marryat novels by Margaret Leek

The Healthy Grave   Raven 1980
We Must Have a Trial   Raven 1980

Stories by Sara Woods

'The Trouble with some Policemen – They Won't Stick to the Facts' (*ES*, 14 Mar. 1963; *Saint* (UK) July 1964 as 'The Trouble with some Policemen')
'Every Tale Condemns Me' (*Winter's Crimes 17*, Macmillan 1985)   *JC*

Margaret Yorke (b. 1924)

Margaret Yorke is a crime novelist who abandoned detective fiction after an attractive series about an Oxford don named Patrick Grant, a handsome, opinionated bachelor with five cases, from *Dead in the Morning* in 1970 to *Cast for Death* in 1976. For *Silent Witness* he goes to Austria and for *Mortal Remains* to Greece; but his promising career stopped dead in 1976, when his author changed direction. The later books are much concerned with irruptions of violence and derangement into tranquil, humdrum lives. A threatening sentence sets the tone: 'Mick liked frightening people.' *Find Me a Villain* offers gentle relief from the prevailing climate of unease and unsettlement: though not a detective story, it is very agreeable.

Patrick Grant's career began with *Dead in the Morning*, published in 1970 by Bles, who issued all but the last of his five cases. It is a black book, with gilt spine lettering, and is not as tall as the books that followed. The orange dust-wrapper by Kaye Bellman shows three members of the household at Pantons, with the half-empty bottle of sodium amytal capsules that despatches the housekeeper. *Silent Witness* is also black and gilt, with black endpapers and a wrapper contrasting the blue of the Alpine sky with the white of the snow. *Grave Matters* has a brown binding, gilt spine lettering, and yellow endpapers; and *Mortal Remains* is orange and gilt, with an attractive wrapper by John Andrews, whose design achieves a classical Greek symmetry.

Cast for Death is a Hutchinson book, black, with white spine lettering and a photographic wrapper. *No Medals for the Major* and *The Small Hours of the Morning* were also published by Bles, alternating with the Grant detective stories. The latter, which appeared when Bles was folding, is taller than the rest of the secondary sequence. The later Hutchinson books are black with silver spine lettering and routine photographic wrappers (though *Find Me a Villain* is again a welcome exception, with its pregnant glimpse of Nina Crowther pulling aside a curtain at Netherton Hall). *Devil's Work* marks the beginning of a taller tertiary sequence.

From 1988 to 1990 the books were published by Mysterious Press, an imprint at that time of Century Hutchinson. In 1991, Hutchinson unalloyed took over again. The three Mysterious books are black and have the standard red endpapers with repetitions of the publisher's logo forming a pattern in black. *Crime in Question* has silver lettering, the others have gilt. *A Small Deceit* is dark blue, *Criminal Damage* black and *Dangerous to Know* red. The earlier pair have gilt spine lettering, *Dangerous to Know* has silver. With *Criminal Damage* the books made yet another leap in size (probably off most collectors' shelves). All Margaret Yorke's books are dated on the copyright page.

Except for *The Point of Murder*, which became *The Come-on*, American titles remain unchanged. Four novels have appeared in America in paperback editions only.

Margaret Yorke's shorter fiction was collected in a Warner-Futura paperback published in 1994, *Pieces of Justice*. The twenty-three stories include a more recent case for Patrick Grant, 'Greek Tragedy'.

Novels

(with Grant as stated)

Dead in the Morning Bles 1970, Bantam 1982 (Grant)
Silent Witness Bles 1972, Walker 1973 (Grant)
Grave Matters Bles 1973, Bantam 1982 (Grant)
No Medals for the Major Bles 1974, Penguin (US) 1987
Mortal Remains Bles 1974 (Grant)
The Small Hours of the Morning Bles 1975, Walker 1975
Cast for Death Hutchinson 1976, Walker 1976 (Grant)

The Cost of Silence Hutchinson 1977, Walker 1977
The Point of Murder Hutchinson 1978
a.k.a. *The Come-on* Harper 1979
Death on Account Hutchinson 1979, Penguin (US) 1988
The Scent of Fear Hutchinson 1980, St Martin's 1981
The Hand of Death Hutchinson 1981, St Martin's 1982
Devil's Work Hutchinson 1982, St Martin's 1982
Find Me a Villain Hutchinson 1983, St Martin's 1983
The Smooth Face of Evil Hutchinson 1984, St Martin's 1984
Intimate Kill Hutchinson 1985, St Martin's 1985
Safely to the Grave Hutchinson 1986, St Martin's 1986
Evidence to Destroy Hutchinson 1987, Viking 1987

MARGARET YORKE
A THRILLER

Speak for the Dead   Mysterious Press 1988, Viking 1988

Crime in Question   Mysterious Press 1989, Viking 1989

Admit to Murder   Mysterious Press 1990, Viking 1990

A Small Deceit   Hutchinson 1991, Viking 1991

Criminal Damage   Hutchinson 1992, Mysterious Press 1993

Dangerous to Know   Hutchinson 1993

Story collection

Pieces of Justice, Warner-Futura 1994 (23 stories)

BP

APPENDIX A.   Subject guide

There have been several lists grouping writers and books by subject and setting: Richard Emery's supplements to *The Poisoned Pen*; the second edition of Allen J. Hubin's bibliography, *Crime Fiction 1794–1980* (Garland 1984); *The Subject is Murder* by Albert Menendez (2 volumes: Garland 1986, 1990); and *Murder by Category* by Tasha Mackler (Scarecrow 1991). Books relating to specialized subject areas include *Locked Room Murders* by Robert Adey (Crossover Press 1992); *Novel Verdicts: A Guide to Courtroom Fiction* by Jon L. Breen (Scarecrow 1985); *College Mystery Novels* by John E. Kramer Jr and John E. Kramer III (Garland 1985); *The Police Procedural* by George N. Dove (Popular Press 1982); and *Mysterium and Mystery: The Clerical Crime Novel* by William David Spencer (UMI Research Press 1989). In addition, each issue of Janet Rudolph's *Mystery Readers Journal* is largely devoted to a single topic. Recent issues have dealt with journalism, religion, art and sport, for example. We give here some slight indication of the importance of particular themes or settings in the work of a small selection of writers.

Historical mysteries

Gwendoline Butler, John Dickson Carr, Lindsey Davis, Lillian de la Torre, P. C. Doherty/Michael Clynes/Paul Harding, Elizabeth Eyre, Richard Falkirk, Ray Harrison, Keith Heller, Evelyn Hervey, John Buxton Hilton, Alanna Knight, Peter Lovesey, Anne Perry, Ellis Peters, Jeremy Potter, Bernard St James, Francis Selwyn/Donald Thomas, Jean Stubbs, Jeremy Sturrock/J. G. Jeffreys, Julian Symons, Leonard Tourney, Robert van Gulik, R. J. White

The humorous mystery

Adrian Alington, Delano Ames, Robert Barnard, George Baxt, Edgar Box, Pamela Branch, Simon Brett, Leo Bruce, Heron Carvic, Hildegarde Dolson, Caroline Graham, Tim Heald, Kenneth Hopkins, Austin Lee, Nancy Livingston, Dick Lochte, Charlotte Macleod, Joyce Porter, Craig Rice, Margaret Scherf, Nancy Spain, Phoebe Atwood Taylor/Alice Tilton, Colin Watson, Donald E. Westlake, David Williams.

Police procedurals

John Ball, Rex Burns, Roger Busby, Michael Gilbert, Laurence Gough, Laurence Henderson, Graham Ison, Bill James, Bill Knox, Elizabeth Linington/Lesley Egan/Dell Shannon, J. J. Marric, William McIlvanney, Lillian O'Donnell, Maurice Procter, Jonathan Ross, Jack Scott, Lawrence Treat, Dorothy Uhnak, John Wainwright, Hillary Waugh, Collin Wilcox

Small-town/village mysteries

Catherine Aird, Leo Bruce, W. J. Burley, John Dickson Carr, Agatha Christie, D. M. Devine/Dominic Devine, Elizabeth Ferrars/E. X. Ferrars, Anthea Fraser, James Fraser, Elizabeth Lemarchand, Emma Page, Sheila Radley, Dorothy Simpson, June Thomson, Patricia Wentworth

Don-detectives

V. C. Clinton-Baddeley, Edmund Crispin, Amanda Cross, Glyn Daniel/Dilwyn Rees, Jocelyn Davey, Eilis Dillon, Timothy Fuller, Jane Langton, Jessica Mann, Simon Nash, Margaret Yorke

Religious detectives

C. A. Alington, Henry Catalan, G. K. Chesterton, H. H. Holmes, Leonard Holton, Harry Kemelman, William X. Kienzle, Ralph McInerny/Monica Quill, Sister Carol Ann O'Marie, Margaret Scherf, Charles Merrill Smith

The 'ethnic' detective

Delano Ames, Pierre Audemars, John Ball, Earl Derr Biggers, Suzanne Blanc, John and Emery Bonett, Bruce Buckingham, E. V. Cunningham, Nicolas Freeling, Richard Grayson, Nan Hamilton, Tony Hillerman, Timothy Holme, Roderic Jeffries, H. R. F. Keating, Maria Lang, John P. Marquand, A. E. W. Mason, James McClure, James Melville, Susan Moody, Magdalen Nabb, James Norman, Fremy Olbrich, David Serafin, Maj Sjöwall and Per Wahlöö, Thomas Sterling, Arthur W. Upfield, Robert van Gulik

Legal mysteries

Michael Gilbert, Cyril Hare, M. R. D. Meek, John Mortimer, Francis M. Nevins Jr, Michael Underwood, Sara Woods

Handicapped detectives

Vicars Bell, Ernest Bramah, Baynard Kendrick, Roy Lewis, John Trench

The world of the theatre

Simon Brett, Jane Dentinger, Ngaio Marsh, Anne Morice, Simon Shaw

The world of antiques

Michael Delving, Jonathan Gash, John Malcolm, Anthony Oliver

A selection of books on specific themes

Locked rooms/impossible crimes

His Burial Too Catherine Aird
Flowers for the Judge Margery Allingham
The Woman in the Wardrobe Peter Antony
The Layton Court Mystery Anthony Berkeley

Suddenly at His Residence Christianna Brand
Case for Three Detectives Leo Bruce
many titles by John Dickson Carr
The Moving Toyshop Edmund Crispin
The End of Andrew Harrison Freeman Wills Crofts
Close Quarters Michael Gilbert
Careless Corpse C. Daly King
The Crime Conductor Philip MacDonald
Through a Glass Darkly Helen McCloy
The Moonflower Beverley Nichols
The Elberg Collection Anthony Oliver
The Chinese Orange Mystery Ellery Queen
Tragedy at the Unicorn John Rhode
Invisible Green John Sladek
Catt Out of the Bag Clifford Witting
many titles by Anthony Wynne

Mysteries set on boats and trains

Murder Sails at Midnight Marian Babson
The Widow's Cruise Nicholas Blake
Dead Man's Shoes Leo Bruce
Death on the Nile Agatha Christie
The Blind Barber John Dickson Carr
Murder on the Orient Express Agatha Christie
Mystery in the Channel Freeman Wills Crofts
A Necessary End Val Gielgud
Obelists at Sea C. Daly King
The False Inspector Dew Peter Lovesey
Singing in the Shrouds Ngaio Marsh
Death on the Boat Train John Rhode
Death Under Sail C. P. Snow
The Wheel Spins Ethel Lina White

Medical/hospital mysteries

Murder in Hospital Josephine Bell
Green for Danger Christianna Brand
Murder M.D. Miles Burton
Upstairs, Downstairs Carol Carnac
Doctors Also Die D. M. Devine
One Foot in the Grave Peter Dickinson
The Attending Physician R. B. Dominic
Victims B. M. Gill
Shroud for a Nightingale P. D. James
A Stitch in Time Emma Lathen
The Nursing Home Murder Ngaio Marsh and Henry Jellett
Death in Harley Street John Rhode

Academic mysteries

Parting Breath Catherine Aird
Little Victims Robert Barnard
Death at Half Term Josephine Bell
Deadly Meeting Robert Bernard
A Question of Proof Nicholas Blake
Death at St. Asprey's School Leo Bruce
A Taste of Power W. J. Burley
Murder in the Coalhole Miles Burton
The Case of the Dead Shepherd Christopher
  Bush
The Dead Man's Knock John Dickson Carr
Cat Among the Pigeons Agatha Christie
Death's Bright Dart V. C. Clinton-Baddeley
Love Lies Bleeding Edmund Crispin
The Theban Mysteries Amanda Cross
Devil At Your Elbow D. M. Devine
The Night of the Twelfth Michael Gilbert
Death Drop B. M. Gill
An Advancement of Learning Reginald Hill
The Weight of the Evidence Michael Innes
Death of an Old Girl Elizabeth Lemarchand
Rest You Merry Charlotte Macleod
Murder at Midyears Marion Mainwaring
Tom Brown's Body Gladys Mitchell
The Cambridge Murders Dilwyn Rees
The Paper Chase Julian Symons
Miss Pym Disposes Josephine Tey
Treasure by Degrees David Williams.

APPENDIX B.   Anthologies of the CWA and MWA

CWA

Butcher's Dozen   Heinemann 1956
Choice of Weapons   Hodder & Stoughton 1958
Planned Departures   Hodder 1958
Some Like them Dead   Hodder 1960
Crime Writers' Choice   Hodder 1964
John Creasey's Mystery Bedside Book   Hodder 1966–75 (10 volumes)
John Creasey's Crime Collection   Gollancz 1977–90 (14 volumes)
Crime Waves 1,   Gollancz 1991
1st Culprit   Chatto & Windus 1992
2nd Culprit   Chatto 1993

MWA

Murder Cavalcade   Duell 1946, Hammond 1953
Murder By Experts   Ziff-Davis 1947, Sampson Low 1950
Four-and-Twenty Bloodhounds   Simon & Schuster 1950, Hammond 1951
20 Great Tales of Murder   Random House 1951, Hammond 1952
Maiden Murders   Harper 1952, Hammond 1953
Crooks' Tour   Dodd, Mead 1953, Macdonald 1954
Butcher, Baker, Murder-Maker   Knopf 1954, Macdonald 1956
Crime for Two   Lippincott 1955, Macdonald 1957
Eat, Drink and Be Buried   Viking 1956
abridged version as *For Tomorrow We Die* Macdonald 1958
Dolls are Murder   Lion 1957 (paperback)
For Love or Money   Doubleday 1957, Macdonald 1959
Big Time Mysteries,   Dodd 1958 (for young adults)
A Choice of Murders   Scribner 1958, Macdonald 1960

The Lethal Sex   Dell 1959 (paperback)
abridged version Collins Crime Club 1962
The Comfortable Coffin   Gold Medal 1960 (paperback)
Tales for a Rainy Night   Holt 1961, Dobson 1967
The Quality of Murder   Dutton 1962 (true crime)
Cream of the Crime   Holt 1962, Harrap 1964
A Pride of Felons   Macmillan 1963, Dobson 1964
Crimes Across the Sea   Harper 1964, Harrap 1965
Masters of Mayhem   Morrow 1965
Sleuths and Consequences   Simon 1966
Murder in Mind   Dutton 1967
With Malice Toward All   Putnam 1968, Macmillan 1969
Merchants of Menace   Doubleday 1969
Crime Without Murder   Scribner 1970, Gollancz 1972
Murder Most Foul   Walker 1971
Dear Dead Days   Walker 1972, Gollancz 1974
Mirror, Mirror, Fatal Mirror   Doubleday 1973
Killers of the Mind   Random House 1974, Gollancz 1975
Every Crime in the Book   Putnam 1975
Tricks and Treats   Doubleday 1976
a.k.a. *Mystery Writers' Choice 1977*   Gollancz 1977
When Last Seen   Harper 1977
a.k.a. *Mystery Writers' Choice 1978*   Gollancz 1978
I, Witness   Times Books 1978 (true crime)
Cop Cade   Doubleday 1978
Women's Wiles   Harcourt Brace 1979
The Edgar Winners   Random House 1980
All But Impossible!   Ticknor & Fields 1981, Hale 1983
A Special Kind of Crime   Doubleday 1982

The Mystery Hall of Fame   Morrow 1984
The Crime of My Life   Walker 1984, Severn
   House 1986
Last Laughs   Mysterious Press 1986
Murder on the Aisle   Simon 1987
Distant Danger   Wynwood 1988
Beastly Tales   Wynwood 1989
The New Edgar Winners   Wynwood 1990

APPENDIX C.   CWA and MWA award winners, for the best novel(s) of each year

CWA

1955	*The Little Walls* Winston Graham
1956	*The Second Man* Edward Grierson
1957	*The Colour of Murder* Julian Symons
1958	*Someone From the Past* Margot Bennett
1959	*Passage of Arms* Eric Ambler
1960	*The Night of Wenceslas* Lionel Davidson
1961	*The Spoilt Kill* Mary Kelly
1962	*When I Grow Rich* Joan Fleming
1963	*The Spy Who Came In from the Cold* John Le Carré
1964	*The Perfect Murder* H. R. F. Keating
1965	*The Far Side of the Dollar* Ross Mac-Donald
	Midnight Plus One Gavin Lyall (Best British novel)
1966	*A Long Way to Shiloh* Lionel Davidson
1967	*Murder Against the Grain* Emma Lathen
	Dirty Story Eric Ambler (Best British novel)
1968	*Skin Deep* Peter Dickinson
	The Private Wound Nicholas Blake (runner-up)
1969	*A Pride of Heroes* Peter Dickinson (Gold Dagger)
	Another Way of Dying Francis Clifford (Silver Dagger)
1970	*Young Man, I Think You're Dying* Joan Fleming
	The Labyrinth Makers Anthony Price
1971	*The Steam Pig* James McClure
	Shroud for a Nightingale P. D. James
1972	*The Levanter* Eric Ambler
	The Rainbird Pattern Victor Canning
1973	*The Defection of A. J. Lewinter* Robert Littell

	A Coffin for Pandora Gwendoline Butler
1974	*Other Paths to Glory* Anthony Price
	The Grosvenor Square Goodbye Francis Clifford
1975	*The Seven-per-cent Solution* Nicholas Meyer
	The Black Tower P. D. James
1976	*A Demon in My View* Ruth Rendell
	Rogue Eagle James McClure
1977	*The Honourable Schoolboy* John Le Carré
	Laidlaw William McIlvanney
1978	*The Chelsea Murders* Lionel Davidson
	Waxwork Peter Lovesey
1979	*Whip Hand* Dick Francis
	Service of All the Dead Colin Dexter
1980	*The Murder of the Maharajah* H. R. F. Keating
	Monk's-Hood Ellis Peters
1981	*Gorky Park* Martin Cruz Smith
	The Dead of Jericho Colin Dexter
1982	*The False Inspector Dew* Peter Lovesey
	Ritual Murder S. T. Haymon
1983	*Accidental Crimes* John Hutton
	The Papers of Tony Veitch William McIlvanney
1984	*The Twelfth Juror* B. M. Gill
	The Tree of Hands Ruth Rendell
1985	*Monkey Puzzle* Paula Gosling
	Last Seen Alive Dorothy Simpson
1986	*Live Flesh* Ruth Rendell
	A Taste for Death P. D. James
1987	*A Fatal Inversion* Barbara Vine
	Presumed Innocent Scott Turow
1988	*Ratking* Michael Dibdin
	Toxic Shock Sara Paretsky
1989	*The Wench is Dead* Colin Dexter
	The Shadow Run Desmond Lowden

1990	*Bones and Silence* Reginald Hill
	The Late Candidate Mike Phillips
1991	*King Solomon's Carpet* Barbara Vine
	Deep Sleep Frances Fyfield
1992	*The Way Through the Woods* Colin Dexter
	Bucket Nut Liza Cody
1993	*Cruel and Unusual* Patricia D. Cornwell
	Fatlands Sarah Dunant

MWA

1953 *Beat Not the Bones* Charlotte Jay
1954 *The Long Goodbye* Raymond Chandler
1955 *Beast in View* Margaret Millar
1956 *A Dram of Poison* Charlotte Armstrong
1957 *Room to Swing* Ed Lacy
1958 *The Eighth Circle* Stanley Ellin
1959 *The Hours Before Dawn* Celia Fremlin
1960 *The Progress of a Crime* Julian Symons
1961 *Gideon's Fire* J. J. Marric
1962 *Death and the Joyful Woman* Ellis Peters
1963 *The Light of Day* Eric Ambler
1964 *The Spy Who Came In from the Cold* John Le Carré
1965 *The Quiller Memorandum* Adam Hall
1966 *King of the Rainy Country* Nicolas Freeling
1967 *God Save the Mark* Donald E. Westlake
1968 *A Case of Need* Jeffrey Hudson
1969 *Forfeit* Dick Francis
1970 *The Laughing Policeman* Maj Sjöwall and Per Wahlöö
1971 *The Day of the Jackal* Frederick Forsyth
1972 *The Lingala Code* Warren Kiefer
1973 *Dance Hall of the Dead* Tony Hillerman
1974 *Peter's Pence* Jon Cleary
1975 *Hopscotch* Brian Garfield
1976 *Promised Land* Robert B. Parker
1977 *Catch Me, Kill Me* William Hallahan
1978 *The Eye of the Needle* Ken Follett
1979 *The Rheingold Route* Arthur Maling
1980 *Whip Hand* Dick Francis
1981 *Peregrine* William Bayer
1982 *Billingsgate Shoal* Rick Boyer
1983 *La Brava* Elmore Leonard
1984 *Briarpatch* Ross Thomas
1985 *The Suspects* L. R. Wright

1986 *A Dark-adapted Eye* Barbara Vine
1987 *Old Bones* Aaron Elkins
1988 *A Cold Red Sunrise* Stuart Kaminsky
1989 *Black Cherry Blues* James Lee Burke
1990 *New Orleans Mourning* Julie Smith
1991 *A Dance at the Slaughter House* Lawrence Block
1992 *Bootlegger's Daughter* Margaret Maron
1993 *The Sculptress* Minette Walters

APPENDIX D.   Specialist dealers

We acknowledge a considerable debt to *TAD* for details of current American dealers

UK

Al Crime Fiction, Westridge, 3 Horsecastles Lane, Sherborne, Dorset DT9 6 DW

R. Andrews, The Barn, Brockhampton, Cheltenham, Glos. GL54 5XL

Black Bird Books, 24 Grampian Gardens, London NW2 1JG

Blythwood Books, 85 Talbot Road, Bournemouth, Hants BH9 2JD

Geoff Bradley, 9 Vicarage Hill, South Benfleet, Essex SS7 1PA

C. R. Ellis, Cherrington, 20A Mayor's Walk, Pontefract, West Yorks WF8 2RR

Ergo Books, 46 Lisburne Road, London NW3 2NR

Ferret Fantasy, at Bell Book & Radmall, 4 Cecil Court, London WC2

Scott Herbertson, 89 Harvest Bank Road, West Wickham, Kent BR4 9DP

Mainly Fiction, 21 Tennyson Road, Cheadle, Cheshire SK8 2AR

Ming Books, 110 Gloucester Avenue, Chalk Farm, London NW1 HAA

Murder One, 71–3 Charing Cross Road, London WC2H OAA

Post Mortem Books, 58 Stanford Avenue, Hassocks, West Sussex BN6 8JH

Donald Rudd, 8 Parkside, Middlesborough, Cleveland TS3 OBP

R. F. Stewart, 151 Berwick Avenue, Heaton Mersey, Stockport SK4 3AT

Jamie Sturgeon, 14 Longlands, Worthing, West Sussex BN14 9NT

Time Enough for Books, 43 Mile End Road, Colchester, Essex CO4 5BU

USA

Steven C. Bernard, 15011 Plainfield Lane, Darnestown, Maryland 20874

Book Carnival, 348, South Tustin Avenue, Orange, California 92666

The Bookshop, 400 West Franklin Street, Chapel Hill, N. Carolina 27514

Dunn & Powell, The Hideaway, Bar Harbor, Maine 04609

Patricia A. Fickes, 1471 Burkhardt Avenue, Akron, Ohio 44301

Gravesend Books, Box 235, Pocono Pines, Pennsylvania 18350

Grounds for Murder, 3858 Fifth Avenue, San Diego, California 92103

The Haunted Bookshop, 100 Elmwood Avenue, Buffalo, New York 14201

Heartland Books, 214 Main Street, Woodstock, Illinois 60098

I Love a Mystery, 1621 New Scotland Road, Slingerlands, New York 12159

Janus Books, PO Box 40787, Tucson, Arizona 85717

Kate's Mystery Books, 2211 Massachusetts Avenue, Cambridge, Massachusetts 02140

Limestone Hills Bookshop, PO Box 1125, Glen Rose, Texas 76043

Maxwell's Bookmark, 2103 Pacific Avenue, Stockton, California 95204

Mitchell Books, 1395E Washington Boulevard, Pasadena, California 91104

Mordida Books, PO Box 79322, Houston, Texas 77279

Murder and Mayhem, 6412 Carrollton Avenue, Indianapolis, Indiana 46220

Murder by the Book, 1574 South Pearl Street, Denver, Colorado 80210

Murder Ink, 2486 Broadway, New York, New York 10025

The Mysterious Bookshop, 129 West 56th Street, New York, New York 10019

The Mysterious Bookshop West, 8763 Beverley Boulevard, West Hollywood, California 90069

Maurice F. Neville Rare Books, 835 Laguna Street, Santa Barbara, California 93101

Oceanside Books Unlimited, 173a Woodfield Road, West Hempstead, New York 11552

Once Upon a Crime, 604 West 26th Street, Minneapolis, Minnesota 55405

Frank S. Pollack, 1214 Green Bay Road, Highland Park, Illinois 60035

Raven Books, PO Box 939, Artesia, California 90702/0939

The Rue Morgue, 942 Pearl Street, Boulder, Colorado 80302

San Francisco Mystery Bookstore, 746 Diamond Street, San Francisco, California 94114

Seattle Book Center, 2231 Second Avenue, Seattle, Washington 98121

Seattle Mystery Bookshop, 117 Cherry St, Seattle, Washington 98104

Second Story Books, 12160 Parklawn Drive, Rockville, Maryland 20852

The Silver Door, PO Box 3208, Redondo Beach, California 90277

Spenser's Mystery Bookshop, 314 Newbury Street, Boston, Massachusetts 02115

Thomolsen Books, Box 24, Bayville, New York 11709

TLC Books, 9 North College Avenue, Salem, Virginia 24153

Uncle Buck's Mysteries, 390 Oak Hill Drive, Belleville, Illinois 62223

West's Booking Agency, PO Box 406, Elm Grove, Wisconsin 53122

CANADA

Sleuth of Baker Street, 1595 Bayview Avenue, Toronto, Ontario MG4 3B5

APPENDIX E.   Glossary of terms used by book collectors and dealers

Association copy: a copy of a book with a unique feature connected in some way with its author

Backstrip: the back of a book, visible when it is stored on the shelf (and more commonly called the spine)

Binding: the covering of a book

Blank: a leaf with no printing on it; also used adjectivally to describe covers with no lettering or decoration

Blind-stamped: impressed on a binding, without subsequent inking or gilding

Boards: the slabs of stiff, compressed paper used in the binding of books

Bookplate: a personal label, often decorative, stuck into the front of a book as a badge of ownership (undesirable unless the owner has some claim to the collector's esteem)

Border: a single line ruled close to each edge of the front cover of a book, jointly framing its main area

Chipped: with small pieces missing from the edges (used of dust-wrappers)

Cloth: the woven material in which many books were bound

Colophon: a publisher's ornamental device, often seen at the base of a book's spine and on its title-page (also known as a logo)

Copyright notice: the attribution to authors of their sole rights in the reproduction of their work, usually featured on the back of the title-page of a book (sometimes loosely called the copyright page)

Dedication copy: the copy of a book in which the author has added a holograph dedication to the printed one

Dust-wrapper: the paper folded round a book for its protection (also known as the dust-jacket); abbreviated to dw or dj in dealer's lists.

Endpapers: the paper sheets forming double leaves at the front and end of a book, used to join the binding to the pages. The outer half of each sheet is pasted to the inside of each cover, and is known as the pastedown. The inner half is known as the free front or rear endpaper.

Ex-library: not just from a library, but defaced by the signs of the library's ownership

First edition: the first appearance of a text in book form

Flyleaf: a blank leaf at the beginning or end of a book

Fore-edge: the combined front edges of the pages of a book

Foxed: discoloured by scattered brown spots, on the pages or edges of a book

Frontispiece: an illustration facing the title-page of a book

Gathering: the folded printed sheets that form a section of a book. The gatherings were indicated in sequence by the letters of the alphabet, known in this context as signatures.

Half-title: the page preceding the title-page, which bears only the title of the book

Hinge: any of the inner folds of the pages, connecting with the flexible joint on the inside of the backstrip of a book

Holograph: written in the author's hand

Lamination: a binding process whereby pictorial boards are coated with a thin plastic covering

Leaf: two pages of a book, the front or recto, and the back or verso

Logo: a publisher's device (*see* Colophon)

Page: one printed side of a leaf

Panel: the area of a dust-wrapper extending over the front or back cover

Pastedown: the inside of the front or back cover (*see* Endpapers)

Pictorial cloth: a cloth binding with a picture printed directly on to it

Preliminaries: the pages of a book that precede the text

Presentation copy: a copy of a book presented by the author, with a holograph inscription

Printer's code: the formula used by the printer of a book to indicate when it was printed, sometimes found on the copyright page and sometimes at the end

Proof copy: an early, uncorrected copy of a book in paper covers, intended to be checked and corrected

quarter-binding: a quarter-bound book has its spine and the adjacent areas in a different, usually superior, material from the boards used for the greater part of the covers. The separate areas have either different colours or sometimes shades of the same colour.

Recto: the right-hand of two pages

Remainder spray: a scattering of tiny dots over the bottom edge of book, applied by some US publishers to their remainder stock (remainders are unsold books offered at a reduced price)

Rubbed: showing signs of wear caused by friction

Rule: a single ruled line

Spine: the backstrip of a book

Tipped in: stuck into a book, to form an additional page after the gatherings have been assembled. Frontispieces and illustrations are often tipped in, and so are cancel pages, replacing pages removed for some reason (before publication).

Title-page: the preliminary page giving the title, author, and publisher of a book, sometimes with the year of publication

Top edge: the combined top edges of the pages of a book

Verso: the left-hand of two pages

APPENDIX F. A selective guide to publishers' practice in designating first editions

It should be possible to formulate rules for the recognition of first editions of all English-language crime fiction – and to list all the exceptions. To do so, however, would entail intensive research in the copyright libraries of Britain and America, and could well occupy a lifetime. What follows is no more than a preliminary stab at such an enterprise, but, since it is based on books we have seen, it is correct as far as it goes.

Ernest Benn: Mid-1920s books have dated title-pages. Later titles have 'First published in –' on reverse of title-page.

Geoffrey Bles: Inconsistent procedure – some books are undated; some have dated title-page; some have 'First published in –', from the 1960s with copyright notice.

Bodley Head: Books have 'First published in –' on reverse of title-page, in more recent years with copyright notice.

Cassell: Books have 'First published in –' on reverse of title-page, from the 1960s with copyright notice. Most Cassell books have a printer's code, at least up to 1970. This features at the end of the book in earlier titles, and on the reverse of the title-page from the 1930s.

Chatto & Windus: Books have dated title-pages, from the late 1950s with copyright notice also.

Collins: Pre-Crime Club books have 'Copyright' with the year in the middle of reverse of title-page, and so do early Crime Club titles. From the mid-1930s, these appear at the foot of the page, sometimes with the author's name. From 1971, 'First published in –' also appears. Rarely, title-pages are dated (1958/9). Two undated titles are known. If a Crime Club book has an asterisk on the spine, above the publisher's name, this indicates an ex-library copy.

Constable: Inconsistent procedure – dated title-pages and 'First published in –' on reverse of title-page both occur, in the 1970s with copyright notices.

Peter Davies: Books have 'First Published in –' on reverse of title-page, with copyright notice after 1958.

Eyre & Spottiswoode: Books have dated title-pages from the 1930s to the 1950s. 'First published in –' began to appear around 1960, at first with dated title-page, but later without. Copyright notices feature from around 1960.

Faber & Faber: 1930s books have 'First published in –' with the month and the year, on reverse of title-page. Later books show the year only. The years appeared in Roman numerals to around 1957, and copyright notices began to appear at this time.

Victor Gollancz: Earlier books have dated title-pages. From around 1947, copyright notices appear on reverse of title-page. From 1985, 'First published in –' also appears.

Robert Hale: Books have 'First published in –' on reverse of title-page, with copyright notice from around 1960. Undated titles from the 1930s and 1950s are known.

Hamish Hamilton: Books have 'First published in –' on reverse of title-page, with or without copyright notice.

Hammond, Hammond: Inconsistent procedure – undated books are known; many have 'First published in –' on reverse of title-page, with or without the copyright notice; and often the copyright notice only appears. From about 1947, the copyright page often has a printer's datecode at the foot.

William Heinemann: Most books have 'First published in –' on reverse of title-page. Undated books are known (1938/9), and one book has 'First published in 1942' on the front free endpaper.

Hodder & Stoughton: Inconsistent procedure – undated books appeared in the 1920s and 1930s; some have dated title-pages; some have 'First published in –' on reverse of title-page; many have 'First printed in –', sometimes with the month as well as the year; some have the copyright notice only (around 1958); and later titles have 'First published in –' with the copyright notice.

Hutchinson: Many earlier books are undated, except at the head of advertisement sections at the end (and sometimes not even there). Early post-war books are also undated. From 1950 'First published in –' appears on reverse of title-page; from the 1960s with the copyright notice.

Michael Joseph: Books have 'First published in –' on reverse of title-page, with copyright notice from around 1957.

Macdonald: Books have 'First published in –' on reverse of title-page, with copyright notice from the 1960s. An undated title is known (1946).

Macmillan: Books have 'First published in –' on reverse of title-page, with copyright notice.

Methuen: Books have 'First published in –' on reverse of title-page, in later years with the copyright notice. Many 1920s and some 1930s books have printer's datecode at the end, which must match the date at the front.

Nicholson & Watson: 1930s books have dated title-pages and 'First published in –' on the reverse. Later books have undated title-pages, but retain the second feature.

Secker & Warburg: 1950s and 1960s books have dated title-pages and 'First published in –' on the reverse, sometimes with the copyright notice as well. Later title-pages are not dated.

Ward Lock: Earlier books are known with dated title-page or 'First published in –' on reverse of title-page. Later books have the latter only.

Weidenfeld & Nicolson: Around 1970, books have copyright notice only on reverse of title-page. 'First published by Weidenfeld & Nicolson' appears later, with the copyright notice

for dating. The date is added to the formula from 1980.

Addendum

In recent years a number of British publishers have begun to use an American-style printer's key, found invariably on the copyright page. A key indicates whether the book is the first edition or a later issue. The lowest digit should be 1 for a book to be the first printing. Harper-Collins Crime Club uses the key 987654321; Headline uses 10987654321; Macmillan uses 987654321 or 135798642; and Viking uses 10987654321 or 13579108642.

APPENDIX G.   Specialist journals

This section is heavily indebted to Geoff Bradley. The publications listed are likely to range over the whole field of crime fiction.

UK

Crime and Detective Stories (*CADS*) 9 Vicarage Hill, South Benfleet, Essex SS7 1PA

A Shot in the Dark 32 High Street, Bonsall, Matlock, Derbyshire DE4 2AR

USA

The Armchair Detective (TAD), 129 West 56th Street, New York, New York 10019

Clues, The Popular Press, Bowling Green State University, Bowling Green, Ohio 43404

The Criminal Record, 3131 Seventh Avenue, Denver, Colorado 80206

Deadly Pleasures, PO Box 839, Farmington, Utah 84025-0839

The Drood Review, 5047 West Main, 110, Kalamazoo, Michigan 49009

Mostly Murder, 2614 Hood Street, Dallas, Texas 75219

Mystery & Detective Monthly (MDM), 5601 North 40th Street, Tacoma, Washington 98407

Mystery News, PO Box 1201, Port Townsend, Washington 98368-0901

Mystery Readers Journal, PO Box 8116, Berkeley, California 94707-8116

Mystery Scene, Mystery Enterprises, PO Box 669, Cedar Rapids, Iowa 52406-0669

Prime Suspect, PO Box 81036, Albuquerque, New Mexico 87198

Australia

Mean Streets, What Goes On Pty Ltd, 214 Hat Hill Road, Blackheath, New South Wales 2785

Canada

The Mystery Review, C. von Hessert & Associates Ltd, PO Box 233, Colborne, Ontario KOK 150

France

Enigmatika (in French), 4 rue de l'Avenir, Les Mesneux, 51500 Rilly le Montagne.

Scandinavia

Guide to Scandinavian Crime and Detection, published by SKS and Antikvariat Pinkerton, Nansensgade 70, DK-1366, Copenhagen K, Denmark, lists eleven magazines, five for Denmark, one for Finland and five for Sweden. The Swedish journal *Dast* tends to have some English content. Its editor is Iwan Morelius, Calle Acacia 801, Pinar de Campo Verde, El Pilar de la Horadada, E-03190 Alicante, Spain. As far as is known, the other magazines listed are wholly in the language of the country of origin.

APPENDIX H. Societies and/or journals/newsletters devoted to individual writers

We are grateful to Roger Johnson for information about Conan Doyle and Sherlock Holmes and, again, to Geoff Bradley, for much we would not otherwise have known.

Margery Allingham

The Margery Allingham Society was founded by Mrs Pat Watt, 3 Corringham Road, Wembley, Middlesex HA9 9PX. Mrs Maryell Cleary is the US secretary and editor: her address is 1183 Arbor Drive, Apt B, East Lansing, Michigan 48823, USA. The journal is *The Bottle Street Gazette*.

Lilian Jackson Braun

The Lilian Jackson Braun Newsletter is available from Helen McCarthy, 4 Tamarack Road, Natick, Massachusettss 01760, USA.

Leo Bruce

The Leo Bruce Fan Club, Japan, is run by Susumu Kobayashi, 4-10-7 Junjoh-Nakahara, Kita-ku, Tokyo 114, Japan. The journal, *Aunt Aurora*, is almost entirely in Japanese.

Leslie Charteris

The address of The Saint Club is c/o Arbour Youth Centre, Shandy Street, Stepney, London E1 4ST. The club journal is *The Epistle*.

G. K. Chesterton

The Chesterton Review is published from St Thomas More College, 1437 College Drive, Saskatoon, Saskatchewan S7N OW6, Canada.

Agatha Christie

The Agatha Christie Society has Rosalind Hicks as President, Mathew Prichard as Chairman and Joan Hickson and David Suchet as Vice-presidents. The journal is the *Christie Chronicle* and the address for correspondence is PO Box 985, London SW1 9XA. The Agatha Christie Appreciation Society – Postern of Murder is run by Dorothy M. Carr and friends. The journal is *The Laurel Lines* and the address is Apt 206, 16 E. Northampton Street, Wilkes-Barre, Pennsylvania 18701-3005, USA.

Wilkie Collins

The President of the Wilkie Collins Society is Kirk H. Beetz, 1307 F Street, Davis, California 95616, USA. The Secretary is Andrew Gasson, 3 Merton House, 36 Belsize Park, London NW3 4EA. A regular newsletter is issued.

A. Conan Doyle

The Baker Street Irregulars is the senior Sherlockian society, founded in 1934. The 'benevolent autocrat' is Thomas L. Stix Jr., 34 Pierson Avenue, Norwood, New Jersey 07684, USA. *The Baker Street Journal* is available to members and non-members. The address is PO Box 465, Hanover, Pennsylvania 17331, USA. Payment by credit card is in order.

The Sherlock Holmes Society of London publishes *The Sherlock Holmes Journal* twice yearly. The membership secretary is Commander G. S. Stavert (RN retired), 3 Outram Road, Southsea, Hants PO5 1QP

The Arthur Conan Doyle Society was founded by Christopher Roden, Ashcroft, 2 Abbottsford Drive, Penyffordd, Chester CH4 OJG. The journal, *ACD*, appears annually.

The Northern Musgraves have two co-presidents: David Stuart Davies, Overdale, 69 Greenhead Road, Huddersfield HD1 4ER, and Kathryn White, 149 Myrtle Terrace, Cross Roads, Keighley, West Yorks BD22 9AJ. The journal, published annually, is *The Musgrave Papers*.

The Franco-Midland Hardware Co. may be reached through the Stockbroker's Clerk at 6 Bramham Moor, Hill Head, Fareham, Hants PO14 6RU. The company publishes an annual report and an interim report. It is also agent for *The Universal Sherlock Holmes*, the updated and greatly expanded version of Ronald Burt de Waal's *World Bibliography of Sherlock Holmes*, originally published in 1974.

Independent Sherlockian journals include *The Baker Street Gazette*, PO Box 221, Alderney, Channel Islands, and *The Baker Street Miscellanea*, The Sciolist Press, PO Box 225, Winnetka, Illinois 60093-0225, USA.

R. Austin Freeman

The Thorndyke File continues under the editorship of John J. McAleer, Mount Independence, 121 Follen Road, Lexington, Massachusetts, 02173, USA. *John Thorndyke's Journal* is published by David Chapman, 55 Highfield Gardens, Aldershot, Hants GU11 3DB.

Erle Stanley Gardner

The National Association for the Advancement of Perry Mason may be reached at 2735 Benvenue 3, Berkeley, California 94705, USA.

Elizabeth Linington

The Linington Line-up is published by Rinehart S. Potts, 1223 Glen Terrace, Glassboro, New Jersey 08028, USA.

John D. Macdonald

The *JDM Bibliophile* is edited by Ed Hirschberg, Department of English, University of Florida, Tampa, Florida 33620, USA.

Charlotte Macleod

The Charlotte Macleod Newsletter is published by Anne Weissman, 23 Van Dam, New York, New York 10013, USA.

Elizabeth Peters

A newsletter, *MPM* (for Mertz, Peters, Michaels), is available from Box 4262, Frederick, Maryland 21705, USA.

Ellis Peters

The Ellis Peters Appreciation Society was founded by Sue Feder, 7815 Daniels Avenue, Parksville, Maryland 21234, USA. The journal is *Most Loving Mere Folly*.

Dorothy L. Sayers

The President of the Sayers Society is Lt.-Col. Ralph Clarke and the Chairman is Christopher Dean, Rose Cottage, Malthouse Lane, Hurstpierpoint, West Sussex BN6 9JY. The Society publishes regular bulletins, a series of *Sidelights on Sayers* and the proceedings of its annual conventions.

Rex Stout

The address for The Wolfe Pack is PO Box 822, Ansonia Station, New York, New York 10023, USA. The Wolfe Pack journal is *The Gazette*.

Edgar Wallace

The Edgar Wallace Society is run by Neil Clark, 9 Hurst Rise Road, North Hinksey, Oxford OX2 9HE. The President of the Society is Penelope Wallace, the author's daughter, and the journal is *The Crimson Circle*.

APPENDIX I.   Other recommended authors

JC recommends:

Herbert Adams; Michael Allen; Pauline Bell;
Margot Bennett; Julie Burrows; Alison Cairns;
Stewart Farrar; Laurence Gough; Ann Granger;
Edward Grierson; Bruce Hamilton; Laurence
Henderson; Margaret Hinxman; Richard Hull;
Bill James; C. H. B. Kitchin; Lynton Lamb;
Kay Mitchell; Simon Nash; Staynes and Storey;
Glen Trevor; Jill Paton Walsh; Jacqueline
Wilson

BP recommends:

Delano Ames; Ralph Arnold; Isaac Asimov;
Maisie Birmingham; Herbert Brean; Barbara
Ninde Byfield; James Byrom; Edward Candy;
Youngman Carter; Heron Carvic; Lettice
Cooper; Guy Cullingford; Jocelyn Davey; Jane
Dentinger; Hildegarde Dolson; Nigel
FitzGerald; Kenneth Giles; Charles A.
Goodrum; M. R. Hodgkin; Timothy Holme;
Kenneth Hopkins; Colin Howard/Howard
Shaw; Stanley Hyland; Mary Kelly; Thomas
Kyd; Lange Lewis; Amanda Mackay; Marion
Mainwaring; Kenneth O'Hara; Sheila Pim;
Robert Player; Helen Robertson; Margaret
Scherf; John Sherwood; Fiona Sinclair; John
Sladek; Richard H. R. Smithies; Thomas
Sterling; James Turner; Mignon Warner;
Audrey Williamson; Barbara Worsley-Gough.

APPENDIX J. A personal choice of books

The reader will observe that the following lists include some authors unrepresented in this book, and also that some who are included in the book are absent from the lists. We take this as an indication that the book tells only part of an infinitely rewarding story.

JC recommends:

A Late Phoenix Catherine Aird
Spence in Petal Park Michael Allen
Death of a Ghost Margery Allingham
Death Walks in Eastrepps Francis Beeding
Trial and Error Anthony Berkeley
Minute for Murder Nicholas Blake
Green for Danger Christianna Brand
Death in a Salubrious Place W. J. Burley
A Coffin from the Past Gwendoline Butler
The Hollow Man John Dickson Carr
Ten Little Niggers Agatha Christie (now known as *And Then There Were None*)
No Case for the Police V. C. Clinton-Baddeley
The Moving Toyshop Edmund Crispin
The Cask Freeman Wills Crofts
The Fifth Cord D. M. Devine
The Silent World of Nicholas Quinn Colin Dexter
The Red Widow Murders Carter Dickson
Something Wicked Elizabeth Ferrars
Every Inch a Lady Joan Fleming
Six Proud Walkers Anthea Fraser
A Cockpit of Roses James Fraser
Well-schooled in Murder Elizabeth George
A Necessary End Val Gielgud
Death of a Favourite Girl Michael Gilbert
The Killings at Badger's Drift Caroline Graham
Tragedy at Law Cyril Hare
Death in the Stocks Georgette Heyer
Recalled to Life Reginald Hill
Malice Aforethought Francis Iles

Death at the President's Lodging Michael Innes
A Taste for Death P. D. James
Murder Gone Mad Philip MacDonald
Scales of Justice Ngaio Marsh
The Murders of Mrs. Austin and Mrs. Beale Jill McGown
Death in the Garden Jennie Melville
Who Saw Her Die? Patricia Moyes
Cover-Up Anthony Oliver
Who Saw Him Die? Sheila Radley
Wolfman Ian Rankin
A Sleeping Life Ruth Rendell
Diminished by Death Jonathan Ross
Murder Must Advertise Dorothy L. Sayers
Last Seen Alive Dorothy Simpson
The Man Who Killed Himself Julian Symons
The Daughter of Time Josephine Tey
Alibi in Time June Thomson
New Graves at Great Norne Henry Wade
Murder in Advent David Williams
Frost at Christmas R. D. Wingfield
Catt Out of the Bag Clifford Witting

BP recommends

More Work for the Undertaker Margery Allingham
Fish and Company Ralph Arnold
No Murder H. C. Bailey
The Poisoned Chocolates Case Anthony Berkeley
The Widow's Cruise Nicholas Blake
Dead Lion John and Emery Bonett
The Case of the Seven of Calvary Anthony Boucher
The Bells at Old Bailey Dorothy Bowers
London Particular Christianna Brand
Wilders Walk Away Herbert Brean
Case With Ropes and Rings Leo Bruce

The Case of the 100% Alibis   Christopher
  Bush
Fire, Burn!   John Dickson Carr
Thus Was Adonis Murdered   Sarah Caudwell
Murder on the Orient Express   Agatha Christie
Love Lies Bleeding   Edmund Crispin
The House Without a Door   Elizabeth Daly
The Naked Villany   Jocelyn Davey
The Chelsea Murders   Lionel Davidson
The Last House-Party   Peter Dickinson
The Judas Window   Carter Dickson
The Horizontal Man   Helen Eustis
The Lift and the Drop   G. V. Galwey
Smallbone Deceased   Michael Gilbert
Victims   B. M. Gill
Gravedigger   Joseph Hansen
Suicide Excepted   Cyril Hare
Dead Indeed   M. R. Hodgkin
Nine Times Nine   H. H. Holmes
Green Grow the Tresses-O   Stanley Hyland
Stop Press   Michael Innes
Shroud for a Nightingale   P. D. James
The Spoilt Kill   Mary Kelly
Dark Nantucket Noon   Jane Langton
The Random Factor   Linda J. LaRosa and
  Barry Tanenbaum
The Nursemaid Who Disappeared   Philip
  MacDonald
Singing in the Shrouds   Ngaio Marsh
Two-thirds of a Ghost   Helen McCloy
Death of a Dancer   Jill McGown
The Elberg Collection   Anthony Oliver
The Knocker on Death's Door   Ellis Peters
The Egyptian Cross Mystery   Ellery Queen
Death and the Maiden   Sheila Radley
Some Lie and Some Die   Ruth Rendell
Dr. Goodwood's Locum   John Rhode
Landscape with Dead Dons   Robert Robinson
The Nine Tailors   Dorothy L. Sayers
Invisible Green   John Sladek
A Coat of Varnish   C. P. Snow
Murder by the Book   Rex Stout
The Franchise Affair   Josephine Tey
A Question of Identity   June Thomson
Docken Dead   John Trench
Bump in the Night   Colin Watson
Unholy Writ   David Williams
Midsummer Murder   Clifford Witting

Recommended collections include:

Mr. Campion and Others   (1950) Margery
  Allingham
Book of Murder   Frederick Irving Anderson
Call Mr. Fortune   H. C. Bailey
Trent Intervenes   E. C. Bentley
Exeunt Murderers   Anthony Boucher
The Eyes of Max Carrados   Ernest Bramah
The Innocence of Father Brown   G. K.
  Chesterton
The Labours of Hercules   Agatha Christie
Beware of the Trains   Edmund Crispin
Dr. Sam: Johnson Detector   Lillian de la Torre
Designs on Life   Elizabeth Ferrars
Game Without Rules   Michael Gilbert
Best Detective Stories of Cyril Hare
Appleby Talking   Michael Innes
Uncle Abner   Melville Davisson Post
Calendar of Crime   Ellery Queen
Lord Peter Views the Body   Dorothy L. Sayers
The Department of Dead Ends   (1949) Roy
  Vickers

337

APPENDIX K. Twenty-five important anthologies

n.d. (1935)
A Century of Detective Stories Hutchinson, introduced by G. K. Chesterton

1936
Tales of Detection Dent, edited by Dorothy L. Sayers

n.d. (1936)
Six Against the Yard Selwyn & Blount, with commentaries by ex-Supt Cornish, CID.

n.d. (1938)
Fifty Famous Detectives of Fiction Odhams, illustrated

1938
Challenge to the Reader Stokes, edited by Ellery Queen

n.d. (1939)
Detection Medley Hutchinson, edited by John Rhode, introduced by A. A. Milne: Detection Club collection

1940
Detective Stories of Today Faber, edited by Raymond Postgate

1944
The Misadventures of Sherlock Holmes Little, Brown, edited by Ellery Queen

1946
To the Queen's Taste Little, Brown, edited by Ellery Queen

1948
Twentieth-Century Detective Stories World, edited by Ellery Queen and including 'Queen's Quorum'

1950
The Evening Standard Detective Book Gollancz

1950
Four-and-Twenty Bloodhounds Simon & Schuster, MWA collection edited by Anthony Boucher with 'Detectives' *Who's Who*'

1951
The Evening Standard Detective Book, Second Series Gollancz

1958
Planned Departures Hodder & Stoughton, CWA collection introduced by Elizabeth Ferrars

1959
Best Detective Stories Faber, edited and introduced by Edmund Crispin

1960
Some Like Them Dead Hodder & Stoughton, CWA collection introduced by Roy Vickers

1960
Great Stories of Detection Barker, edited by R. C. Bull

1979
Verdict of Thirteen Faber, Detection Club collection introduced by Julian Symons

1985
The Further Adventures of Sherlock Holmes Penguin, edited and introduced by Richard Lancelyn Green

1988
Crime at Christmas Equation, edited with introductions by Jack Adrian, illustrated by Brian Denington

1989
Winter's Crimes 21 Macmillan, edited by Hilary Hale

1990
A Classic English Crime Pavilion, edited by Tim Heald, CWA collection to honour Agatha Christie

1990
A Suit of Diamonds Collins Crime Club, Crime Club Diamond Jubilee collection

1992
The Man Who... Macmillan, edited and introduced by H. R. F. Keating, Detection Club collection to honour Julian Symons

1992
1st Culprit Chatto & Windus, CWA collection edited by Liza Cody and Michael Z. Lewin

APPENDIX L.   Dust-wrapper artists

Many graphic artists made important contributions to the dust-wrapper art of detective fiction. Listed here are twenty of the best known, with brief accounts of their work in the field.

S. Abbey

Leading designer with two Sherlock Holmes titles to his credit: *His Last Bow* and *The Case-Book*. Also designed for H. C. Bailey (*Mr. Fortune Explains*), John Dickson Carr (*The Crooked Hinge, The Black Spectacles*), Gordon Daviot (*The Man in the Queue*) and John Rhode (*The Ellerby Case*)

J. Z. Atkinson

Designer with strong, distinctive style. Best known for Agatha Christie's *Towards Zero*: also A. Fielding's *Pointer to a Crime* and two by E. C. R. Lorac (*Fell Murder* and *Checkmate to Murder*).

Barbosa

Stylish designer famous for designing Georgette Heyer's historical novels. Criminous work includes *Gold and Gaiters* (C. A. Alington), *Let's Kill George* (Lucy Cores), *Fear is the Same* (Carter Dickson) and *Death Is No Sportsman* (Cyril Hare).

C(ecil) W(alter) Bacon

A major figure with much fine work to his credit. Designed, among others, for: Margery Allingham (*Traitor's Purse*), Ralph Arnold (*Fish and Company, Skeletons and Cupboards*), Herbert Brean (*Wilders Walk Away, Hardly a Man is now Alive*), Christopher Bush (*The Case of the Burnt Bohemian/Red Brunette*), John Dickson Carr (*Below Suspicion, Patrick Butler for the Defence*), Raymond Chandler (*The Little Sister*), Georgette Heyer (*Duplicate Death*), P. M. Hubbard (*Cold Waters*), Richard Hull (*The Ghost It Was*), Elspeth Huxley (*Death of an Aryan*) and Gladys Mitchell (*Brazen Tongue*).

Biro

Another major figure, esteemed for the uniform series he designed for Leo Bruce's Carolus Deene novels from Peter Davies. Also drew memorable portraits of Dr Fell for *The Dead Man's Knock* and Leonidas Witherall for *The Hollow Chest*. Other work includes Alex Atkinson's *Exit Charlie*, Margot Bennett's *The Man Who Didn't Fly*, both 'Sebastian Fox' titles (*One Man's Poison, Odd Woman Out*), several titles by Max Murray and further Carr titles (*The Third Bullet, The Demoniacs, Most Secret*, etc.).

(Philip) Youngman Carter

Prolific designer, elegant and meticulous. Husband of Margery Allingham and designer for some twenty of her books, notably *Mystery Mile, Police at the Funeral, Death of a Ghost, Mr. Campion and Others* and *The Beckoning Lady*. Also designed for Leo Bruce (*Case with Ropes and Rings*), Raymond Chandler (*The Smell of Fear*), Carter Dickson (*The Bowstring Murders, The Magic Lantern Murders, The Judas Window*), E. C. R. Lorac (*The Case of Colonel Marchand*), Gladys Mitchell (*Printer's Error*), Helen McCloy (*Design for Dying*), John Rhode (*Poison for One*), Henry Wade (*Constable, Guard Thyself*) and a long series for Simenon.

Ellen Edwards

Designer for *The Murder of Roger Ackroyd* and something of a specialist in worried women. Examples appear on her wrappers for *The Specimen Case* (Ernest Bramah), *Colonel Gore's Second Case* (Lynn Brock), *Murders in Volume 2* (Elizabeth Daly), *Helen Vardon's Confession* (R. Austin Freeman) and *The Body on the Beam* (Anthony Gilbert).

Kenneth Farnhill

Prolific designer in a variety of styles from austere to ornate. Much employed by the Crime Club, designing for Nicholas Blake (*A Tangled Web*), Agatha Christie (*Third Girl, Endless Night*), D. M. Devine (*The Fifth Cord*), Nigel FitzGerald (*Affairs of Death*), Ngaio Marsh (*Death at the Dolphin*), Patricia Moyes (*Murder Fantastical*), Ellis Peters (*The Piper on the Mountain*), Rex Stout (*A Right to Die*) and Julian Symons, (*The Man Who Lost His Wife*). Also worked for Michael Joseph: P. M. Hubbard's *Flush as May* and *Picture of Millie*, Barbara Worsley-Gough's *Lantern Hill* and a memorable series for Gladys Mitchell, from *The Twenty-Third Man* to *Adders on the Heath*. Uniform run for Nancy Spain (Hutchinson), more pictorial than usual.

Jarvis

Worked for Hodder & Stoughton, designing for Delano Ames (*The Body on Page One* and others), Freeman Wills Crofts (*Anything to Declare?*) Michael Gilbert (*Death has Deep Roots*), John Sherwood (*Two Died in Singapore*), Patricia Wentworth (*Anna, Where Are You?* and others) and the CWA (*Choice of Weapons, Planned Departures*).

Broom Lynne

Major figure, very prolific, often very stylish. Worked for Joseph, Heinemann and Macdonald: Mary Kelly (*The Spoilt Kill* and others), Jennie Melville (*Come Home and Be Killed* and others), Gladys Mitchell (*The Croaking Raven* and others) and C. E. Vulliamy (*Cakes For Your Birthday* and others); Matthew Head (*Murder at the Flea Club*) and Edith Pargeter (*Fallen into the Pit*); and Helen Robertson (*The Winged Witnesses* and others), John Trench (*Docken Dead, Dishonoured Bones*) and Mary Fitt (ten titles from *A Fine and Private Place*).

Denis McLoughlin

Esteemed for the long series of wrappers designed for Boardman, publisher of 'hard-boiled' crime. Four wrappers for Louisa Revell, a rare exception – also three for P. W. Wilson.

Freda Nichols

Attractive designer, worked for Joseph. Designs include two for Gladys Mitchell (*Tom Brown's Body, Groaning Spinney*), three for Max Murray (*The Right Honourable Corpse, The Neat Little Corpse, No Duty on a Corpse*), Jonathan Stagge's *The Three Fears* and Barbara Worsley-Gough's *Alibi Innings*. Also Clara Stone's *Death in Cranford*, for Hutchinson.

Nicholson

Like Jarvis, worked much for Hodder. Designed, among others, for Delano Ames (*She Shall Have Murder* and others), Dorothy Bowers (*A Deed Without a Name*), J. J. Connington (*No Past is Dead* and others), Freeman Wills Crofts (*Death of a Train, Silence for the Murderer*), Patricia Wentworth (*Lonesome Road, The Chinese Shawl* and others) and Clifford Witting (*Catt Out of the Bag*).

Bip Pares

Distinguished woman designer, much employed by Hodder; for Freeman Wills Crofts (*Murderers Make Mistakes*), Michael Gilbert (*Close Quarters, They Never Looked Inside, The Doors Open*), Ronald A. Knox (*The Body in the Silo, Still Dead, Double Cross Purposes*), Sheila Pim (*Creeping Venom*) and John Sherwood (*The Disappearance of Dr. Brudenstein*). Also Brahms and Simon's *A Bullet in the Ballet*, for Joseph.

Salim Patel

A more recent artist with an attractive style. Designed for Gwendoline Butler (*A Coffin from the Past*), Heron Carvic (*Miss Seeton Bewitched*, with a fine portrait), Peter Dickinson (*Skin Deep*) and, especially, Colin Watson (three of the Flaxborough novels and the omnibus with its map of the town). The artist matches visually the wit and verve of Watson's text.

William Randell

Prolific designer much employed by the Crime Club. Also worked for Hutchinson and was Ruth Rendell's designer during her John Long phase. Bold pictorial style, usually instantly recognizable. Designed extended run for Miles Burton's later career, all vivid, some powerful (*Bones in the Brickfield, Death Takes a Detour*). Also multiple titles for Carol Carnac (*Death of a Lady Killer*, etc.), Nigel FitzGerald (*Imagine a Man*, etc.) and E. C. R. Lorac *Dishonour Among Thieves*, etc.). Drew Nero Wolfe twice, for *Crime and Again* and with Archie for *The Black Mountain*. Designs range from inspired (Ellis Peters' *Death Mask*) to inept (Ruth Rendell's *Vanity Dies Hard*).

J(ohn) Morton Sale

Distinguished designer of pictorial wrappers. Designs include E. H. Clements' *Berry Green*, Freeman Wills Crofts' *Fatal Venture*, Elizabeth Ferrars' *Your Neck in a Noose*, E. C. R. Lorac's *Murder on the Burrows*, Henry Wade's *The Duke of York's Steps* and Clifford Witting's *Measure for Murder*.

Sax

A most attractive artist, popular with Hammond, Hale and Jenkins. Lively pictorial style – not for nothing was he chosen to illustrate P. G. Wodehouse. Designed distinguished runs for Pamela Branch (*Lion in the Cellar* et al.) Guy Cullingford (*Post Mortem* and four others), Margaret Erskine (*Death of Our Dear One* et al.) and Craig Rice (*The Fourth Postman* et al.). Notable portrait of John J. Malone for *The Name is Malone*. Also Elizabeth Daly's *The Book of the Lion*, Austin Lee's *Miss Hogg and The Squash Club Murder*, Philip MacDonald's *Guest in the House*, Joanna Pullein-Thompson's *Gin and Murder* and Roy Vickers' *Eight Murders in the Suburbs*.

(Leslie Leonard) Stead

Prolific, versatile artist, always reliable. Worked for Hodder (Freeman Wills Crofts' *Enemy Unseen*, Georgette Heyer's *No Wind of Blame* and *Envious Casca*, A. E. W. Mason's *The House in Lordship Lane*, R. A. J. Walling's *More Than One Serpent* and *Dust in the Vault*, Patricia Wentworth's *Red Stefan* and Clifford Witting's *Subject: Murder* and *Let X be the Murderer*); and for the Crime Club (Miles Burton's *Death Takes the Living*, Agatha Christie's *The Body in the Library*, and *Sparkling Cyanide*, Leslie Ford's *The Philadelphia Murder Story*, E. C. R. Lorac's *Case in the Clinic, Still Waters* and others, and Ngaio Marsh's *Surfeit of Lampreys* and *Death and the Dancing Footman*).

Stein

Prolific designer in a rough-and-ready style, effective at its best, disastrous at its worst. Worked for many publishers. Notable designs include H. C. Bailey's final run from Macdonald, Gladys Mitchell's *Death and the Maiden*, Georgette Heyer's *Detection Unlimited* and the complete run of Kenneth Hopkins' seven novels. He also designed for Herbert Adams (*Exit the Skeleton, Crime Wave at Little Cornford*), Douglas G. Browne (*Too Many Cousins, What Beckoning Ghost, Death in Seven Volumes*), Carol Carnac (*The Striped Suitcase, Upstairs, Downstairs, Over the Garden Wall*), Carter Dickson (*Night at the Mocking Widow*), Mary Fitt (*Case for the Defence*), Joan Fleming (*The Good and the Bad, He Ought to be Shot*), Selwyn Jepson (three Eve Gill titles), Mary Kelly (*The Christmas Egg*) and Austin Lee (*Miss Hogg and the Missing Sisters*). See him at his worst on E. H. Clements' *Over and Done With*, Margaret Erskine's *The Disappearing Bridegroom* and, rock-bottom, Kathleen Freeman's *Gown and Shroud*.

John French

Simon Brett

A. B. Cox
(Francis Iles)

John Rhode

Jaques Charles

Gil North

Margaret Yorke

Gwendoline Butler

Harry Keating

Jennie Melville

Peter Deloion

Gladys Mitchell

Cyril Hare

Agatha Christie

Anthony ...

Joyce Porter

E. J. Newshore

John Watson

Ellery Queen

Catherine Aird

AMANDA CROSS

Beverley Nichols

and Carolyn Heilbrun

S. S. Van Dine

H. C. Bailey

Lillian de la Torre

Ruth Rendell

Patricia Wentworth

Clemence Dane

Henry Wade

Elizabeth Lemarchand

JOHN ROSSITER
aka
JONATHAN ROSS.

Sheila Radley

June Thomson

Margaret Erskine

Antonia Fraser